ALWD Guide to Legal Citation

FREE ACCESS to the **ALWD Online Companion**

to accompany the ALWD Guide to Legal Citation, Fifth Edition

Your Access Code:

To redeem:

1. Go to aspenlaw.com and log in or create an account.
2. Once logged in, go to My Account / Redeem an Access Code.
3. Enter the access code listed above.
4. Go to www.alwdonline.com and log in with your aspenlaw.com credentials.

For Technology Support:
Email: supportservices@loislaw.com
Phone: 1.877.471.5632
Reference: ALWD Online
Hours: Monday-Friday 3 a.m. −10 p.m. CST

Kimberly

Aspen
Coursebook
Series

ALWD Guide to Legal Citation

Fifth Edition

Association of Legal Writing Directors

and

Coleen M. Barger

Professor of Law
University of Arkansas at Little Rock
William H. Bowen School of Law

Wolters Kluwer
Law & Business

Dedicated to Marijean Oliver Voss (1952–2013)

ISBN 978-1-4548-2875-4

Library of Congress Cataloging-in-Publication Data

ALWD citation manual.
    ALWD guide to legal citation / Association of Legal Writing Directors and Coleen M. Barger, professor of law, University of Arkansas at Little Rock, William H. Bowen School of Law. — Fifth edition.
        pages cm. — (Aspen coursebook series)
    Includes bibliographical references and index.
    ISBN 978-1-4548-2875-4 (alk. paper)
    1. Citation of legal authorities--United States. 2. Annotations and citations (Law) — United States. I. Barger, Coleen M., 1953- author. II. Association of Legal Writing Directors, author. III. Title.
    KF245.A45 2014
    808.02'7 — dc23
                                                        2013049517

About Wolters Kluwer Law & Business

Wolters Kluwer Law & Business is a leading global provider of intelligent information and digital solutions for legal and business professionals in key specialty areas, and respected educational resources for professors and law students. Wolters Kluwer Law & Business connects legal and business professionals as well as those in the education market with timely, specialized authoritative content and information-enabled solutions to support success through productivity, accuracy and mobility.

Serving customers worldwide, Wolters Kluwer Law & Business products include those under the Aspen Publishers, CCH, Kluwer Law International, Loislaw, ftwilliam.com and MediRegs family of products.

CCH products have been a trusted resource since 1913, and are highly regarded resources for legal, securities, antitrust and trade regulation, government contracting, banking, pension, payroll, employment and labor, and healthcare reimbursement and compliance professionals.

Aspen Publishers products provide essential information to attorneys, business professionals and law students. Written by preeminent authorities, the product line offers analytical and practical information in a range of specialty practice areas from securities law and intellectual property to mergers and acquisitions and pension/benefits. Aspen's trusted legal education resources provide professors and students with high-quality, up-to-date and effective resources for successful instruction and study in all areas of the law.

Kluwer Law International products provide the global business community with reliable international legal information in English. Legal practitioners, corporate counsel and business executives around the world rely on Kluwer Law journals, looseleafs, books, and electronic products for comprehensive information in many areas of international legal practice.

Loislaw is a comprehensive online legal research product providing legal content to law firm practitioners of various specializations. Loislaw provides attorneys with the ability to quickly and efficiently find the necessary legal information they need, when and where they need it, by facilitating access to primary law as well as state-specific law, records, forms and treatises.

ftwilliam.com offers employee benefits professionals the highest quality plan documents (retirement, welfare and non-qualified) and government forms (5500/PBGC, 1099 and IRS) software at highly competitive prices.

MediRegs products provide integrated health care compliance content and software solutions for professionals in healthcare, higher education and life sciences, including professionals in accounting, law and consulting.

Wolters Kluwer Law & Business, a division of Wolters Kluwer, is headquartered in New York. Wolters Kluwer is a market-leading global information services company focused on professionals.

Table of Contents

About the Authors

The Association of Legal Writing Directors is a learned society for professors who coordinate legal writing instruction in legal education. ALWD members teach at nearly all American law schools. ALWD is headquartered at the University of Michigan Law School, 625 South State Street, Ann Arbor, MI 48109-1215.

Coleen M. Barger is Professor of Law at the University of Arkansas at Little Rock William H. Bowen School of Law, where she has taught legal writing, legal research, and appellate advocacy courses since 1992. She is a co-founder and Developments Editor of the *Journal of Appellate Practice and Process*, a faculty-edited law review that has used ALWD citation format since 2000. Coleen is a member of the Legal Writing eJournal Advisory Board for the SSRN Legal Scholarship network. She has served as a co-editor of the *Legal Writing Prof Blog*, and she has been a member of the Board of Directors for both the Association of Legal Writing Directors and the Legal Writing Institute. She and Professor Brooke Bowman are co-authors of the *ALWD Companion*.

Preface

Legal citations serve many purposes. They record the sources selected by writers to support their statements concerning the law. They provide readers with the information they'll need to access those sources. They signify the weight, the relevance, and even the influence that a particular source possesses. They give credit to the original authors of text and ideas. And they even tell us something about the legal writers who drafted them—including how current, how extensive, and how careful their research was—and consequently, the degree to which the writers' work will be perceived as trustworthy, complete, accurate, and ethical.

In the late 1990s, the Association of Legal Writing Directors determined that legal writing professionals were in the best position to create a legal citation textbook that would clearly explain and abundantly illustrate the fundamentals as well as the more subtle nuances of legal citation. The *ALWD Citation Manual* was the result, written by Darby Dickerson and published in its first edition in 2000. Dean Dickerson's goals were to write a text that was easy to use, easy to teach from, and easy to learn from, and she succeeded in all three respects. This new text was also innovative, as it focused on the citation formats used in everyday law practice, rather than in scholarly footnotes, and as it urged a single consistent set of rules and abbreviations to operate in both settings.

A dozen years later, ALWD's members requested a major revision of the textbook, then in its fourth edition. Feedback from membership surveys pointed to the staying power of certain scholarly traditions in legal citation and urged that ALWD modify its rules to acknowledge those traditions. The surveys also indicated that users wanted a shorter, more streamlined text, but that they didn't want to give up the clear explanations and abundant illustrations that made the *ALWD Citation Manual* so helpful to novice legal writers.

To meet its users' concerns and needs, the fifth edition required significant revisions and reorganization. The *ALWD Guide to Legal Citation* has the following goals:

- To help beginning law students learn the conventions of legal citation, both for constructing citations and for understanding citations written by others;

- To explain the functions of the specific components for citations to various types of legal sources;

- To give students a text that makes sense and that provides a step-by-step guide to constructing accurate citations;

- To offer legal writing and research professors a text that is easy to use, well organized, and self contained;

- To arrange the contents so that legal professionals can easily find what they need to construct the citations they'll use every day in practice-based documents; and

- To identify and make easy to find the small changes needed to modify citations for the constraints of scholarly writing in academic journals.

To that end, we reexamined each rule and example. We combined some rules relating to similar sources (e.g., combining federal and state legislative materials into a single rule). We added dozens of new examples, and we updated others. To help users recognize formats and short citation practices that apply only to academic footnotes, we added new subsections to affected source rules, indicated by the (FN) suffix and an academic formatting icon. We revised and updated the Appendices, adding new subsections to Appendix 3. The fifth edition covers more, but it does so with fewer rules, more examples, and a focus on the rules practitioners use—while also providing guidance on scholarly citation modifications. The *ALWD Guide to Legal Citation* ably serves all the needs of law students, law professors, practicing attorneys, and courts. Even with these changes, the *ALWD Guide* remains true to its roots and its pedagogical strengths. Each student who purchases the *ALWD Guide* will receive access to the online *Companion,* an interactive program designed to guide users in recognizing and constructing accurate citations in context.

⚠ ACADEMIC
FORMATTING

Academic
formatting icon

Acknowledgments to the First Edition

I would like to thank and recognize the following people and organizations without whom the ALWD Citation Manual would not have become a reality:

The Association of Legal Writing Directors (ALWD), whose officers and directors conceived the idea of a new citation system and provided guidance and support throughout the process.

Members of the ALWD Citation Manual Advisory Committee who reviewed draft manuscripts and provided valuable input, support, and suggestions: Coleen Barger, Mary Beth Beazley, Maria Ciampi, Eric B. Easton, Ruth AnnMcKinney, Craig T. Smith, Kathleen Elliott Vinson, Marilyn R. Walter, and Ursula H. Weigold.

Special thanks to the co-chairs of the ALWD Citation Manual Advisory Committee, Steven D. Jamar and Amy E. Sloan, to Richard K. Neumann, Jr., who served as a liaison between ALWD and the publisher and provided invaluable assistance and advice from the beginning of the project through the end, and to Jan Levine, who conceived the idea of the Manual and supported and contributed to it throughout the process.

The four presidents of ALWD who served during the pendency of this project and who helped facilitate its completion: Jan Levine, Katie McManus, Maureen Straub Kordesh, and Sue Liemer.

The other ALWD officers, including Molly Warner Lien, who supported and nurtured the project.

Henry T. Wihnyk: for participating in the initial stages of the project.

Joe Kimble and Christy B. Nisbett for providing insightful and detailed comments on a prior draft of the Manual.

The anonymous reviewers who provided helpful critiques of earlier drafts of the Manual.

The administration and faculty of Stetson University College of Law for providing generous financial support and ongoing encouragement for the project.

Professor Peter L. Fitzgerald for sharing his knowledge about international treaties and Internet sources.

The Stetson University College of Law Reference Librarians—Pamela Burdett, Dorothy Clark, Michael Dahn, Earlene Kuester, Madison Mosley, and Sally Waters—for locating difficult-to-find material, processing many interlibrary loan requests, and serving as excellent sources of bibliographic information.

The Stetson University College of Law Faculty Support Services Department, headed by Connie P. Evans, for superb clerical services and moral support.

The following Stetson University College of Lawstudentswhoprovided top-notch research assistance: Robert Taylor Bowling, Christopher H. Burrows, Victoria L. Cecil, David F. Chalela, Julianne J. Flynn, Darren D. McClain, Ashkan Najafi, Nicole D. Quinn, Tyra Nicole Read, Jeffrey P. Rosato, and Debra A. Tuomey.

Students Victoria J. Avalon, Danielle M. Bonett, Pamela H. Cazares, and Kevin M. Iurato deserve special recognition for their painstaking and detail-oriented work on several appendices and other portions of the Manual.

Aspen Law & Business for recognizing the value of this project and enhancing the quality of the manuscript. Within Aspen, I would like to specifically recognize Dan Mangan, Melody Davies, Ellen Greenblatt, Carol McGeehan, and Linda Richmond for their creativity, persistence, and hard work.

Finally, a special thanks to my husband, Michael P. Capozzi, for understanding why I have not been around much during the last year.

Darby Dickerson
Associate Dean, Professor of Law, and
Director, Legal Research and Writing
Stetson University College of Law
St. Petersburg, Florida
April 2000

Acknowledgments to the Second Edition

As with many projects, there are so many people to thank and such little space in which to express that thanks. Over the years, many individuals and organizations have contributed to the production and success of the *ALWD Citation Manual*. In addition to those recognized in the *Manual's* first edition, I would like to thank the following for their assistance with the second edition:

The Association of Legal Writing Directors (ALWD), and its officers, directors, and members, who have supported this project from the beginning.

Specifically, I would like to thank the following ALWD presidents who have served since the first edition was published and while the second edition was being prepared: Sue Liemer, Pamela Lysaght, Nancy Schultz, and Amy Sloan.

The members of the *ALWD Citation Manual* Advisory Committee for the Second Edition, who provided invaluable input and guidance: Tracy L. Bach, Coleen Barger, Jan Levine, Tracy McGaugh, Judith Rosenbaum, Arnold I. Siegel, and Grace Tonner.

Richard K. Neumann, Jr. and Jan Levine, who conceived the idea of the *Manual* and have provided input, suggestions, and support since that time.

Members of the *ALWD Citation Manual* Adoption Committee for their work in spreading the word about the *Manual*. Special thanks goes to co-chairs Coleen Barger, Wayne Schiess, and Hether Macfarlane.

My former student and now colleague Brooke J. Bowman for her assistance with so many of the painstaking details.

The following current and former Stetson University College of Law students who provided excellent research assistance: Irene Bosco, Tracy Carpenter, Catherine Shannon Christie, Tanya Dentamaro, Dale Goerne (tax appendix), Moein Marashi, Susan St. John, Bridget Remington, and Natsha Wolfe.

Stetson University College of Law, for continued support and resources

The anonymous reviewers of the new tax appendix.

The many law librarians and state reporters of decisions who took time to complete surveys regarding the *Manual*.

The many users who took the time to write with comments and changes. A special thanks goes to C. Edward Good for his comments.

The many research and writing professionals who took the time to write reviews of the first edition.

Aspen Publishers, for helping in so many ways to make the *Manual* a success. I would like to extend special thanks to Dan Mangan, Melody Davies, Carol McGeehan, Michael Gregory, Barbara Lasoff, and Paul Sobel for their hard work on this project.

Despite all of the help, all errors remain my own.

Darby Dickerson Stetson
University College of Law
Tampa Bay, Florida
November 2002

Acknowledgments to the Third Edition

To be a success, a project the magnitude of the *ALWD Citation Manual* requires the expertise and assistance of many people. As with the first two editions, I have many people to thank for helping to bring the third edition to fruition, including the following:

The Association of Legal Writing Directors (ALWD) and its officers, directors, and members for continuing to support this project.

The ALWD presidents who have served and supported the *Manual* since the second edition was printed: Jo Anne Durako, Brad Clary, and Kristin Gerdy.

The members of the *ALWD Citation Manual* Advisory Committee, who provided outstanding advice and guidance: Pam Armstrong, Brooke J. Bowman, Pamela Lysaght, Tracy McGaugh, Amy E. Sloan, Tracy Weissman, and Melissa H. Weresh.

The members of the *ALWD Citation Manual* Adoptions Committee who have generated many creative ideas over the years. A special thanks goes to Hether Macfarlane, who has chaired that committee for many years.

Molly Lien, for providing material on foreign and international citations for Rule 21.

My Stetson colleague Brooke J. Bowman, who helped to update several rules and appendices, and was a source of constant support and encouragement during this project.

My assistants Roxane Latoza and Vicky Baumann, for managing the office while I was locked away preparing this edition.

Stetson law students Paula Bentley, Sarah Lahlou-Amine, and Josephine Thomas for their assistance in updating rules and examples.

The Stetson reference librarians, and particularly Sally G. Waters, who helped to locate sources and materials for this edition.

Members and editors of the *Stetson Law Review* for passing along suggestions to help improve the *Manual*.

Stetson University and Stetson University College of Law for continued support and resources.

The many users who took the time to write with questions, ideas, and suggestions.

The research and writing professionals who took the time to write reviews of the first and second editions, and who showed confidence in the *Manual* by adopting it in their classes.

Aspen Publishers, for its continued efforts to make the *Manual* a success. I would like to extend special thanks to Carol McGeehan, Melody Davies, Barbara Lasoff, Laurel Ibey, Michael Gregory, and George Serafin for their help over the years and for their hard work on the third edition.

And, as usual, despite all of the help, all errors remain my own.

Darby Dickerson
Stetson University College of Law
Tampa Bay, Florida
November 2005

Acknowledgments to the Fourth Edition

As we celebrate the *ALWD Citation Manual*'s tenth anniversary, I thank all of the faculty members, attorneys, judges, students, and other individuals who have used the *Manual*. Your support has been critical to the book's continued success and improvement. I send a heartfelt thanks to the professors who adopted the *Manual*, sometimes at risk to their own careers, because they believe it is the best teaching tool for legal citation.

I reserve special thanks for two individuals who made the fourth edition a better product because of their effort: Professor Coleen Barger and Professor Brooke J. Bowman, co-authors of *The ALWD Companion: A Citation Practice Book*, which will be published soon after this fourth edition. Professor Bowman is my former student and current Stetson Law colleague. She is passionate (yes . . . that's correct) about legal citation and has contributed outstanding suggestions, eagle eyes, and valuable time to this edition. Professor Barger is a nationally recognized expert on legal writing and citation who has served as a reviewer for every edition. I'm thrilled that she was able to join us as a Visiting Professor at Stetson in Fall 2009. As I've come to expect, Professor Barger offered fabulous ideas, was willing to ask the tough questions, and combed through the *Manual* multiple times to help think about what should be updated, added, or revised.

Once again, I could not have updated the appendices without tremendous help from the Stetson Law Librarians. Professor and Law Library Director Rebecca Trammell assisted with Appendices 5 and 7, among others. Pamela Burdett, Whitney Curtis, Alyssa Folse, Earlene Kuester, Wanita Scroggs, Jules Stevens, and Sally ("Queen of Reference") Waters helped check and re-check sources for accuracy and track down difficult-to-locate sources. Thank you for all that you do!

The Association of Legal Writing Directors (ALWD) has been an outstanding partner for this project, and I again thank its officers, directors, and members for their continuing support. The ALWD presidents who have served and supported the *Manual* since the third edition was printed are Craig Smith, Terrill Pollman, Judy Stinson, and Mary Beth Beazley.

My student assistant Stephanie Sawchuk performed assignments admirably and completed less-than-glamorous tasks professionally and cheerfully. Thanks also go to Stetson Law student Kaleena Barnes for helping with various projects. Among other things, she gamely tested draft rules for some of the "new media" sources.

My assistants Roxane Latoza and Charmaine Rushing were, as always, amazing throughout the updating process.

I am grateful to Stetson University and Stetson University College of Law for providing support and resources for me to complete this and earlier editions.

Finally, thanks go to the talented staff at Wolters Kluwer/Aspen Publishers for their patience, hard work, and determination to make the fourth edition as perfect as possible. They truly have added great value to this project. Carol McGeehan, Melody Davies, Michael Gregory, and George Serafin have been with the project since inception. They have all become friends and treasured colleagues who always have great ideas and sage advice. And it has been a great pleasure to work with Barbara Roth, Darren Kelly, and Lisa Wehrle to prepare this edition for publication. I know that working with a sitting law dean who travels constantly was not the easiest assignment. You deserve great credit for bringing the project to successful conclusion.

As always, all errors are mine. If you see any, please let me know!

Darby Dickerson
darby@law.stetson.edu
Stetson University College of Law
Tampa Bay, Florida
March 2010

Acknowledgments to the Fifth Edition

The fifth edition of the *ALWD Guide to Legal Citation* was inspired by and owes its development to many people, without whom it could not have come into being. I thank the officers, directors, and membership of the Association of Legal Writing Directors, who recognized the direction in which the *Guide* needed to go and who have been so supportive. In particular, I wish to thank the three ALWD presidents under whose watch I've worked on this project: J. Lyn Entrikin, Anthony Niedwiecki, and Kathleen Elliott Vinson.

I am so fortunate for the guidance and suggestions of the members of the ALWD Citation Advisory Committee: Professors Cindy Archer, Mary Beth Beazley, Luellen Curry, Jan Levine, Deborah Panek Paruch, Mary Rose Strubbe, and Dean Maria Perez Crist. The project has also enjoyed the support of ALWD Publication Committee chairs J. Lyn Entrikin and Ted Becker. And for those times when the project seemed daunting, I appreciate the encouragement of Professors Richard Neumann and Grace Tonner.

Three people provided extraordinary levels of help and feedback during the editing process: Professors Jessica Clark, Jan Levine, and Samantha Moppett. Thank you, guys. I would also like to thank Professor Brooke Bowman and the *ALWD Companion* scholars, updating its exercises to guide law students in mastering legal citation: Professors Jessica Clark (again!), Cassandra Hill, Erin Karsman, and Samantha Moppett.

At UALR, I owe so many thanks to my student research assistants: Luke Burton, Kayleigh Collins Dulaney, Katie Beck, and Kristen Garner. My faculty assistant, Colleen Godley, was a great help in updating several sources' Snapshots. Thank you to UALR law librarians Jessie Burchfield and Melissa Serfass for your wise advice. And of course, I couldn't have done this without the generous research support and personal encouragement of UALR deans John DiPippa, Paula Casey, and Michael Hunter Schwartz.

At Aspen, special thanks go to Carol McGeehan, Christine Hannan, Aaron Reid, Dana Wilson, and Susan Junkin. Additional thanks go to talented book designer Claire Seng-Niemoeller.

I owe a mountainous debt of gratitude to Dean Darby Dickerson, who created the original *ALWD Citation Manual* and whose clear explanations, sensible organization, remarkable consistency, and generous examples in the four earlier editions continue to inspire this book.

Finally, thanks go to my husband, Gary Barger, for his patience, wisdom, and unwavering support, and for listening to hours of citation minutiae during our walks!

Please let me know your suggestions, and without question, let me know if you find problems. My email address is below.

Coleen M. Barger
cmbarger@ualr.edu
University of Arkansas at Little Rock,
William H. Bowen School of Law
Little Rock, Arkansas
February 2014

Part 1
Introductory Material

Purposes and Uses of Citations

A legal citation is a shorthand reference to a specific source that its writer wants to bring to a reader's attention. The sources used in legal writing are primary and secondary authorities. A primary authority is *the law itself* as determined by one of the three branches of government (judicial, legislative, and executive/administrative). Within the jurisdiction of the governmental body that issued it, a primary authority is mandatory until it is changed by subsequent governmental action (e.g., repeal of a statute, overruling of a case). A secondary authority, in contrast, is a source that *talks about* the law (or some other topic); unlike a primary authority, it has no force of law.

While citations vary, depending on the nature of the source, a legal citation typically provides the name of the source's author, its title, the location of pertinent data within the source (such as a volume, page, or paragraph number), and its date of publication.

Legal citations serve many purposes. For one thing, by indicating **the nature** of a source, a legal citation tells law-trained readers **where to find the source**, such as within a set of statutes or a volume of a law review. A citation's format also indicates to law-trained readers whether the source is in print or online. Because readers often want to review the source, whether to verify what it says or to learn additional details, its citation should provide all the information necessary to locate both the source and any internal reference within it.

Second, law-trained readers can determine much about a source's **weight and persuasiveness** from reading its citation. For example, when encountering a case citation in a brief, a reader would be able to tell whether the case is mandatory authority (i.e., whether the court must adhere to that case's holding) or whether it is merely persuasive authority (e.g., a case from another jurisdiction). A legal citation may reveal many other relevant facts about a source's influential value, such as its author's identity, its age, its hierarchical position among other relevant authorities, and its current validity.

Third, a citation conveys the **type and degree of support** that the source provides for a particular proposition. For example, through the use of signals, a citation can show whether a case provides strong, direct support for the writer's assertion or support that is more indirect; in another situation, a citation can indicate that an authority contradicts or challenges an opponent's assertion. Law-trained readers can discern the type and degree of support from the citation itself and from the signal used to introduce it.

In addition, attorneys use citations to **demonstrate that their positions are well researched and well supported**. Law-trained readers expect to see evidence that writers have thoroughly researched the authorities for and against particular propositions. Careful writers therefore document their research by citing the sources that support their assertions and by citing other relevant sources they have consulted.

Legal writers also use citations to **give credit** to those who originated ideas that the writers are borrowing. The principles of effective and ethical legal writing and legal citation demand that legal writers give proper attribution to those whose words and ideas have informed them.

B How to Use the *ALWD Guide*

The fifth edition of the *ALWD Guide to Legal Citation* assists writers in developing citations to the sources they are using in their legal writing. The *ALWD Guide* codifies the most commonly followed rules for legal citation. While no citation system can anticipate every source a writer might need or choose to cite, the system presented here provides rules and examples for the most frequently cited materials, as well as guidelines for citing new or less familiar materials.

The *ALWD Guide* focuses on sources of United States law, both federal and state. It does not address international or foreign sources, except for treaties binding on the United States. If you need to cite a legal source from another country or an international law source, consult the *Guide to Foreign and International Legal Citations* (2d ed. 2009), prepared by the editors of New York University School of Law's *Journal of International Law and Politics*.

The citation system presented in the *ALWD Guide* applies to all forms of legal writing, both practice-based and scholarly writing. Where scholarly writing requires some modifications to citation format, the *ALWD Guide* identifies those modifications and provides examples.

1 Overall Organization

The *ALWD Guide* is organized into seven parts:

- **Part 1**, "Introductory Material," contains an overview of the contents and organization of the *ALWD Guide*, an introduction to the operation and features of rules for citing specific sources, a discussion of the ways a word processor may automatically alter your citations in unintended ways (which you can override), and advice for dealing with nonconforming citations you may encounter in different contexts.

- **Part 2**, "Citation Basics," addresses key concepts you will use when citing most types of legal sources. Consult Part 2 before beginning to cite any particular source, particularly if it is not a source you frequently cite.

- **Part 3**, "Citing Specific Sources," provides citation formats for print and certain electronic versions of primary and secondary authorities. Although online versions of many print sources are widely available, current citation norms favor citation to print sources. Use the rules in Part 3 to determine how to cite a specific type of source, such as a case, a statute, a regulation, a treatise, or an article.

- **Part 4**, "Electronic Sources," addresses citation of electronic sources not already covered in Part 3, including sources available on the World Wide Web, on commercial databases such as Bloomberg BNA, Lexis

Advance, and WestlawNext, and other electronic media such as email, listserv postings, e-books, and other new media sources.

▪ **Part 5**, "Incorporating Citations into Documents," explains and illustrates several principles governing the use of citations in legal text. For example, it discusses the placement of citations in text, including the use of citation sentences, citation clauses, embedded citations, and citations in academic footnotes. It provides guidance for choosing which authorities to cite and for organizing citations to multiple authorities. It addresses important concepts for constructing legal citations, such as the uses of signals and explanatory parentheticals.

▪ **Part 6**, "Quotations," explains the essentials for correctly using quotations in legal documents, including correct punctuation and formatting. It also demonstrates the correct ways to make alterations to or indicate omissions from quoted text.

▪ **Part 7**, "Appendices," collects essential information needed for various components of legal citations, including general and specialized abbreviations, court names, legal periodicals, and for both federal and state jurisdictions, their primary sources and local rules affecting citations.

▉ 2 ▉ Organization Within Each Part of the *ALWD Guide*

Parts **2** through **6** of the *ALWD Guide* are divided into forty rules. Each rule is, in turn, divided into subsections. Each rule provides detailed explanations for citing a particular source or applying a particular concept. Examples illustrate key points as well as exceptions to the general rules.

Rules for citing a particular source begin by identifying and illustrating the required components of a full citation to that source. A full citation is required the first time a source is cited in a legal text; it includes every citation component a reader would need to locate and evaluate the source. (For more information about full citations, see **Rule 11.1**.) The illustrations use a vertical line (|) to separate the components; the line does not, however, indicate a necessary space. Instead, the *ALWD Guide* uses colored triangles (▲) in its examples to designate required spaces. Using ordinary type, *italics*, or Large and Small Capitals, the illustrations indicate citation components that must be rendered in those typefaces. Finally, the illustrations show the placement of necessary punctuation such as commas or parentheses.

The following example of an illustration is from **Rule 12, Cases:**

Case name, | Reporter volume | Reporter abbreviation | Initial page, |
Pinpoint page(s) | (Court abbreviation | Date), | *Subsequent history
designation,* | Subsequent history citation.

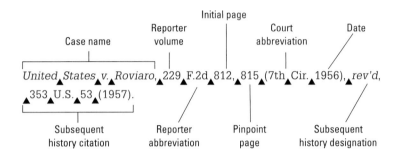

Following the illustration, the rule explains in detail each component of the
full citation and provides additional examples.

Rules 12 through **29** and **Rules 31** through **33** begin with "Fast Formats,"
tables containing representative citations for the commonly cited materials
covered by each rule. Consult a rule's Fast Formats to get a quick preview of the
basic citation components or to refresh your memory when you have not used
the rule for a particular source in some time.

"Snapshots" at the beginning of many rules provide further assistance in
crafting citations to those sources. The photographs reflect portions of the
source from which elements of the citation are drawn, with notations tied to
elements of the citation format.

Finally, throughout the *ALWD Guide,* you will encounter "Sidebars" presenting useful background information about particular publications, caveats
about common mistakes, and tips for citing particular sources.

3   Citations in Text or in Footnotes

A distinctive feature of legal writing is its preference for placement of citations in the body of the text itself. In some contexts, however, such as scholarly
writing, the convention is to place citations in footnotes, and for some kinds
of sources, footnote placement will require changing the typeface of certain
words into large and small capital letters, a minor change of formatting. The
ALWD Guide addresses the construction and format of citations appearing
both in the body of the text and in academic footnotes. Academic footnoting
rules are easy to find; the rule numbers end with the abbreviation FN. (Note:
The *ALWD Guide's* formatting rules for academic footnotes apply equally to
academic endnotes.)

4   Automatic Formatting in Your Word-Processing Software

Preexisting settings in your word-processing software can adversely affect the formatting of citations you type. Unless modified or disabled, default settings and quick-correct or auto-correct features can make changes you did not intend and, consequently, create errors in your citations. For example, your software may automatically insert one or two spaces after a period, even though you are trying to type a citation component that uses no spaces after periods (e.g., U.S.C.). It may recognize your attempt to type an ellipsis to indicate an omission, yet convert your correctly spaced ellipsis points to three unspaced periods (e.g., from . . . to ...). It may erroneously convert some ordinal contractions to superscript (e.g., 4th to 4th) while leaving others alone (e.g., 2d and 3d). It may automatically convert some pinpoint references to other symbols, such as converting (c) to ©. And if you type an Internet address, the software may automatically convert the URL (Uniform Resource Locator) to a hyperlink, underlined and in a different color.

Test your software to see whether it makes these kinds of unwanted changes. If it does, consult the developer's website for help in modifying, turning off, or disabling these features.

5   Finding Tools

To understand the *ALWD Guide*'s overall organization and to quickly locate rules on the major sources of law, check the Table of Contents. To find a rule covering a specific source or concept, look for its topic in the Index. Use the tabs supplied inside the *ALWD Guide*'s back cover to mark pages you frequently consult.

6   Citing Sources Not Covered in the *ALWD Guide*

If your writing requires citation to a source not covered in the *ALWD Guide*, do not be distressed. In the absence of a rule exactly on point, use the rule for the source most analogous to the source you have found. Remember, the primary goal of legal citation is to lead the interested reader to the cited source. By analogizing to the most similar type of source, you stand the best chance of providing readers with the information they need to find the source.

7   Caveats

Citation rules and practices evolve over time, and writers always seek guidance in constructing citations to new types of sources. In your research, you may encounter citations that are inconsistent with what you see in the *ALWD Guide*.

Those citations may be different because they reflect older or superseded rules and practices. Many courts have their own citation requirements that attorneys must follow when submitting documents to those courts (known as *local rules*; see **Appendix 2**). In addition, many legal publishers employ their own unique citation formats in specific contexts (such as the running header of a case reporter). Unless you are following a court's local rules in a document to be submitted to that court, when you find nonconforming citations, do not copy them as shown. Instead, look up the relevant rules in the *ALWD Guide* and revise the citations to conform to current citation standards.

8 Sources for Additional Guidance

For more guidance on matters of capitalization, punctuation, style, and special citation formats not addressed in the *ALWD Guide*, consult the most recent editions of the following works:

▪ *United States Government Printing Office Style Manual* (2008), available for free download from http://www.gpo.gov/fdsys/pkg/GPO-STYLEMANUAL-2008/content-detail.html.

▪ *The Chicago Manual of Style* (16th ed. 2010), available online at http://www.chicagomanualofstyle.org/home.html.

▪ Bryan A. Garner, *The Redbook: A Manual on Legal Style* (3d ed. 2013).

9 Online *ALWD Companion*

The *ALWD Companion* is an online counterpart to the *ALWD Guide*, available at http://www.alwdonline.com. Designed to help legal writers become proficient in citing the most common forms of legal sources and coordinated with the fifth edition of the *ALWD Guide*, the *Companion* contains a variety of exercises, from simple learning drills to creating and correcting citations in context. With exercises progressing through basic, intermediate, and expert levels, the *Companion* builds skills and confidence in legal writers to create clear and accurate legal citations.

10 Citing the *ALWD Guide*

Cite this book as ALWD & Coleen M. Barger, *ALWD Guide to Legal Citation* (5th ed. 2014).

Part 2
Citation Basics

1   Typeface for Citations

1.1   Typeface Choices

Legal citations use the following typefaces: ordinary type, *italics* (or its equivalent, underlining), and LARGE AND SMALL CAPITAL LETTERS (also known as "small caps").

1.2   When to Use Ordinary Type

Ordinary type consists of uppercase and lowercase letters without any enhancement. You will use ordinary type for most components of legal citations. Use ordinary type for everything not listed below in **Rule 1.3** or **Rule 1.4**.

1.3   When to Use Italics (or Underlining)

1.3(a)   Components to italicize

Represent italicized words with *slanted* type. In practice-based documents, underlining is an alternative to italicizing, and some local court rules require its use in briefs submitted to those courts. When the *ALWD Guide* directs the use of italics, you should substitute underlining if required to use that format by a local court rule or a professor's course requirements. Therefore, in those situations, any rule in the *ALWD Guide* that specifies the use of italics will be satisfied with underlining. In academic footnotes, however, always use italics. **Chart 1.1** identifies citation components that should be italicized.

1.3(b)   Italicized punctuation

Italicize (or underline) punctuation marks such as commas and periods when they are located *within* other italicized components of the citation (e.g., a case name or the title of a law review article). Do not italicize commas that *follow* case names, titles, or other italicized components.

Examples (italicized or underlined punctuation in red)

> *Tomlinson v. Goldman, Sachs & Co.*, 682 F. Supp. 2d 845, 848 (N.D. Ill. 2009), *aff'd sub nom. Premium Plus Partners, L.P. v. Goldman, Sachs & Co.*, 648 F.3d 533 (7th Cir. 2011).

> Tomlinson v. Goldman, Sachs & Co., 682 F. Supp. 2d 845, 848 (N.D. Ill. 2009), aff'd sub nom. Premium Plus Partners, L.P. v. Goldman, Sachs & Co., 648 F.3d 533 (7th Cir. 2011).

> *See id.* at 847.

> See id. at 847.

10

CHART 1.1	Citation Components to *Italicize*	

Component	Rule(s)
Signals (such as *see, cf.*)	35
Internal cross-references *supra* and *infra*	10
Case names in full citation format, unless the citations are in academic footnotes	12.2(a), 18.5(a)
Case names in short citation format	12.19
Phrases indicating subsequent or prior history of a case (such as *aff'd, cert. denied*)	12.8, 12.9
Titles of congressional hearings, unless the citations are in academic footnotes	15.7
Titles of books, treatises, other nonperiodic materials, and forthcoming works, unless the citations are in academic footnotes	20.1(c), 22.1(a)
Titles of works published in periodicals	21.2(c), 21.3(b)
Topics or titles in annotations and legal encyclopedias	22.3(c), 22.6(b)
Titles of presentations, videos, visual programs, and audio recordings	28.1(a), 28.3(b)
Titles of websites	31.2(b)
Titles of individual postings on blogs	31.3
The short citation forms *id.* and *supra*	11.3, 11.4

1.3(c) Possessive endings of italicized material

Do not italicize possessive endings ('s) of case names, publication names, or similar citation components.

Examples

Counsel for the petitioner argued that *Tinker*'s protection of student free speech did not apply to teachers while they were in the classroom.

The court adopted Black's Law Dictionary's definition of "affiliate."

1.3(d) Italicized material within italicized material

When words that would have been italicized under a rule in the *ALWD Guide* appear *within* italicized material (e.g., a case name in the title of a law review article), present those words in ordinary type.

Examples

Zachary M. Vaughn, Note, *The Reach of the Writ:* Boumediene v. Bush *and the Political Question Doctrine*, 99 Geo. L.J. 869, 872 (2011).

Rob Atkinson, *Liberating Lawyers: Divergent Parallels in* Intruder in the Dust *and* To Kill a Mockingbird, 49 Duke L.J. 601, 647 (1999).

Nina W. Tarr, <u>A Different Ethical Issue in</u> Anatomy of a Murder<u>: Friendly Fire from the Cowboy-Lawyer</u>, 32 J. Legal Prof. 137, 157–58 (2008).

1.3(e) Italicizing for emphasis

Emphasize words by italicizing (or underlining) them, but use this technique sparingly. When you add emphasis to words in quotations, append a parenthetical note to the quoted source's citation to indicate the added emphasis. Read **Rule 39.4** for more guidance. It is not necessary to parenthetically note emphasis appearing in a source's original language.

Example

"A written provision in any maritime transaction or a contract evidencing a transaction involving commerce to settle by arbitration a controversy thereafter arising out of such contract . . . shall be valid, irrevocable, and enforceable, *save upon such grounds as exist at law or in equity for the revocation of any contract.*" 9 U.S.C. § 2 (2012) (emphasis added).

1.3(f) Italicizing foreign words and abbreviations

You may italicize (or underline) foreign words that have not been incorporated into everyday English. Many law terms in Latin, however, are so common in legal writing that they are not italicized. **Chart 1.2** sets out words and abbreviations from legal Latin that should not be italicized unless they are used within a citation component that itself requires italics, such as a case name or the title of a law review article. To determine whether to italicize other foreign words or abbreviations, consult the current edition of *Black's Law Dictionary*.

CHART 1.2	**Words and Abbreviations Ordinarily Not Italicized in Legal Writing Text**	
ad hoc	en banc	in rem
amicus curiae	et al.	inter alia
certiorari	et seq.	prima facie
de facto	etc.	quid pro quo
de novo	habeas corpus	res gestae
dicta, dictum	i.e.,	res ipsa loquitur
e.g.,	in personam	res judicata

1.4(FN) Using Large and Small Capital Letters

⚠ ACADEMIC FORMATTING

Use large and small capital letters only for citations placed in academic footnotes, such as the footnotes found in books, treatises, and law review articles. For footnotes in any other context, such as in a memorandum of authorities or an appellate brief, use ordinary type and italics (or its equivalent, underlining) for citation components. (Note: As you see in the number for this rule, the *ALWD Guide* uses the abbreviation "FN" to mark rules concerning format for academic footnotes.)

Do not use large and small capital letters for any citation in the body of the text or for any citation used as a part of speech (also known as an "embedded citation" and discussed in **Rule 34.1(c)**). **Chart 1.3** identifies the citation components that in academic footnotes require use of large and small capital letters.

CHART 1.3	Components Using LARGE AND SMALL CAPITAL LETTERS in Academic Footnotes
Component	**Rule(s)(FN)**
Abbreviated names of constitutions	13.2(e)
Abbreviated names of statutory codes	14.2(h), 14.4(c), 14.5(c)
Authors, titles, and abbreviations of numbered congressional reports, documents, and prints	15.7(g), 15.9(b), 15.10(a)(6), 15.10(b)(3), 15.10(c)(2), 15.10(d)(3), 15.11(b), 15.11(c)(3), 15.17(g), 15.18(g), 15.19(b), 15.20(c)
Declaration of Independence	15.12(b)
Abbreviated names of court rules, jury instructions	16.1(e), 16.3(b), 16.3(d)
In codified ordinances, names of political subdivisions and codes	17.3
Names of authors and titles of books, treatises, and other non-periodic materials	20.1(f), 20.3(e), 20.6(d)
Abbreviated names of periodicals	21.6
Names of dictionaries, encyclopedias, and annotation series	22.1(b), 22.3(f), 22.6(g)
Titles of Restatements, model codes, uniform laws, and sentencing guidelines	23.1(e), 23.3(b), 23.5(c), 23.7(b)

Examples

---

[11] U.S. CONST. art. IV.

[12] OR. REV. STAT. § 215.080 (2011).

[13] S. REP. NO. 112-202, at 8 (Aug. 2, 2012).

[14] 8TH CIR. R. 28A(i).

[15] LOUDON CNTY., VA., CODIFIED ORDINANCES § 684.03 (2009).

[16] STEPHEN BREYER, MAKING OUR DEMOCRACY WORK: A JUDGE'S VIEW 42–44 (2010).

[17] Andrew Jay McClurg, *Fight Club: Doctors vs. Lawyers—A Peace Plan Grounded in Self-Interest*, 83 TEMP. L. REV. 309, 345 (2011).

[18] ALAN GILPIN, DICTIONARY OF ENVIRONMENTAL LAW 42 (2001).

[19] RESTATEMENT (SECOND) OF PROP.: LANDLORD AND TENANT §§ 1.4–1.8 (1977).

2 Abbreviations

2.1 Using Abbreviations

2.1(a) Standard and non-standard abbreviations

Legal writers use abbreviations to shorten words in many citation components, such as case names, court names, and periodical names. The **Appendices** in **Part 7** contain tables of standard abbreviations used in legal citations. Note that while most abbreviations end in a period, many standard abbreviations in legal writing are actually contractions that are formed with apostrophes; such abbreviations do not end with a period.

Be aware that in your research, you may encounter non-standard abbreviations or abbreviations that are no longer used. Look for their counterparts in the appendices, and substitute the abbreviations shown there for the non-standard forms. If a word does not appear in one of the appendices in the *ALWD Guide*, or if the relevant appendix does not permit you to create abbreviations of longer words, spell it out. Do not use another abbreviation unless a local court rule requires you to do so in documents submitted to that court.

2.1(b) Abbreviations used for multiple words

As you will see in the appendices, a few abbreviations stand for multiple words or multiple forms of a word. For example, "J." is an abbreviation for "Joint," "Journal," "Judge," or "Justice," depending on the source or context, and "Elec." stands for "Electric," "Electrical," "Electricity," or "Electronic."

2.2 Spacing for Abbreviations

2.2(a) Spaces between abbreviations

When a citation uses two or more adjacent abbreviations, insert a space between the abbreviations, unless they consist of single letters. (Note: Many of the examples in the *ALWD Guide* and all of the abbreviations in Appendices 1, 3, 4, 5, and 7 illustrate required spaces with a triangle (▲).)

2.2(b) Single-letter abbreviations

When an abbreviation has consecutive single letters, omit the spaces between them, except when abbreviating the name of a periodical, as provided in **Rule 2.2(c)**.

Examples

N.C.	H.R.
U.S.C.	S.D.N.Y.

2.2(c) Abbreviations in periodical names

In citations to publications in periodicals, set off the institutional or geographic abbreviation from other parts of the periodical abbreviation. Thus, insert a space before and after a group of consecutive single letters that denotes an institutional or geographic entity. (Note: Find periodical abbreviations in **Appendix 5**.)

Examples (spaces denoted by ▲)

B.U.▲J.▲Sci.▲&▲Tech.▲L.

S.C.▲L.▲Rev.

U.S.F.▲Mar.▲L.J.

2.2(d) Ordinal contractions treated as single-letter abbreviations

Treat an ordinal contraction, such as 2d or 5th, as a single letter. For more information about ordinal contractions, see **Rule 4.3(b)**.

Examples (spaces denoted by ▲)

1st	3d
5th	13th
20▲P.3d▲100	L.▲Ed.▲2d

2.2(e) Symbols

Do not treat an ampersand (&), a single section symbol (§), or a single paragraph symbol (¶) as a single letter; instead, always insert a space before and after the symbol. While you should also insert a space before and after double section (§§) or paragraph (¶¶) symbols, *do not* insert a space between them.

Examples (spaces denoted by ▲)

N.D.▲Cent.▲Code▲§▲14-18-05▲(2009).

3▲Jack▲B.▲Weinstein▲&▲Margaret▲A.▲Berger,▲*Weinstein's*▲*Federal*▲ *Evidence*▲¶¶▲502–504▲(2005).

2.3   Referring to Cases in Textual Sentences

In general, do not abbreviate words in a case name used as a part of speech in a textual sentence (e.g., a case name used as object of a preposition), including a case name in an embedded citation. For more information about embedded citations, see **Rule 34.1(c)**.

It is nonetheless permissible to use well-known acronyms (e.g., FBI, NAACP) in case names in textual sentences. (For guidance on using acronyms in case names, see **Rule 12.2(e)(3)**.) In addition, if one of the following words in **Chart 2.1** appears in a case name in a textual sentence *or* in an embedded citation, you may abbreviate it as shown below and in **Appendix 3(E)**.

CHART 2.1	Words to Abbreviate in Textual Sentences and Embedded Citations
and	&
Association	Ass'n
Brothers	Bros.
Company	Co.
Corporation	Corp.
Incorporated	Inc.
Limited	Ltd.
Number	No.

Examples

Correct: In *Performance Coal Co. v. Federal Mine & Health Review Commission*, the court disagreed with the government's interpretation of the statute.

Incorrect: In *Performance Coal Co. v. Federal Mine & Health Review Comm'n*, the court disagreed with the government's interpretation of the statute.

Do not, however, confuse references to case names within textual sentences with references to case names in citation clauses, which are set off from the text by commas and which are not grammatical elements of those sentences. (See **Rule 34.1(b)** for more information about citation clauses.) For case names in citation clauses, always abbreviate any words found in **Appendix 3(E)**.

Examples

Case name reference in textual sentence (no abbreviations):

In *Mississippi University for Women v. Hogan*, the Court stressed that a gender-based policy "must be applied free of fixed notions concerning the roles and abilities of males and females." 458 U.S. 718, 724–25 (1982).

Case name reference in embedded citation in textual sentence (no abbreviations):

In *Mississippi University for Women v. Hogan*, 458 U.S. 718, 724–25 (1982), the Court stressed that a gender-based policy "must be applied free of fixed notions concerning the roles and abilities of males and females."

Case name reference in textual sentence (no abbreviations), citation in academic footnote:

While the Supreme Court in *Mississippi University for Women v. Hogan* stated that a gender-based policy "must be applied free of fixed notions concerning the roles and abilities of males and females,"[65] the statute at issue here does not materially affect a woman's ability to obtain employment in a male-dominated field.

––––––––––––––––––

[65] 458 U.S. 718, 724–25 (1982).

Case name reference in citation clause (abbreviations):

While the Supreme Court has stated that a gender-based policy "must be applied free of fixed notions concerning the roles and abilities of males and females," *Miss. Univ. for Women v. Hogan*, 458 U.S. 718, 724–25 (1982), the statute at issue here does not materially affect a woman's ability to obtain employment in a male-dominated field.

3 Spelling and Capitalization

3.1 Spelling in Source Titles and Text

Do not alter a source's original spelling of words in its title or subtitle. When quoting a source with spelling errors in the *text*, however, it is your choice whether to reproduce the errors or to correct them. See **Rule 39.6** for guidance on indicating errors in the original or making corrections.

3.2 Capitalization in Source Titles and Subtitles

3.2(a) General rule for capitalizing source titles and subtitles

Capitalize the first letter of the following words in source titles (and subtitles):

- The first word;
- The first word after a colon or dash;
- All other words *except* articles ("a," "an," "the"); coordinating conjunctions ("and," "but," "for," "or," "nor"); prepositions of four or fewer letters (e.g., "in," "from," "of," "to"); and "to" when used in an infinitive (e.g., "to decide," "to reconsider").

Examples (titles and subtitles in practice-based document text and in academic footnotes)

> Tomiko Brown-Nagin, *Courage to Dissent: Atlanta and the Long History of the Civil Rights Movement* 338 (2011).

> Lainie Rutkow & Stephen P. Teret, *The Potential for State Attorneys General to Promote the Public's Health: Theory, Evidence, and Practice*, 30 St. Louis U. Pub. L. Rev. 267, 287–88 (2011).

> [17] Tomiko Brown-Nagin, Courage to Dissent: Atlanta and the Long History of the Civil Rights Movement 338 (2011).

⚠ACADEMIC FORMATTING

> [25] Lainie Rutkow & Stephen P. Teret, *The Potential for State Attorneys General to Promote the Public's Health: Theory, Evidence, and Practice*, 30 St. Louis U. Pub. L. Rev. 267, 287–88 (2011).

SIDEBAR 3.1   Common Prepositions

The list below contains commonly used prepositions; it is not exhaustive. If you are uncertain whether a word is a preposition, consult a dictionary or style manual. In titles and subtitles, capitalize the first letter of prepositions that have five or more letters (whether or not in this list).

about	beside	inside	through
above	besides	into	throughout
across	between	like	till
after	beyond	near	to
against	by	of	toward
around	down	off	under
at	during	on	up
before	except	out	upon
behind	for	outside	versus
below	from	over	with
beneath	in	since (indicating time)	without

3.2(b) Capitalizing hyphenated words in source titles and subtitles

When words in a source's title or subtitle are joined by a hyphen, capitalize the first letter of the first word in the hyphenated phrase. Capitalize the first letter of a word *following* a hyphen *unless* it is an article, preposition, coordinating conjunction, or a modifier for a musical term (e.g., "flat," "sharp"). If a title uses spelled-out numbers or fractions, capitalize words on either side of the hyphen (e.g., "Twenty-Second," "Three-Fourths").

Examples

Shyamkrishna Balganesh, *Quasi-Property: Like, but Not Quite Property*, 160 U. Pa. L. Rev. 1889, 1909 (2012).

Lynn Foster, *Fifty-One Flowers: Post-Perpetuities War Law and Arkansas's Adoption of USRAP*, 29 U. Ark. Little Rock L. Rev. 411, 426 (2007).

[65] Christopher J. Peters, *Under-the-Table Overruling*, 54 Wayne L. Rev. 1067, 1090 (2008).

[84] Scott W. McKinley, Comment, *The Need for Legislative or Judicial Clarity on the Four-Fifths Rule and How Employers in the Sixth Circuit Can Survive the Ambiguity*, 37 Cap. U. L. Rev. 171, 176–77 (2008).

3.3 Capitalization in Text

3.3(a) Capitalizing proper nouns

Capitalize proper nouns, including the names of people, entities, organizations, and places. Capitalize the shortened form of a proper noun.

Examples

Hillary Rodham Clinton	the Library of Congress
Heifer International	Niagara Falls
the Iowa General Assembly	the General Assembly

3.3(b) Capitalizing proper adjectives

Capitalize adjectives derived from words that exist solely as proper nouns (e.g., American, Lincolnesque). However, when a word does not exist exclusively as a proper noun, do not capitalize the adjective derived from it (e.g., congressional, presidential). Unless an ordinal number is part of a proper noun phrase, do not capitalize the number when it is used as an adjective.

Examples

European	Third Reich
constitutional	twenty-first century

3.3(c) Capitalizing defined terms

Once a term is defined in a document, it becomes a proper noun that should subsequently be capitalized.

Example

Jackson Elementary School ("Buyer") agrees to purchase five hundred half-pint cartons of milk each week from Smart Dairy, Inc. ("Seller"). Buyer will pay Seller within thirty days of receiving an invoice from Seller.

3.3(d) Capitalizing professional and honorific titles of persons

Capitalize a person's professional title or a title of honor or respect that immediately precedes or follows the person's name or that substitutes for the name. Capitalize titles presented in the second person (e.g., Your Honor) or third person (e.g., His Majesty).

Examples

Senator John McCain	Justice Earl Warren
the President	Saint Peter
the Duchess of Windsor	His Eminence Archbishop Demetrios

3.4   Capitalizing Specific Words

Capitalize words shown below in **Chart 3.1** when they are used in the contexts described. For capitalization of words not listed here or not covered by **Rules 3.2** and **3.3**, consult the most recent edition of the *United States Government Printing Office Style Manual*, *The Chicago Manual of Style*, or *The Redbook: A Manual on Legal Style*.

CHART 3.1	Capitalization of Specific Words
Act	Capitalize when referring to a specific legislative act or when making a subsequent reference to a previously named act
Examples	The Americans with Disabilities Act requires . . .
	Interpreting that provision of the Act, the trial court . . .
Appellant, Appellee	Capitalize when submitting a document to a court (such as a brief) and that document refers to a party in the pending case.
Examples	As for whether the condition was met, Appellant incorrectly argues . . .
	Court rules require an appellant's opening brief to contain . . .
Board, Commission, Department	Capitalize when used in a proper name or when referring to a governmental entity.
Examples	Members of the Board of Visitors of George Mason University are appointed by . . .
	The chair of the department called a meeting for . . .
Circuit	Capitalize when used with a circuit number.
Examples	Eleventh Circuit
	The circuit court held . . .
Code	Capitalize when referring to a named code.
Examples	United States Code, Code of Federal Regulations, Indiana Code
	Many states have codes that address . . .

(*Continued*)

CHART 3.1	**Capitalization of Specific Words, CONTINUED**
Committee, Subcommittee	Capitalize when used in a proper name or when referring to a governmental committee.
Examples	Committee for Education Funding, Senate Committee on Armed Services, Subcommittee on Personnel
	The bill was blocked in committee.
Commonwealth, People, State	Capitalize when part of the full name of a state or federation of states or when referring to a state or federation of states as a governmental actor or party to litigation.
Examples	State of Tennessee, Commonwealth of Virginia
	The People argued that the conviction was . . .
	As a commonwealth develops politically, it often develops economically as well.
Constitution, Article, Amendment	Capitalize when naming any constitution in full or when referring to the United States Constitution. Capitalize names of parts of the United States Constitution.
Examples	Texas Constitution, First Amendment, Equal Protection Clause
	The attorney general argued that the state's constitution did not authorize . . .
Court	Capitalize when naming any court in full, when referring to the United States Supreme Court, or when directly addressing a specific court, no matter what its level.
Examples	Ohio Supreme Court, West Virginia Court of Claims
	Defendant asks this Court to certify . . .
	The executor filed a petition with the probate court.
Defendant, Plaintiff	Capitalize within a court document (such as a complaint, a motion, or a brief) when referring to a party in the pending case.
Examples	Plaintiff requests that the Court grant his motion to . . .
	In *State v. Hudson*, the defendant argued that . . .

(*Continued*)

CHART 3.1	**Capitalization of Specific Words,** CONTINUED
Federal	Capitalize when the word it modifies is capitalized.
Examples	Federal Aviation Administration, Federal Rules of Evidence
	The federal government
Judge, Justice	Capitalize when used as a title or when referring to a Justice of the United States Supreme Court.
Examples	Judge Rhonda Wheeler, Chief Justice Rehnquist
	The circuit judge recused herself due to a conflict of interest.
Nation, National	Capitalize "Nation" when used as part of a proper name or as a synonym for the United States of America. Capitalize "National" when the word it modifies is capitalized.
Examples	United Nations, Cherokee Nation, National Guard
	The ambassadors of several nations gathered at . . .
President, Vice President	Capitalize when used as a title or when referring to a head or vice head of state.
Examples	President Truman, Vice President
	The Vice President campaigned in Florida last night.
	Mr. Jones serves as vice president of the club.
Secretary	Capitalize when used as a title or when referring to a cabinet-level official of the United States government.
Examples	Secretary of Defense Leon Panetta
	The Secretary traveled to Beijing in order to . . .
	The secretary contacted the judge's clerk to ask . . .

4 Numbers

4.1 Numbers in Citations

Present numbers within citations as numerals, unless the number appears in a title or subtitle. In titles and subtitles, reproduce the number as it appears in the original source, whether it is spelled out or shown as a numeral.

In citations using numbers of five digits or more (i.e., 10,000 and above), divide such large numbers into three-digit groups with commas (e.g., 12,843). Do not, however, use commas to set off three-digit groups in citations' references to statutory sections, database identifier numbers, or docket numbers.

Examples

11 U.S.C. § 510(c).

Fed. R. Civ. P. 45.

Ruthann Robson, *Thirteen False Blackbirds*, 37 N.Y.U. Rev. L. & Soc. Change 315, 318 (2013).

Max Stul Oppenheimer, *Patents 101: Patentable Subject Matter and Separation of Powers*, 15 Vand. J. Ent. & Tech. L. 1, 30–31 (2012).

Enhancing Airline Passenger Protections, 76 Fed. Reg. 23,110, 23,166 (Apr. 25, 2011) (to be codified at 14 C.F.R. pt. 399).

4.2 Numbers in Text

4.2(a) Representing numbers as words or numerals

When referring to numbers in text, most legal writers spell out the numbers zero to ninety-nine and round numbers (e.g., one thousand, two million), and they use numerals (e.g., 125, 476) for everything else. In non-legal settings, in contrast, the preference is to spell out zero through nine and use numerals for everything else. In either setting, however, some contexts call for numbers to be treated in a particular manner, as explained in the subsections below. If you are dissatisfied with the appearance of a number as a word or a numeral, consider revising the sentence structure to accommodate your preference.

Examples

The court listed five reasons for denying the motion.

The jury awarded the plaintiff compensatory damages of more than one million dollars.

Even though the firm logged 735 billable hours in preparing for trial, its bill was too high.

4.2(b) Numbers that begin a sentence

Always spell out a number that begins a sentence. If the number is part of an embedded citation, construct the sentence to prevent misreading. For statutes beginning with a number, use an appropriate noun indicating the statute's relative position within the code in which it appears (e.g., title, section).

Examples

One hundred thirty-five prisoner petitions are pending before the court.

Section 26-10C-1 describes the state's putative father registry.

Title 18 U.S.C. § 922 prohibits certain individuals from possessing firearms, ammunition, or explosives.

4.2(c) Arabic and roman numerals

In general, use arabic numerals (1, 4, 25) in preference to roman numerals (I, IV, XXV). (See, for example, **Rule 20.1(a)**, to indicate the volume number of a book within a multi-volume work.) However, use capitalized roman numerals in the names of monarchs, popes, and similar persons; in personal names; in names of certain events; and in names of vehicles or vessels. Use lowercase roman numerals for page numbers in the front matter of a book or an appellate brief.

Examples

Chapter 13 bankruptcy	Appendix 3	Interstate 40
Queen Elizabeth II	World War I	Thomas Michael Adams IV

4.2(d) Additional information on using numbers in text

For more guidance on using numbers in text, see the most recent edition of the *United States Government Printing Office Style Manual*, *The Chicago Manual of Style*, or *The Redbook: A Manual on Legal Style*.

◼ 4.3 ◼ Ordinal Numbers

4.3(a) Ordinal numbers in general

An ordinal number designates a position in a series, whether spelled out (e.g., first, fiftieth) or within an ordinal contraction using numbers and letters (e.g., 3d, 21st, 75th). Represent ordinal numbers as words or numbers according to the principles set out in **Rule 4.2(a)**.

Examples

The court agreed with the appellant's fifth argument.

Robert Wolfe, *The OECD Contribution to the Evolution of Twenty-First Century Trade Law*, 43 Geo. Wash. Int'l L. Rev. 277, 284–85 (2011).

Michael A. Olivas, *Commemorating the 50th Anniversary of* Hernandez v. Texas, 25 Chicano-Latino L. Rev. 1, 4 (2005).

4.3(b) Ordinal contractions

Ordinal contractions appear in a variety of legal citation references, such as abbreviations for publications issued in series (e.g., Am. Jur. 2d, F.3d) and court name abbreviations (e.g., 2d Cir., 9th Cir.). Legal citation uses just the letter "d" to represent the "nd" and "rd" endings of ordinal contractions for "second" and "third" (e.g., 3d, 22d). Ordinal contractions should not end with a period (i.e., write 3d rather than 3d.).

Avoid using superscript to represent the letters in ordinal contractions (e.g., write 21st rather than 21st); if necessary, disable the automatic superscript feature of your word-processing software. Do not use ordinal numbers in dates (e.g., write June 17 rather than June 17th).

Examples of ordinal contractions

First:	1st	**Fourth:**	4th
Second:	2d	**Twenty-second:**	22d
Third:	3d	**Forty-third:**	43d

5 Page Numbers

5.1 Initial Pages

5.1(a) Definition of "initial page"

The "initial page" is the page on which a cited source begins. For example, the initial page of a case is the page on which the caption appears; the initial page of a law review article is the page showing the title and author.

5.1(b) When to refer to initial page

To assist readers in locating a paginated source that is one of several sources published within a larger work (e.g., a case within a regional reporter, an article within an issue of a periodical), always provide the initial page of the source in its full citation. On the other hand, when you cite a paginated source that stands on its own (e.g., a book, a treatise, a pamphlet), there is no need to refer to the initial page of that source.

Examples (initial page, where required, in red)

Teen Ranch v. Udow, 389 F. Supp. 2d **827**, 831 (W.D. Mich. 2005).

Steven K. Green, *Federalism and the Establishment Clause: A Reassessment*, 38 Creighton L. Rev. **761**, 764–65 (2005).

Akhil Reed Amar, *The Bill of Rights: Creation and Reconstruction* 277 (1998).

5.1(c) Abbreviations "p." and "pp."

Do not use the abbreviations "p." or "pp." before page numbers in a citation. Use these abbreviations only in a document's internal cross-references to its own pages (see **Rule 10.2(a)**).

5.2 Pinpoint Pages

5.2(a) Definition of "pinpoint page"

The *ALWD Guide* uses the term "pinpoint page" to refer to the specific page(s) of a cited source on which a quotation or relevant passage appears. Other terms for such references include "pincite," "jump citation," "jump cite," and "jump page."

5.2(b) When to refer to pinpoint pages

Pinpoint pages indicate the exact location of cited material within a paginated source. Whether you are quoting from the source or otherwise referring to specific information within that source, always add a pinpoint page reference to the citation. For example, if the text refers to the holding of a case, the citation should indicate the page(s) on which the holding appears.

Examples (pinpoint pages in red)

> *Teen Ranch v. Udow*, 389 F. Supp. 2d 827, **832** (W.D. Mich. 2005).

> Steven K. Green, *Federalism and the Establishment Clause: A Reassessment*, 38 Creighton L. Rev. 761, **764–65** (2005).

> Akhil Reed Amar, *The Bill of Rights: Creation and Reconstruction* **277** (1998).

If the pinpoint page number is also the initial page of the cited source, set it out twice; doing so unambiguously tells readers that the cited material not only begins on the cited page but is also found on that page.

Example (pinpoint page in red)

> *P.D.T. v. State*, 996 So. 2d 919, **919** (Fla. Dist. Ct. App. 2008).

5.2(c) Preventing confusion in references to numbers in titles

When the title of a cited source ends in a number, to prevent confusion whether the number is part of the title or a pinpoint page reference, you may insert the preposition "at" before the citation's pinpoint page reference.

Examples

> John C. Maxwell, *Attitude 101*, at 56–57 (2003).

> Constance Backhouse, *Carnal Crimes: Sexual Assault Law in Canada, 1900–1975*, at 276 (2008).

5.3 Consecutive Pages

When providing pinpoint references to material on consecutive pages (also known as a "page span"), set out the beginning and ending page numbers of the span, joined by a hyphen (-), an en dash (–), or the word "to." (**Sidebar 5.2**

SIDEBAR 5.1   **Importance of Using Pinpoint References**

Pinpoint references are essential. Readers are frustrated when citations do not indicate specific pages or other subdivisions where the referenced material appears. And if a judge or judicial law clerk cannot locate support for your position, you may lose credibility with the court, or the court may discount your position. Accordingly, always spend the extra time it takes to insert a pinpoint reference.

contains guidance on using hyphens, en dashes, and "to" in citations.) If pages in the span are numbered 100 or higher, drop repetitious digits, but retain the last two digits for the ending page number.

Examples (page spans in red)

State v. Spikes, 961 A.2d 426, **434–35** (Conn. App. Ct. 2008).

Cynthia S. Duncan, Note, *The Need for Change: An Economic Analysis of Marijuana Policy*, 41 Conn. L. Rev. 1701, **1736–38** (2009).

5.4 Scattered Pages

When providing a pinpoint reference to multiple pages that are not consecutive, separate the page numbers by a comma and one space. Do not use an ampersand (&) or the word "and" before the final page number in the group.

Examples

Correct: 5, 14, 26

Incorrect: 5, 14 & 26

                 5, 14, and 26

SIDEBAR 5.2	**Using Hyphens, En Dashes, and "To" for Spans**

Denote a span of pages or other subdivisions by using a hyphen (-), an en dash (–), or the word "to."

In everyday documents prepared on keyboards, such as memoranda or briefs, most writers use a hyphen to denote such spans. In published materials, however, such as law review articles and books, page spans are normally denoted with an en dash. What's the difference? The length: The en dash is the width of the letter N and the hyphen is shorter. (The "em dash" is the long dash used in punctuation whose length is based on the width of the letter M. Don't use it here.)

Substitute the word "to" for a hyphen or an en dash when it will avoid ambiguity or confusion. For example, some publications use hyphenated numbers to indicate pages or sections (e.g., 53-01, 53-02). In citations to such publications, using a hyphen or en dash to denote a span could confuse readers (53-01–53-02); therefore, most writers will instead use "to" in indicating the span (53-01 to 53-02).

5.5 Star Pagination

5.5(a) Definition of "star pagination"

The terms "star pagination" and "star page" typically indicate page numbering inserted by a publisher that refers the reader to the page numbering used in a different source containing the same material, preceded by one or more asterisks. For example, an unofficial reporter may contain star pagination to a case's page numbering in the official reporter. The terms are also used to describe virtual page numbering displayed in an online source.

5.5(b) Star pages in online databases that reflect pages in print sources

Commercial databases like Lexis Advance, WestlawNext, and Bloomberg BNA often insert star pagination to indicate the beginning of a page in one or more print versions of the same source (e.g., a case published in official and unofficial reporters). Depending on the number of available sources, a publisher's online version may use one asterisk before a numeral to indicate a pinpoint page in the first print source, two asterisks before a numeral to indicate a page in the second print source, and so on. While you may rely on star pagination to locate a page in a print source, when you provide the pinpoint reference in the citation, omit the asterisk(s). Other publishers may place brackets around star pages (e.g., [34]); omit the brackets.

Examples

Caption from case in WestlawNext:

Gideon v. Wainwright
Supreme Court of the United States   March 18, 1963   372 U.S. 335   83 S.Ct. 792 *(Approx. 11 pages)*

Document   Filings (12)   Negative Treatment (123)   History (4)   Citing References (23,138)   *Powered by* KeyCite

Abrogation Recognized by Pueblo v. Dolce, P.R., December 13, 1976

Original Image of 83 S.Ct. 792 (PDF)

83 S.Ct. 792
Supreme Court of the United States

Clarence Earl GIDEON, Petitioner,

v.

Louie L. WAINWRIGHT, Director, Division of Corrections.

No. 155.   Argued Jan. 15, 1963.   Decided March 18, 1963.

Excerpt from WestlawNext displaying star pages (in bold red):

*341 We think the Court in Betts had ample precedent for acknowledging that those guarantees of the Bill of Rights which are fundamental safeguards of liberty immune from federal abridgment are equally protected against state invasion by the Due Process Clause of the Fourteenth Amendment. This same principle was recognized, explained, and applied in Powell v. Alabama, 287 U.S. 45, 53 S. Ct. 55, 77 L. Ed. 158 (1932), a case upholding the right of counsel, where the Court held that despite sweeping language to the contrary in ****795** Hurtado v. California, 110 U.S. 516, 4 S. Ct. 292, 28 L. Ed. 232 (1884), the . . .

Explanation: Look at the caption, and find the references to the reporters in which this case is printed. Star page ***341** reflects the beginning of page 341 in volume 372 of the official *United States Reports* print version of the case. Star page ****795** indicates the beginning of page 795 in volume 83 of the unofficial *Supreme Court Reporter* print version. **Rule 12.4(c)** requires citation to the official reporter where available, so the citation should use star page 341.

(Note: Case names in commercial database text are often not italicized, as the example above demonstrates, or an entire citation may be underlined. Be prepared to make corrections to typeface in your citations and quotations.)

Citation: *Gideon v. Wainwright*, 372 U.S. 335, 341 (1963).

Caption from case in Lexis Advance:

△ Foster v. Winston-Salem Joint Venture, 281 S.E.2d 36 (Copy citation)

Supreme Court of North Carolina
August 17, 1981, Filed
No. 124

Reporter: 303 N.C. 636 | 281 S.E.2d 36 | 1981 N.C. LEXIS 1205

IRENE B. FOSTER v. WINSTON-SALEM JOINT VENTURE, a general partnership; JACOBS, VISCONSI & JACOBS COMPANY; CENTER RIDGE CO.; BELK-HENSDALE COMPANY OF FAYETTEVILLE, N.C., INC.; SEARS, ROEBUCK AND COMPANY; and J. C. PENNEY PROPERTIES, INC.

Reprinted, by permission, from Lexis Advance © LexisNexis.

Excerpt from Lexis Advance displaying star pages (in bold red):

[37] Plaintiff presents two issues for our determination; first, whether plaintiff has a cause of action against defendants in negligence for their alleged failure to provide adequate security in the Hanes Mall parking lot, and second, if it is determined that plaintiff has stated a claim for relief, whether she has presented sufficient evidence in support of her claim to withstand **[38]** defendants' motion for summary judgment. For the reasons stated below, we affirm that portion of the Court of Appeals' decision which held that plaintiff had stated a proper claim for relief, reverse that portion of the decision which found that plaintiff had failed to present sufficient evidence to withstand defendants' motion for summary judgment, and remand for a trial on the merits.

Explanation: Lexis Advance encloses star pages in square brackets. Star page **[37]** reflects the beginning of page 37 in volume 281 of the unofficial *South Eastern Reporter, Second Series* print version of the case. Depending on the reporter you select, the star paging will vary, both in placement and in the numbers themselves. Look at the caption again. The *North Carolina Reports* version of this case begins on page 636 and ends on page 647; were you viewing that version, you would see star page **[638]** at the beginning of the same excerpt shown above. To cite this state case in an office memorandum, follow **Rule 12.4(b)**, which requires citation to the regional reporter where available.

Citation: *Foster v. Winston-Salem Joint Venture*, 281 S.E.2d 36, 37–38 (N.C. 1981).

5.5(c) Star pages in unofficial print reporters that reflect pages in official print reporters

Legal publisher Thomson West uses star pagination in many of its unofficial print reporters to indicate the beginning of pages in the official reporter. While you may rely on star pagination to locate a page in an official print reporter, when you provide the pinpoint reference in the citation, omit the asterisk(s).

5.5(d) Star pages in online sources that do not appear in print

Some online databases use star pagination in sources that appear *only* in electronic format. For example, the database may employ star pagination to reflect the top of a page in an unpublished case (addressed in **Rule 12.13(b)**). Depending on the nature of the online source, retain the asterisk before any reference to an initial page or to the first page of a consecutive span of pages, and before reference to each page of scattered references.

Examples

Jones v. Scotti, No. 11-2213, 2012 WL 4373655, at *4–5 (1st Cir. Sept. 26, 2012).

Goodman v. Genesee Cnty., 2008 Mich. App. LEXIS 161, at *14, *19 (Mich. Ct. App. Jan. 24, 2008).

5.5(e) Star pages in star editions

Many classic sources, such as William Blackstone's *Commentaries* (published in 1765–1769 and whose original edition is consequently not easily accessed), have been republished in later "star editions" whose page numbering reflects that of the original work. When working with a star edition, follow **Rule 20.2** to format page numbers.

5.6   *Passim*

When pinpoint references in a citation would be so numerous as to be unwieldy, you may use the italicized word *passim* to indicate that the references can be found at various places in the cited source. Similarly, you may use *passim* in a brief's table of authorities to indicate a source that is cited repeatedly. Because *passim* does not tell the reader exactly where to find the references, be sure that its use is warranted.

Examples

For a defense of Judge Arnold's conclusions, see Polly J. Price, *Precedent and Judicial Power After the Founding*, 42 B.C. L. Rev. 81 *passim* (2001).

In table of authorities:

Sutton v. United Airlines, Inc., 527 U.S. 471 (1999). . . . . *passim*

6 Sections and Paragraphs

6.1 General Rules for Citing Sections and Paragraphs

Like pinpoint page references **(Rule 5.2)**, citations to sources divided by sections or paragraphs should indicate, to the extent possible, the exact location of the cited material.

6.1(a) Sources divided solely by sections or paragraphs

If a source is divided solely by sections or by paragraphs, provide a pinpoint reference to the relevant subdivisions, including subsections or subparagraphs, if any.

To denote subsections or subparagraphs, use the punctuation or formatting shown in the original source to differentiate main sections or paragraphs from their subdivisions. Section designations sometimes include letters as well as numbers (e.g., "2000e-2"). Because these letters do not refer to subsections, do not use separating punctuation. Omit reference to subsections or subparagraphs when the cited material refers to a higher level that encompasses all such subdivisions.

Examples

> Fed. R. Civ. P. 26(a)(1)(D).
>
> 7 C.F.R. §§ 15d.1–15d.3 (2014).

If the original source does not display any specific punctuation or formatting to differentiate numbered or lettered subdivisions from the main text, place the subdivision designations in parentheses.

Avoid using the preposition "at" before a section or paragraph symbol, even in a short citation.

Examples

| **Correct:** | *Id.* § 35. |
| **Incorrect:** | *Id.* at § 35. |

6.1(b) Sources divided both by pages and by sections or paragraphs

If a source is divided both by pages and by sections or paragraphs, refer to both the page and the section or paragraph in the citation, unless the citation refers to an entire section or paragraph. Set out the section or paragraph number first, followed by a comma and space, followed by the page number on which the cited material appears.

Example

> Julian Conrad Juergensmeyer & Thomas E. Roberts, *Land Use Planning and Control Law* § 10.4, 425 (2d ed. 2007).

Although you should not use the preposition "at" before a pinpoint reference to a section or paragraph **(Rule 6.1(a))**, if it might be unclear whether a citation refers to a paragraph or section number or to a page number, you may insert ", at" before a pinpoint *page* number. For example, a citation might be interpreted as referring to scattered section numbers when in fact it was intended to refer to certain sections on a given page.

Example

> Bernard J. Hibbitts, *The Technology of Law*, 102 Law Libr. J. ¶¶ 25–28, at 105–06 (2010).

6.2 Spacing with Section and Paragraph Symbols

Insert a space between a section (§) or paragraph (¶) symbol and the number or letter that follows. Do not insert a space between a main section and its own subdivision(s). Do not insert a space between two section symbols (§§) or two paragraph symbols (¶¶).

Examples (spaces denoted by ▲)

§▲1710(b)(3)

¶¶▲A–C

§§▲22.05(a),▲22.07

6.3 Consecutive Sections or Paragraphs

6.3(a) Indicating span of specific sections or paragraphs

To provide a pinpoint reference to a span of consecutive sections or paragraphs, set out the beginning and ending subdivisions of the span, separated with a hyphen (-), an en dash (–), or the word "to." Use two section (§§) or paragraph (¶¶) symbols, even if the span contains more than two sections or paragraphs. While you should ordinarily retain all digits or letters on either side of the span, you may omit identical digits or letters that *precede* a punctuation mark if doing so will not be confusing to the reader.

Examples

§§ 1–55   §§ 1961–1965

¶¶ 73–107   ¶¶ 14.30–.50

6.3(b) *Et seq.*

Avoid using the abbreviation "*et seq.*" to denote a span of sections. "*Et seq.*" is not a helpful reference; it simply means "and the following ones." Set out the actual span.

Examples

Correct:	15 U.S.C. §§ 2301–2310 (2012).
Incorrect:	15 U.S.C. §§ 2301 *et seq.* (2012).

6.3(c) Indicating consecutive subdivisions within a single section or paragraph

To provide a pinpoint reference to multiple subsections or subparagraphs that fall within a single section or paragraph, follow **Rule 6.4(a)**, but use a single section (§) or paragraph (¶) symbol.

Examples (spaces denoted by ▲)

§▲22(a)–(c)

¶▲3601(a)–(c)

¶▲3601(a)▲to▲(c)

6.4 Scattered Sections or Paragraphs

6.4(a) Indicating scattered sections or paragraphs

To provide a pinpoint reference to multiple, nonconsecutive sections or paragraphs, use two section (§§) or paragraph (¶¶) symbols followed by a space and by the section or paragraph numbers, separated by commas and spaces. Do not use an ampersand (&) or the word "and" before the final number.

Examples (spaces denoted by ▲)

§§▲1961,▲1963,▲1965

¶¶▲47(c),▲58(m),▲107(a)

¶¶▲33(b)(7),▲33(c)(5)

6.4(b) Indicating scattered subdivisions within a single section or paragraph

To provide a pinpoint reference to multiple, nonconsecutive subdivisions located within a single section or paragraph, follow **Rule 6.4(a)**, but use a single section (§) or paragraph (¶) symbol.

Examples (spaces denoted by ▲)

§▲1961(a),▲(c),▲(e)

¶▲47(c),▲(m)

6.5   Unnumbered Paragraphs

For sources containing indented, but unnumbered, paragraphs, use the abbreviation "para." (plural, "paras.") rather than the paragraph symbol.

Example

18 U.S.C. § 1546(a) para. 3 (2012).

6.6   Referring to Sections and Paragraphs in Text

To refer to a specific section or paragraph in text, use the symbol (§ or ¶) or spell out the word ("section" or "paragraph"). Never begin a sentence with a symbol.

Examples

The police officers sought immunity under § 1983.

The police officers sought immunity under section 1983.

Section 1983 might provide a defense for police officers charged with conducting an illegal search.

The agency asserted that it had jurisdiction under ¶¶ 10–12.

The complaint alleged the defendant had violated Title 18 United States Code, Sections 1591 and 1594(a).

7 Footnotes and Endnotes

7.1 General Rules for Citing Footnotes and Endnotes Within a Source

To cite a footnote or an endnote within a source, set out the page of the source on which the note begins (even if it spans two or more pages), followed by the abbreviation "n." (plural, "nn.") and the note number(s), *with no intervening space between them.* Use this method as well to cite consecutive notes on a single page. For endnotes, cite the actual page on which the endnote appears, not the page containing its note reference. To cite specific pages of a footnote or endnote that spans multiple pages, set out only those specific pages. Note that if you perform your research in an online database, depending on the source, it can be difficult, if not impossible, to determine whether a note spans multiple pages. For that reason, consult a print copy of the source if it is available.

Examples

Citation to a single footnote:	Sarah Howard Jenkins, *Application of the U.C.C. to Nonpayment Virtual Assets or Digital Art*, 11 Duq. Bus. L.J. 245, 248 n.8 (2009).
	Sanders v. Mountain Am. Fed. Credit Union, 689 F.3d 1138, 1142 n.2 (10th Cir. 2012).
Citation to consecutive notes on a single page:	John J. Brunetti, *Searching for Methods of Trial Court Fact-Finding and Decision-Making*, 49 Hastings L.J. 1491, 1494 nn.15–17 (1998).
Citation to single note that spans multiple pages:	Howard J. Bashman, *Recusal on Appeal: An Appellate Advocate's Perspective*, 7 J. App. Prac. & Process 59, 64–65 n.9 (2005).

To cite scattered notes on a single page, join the final two note numbers with an ampersand (&). To cite both a page in the source and a note on that page, set out the page number, followed by an ampersand, the abbreviation "n." (or "nn."), and the note number(s).

Examples

Citation to scattered notes on a single page:	Susanna L. Blumenthal, *Law and the Creative Mind*, 74 Chi.-Kent L. Rev. 151, 158 nn.20, 21 & 23 (1998).
Citation to consecutive notes on span of pages:	*World Wide Minerals, Ltd. v. Republic of Kaz.*, 296 F.3d 1154, 1166–67 nn.19–22 (D.C. Cir. 2002).

| Citation to scattered notes on nonconsecutive pages: | John H. Langbein, *Chancellor Kent and the History of Legal Literature*, 93 Colum. L. Rev. 547, 567 n.100, 569 n.108 (1993). |
| Citation to page in text and note on same page: | Roy Stuckey et al., *Best Practices for Legal Education: A Vision and a Road Map* 110 & n.323 (2007). |

7.2 Preventing Confusion in a Single Citation's References to Notes and Pages

You may need to deviate from the general rules to ensure that the reader will not be confused about which numbers in a citation refer to pages and which refer to notes. For example, in following the general rules to cite footnotes 2 and 5 on page 16 of an article, as well as material on page 18 of that same article, the citation's pinpoint reference would appear as follows: 16 nn.2, 5, 18. A reader might think, however, that "18" refers to a third footnote instead of the later page. The simplest way to resolve this dilemma is to provide two citations, one to the referenced notes and the next to the later page, as shown in the example below.

Example

Harold J. Berman, *The Historical Foundations of Law*, 54 Emory L.J. 13, 16 nn.2–5 (2005); *id.* at 18.

7.3 Citing Footnotes and Endnotes in Short Citations

Short citation formats are discussed generally in **Rule 11.2** and are discussed specifically within each rule that addresses a particular type of source.

Writers sometimes are unsure how best to provide pinpoint references to footnotes or endnotes when *id.* is the short citation. There are two alternatives for handling this situation, as shown below. (Note: Although the examples are from academic footnotes, the *short citations* would be formatted the same in a practice-based document.)

First alternative

> [5]Harold J. Berman, *The Historical Foundations of Law*, 54 EMORY L.J. 13, 16 nn.2–5 (2005).

⚠ACADEMIC FORMATTING

> [6] *Id.* at 16 n.4.

> [7] *Id.* at 18 n.7.

Second alternative

> [5]Harold J. Berman, *The Historical Foundations of Law*, 54 EMORY L.J. 13, 16 nn.2–5 (2005).

⚠ACADEMIC FORMATTING

> [6] *Id.* at n.4.

> [7] *Id.* at 18 n.7.

In the first alternative, footnote 6 includes the pinpoint page from the previous footnote, while in the second alternative, footnote 6 does not repeat the page. The second alternative is technically more accurate under **Rule 11.3**, but many writers prefer the first alternative. Once you select an alternative, use it consistently.

8   Supplements

Many legal texts are regularly updated by pocket parts or supplemental pamphlets. The material to be cited may be located solely in the supplement, solely in the main volume, or in both the main volume and the supplement. Use this rule to indicate the location of the material by modifying the citation's date parenthetical, as shown below.

8.1   Sources Found Only in Supplements

To indicate a source that appears solely in a supplement, insert the abbreviation "Supp." after the opening parenthesis of the citation's date parenthetical. If the supplement is numbered or its name is otherwise modified, include that information as well. Set out the year of the supplement's publication, and close the parentheses.

Examples

18 U.S.C. § 1965 (Supp. 2010).

42 U.S.C. § 3796hh (Supp. I 2001).

Or. Rev. Stat. Ann. § 540.520 (West Supp. 2009).

If the supplement updates a later edition of the main work, insert the abbreviation "Supp." and its publication date after the edition.

Example

John Wesley Hall, Jr., *Professional Responsibility in Criminal Defense Practice* § 9:3.50 (3d ed. Supp. 2012).

8.2   Sources Found Only in Main Volume of a Supplemented Work

To indicate a source that appears solely in the main volume of a work with supplements, use only the publication date of the main volume in the date parenthetical. Omit reference to the supplement. Consult the rule for the specific source being cited (e.g., **Rule 14.2(h)** for statutes; **Rule 20.1(e)(5)** for books).

Examples

18 U.S.C. § 1965 (2012).

John Wesley Hall, Jr., *Professional Responsibility in Criminal Defense Practice* § 14:2 (3d ed. 2005).

8.3   Sources Found in Both a Main Volume and a Supplement

To indicate a source that appears in both a main volume and its supplement, use both dates in the date parenthetical. Set out the date of the main volume first, followed by an ampersand (&) and a reference to the supplement and its date.

Examples

> 18 U.S.C. § 1965 (2000 & Supp. IV 2004).
>
> John Wesley Hall, Jr., *Professional Responsibility in Criminal Defense Practice* § 28:19 (3d ed. 2005 & Supp. 2012).

8.4   Sources Found in Multiple Supplements

If a cited source appears in multiple supplements, cite the supplements in chronological order.

Examples

Multiple supplements, different years:	(Supps. IV 1999 & V 2000).
Multiple supplements, same year:	(Supps. IV & V 1994).
Main volume and supplements in different years:	(1988 & Supps. I 1989, II 1990, III 1991, IV 1992, V 1993).
Supplements to later edition:	(2d ed. Supps. 1994 & 1996).

9 Graphical Material, Appendices, and Other Subdivisions

9.1 Graphical Material

To cite graphical material such as tables, charts, figures, graphs, or illustrations, set out the pinpoint page number on which the graphical material begins, the abbreviation from **Appendix 3(C)** (if any) for the particular type of graphical material cited, and the number, letter, or other designation for the graphical material, if any. For several abbreviations in **Appendix 3(C)** (e.g., **fig.**, **rptr.**, **nn.**), a note instructs you to omit any space between the abbreviation and a number following it. To cite multiple graphics, analogize to citing multiple sections or paragraphs (see **Rules 6.3** and **6.4**).

Examples

Bryan A. Garner, *The Winning Brief* 413 chart (2d ed. 2004).

[87] Gary L. Blasi, *What Lawyers Know: Lawyering Expertise, Cognitive Science, and the Functions of Theory*, 45 J. Leg. Educ. 313, 370 fig.4 (1995).

⚠ ACADEMIC FORMATTING

9.2 Preventing Confusion in References to Graphical Material

You may need to deviate from the general rules to prevent reader confusion about which numbers refer to pages, sections, or paragraphs and which refer to graphical material. In such instances, analogize to the solutions presented in **Rules 6.1(b)** and **7.2**.

9.3 Appendices

9.3(a) Entire appendix

To cite an entire appendix, determine whether the appendix belongs to the entire source (e.g., an appendix to a law review article) or to a specific portion of the source (e.g., an appendix to a book chapter), and place a comma, one space, and the abbreviation "app." immediately following the appropriate component of the citation. For example, if an appendix is attached to a law review article, provide the initial page of the law review article and then designate the appendix. If the appendix is attached to a particular chapter of a book, provide the book's chapter number, and then refer to the appendix.

If the appendix has a designation, such as a number or letter, insert one space between "app." and the designation. The abbreviation for multiple appendices is "apps." To cite multiple appendices, analogize to citing multiple sections and paragraphs (**Rules 6.4** and **6.5**).

Examples

Federal Advisory Committee Act, 5 U.S.C. app. (2012).

M.H. Sam Jacobson, *Providing Academic Support Without an Academic Support Environment*, 3 Leg. Writing 241, app. B (1997).

Thompson v. Oklahoma, 487 U.S. 815, apps. A–F (1988).

9.3(b) Material within an appendix

To provide a pinpoint reference to specific material within an appendix, place a comma and one space after the appendix designation; then insert the pinpoint reference.

Examples

Federal Advisory Committee Act, 5 U.S.C. app., § 4 (2012).

M.H. Sam Jacobson, *Providing Academic Support Without an Academic Support Environment*, 3 Leg. Writing 241, app. B, 261–63 (1997).

9.4 Other Subdivisions

To cite a subdivision not specifically described in **Rules 5** through **9.3**, use the most similar subdivision as an analogy. Consult **Appendix 3(C)** for the appropriate abbreviation (if any) for the subdivision.

Examples

Chapter:	Philip C. Kissam, *The Discipline of Law Schools: The Making of Modern Lawyers* ch. 3 (2003).
Comment:	Model Rules of Prof'l Conduct R. 7.3 cmt. 5 (2013).
Historical notes:	Mass. Gen. Laws Ann. ch. 211, § 2A hist. nn. (West 2005 & Supp. 2013).

10 Internal Cross-References

10.1 Definition of "Internal Cross-Reference"

An "internal cross-reference" refers readers to material located in another part of the document they are reading, such as text, appendices, footnotes, or pages. Internal cross-references are most commonly used in academic footnotes or endnotes, but you may encounter them in other kinds of sources, such as judicial opinions. Most attorneys do not use internal cross-references in documents without footnotes or endnotes. Do not use an internal cross-reference to cite a previously cited source outside the document, such as a case or a statute; instead use an appropriate short citation to that source. Short citations are addressed in **Rules 11.2** through **11.4**.

10.2 (FN) Constructing an Internal Cross-Reference

10.2(a)(FN) Indicating location of cross-references with *supra* and *infra*

⚠ ACADEMIC FORMATTING

Provide the most specific reference possible, and if warranted, introduce the cross-reference with a signal **(Rule 35)**. To cross-reference material that appears earlier in the document, use the appropriate signal before the italicized term *supra* (meaning "above"), followed by a reference to the specific location of the material. For material appearing later in the document, use the appropriate signal and the italicized term *infra* ("below"). (For information about using *supra* in a short citation, rather than as a cross-reference, see **Rule 11.4**.)

Unless cross-referencing specific pages within a document, spell out cross-references to its footnotes, tables, figures, appendices, and other internal subdivisions. To cross-reference the document's own pages, use the abbreviations "p." or "pp." before the page number(s).

Examples

Cross-referencing an earlier discussion:	[125]*See supra* text accompanying note 75.
Cross-referencing a later portion of document:	[133]*See infra* Part IV.
Cross-referencing specific pages:	[88]*See infra* pp. 25–26.

10.2(b)(FN) Adding explanatory parentheticals to cross-references

⚠ ACADEMIC FORMATTING

If the accompanying text or citation does not adequately identify the subject of the cross-reference, add an explanatory parenthetical. For more information about using explanatory parentheticals, see **Rule 37.**

Examples

[34] *See supra* notes 20–31 (examining history of Supreme Court's decisions on attorney advertising).

[47] *See infra* Part C(1) (explaining proper deposition objections).

11 Full and Short Citation Formats

11.1 Full Citation Format

11.1(a) Definition of "full citation"

A "full citation" is one that includes each component required for the first reference to a particular source. It gives readers necessary and sufficient information to locate that source in print or in an electronic version.

11.1(b) Components of a full citation

The components of a full citation to each type of source are illustrated in **Rules 12** through **29**. The information provided in a full citation typically includes the author's name (if any); the title or name of the source; a specific reference to the volume, page, section, or other subdivision within which the referenced material is located; and the date.

11.1(c) Frequency of full citation to source in practice-based document

In practice-based documents, provide a full citation to a source the first time it is cited. If desired, however, or if required by local court rule (see **Appendix 2**), you may cite a source in full more frequently, such as each time the source is cited for the first time in a new section of the document.

11.1(d)(FN) Frequency of full citation to source in academic footnotes

⚠ ACADEMIC FORMATTING

In documents with academic footnotes, always repeat the full citation to a *primary authority* if the authority has not been cited in full or in short form (including *id.*) in one of the previous five footnotes. It is not necessary to repeat full citations to secondary materials and other non-primary sources cited in documents with academic footnotes; instead, use the *supra* short citation to send readers to the original footnote containing the source's full citation (see **Rule 11.4**).

11.2 Short Citation Format

Once a source has been cited in full, the writer may generally use a short citation thereafter to refer to the source. A short citation omits some of the required components of a source's full citation components, while still providing enough information for readers to identify the source and relate it to the earlier full citation. Short citations save space and are less disruptive to the flow of text than are full citations.

Use short citations when the reader will neither be confused about the source being referenced nor have trouble quickly locating the source's full citation. The type of short citation to use will vary depending on the nature of the source, the location of the short citation in relation to the full citation, and whether the citation appears in a practice-based document, such as an office memorandum or a brief, or in an academic footnote, such as those used in law review articles and treatises.

Each rule in the *ALWD Guide* for a specific source contains in-depth information on its full and short citation formats. Accordingly, consult a source's rule for an explanation and examples of its short citation formats. The remainder of **Rule 11** deals with short citations that may be used for most types of sources.

11.3 *Id.* as a Short Citation

11.3(a) Definition of "*id.*"

"*Id.*" is the abbreviation for the Latin word "*idem*," meaning "the same." *Id.* refers to everything that is *id*entical to the previous citation, including the page number or other pinpoint reference, if it has not changed. *Id.* tells readers that you are citing the same source just cited. Where it is appropriate, *id.* is the preferred short citation.

11.3(b) Typeface and capitalization of *id.*

Italicize *id.* and its period. If you use underlining, be sure to underline the period (id.). When the word *id.* begins a citation, capitalize the letter "I." If *id.* is not the first word in a citation, however, use a lowercase "i."

Examples

Any object may suffice as a simulated deadly weapon, provided the victim reasonably perceives it to be an actual weapon. State v. Felix, 737 P.2d 393, 394 (Ariz. Ct. App. 1986). When the defendant in *Felix* pressed a nasal inhaler against his victim's back, declaring that he had a gun, the victim was convinced that the object he felt was a gun. Id. at 396. On these facts, the court had no difficulty in ruling that the defendant had simulated a deadly weapon. See id.

[18] Nollan v. Cal. Coastal Comm'n, 483 U.S. 825, 834 (1987). ⚠ ACADEMIC FORMATTING

[19] *Id.*

[20] *See id.* at 835.

11.3(c) Appropriate uses of *id.*

Use *id.* to cite the same material just cited in the immediately preceding citation, whether it appears in text or in an academic footnote. (Note: *Id.* is used in legal citations the same way *ibid.* is used in non-legal citation systems.) Because *id.* refers to the identical source, do not use this short form if the previous textual citation or academic footnote refers to two or more sources.

You may use *id.* as a short citation for any source except an appellate record (**Rule 25.6**) or an internal cross-reference (**Rule 10**). In a parallel case citation, *id.* replaces the first cited source, but not the second (see **Rule 12.19(e)** for more information).

Examples (in practice-based documents)

Some states have enforced surrogacy agreements. For example, the California Supreme Court held that surrogacy contracts do not violate the policies governing the termination of parental

Full citation for first ——— rights. *Johnson v. Calvert*, **851 P.2d 776, 784**
reference to *Johnson* **(Cal. 1993).** The court reached this ruling because the contract was based on services, not on the termination of parental rights.

Id. refers to same case ——— *Id.* Other states, however, have refused
and page of *Johnson* to enforce surrogacy agreements. The Massachusetts Supreme Court, for example, held that a contract in which the birth mother receives payment for her services is not enforceable if the payment is used to influence her decision to relinquish custody.

Full citation for first ——— *R.R. v. M.H.*, **689 N.E.2d 790, 796 (Mass.**
reference to *R.R.* **1998).** In *R.R.*, the surrogate was artificially inseminated with the intended father's

Id. refers to *R.R.* but to ——— sperm. *Id.* **at 791.** Because the contract
page 791 indicated that the surrogate would receive $10,000 for delivering the child, the court refused to enforce the contract, reasoning

Id. refers to page 796 of *R.R.* ⟍ that the payment vitiated the surrogate's
⟍ intent. *Id.* **at 796.**

Reference to *Johnson* does not The California court gave several public
use *id.* because *R.R.* was last ⟍ policy reasons why surrogacy contracts
source cited ⟍ should be enforced. *Johnson*, **851 P.2d at 784.**

In a string citation (multiple sources cited to support the same proposition), *id.* cannot be used to refer to the entire string or to any source cited in the string. Instead, the subsequent citations to these cases use a short form other than *id.*

The problems of sexual assault at colleges and universities—usually fueled by alcohol—have continued to vex courts. Two important decisions have occurred since 1999 that are potentially reconcilable with our theory: *Freeman v. Busch*, 349 F.3d 582 (8th Cir. 2003); *Stanton v. Univ. Me. Sys.*, 773 A.2d 1045 (Me. 2001). Both cases involved female students being sexually assaulted in residence halls. *Freeman*, 349 F.3d at 585; *Stanton*, 773 A.2d at 1047–48.

11.3(d) *Id.* followed by pinpoint reference

When citing a source whose pinpoint reference *has not* changed from the immediately preceding citation, use *id.* by itself to refer both to the source and to the pinpoint reference. If the source is the same but the pinpoint reference *has* changed, use *id.* followed by the new pinpoint reference. When citing a source whose pinpoint references are *page numbers*, insert the preposition "at" between *id.* and the new page number. Do not use "at" before other types of pinpoint references.

Examples

Page number:	*Id.* at 321.
Section number:	*Id.* § 14.3.
Paragraph number:	*Id.* ¶ 6-6.
Other reference:	*Id.* app. 1.

11.3(e) Using *id.* to refer to a shorter work within a collection

When citing a shorter work in a collection, use *id.* to refer to the shorter work, not to the overall collection. For examples, see **Rule 20.6(c)**.

11.3(f) Intervening sources

Sources referenced in an explanatory parenthetical (**Rule 37**), a subsequent history designation (**Rule 12.8**), or a prior history designation (**Rule 12.9**) are not considered intervening sources for purposes of determining whether to use *id.* The following examples reflect the correct use of *id.*

Examples

<table>
<tr>
<td>Practice-based document</td>
<td>An abuse of discretion standard applies to the district court's failure to conduct a mental competency hearing. United States v. Ruston, 565 F.3d 892, 901 (5th Cir. 2009) ("Whether the district court erred in not sua sponte holding a competency hearing is reviewed for abuse of discretion."); United States v. Messervey, 317 F.3d 457, 463 (5th Cir. 2002). The Fifth Circuit acknowledges that " '[t]he district court is in the best position to determine the need for a competency hearing.' " Ruston, 565 F.3d at 901 (citation omitted). It is clear, however, that "[i]n determining whether [it] should order a mental competency hearing, the court must consider three factors: (1) the existence of a history of irrational behavior, (2) the defendant's demeanor at trial, and (3) prior medical opinion on competency." Id. at 902 (citing Messervey, 317 F.3d at 463). Although all three factors are relevant to determining whether further inquiry is warranted, under certain circumstances, "even one of these factors standing alone" may be sufficient. Id.</td>
</tr>
<tr>
<td>Document with academic footnotes</td>
<td>

[100] Haw. Hous. Auth. v. Midkiff, 467 U.S. 229, 241 (1984) (quoting United States v. Gettysburg Elec. Ry., 160 U.S. 668, 680 (1896)).   ⚠ ACADEMIC FORMATTING

[101] **_Id._ at 242.**

[102] 634 N.Y.S.2d 740 (App. Div. 1995), aff'd, 679 N.E.2d 1035 (N.Y. 1997).

[103] **_Id._ at 741.**

</td>
</tr>
</table>

11.4 *Supra* in a Short Citation

11.4(a) Definition of "*supra*"

The term "*supra*," which means "above," indicates that a full citation to the cited source can be found earlier in the document. This use of *supra* is different from the internal cross-reference use of *supra* described in **Rule 10.2(a)(FN)**.

11.4(b) Appropriate uses of *supra* in practice-based documents

The *supra* citation format cannot be used for every type of source or cross-reference. Do not use *supra* to refer to an earlier citation of the following primary sources of law: cases, statutes, session laws, ordinances, legislative materials (other than hearings), constitutions, or administrative regulations. You may, however, use it to refer to earlier full citations of secondary sources such as books, treatises, and periodicals.

As with any short citation, use *supra* only after the source has been cited once in full citation format. Do not use *supra* if *id.* would be appropriate.

11.4(c) Format of short citations using *supra* in practice-based documents

For the *supra* short citation in a practice-based document, use the following format:

> **Author's last name (or if no author, the title of the work), | *supra*, | [at] | Pinpoint reference.**

If the pinpoint reference is a page of the cited work, insert the preposition "at" before the new page number. Do not insert "at" before paragraph or section symbols.

Example

> Since the days of the Salem witch trials, the accuracy of children's testimony has been suspect. Michelle L. Morris, *Li'l People, Little Justice: The Effects of the Witness Competency Standard in California on Children in Sexual Abuse Cases*, 22 J. Juv. L. 113, 114 (2001–2002). The reason, however, is not the child's age. Even in the late nineteenth century, the United States Supreme Court upheld the competency of children as witnesses and stated that there is no minimum age for child competency. *See Wheeler v. United States*, 159 U.S. 523, 526 (1895). Addressing whether a five-year-old was competent to testify in a murder trial, the Court stated "that the boy was not by reason of his youth, as a matter of law, absolutely disqualified as a witness . . . . While no one would think of calling an infant of only two or three years old, there is no precise age which determines the question of competency." *Id.* However, a judge must still assess the child's qualifications for testifying. "This was a conditional competency standard, not a per se rule declaring children competent to testify." **Morris, *supra*, at 114.**

11.4(d)(FN)   Appropriate uses of *supra* in academic footnotes

⚠ ACADEMIC FORMATTING

In academic writing, *supra* is appropriate only for a reference to the source's full citation in an earlier footnote. Even in academic footnotes, however, do not use *supra* for short citation references to the following primary sources of law: cases, statutes, session laws, ordinances, legislative materials (other than hearings), constitutions, or administrative regulations. Use *supra* for short citation references to other administrative, legislative, or executive materials and for references to secondary sources such as books, law review articles, and web sites.

11.4(e)(FN)   Format of short citations using *supra* in academic footnotes

⚠ ACADEMIC FORMATTING

For the *supra* short citation in an academic footnote, use the following format:

Author's last name (or if no author, the title of the work), | *supra* | note | [number of footnote containing full citation to source] | [at] | Pinpoint reference.

If the pinpoint reference is to a page of the cited work, insert the preposition "at" before the new page number. Do not insert "at" before paragraph or section symbols.

Examples

[45] Kristen David Adams, *Do We Need a Right to Housing?*, 9 Nev. L.J. 275, 303 (2009).

.   .   .

[57] Adams, *supra* note 45, at 318.

.   .   .

[84] Joshua Dressler, Understanding Criminal Law § 10.04[A][1] (3d ed. 2001).

.   .   .

[95] Dressler, *supra* note 84, § 10.03.

11.5   Designating a Shortened Reference with "Hereinafter"

11.5(a)   Function of "hereinafter" designation

The "hereinafter" designation appended to a full citation alerts readers that the writer will use a shortened reference to the cited source in subsequent citations. It can be used to provide a shorter *supra* citation or to shorten a long title that would otherwise be used in the short citation format. While it may be used in practice-based documents, its primary use is in academic footnotes, as you will see in the examples in **Rule 11.5(c)(FN)**.

11.5(b) Format of "hereinafter" designation

Immediately following the first full citation to the source, insert one space and an opening square bracket, followed by the word "hereinafter," in ordinary type, one space, the shortened reference, and a closing square bracket. Depending on the nature of the source, the shortened reference may be an author's surname and a shortened version of the title, or if the full citation did not have an author, just a shortened title. Present the information following "hereinafter" in the same typeface as the material appears in its full citation. Place the "hereinafter" information before any explanatory parenthetical.

Example

As a general matter, "courts have had a fair amount of trouble developing standards for distinguishing frivolous cases from ordinary losers." Charles M. Yablon, *The Good, the Bad, and the Frivolous Case: An Essay on Probability and Rule 11*, 44 U.C.L.A. L. Rev. 65, 66, 94 (1996) [hereinafter Yablon, *Essay on Probability*]. A study of Rule 11 reversals by the federal courts of appeals revealed that in 19 percent of those cases, the appellate courts concluded that the cases had merit, even though the district courts had not viewed them as such. Federal Judicial Ctr., *Rule 11: Final Report to the Advisory Committee on Civil Rules of the Judicial Conference of the United States* 21 (1991). Certainly this statistic shows that courts can disagree about what makes a case frivolous. Yablon, *Essay on Probability*, 44 U.C.L.A. L. Rev. at 94.

11.5(c)(FN) Appropriate use of "hereinafter" designation in academic footnotes

⚠ ACADEMIC FORMATTING

Use "hereinafter" in the following circumstances:

★ When the cited source has no author and the title is long.

Example

[65] *Terrorism: Victims' Access to Terrorist Assets: Hearing Before the Senate Committee on the Judiciary*, 106th Cong. 17 (1999) [hereinafter *Terrorism Hearing*].

. . .

[74] *Terrorism Hearing, supra* note 65, at 19.

★ When full citations to two or more works from the *same* author appear in the same academic footnote (to prevent confusion in subsequent short citations over which of the author's works is being cited).

Example

> [5] Lani Guinier, *Lessons and Challenges of Becoming Gentlemen*, 24 N.Y.U. REV. L. & SOC. CHANGE 1, 11 (1998) [hereinafter Guinier, *Lessons*]; Lani Guinier, *Reframing the Affirmative Action Debate*, 86 KY. L.J. 505, 517–18 (1997–1998) [hereinafter Guinier, *Reframing Debate*].
>
> . . .
>
> [18] Guinier, *Lessons*, *supra* note 5, at 12–15.
>
> [19] *Id.* at 13, 17.
>
> [20] Guinier, *Reframing Debate*, *supra* note 5, at 520.

★ When the regular shortened form might confuse the reader, or when the "hereinafter" designation would help readers more easily recognize the source.

> [84] Memorandum for the Heads of Executive Departments and Agencies, 28 Fed. Reg. 10,943 (Oct. 12, 1963), 3 C.F.R. § 861 (1959–1963) [hereinafter Kennedy Memo].
>
> . . .
>
> [93] Kennedy Memo, 28 Fed. Reg. at 10,943.

Part 3
Citing Specific Sources

12 Cases

Fast Formats

	Cases
United States Supreme Court	*Citizens United v. Fed. Election Comm'n*, 558 U.S. 310, 365–66 (2010).
United States Court of Appeals	*United States v. Mahin*, 668 F.3d 119, 123 (4th Cir. 2012).
	Bradley v. Looten, 450 F. App'x 558, 559 (8th Cir. 2012).
United States District Court	*Woollard v. Sheridan*, 863 F. Supp. 2d 462, 469 (D. Md. 2012).
State supreme court	*Firstland Vill. Assocs. v. Lawyer's Title Ins. Co.*, 284 S.E.2d 582, 584 (S.C. 1981).
State intermediate appellate court	*Oberlander v. Handy*, 913 N.E.2d 734, 738 (Ind. Ct. App. 2009).
Parallel citation	*Walder v. Lobel*, 339 Pa. Super. 203, 211–12, 488 A.2d 622, 626 (1985).
Non-majority opinion	*Polsky v. Virnich*, 804 N.W.2d 80, 81 (Wis. 2011) (Abrahamson, C.J., dissenting).
Unpublished opinion	*In re Weisinger*, No. 14-12-00558-CV, 2012 WL 3861960 (Tex. App. Sept. 6, 2012).
Case cited in academic footnote	[153] *See* Quan v. Gonzales, 428 F.3d 883, 888–89 (9th Cir. 2005).
Short citations	913 N.E.2d at 737.
	Oberlander, 913 N.E.2d at 736.
	Id. at 213, 488 A.2d at 627.
	[155] *Quan*, 428 F.3d at 889.

Snapshot
CASES

Before we can order the release of a state prisoner for failure to obtain a "speedy trial," we must be convinced that the failure resulted in the taking of the prisoner's liberty or property without due process of law.

[11, 12] The right to a speedy trial is relative and must always be judged by the surrounding circumstances. Beavers v. Haubert, 198 U.S. 77, 25 S.Ct. 573, 49 L.Ed. 950; United States ex rel. Hanson v. Ragen, 7 Cir., 166 F.2d 608. Under the circumstances shown by the record in this case the delay in bringing Sawyer to trial was not so unreasonable as to contravene his Constitutional rights.

The record shows that Sawyer was indicted on April 25, 1950, and the following day was released on bail. He has been at liberty on bail ever since, so that the delay in bringing him to trial has not resulted in any additional imprisonment.

Sawyer was arraigned on May 5, 1951, more than a year after he was indicted. This is not an unreasonable amount of time considering the fact that Sawyer filed an affidavit of prejudice against the Municipal Judge necessitating the appointment of a special judge, and the fact that Sawyer twice moved to dismiss the indictment listing sixteen grounds.

The state elected to try Krause first on charges that did not involve Sawyer. Krause was convicted and appealed to the Supreme Court of Wisconsin. His principal argument on appeal was that the grand jury, which had indicted both him and Sawyer, had been unlawfully constituted. If the court had upset Krause's indictment, it would have upset Sawyer's as well. It was only reasonable for the state to wait until the validity of the grand jury's action had been determined by the Supreme Court of Wisconsin before going to trial with the Sawyer case.

The only request for extra time made by the state was made on June 5, 1951, when it decided to try Krause first and Sawyer later. This delay was reasonable since the prosecutor could not try them both at the same time, and Krause had been indicted first.

[13] Not only has Sawyer failed to show that the delay in bringing him to trial was unreasonable, but also he failed to ask the court before which his case was pending for an immediate trial. Acquiescence in the delay, by failing to ask the court for immediate trial, waives the right to speedy trial. Miller v. Overholser, 92 U.S.App.D.C. 110, 206 F.2d 415; Fowler v. Hunter, 10 Cir., 164 F.2d 668; Shepherd v. United States, 8 Cir., 163 F. 2d 974; United States v. Albrecht, 7 Cir., 25 F.2d 93. Also see Annotation 129 A.L.R. 572.

Since it involves no prejudicial error, the judgment of the District Court is

Affirmed.

The UNITED STATES of America, Plaintiff-Appellee,

v.

Albert ROVIARO, Defendant-Appellant.

No. 11616.

United States Court of Appeals Seventh Circuit.

Feb. 7, 1956.

Rehearing Denied March 7, 1956.

Defendant was convicted of illegal sale of narcotics and of illegal carriage and possession of same. The United States District Court for the Northern District of Illinois, Eastern Division, Win G. Knoch, J., rendered judgment, and defendant appealed. The Court of Appeals, Lindley, Circuit Judge, held, inter alia, that where there was evidence, without disclosure of identity of informer, to sustain conviction on second count and guilt under second count was suffi-

First party's name: Use Rule 12.2(g) for United States.

Second party's name: Use Rule 12.2(d) for an individual.

Court: Use Appendix 4 to determine abbreviation.

Date of decision: Use Rule 12.7. Ignore the date the rehearing was denied.

Snapshot
CASES

reporter
abbreviation

reporter
volume

UNITED STATES v. ROVIARO   813

Cite as 229 F.2d 812

initial
page
numb

cient to support sentence imposed, disclosure of identity of informer was not necessary, although he was named as purchaser in the first count.

Judgment affirmed.

1. Indictment and Information ⟐121(1)
Witnesses ⟐268(1)
If a person is named in an indictment as an informer and nothing more, defendant is not entitled to have his identity disclosed by bill of particulars or cross-examination.

2. Poisons ⟐9
In prosecution for illegal possession and carriage of narcotics, proof of possession and carriage alone furnished prima facie evidence of guilt, and left defendant with burden to prove that he possessed the narcotics lawfully. Narcotic Drugs Import and Export Act, § 2(c) as amended 21 U.S.C.A. § 174.

3. Poisons ⟐9
In respect to prosecution for illegal possession and carriage of narcotics, wherein there was testimony by government agent that they saw defendant pick up and carry package of narcotics, proof of identity of person to whom defendant sold narcotics was not involved, and disclosure of this person's identity was not required. Narcotic Drugs Import and Export Act, § 2(c) as amended 21 U.S.C.A. § 174.

4. Criminal Law ⟐1177
Where a sentence does not exceed that which may lawfully be imposed under any single count, judgment must be affirmed if evidence is sufficient to sustain any one of the counts.

5. Criminal Law ⟐1177
In prosecution for illegal sale of narcotics and illegal possession and carriage thereof, wherein there was evidence, without disclosure of identity of informer, to sustain conviction on second count and guilt under second count was sufficient to support sentence imposed, disclosure of identity of informer was not necessary, although he was named as

purchaser in the first count. 26 U.S.C.A. (I.R.C.1939) § 2554(a); Narcotic Drugs Import and Export Act, § 2(c) as amended 21 U.S.C.A. § 174.

6. Criminal Law ⟐627½
In narcotics prosecution, wherein there was testimony that several arresting officers participated in the discovery of narcotics in an automobile and wherein one officer testified that he found a package, envelope in which package was preserved and which bore label stating that narcotics had been found by a different participating officer was not required to be produced.

7. Criminal Law ⟐627½
Where a witness does not use his notes or memoranda in court, a party has no absolute right to have them produced and to inspect them, and trial judge has a large discretion in this respect.

———◆———

Maurice J. Walsh, Chicago, Ill., for appellant.

Robert Tieken, U. S. Atty., John Peter Lulinski, Asst. U. S. Atty., Chicago, Ill., Chester E. Emanuelson Asst. U. S. Atty., Chicago, Ill., of counsel, for appellee.

Before FINNEGAN, LINDLEY and SCHNACKENBERG, Circuit Judges.

LINDLEY, Circuit Judge.

In a trial before the court without a jury, defendant was found guilty upon the two counts of an indictment charging that he (1) on August 12, 1954, sold to one John Doe heroin in violation of 26 U.S.C. § 2554(a), and (2) on the same date, in the city of Chicago, knowingly received, concealed and facilitated the transportation, after importation, of heroin in violation of 21 U.S.C.A. § 174. The court entered a general sentence, ordering defendant imprisoned for two years and fined.

Upon appeal, defendant aserts error in that the court (1) denied his petition for a bill of particulars disclosing the home address and occupation of John Doe; (2) unduly limited the cross-examination concerning the identity of the said Doe;

Reprinted, by permission, from *Federal Reporter Second Series* ©
Thomson Reuters/West.

60

12.1 Full Citation Format for Cases

Depending on the publication source(s) and the history of a case, a full case citation may contain up to nine components; many case citations, however, have fewer components.

> *Case name,* | Reporter volume | Reporter abbreviation | Initial page, | Pinpoint page(s) | (Court abbreviation | Date), | *Subsequent history designation,* | Subsequent history citation.

Example

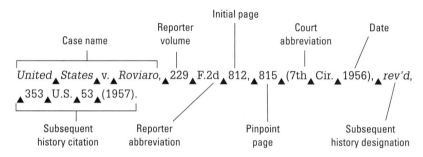

12.2 Case Name

To construct a case name, examine the caption at the top of the case. (A caption is a heading at the top of a court document indicating the presiding court, the parties, the case's identification number, and the nature of the document.) The case name component originates in the caption created for the case's initial pleading (e.g., a plaintiff's complaint, an appellant's notice of appeal). In constructing the case name component, your job is to represent the caption the case bears, but in abbreviated form and in accordance with the subsections of **Rule 12.2(b)** set out below. Do not rely on the case name or abbreviations represented in a running header displayed in the source; they may not comply with these rules.

12.2(a) Typeface for case names

12.2(a)(1) Typeface for case names in practice-based documents
When citing a case within a practice-based document (e.g., an office memorandum or an appellate brief), present the case name and any internal punctuation *within* the case name in *italics* (or <u>underlining</u>, if you have been directed by a court rule or other instruction to use that formatting). Use this typeface regardless whether the citation appears in a full citation or a short citation and whether it appears in a citation sentence, a citation clause, or an embedded

citation (**Rule 34.1**). Use ordinary type for the comma that separates the case name from the remainder of the citation.

Examples (case names in practice-based document citations)

Singh v. Ashcroft, 393 F.3d 903, 905 (9th Cir. 2004).

Locke v. Davey, 540 U.S. 712, 720 (2004).

State ex rel. Gallwey v. Grimm, 48 P.3d 274, 286 (Wash. 2002).

Singh, 393 F.3d at 904.

12.2(a)(2)(FN) Typeface for case names in academic footnotes
⚠ ACADEMIC FORMATTING

When presenting a *full case citation* in an academic footnote, use ordinary type—*not* italics—for the case name and its internal punctuation, if any, but italicize any procedural phrases that may be in the name. (For more information about procedural phrases, see **Rules 12.2(o)** and **Rule 12.2(p)**.)

However, when an academic footnote refers to a case in a *short citation*, italicize the case name reference (see **Rule 12.19(g)**). Use ordinary type for the comma that separates the case name from the remainder of the citation.

Examples (case names in academic footnote citations)

[5] Singh v. Ashcroft, 393 F.3d 903, 905 (9th Cir. 2004).

[6] Locke v. Davey, 540 U.S. 712, 720 (2004).

[7] State *ex rel.* Gallwey v. Grimm, 48 P.3d 274, 286 (Wash. 2002).

[8] *Singh*, 393 F.3d at 904.

12.2(b) Consolidated cases and cases with two names

If a caption displays two or more cases that have been consolidated for the opinion, cite only the first case listed. If a single case has two different names, use the name shown first, unless it is a bankruptcy case. Bankruptcy cases with two names are governed by **Rule 12.2(p)(2)**.

Caption:	Case name:
VIKING PUMP, INC., Plaintiff, v. CENTURY INDEMNITY COMPANY, et al., Defendants. Warren Pumps LLC, Third-Party Plaintiff, v. Century Indemnity Company, et al., Third-Party Defendants. Viking Pump, Inc., Third-Party Plaintiff, v. John Crane, Inc., Houdaille Industries, Inc., Third-Party Defendants	*Viking Pump, Inc. v. Century Indem. Co.,*

SIDEBAR 12.1	**Distinguishing Case Names from Party Names**

In a textual sentence, use *italics* (or <u>underlining</u>) to refer to a case name, but use ordinary type to refer to the person after whom the case is named.

Case name: In *Smith*, the court imposed a ten-year sentence on the defendant.

Person: Smith was sentenced to ten years.

12.2(c) Parties cited

Cite the first-listed party on each side of the case, beginning with the first-listed relator, if any. (A relator is a person or entity who sues or defends on behalf of another interested party or entity, such as a guardian acting on behalf of a minor or an incapacitated ward or a government acting on behalf of a private citizen. See **Rule 12.2(o)** for guidance on indicating relators.)

Some reporters and electronic databases display the first-named party in all capital letters; despite that presentation, capitalize only the first letter of each word used in the party's name. If "v." or "versus" is displayed in the caption, place a lowercase "*v.*" between the names of opposing parties. Omit phrases such as "*et al.*" ("and others"), "*et ux.*" ("and spouse"), or other terms that designate additional or unnamed parties. Omit a caption's references to parties' designations or roles, such as plaintiff, defendant, appellant, appellee, petitioner, respondent, intervenor, administrator, executor, guardian, licensee, or trustee. If a party's name is exceptionally long, you may drop words not essential to its representation.

Examples

Caption:	Case name:
Robert J. Tarbox et al. v. Stephen W. Blaisdell et al.	*Tarbox v. Blaisdell,*
Kathy SMITH, as Executrix for the Estate of Kenneth Smith, Deceased, and Kathy Smith, Individually, Appellant, v. Linda ROHRBAUGH, Appellee	*Smith v. Rohrbaugh,*

12.2(d) Individual as party

12.2(d)(1) Surname

When a case name refers to an individual, use only that person's surname as it is spelled in the caption. Retain all words in the surname, even if it is hyphenated or contains two or more words. Omit surname suffixes such as "Jr." and "III." Omit alternative names for the party introduced by phrases such as "a/k/a" or "aka" ("also known as"). If you are unsure whether a word in a caption is part of an individual's surname, consult the index to the reporter in which the case appears; cases are indexed by surnames. Do not use **Appendix 3** to abbreviate an individual's surname, even if one or more words in that surname appear in **Appendix 3**.

For public officials individually named as parties, see **Rule12.2(m)**.

Examples

Caption:	Case name:
Juma Mussa v. Nikki Palmer-Mussa	*Mussa v. Palmer-Mussa,*
William S. Bailey v. Vernon L. Lanou, Jr.	*Bailey v. Lanou,*

12.2(d)(2) Family names

If a caption displays a party's family name preceding the party's given name, as may be the case for parties of Asian heritage (e.g., Chinese, Korean, Vietnamese), set out the full name of the party as shown in the caption. If the caption displays a party name consisting of two family names, one representing each parent, as may be the case for parties of Portuguese or Spanish heritage, set out both family names as shown in the caption (whether hyphenated or joined by the conjunction "y"). Do not capitalize "y" in a family name. (Hint: If unsure, look at the name in the caption shown in the reporter; if all of a party's names are in capital letters, keep them. Alternatively, consult the index to the reporter in which the case appears, and use the names shown there.)

Examples

Caption:	Case name:
TUAN AHN DU, Plaintiff-Appellant, v. Michael J. ASTRUE, Commissioner of Social Security, Defendant-Appellee	*Tuan Ahn Du v. Astrue,*
The PEOPLE of the State of New York, Respondent, v. Pedro Luis RODRIGUEZ Y PAZ, Appellant	*People v. Rodriguez y Paz,*

12.2(d)(3) Initials of individual

Case captions may use initials to refer to a party whose identity is being shielded (typically because the individual is a juvenile). If a party is designated solely by initials, use all of them as the party name, omitting spaces between consecutive capital letters (see **Rule 2.2(b)**). If a party is represented with a first name and an initial for the surname, retain both the first name and the initial.

Examples

Caption:	Case name (spaces denoted by ▲):
D.P.G., Plaintiff-Appellant, v. L.G., Defendant-Respondent	*D.P.G.*▲*v.*▲*L.G.,*

Ruben M., Appellant, v. Arizona Department of Economic Security, Latina M., Isaiah M., Reynaldo M., Estella T., Appellees	*Ruben▲M.▲v.▲Ariz.▲Dep't▲of▲ Econ.▲Sec.,*

12.2(e) Organization as party

12.2(e)(1) Name of organization

Organizations include legally recognized entities such as companies, corporations, firms, partnerships, airlines, railroads, associations, syndicates, and similar groups. Set out the full name of the organization as shown in the caption, even if the organization is named after a person, abbreviating words as described in **Rule 12.2(e)(2)**.

The name of an organization typically ends with a business designation (e.g., Ass'n, Co.). If an organization's name contains two business designations, delete the second. See **Chart 12.1** for a list of common business designations and their abbreviations; for abbreviations for other business designations, see **Appendix 3(E)**.

Omit "the" as the first word of an organization's name (see also **Rule 12.2(r)**). Omit phrases that come after the organization's name such as "d/b/a" or "dba" ("doing business as"), "f/k/a" ("formerly known as"), and the words following such phrases.

Examples

Caption:	Case name:
Margaret HOWARD and Robert Howard, Co-Executors of the Estate of John C. Ravert, Deceased v. A.W. CHESTERTON CO., Ace Hardware Corp., Monsey Products Co., Pecora Corp. and Union Carbide Corp.	*Howard v. A.W. Chesterton Co.,*
Theresa Rivernider, Appellant, v. Buena Vida Homeowners Association, Inc., a Florida Corporation, Appellee	*Rivernider v. Buena Vida Homeowners Ass'n,*
Goodwyn, Mills & Cawood, Inc., a corporation, Plaintiff, v. Black Swamp, Inc. d/b/a Black Swamp Mitigation Bank, a corporation, and Murphree Evans, an individual, Defendants	*Goodwyn, Mills & Cawood, Inc. v. Black Swamp, Inc.,*

12.2(e)(2) Abbreviated words in organization name

Abbreviate any words in an organization's name that appear in **Appendix 3(E)**. (Note: It may be necessary to modify an abbreviation shown in a caption in order to comply with the word's abbreviation shown in **Appendix 3(E)**.)

Unless otherwise indicated in **Appendix 3(E)**, form an abbreviation's plural by adding "s." You may abbreviate other words of eight or more letters if the abbreviation will save substantial space in the case name and will be easily understood by readers.

Examples

Caption:	Case name:
Ronald M. Bendalin, Appellant, v. Youngblood & Associates, a Texas General Partnership, Eldon L. Youngblood, Hilary Youngblood, and David Pederson, Appellees	*Bendalin v. Youngblood & Assocs.*,
MEDIA GENERAL CABLE OF FAIRFAX, INC., Plaintiff-Appellant, v. SEQUOYAH CONDOMINIUM COUNCIL OF CO-OWNERS; AMSAT Communication, Incorporated, Defendants-Appellees	*Media Gen. Cable of Fairfax, Inc. v. Sequoyah Condo. Council of Co-Owners,*

12.2(e)(3) Commonly known initials in organization name

"Commonly known initials" are a form of abbreviation that people tend to use—in ordinary speech—in place of an organization's full name (e.g., ACLU, NBC, NAACP). When there is no danger of confusion, you may substitute commonly known initials for a party's complete name. Do not insert periods or spaces between commonly known initials. If you are uncertain whether the initials are commonly known, use the organization's complete name, abbreviating any words that appear in **Appendix 3(E)**.

Example

Caption:	Case name:
Alliance for Community Media, et al., Petitioners, v. Federal Communications Commission, et al., Respondents	*Alliance for Cmty. Media v. FCC,*

12.2(f) Union as party

Indicate the name of a union as it is shown in the caption, but if the party is a local unit of the union, omit the caption's subsequent references to larger affiliations (e.g., AFL-CIO), and omit all prepositional phrases indicating location. Otherwise, follow **Rule 12.2(e)** for organization names.

Examples

Caption:	Case name:
Road Sprinkler Fitters Local Union No. 669, U.A., AFL-CIO, Plaintiff-Appellant, v. Dorn Sprinkler Company; Dorn Fire Protection, LLC; Christopher Dorn; David Dorn, Defendants-Appellees	*Road Sprinkler Fitters Local Union No. 669 v. Dorn Sprinkler Co.,*
Jesse James, Plaintiff, v. Enterprise Association of Steamfitters Local 638 of the United Association of Steam, Hot Water, Hydraulic and General Pipe Fitters of New York and Vicinity, Defendant	*James v. Enter. Ass'n of Steamfitters Local 638,*

CHART 12.1	Common Business Designations

Where the chart indicates options between abbreviations with and without periods, select the option shown in the party's name in the case caption. For other business designation abbreviations, see **Appendix 3(E)**.

Business designation:	Abbreviation:
Association	Ass'n
Company	Co.
Corporation	Corp.
Federal Savings Bank	F.S.B.
Incorporated	Inc.
Limited Liability Company	LLC *or* L.L.C.
Limited Liability Limited Partnership	LLLP *or* L.L.L.P.
Limited Liability Partnership	LLP *or* L.L.P.
Limited Partnership	LP *or* L.P.
National Association	N.A.
National Trust and Savings Association	NT & SA *or* N.T. & S.A.
Professional Association	PA *or* P.A.
Professional Corporation	PC *or* P.C.
Professional Limited Liability Company	PLLC *or* P.L.L.C.
Registered Limited Liability Partnership	RLLP *or* R.L.L.P.
Railroad	R.R.
Railway	Ry.
Sociedad Anónima, Société Anonyme	SA *or* S.A.
Societa per Azioni, Sociedad por acciones	S.p.A.

12.2(g) United States as party

When the government of the United States of America is a party, refer to it as "United States"; do not abbreviate it as "US" or "U.S.," regardless of how it may appear in the caption. If the words "of America" are displayed in the caption, omit them. When the words "United States" are used as part of the name of a federal department or agency (**Rule 12.2(k)**) or part of an organization's name (**Rule 12.2(e)**), however, abbreviate them as "U.S."

Examples

Caption:	Case name:
United States of America, Plaintiff-Appellee, v. Johnny E. Hatcher, Defendant-Appellant	*United States v. Hatcher,*
UNITED STATES DEPARTMENT OF COMMERCE, et al., Appellants v. MONTANA, et al., Appellees	*U.S. Dep't of Commerce v. Montana,*
Toth v. United States Steel Corp.	*Toth v. U.S. Steel Corp.*

12.2(h) State or commonwealth as party

When one of the fifty states in the United States is a party, examine the case caption to determine whether the case was decided by a *court of the same state* (e.g., the State of Texas in a case decided by the Texas Supreme Court; the People of Colorado in a case decided by the Colorado Court of Appeals) or by a *court in a different jurisdiction* (e.g., the State of Texas in a case decided by the United States Court of Appeals for the Fifth Circuit; the People of Colorado in a case decided by the United States Supreme Court).

If citing a decision of the *state's own court*, retain only the word "State," "Commonwealth," or "People," depending on which noun appears in the case caption. Omit the prepositional phrase containing the state's name.

If citing a decision of a *different jurisdiction's court*, retain the state's full name but omit the phrase "State of," "Commonwealth of," or "People of." Do not abbreviate the state's name.

Examples

Caption (indicating court):	Case name:
Commonwealth Court of Pennsylvania.	*Commonwealth v. Reynolds,*
Commonwealth of Pennsylvania v. Sandra Reynolds, Appellant	

United States Court of Appeals, Ninth   *Sharer v. Oregon,*
Circuit.

Lois Sharer; Steven Humber,
Plaintiffs-Appellants,
v.
State of Oregon; Peter Ozanne; Peter
Gartlan, Defendants-Appellees

12.2(i) Other geographical references in party names

Many party names contain geographical references. Retain the first geographical reference in a party's name, and abbreviate any of its words that appear in **Appendix 3(B)**; omit any subsequent geographical references in the party name. A practical guide is to omit words following the first comma in the party's name. Omit the word "the" if it appears before a geographical location (**Rule 12.2(r)**).

Follow **Rule 12.2(g)** if the United States of America is itself a party; **Rule 12.2(h)** if a state or commonwealth is a party; and **Rule 12.2(j)** if a city or municipality is a party.

Examples

Caption: **Case name:**

Luana B. OHMER, Petitioner, v.   *Ohmer v. Super. Court of Cal.,*
SUPERIOR COURT OF CALIFORNIA,
COUNTY OF LOS ANGELES,
Respondent

TENNESSEE VALLEY AUTHORITY,   *Tenn. Valley Auth. v. Hill,*
Petitioner, v. Hiram G. HILL, Jr., et al.,
Respondent

12.2(j) City or municipality as party

When a city or municipality is a party, set out its full name, omitting "the" if that article is the first word of the party's name (**Rule 12.2(r)**) and omitting any larger geographical designations following the name (e.g., a county name or a state name).

Examples

Caption: **Case name:**

HISTORIC CHARLESTON FOUNDATION   *Historic Charleston Found. v.*
and Preservation Society of Charleston,   *City of Charleston,*
Respondents, v. The CITY OF
CHARLESTON, The City of Charleston
City Council and Library Associates,
LLC, Appellants

Mary Peters SCHRAMEL, et al.,   *Schramel v. Collegeville*
Appellants, v. Collegeville Township,   *Twp.,*
Minnesota, Respondent

12.2(k) Other governmental entity as party

When a governmental entity such as an agency or department is the first-named party on either side of a case, follow **Rule 12.2(e)** and cite the name of that entity as you would that of an organization. Represent the party's name as it appears in the caption, but abbreviate any words appearing in **Appendix 3(B)** or **Appendix 3(E)**.

When there is no danger of confusion, you may substitute commonly known initials (e.g., FAA, NLRB, OSHA, SEC) for the entity's name, as explained in **Rule 12.2(e)(3)**.

Examples

Caption:	Case name:
Sylvester Grandberry, Petitioner, v. Department of Homeland Security, Respondent	*Grandberry v. Dep't of Homeland Sec.,*
UNITED STATES DEPARTMENT OF JUSTICE, et al., Petitioners, v. REPORTERS COMMITTEE FOR FREEDOM OF THE PRESS, et al., Respondents	*U.S. Dep't of Justice v. Reporters Comm. for Freedom of the Press*

12.2(l) Commissioner of Internal Revenue as party

When the Commissioner of Internal Revenue is listed as a party, abbreviate the word "Commissioner" as "Comm'r"; omit the prepositional phrase "of Internal Revenue."

Example

Caption:	Case name:
Lawrence VIVENZIO and Gloria E. Vivenzio, Petitioners, v. COMMISSIONER OF INTERNAL REVENUE, Respondent	*Vivenzio v. Comm'r,*

12.2(m) Public official as party

When an individual who is a public official is the first-named party on either side of a case, follow **Rule 12.2(d)** to refer to him or her by surname, and omit reference to the person's governmental title. See **Sidebar 12.2** for guidance in citing cases in which a public official is replaced by a successor.

Example

Caption:	Case name:
Ralph E. Price, Plaintiff-Appellant, v. Leon E. Panetta, Secretary of Defense, Department of Defense, and United States, Defendants-Appellees	*Price v. Panetta,*

12.2(n) Real or personal property as party

When a caption lists real or personal property as a party, cite only the first-listed item of such property. If the caption displays a street address for real property, use only that address and omit what follows. Also omit words following the first comma in the party's name, such as larger geographical designations or vehicle identification numbers, for example. Abbreviate any words found in **Appendix 3(E)**.

Examples

Caption:	Case name:
UNITED STATES of America, Plaintiff, v. REAL PROPERTY LOCATED AT 6415 NORTH HARRISON AVE., FRESNO COUNTY, et al., Defendants	*United States v. 6415 N. Harrison Ave.,*
United States of America, Plaintiff, v. One 1987 Chevrolet Corvette, VIN 1G1YY3189H5125250, Defendant	*United States v. One 1987 Chevrolet Corvette,*

SIDEBAR 12.2   Public Official Named as Party

When a federal public official is a party to an action in his or her official capacity and the official leaves office during the pendency of the case, the case name changes to that of the successor. Fed. R. Civ. P. 25(d). Many state rules of civil procedure contain similar provisions about substituting public officials.

For example, although Mickey Kantor was Secretary of Commerce at the time Abraham Friedman brought suit in the Court of International Trade in 1996, by the time the case was appealed to the Federal Circuit, William Daley was the Secretary of Commerce. Thus the case *Friedman v. Kantor*, 977 F. Supp. 1242 (Ct. Int'l Trade 1997), was affirmed on appeal *sub nom. Friedman v. Daley*, 156 F.3d 1358 (Fed. Cir. 1998). (See **Rule 12.8(d)** for more about "*sub nom.*," a Latin abbreviation meaning "under the name of.")

12.2(o) Relator as party; procedural phrase *ex rel.*

A relator is a person or entity who sues or defends on behalf of another interested party or entity, such as a parent on behalf of a minor child, a guardian on behalf of a ward. The procedural phrase "*ex rel.*" (abbreviating "*ex relatione*") indicates that a relator is involved in the case. These relationships are also indicated by phrases in a caption such as "by and through," "for the use of," "on behalf of," and "on the relation of," to name a few.

Begin with the *relator's* name, followed by the procedural phrase *ex rel.* (which replaces any other relationship phrase used in the case name) and then the name of the interested party or entity.

If a caption shows multiple relators or interested parties, cite only the first-listed relator or interested party per side. If a caption lists the interested party first, change the order to begin the case name with the relator. If a caption identifies a party as participating both individually and as a relator, use the party's first-listed status; thus, if a person is first identified as acting individually, omit reference to the person as a relator.

Examples

Caption:	Case name:
Wayne MYLES, Appellant, v. FLORIDA DEPARTMENT OF REVENUE on behalf of Natricia A. BATCHELOR, Appellee	*Myles v. Fla. Dep't of Revenue ex rel. Batchelor,*
Nydreeka Williams, by and through her Mother and next friend, Theresa Raymond, and Theresa Raymond, as Administrator of the Estate of Robert Earl Williams, Deceased v. Wal-Mart Stores East, L.P., and Martha Parker	*Raymond ex rel. Williams v. Wal-Mart Stores E., L.P.,*
Keisha Hunt, Individually and on Behalf of her Minor Child, M.H. v. McNeil Consumer Healthcare, et al.	*Hunt v. McNeil Consumer Healthcare,*

12.2(p) Procedural phrases *in re* and *ex parte*; procedural phrases in bankruptcy case names

12.2(p)(1) Procedural phrases *in re* and *ex parte* in general

Use the procedural phrases "*in re*" and "*ex parte*" when they or their synonyms appear in case names.

"*In re*" means "regarding." It labels a proceeding with no adversarial parties, but which involves a thing or a status, such as a bankrupt's estate or a proposed public project. "*In re*" replaces synonymous phrases such as "in the matter of," "matter of," "petition of," and "application of."

"*Ex parte*" means "from or on behalf of only one side to a lawsuit." It labels an action made by, for, or on behalf of one party, often without notice to or contest by the other side. For example, an *ex parte* divorce hearing is one in which only one spouse participates and the other does not appear. Habeas corpus proceedings for wrongful convictions often display "*ex parte*" case names on behalf of the prisoner.

If a procedural phrase is used before an adversarial party name (look for the "v."), drop the procedural phrase. Phrases such as "Estate of" and "Will of" are not treated as or replaced by procedural phrases; retain them in the case name. If a caption displays more than one procedural phrase, use only the first. For bankruptcy cases, see **Rule 12.2(p)(2).**

Examples

Caption:	Case name:
Ex parte Sherman D. GEORGE	*Ex parte George,*
In the Matter of the Adoption of F.I.T.	*In re Adoption of F.I.T.,*
In the Matter of the ESTATE OF Kenneth Alexander TAYLOR, Deceased	*In re Estate of Taylor,*
Ex parte TYSON FOODS, INC., et al. (In re Reba Kirkley, as administratrix of the estate of Allen Hayes, deceased v. Tyson Foods, Inc., et al.)	*Ex parte Tyson Foods, Inc.*
In re L. Dennis KOZLOWSKI, Petitioner-Respondent, v. NEW YORK STATE BOARD OF PAROLE, Respondent-Appellant	*Kozlowski v. N.Y. State Bd. of Parole,*

12.2(p)(2) Procedural phrases in bankruptcy case names

Captions for bankruptcy cases often display two names, one adversarial (Party v. Party) and one non-adversarial (typically using "*in re*"). If the caption for a bankruptcy case displays two names, use the adversarial name, even if it is not listed first. If desired, you may supply the non-adversarial name in parentheses following the adversarial case name.

Example

Caption:	In re Frank Lamont Swain and Esther Marie Swain, Debtors Frank Lamont Swain and Esther Marie Swain, Plaintiffs-Appellants v. Dredging, Inc., d/b/a Scott's Concrete and Jane Ellen Martin, Defendants-Appellees
Case name:	*Swain v. Dredging, Inc.,*
Alternative:	*Swain v. Dredging, Inc. (In re Swain),*

12.2(q) Case known by popular name

A case occasionally becomes well known by a popular name, as opposed to the formal name that appears in its caption. If a case is always referred to in the literature by its popular name, the popular name may replace the formal name that appears in the reporter or may be added parenthetically after the case's formal name. However, if the case is often referred to by its formal name as well as its popular name, use the formal name for the citation; you may then parenthetically indicate the popular name, if desired.

Example

Caption:	UNITED STATES v. STANLEY.; UNITED STATES v. RYAN.; UNITED STATES v. NICHOLS.; UNITED STATES v. SINGLETON.; ROBINSON & Wife v. MEMPHIS AND CHARLESTON RAILROAD COMPANY.
Case name:	*The Civil Rights Cases,*
	or
	United States v. Stanley (The Civil Rights Cases),

12.2(r) "The" as first word of party's name

Omit "the" if it is the first word in a party's name, unless it is part of the name of an object in an *in rem* action (see **Rule 12.2(p)**), it refers to an established popular name (see **Rule 12.2(q)**), or it refers to "The King" or "The Queen" as a party.

Examples

Caption:	Case name:
The New Yorker Magazine, Inc., Appellant, v. Lawrence E. Gerosa, Comptroller of the City of New York, and George M. Bragalini, Treasurer of the City of New York	*New Yorker Magazine, Inc. v. Gerosa,*
In re The EXXON VALDEZ	*In re The Exxon Valdez,*
Barry Victor Randall, Appellant, v. The Queen, Respondent	*Randall v. The Queen,*

12.2(s) Cases with multiple decisions

When multiple decisions have been issued in a single case, it may help readers to provide a case name identifier for each decision. The identifier is typically the short case name followed by a roman numeral. The identifier may either be embedded within non-italicized parentheses following the formal case name or set out in a "hereinafter" construction following the court/date parenthetical (**Rule 11.5**). The identifier may be used in textual sentences.

Examples

In 1999, the Tenth Circuit Court of Appeals vacated its 1998 decision in the same case. In writing about both decisions, an author could add identifiers to differentiate the cases, as shown below.

Case reference options: *United States v. Singleton*, 144 F.3d 1343 (10th Cir. 1998) (*Singleton I*).

United States v. Singleton, 165 F.3d 1297 (10th Cir. 1999) [hereinafter *Singleton II*].

Textual reference: In *Singleton II*, the court held . . .

12.3 Reporter Volume

A case is customarily cited to its appearance in a print reporter, even when the researcher has located the case through an online database or other source. Following the italicized case name and its concluding comma in ordinary type, insert the volume number of the cited reporter, formatted in ordinary type and set off with a space on either side.

Example (reporter volume in red)

Jenkins v. Hestand's Grocery, Inc., **898** S.W.2d 30 (Ark. 1995).

12.4 Reporter Name

12.4(a) Abbreviation and series

Following the reporter volume number, insert the abbreviation for the name of the reporter (**Rule 12.4(b)**), formatted in ordinary type and followed by one space. **Chart 12.2** shows abbreviations for the most commonly used reporters. (For abbreviations to print reporters containing a specific jurisdiction's cases, consult the jurisdiction's entry in **Appendix 1**.)

Once a reporter reaches a set number of volumes (typically 999, but sometimes fewer), its publisher issues a new series and begins numbering the volumes again. For series subsequent to the first, add the series number to the reporter abbreviation, using an ordinal contraction (**Rule 4.3(b)**). If the ordinal contraction follows a single-letter abbreviation, omit space between the abbreviation and the ordinal contraction, as shown in **Chart 12.2**.

CHART 12.2	Reporter Name Abbreviations		

Reporter names:	Abbreviations and series (spaces denoted by ▲):	Reporter names:	Abbreviations and series (spaces denoted by ▲):
United States Reports	U.S.	New York Supplement	N.Y.S.
Supreme Court Reporter	S.▲Ct.		N.Y.S.2d
United States Supreme Court Reports, Lawyers' Edition	L.▲Ed. L.▲Ed.▲2d	North Eastern Reporter	N.Y.S.3d N.E. N.E.2d
United States Law Week	U.S.L.W.		N.E.3d
Federal Reporter	F.	North Western Reporter	N.W.
	F.2d		N.W.2d
	F.3d		N.W.3d
Federal Appendix	F.▲App'x	Pacific Reporter	P.
Federal Supplement	F.▲Supp.		P.2d
	F.▲Supp.▲2d		P.3d
	F.▲Supp.▲3d	South Eastern Reporter	S.E.
Federal Rules Decisions	F.R.D.		S.E.2d
Bankruptcy Reporter	B.R.		S.E.3d
Atlantic Reporter	A.	South Western Reporter	S.W.
	A.2d		S.W.2d
	A.3d		S.W.3d
California Reporter	Cal.▲Rptr.	Southern Reporter	So.
	Cal.▲Rptr.▲2d		So.▲2d
	Cal.▲Rptr.▲3d		So.▲3d

12.4(b) Reporter selection

Unless a case is published in only one reporter, select the most appropriate reporter version to cite, considering the type of document you are drafting, the availability of the desired version, the identity of the court issuing the opinion, and the requirements or expectations of your readers. For cases that will be published in a print reporter but are not yet available there, see **Rule 12.12**.

12.4(b)(1) Selecting reporter for citation in court documents
In documents submitted to *federal* or *state courts*, such as motions and briefs, cite cases to the reporter(s) required by the court's *local rule*, if any. (For citations and links to local rule sources, see **Appendix 2**.) Many state court rules require parallel citations, that is, citation to both the official and unofficial reporters in which a case is published (addressed in **Rule 12.4(c)**). In the absence of such local rules, select the reporter following the order of preference set out for non-court documents in **Rule 12.4(b)(2)**.

12.4(b)(2) Selecting reporter for citation in non-court documents
In citations appearing in *non-court documents* such as office memoranda or academic footnotes in law review articles, when selecting a reporter, differentiate between cases from the United States Supreme Court and cases from lower federal courts or state courts.

Cite a **United States Supreme Court** case decided *since 1874* to a single reporter, in the order of preference set out below:

▪ *United States Reports*;

▪ *Supreme Court Reporter*;

▪ *United States Supreme Court Reports, Lawyers' Edition*; or

▪ An online source (e.g., a commercial database such as Bloomberg BNA, Lexis Advance or WestlawNext, or a reliable site on the World Wide Web).

To cite reporters for United States Supreme Court cases decided *before 1874*, see **Sidebar 12.3** and **Rule 12.4(b)(4)**.

Unless the case has been reported under an *official* neutral citation (addressed in **Rule 12.17**), cite a **lower federal case or a state case** to a single reporter, according to its availability there, in the following order of preference:

▪ A West federal (e.g., F.3d, F. Supp. 2d) or regional reporter (e.g., A.3d, N.W.2d);

▪ Another print reporter in which the case appears (e.g., a state-specific unofficial reporter such as N.Y.S.2d or an official reporter such as Ohio App. 3d);

▪ A commercial database (see **Rule 12.13(b)**);

▪ A looseleaf reporter (see **Rule 24.1**); or

▪ Any other source in which the case appears (e.g., a legal newspaper or a reliable site on the World Wide Web).

12.4(b)(3) Cases in both West's regional and state-specific reporters
When citing a case that appears both in West's *Pacific Reporter* and the *California Reporter*, or both in West's *North Eastern Reporter* and the *New York*

Supplement, cite the *Pacific Reporter* or *North Eastern Reporter* version. If you are in California or New York, however, where attorneys prefer citations to the state-specific reporters, you may cite the state-specific reporter instead of the regional reporter.

12.4(b)(4) Cases in nominative reporters

The first ninety volumes of the *United States Reports* and a few states' early case reports were named for the editors who compiled the cases for publication (i.e., the "reporters"). Citations to cases in those reporters should include a parenthetical reference to the volume and number of the nominative reporter, as shown below. See **Sidebar 12.3** for the names, dates, and abbreviations (if any) to use for nominative reporters of United States Supreme Court cases. If the page numbering in the nominative reporter differs from that in the *United States Reports* or the state reporter, present the two reporters as parallel citations, following **Rule 12.4(c)**.

Examples

United States v. Hudson, 11 U.S. (7 Cranch) 32, 34 (1812).

Trs. of Dartmouth Coll. v. Woodward, 17 U.S. (14 Wheat.) 518, 644 (1819).

SIDEBAR 12.3	**Names and Dates of Early United States Supreme Court Nominative Reporters**

Nominative Reporter (Abbreviation):	Corresponding U.S. Volumes:	Years of Publication:
Dallas (Dall.)	1–4	1789–1800
Cranch (Cranch)	5–13	1801–1815
Wheaton (Wheat.)	14–25	1816–1827
Peters (Pet.)	26–41	1828–1842
Howard (How.)	42–65	1843–1860
Black (Black)	66–67	1861–1862
Wallace (Wall.)	68–90	1863–1874

The first 107 volumes of *United States Reports* (through the 1882 term) generally do not provide the date of the decision. Because a case citation requires a date (**Rule 12.7**), consult another source for that information, such as the official website of the United States Supreme Court, http://www.supremecourtus.gov.

SIDEBAR 12.4	Locating Parallel Citations and Determining Pagination

Because a case may be published in only one reporter, not every case has a parallel citation. When court rules require you to provide a parallel citation, you may be able to find references to other reporters by consulting one or more of the following:

★ the first page of the West reporter version;

★ the first page of the official reporter version;

★ the running head or caption of the Lexis Advance or WestlawNext version;

★ the case's entry in West's *KeyCite* citator; and

★ the case's entry in the print or Lexis Advance version of *Shepard's* citators.

It may not be necessary to consult both versions of the case to determine internal pagination; some reporters embed pagination for the parallel reporter within the text of the case. See **Rule 5.5** for more information about star pagination. For example, opinions in permanent versions of the *Supreme Court Reporter* and the *Lawyers' Edition* include references to case pagination in the *United States Reports*. In the *Supreme Court Reporter*, the *United States Reports* page numbers appear as subscript numbers (e.g., $\perp_{188}$). In the *Lawyers' Edition, United States Reports* numbers appear in bolded superscript, enclosed in brackets (e.g., [513 U.S. 1304]).

12.4(c) Indicating reporters in parallel citations

A parallel citation displays two or more sources for the same case, typically one published in an official print reporter and another published in an unofficial print reporter. Do not provide parallel citations unless required to do so by local rule (see **Appendix 2**). See **Sidebar 12.4** for information about locating parallel citations.

When citing a case to parallel reporters, cite the *official* reporter first. If there are two official reporters, cite the government-published reporter first. Except as required by **Rule 12.4(b)(2)** for United States Supreme Court cases, if there are two *unofficial* reporters, the West reporter comes last. Consult **Appendix 1** to determine which reporters are official and which are unofficial. For courts using neutral parallel citations, see **Rule 12.17.**

Examples

> *O'Connell v. Kirchner,* 513 U.S. 1303, 1304, 115 S. Ct. 891, 892, 130 L. Ed. 2d 873, 875 (1995).
>
> *People v. Sargent,* 19 Cal. 4th 1206, 1215, 970 P.2d 409, 414, 81 Cal. Rptr. 2d 835, 840, (1999).
>
> *In re Estate of Netherton,* 62 Ill. App. 3d 55, 57–58, 378 N.E.2d 800, 802 (1978).

12.5 Page Numbers

Citations to cases should indicate the initial page number of the reporter on which the case begins, and if possible, a pinpoint page reference to the specific material cited. For general information about page number references, see **Rule 5**.

12.5(a) Initial page number

Following the reporter abbreviation, insert a space followed by the case's initial page number, that is, the page on which the case begins in that reporter. In parallel citations, provide the initial page for the case in each reporter, immediately after each reporter's abbreviation. (See examples in **Rule 12.5(c)**.)

12.5(b) Pinpoint references in general

When you refer to specific material in a case, add a comma after the initial page, a space, and a pinpoint page reference, as described in **Rule 5.2**. If the pinpoint reference spans more than one page, indicate the span of pages, dropping all repetitive digits but the final two.

Examples

> *Chambers v. Bowersox,* 157 F.3d 560, 566 (8th Cir. 1998).
>
> *In re Estate of Hewitt,* 721 A.2d 1082, 1085–86 (Pa. 1998).

12.5(c) Pinpoint references in parallel citations

In a parallel citation (**Rule 12.4(c)**), provide pinpoint references for pages in the West reporter, at a minimum. Other pinpoint references are optional, but you may anticipate that readers will have ready access to West's National Reporter System and to official reporters for the state in which they work. See **Sidebar 12.4** for information about locating pinpoint references for parallel citations.

Examples

> *Williams v. State,* 321 Ark. 344, 349, 902 S.W.2d 767, 770 (1995).
>
> *Commonwealth v. Sell,* 504 Pa. 46, 65, 470 A.2d 457, 467 (1983).

12.5(d) Pinpoint references in dissenting or concurring opinions

Following reference to the initial page of the case (**Rule 12.5(a)**), insert a pinpoint reference to the page(s) of the dissenting or concurring opinion containing the cited material. See **Rule 12.10(a)** for additional requirements in citing dissenting or concurring opinions.

Example

> *Purkett v. Elam*, 514 U.S. 765, 775 (Stevens & Brennan, JJ., dissenting).

12.6   Court Abbreviation

12.6(a) General rule for identifying court of decision

Each case citation must identify, in some form, the court who decided the matter. You typically will do so in a court/date parenthetical that immediately follows the initial page and pinpoint page references. To create the parenthetical, insert an opening parenthesis, followed by the abbreviation for the court's name, as shown in **Appendix 1** or **Appendix 4**. (Note: Close the parentheses after inserting the date of decision (**Rule 12.7**).)

Examples

> *Howard v. Wal-Mart Stores, Inc.*, 160 F.3d 358, 360 (7th Cir. 1998).
>
> *Webb v. Dixie-Ohio Express Co.*, 165 S.W.2d 539, 541 (Ky. 1942).

12.6(b) Identifying United States Supreme Court

If citing a case to a reporter that publishes only cases from the United States Supreme Court, there is no question which court decided the case. Therefore, omit the court abbreviation from the court/date parenthetical. Identify the court, however, if citing the case in *United States Law Week* (U.S.L.W.), a looseleaf service that publishes, among other things, the decisions of multiple courts.

Examples

Correct:	*Penry v. Lynaugh*, 492 U.S. 302 (1989).
Incorrect:	*Penry v. Lynaugh*, 492 U.S. 302 (U.S. 1989).
Correct:	*Kloeckner v. Solis*, 81 U.S.L.W. 4018 (U.S. Dec. 10, 2012).
Incorrect:	*Kloeckner v. Solis*, 81 U.S.L.W. 4018 (Dec. 10, 2012).

12.6(c) Additional jurisdictional information in court name

12.6(c)(1) State court abbreviations

When citing a case decided by a court other than the state's highest court, use the abbreviation shown in that state's entry in **Appendix 1** or **Appendix 4**, if therein. Omit reference to departments, districts, or other subdivisions unless the information is highly relevant. If so, present the information in the order and numerical style used by the particular court, abbreviating any words shown in **Appendix 3(G)**.

Examples

Griffin v. Paul, 901 So. 2d 1034, 1034 (Fla. Dist. Ct. App. 2005).

Griffin v. Paul, 901 So. 2d 1034, 1034 (Fla. 2d Dist. Ct. App. 2005).

12.6(c)(2) Federal courts in general

Except as noted in **Rules 12.6(c)(3)** and **12.6(c)(4)**, omit reference to divisions or units of federal district courts or courts of appeal. When identifying a court of the United States Courts of Appeals, always omit reference to the state in which the case originated.

Examples

Correct:	Lipford v. Carnival Corp., 346 F. Supp. 2d 1276, 1278 (S.D. Fla. 2004).
Incorrect:	Lipford v. Carnival Corp., 346 F. Supp. 2d 1276, 1278 (S.D. Fla. Miami Div. 2004).
Correct:	Ezell v. City of Chi., 651 F.3d 684, 704 (7th Cir. 2011).
Incorrect:	Ezell v. City of Chi., 651 F.3d 684, 704 (7th Cir. (Ill.) 2011).

12.6(c)(3) Fifth Circuit split

The United States Court of Appeals for the Fifth Circuit was divided to create two circuits, the Fifth and the Eleventh, on October 1, 1981. If the caption for a former Fifth Circuit case indicates "Unit A" or "Unit B," add that information following the "5th Cir." abbreviation. For cases decided in 1981, add the abbreviated month of decision (**Appendix 3(A)**). If the caption contains a "Former Fifth Circuit" reference but no unit information *and* the case was decided after September 30, 1981, use "Former 5th Cir." as the court abbreviation.

Examples

Gullatte v. Potts, 654 F.2d 1007, 1012 (5th Cir. Unit B Aug. 1981).

United States v. Flynn, 664 F.2d 1296, 1299 (Former 5th Cir. 1982).

12.6(c)(4) Historic federal courts

In the original districts of Maine and Kentucky, and in many states admitted during the nineteenth century, until a district was incorporated into a specific judicial circuit, the United States district court also exercised the jurisdiction of the United States circuit court of appeals. Only in 1889 did Congress finally provide a circuit court of appeals for every judicial district in the nation, which then ended the expanded jurisdiction of certain district courts. When citing a case from an early federal district court exercising circuit court jurisdiction, add the abbreviation "C.C." before the district court abbreviation, and if the caption shows the case number, put that number in a parenthetical following the court/date parenthetical.

Examples

Pierson v. Philips, 36 F. 837 (C.C.E.D. Tex. 1888).

United States v. Burr, 25 F. Cas. 55, 56–57 (C.C.D. Va. 1807) (No. 14,693).

Similarly, when citing cases from the old federal circuits, which were abolished on June 1, 1912, follow the format for current United States Court of Appeals cases, but use the abbreviation "C.C." instead of "Cir."

Example

United States ex rel. Stokes v. Kendall, 26 F. Cas. 702, 713 (C.C.D.C. 1837) (No. 15,517), *aff'd*, 37 U.S. (12 Pet.) 524 (1838).

For other early courts whose names may differ from that of the modern court that serves the particular jurisdiction, abbreviate the court name as it appears in the caption, analogizing to court abbreviations shown in **Appendix 1**.

Example

Glenn v. United States, 10 F. Cas. 472, 475 (D. Ark. 1849) (No. 5481), *aff'd*, 54 U.S. (13 How.) 250 (1851).

12.6(d) Parallel citations and court abbreviations

In parallel citations, omit all or part of the court abbreviation in the court/date parenthetical if the name of any cited reporter or database clearly indicates the state or court of decision (e.g., Iowa Reports, North Carolina Court of Appeals Reports, Miss. App. LEXIS).

Examples

Miller v. Commonwealth, 5 Va. App. 22, 25, 359 S.E.2d 841, 842 (1987).

State v. Davis, 283 Conn. 280, 299, 929 A.2d 278, 313 (2007).

People v. Albanese, 38 A.D.3d 1015, 1017, 831 N.Y.S.2d 280, 283 (2007).

Westphal v. City of St. Petersburg, No. 1D12-3563, 2013 Fla. App. LEXIS 15084 (Sept. 23, 2013).

12.7 Date of Decision

Within the same parenthetical as the court abbreviation (if any), set out the date on which the case was decided. For cases cited to print reporters, provide only the year of the decision. For unpublished cases and cases available only in online databases or looseleaf services, provide the exact date (Month Day, Year) of the decision; abbreviate the month according to **Appendix 3(A)**.

Examples

> *Guinan v. Tenet Healthsystems of Hilton Head, Inc.*, 677 S.E.2d 32, 36 (S.C. Ct. App. 2009).
>
> *Allen v. Adams*, 2004 U.S. Dist. LEXIS 6313, at *4 (W.D. Tex. Mar. 30, 2004).
>
> *Collins v. Vill. of Woodridge*, 84 Fair Empl. Prac. Cas. (BNA) 787, 788 (N.D. Ill. Oct. 19, 1999).

12.8 Subsequent History

An essential step in legal research is determining whether anything significant has happened to affect the precedential value of a case since it was decided. Use tools like *Shepard's* or *KeyCite* to check a case's subsequent history. Add subsequent history to the full citation of a case if the form of history—or an analogous form of history having similar effect—is addressed in **Rule 12.8(a)** and **Chart 12.3**. Some forms of subsequent history may be ignored, as explained in **Rule 12.8(b)**. For information on citing a case's *prior* history, see **Rule 12.9**.

12.8(a) Subsequent history to include

Use the italicized abbreviations in **Chart 12.3** below to denote certain dispositions and rulings, or those with similar effect. Forms of subsequent history marked below with an asterisk (*) should be provided only if the cited case— not the disposition or ruling indicated in the history—was decided within the last two years *or* if that case's history is particularly important to the discussion. See **Sidebar 12.5** for a discussion of what is considered "particularly important." Forms of subsequent history marked in **Chart 12.3** with a dagger (†) should be ignored after a *higher* court later makes some disposition of the cited case.

The subsequent history phrase may include an explanation for the disposition, such as *vacated as moot*, *rev'd without opinion*, or *aff'd by an equally divided court*.

12.8(b) Subsequent history to ignore

Ignore history concerning remands, rehearings, rehearings en banc, and similar matters unless the history is particularly relevant to the purpose for which

CHART 12.3	Subsequent History Designations

Disposition or ruling:	Abbreviation:
Abrogated	*abrogated by*
Affirmed	*aff'd,*
Affirmed in part and reversed in part	*aff'd in part, rev'd in part,*
Affirmed on other grounds	*aff'd on other grounds,*
Affirmed on rehearing	*aff'd on reh'g,*
Amended by	*amended by*
*Appeal denied	*appeal denied,*
*Appeal dismissed	*appeal dismissed,*
†Appeal docketed	*appeal docketed,*
†Appeal filed	*appeal filed,*
*Certiorari denied	*cert. denied,*
*Certiorari dismissed	*cert. dismissed,*
†Certiorari granted	*cert. granted,*
Certifying question to	*certifying question to*
Depublished by	*depublished by*
Dismissing appeal from	*dismissing appeal from*
Enforced	*enforced,*
Invalidated by	*invalidated by*
Mandamus denied	*mandamus denied,*
Modified	*modified,*
Overruled by	*overruled by*
*Permissive appeal denied	*perm. app. denied,*
†Permissive appeal granted	*perm. app. granted,*
†Petition for certiorari filed	*petition for cert. filed,*
Probable jurisdiction noted	*prob. juris. noted,*
Reversed	*rev'd,*
Reversed in part and affirmed in part	*rev'd in part, aff'd in part,*
Superseded	*superseded by*
Vacated	*vacated,*
Withdrawn	*withdrawn,*

the case is cited. Similarly, unless it is relevant to the proposition for which a case is cited, ignore a denial of certiorari when more than two years have passed since the case's date of decision. (For more information about denials of certiorari, see **Sidebar 12.5**.)

12.8(c) Placement, format, and components of subsequent history designation

Indicate subsequent history as defined in **Rule 12.8(a)** whenever citing a case in full. Never attach subsequent history to a short citation.

SIDEBAR 12.5   Information about Denials of Certiorari

A writ of certiorari is a device used by courts of last resort, such as the United States Supreme Court, that have discretion to select the cases they want to hear. If the party who lost in the court below seeks review in a court that has discretion to hear the appeal, that party files a "Petition for Writ of Certiorari." If the court grants the petition, it will hear the appeal. If the court denies the petition, it will not hear the appeal.

Do not copy *"cert. denied"* information from other citation sources, as they may not follow **Rule 12.8** or otherwise may not reflect the current status of a case.

Precedential Value

Denials of certiorari carry no precedential value and do not indicate that the higher court agreed with the lower court's decision. Accordingly, denials of certiorari typically are not included as subsequent history. However, because denials inform readers that the lower court's decision has become final, provide the information when the cited lower court decision is two years old or less at the time of your document's preparation. Two years reflects the time within which most cases are resolved on appeal.

"Particularly Important"

The denial also should be included if the case is particularly important to the writer's topic or argument. A denial of certiorari is important if the case is the focus of the discussion. It also is important when the higher court issues an opinion explaining why a petition for certiorari was denied or when a judge issues a dissenting opinion concerning the denial of certiorari.

Insert the subsequent history designation after the court/date parenthetical. Italicize everything within the history phrase but not the commas (if any) that precede or follow it.

If the case name in the history case is the same as the cited case, if the parties' names are merely reversed, or if the subsequent history consists solely of a denial of certiorari, omit the case name from the history; set out just the volume, reporter abbreviation, initial page, and court/date parenthetical for the history case. If the subsequent history is something other than a denial of certiorari and the case name changed on appeal, however, follow **Rule 12.8(d)**.

If a case's history is not separately reported but is denoted in the case's caption, set out the appropriate history phrase followed by a parenthetical with the court abbreviation and exact date (Month Day, Year) of the disposition; there will not be an additional reporter to cite.

If the history itself has history, set it out using another history designation. Connect multiple decisions by a *single* court with the italicized word "*and*."

Examples

> *Saregama India Ltd. v. Mosley*, 687 F. Supp. 2d 1325 (S.D. Fla. 2009), *aff'd*, 635 F.3d 1284(11th Cir.2011).

> *McHenry v. Fla. Bar*, 808 F. Supp. 1543 (M.D. Fla. 1992), *aff'd*, 21 F.3d 1038 (11th Cir. 1994), *rev'd sub nom. Fla. Bar v. Went For It, Inc.*, 515 U.S. 618 (1995).

> *EEOC v. Ilona of Hungary, Inc.*, 108 F.3d 1569, 1574–75 (7th Cir. 1996, *modified on reh'g en banc*, Mar. 6, 1997).

> *Shell Oil Co. v. Meyer*, 684 N.E.2d 504 (Ind. Ct. App. 1997), *vacated*, 698 N.E.2d 1183 (Ind.), *and aff'd in part, vacated in part*, 705 N.E.2d 962 (Ind. 1998).

12.8(d) Case name changed on appeal

When the subsequent history of a case indicates that its name changed in later proceedings, indicate the new case name in the subsequent history phrase by using the italicized abbreviation "*sub nom.*" (meaning "under the name of"). Insert "*sub nom.*" and the new case name immediately after the history designation, followed by the rest of the subsequent history case components.

Examples

> *Macias v. Mine Safety Appliances Co.*, 244 P.3d 978 (Wash. Ct. App. 2010), *rev'dsub nom. Macias v. Saberhagen Holdings, Inc.*, 282 P.3d 1069 (Wash. 2012).

> *In re Iraq & Afg. Detainees Litig.*, 479 F. Supp. 2d 85, 105 (D.D.C. 2007), *aff'd sub nom. Ali v. Rumsfeld*, 649 F.3d 762 (D.C. Cir. 2011).

Do not indicate a different case name in the following situations:

- When the only change is a reversal of the parties' names;
- When the designation of a state shifts between "Commonwealth," "People," or "State," and the state's proper name (e.g., when a federal court hears an appeal from a case previously decided by a state court); or
- When the subsequent history is solely a denial of certiorari.

12.8(e) Abrogated, overruled, and superseded cases

The precedential effect of a case may be directly or indirectly altered by the subsequent actions of courts or legislatures. For example, a court may explicitly overrule one of its earlier cases, or it may abrogate one of its earlier decisions by deciding an outcome that is inconsistent with its prior decisions on the issue. A statute may be enacted or a constitutional amendment may be approved in order to supersede the common law in a specific judicial decision. These actions must be treated as subsequent history appended to the full citation of the case.

Do not use the phrase "*sub nom.*" before the name of a history case that overrules or abrogates the case you are citing; two different cases are involved, and the second case is not an appeal from the first.

Examples

Baldasar v. Illinois, 446 U.S. 222 (1980), *overruled by Nichols v. United States*, 511 U.S. 738 (1994).

United States v. Barrett, 198 F. Supp. 2d 1046 (S.D. Iowa 2002), *abrogated by United States v. Griner*, 358 F.3d 979 (8th Cir. 2004).

Sutton v. United Air Lines, Inc., 527 U.S. 471 (1999), *superseded by statute*, ADA Amendments Act of 2008, Pub. L. No. 110-325, 122 Stat. 3553 (2008), *as recognized in Allen v. SouthCrest Hosp.*, 455 Fed. App'x 827 (10th Cir. 2011).

12.8(f) Subsequent history in same year as original decision

When citing a case that has subsequent history in the same year the case was originally reported, omit the date from the cited case's court/date parenthetical, and instead, set out the year solely in the court/date parenthetical for the more recent history disposition.

Examples

Natural Res. Def. Council, Inc. v. Winter, 518 F.3d 658 (9th Cir.), *rev'd*, 555 U.S. 7 (2008).

United States v. Vargas, 689 F.3d 867, 875 (7th Cir.), *cert. denied*, 133 S. Ct. 804 (2012).

12.8(g) Relation to parenthetical information

Follow **Rule 37** regarding placement of explanatory parenthetical information. Thus, if the parenthetical concerns the lower court case, it should follow the lower court case citation. If the parenthetical concerns the higher court history case, it should follow the higher court case citation.

Examples

Parenthetical relates to lower court case:	*Mapp v. Ohio*, 166 N.E.2d 387 (Ohio 1960) (holding that contraband obtained by an unlawful search is admissible evidence), *rev'd*, 347 U.S. 643 (1961).
Parenthetical relates to higher court case:	*Mapp v. Ohio*, 166 N.E.2d 387 (Ohio 1960), *rev'd*, 347 U.S. 643 (1961) (holding that evidence obtained by an unconstitutional search is not admissible).

12.9 Prior History

Prior history refers to rulings in and dispositions of a case before the cited opinion was issued. Add prior history to a citation only when it is significant to a point addressed in the document. For example, a law review article might include a discussion about what happened when a case was in the lower courts; in that instance, the writer might add prior history to the citation of the cited case. On the other hand, in a more extended discussion of a case's early history, it might be better to cite earlier rulings directly.

Insert prior history after a full citation in the same manner as subsequent history (**Rule 12.8(c)**). *Do not* attach prior history to a short citation. For prior history phrases, refer to the examples shown in **Chart 12.4** below or modify abbreviations shown in **Chart 12.3**.

If citing both prior and subsequent histories, provide the *prior* history *first*. Insert a comma followed by the italicized word "*and*" before the subsequent history.

Examples

Prior history in citation:	*Edwards v. Nat'l Audubon Soc'y, Inc.*, 556 F.2d 113 (2d Cir. 1977), *rev'g* 423 F. Supp. 516 (S.D.N.Y. 1976).
Prior history and subsequent history in same citation:	*McHenry v. Fla. Bar*, 21 F.3d 1038 (11th Cir. 1994), *aff'g* 808 F. Supp. 1543 (M.D. Fla. 1992), *and rev'd sub nom. Fla. Bar v. Went For It, Inc.*, 515 U.S. 618 (1995).

CHART 12.4	Prior History Designations
Disposition or ruling:	**Abbreviation:**
Acquiescing	*acq.*
Acquiescing in result	*acq. in result*
Affirming	*aff'g*
Enforcing	*enforcing*
Modifying	*modifying*
Reversing	*rev'g*
Vacating	*vacating*
Vacating as moot	*vacating as moot*

12.10 Parenthetical Information

12.10(a) Dissenting, concurring, and plurality opinions

Identify a citation to a non-majority opinion (e.g., a dissent or a concurrence) in a parenthetical that follows either the case's full citation or its short citation (including *id.*). For dissents and concurrences, set out the last name(s), a comma, and the title abbreviation(s) of all justices or judges who participated in the minority decision. List names in the order they appear in the non-majority opinion. See **Chart 12.5** for abbreviations for judicial titles. Following the judicial title abbreviation, add a comma, and indicate the type of opinion (e.g., "concurring," "concurring in part," "dissenting," "dissenting from Parts II and III of the opinion"). For plurality opinions, simply state "plurality" in the parenthetical, and omit reference to the judges' or justices' names and judicial titles.

Examples

United States v. Anderson, 895 F.2d 641, 647 (9th Cir. 1990) (Kozinski, J., dissenting).

Johnson v. Carroll, 658 F.3d 819, 830 (8th Cir. 2011) (Gruender, J., concurring in part and dissenting in part).

Nat'l Fed'n of Indep. Bus. v. Sebelius, 132 S. Ct. 2566, 2623 (2012) (Ginsburg, J., with Breyer, Sotomayor, and Kagan, JJ., concurring in part, concurring in the judgment in part, and dissenting in part).

Missouri v. Seibert, 542 U.S. 600, 606 (2004) (plurality).

CHART 12.5	Abbreviations for Titles of Judges and Other Judicial Officials
Administrative Law Judge	A.L.J.
Arbitrator	Arb.
Chancellor	C.
Chief Judge, Chief Justice	C.J.
Commissioner	Comm'r
Judge, Justice	J.
Judges, Justices	JJ.
Magistrate, Magistrate Judge	Mag.
Mediator President	Med. Pres.
Referee	Ref.
Vice Chancellor	V.C.

When citing different opinions within the same case, provide a designating parenthetical each time you switch opinions. As illustrated below, if you use *id.* to refer successively to the same non-majority opinion within the case, you need not repeat the parenthetical. When citing the majority opinion immediately after a non-majority opinion, indicate the majority parenthetically. Although the illustration below is from a document with academic footnotes, the rule also applies to citations in practice-based documents.

Examples

[59] *Id.* at 381 (Alito, J., concurring).   ⚠ACADEMIC FORMATTING

[60] *Id.*

[61] *Id.* at 387 (Scalia, J., dissenting).

[62] *Id.* at 382 (Alito, J., concurring).

[63] *Id.* at 369 (majority opinion).

[64] *Id.* at 371.

12.10(b) Parenthetical reference to weight of authority

You may always parenthetically provide information about the weight of the case. Such an explanatory parenthetical may indicate a variety of things. For example, it may identify an en banc decision or a per curiam opinion; identify the split among the judges who decided the case; label the cited proposition as dictum as opposed to holding; or state whether a case was decided without an opinion, a disposition known as a "memorandum opinion" (abbreviated "mem.").

Examples

> *Ellis v. Anderson Tully Co.*, 727 So. 2d 716 (Miss. 1998) (en banc).
>
> *Aguilar v. Felton*, 473 U.S. 402 (1985) (affirming 5–4).
>
> *Beer v. United States*, 131 S. Ct. 2865, 2865-66 (2011) (mem.).

12.10(c) Other uses for explanatory parentheticals

When a cited case is not extensively discussed in the text, it may be useful to provide an explanatory parenthetical, appended to the citation, summarizing the holding of the cited case, explaining its relevance, or providing a pertinent quotation. See **Rule 37** for more information about explanatory parentheticals.

12.11 Table Cases

If a case is listed in a reporter table without opinion, cite it using the format for published cases. Following the court/date parenthetical, insert one space and the parenthetical notation "(table)."

If a table case's opinion, as opposed to just its disposition, is available online, insert "(table)" after the initial page number and add the database identifier and court/date parenthetical. (see **Rule 12.13(b)**).

Examples (fictitious)

If table case opinion is not available online:

Dominik v. Illinois, 704 F.3d 429 (7th Cir. 2016) (table).

If table case opinion is available online:

Dominik v. Illinois, 704 F.3d 429 (table), 2016 WL 823751 (7th Cir. 2016).

12.12 Cases Not Yet Available in Print Reporter

If a case will be printed in a print reporter but the volume and page numbers are not yet available, immediately after the case name, insert the docket number (also referred to as a "case number," "file number," or "record number") as shown in the caption. Replace both the volume number of the reporter and the initial page number with three underlined spaces, add a parallel citation to its version in a commercial database such as Bloomberg BNA, Lexis Advance, or WestlawNext if available, and in the court/date parenthetical, provide the court abbreviation (if not apparent from the database identifier) and the exact date (Month Day, Year). Abbreviate the month as indicated in **Appendix 3(A)**.

Examples (fictitious)

> *In re Sofia B.*, No. 2-15-1816, ___ N.E.2d ___, 2015 Ill. App. LEXIS 52006 (May 20, 2015).

> *Dahlberg v. Miller*, No. 74-cv-1951-GCB, ___ F. Supp. 2d ___, 2016 WL 72113 (E.D. Ark. Aug. 15, 2016).

12.13 Non-Precedential or "Unpublished" Cases

A significant number of appellate court opinions (and almost all trial court opinions) are never published in print, either because they are not binding precedent or because, in the court's estimation, they do not add anything of value to the existing body of authority in the jurisdiction. Despite their "unpublished" status, such cases are often available in online media, whether on a court's website or in commercial databases such as Bloomberg BNA, Lexis Advance, and WestlawNext. In addition, Thomson West collects many cases not designated for publication by federal appellate courts and prints them in its unofficial *Federal Appendix* reporter.

Although the general rule is that unpublished cases are not binding precedent and therefore should not be cited, with the adoption of Federal Rule of Appellate Procedure 32.1 (applicable to cases decided on or after January 1, 2007), federal courts no longer prohibit their citation. Many state courts have begun to permit their citation as well. (For more information about citing unpublished cases, see **Sidebar 12.6**.)

For cases that will in fact be published but are *not yet* available in a print reporter, follow **Rule 12.12**. When such cases appear in online databases, the headers typically show underlined spaces before and after the reporter abbreviation, representing the as-yet-unassigned volume number and initial page number.

12.13(a) Unpublished cases available in the *Federal Appendix* reporter

If an unpublished case appears in the *Federal Appendix*, cite it to this print reporter in preference to another source in which it may be available. Follow the format for citing cases from the United States Courts of Appeals, using the abbreviation "Fed. App'x" for the reporter name.

Example

> *Scarborough v. Morgan*, 21 Fed. App'x 279, 280 (6th Cir. 2001).

12.13(b) Unpublished cases available in commercial databases

When a case is not published in a reporter but is available online in a commercial database such as Bloomberg BNA, Lexis Advance, or WestlawNext, its full citation consists of the case name (**Rule 12.2**); its docket number (also referred to as a "case number," "file number," or "record number") as it is shown in the caption, preceded by the abbreviation "No."; its database identifier as shown in the caption; and a court/date parenthetical. Do not cite a case to a commercial database if it is presently available in a print reporter. For cases that will be published in a reporter but are not yet available, see **Rule 12.12**.

The database identifier in Bloomberg BNA consists of the year, the abbreviation BL, and a document number. Similarly, the database identifier in WestlawNext consists of the year, the abbreviation WL, and a document number. The database identifier in Lexis Advance consists of the year, an abbreviation for the issuing court, and a document number.

SIDEBAR 12.6	**Court Rules Prohibiting or Limiting Citation of Unreported Cases**

Although cases designated as "unpublished" do not appear in reporters, they may be available online or through other sources. Courts have differing rules on whether litigants may cite unpublished cases in briefs or other documents presented to them. While some courts permit these cases to be cited in court documents, others prohibit such citation or limit the precedential value they carry.

In a document to be submitted to a court, before citing an opinion designated as "unpublished," check controlling court rules. Federal Rule of Appellate Procedure 32.1, applying to cases issued on or after January 1, 2007, provides that a federal court of appeals "may not prohibit or restrict the citation" of federal judicial decisions that have been "designated as 'unpublished,' 'not for publication,' 'non-precedential,' 'not precedent,' or the like." As for pre-2007 federal appellate unpublished decisions, court rules differ from circuit to circuit. While many local rules permit their citation (e.g., 3d Cir. I.O.P. 5.7), others explicitly label the practice as "disfavored" (e.g., 4th Cir. R. 32.1). Some expressly declare that unpublished cases are "not precedent" (e.g., 8th Cir. R. 32.1A). Similarly, local rules for state courts vary with regard to their treatment of unpublished cases.

If you are considering citing an unpublished case in a brief or other court document, always consult the local rules for that court to determine its practices and restrictions. See **Appendix 2** for citations to local court rules and links to rules on court websites.

If the database identifier clearly indicates which court decided the case, omit redundant aspects of the court abbreviation in the court/date parenthetical. Indicate the exact date of the decision (Month Day, Year), abbreviating the month as shown in **Appendix 3(A)**.

Omit reference to an initial page number. For a pinpoint page reference, insert a comma and the word "at" after the database identifier, followed by a space, one asterisk, and the page number(s). If the database source indicates pagination to several different sources, carefully determine which page numbers belong to the online database.

Examples

Va. Dep't of Transp. v. EPA, No. 1:12-CV-775, 2013 BL 2384, at *3–4 (E.D. Va. 2012).

Radar Rim, Inc. v. CMB Mortg. Servs., Inc., No. 04 C 1945, 2004 U.S. Dist. LEXIS 21431, at *1 (N.D. Ill. Oct. 21, 2004).

Clohset v. No Name Corp., No. 301681, 2013 Mich. App. LEXIS 1549, at *10 (Oct. 1, 2013).

United Parcel Serv., Inc. v. Giatas, No. 0308-09-4, 2009 WL 1748546, at *1 (Va. Ct. App. June 23, 2009).

12.14 Cases Published Only in Looseleaf Services

Do not cite a case in a looseleaf service if it has since become available in a reporter or in a commercial database. To cite a case in a looseleaf service, follow the format shown in **Rule 24.1**.

12.15 Cases Available Only in Slip Opinions

A "slip opinion" is the first public issuance of a court's decision, typically printed in pamphlet form, prior to the decision's being published in a reporter. When citing a case that is available only in a slip opinion, following the case name, insert the docket number (also referred to as a "case number," "file number," or "record number"), and in the court/date parenthetical, provide the exact date (Month Day, Year) of the disposition, abbreviating the month as shown in **Appendix 3(A)**.

To add a pinpoint page reference, immediately after the docket number insert a comma, the phrase "slip op. at," and the number(s) of the cited page or pages (**Rule 12.5**). If the date reference is not the date of disposition, indicate its significance by inserting an appropriate description between the court abbreviation and the date in the court/date parenthetical.

Examples

In re Hostess Brands, Inc., No. 12-22052 (RDD), slip op. at 11–13 (Bankr. S.D.N.Y. Jan. 7, 2013).

Woods v. Wyeth Labs. Inc., No. 94-1493, slip op. at 1 (W.D. Pa. filed Sept. 1, 1994).

12.16 Cases on the World Wide Web

Do not cite a case to a non-judicial source on the World Wide Web if it is available in a print reporter, a commercial database such as WestlawNext, Lexis Advance, or Bloomberg BNA, or a looseleaf service. The World Wide Web may be a useful resource, however, for examples such as locating recent slip opinions, opinions of lower courts whose decisions are not published, or cases from other countries.

To cite a case published on the World Wide Web, provide the case name as required by **Rule 12.2**, the docket number (if apparent), and a parenthetical with the court abbreviation and exact date (Month Day, Year), abbreviating the month as shown in **Appendix 3(A)**. Following the court/date parenthetical, add a comma, the italicized phrase *"available at"* and the URL for the website. For more information on citing sources on the World Wide Web, see **Rule 31.0**.

Example

Menna v. Walmart, No. 08-2610 (N.Y. Sup. Ct. Suffolk Cnty. July 10, 2013), *available at* http://www.nycourts.gov/reporter/3dseries/2013/2013_51255.htm.

It may not be possible to provide pinpoint references for court decisions published on the World Wide Web. Some courts, however, provide page or paragraph numbering in the opinion. If the opinion displays page numbers, insert the preposition "at" before the pinpoint page reference. If the opinion displays paragraph numbers, do not use the preposition "at," but simply insert the paragraph symbol ¶ or ¶¶ before the cited paragraph(s).

Examples

Page number:

In re Russell, No. SC-11-1, slip op. at 3–4 (N.C. Cherokee Ct. Aug. 15, 2011), *available at* http:// turtletalk.files.wordpress.com/2011/08/in-re-russell.pdf.

Paragraph number:

El-Masri v. Former Yugoslav Republic of Maced., 66 Eur. Ct. H.R. ¶¶ 79–90 (2012), *available at* http://hudoc.echr.coe.int/sites/eng/pages/search.aspx?i=001-115621.

12.17 Neutral Citations

Neutral citations are case citations that do not refer to a particular vendor's source (such as West regional reporters) or to a particular type of source (such as a reporter, a database such as Lexis Advance, or a site on the World Wide Web). They are alternatively labeled as "medium-neutral," "vendor-neutral," "universal," or "public domain" citations.

Always use neutral citations when required by local court rule. Consult **Appendices 1 and 2** to determine whether a particular court requires neutral citations and the specific format, if any, that it requires. Even in non-court documents, however, if the case you wish to cite has an officially assigned neutral citation, include it as a parallel citation to a print reporter citation, as explained below.

If the court does not dictate the format, or the neutral citation is in a document not being submitted to a court, use the following components:

Case name, | Year of decision | State's two-letter postal code abbreviation | Court abbreviation (if decided by a court other than state's highest) | Opinion number [followed by letter "U" if unpublished], | Pinpoint reference.

Examples

*Johnson▲v.▲Traynor,▲*1998▲ND▲115,▲¶¶▲8–9.

*Anderson▲v.▲State,▲*2009▲AR▲Ct.▲App.▲230U,▲at▲6–7.

Include a pinpoint reference whenever possible. Most neutral citation formats use a paragraph number instead of a page number as the pinpoint reference. If the opinion displays page numbers, insert the preposition "at" before the pinpoint page reference. If the opinion displays paragraph numbers, do not use the preposition "at," but simply insert the paragraph symbol ¶ or ¶¶ before the cited paragraph(s).

Examples

Gen. Steel Domestic Sales, LLC v. Bacheller, 2012 CO 68, ¶ 3.

Meleski v. Schbohm LLC, 2012 WI Ct. App. 63, ¶ 6, 341 Wis. 2d 716, 720, 817 N.W.2d 887, 889.

12.18 Court Documents in a Case

Follow this rule to cite court documents or other materials filed in connection with a case *other than* the same case for which the writer is currently writing a document. To cite documents or other materials filed earlier in the *same case* (e.g., in an appellate brief, referring to the trial court's order), follow **Rule 25**.

Set out, in ordinary type, the title of the court document as identified on its cover or first page, followed by a pinpoint reference, if relevant, to specific pages or subdivisions within the document. Do not abbreviate words in the document's title unless they are listed in **Rule 2.3**.

Add a full citation, if available, to the case's publication in a reporter, an online database, or a website, including a court/date parenthetical. If the case is still pending, the date in the parenthetical should reflect the date of the document's filing. In either case, following the court/date parenthetical, add a second parenthetical containing the case's docket number.

Examples

> Complaint ¶¶ 84–88, *United States v. Huseby*, 862 F. Supp. 2d 951 (D. Minn. 2012) (No. 009CV03737).

> Brief for Respondent at 23, *Lozman v. City of Riviera Beach*, http:// www.americanbar.org/ content/dam/aba/publications/ supreme_court_preview/briefs/11-626_respondent.authcheckdam.pdf (U.S. July 12, 2012) (No. 11-626).

12.19 Short Citation Formats for Cases

12.19(a) *Id.* as the preferred short citation

Use *id.* only to refer to the case cited in the immediately preceding citation. That preceding citation must not refer to more than one case, although it may contain a subsequent history phrase (see **Rule 12.8**). Never use *id.* when the preceding citation contains a string citation (see **Rule 34.3**). When *id.* is appropriate, use it as the preferred short citation.

If *id.* is not appropriate, use a citation format from those described below in **Rules 12.19(b)** through **12.19(g)**. See **Rules 11.2** and **11.3** for more information on *id.* and other short citations.

12.19(b) Short citation format when textual sentence has no reference to case name

When the textual sentence supported by the citation does *not* contain a reference to all or part of the cited case's name, use the following short citation format, including reference to the volume and reporter:

Single party's name, | Reporter volume | Reporter abbreviation | at | Pinpoint reference.

Example (short citation in red)

> A trial court generally has discretion whether to grant a motion for a continuance. *Seel v. Van Der Veur*, 971 P.2d 924, 926 (Utah 1998). "[T]o constitute reversible error, the error complained of must be sufficiently prejudicial that there is a reasonable likelihood of a more favorable result for the defendant in its absence." *State v. Featherson*, 781 P.2d 424, 431 (Utah 1989). Where the record supports a conclusion that the trial's outcome would be no different had the continuance been granted, a defendant has not been denied due process of law. ***Seel, 971 P.2d at 927.***

> ***Incorrect:*** *Seel*, at 926.

Use the *first party's* name for the short citation unless that name would cause confusion; if so, use the second party's name. For example, the first party's name would cause confusion if the document cited two or more cases in which the first party's name was Smith; similarly, the first name may cause confusion if the party is a geographic or governmental entity, for example, Massachusetts, United States, People, State.

Example

Full citation:	*United States v. Chairse*, 18 F. Supp. 2d 1021, 1023 (D. Minn. 1998).
Short citation:	*Chairse*, 18 F. Supp. 2d at 1024.

If the party's name is particularly long, include enough of it for a reader to recognize the case. **Rule 12.2(e)** describes ways to shorten an organizational party's name in a full citation.

Example

Full citation:	*Metro E. Ctr. for Conditioning & Health v. Qwest Commc'ns Int'l, Inc.*, 294 F.3d 924, 929 (7th Cir. 2002).
Short citation:	*Metro E. Ctr.*, 294 F.3d at 928.

12.19(c) Short citation format when textual sentence includes all or part of case name

When all or part of the case name is used in the textual sentence supported by the citation, it is unnecessary to repeat the case name in the short citation. Use only the following components:

Volume number | Reporter abbreviation | at | Pinpoint page(s).

Example (short citation in red)

> The decision in *International Shoe* specifically addressed minimum contacts relating to *in personam* jurisdiction. **326 U.S. at 316.**

12.19(d) Short citation format for cases in parallel citations

When the full citation uses parallel citations, *id.* alone is not an appropriate short citation because *id.* refers to a single preceding publication source while a parallel citation refers to two or more publication sources. However, unless a local court rule prohibits your doing so, use *id.* to refer to the *first* source in the parallel citation. For the second source in the parallel citation, provide the volume number, reporter abbreviation, and pinpoint reference.

Example

Full citation:	*Dow Chem. Co. v. Mahlum*, 114 Nev. 1468, 970 P.2d 98 (1998).
Short citation:	*Id.* at 1469, 970 P.2d at 99.

Where you cannot use *id.*, consult **Rules 12.19(b)** and **12.19(c)** to determine whether the short form needs a party name. If it does, select a single party name (following the guidance in **Rule 12.19(b)**). For the first-cited reporter, set out its volume number, reporter abbreviation, and the preposition "at" followed by a pinpoint page reference. Then add a comma, one space, and for the second-cited reporter, its volume number, reporter abbreviation, "at" and a pinpoint page reference. If a pinpoint page reference is not available, use three underlined blank spaces to represent the unavailable page.

Examples

Full citation:	*Abel v. Fox*, 247 Ill. App. 3d 811, 654 N.E.2d 591, 593, 221 Ill. Dec. 129, 131 (4th Dist. 1995).
Short citation:	*Abel*, 247 Ill. App. 3d at 813, 654 N.E.2d at 593, 221 Ill. Dec. at 131.
Full citation:	*Minneci v. Pollard,* ___ U.S. ___, 132 S. Ct. 617, 181 L. Ed. 2d 606 (2012).
Short citation:	*Minneci,* ___ U.S. at ___, 132 S. Ct. at 626, 181 L. Ed. 2d at 616–17.

12.19(e) Short citation format for cases in commercial databases

Select a single party name (following the guidance in **Rule 12.19(b)**). Omit the docket number, and substitute the database identifier for the reporter volume and abbreviation. For a pinpoint reference, use the preposition "at," one space, and a single asterisk, with no space, before the pinpoint page number(s).

Example

Full citation:	*State ex rel. Knotts v. Facemire*, No. 34647, 2009 W. Va. LEXIS 50, at *16 (June 5, 2009).
Short citation:	*Facemire*, 2009 W. Va. LEXIS 50, at *19–20.

12.19(f) Short citation format for slip opinions

Select a single party name (following the guidance in **Rule 12.19(b)**). In place of a reporter reference, use the phrase "slip op. at" before the pinpoint page number(s).

Example

Full citation:	*St. Joseph Abbey v. Castille*, No. 11-30756, slip op. at 10 (5th Cir. Oct. 23, 2012).
Short citation:	*St. Joseph Abbey*, slip op. at 9.

12.19(g)(FN) Short citation format for cases in academic footnotes

⚠ ACADEMIC FORMATTING

In academic footnotes, use *id.* to refer to a single case (including its subsequent history, if any) previously cited within the *same* footnote or cited in the immediately preceding footnote.

Where you cannot use *id.*, consult **Rules 12.19(b)** and **12.19(c)** to determine whether the short form needs a party name. If it does, select a single party name (following the guidance in **Rule 12.19(b)**) and present it *in italics*. (Reminder: Full case names in academic footnotes are presented in ordinary type. **Rule 12.2(a)(2)(FN)**.) Present the rest of the short citation in accordance with **Rule 12.19(b), (c), (d), (e)**, or **(f)**, as applicable.

If the case has not previously been cited in the same footnote or in any of the five immediately preceding footnotes, however, do not use a short form. Repeat the full citation. Never use *supra* as a short citation format for a case.

Example

The wave of post-*Chevron* deference arguably crested in 1997 with *Auer v. Robbins*,[256] a unanimous decision authored by Justice Scalia.[257] . . . The dispute in *Auer* involved a claim by St. Louis police officers that the City had erroneously designated them "exempt" from the wage and hour provisions of the Fair Labor Standards Act (FLSA).[263] The Secretary of Labor, carrying out specific rulemaking authority conferred by the FLSA,[264] had issued regulations defining the scope of the exemption,[265] which in part turned on the outcome of the "salary basis test,"[266] defined in the agency's regulations.[267] As one condition for exempt status, an employee's salary could not be subject to reduction for variations in "work performance."[268] The officers argued that the mere possibility that their salaries might be reduced was sufficient to defeat exempt status. The City argued that to be nonexempt, the officers had to be realistically vulnerable to an actual pay reduction; a theoretical possibility was not enough.[269]

[256] 519 U.S. 452 (1997).

[257] *Id.* at 454.

. . .

[263] Auer v. Robbins, 519 U.S. 452, 455 (1997).

[264] 29 U.S.C. § 213(a)(1) (2006).

[265] *Auer*, 519 U.S. at 456.

[266] *Id.* at 456–57.

[267] *See* 29 C.F.R. §§ 541.1(f), 541.2(e), 541.3(e) (1996).

[268] *Auer*, 519 U.S. at 456 (citing 29 C.F.R. § 541.118(a) (1996)) (defining "salary basis" test).

[269] *Id.* at 459.

13 Constitutions

Fast Formats

Constitutions	
United States Constitution (provision currently in force)	U.S. Const. art. IV, § 5(b).
United States Constitution (provision not currently in force)	U.S. Const. amend. XVIII (repealed 1933).
State constitutions (provisions currently in force)	Conn. Const. art. XIII, § 1. N.J. Const. art. I, ¶ 9.
State constitutions (provision not currently in force)	Cal. Const. art. XVII, *repealed by* Cal. Const. art. XXI.
Constitution cited in academic footnote	[42]U.S. CONST. art. II, § 4.
Short citation	*Id.* amend. V.

13.1 Which Source to Cite

Typically cite the constitution currently in force, using a print source. For citations to constitutions in official websites or electronic databases, see **Rule 13.2(d)**. For citations to historical constitutional provisions, see **Rule 13.3**.

13.2 Full Citation Format for Constitutions Currently in Force

A full citation to a print source of a constitution currently in force contains only two components, its abbreviated name and a pinpoint reference.

> Abbreviated name of constitution | Pinpoint reference.

Example (spaces denoted by ▲)

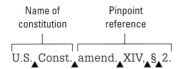

Name of constitution	Pinpoint reference

U.S.▲Const.▲amend.▲XIV,▲§▲2.

13.2(a) Name of constitution

A constitution's name uses the abbreviation of its jurisdiction (U.S. or a state's abbreviation, as shown in **Appendix 3(B)**), a space, and the abbreviation "Const.," all in ordinary type.

Examples (spaces denoted by ▲)

> U.S.▲Const.▲amend.▲XXVI.
>
> N.J.▲Const.▲art.▲XI,▲§▲7.

13.2(b) Pinpoint references in citations to constitutions

Following the abbreviated name of the constitution, set out the relevant pinpoint reference. Use the subdivision abbreviations in **Appendix 3(C)**. When citing the United States Constitution, use roman numerals for articles and amendments; use arabic numbers for smaller subsections, such as sections and clauses. For a state constitution, follow the numbering system shown in the cited source. For more information on numbers, see **Rule 4**; for more information on citing subdivisions, see **Rule 6**.

Examples (spaces denoted by ▲)

> U.S.▲Const.▲art.▲I,▲§▲9,▲cl.▲2.
>
> U.S.▲Const.▲pmbl.
>
> Fla.▲Const.▲art.▲X,▲§▲2(a)–(b).
>
> Ga.▲Const.▲art.▲I,▲§▲1,▲¶▲16.
>
> Kan.▲Const.▲Bill▲of▲Rights▲§▲15.

13.2(c) Date references in citations to constitutions

Citations to constitutional provisions currently in force ordinarily omit date references. However, if information about a date is relevant to the point for which the constitution is being cited (e.g., date of an amendment's adoption), you may include it parenthetically. See **Rule 13.3** for citing relevant dates of former constitutional provisions.

Examples

> U.S. Const. amend. XIV, § 2.
>
> Iowa Const. art. I, § 1 (amended 1998).

13.2(d) Constitution published in commercial database or official website

To cite a constitutional provision published in a commercial database such as WestlawNext, Lexis Advance, or Bloomberg BNA, add a parenthetical identifying the database and its currency, as indicated by the database itself.

Example (spaces denoted by ▲)

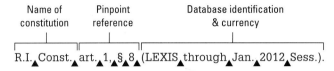

Name of   Pinpoint   Database identification
constitution   reference   & currency

R.I.▲Const.▲art.▲1,▲§▲8▲(LEXIS▲through▲Jan.▲2012▲Sess.).

If a version of a constitution on the World Wide Web is published, edited, or compiled by or under the supervision of governmental officials, no parenthetical is needed; cite the constitution the same as its print version.

13.2(e)(FN) Citing constitutions in academic footnotes

⚠ ACADEMIC FORMATTING

When citing a constitution in an academic footnote, use large and small capital letters for the name of the constitution, and use ordinary type for subdivisions such as articles, amendments, and clauses.

Examples

   [23] U.S. CONST. amend. XXVI.

   [64] N.J. CONST. art. XI, § 7.

13.3   Full Citation Format for Constitutions or Specific Constitutional Provisions No Longer in Force

13.3(a) Historical constitutions

When citing a historical constitution that has been completely superseded or is otherwise no longer in force, set out the abbreviated name of the constitution followed by the preposition "of" and the year of that constitution's adoption. You may add a pinpoint reference to a particular provision of the historical constitution.

Examples

  Ind. Const. of 1816.

  Ga. Const. of 1777, art. IX, § 1.

13.3(b) Constitutional provisions no longer in force

When citing a particular constitutional provision that is no longer in force (e.g., one that has been amended, repealed, or superseded), use the citation format for the current constitution and the pinpoint reference, but add a parenthetical, in ordinary type, stating the reason the provision is no longer in force and the year the provision lost effect.

If the provision was repealed, refer to the year of repeal. If the provision was amended, refer to the year of amendment. Alternatively, you may append a clause with an italicized reference to the action affecting the provision, followed by a full citation to the repealing or amending provision.

Examples

U.S. Const. amend. XVIII (repealed 1933).

Cal. Const. art. XXV (repealed 1949).

U.S. Const. amend. XVIII, *repealed by* U.S. Const. amend. XXI.

La. Const. art. I, § 6 (1921), *superseded by* La. Const. art. I, § 22.

13.4 Short Citation Format for Constitutions

When appropriate, use *id.* as a short-form citation for constitutional provisions (whether current or no longer in force). See **Rule 11.3** for more information on using *id.* If *id.* is not appropriate, repeat the full citation.

Example

Full citation:	U.S. Const. art. I, § 10, cl. 3.
Short citation:	*Id.* art. VI, cl. 2.

SIDEBAR 13.1   Referring to Constitutions in Text

When referring to a constitutional provision in a textual sentence, do not use the citation format; instead, spell out the provision. Even though they are not capitalized within a citation, capitalize textual references to subdivisions of the United States Constitution. Do not capitalize a textual reference to a state constitution's subdivision unless it is the first word of a sentence.

Examples

Impeachment of the President is treated in Article II, Section 4.

The argument centered on the Privileges and Immunities Clause of the Fourteenth Amendment.

Article IX, section 1, of the Florida Constitution provides that "[a]dequate provision shall be made by law for a uniform system of free public schools."

14 Statutory Codes and Session Laws

Fast Formats

Statutory Codes and Session Laws	
Full citation format for *United States Code*	19 U.S.C. § 2411 (2012).
Full citation format for *United States Code Annotated* (citing a supplement)	5 U.S.C.A. § 552 (West Supp. 2013).
Full citation format for *United States Code Service* (citing main volume and a supplement)	17 U.S.C.S. § 115 (LexisNexis 2008 & Supp. 2013).
Full citation format for state statute (consult Appendix 1 for each state's format)	Wyo. Stat. Ann. § 4-10-902 (2011). N.Y. Exec. Law § 63-b (McKinney 2010). Conn. Gen. Stat. Ann. § 9-325 (West 2009).
Statute in commercial database	Or. Rev. Stat. Ann. § 258.036 (West, WestlawNext through Ch. 570 of 2013 Reg. Sess.). Mass. Ann. Laws ch. 56, § 59 (LexisNexis, Lexis Advance through Act 29 of 2013 Legis. Sess.).
Statute cited in academic footnote	[33] 18 U.S.C. § 2314 (2012). [119] Mo. Rev. Stat. § 287.835 (2011).
Short citation formats for federal and state statutes	*Id.* § 2412. 19 U.S.C. § 2412. Or. Rev. Stat. Ann. § 258.036.
Federal session law	Pub. L. No. 109-2, 119 Stat. 12 (2005). Economic Espionage Act of 1996, Pub. L. No. 104-294, § 201, 110 Stat. 3488, 3491.
State session law (consult Appendix 1 for each state's format)	1985 N.J. Laws 308.
Short citation formats for session laws	119 Stat. at 13. Economic Espionage Act § 201. § 201, 110 Stat. at 3492. 1996 Alaska Sess. Laws at 53.

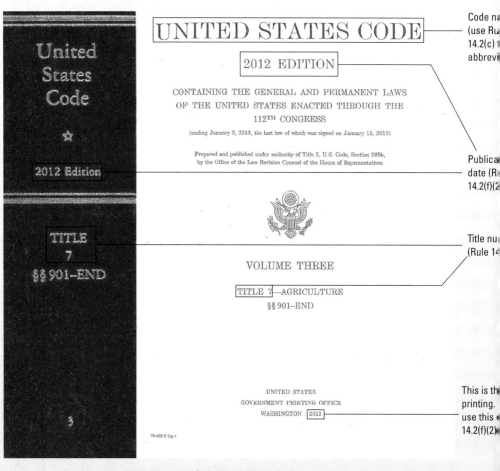

Spine and Title Page

Spine:

United
States
Code

☆

2012 Edition

TITLE
7
§§ 901–END

3

Title Page:

UNITED STATES CODE

2012 EDITION

CONTAINING THE GENERAL AND PERMANENT LAWS
OF THE UNITED STATES ENACTED THROUGH THE
112TH CONGRESS

(ending January 2, 2013, the last law of which was signed on January 15, 2013)

Prepared and published under authority of Title 2, U.S. Code, Section 285b,
by the Office of the Law Revision Counsel of the House of Representatives

VOLUME THREE

TITLE 7—AGRICULTURE
§§ 901–END

UNITED STATES
GOVERNMENT PRINTING OFFICE
WASHINGTON : 2013

78-402 D Sig-1

Annotations (right margin):

Code na
(use Ru
14.2(c)
abbrev

Publica
date (R
14.2(f)(2

Title nu
(Rule 14

This is th
printing.
use this
14.2(f)(2)

Snapshot
UNITED STATES CODE

§ 1736e

Section number (Rule 14.2(d)). Use only the section number, not the subtitle that follows it.

ducted under subchapters I, III, and III–A of this chapter, and that such evaluations cover no fewer than five countries sampled from the developing regions (Asia, Africa, Latin America, and Caribbean), and assess the nutritional and other impacts, achievements, problems, and future prospects for programs thereunder, for provisions that, not later than November 1 of each calendar year the President submit to the House Committee on Agriculture, the House Committee on International Relations, the Senate Committee on Agriculture and Forestry, and the Senate Committee on Foreign Relations a revised global assessment of food production and needs, and revised planned programming of food assistance for the current fiscal year, to reflect, to the maximum extent feasible, the actual availability of commodities for food assistance.

Subsecs. (d), (e). Pub. L. 95–113 added subsecs. (d) and (e).

1975—Pub. L. 94–161 designated existing provisions as subsec. (a), substituted "fiscal" for "calendar" in first sentence, and added subsecs. (b) and (c).

EFFECTIVE DATE OF 2008 AMENDMENT

Amendment by Pub. L. 110–246 effective May 22, 2008, see section 4(b) of Pub. L. 110–246, set out as an Effective Date note under section 8701 of this title.

EFFECTIVE DATE OF 1990 AMENDMENT

Amendment by Pub. L. 101–624 effective Jan. 1, 1991, see section 1513 of Pub. L. 101–624, set out as a note under section 1691 of this title.

EFFECTIVE DATE OF 1985 AMENDMENT

Amendment by Pub. L. 99–83 effective Oct. 1, 1985, see section 1301 of Pub. L. 99–83, set out as a note under section 2151–1 of Title 22, Foreign Relations and Intercourse.

EFFECTIVE DATE OF 1981 AMENDMENT

Amendment by Pub. L. 97–98 effective Dec. 22, 1981, see section 1801 of Pub. L. 97–98, set out as an Effective Date note under section 4301 of this title.

EFFECTIVE DATE OF 1977 AMENDMENTS

Amendment by Pub. L. 95–113 effective Oct. 1, 1977, see section 1901 of Pub. L. 95–113, set out as a note under section 1307 of this title.

Amendment by Pub. L. 95–88 effective Oct. 1, 1977, see section 215 of Pub. L. 95–88, set out as a note under section 1702 of this title.

EFFECTIVE DATE

Section effective Jan. 1, 1967, see section 5 of Pub. L. 89–808, set out as an Effective Date of 1966 Amendment note under section 1691 of this title.

§§ 1736c, 1736d. Repealed. Pub. L. 104–127, title II, §§ 218, 219, Apr. 4, 1996, 110 Stat. 957

Section 1736c, act July 10, 1954, ch. 469, title IV, § 409, as added Nov. 11, 1966, Pub. L. 89–808, § 2(E), 80 Stat. 1537; amended July 29, 1968, Pub. L. 90–436, § 1, 82 Stat. 450; Nov. 30, 1970, Pub. L. 91–524, title VII, § 701, 84 Stat. 1379; Aug. 10, 1979, Pub. L. 92–96, § 1(26), 87 Stat. 237; Sept. 29, 1977, Pub. L. 95–113, title XII, § 1208, 91 Stat. 957; Dec. 22, 1981, Pub. L. 97–98, title XII, § 1216, 95 Stat. 1282; Dec. 23, 1985, Pub. L. 99–198, title XI, § 1105, 99 Stat. 1466; Nov. 28, 1990, Pub. L. 101–624, title XV, § 1512, 104 Stat. 3653; Dec. 13, 1991, Pub. L. 102–237, title III, § 322, 105 Stat. 1857, required promulgation of regulations to implement chapter not later than 180 days after Nov. 28, 1990.

Section 1736d, act July 10, 1954, ch. 469, title IV, § 410, as added Nov. 11, 1966, Pub. L. 89–808, § 2(E), 80 Stat. 1538; amended Nov. 28, 1990, Pub. L. 101–624, title XV, § 1512, 104 Stat. 3653; Dec. 13, 1991, Pub. L. 102–237, title III, § 322, 105 Stat. 1857, provided for independent evaluation of programs under subchapters II, III, and III–A of this chapter and report to Congress.

§ 1736e. Debt forgiveness

(a) Authority

The President, taking into account the financial resources of a country, may waive payments of principal and interest that such country would otherwise be required to make to the Commodity Credit Corporation under dollar sales agreements under subchapter II of this chapter if—

(1) that country is a least developed country; and

(2) either—

(A) an International Monetary Fund standby agreement is in effect with respect to that country;

(B) a structural adjustment program of the International Bank for Reconstruction and Development or of the International Development Association is in effect with respect to that country;

(C) a structural adjustment facility, enhanced structural adjustment facility, or similar supervised arrangement with the International Monetary Fund is in effect with respect to that country; or

(D) even though such an agreement, program, facility, or arrangement is not in effect, the country is pursuing national economic policy reforms that would promote democratic, market-oriented, and long term economic development.

(b) Request for debt relief by President

The President may provide debt relief under subsection (a) of this section only if a notification to Congress is submitted at least 10 days prior to providing the debt relief. Such a notification shall—

(1) specify the amount of official debt the President proposes to liquidate; and

(2) identify the countries for which debt relief is proposed and the basis for their eligibility for such relief.

(c) Appropriations action required

Subsection (Rule 14.2(d))

The aggregate amount of principal and interest waived under this section may not exceed the amount approved for such purpose in an Act appropriating funds to carry out this chapter.

(d) Limitation on new credit assistance

If the authority of this section is used to waive payments otherwise required to be made by a country pursuant to this chapter, the President may not provide any new credit assistance for that country under this chapter during the 2-year period beginning on the date such waiver authority is exercised, unless the President provides to the Congress, before the assistance is provided, a written justification for the provision of such new credit assistance.

(e) Applicability

The authority of this section applies with respect to credit sales agreements entered into before November 28, 1990.

(July 10, 1954, ch. 469, title IV, § 411, as added Pub. L. 91–524, title VII, § 704, Nov. 30, 1970, as added Pub. L. 93–86, § 1(26), Aug. 10, 1973, 87 Stat. 237; amended Pub. L. 101–624, title XV, § 1512, Nov. 28, 1990, 104 Stat. 3654; Pub. L. 102–237, title

Inside Page

109

14.1 Sources of Statutory Law

Federal statutes are preferably cited either to the official print version of the *United States Code* (even though it is rarely up to date (see **Sidebar 14.1**)) or to the authenticated online version of the code in the Government Printing Office's Federal Digital System ("FDsys"). Authenticated online content is identified with the Government Printing Office's seal of authenticity, a graphic of an eagle beside the phrase "Authenticated U.S. Government Information." Cite an authenticated federal statute in FDsys exactly the same way you cite it in the official print source (**Rule 14.2**).

Similarly, cite official versions of state statutes if possible. Official print compilations of state statutes are indicated with a star (★) in **Appendix 1(B)**. A few states publish authenticated versions of their statutes online, and these kinds of official online compilations are certain to become more common. Do not assume that an online compilation is official, even if on a governmental website; look for specific language indicating its status as official or authenticated.

For federal or state statutes, if the official or authenticated code is not readily available or does not yet contain the cited statute, cite the statute in other sources according to the following order of preference:

▪ Unofficial code in print;

▪ Official session laws in print;

▪ Unofficial session laws in print;

▪ Commercial database;

▪ Looseleaf service;

▪ Unofficial source on World Wide Web; or

▪ A newspaper.

(Note: If you want readers to view a statute in the form enacted by the legislature, cite the session law. See **Rule 14.6**.)

14.2 Full Citation Format for Federal Statutes Currently in Force

A full citation to a federal statute currently in force has five to seven components, depending on whether it has an official name, whether the cited source of the code is official or unofficial, and whether the source is in print or online.

[Official name (if any),] | Title number | Code abbreviation | §[§] | Section number(s) (including pinpoint subdivision, if any) | ([Publisher if citing unofficial code] | Publication date [or Database | through | Currency information]).

Examples (spaces denoted by ▲)

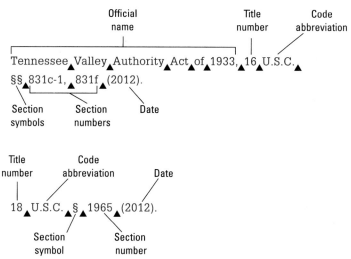

14.2(a) Official or popular name of statute

If a statute is commonly referenced by its name, or if providing the name of a cited statute would assist your readers in identifying it, you may begin the citation with the statute's official name, popular name, or both, set out in ordinary type. Capitalize words in the name according to the guidelines in **Rule 3.2**. If the statute's official name includes reference to a year, keep it. If the statute is typically cited with its original section number, add that reference to the title as well. Omit "The" when it begins a statute's name. You can find official and popular name tables at the end of the general indexes to the *United States Code* and the two unofficial codes.

Examples

Americans with Disabilities Act of 1990, 42 U.S.C. §§ 12101–12117 (2012).

Securities Exchange Act of 1934 § 10(b), 15 U.S.C. § 78j(b) (2012).

Marine Mammal Rescue Assistance Act of 2000, 16 U.S.C.A. § 1421f-1 (West 2010).

14.2(b) Title number

Federal statutes are grouped within numbered titles. The *United States Code* has fifty-one titles, each addressing specific topics. If the citation begins with the name of the statute, add a comma and one space, followed by the title number and a space. If you are not providing the name of the statute, begin the citation with the title number, followed by a space.

Title 26 is the Internal Revenue Code; in citations to that title, you may substitute the abbreviation "I.R.C." for "26 U.S.C."

14.2(c) Abbreviated name of code

Following the title number, insert the abbreviated name of the code, in ordinary type, followed by a space. The official code for federal statutes is the *United States Code* ("U.S.C."), whether in print or in the authenticated online FDsys (see **Rule 14.1**).

The two unofficial codes are the *United States Code Annotated* ("U.S.C.A.") and the *United States Code Service* ("U.S.C.S."), available in print and in their publishers' commercial databases (**Rule 14.2(f)**).

14.2(d) Sections and subsections in federal statutes

Following the code abbreviation, insert one or two section symbols (§ or §§), depending on whether the citation refers to a single section or multiple sections of the code. Insert a space after the final symbol; avoid putting a space *between* two section symbols.

Following the section symbol(s), set out the section number(s) and subsection(s) you are citing, making as specific a reference as possible. Some sections of the *United States Code* are designated by numbers plus one or more letters (which may be uppercase or lowercase); do not treat these letters as subsections, and do not insert a space before them. Omit references to subtitles, parts, chapters, or subchapters of the *United States Code*. See **Rule 6** for more information on citing sections and subsections, particularly when citing consecutive or scattered subsections.

Examples (spaces denoted by ▲):

Single section:	28▲U.S.C.▲§▲2671▲(2012).
	18▲U.S.C.▲§▲1593(b)(3)▲(2012).
Section designated by number and letters:	18▲U.S.C.▲§▲3600A▲(2012).
Consecutive sections:	21▲U.S.C.▲§§▲2001–2003▲(2012).
Consecutive subsections:	28▲U.S.C.▲§▲2631(a)–(c)▲(2012).
	6▲U.S.C.▲§▲195a(b)(1)–(2)▲(2012).
Scattered sections:	15▲U.S.C.▲§§▲291,▲297▲(2012).
Scattered subsections:	18▲U.S.C.▲§▲1962(a),▲(d)▲(2012).
	5▲U.S.C.▲§▲305(a)(1),▲(4),▲(7)▲(2012).

14.2(e) Statutory appendices and other subdivisions

To cite material in a statutory appendix, insert the abbreviation "app." immediately following the title number and code abbreviation, followed by a pinpoint reference to relevant section(s) and subsection(s), if any.

Example

46 U.S.C. app. §§ 1300–1315 (1994).

To cite notes or other types of information accompanying a statute, insert the word "note" or, if applicable, an abbreviation from **Appendix 3(C)** for the specific subdivision immediately following the section number. You may use a parenthetical to identify one of multiple named notes beneath a section, as illustrated in the third example below.

Examples

5 U.S.C. § 801 note (2006).

49 U.S.C. § 40105 hist. nn. (2006).

15 U.S.C. § 78s note (2006) (Construction of 1993 Amendment).

14.2(f) Publication parenthetical

A statute's publication parenthetical immediately follows the statute's section number(s) and pinpoint references. Citations to statutes in official codes do not indicate the name of a publisher; they identify only the date of publication. In practice-based documents, if you are using the abbreviation "I.R.C." in place of "26 U.S.C." in the current official code, you may drop the publication parenthetical otherwise required by this rule.

Example

Internal Revenue Code section: 26 U.S.C. § 1402(b) (2012).

or

I.R.C. § 1402(b).

When citing a statute in an unofficial version of the code, however, indicate the code's publisher, as well as the name of the commercial database, where applicable, as explained in **Rule 14.2(f)(1)**.

Whether you are citing an official or an unofficial code, the publication parenthetical must also indicate the publication date of the particular source, as explained in **Rule 14.2(f)(2)**.

14.2(f)(1) Code publisher; commercial database name

Citations to statutes in the official *United States Code*, including citations to FDsys (see **Rule 14.1**), *do not* refer to a publisher. In citations to unofficial print or online codes, however, the publication parenthetical begins with the name of the publisher, followed by one space. If citing a statute to a commercial database (**Rule 14.2(g)**), start the parenthetical with the name of the publisher, followed by the database name, followed by a space.

Examples

> 10 U.S.C. § 2358 (2012).
>
> 10 U.S.C.A. § 2358 (West 2010).
>
> 10 U.S.C.S. § 2358 (LexisNexis, Lexis Advance through Pub. L. No. 113-22, approved July 25, 2013).

14.2(f)(2) Publication date of main volume or supplement; database currency

Every publication parenthetical must indicate the statute's publication date *in the particular source* being cited, whether official or unofficial, whether in print or online. The publication date indicates the currency of the source you cited for the statute. Insert the publication date immediately after the publisher and database name, if any, as shown in the examples below.

For print sources, you may need to provide the publication date for the main volume, a supplement (abbreviated "Supp." whether separately bound or a pocket part), or both. Depending on what is available in the cited source, use the date shown on the spine of the volume, the title page, or the copyright page, in that order. For more information on citing supplements, see **Rule 8**. For more information about publication dates of the *United States Code*, see **Sidebar 14.1**. For citations to the *United States Code* in FDsys, use the publication date of the analogous print version.

When citing a statute in a commercial database, provide the date through which the statute is current in that database. Use the date information as provided by the database itself, which may be a year, an exact Month Day, Year, a particular legislative enactment, a legislative session, a date within a legislative session, or some combination thereof. Abbreviate months as shown in **Appendix 3(A)**.

Examples

Cited material appears only in main volume:	18 U.S.C. § 1965 (2012).
Cited material appears only in supplement:	12 U.S.C. §§ 5381–5394 (Supp. V 2011).
Cited material appears in both main volume and supplement:	17 U.S.C. § 503 (2006 & Supp. V 2011).
Cited material appears in commercial database:	42 U.S.C.A. § 1751 (West, WestlawNext through Pub. L. No. 113-13, approved June 3, 2013).
	42 U.S.C.S. § 1751 (LexisNexis, Lexis Advance through Pub. L. No. 113-22, approved July 25, 2013).

SIDEBAR 14.1	**Publication Dates of Official and Unofficial Versions of the _United States Code_**

A new edition of the official _United States Code_ is published every six years. All titles in the most recent edition were published in 2012. Use the 2012 version of the official code (or its supplements) unless you are doing historical research and need to cite a statute that no longer appears in the current official code.

In contrast, individual volumes of the unofficial _United States Code Annotated_ and the _United States Code Service_ are republished as needed (e.g., when a pocket part becomes too large to fit within the volume's back cover); thus, different volumes of these unofficial codes are likely to have different publication dates.

Similarly, commercial databases update their statutory collections on their own schedules, and they do so more frequently than their print counterparts. Do not assume that the date through which an online statute is current will be the same as its print counterpart or as its counterpart in a different database.

14.2(g) Explanatory parentheticals in statutory citations

To any statute's citation, you may append a separate explanatory parenthetical to indicate the significance of the source. Following the date parenthetical, insert one space and begin a new parenthetical containing the explanation. For more information about explanatory parentheticals, see **Rule 37.**

Examples

35 U.S.C. § 1 (2012) (enacted under Patent Act of 1952, 66 Stat. 792 (1952)).

17 U.S.C. § 109(a) (2012) (providing that "the owner of a particular copy . . . lawfully made under this title, or any person authorized by such owner, is entitled, without the authority of the copyright owner, to sell or otherwise dispose of the possession of that copy").

14.2(h)(FN) Full citations to federal statutes in academic footnotes

⚠ ACADEMIC FORMATTING

In an academic footnote, use large and small capital letters for the abbreviated name of the code, and use ordinary type for everything else. In an academic footnote, if the citation uses the abbreviation "I.R.C." in place of "26 U.S.C.," it must include a publication parenthetical.

Examples

[155] 11 U.S.C. § 721 (2012).

[162] Securities Exchange Act of 1934 § 10(b), 15 U.S.C. § 78j(b) (2012).

14.3 Full Citation Format for Federal Statutes No Longer in Force

14.3(a) Federal statutes repealed or amended

If citing a federal statute that is no longer in force because it was repealed or amended, follow the basic citation format set out in **Rule 14.2**, adding a parenthetical indicating the fact of repeal or amendment, followed by the year of the repeal or amendment. Alternatively, you may append a clause with an italicized reference to the repeal or amendment, followed by a full citation to the repealing or amending statute or session law; for citations to federal session laws, see **Rules 14.6** and **14.7**.

If desired, you may add a parenthetical setting out the year in which the repealed or amended statute was enacted; including this date is important if a more current provision uses the same pinpoint reference (e.g., article number or amendment number). Including the date also can help a reader locate the original provision.

Examples

26 U.S.C. § 1071(a) (repealed 1995).

26 U.S.C. § 1071(a), *repealed by* Act of Apr. 11, 1995, Pub. L. No. 104-7, § 2(a), 109 Stat. 93.

14.3(b) Federal statutes invalidated or declared unconstitutional

If citing a federal statute that is no longer in force because it has been invalidated or held unconstitutional by a court, follow the basic citation format set out in **Rule 14.2**, and append a clause with an italicized reference to the court's action, followed by a full citation to the case.

Example

Flag Protection Act of 1989, 18 U.S.C. § 700 (2006), Pub. L. No. 101-131, 103 Stat. 777, *held unconstitutional by United States v. Eichman*, 496 U.S. 310 (1990).

14.4 Full Citation Format for State Statutes

14.4(a) Components of full citation to state statute

Each state has at least one code containing its statutes. The elements and arrangement of state statutory citations vary widely. Always consult the jurisdiction's entry in **Appendix 1** for its specific components, format, order, and abbreviations. If citing a state statute that is no longer in force, analogize to **Rule 14.3**.

To the extent consistent with the state's entry in **Appendix 1**, analogize to similar components in the rules for federal statutes:

Component:	Rule:
Official or popular name of statute	14.2(a)
Section symbols and section numbers	14.2(d)
Appendices and other subdivisions	14.2(e)
Publisher or commercial database	14.2(f)(1)
Publication date or current-through information	14.2(f)(2)
Explanatory parentheticals	14.2(g)

Examples

Del. Code Ann. tit. 13, § 711A (2012).

Fla. Stat. Ann. § 608.4225(1)(b) (West 2007).

65 Ill. Comp. Stat. 5/11-61-2 (2006).

Ariz. Rev. Stat. § 8-303 (West, WestlawNext through 1st Reg. & 1st Spec. Sess. of 51st Leg.).

Haw. Rev. Stat. Ann. § 201B-1 (LexisNexis, Lexis Advance through Act 110 of 2013 Reg. Sess.).

14.4(b) State code with subject-matter designations

As shown in their states' entries in **Appendix 1(B)**, a few state codes use subject-matter designations. If citing a statute from a subject-matter code, use the abbreviations shown in the jurisdiction's entry in **Appendix 1(B)**.

Examples

Cal. Prob. Code § 4264(c) (West 2009).

N.Y. Gen. Oblig. Law § 5-1501 (McKinney 2011 & Supp. 2013).

14.4(c)(FN) Full citations to state statutes in academic footnotes

⚠ ACADEMIC FORMATTING

In an academic footnote, use large and small capital letters for the abbreviated name of the state code, and use ordinary type for everything else.

Examples

> 11 TENN. CODE ANN. § 55-50-405(a)(1)(C) (2012).

> 42 MO. ANN. STAT. § 404.710.6(3) (West 2011 & Supp. 2013).

14.5 Short Citation Formats for Federal and State Statutes

14.5(a) Appropriate use of *id.* as short citation for federal or state statute

If a citation refers to a statute *within the same title, chapter, or part* as a statute cited in the citation immediately previous, use *id.* as the preferred short citation format, changing the section number as needed (see **Rule 11.3**).

14.5(b) Other short citation formats for federal or state statutes

If *id.* is not appropriate, use one of the short citation formats illustrated below. In selecting a format, choose one with enough information for the reader to easily recognize the source.

Examples

Full citation (federal):	42 U.S.C. § 12101 (2012).
Short citation options:	42 U.S.C. § 12101.
	§ 12101.
Full citation (named statute):	Administrative Procedure Act § 5(d), 5 U.S.C. § 554(e) (2012).
Short citation options:	Administrative Procedure Act § 5(d).
	§ 5(d).
	5 U.S.C. § 554(e).
	§ 554(e).

Full citation (state):	Okla. Stat. Ann. tit. 22, § 258 (2003 & Supp. 2012).
Short citation options:	Okla. Stat. Ann. tit. 22, § 258.
	Tit. 22, § 258.
	§ 258.

14.5(c)(FN) Short citation formats for federal and state statutes in academic footnotes

⚠ ACADEMIC FORMATTING

In documents with academic footnotes, if *id.* is not appropriate (see **Rules 11.1(c)**, **11.3(c)**, and **11.3(f)**), you may use all required components of the full citation, omitting the date, or you may use one of the formats illustrated in **Rule 14.5(b)**, presenting the abbreviated name of the code in large and small capital letters. However, if the statute has not previously been cited in the same footnote or in any of the five previous footnotes, do not use a short form. Repeat the full citation. Do not use *supra* as a short citation format for a statute.

Examples

Federal:

[121] 18 U.S.C. § 1965 (2012).

[122] *Id.* § 1961.

   .   .   .

[124] § 1965.

   .   .   .

[138] 18 U.S.C. § 1965 (2012).

State:

[73] MICH. COMP. LAWS § 445.84 (2008).

[74] *Id.* § 445.86.

   .   .   .

[87] MICH. COMP. LAWS § 445.86 (2008).

   .   .   .

[90] § 445.86.

14.6 Full Citation Format for Federal Session Laws Currently in Force

Once a legislative enactment has been signed into law, but before it is codified, it is cited as a session law (also referred to in the singular as a "slip law"). A full citation to a federal session law currently in force contains the following components. Additional information may be added parenthetically, as indicated below.

> Title of act, if available, | Law abbreviation | No. | Law number, | Pinpoint reference, | Volume number | Stat. | Initial page, | Pinpoint page(s) | (Date).

Example

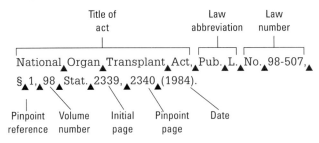

14.6(a) Title of act

Begin the citation with the title or popular name of the act, if it has one, omitting "the" if the first word. If the act is not titled, identify it by referring to its date of enactment or date of effectiveness, using the abbreviated Month Day, and Year. Insert a comma and one space after the title. Present the title in ordinary type. Follow **Rule 3.2** for capitalization and **Appendix 3(A)** for calendar abbreviations.

Examples

Jumpstart Our Business Startups Act, Pub. L. No. 112-106, 126 Stat. 306, 307–08 (2012).

Act of Nov. 7, 2011, Pub. L. No. 112-45, 125 Stat. 535, 536–37.

14.6(b) Abbreviations for public laws and private laws

Federal laws are enacted either as public laws (abbreviated "Pub. L."), which apply generally to all persons, or as private laws (abbreviated "Priv. L."), which apply only to specific individuals or groups. Select the appropriate law abbreviation for the act, in ordinary type, followed by one space.

14.6(c) Public or private law number

After the law abbreviation, set out the abbreviation "No." followed by a space and the number of the public or private law. Federal law numbers are hyphenated (e.g., 107-49). The number preceding the hyphen identifies the Congress that enacted the law (e.g., the 107th Congress). The number following the hyphen indicates the sequential order of the enactment (e.g., the 49th law enacted by the 107th Congress). Insert a comma and one space after the law number.

Example

Priv. L. No. 112-1,

14.6(d) *Statutes at Large*

At the end of each session of Congress, the individual slip laws are compiled as session laws and collectively published in *United States Statutes at Large* (abbreviated "Stat."). Following the law number, set out the volume number of *Statutes at Large* in which the cited session law is published, if available. Insert one space after the volume number, followed by the abbreviation "Stat.," in ordinary type, and one space.

Example

> Credit Card Accountability Responsibility and Disclosure Act of 2009, Pub. L. No. 111-24, § 148(b)(1), 123 Stat. 1734, 1738.

If the statute is not yet available in print in *Statutes at Large*, cite its authenticated online version in the Federal Digital System (FDsys) exactly as you would cite the print source. Alternatively, you may cite a commercial source for advance session laws, such as West's *United States Code Congressional and Administrative News* (abbreviated "U.S.C.C.A.N."), the advance pamphlets of LexisNexis's *United States Code Service*, *United States Law Week*, or a commercial database from publishers such as Lexis Advance, WestlawNext, or Bloomberg BNA.

14.6(e) Initial page and pinpoint references

After "Stat.," insert the initial page of the cited law. If citing specific sections of a session law, indicate them with section numbers and provide corresponding page numbers from *Statutes at Large*. See **Rule 5.2** for more information on pinpoint references.

Example

> Economic Espionage Act of 1996, Pub. L. No. 104-294, § 201, 110 Stat. 3488, 3491.

14.6(f) Enactment or effective date

Following the page reference(s), set out in parentheses the year of the session law's enactment, or if no enactment date is available, the law's effective date. Omit this date reference if the year is part of the session law's title.

Examples

> Air Carriage of International Mail Act, Pub. L. No. 110-405, § 2(a), 122 Stat. 4287, 4287–90 (2008).
>
> Act of Aug. 16, 2012, Pub. L. No. 112-170, 126 Stat. 1303, 1304.

14.6(g) Information regarding codification of session law

If available, indicate parenthetically the statutory code in which the session law has been or will be codified.

Example

> Cruise Vessel Security and Safety Act of 2010, Pub. L. No. 111-207, § 3, 124 Stat. 2243, 2244–51 (codified as 46 U.S.C. §§ 3507–3508 (2012)).

14.6(h)(FN) Full citations to federal session laws in academic footnotes ⚠ ACADEMIC FORMATTING

There are no differences between citations to federal session laws in academic footnotes and those in practice-based documents.

14.7 Full Citation Format for Federal Session Laws No Longer in Force

When citing a session law for a federal statute that is no longer in force, follow **Rule 14.6**, but add a parenthetical notation regarding the date that the statute was repealed or superseded.

Example

> Pub. L. No. 87-301, § 5, 75 Stat. 650, 651–53 (1961) (repealed 1996).

14.8 Full Citation Format for State Session Laws

To cite state session laws, follow the formats and use the abbreviations shown in the state's entry in **Appendix 1**, setting out all components in ordinary type. To the extent the state session law's components are comparable to federal session law components, analogize to **Rule 14.6**. If a state session law is no longer in force, analogize to **Rule 14.7**. Whether you are citing a state session law in print or in electronic format, the citation form is the same. You may indicate parenthetically information about finding the source.

Examples of state session laws

> 2009 S.D. Sess. Laws 69, 71.

> 2002 Mich. Pub. Acts 389, 392 (codified at Mich. Comp. Laws § 15.243(1)(y) (West 2004)).

14.9 Short Citation Formats for Federal and State Session Laws

14.9(a) Appropriate use of *id.* as short citation for session law

If a citation refers to the same session law as in the citation immediately previous, use *id.* as the preferred short citation format, changing the section number or pinpoint pages as needed. See **Rule 11.3** for more information on *id.*

14.9(b) Other short citation formats for session laws

In practice-based documents, if *id.* is not appropriate, use one of the following short citation formats listed below. In selecting a format, ensure that the short citation will not confuse the reader.

Examples

Full citation (with title of act):	Economic Espionage Act of 1996, Pub. L. No. 104-294, § 201, 110 Stat. 3488, 3491.
Short citation options:	§ 201.
	Economic Espionage Act § 201.
	§ 201, 110 Stat. at 3491.
Full citation:	1996 Alaska Sess. Laws 52.
Short citation:	1996 Alaska Sess. Laws at 53.

14.9(c)(FN) Short citation formats for session laws in academic footnotes

⚠ ACADEMIC FORMATTING

In documents with academic footnotes, if *id.* is not appropriate (see **Rules 11.1(c)**, **11.3(c)**, and **11.3(f)**), you may use all required components of the full citation, omitting the date, or you may use one of the formats illustrated in **Rule 14.9(b)**. There are no differences in typeface.

However, if the session law has not previously been cited in the same footnote or in any of the five previous footnotes, do not use a short form. Repeat the full citation. Do not use *supra* as a short citation format for a session law.

Examples (document with academic footnotes)

[45] Rosa's Law, Pub. L. No. 111-256, § 4, 124 Stat. 2643, 2645 (2010).

[46] *Id.* § 3, 124 Stat. at 2645.

. . .

[49] § 2, 124 Stat. at 2643–44.

[50] *Id.*

. . .

[61] Rosa's Law, Pub. L. No. 111-256, § 4, 124 Stat. 2643, 2645 (2010).

15 Other Legislative Materials

Fast Formats

Other Legislative Materials

House bill	H.R. 6, 109th Cong. § 142 (2005).
Senate simple resolution	S. Res. 262, 103d Cong. (1994).
House concurrent resolution	H.R. Con. Res. 133, 112th Cong. (2012).
House joint resolution	H.R.J. Res. 2, 113th Cong. (2013).
Bill cited in academic footnote	[24] Social Security Solvency and Sustainability Act, S. 804, 112th Cong. § 3 (2011).
Congressional hearing	*Department of Defense Mustard Gas Testing: Hearing Before the Subcomm. on Compensation, Pension & Ins. of the H.R. Comm. on Veterans' Affairs*, 102d Cong. 12–16 (1993) (statement of Constance M. Pechura).
Congressional report	S. Rep. No. 113-9, at 6–7 (2013).
Congressional report cited in academic footnote	[109] S. Rep. No. 113-9, at 6–7 (2013).
Congressional debate, permanent edition	147 Cong. Rec. 13,463 (2001).
Congressional debate, permanent edition, cited in academic footnote	[68] 147 Cong. Rec. 13,463 (2001).
Congressional debate, daily edition	158 Cong. Rec. H1923 (daily ed. Apr. 18, 2012).
Unenacted state house bill	H.R. 4660, 97th Leg., 1st Sess. § 31 (Mich. 2013).
State senate resolution	S. Res. 76, 130th Gen. Assemb., Reg. Sess. (Ohio 2013).

State legislative hearing	*Hearing to Evaluate Governor's Program Bill 44 Before the S. Standing Comm. on Banks,* 2008 Leg., 232d Sess. 11, 17 (N.Y. 2008) (prepared testimony of Paul J. Richman, vice president of state government affairs, Mortgage Bankers Ass'n).
State legislative report or document	S. Rules Comm. Office of S. Floor Analyses, *Report on Senate Bill No. 1471,* 1995–1996 Reg. Sess. 2–3 (Cal. 1996).
State legislative report or document cited in academic footnote	[49] FINAL LEGIS. REP., 57th Leg. 198 (Wash. 2001).

15.1 Full Citation Format for Federal Unenacted Measures

A full citation to an unenacted measure of the United States Senate or House of Representatives contains up to seven components. Congress uses four types of measures: the bill, the simple resolution, the concurrent resolution, and the joint resolution. The first three are treated here in **Rule 15.1**; for enacted federal bills and joint resolutions, see **Rule 15.3**.

Title of measure, | Designation of measure | Measure number, | Congress number | Pinpoint reference | [(Session number (for older measures)] | Year).

Example (House bill)

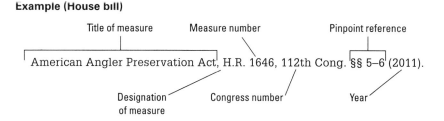

American Angler Preservation Act, H.R. 1646, 112th Cong. §§ 5–6 (2011).

Title of measure   Measure number   Pinpoint reference

Designation of measure   Congress number   Year

Other examples (spaces denoted by ▲)

House simple resolution:	H.R. ▲Res. ▲438, ▲109th ▲Cong. ▲(2005).
House concurrent resolution:	H.R. ▲Con. ▲Res. ▲6, ▲111th ▲Cong. ▲(2009).
Senate bill (with title):	Border ▲Security, ▲Economic ▲Opportunity, ▲and ▲Immigration ▲Modernization ▲Act, ▲S. ▲744, ▲113th ▲Cong. ▲§ ▲2101 ▲(2013).
Senate simple resolution:	S. ▲Res. ▲262, ▲103d ▲Cong. ▲(1994).
Senate concurrent resolution:	S. ▲Con. ▲Res. ▲37, ▲110th ▲Cong. ▲(2007).
Senate bill (with session reference):	S. ▲109, ▲25th ▲Cong. ▲(3d ▲Sess. ▲1839).

15.1(a) Title of measure

Every measure bears what is known as a "long title," beginning with words identifying it as a bill or a form of resolution and serving as the official name of the measure. Citations to legislative measures do not ordinarily refer to their long titles. However, many measures are given a "short title" intended as a briefer and more memorable reference to the measure. If desired, begin the citation to a measure with its short title, if any, followed by a comma and one space. Set out the title in ordinary type. Capitalize words according to **Rule 3.2**.

Example

> Puppy Uniform Protection and Safety Act, S. 395, 113th Cong. (2013).

15.1(b) Designation of measure

Each measure is designated using an abbreviation indicating the chamber in which it was introduced and the form of the measure, presented in ordinary type. Insert one space after the abbreviation. For more information on forms of legislative measures, see **Sidebar 15.1**.

Designation of measure:	Abbreviation (spaces denoted by ▲):
House Bill	H.R. ▲
House Resolution	H.R. ▲Res. ▲
House Concurrent Resolution	H.R. ▲Con. ▲Res. ▲
House Joint Resolution	H.R.J. ▲Res. ▲
Senate Bill	S. ▲

Senate Resolution	S.▲Res.▲
Senate Concurrent Resolution	S.▲Con.▲Res.▲
Senate Executive Resolution	S.▲Exec.▲Res.▲
Senate Joint Resolution	S.J.▲Res.▲

15.1(c) Number of measure

Following the abbreviation for the measure's designation, insert its number, followed by a comma and one space.

15.1(d) Congress number

Following the number of the measure, designate the Congress in which the measure was introduced, in ordinary type, using an ordinal contraction for the Congress number. (See **Rule 4.3** for more information on ordinals.) Then insert a space and the abbreviation "Cong." (e.g., 103d Cong., 111th Cong.), followed by another space.

SIDEBAR 15.1 Forms of Legislative Measures

Legislative measures are presented in one of four forms: the bill, the joint resolution, the concurrent resolution, and the simple resolution. The most common form is the bill. Once a bill has been approved by the chamber in which it was introduced, it goes to the other chamber for consideration. When it has been approved in identical form in both chambers, it goes to the president for signature, and if signed, becomes law. Alternatively, it may become law if the president fails to veto it within ten days after receiving it, or if vetoed, by a two-thirds override vote of each of the two chambers. Similarly, a joint resolution must be approved by both chambers and the president in order to become law. Joint resolutions typically deal with limited matters such as proposed amendments to the Constitution or specific appropriations.

Concurrent and simple resolutions, in contrast, deal with the rules and procedures that concern Congress itself. A concurrent resolution requires the agreement of both chambers, but it is not signed by the president. A simple resolution applies only to the chamber that proposed and passed it.

For descriptions of the various versions of bills and resolutions as they move through the legislative process, visit the Government Printing Office, *About Congressional Bills*, http://www.gpo.gov/help/index.html#about_congressional_bills.htm (last visited Aug. 7, 2013).

15.1(e) Pinpoint references

When referring to only a portion of a measure, provide a pinpoint reference to the specific subdivision of the measure immediately following the Congress number. Bills and resolutions are typically divided into sections. Insert one space after the subdivision information. (For more information on citing sections and other subdivisions, see **Rule 6**.)

Examples (spaces denoted by ▲)

S. ▲3978, ▲109th ▲Cong. ▲§§ ▲2–3 ▲(2005).

H.R. ▲Res. ▲97, ▲110th ▲Cong. ▲§ ▲1(B) ▲(2007).

15.1(f) Year of publication, version of measure, and session number

At a minimum, indicate the cited measure's year of publication, placed in a parenthetical following the Congress number and the pinpoint reference, if any. Depending on the age of the measure, the parenthetical may also need to indicate the session of Congress in which the measure was introduced.

In modern times, each Congress meets for two sessions. In the past, however, the Congress met in three sessions. When citing a House or Senate bill or resolution published before the 60th Congress (1907), indicate in the date parenthetical whether the measure was introduced during that Congress's first, second, or third session. For later Congresses, the session can be inferred from the year and thus should not be included. When needed, place the session designation in the date parenthetical, preceding the year of publication. Use an ordinal contraction for the session ("1st," "2d," or "3d"), followed by a space and the abbreviation "Sess."

Examples

Nonprofit Energy Efficiency Act, S. 717, 113th Cong. (2013).

H.R. Res. 88, 39th Cong. (1st Sess. 1866).

Because legislative measures often go through multiple versions as they move through the political process, when citing a particular version (or if the information would otherwise be helpful to your readers), you may indicate parenthetically the version of the measure or its status on a particular date (e.g., "as introduced," "as passed by the Senate [on Month Day, Year]," "as reported by H.R. Comm. on Ways & Means [on Month Day, Year]"), in place of the year of publication. In referring to names of congressional committees and subcommittees, you may abbreviate words appearing in **Appendix 3(F)** (Legislative Terms).

Examples

> H.R. 203, 107th Cong. § 6 (as introduced, Jan. 3, 2001).
>
> H.R. 203, 107th Cong. § 6 (as reported by House Comm. on Small Bus., Sept. 21, 2001).
>
> H.R. 203, 107th Cong. § 6 (as passed by House, Oct. 2, 2001).

15.1(g) Parallel citations to other publication sources of legislative measures

Where possible, cite an official version of a legislative measure, in print or online. Official electronic versions of congressional measures are available from the Government Printing Office's Federal Digital System (FDsys) website, http://www.gpo.gov/fdsys/search/home.action. Cite an official electronic version in the same manner as its print counterpart. If desired, you may append a parallel citation containing the URL.

Example

> National Small Business Regulatory Assistance Act of 2001, H.R. 203, 107th Cong. (2001), http://www.gpo.gov/fdsys/pkg/BILLS-107hr203ih/pdf/BILLS-107hr203ih.pdf.

To assist readers in locating the measure, you may also provide a parallel citation to a published committee hearing (**Rule 15.5**), a committee report (**Rule 15.7**), or a congressional debate (**Rule 15.10**).

Example (with parallel citation to committee report)

> Sleeping Bear Dunes National Lakeshore Conservation and Recreation Act, S. 140, 112th Cong. (2011), S. Rep. No. 112-104 (2012).

When citing a measure to its version in a commercial database, provide a parallel citation to its unique database identifier, if any, and add a parenthetical with the name of the database provider, if it is not clear from the database identifier.

Example

> Sleeping Bear Dunes National Lakeshore Conservation and Recreation Act, S. 140, 112th Cong. (2011), 2011 CONG US S 140 (WestlawNext).

15.2 Short Citation Formats for Federal Unenacted Measures

15.2(a) Appropriate use of *id.* as short citation for unenacted measure

Use the short form *id.* to cite the same unenacted measure just cited in the immediately preceding citation, even if the pinpoint reference has changed.

Do not use *id.* if the previous citation was a string citation referring to the unenacted measure and one or more other sources (**Rule 34.3**). See **Rule 11.3** for more information on *id.* For materials divided by sections, see **Rule 6.0** for guidance on pinpoint references.

15.2(b) Other short citation format for unenacted measure

If *id.* is not an appropriate short citation to an unenacted measure, omit the title of the measure, the number of the Congress, the date parenthetical, and any parallel citation or parenthetical appended to the full citation. Keep the designation of the measure and its number. Change the pinpoint reference if necessary.

Example

Full citation:	H.R. 988, 109th Cong. § 702 (2005).
Short citation:	H.R. 988 §§ 701–703.

15.2(c)(FN) Short citation formats for federal unenacted measures in academic footnotes

⚠ ACADEMIC FORMATTING

In documents with academic footnotes, always repeat the full citation if the legislative material has not been cited, in full or in short form (including *id.*), in the same footnote or one of the previous five footnotes. Otherwise, use the applicable short citation format described in **Rules 15.2(a)** or **15.2(b)**.

Examples

[59] Graduation for All Act, H.R. 547, 109th Cong. §§ 201–203 (2005).

[60] *Id.*

. . .

[63] H.R. 547 § 202.

. . .

[77] Graduation for All Act, H.R. 547, 109th Cong. §§ 201–203 (2005).

15.3 Citation Formats for Federal Enacted Bills and Joint Resolutions

15.3(a) Full citation format for federal enacted bills and joint resolutions

Cite enacted federal bills and joint resolutions as statutes pursuant to **Rule 14**, except when using the bill or joint resolution to document legislative history. In such instances, cite the bill or resolution following **Rule 15.1**.

Examples

House Joint Resolution:	H.R.J. Res. 75, 107th Cong. (2001).
Senate Joint Resolution:	S.J. Res. 23, 110th Cong. (2007).

15.3(b) Short citation formats for federal enacted bills and joint resolutions

15.3(b)(1) Appropriate use of *id.* as short citation for enacted bill or joint resolution

Follow **Rule 15.2(a)**.

15.3(b)(2) Other short citation format for enacted bill or joint resolution

If *id.* is not an appropriate short citation, omit the number of the Congress and the date parenthetical, but keep all other components of the full citation. Change the pinpoint reference if necessary.

Example

Full citation:	S.J. Res. 5, 106th Cong. §§ 1–4 (2000).
Short citation:	S.J. Res. 5 § 1.

15.3(b)(3)(FN) Short citation formats for enacted bills or joint resolutions in academic footnotes

⚠ ACADEMIC FORMATTING

In documents with academic footnotes, always repeat the full citation if the legislative material has not been cited, in full or in short form (including *id.*), in the same footnote or one of the previous five footnotes. Otherwise, use the applicable short citation format described in **Rules 15.3(b)(1)** or **15.3(b)(2)**.

Examples

[20] H.R.J. Res. 110, 112th Cong. § 1 (2012).

[21] *Id.* § 3.

. . .

[24] H.R.J. Res. 110 § 3.

. . .

[38] H.R.J. Res. 110, 112th Cong. §§ 1, 3 (2012).

15.4 Citation Formats for Federal Enacted Simple and Concurrent Resolutions

15.4(a) Full citation format for federal enacted simple and concurrent resolutions

Cite an enacted simple or concurrent resolution of either chamber in the same manner as an unenacted bill or resolution under **Rule 15.1**, but add a parenthetical containing the term "enacted."

Examples

> H.R. Res. 723, 108th Cong. (2004) (enacted).
>
> S. Con. Res. 115, 108th Cong. (2005) (enacted).

When possible, provide a parallel citation to the *Congressional Record* (for simple resolutions) or *Statutes at Large* (for concurrent resolutions), as illustrated below. Because only enacted resolutions are printed in *Statutes at Large*, omit the "(enacted)" parenthetical when providing a parallel reference to *Statutes at Large*, and indicate the year of publication of the *Statutes at Large* volume.

Examples

> **With reference to *Congressional Record* (daily edition):**
>
> H.R. Res. 188, 109th Cong. (2005) (enacted), *reprinted in* 151 Cong. Rec. H1802 (daily ed. Apr. 6, 2005).
>
> **With reference to *Statutes at Large*:**
>
> H.R. Con. Res. 464, 107th Cong., 116 Stat. 3150 (2002).

15.4(b) Short citation formats for federal enacted simple and concurrent resolutions

15.4(b)(1) Appropriate use of *id.* as short citation for enacted simple or concurrent resolution

Follow **Rule 15.2(a)**.

15.4(b)(2) Other short citation format for enacted simple or concurrent resolution

If *id.* is not an appropriate short citation, use the full citation format, but omit the number of the Congress, the date parenthetical, and any parallel citation or parenthetical included with the full citation.

Example (enacted simple or concurrent resolution)

Full citation: S. Con. Res. 8, 109th Cong. § 1 (2005) (enacted), *reprinted in* 151 Cong. Rec. S825 (daily ed. Feb. 1, 2005).

Short citation: S. Con. Res. 8 § 1.

15.4(b)(3)(FN) Short citation formats for enacted simple or concurrent resolutions in academic footnotes

⚠ ACADEMIC FORMATTING

In documents with academic footnotes, always repeat the full citation if the legislative material has not been cited, in full or in short form (including *id.*), in the same footnote or one of the previous five footnotes. Otherwise, use the applicable short citation format described in **Rules 15.4(b)(1)** or **15.4(b)(2)**.

15.5 Full Citation Format for Congressional Hearings

A full citation to a congressional hearing contains a minimum of four components, including the full title of the hearing; the name of the subcommittee and/or committee conducting the hearing; the Congress number; and the year of publication. If the hearing concerns a pending measure, also include the designation of the measure and its number.

Full title: | *Hearing* [*on Designation of Measure and Measure number (if any)*] | *Before the* | *Name of Subcommittee (if any) and/or Committee,* | **Congress number** | **Pinpoint reference** | **([Session number (if applicable)])** | **Year of publication).**

Example

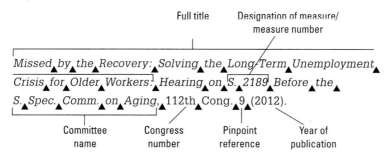

15.5(a) Title of committee hearing, designation of measure, and measure number

Begin the citation with the full title as it appears on the cover of the published hearing, followed by a colon and one space, and if the hearing refers to a measure, the designation of that measure and its number. Present the title of the hearing in italics, as well as the designation of the measure and the measure number (if relevant), followed by a comma and one space.

Example

> *Junk Fax Prevention Act of 2004: Hearing Before the H. Subcomm. on Telecomm. & Internet of Comm. on Energy & Commerce*, 108th Cong. 3–5 (2004).

15.5(b) Name of committee or subcommittee

Provide the abbreviated name of the committee before which the hearing was held. If the hearing was before a subcommittee, also indicate the name of the committee to which it is subordinate. To conserve space, you may abbreviate any words in the committee or subcommittee name that are listed in **Appendix 3(F)**. Insert a comma and one space after the abbreviated name(s) of the committee(s).

15.5(c) Congress number

Follow **Rule 15.1(d)**.

15.5(d) Pinpoint references

Follow **Rule 15.1(e)**.

15.5(e) Year of publication; session number

Follow **Rule 15.1(f)**.

15.5(f) Parenthetical information about congressional hearings

You may include any explanation after the citation that will clarify the reference or otherwise assist readers; for example, you might identify the person testifying before the committee. See **Rule 37** regarding explanatory parentheticals.

Example

> *Impeachment Inquiry: William Jefferson Clinton, President of the United States: Hearing Before the H. Comm. on the Judiciary*, 105th Cong. 19–21 (1998) (statement of Kenneth W. Starr, Independent Counsel).

15.6 Short Citation Formats for Congressional Hearings

15.6(a) Appropriate use of *id.* as short citation for congressional hearing

Follow **Rule 15.2(a)**.

15.6(b) Other short citation format for congressional hearing

If *id.* is not an appropriate short citation to a congressional hearing, set out the hearing title (or a shortened version thereof), omit the date parenthetical, and insert the preposition "at" before the pinpoint reference. Change the pinpoint reference if necessary.

Example

Full citation:	Roundtable Discussions on Comprehensive Health Care Reform: Hearings Before the S. Comm. on Fin., 111th Cong. 120 (2009)[hereinafter Roundtable Discussions].
Short citation:	Roundtable Discussions, 111th Cong. at 137 (testimony of Edward Kleinbard, Chief of Staff, Joint Comm. on Taxation).

15.6(c)(FN) Short citation formats for congressional hearing in academic footnotes

⚠ ACADEMIC FORMATTING

In a document with academic footnotes, if *id.* is not appropriate, use the *supra* format that follows, referring the reader to the footnote containing the full citation, but indicating the new pinpoint reference. See **Rule 11.4** for more information on *supra*.

Hearing title, | *supra* | note | Note number, | at | Pinpoint reference.

Example

[19] *Health Care Reform: Recommendations to Improve Coordination of Federal and State Initiatives: Hearing Before the Subcomm. on Health, Emp't, Labor & Pensions of the H. Comm. on Educ. & Labor,* 110th Cong. 46 (2007) [hereinafter *Health Care Reform*].

．　．　．

[25] *Health Care Reform, supra* note 19, at 44.

15.7 Full Citation Format for Numbered Congressional Reports and Documents

Congressional reports address proposed legislation and issues under a committee's investigation. Senate executive reports relate to nominations of individuals or to treaties between the United States and other countries. House and Senate documents address a variety of materials that Congress has ordered to be printed. Senate treaty documents contain treaty text as submitted to the Senate for presidential ratification.

Because numbered congressional reports and documents are most easily accessed by their numbers, a full citation contains a minimum of five components, including the type of report or document (which includes an abbreviation for the chamber in which it originated); its number; a pinpoint reference; and the year of publication.

[Author,] | [*Title,*] | Abbreviation for type of document | No. | Report or document number, | at | Pinpoint reference | ([Session (if applicable)] | Year of publication).

Example (House Report)

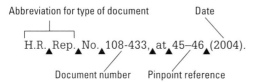

15.7(a) Author and title option

If desired, you may begin the citation with the author and title of the report or document. Do not indicate a title without also giving the name of the author. For an institutional author, follow **Rule 20.1(b)(3)**, abbreviating words in **Appendix 3(E)** and **Appendix 3(F)**. Use ordinary type for the name of the author and italics for the title.

Example

> Permanent Subcomm. on Investigations of the S. Comm. on Governmental Affairs, *Phony Identification and Credentials via the Internet*, S. Rep. No. 107-133, at 25–29 (2002).

15.7(b) Abbreviation for numbered report or document

Following the author and title, if any, or as the first component of the citation, abbreviate the type of numbered report or document, including an abbreviation for the chamber in which it originated, followed by one space. Indicate conference reports by adding a parenthetical with the abbreviation "Conf. Rep." after the date parenthetical (example in **Rule 15.7(d)**).

Type of document:	Abbreviation (spaces denoted by ▲):
House Report	H.R.▲Rep.▲No.▲
House Document	H.R.▲Doc.▲No.▲
House Miscellaneous Document	H.R.▲Misc.▲Doc.▲No.▲
Senate Report	S.▲Rep.▲No.▲
Senate Executive Report	S.▲Exec.▲Rep.▲No.▲
Senate Document	S.▲Doc.▲No.▲
Senate Treaty Document	S.▲Treaty▲Doc.▲No.▲

15.7(c) Report or document number

To create the report or document number, insert the Congress number, a hyphen, and the number shown on the report or document, followed by one space. If the document or report does not have a number, follow **Rule 15.9**.

Example

103-42 ——— Report or document number
|
Congress number

15.7(d) Pinpoint references

If referring to only *part* of the report or document, indicate the subdivision. Use ", at" only before a reference to one or more *pages*; the preposition "at" lets readers know that what follows is not part of the title, but rather a reference to specific page numbers within. For more information on pinpoint subdivisions, see **Rule 5.2**. Insert one space after the pinpoint information.

Examples

H.R. Doc. No. 111-113, at 7–9 (2010).

S. Treaty Doc. No. 111-5, pt. 4, at 63–64 (2010).

H.R. Rep. No. 110-803 § 113 (2008) (Conf. Rep.).

15.7(e) Year of publication; session designation for older Congresses

Indicate the year in which the report, document, or print was ordered to be printed, enclosed in parentheses.

In a citation to a House Report published before the 47th Congress (1881), or a Senate Report published before the 40th Congress (1867), the parenthetical should indicate whether the measure was introduced during that Congress's first, second, or third session. For later Congresses, the session can be inferred from the year and thus should not be included. Place the session designation before the year of publication. Use an ordinal contraction for the session ("1st," "2d," or "3d"), followed by a space and the abbreviation "Sess."

15.7(f) Parallel citation to U.S.C.C.A.N. or other sources

Provide a parallel citation to the report or document, if possible, in the permanent edition of *United States Code Congressional and Administrative News* ("U.S.C.C.A.N."), introduced by the italicized phrase *"reprinted in."* U.S.C.C.A.N. is available in WestlawNext.

Example

> H.R. Rep. No. 94-1487, at 7 (1976), *reprinted in* 1976 U.S.C.C.A.N. 6604, 6605–06.

Federal committee reports within the fairly recent past are available on Congress.gov (http://beta.congress.gov/congressional-reports) (beginning with the 104th Congress) and FDsys (http://www.gpo.gov/fdsys/) (also from the 104th Congress onward).

Example

> H.R. Rep. No. 111-13, at 7 (2009), *available at* http://www.gpo.gov/fdsys/pkg/ CRPT-111hrpt13/pdf/CRPT-111hrpt13.pdf.

15.7(g)(FN) Full citation format for numbered congressional report or document in academic footnotes

⚠ ACADEMIC FORMATTING

In academic footnotes, use large and small capital letters for the abbreviation of the report or document and the abbreviation "No.," as shown below. If the citation includes an author name and a title, they should be presented in large and small capital letters as well.

Examples

> [68] H.R. REP. NO. 108-724, pt. 3 (2004) (Conf. Rep.).

> [113] GEORGE W. BUSH, STATE OF THE UNION MESSAGE, H.R. DOC. NO. 109-3 (2005).

15.8 Short Citation Formats for Numbered Congressional Reports and Documents

15.8(a) Appropriate use of *id.* as short citation for numbered congressional report or document

Follow **Rule 15.2(a)**.

15.8(b) Other short citation format for numbered congressional report or document

If *id.* is not appropriate, omit the date parenthetical, but keep all other elements of the full citation.

Example

Full citation:	H.R. Conf. Rep. 109-123 §§ 2–4 (2005).
Short citation:	H.R. Conf. Rep. 109-123 § 3.

15.8(c)(FN) Short citation formats for numbered congressional report or document in academic footnotes

⚠ ACADEMIC FORMATTING

In documents with academic footnotes, always repeat the full citation if the numbered report or document has not been cited, in full or in short form (including *id.*), in the same footnote or one of the previous five footnotes. Otherwise, use the formats described in **Rules 15.10(a)** and **15.10(b)**.

Example

[33] S. Rep. No. 94-755, at 81 (1976).

[34] *Id.*

. . .

[41] S. Rep. No. 94-755, at 80 (1976).

15.9 Full Citation Format for Unnumbered Reports, Documents, and Committee Prints

15.9(a) Institutional author and title

Begin the citation with the name of the congressional entity who wrote the unnumbered report, document, or committee print. Treat the entity as an institutional author under **Rule 20.1(b)(3)**, abbreviating any words in **Appendix 3(E)** or **Appendix 3(F)**, and include the Congress number as part of the author's name. Use ordinary type for the author's name. Italicize the title. For pinpoint references, follow **Rule 15.7c)**. To the beginning of the date parenthetical, add an abbreviation for the type of document.

Example

> Staff of S. Comm. on Banking, Hous. & Urban Affairs, 94th Cong., *Report of the Securities and Exchange Commission on Questionable and Illegal Corporate Payments and Practices* 2–3 (Comm. Print 1976).

15.9(b)(FN)   Full citation format for unnumbered report, document, or committee print in academic footnotes

⚠ ACADEMIC FORMATTING

In academic footnotes, follow **Rule 15.9(a)**, but use large and small capital letters for both the name of the author and the title.

Example

> [23] STAFF OF S. COMM. ON BANKING, HOUS. & URBAN AFFAIRS, 94TH CONG., REPORT OF THE SECURITIES AND EXCHANGE COMMISSION ON QUESTIONABLE AND ILLEGAL CORPORATE PAYMENTS AND PRACTICES 2–3 (Comm. Print 1976).

15.10   Citation Formats for Congressional Debates

15.10(a)   Full citation format for post-1873 congressional debates

Cite congressional debates occurring *after* 1873 to the *Congressional Record*. (For earlier debates, see **Rule 15.10(c)** below.) The *Congressional Record* is published daily while either house is in session. At the end of each congressional session, a bound volume of the *Congressional Record*, known as the "permanent edition," is published. The permanent edition is the preferred source. Cite the daily edition only for material not yet available in the permanent edition.

A full citation to a post-1873 congressional debate contains four to six components, depending on whether the citation includes the debate's title and whether the citation refers to the daily edition or the permanent edition of the *Congressional Record*.

Examples

| Permanent edition: | [*Title*,] | Volume number | Cong. Rec. | Pinpoint page | (Year). |

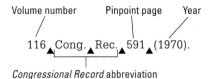

Volume number   Pinpoint page   Year

116 Cong. Rec. 591 (1970).

Congressional Record abbreviation

Daily edition: [*Title*,] | Volume number | Cong. Rec. | Pinpoint
page | (daily ed. | Exact date).

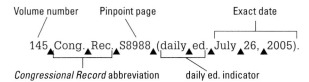

Volume number   Pinpoint page   Exact date

145 Cong. Rec. S8988 (daily ed. July 26, 2005).

Congressional Record abbreviation   daily ed. indicator

15.10(a)(1) Title of debate

If desired, you may begin the citation with the title of the debate, in italics.
Capitalize words according to **Rule 3**.

Example

Suicide Prevention, 155 Cong. Rec. S7446 (daily ed. July 14, 2009).

15.10(a)(2) Volume number and abbreviation for *Congressional Record*

Following the title (if any), indicate the volume number of the *Congressional
Record* in which the debate appears, followed by one space and the abbreviation "Cong. Rec." in ordinary type.

15.10(a)(3) Pinpoint pages

After "Cong. Rec." insert one space and the page number(s) on which the
debate appears. Note that the daily and permanent editions use different systems of pagination. In the daily edition, page numbers are preceded by single-letter prefixes corresponding to one of the four sections published in each
issue: H for proceedings of the House of Representatives, S for proceedings
of the Senate, E for Extensions of Remarks, and D for the Daily Digest (e.g.,
H____, S____, E____, D___). Each section is separately paginated. The permanent edition uses continuous pagination and drops the prefixes.

For guidance on citing consecutive or scattered pages, see **Rules 5.3** and **5.4**.

Examples

| Permanent edition: | 124 Cong. Rec. 32408 (1978). |
| Daily edition: | 149 Cong. Rec. H9748–50 (daily ed. Oct. 21, 2003). |

15.10(a)(4) Edition and date

When citing the permanent edition, set out the year of publication in a date parenthetical. When citing the daily edition, begin the date parenthetical with the phrase "daily ed." followed by one space and the exact date (Month Day, Year) of the issue. Abbreviate the month according to **Appendix 3(A)**.

Examples

| Permanent edition: | 124 Cong. Rec. 32408 (1978). |
| Daily edition: | 150 Cong. Rec. S11653–60 (daily ed. Nov. 19, 2004). |

15.10(a)(5) Parenthetical information

You may include parenthetically any other information that might assist readers, such as the name of the cited speaker or where the reader can locate the cited source. Abbreviate words appearing in **Appendix 3(F)**. See **Rule 37** regarding explanatory parentheticals.

Example

51 Cong. Rec. S546–47 (daily ed. Jan. 26, 2005) (statement of Sen. Jeff Bingaman).

15.10(a)(6)(FN) Full citation format for post-1873 congressional debate in academic footnotes

⚠ ACADEMIC FORMATTING

In academic footnotes, follow **Rule 15.10(a)(1)** through **(5)**, but abbreviate *Congressional Record* using large and small capital letters ("Cong. Rec.").

Examples

[145] *Suicide Prevention*, 155 Cong. Rec. S7445, S7446 (daily ed. July 14, 2009).

[152] *Partial-Birth Abortion Ban Act of 2000*, 146 Cong. Rec. 4491, 4501 (2000) (speech by Rep. DeLay), http://www.gpo.gov/fdsys/pkg/CRECB-2000-pt4/pdf/CRECB-2000-pt4-Pg4491.pdf.

15.10(b) Short citation formats for post-1873 congressional debates

15.10(b)(1) Appropriate use of *id.* as short citation for post-1873 congressional debate

Follow **Rule 15.2(a)**.

15.10(b)(2) Other short citation format for post-1873 congressional debate

If *id.* is not appropriate, keep all components except the date parenthetical, and insert "at" before the pinpoint page(s).

Example

Full citation:	124 Cong. Rec. 32,408 (1978).
Short citation:	124 Cong. Rec. at 32,409.

15.10(b)(3)(FN) Short citation formats for post-1873 congressional debate in academic footnotes

⚠ ACADEMIC FORMATTING

In documents with academic footnotes, abbreviate *Congressional Record* using large and small capital letters ("Cong. Rec."). Always repeat the full citation if the congressional debate has not been cited, in full or in short form (including *id.*), in the same footnote or one of the previous five footnotes. Otherwise, use the formats described in **Rules 15.10(b)(1)** and **15.10(b)(2)**.

Example

[29] 150 Cong. Rec. S11,653 (daily ed. Nov. 19, 2004).

[30] *Id.*

. . .

[33] 150 Cong. Rec. at S11,653.

15.10(c) Full citation format for pre-1874 congressional debates

15.10(c)(1) Publication sources and formats

For congressional debates taking place *up to and through* 1873, there are three publication sources, covering different periods and different Congresses, the *Annals of Congress*, the *Register of Debates*, and the *Congressional Globe*, with a few years' overlap in coverage by the latter two. Use the format shown below for the specific publication source being cited. Represent all components of the citation in ordinary type.

Annals of Congress (1st Cong. to 18th Cong., 1st Sess., 1789–1824):

Volume number | Annals of Cong. | Pinpoint page(s) | (Year).

Example

18 Annals of Cong. 1766 (1819).

Register of Debates (18th Cong., 2d Sess., to 25th Cong., 1st Sess., 1824–1837):

Volume number | Reg. Deb. | Pinpoint page(s) | (Year).

Example

11 Reg. Deb. 130 (1835).

Congressional Globe (23d Cong., 1st Sess., to 42d Cong., 2d Sess., 1833–1873):

Cong. Globe, | Congress number | Cong., | Session number | Pinpoint page(s) | (Year).

Example

Cong. Globe, 41st Cong., 1st Sess. 500–01 (1869).

15.10(c)(2)(FN) Full citation format for pre-1874 congressional debate in academic footnotes

In academic footnotes, follow the format shown in **Rule 15.10(c)(1)**, but use large and small capital letters for the abbreviated name of the publication source.

Examples

[56] 37 ANNALS OF CONG. 47 (1820).

[64] 12 REG. DEB. 2331 (1836).

[198] *See* CONG. GLOBE, 26th Cong., 1st Sess. 150–51 (1840).

15.10(d) Short citation formats for pre-1874 congressional debates

15.10(d)(1) Appropriate use of *id.* for pre-1874 congressional debate

Follow **Rule 15.2(a)**.

15.10(d)(2) Other short citation format for pre-1874 congressional debate

Follow **Rule 15.10(b)(2)**.

Example (pre-1874 congressional debate)

Full citation:	18 Annals of Cong. 1766 (1819).
Short citation:	18 Annals of Cong. at 1766.

15.10(d)(3)(FN) Short citation formats for pre-1874 congressional debate in academic footnotes

⚠ ACADEMIC FORMATTING

In documents with academic footnotes, use large and small capital letters for the abbreviated name of the publication source. Always repeat the full citation if the congressional debate has not been cited, in full or in short form (including *id.*), in the same footnote or one of the previous five footnotes. Otherwise, use the formats described in **Rules 15.10(d)(1)** and **15.10(d)(2)**.

Example

[59] CONG. GLOBE, 41st Cong., 1st Sess. 500–01 (1869).

[60] *Id.*

. . .

[73] CONG. GLOBE, 41st Cong., 1st Sess. 500 (1869).

15.11 Citation Formats for Congressional Journals

15.11(a) Components of full citation to congressional journal

Both the House of Representatives and the Senate publish official proceedings in journals at the end of each session. The journals record motions, actions taken, and roll-call votes but not the text of debates or other proceedings.

A full citation to a congressional journal contains six components, all rendered in ordinary type. Although the word "Journal" is abbreviated in other citation contexts, to avoid possible confusion with joint resolutions, do not abbreviate the word in this context.

Chamber abbreviation | Journal, | Congress number, | Session number | Pinpoint page(s) | (Year of publication).

Example

Chamber abbreviation	Congress number	Year of publication

H.R. Journal, 105th Cong., 2d Sess. 2755–86 (1998).

Session number   Pinpoint pages

15.11(b)(FN) Full citation format for congressional journal in academic footnotes

⚠ ACADEMIC FORMATTING

In academic footnotes, use the components shown in **Rule 15.11(a)**, but for the chamber abbreviation and journal, use large and small capital letters.

Example

[79] S. JOURNAL, 34th Cong., 3d Sess. 132 (1857) (petition for relief of shipwrecked mariners).

15.11(c) Short citation formats for congressional journals

15.11(c)(1) Appropriate use of *id.* as short citation for congressional journal

Follow **Rule 15.2(a)**.

15.11(c)(2) Other short citation format for congressional journal
Follow **Rule 15.10(b)(2)**.

Example

| Full citation: | S. Journal, 38th Cong., 1st Sess. 51–55 (1863). |
| Short citation: | S. Journal, 38th Cong., 1st Sess. at 54. |

15.11(c)(3)(FN) Short citation formats for congressional journal in academic footnotes

⚠ ACADEMIC FORMATTING

In documents with academic footnotes, use large and small capital letters for the abbreviated name of the journal. Always repeat the full citation if the congressional journal has not been cited, in full or in short form (including *id.*), in the same footnote or one of the previous five footnotes. Otherwise, use the formats described in **Rules 15.11(c)(1)** and **15.11(c)(2)**.

Example

[96] S. JOURNAL, 1st Cong., 1st Sess. 117 (1789).

[97] *Id.*

. . .

[108] S. JOURNAL, 1st Cong., 1st Sess. 118 (1789).

15.12 The Declaration of Independence

15.12(a) Components of citation to *The Declaration of Independence*

A full citation to *The Declaration of Independence* includes its italicized title, a pinpoint reference, and a parenthetical with its date (1776). If it might be unclear whether the citation refers to the *Declaration* of the United States or that of another country, add the abbreviation "U.S." to the date parenthetical, before the year. Because the *Declaration* uses indented but unnumbered paragraphs, use the abbreviation "para." instead of a paragraph symbol. See **Rule 6.3**. For short forms, where *id.* is not appropriate, omit the date parenthetical, and change the pinpoint reference if necessary.

Example

> *The Declaration of Independence* para. 1 (1776).

15.12(b)(FN) Citation to *The Declaration of Independence* in academic footnotes

⚠ ACADEMIC FORMATTING

In academic footnotes, follow **Rule 15.12(a)**, but put the title in large and small capital letters.

Example

> [80] THE DECLARATION OF INDEPENDENCE para. 2 (U.S. 1776).

15.13 Full Citation Format for State Unenacted Measures

A full citation to an unenacted measure from a state legislative body is similar to its federal counterpart (**Rule 15.1**), but it may contain additional components. Moreover, while many state measures have names similar to those used by the U.S. Congress, you may encounter measure names that differ (e.g., a "file" instead of a "bill"). Similarly, you may find that the names of legislative bodies differ from those referring to congressional chambers (e.g., Assembly, House of Delegates). To the extent the information is available or applicable, the basic full citation will use the following components.

[Title of measure,] | Designation of measure | Measure number, | Legislature number, | Session designation (if any) | Pinpoint reference (if any) | (State abbreviation | Year).

Example (Alaska House Bill)

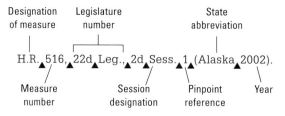

Other examples (spaces denoted by ▲)

Arizona Senate Bill:	S. ▲6114, ▲46th ▲Leg., ▲2d ▲Reg. ▲Sess. ▲(Ariz. ▲2004).
Nebraska Legislative Resolution:	Legis. ▲Res. ▲100, ▲101st ▲Leg., ▲1st ▲Reg. ▲Sess. ▲(Neb. ▲2009).
Wisconsin Assembly Bill:	Assemb. ▲15, ▲2013–2014 ▲Leg., ▲2013 ▲Reg. ▲Sess. ▲§ ▲11 ▲(Wis. ▲2013).

15.13(a) Title of state measure

If desired, you may begin the citation with the state measure's "short title," if any, in ordinary type, followed by a comma and one space. For more information about measure titles, see **Rule 15.1(a)**. Capitalize words in the title according to **Rule 3**.

Example

Arkansas Capital Gains Reduction Act of 2013, H.R. 1007, 89th Gen. Assemb., 2013 Reg. Sess. (Ark. 2013).

15.13(b) Designation and number of state measure

Each measure is designated with an abbreviation for the chamber in which it was introduced and the form of the measure, presented in ordinary type. If a word is not listed below or in **Appendix 3(F)**, spell it out. Note that some states use the word "Assembly" to refer to the lower chamber of the legislature (e.g., California State Assembly, Wisconsin State Assembly), while in others, it refers to the entire legislature (e.g., Indiana General Assembly, Maryland General Assembly).

After the designation, insert the measure's number, followed by a comma and one space.

Designation of measure	Abbreviation (spaces denoted by ^)
Assembly bill	Assemb.▲
Concurrent resolution	Con.▲Res.▲
House of Delegates Bill	H.D.▲
House of Representatives Bill	H.R.▲
House of Representatives Resolution	H.R.▲Res.▲
Joint Resolution	J.▲Res.▲
Legislative Resolution	Legis.▲Res.▲
Resolution	Res.▲
Senate bill	S.▲
Senate joint resolution	S.J.▲Res.▲

Examples (spaces denoted by ▲)

Delaware House concurrent resolution: H.R.▲Con.▲Res.▲29,▲146th▲
Gen.▲Assemb.▲(Del.▲2012).

Wisconsin Senate bill: S.▲73,▲2011–2012▲Leg.,▲100th▲
Reg.▲Sess.▲§▲2▲(Wis.▲2011).

15.13(c) State legislature and session designations

Following the number of the measure, identify the legislature in which the measure was introduced. If the state numbers its legislature or assembly (e.g., 107th General Assembly), begin with an ordinal contraction (**Rule 4.3**) for the legislature or assembly number. If the state does not number its legislature or assembly, look for any other description used by the state (e.g., 2010–2011 Legislature).

When it is available, identify the legislative session. Designate a numbered session with an ordinal contraction (**Rule 4.3(b)**), or designate it with the description used by the state. Insert one space after the session designation. For both the legislature and the session, abbreviate any words listed in **Appendix 3(F)**.

Examples

H.R. 2192, 79th Gen. Assemb., 2d Sess. (Iowa 2002).

S. 10, 47th Leg., 1st Spec. Sess. (Okla. 1999).

15.13(d) Pinpoint references

When referring to only a portion of a measure, provide a pinpoint reference to the particular subdivision, such as a section number or a page, followed by one space. (For more information on citing pages, sections, and other subdivisions, see **Rules 5** through **9**.)

15.13(e) State and date parenthetical

In a parenthetical, set out the abbreviation of the state, as shown in **Appendix 3(B)**, followed by one space and the year in which the measure was enacted, or if unenacted, the year it was published.

15.13(f) Parallel citations to official online or unofficial commercial database sources

Cite an official electronic version of a state legislative measure in the same manner as its print counterpart, but append a parallel citation containing the URL.

Example

> S. 1105, 89th Gen. Assemb., Reg. Sess. (Ark. 2013), *available at* http://www.arkleg.state.ar.us/assembly/2013/2013R/Bills/SB1105.pdf.

When citing a measure to its version in a commercial electronic database, provide a parallel citation to its unique database identifier, as illustrated below, adding a parenthetical with the name of the provider, if it is not clear from the database identifier.

Example

> S. 1105, 89th Gen. Assemb., Reg. Sess. (Ark. 2013), 2013 Bill Text AR S.B. 1105 (Lexis Advance).

15.14 Short Citation Formats for State Unenacted Measures

15.14(a) Appropriate use of *id.* as short citation for state unenacted measure

Follow **Rule 15.2(a)**.

15.14(b) Other short citation format for state unenacted measure

For short citations to state unenacted measures, place the state abbreviation *before* the abbreviated name of the measure, using **Appendix 3(B)** and **Appendix 3(F)**. Omit reference to numbers of the legislative body or the legislative session, and omit the date parenthetical. Change the pinpoint reference as needed; insert "at" before a pinpoint page reference.

Example

Full citation: S. 1359, 1999 Reg. Sess. 2 (Conn. 1999).

Short citation: Conn. S. 1359, at 2.

15.14(c)(FN) Short citation formats for state unenacted measure in academic footnotes

⚠ ACADEMIC FORMATTING

In documents with academic footnotes, always repeat the full citation if the measure has not been cited, in full or in short form (including *id.*), in the same footnote or one of the previous five footnotes. Otherwise, use the short citation formats described in **Rules 15.17(a)** and **15.17(b)**.

15.15 Citation Formats for State Enacted Measures and Joint Resolutions

15.15(a) Full citation formats for state enacted measures and joint resolutions

Cite state enacted measures and joint resolutions as statutes pursuant to **Rule 14.4**, except when using the measure to document legislative history. In that case, analogize to **Rule 15.3**.

Example

S.J. Res. 07-037, 66th Gen. Assemb., 1st Reg. Sess. (Colo. 2007).

15.15(b) Short citation formats for state enacted measures and joint resolutions

Follow **Rule 15.14**.

Example

Full citation: S.J. Res. 07-037, 66th Gen. Assemb., 1st Reg. Sess. (Colo. 2007).

Short citation: Colo. S.J. Res. 07-037, at 1.

15.16 Citation Formats for State Legislative Hearings

15.16(a) Components of full citation to state legislative hearing

A full citation to a state legislative hearing follows the format for federal committee hearings (**Rule 15.5**) but substitutes the legislature's number for the number of Congress and identifies the legislative session. It also inserts the state abbreviation (**Appendix 3(B)**) in the date parenthetical.

15.16(b) Short citation formats for state legislative hearing

For short citations to state legislative hearings, analogize to **Rules 15.6(a)** and **15.6(b)**.

Example

Full citation:	*Section 71.051 Forum Non Conveniens: Hearing on S. 2 Before the S. Econ. Dev. Comm.*, 73d Leg., Reg. Sess. 73 (Tex. 1993).
Short citation:	*Section 71.051 Forum Non Conveniens*, 73d Leg., Reg. Sess. at 74.

15.16(c)(FN) Short citation formats for state legislative hearing in academic footnotes

⚠ ACADEMIC FORMATTING

To cite a state legislative hearing in an academic footnote, analogize to **Rule 15.6(c)(FN)**.

15.17 Full Citation Format for State Legislative Reports and Documents

A full citation to a state legislative report or document contains a minimum of six components, including the abbreviated name for the type of report or document; the number of the legislature combined with the number, if any, of the report or document; the number of the legislative session, if available; a pinpoint reference; the state's abbreviation; and the year of publication.

[Committee or author name,] | [*Title,*] | Abbreviation for type of document | [No.] | [Legislature–Document number (if any),] | [Session designation (if any)] | Pinpoint reference | (State abbreviation | Year of publication).

Example

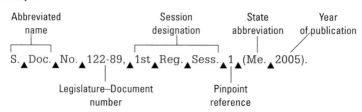

15.17(a) Committee name, author, and title option

If desired, you may begin the citation with the committee name, author's name, and the title. For an institutional author, follow **Rule 20.1(b)(3)**, abbreviating words in **Appendix 3(F)**. Use ordinary type for the author name and italics for the title. See **Rule 15.7(a)** for an analogous example. If the name of the state is clear from the title or author, omit the state's abbreviation from the date parenthetical (**Rule 15.17(e)**).

Example

> S. Comm. on Children, Families & Elder Affairs, *Review of the Baker Act*, Interim S. Rep. No. 2009-15, at 2 (Fla. 2008).

15.17(b) Abbreviation for type of report or document

Abbreviate the type of report or document (using **Appendix 3(F)**), including an abbreviation for the chamber in which the report or document originated, followed by one space, and if the report or document is numbered, the abbreviation "No."

Type of document:	Abbreviation (spaces denoted by ^):
House Report	H.R. ▲ Rep. ▲ No. ▲
Joint Report	J. ▲ Rep. ▲ No. ▲
Assembly Document	Assemb. ▲ Doc. ▲ No. ▲

15.17(c) Legislature-document number

If the report or document is numbered, create a legislature-document number by combining the number of the legislature with the number of the report or document. For more information about legislature numbers, see **Rule 15.13(c)**.

Example

Legislature and report numbers:	105th Legislature, Report No. 97
Legislature-document number:	No. 105-97

15.17(d) State session designation

Follow **Rule 15.13(c)**.

15.17(e) Pinpoint references

If referring to only part of the report or document, cite the particular subdivision. For more information on subdivisions, see **Rules 5, 6**, and **9**. Insert one space after the subdivision information.

15.17(f) State and date parenthetical

Unless the name of the state appears in the segment for the author or title, begin the date parenthetical with its abbreviation (**Appendix 3(B)**), followed by one space. In the same parenthetical, indicate the year of the report's or document's publication.

15.17(g)(FN) Full citation format for state legislative report or document in academic footnotes

⚠ ACADEMIC FORMATTING

In academic footnotes, use large and small capital letters for the name of the committee, author, and title, if any, the abbreviation of the report or document, and the abbreviation "No.," if present.

Example

⁵⁶ S. COMM. ON CHILDREN, FAMILIES & ELDER AFFAIRS, REVIEW OF THE BAKER ACT, INTERIM S. REP. NO. 2009-15, at 2 (Fla. 2008).

15.18 Full Citation Format for State Legislative Debates

A full citation to a state legislative debate contains the following components, depending on whether the debate is published and the type of legislature and session designations, if any, used in the state.

Chamber abbreviation, | *Title or description of debate*, | *Publication source* (if any), | Legislature designation (if any), | Session designation (if any) | Pinpoint reference (if any) | (State abbreviation | Year) | [(Location of transcript or recording)].

Examples

Published debate:

Chamber abbreviation   Description of debate   Legislature designation

H.R., *158th Legislative Day, House Transcripts*, 97th Gen. Assemb., Reg. Sess. 3–4 (Ill. 2012).

Session designation   Pinpoint reference   State abbreviation   Year of publication

Unpublished debate:

Chamber abbreviation   Description of debate   Legislature designation   Session designation   State abbreviation   Exact date

H.R., *Floor Debate*, 51st Leg., Gen. Sess. (Utah Feb. 27, 1995) (House recording tape no. 2, side A).

Location parenthetical

15.18(a) Chamber abbreviation

Begin the citation with an abbreviation for the legislative chamber in which the debate took place (**Appendix 3(F)**), followed by a comma and one space.

15.18(b) Title or description of debate; publication source

If the debate is published, provide its title, in italics, and the name of the source in which it is contained, also in italics, followed by a comma and one space. If the debate is not published, provide a concise description of the debate, in italics (e.g., *Floor Debate, Debate on H.R. 1731*). If providing both a description and the source, put the description first.

Example

> N.Y. Assemb., *Debate on Bill 4843, Record of Proceedings* 474 (Mar. 6, 1995).

15.18(c) State legislature and session designations

Follow **Rule 15.13(c)**.

15.18(d) Pinpoint references

Follow **Rule 15.13(d)**.

15.18(e) State and date parenthetical

Begin the parenthetical with the state's abbreviation (**Appendix 3(B)**), and if available, provide the exact date (Month Day, Year) of the debate, abbreviating the month according to **Appendix 3(A)**. If the exact date is not available, provide at least the year.

15.18(f) Location of transcript or recording of unpublished debate

If the debate is not published, add a second parenthetical indicating where a transcript or audio recording of the debate is located.

Example

> S., *Debate on S. 31*, 74th Leg., Reg. Sess. 1 (Tex. Feb. 1, 1995) (transcript available from Senate Staff Services Office).

15.18(g)(FN) Full citation format for state legislative debate in academic footnotes

⚠ ACADEMIC FORMATTING

In an academic footnote, use large and small capital letters for the chamber abbreviation and the title.

Example

[115] S., DEBATE ON S. 31, 74th Leg., Reg. Sess. 1 (Tex. Feb. 1, 1995) (transcript available from Senate Staff Services Office).

15.19 Short Citation Formats for State Legislative Debates

15.19(a) Short citation using *id.* and other formats

Id. may be used as the short citation. If *id.* is not appropriate, keep all citation components except the state/date parenthetical. Move the state's abbreviation to precede the name of the chamber.

Example

Full citation: S., *Debate on S. 31*, 74th Leg., Reg. Sess. 1 (Tex. Feb. 1, 1995) (transcript available from Senate Staff Services Office).

Short citation: Tex. S., *Debate on S. 31*, 74th Leg., Reg. Sess. at 2.

15.19(b)(FN) Short citation formats for state legislative debate in academic footnotes

⚠ ACADEMIC FORMATTING

In documents with academic footnotes, always repeat the full citation if the debate has not been cited, in full or in short form (including *id.*), in the same footnote or one of the previous five footnotes. Otherwise, omit the state/date parenthetical, but put the state abbreviation before the abbreviated name of the chamber, rendering both in large and small capital letters.

Example

[115] S., DEBATE ON S. 31, 74th Leg., Reg. Sess. 1 (Tex. Feb. 1, 1995) (transcript available from Senate Staff Services Office).

[116] *Id.* at 3.

. . .

[119] TEX. S., DEBATE ON S. 31, 74th Leg., Reg. Sess. at 2.

15.20 Citation Formats for State Legislative Journals

15.20(a) Components of full citation to state legislative journal

Cite state legislative journals using the following format.

> Chamber abbreviation | Journal, | Legislature designation (if any), | Session designation (if any) | Pinpoint reference | (State abbreviation | Year).

Examples (spaces denoted by ^)

S. ▲Journal, ▲81st ▲Gen. ▲Assemb., ▲Reg. ▲Sess. ▲69 ▲(Iowa ▲2005).

H. ▲Journal, ▲17th ▲Leg., ▲Reg. ▲Sess. ▲1467 ▲(Haw. ▲1993).

15.20(b) Short citation formats to state legislative journal

Id. may be used as the short citation. If *id.* is not appropriate, place the state abbreviation before the abbreviated name of the journal. Omit the state/date parenthetical. Provide a pinpoint reference if available.

Examples

Iowa S. Journal, 81st Gen. Assemb., Reg. Sess. at 70.

Haw. H. Journal, 17th Leg., Reg. Sess. at 1469.

15.20(c)(FN) Short citation formats to state legislative journal in academic footnotes

⚠ ACADEMIC FORMATTING

In documents with academic footnotes, always repeat the full citation if the journal has not been cited, in full or in short form (including *id.*) in the same footnote or one of the previous five footnotes. Otherwise, omit the state/date parenthetical, but put the state abbreviation before the abbreviated name of the journal, rendering both in large and small capital letters.

Examples

[92] S. DAILY JOURNAL, 2009–2010 Leg., Reg. Sess. 2332–33 (Cal. 2009).

[93] *Id.* at 2333.

[94] H. JOURNAL, 161st Gen. Assemb., Reg. Sess., vol. 5, at 3663–64 (Pa. 1978).

[95] CAL. S. DAILY JOURNAL, 2009–2010 Leg., Reg. Sess. at 2334.

[96] PA. H. JOURNAL, 161st Gen. Assemb., Reg. Sess., vol. 5, at 3664.

16 Court Rules, Ethics Opinions, and Jury Instructions

Fast Formats

Court Rules, Ethics Opinions, and Jury Instructions	
Federal Rule of Civil Procedure	Fed. R. Civ. P. 56.
Federal Rule of Criminal Procedure	Fed. R. Crim. P. 21(a).
Federal Rule of Evidence	Fed. R. Evid. 801.
State rule of procedure	Mo. R. Civ. P. 56.01(b)(3).
Ethics opinion	ABA Standing Comm. on Ethics & Prof'l Responsibility, Formal Op. 07-446 (2007).
Pattern jury instruction	*Ill. Pattern Jury Instr. Crim.* 1.01 (4th ed. 2000).
Citations in academic footnotes	[21] FED. R. CRIM. P. 21(a).
	[22] ABA Standing Comm. on Ethics & Prof'l Responsibility, Formal Op. 07-446 (2007).
	[23] 11TH CIR. PATTERN JURY INSTR. § 6 (2000).
Short citations	Fed. R. Civ. P. 56.
	ABA Standing Comm. on Ethics & Prof'l Responsibility, Formal Op. 07-446, at 3–4.

16.1 Court Rules

Court rules govern the operation of courts and an array of judicial processes. Court rules may apply broadly to all courts within a given jurisdiction (e.g., a state's rules of civil procedure), or they may have more limited application to particular courts (e.g., bankruptcy courts) or to a single court (e.g., rules of a local court). If you are citing a court rule in a document to be submitted to a court, follow that court's local rules governing citation, if any (see the jurisdiction's entry in **Appendix 2**). For citing uniform or model rules, see **Rule 23.0**.

16.1(a) Full citation format for court rules currently in force

A full citation to a court rule currently in force contains two components.

Code or Rule compilation abbreviation | Rule number.

Example

Rule compilation abbreviation   Rule number (with subdivision)

Fed.▲R.▲Civ.▲P.▲11(a).

16.1(b) Code or rule compilation abbreviation

Unless you are citing a rule of the United States Supreme Court, begin with a reference to the relevant jurisdiction or court, followed by the abbreviation for the code or rule compilation that contains the cited rule. When citing a rule of the United States Supreme Court, omit the jurisdictional reference. For references to other jurisdictions or courts, use abbreviations in **Appendix 3(B)** (states, territories, major cities) or ordinal contractions (**Rule 4.3(b)**) (e.g., 9th instead of Ninth).

Use **Appendices 3(C)**, **3(E)**, and **3(G)** for abbreviations to other words in the name of the code or compilation (e.g., abbreviating "Supreme" as "Sup."). See **Rule 2.2** for guidance on spacing abbreviations. Omit prepositions (e.g., "of," "on") and articles ("a," "an," "the"). Use ordinary type for all components. Insert one space between the abbreviation and the rule number.

Examples (spaces denoted by ▲)

Sup.▲Ct.▲R.▲37.2(b).

Fed.▲R.▲Crim.▲P.▲21(a).

Fla.▲R.▲Crim.▲Evid.▲3.380.

8th▲Cir.▲R.▲30A(a)(2).

Nev.▲Sup.▲Ct.▲R.▲42.

16.1(c) Rule number and subdivisions

Following the code or compilation abbreviation, insert the rule number and a pinpoint reference to its relevant subdivisions, if any. Insert references to internal operating procedures (abbreviated "I.O.P.") and similar information immediately after the rule number.

Examples (spaces denoted by ▲)

Mo.▲R.▲Civ.▲P.▲56.01(b)(3).

Iowa▲Code▲Prof'l▲Responsibility▲DR▲2-101(A).

11th▲Cir.▲R.▲34-4▲I.O.P.▲2(b).

16.1(d) Court rules no longer in force

To cite a court rule that is no longer in force, follow the format shown in **Rule 16.1(a)** through **(c)**, but add a parenthetical with the date of the most recent official source in which the rule appears, and either:

(1) add a second parenthetical indicating the date of the repeal; or

(2) add a comma, one space, the italicized phrase "*superseded by*," and a full citation to the superseding rule.

Examples

Fed. R. Civ. P. 34 (1948) (repealed 1970).

Ohio Code Prof'l Responsibility DR 7-103 (1970), *superseded by* Ohio R. Prof'l Conduct 3.8.

16.1(e)(FN) Full citation format for court rule in academic footnotes

⚠ ACADEMIC FORMATTING

In documents with academic footnotes, use large and small capital letters for the name of the code or rule compilation; the remainder of the citation should be in ordinary type.

Examples

[2] FED. R. EVID. 1006.

[13] FLA. R. CRIM. EVID. 3.380.

[21] WIS. STAT. R. 809.19(2)(b).

16.1(f) Short citation formats for court rules

When appropriate, use *id.* as a short-form citation for court rules, whether current or no longer in force. See **Rule 11.3** for more information on using *id.* If *id.* is not appropriate, use all the components of the full citation.

16.2 Ethics Opinions

16.2(a) Full citation format for ethics opinions

A full citation to an ethics opinion contains four or five components, depending on whether a pinpoint reference is available.

Abbreviated name of issuing entity, | Type of opinion | Opinion number | [, at] | Pinpoint reference (if any) | (Year).

Refer to **Appendices 3(B), 3(E)**, and **3(G)** to abbreviate the name of the entity issuing the opinion and the type of opinion. Present the opinion number as it is displayed in the source. Use ordinary type for all components of the citation.

Example (spaces denoted by ▲)

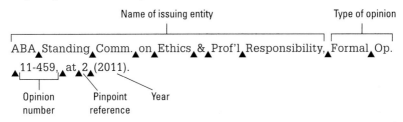

Where possible, provide a pinpoint reference after the opinion number. See **Rules 5, 6, 7**, and **9** for more information about pinpoint references.

To cite an opinion that has been superseded or withdrawn, analogize to **Rule 16.1(d)**. If an opinion has been revised, note that information parenthetically.

Examples

Ohio Bd. of Comm'rs on Grievances & Discipline, Op. 2001-6, at 3–4 (2001).

ABA Standing Comm. on Ethics & Prof'l Responsibility, Informal Op. 1414 (1978), *superseded by* ABA Standing Comm. on Ethics & Prof'l Responsibility, Formal Op. 07-446 (2007).

16.2(b) Short citation formats for ethics opinions

When appropriate, use *id.* as a short-form citation for ethics opinions. See **Rule 11.3** for more information on using *id.* If *id.* is not appropriate, use all the components of the full citation except the date parenthetical.

Example

Full citation:	Or. Bar Ass'n, Formal Op. 2005-164, at 452 (2005).
Short citation:	Or. Bar Ass'n, Formal Op. 2005-164, at 453–54.

▋16.3▋ Jury Instructions

16.3(a) Full citation format for pattern, standard, or approved instructions

A full citation to a pattern, standard, or approved set of jury instructions may contain up to five components, depending on whether the instructions are published in a single volume or a multi-volume set and whether they are published in an edition subsequent to the first.

Example

Volume number [if multi-volume set]   Rule or section number

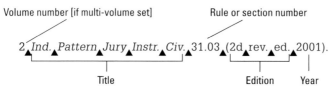

2 *Ind. Pattern Jury Instr. Civ.* 31.03 (2d rev. ed. 2001).

          Title   Edition   Year

Abbreviate words in the title of the instructions, using **Appendices 3(B)** and **3(G)**, and italicize the title. Set out the rule or section number as shown in the source. Add a parenthetical with the edition number, if any, and the year of publication. If the instructions are from a multi-volume set, set out the volume number before the name of the instructions, analogizing to **Rule 20.1(a)**.

Examples

Ill. Pattern Jury Instr. Crim. 1.01 (4th ed. 2000).

11th Cir. Pattern Jury Instr. § 6 (2000).

16.3(b)(FN) Full citation format for pattern, standard, or approved instructions in academic footnotes

⚠ ACADEMIC FORMATTING

To cite pattern, standard, or approved instructions in academic footnotes, use the components described in **Rule 16.3(a)**, but instead of italics, use large and small capital letters for the title.

Examples

[14] ILL. PATTERN JURY INSTR. CRIM. 1.01 (4th ed. 2000).

[23] 11TH CIR. PATTERN JURY INSTR. § 6 (2000).

16.3(c) Full citation format for unofficial jury instructions

Cite unofficial jury instructions, including model instructions, in the same manner as a book, including volume, if any, author, title, and publication data (**Rule 20.1**). *Do not abbreviate* words in the author name or the title. Use ordinary type for the author name and italics for the title. Include pinpoint references where possible.

Example

2 Kevin F. O'Malley et al., *Federal Jury Practice and Instructions* § 23.05 (6th ed. 2006).

16.3(d)(FN) Full citation format for unofficial jury instructions in academic footnotes

⚠ ACADEMIC FORMATTING

To cite unofficial jury instructions in academic footnotes, follow **Rule 16.3(c)**, but use large and small capital letters for both the author name and the title.

Example

> [37] 2 KEVIN F. O'MALLEY ET AL., FEDERAL JURY PRACTICE AND INSTRUCTIONS § 23.05 (6th ed. 2006).

16.3(e) Short citation formats for jury instructions

For any type of jury instruction, use *id.* as a short form when appropriate (**Rule 11.3**). If *id.* is not appropriate, for standard, pattern, or approved jury instructions, use the components shown in **Rule 16.3(a)**, but omit the publication parenthetical. For unofficial jury instructions, analogize to the short citation formats shown in **Rule 20.6(a)**.

Examples

Pattern instructions:	*11th Cir. Pattern Jury Instr.* § 6.
Unofficial instructions:	O'Malley, *supra*, § 23.03.

16.3(f)(FN) Short citation formats for jury instructions in academic footnotes

⚠ ACADEMIC FORMATTING

In documents with academic footnotes, use *id.* if appropriate (**Rule 11.3**). If *id.* is not appropriate, set out the volume number (if applicable) and the author's surname, followed by a *supra* cross-reference to the earlier footnote containing the full citation (**Rule 11.4**) and a pinpoint reference.

Examples

> [37] 2 KEVIN F. O'MALLEY ET AL., FEDERAL JURY PRACTICE AND INSTRUCTIONS § 23.05 (6th ed. 2006).
>
> [38] *Id.* § 23.04.
>
> . . .
>
> [45] O'MALLEY, *supra* note 37, § 23.03.

17 Ordinances

Fast Formats

Ordinances	
Codified ordinance	Village of Richfield, Ohio, Codified Ordinances § 1513.05(f) (2011).
Uncodified ordinance	Moreno Valley, Cal., Ordinance No. 556 (Dec. 14, 1999).
Citations in academic footnotes	[56] VILLAGE OF RICHFIELD, OHIO, CODIFIED ORDINANCES § 1513.05(f) (2011). [71] MORENO VALLEY, CAL., ORDINANCE NO. 556 (Dec. 14, 1999).
Short citations	Village of Richfield, Ohio, Codified Ordinances § 1513.05(f). *Id.* § 1513.05(e).

17.1 Full Citation Format for Codified Ordinances

A full citation to a codified ordinance contains five components.

Name of political subdivision, | State abbreviation, | Name of code | Pinpoint reference | (Publication date).

Example

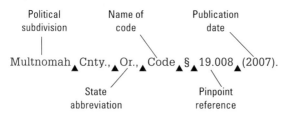

Political subdivision   Name of code   Publication date

Multnomah▲Cnty.,▲Or.,▲Code▲§▲19.008▲(2007).

State abbreviation   Pinpoint reference

17.1(a) Names of political subdivision and code

Begin the citation with the name of the municipality, county, or other political subdivision enacting the ordinance, followed by a comma, a space, and the abbreviated name of the state; use abbreviations shown in **Appendix 3(B)** for city names and states. Following the state abbreviation, insert a comma, a space, and the name of the code containing the cited ordinance, abbreviating any words found in **Appendix 3(E)**. Omit articles ("a," "an," "the") and prepositions (e.g., "of," "for"). Use ordinary type for the name of the political subdivision and code.

Example (spaces denoted by ▲)

Allentown,▲Pa.,▲Codified▲Ordinances▲§▲710.02▲(2013).

17.1(b) Pinpoint references

Provide a pinpoint reference to the specific subdivision(s) of the code containing the cited ordinance, followed by a space. Codified ordinances may be designated by sections, articles, chapters, or other subdivisions. See **Rules 5**, **6**, and **9** for guidance on citing specific types of subdivisions.

17.1(c) Publication parenthetical; official and unofficial online sources

In parentheses, indicate the publication date of the source to which you are citing the ordinance, analogizing to **Rule 14.2(f)(2)**.

Example

Loudon Cnty., Va., Codified Ordinances § 684.03 (2009).

If citing an ordinance from an *official online source*, begin with the preposition "through" followed by the date through which the ordinance is shown to be current in the source. Immediately following the publication parenthetical, insert a comma and one space, followed by the source's URL.

If citing an ordinance from an *unofficial online source*, the publication parenthetical should provide both the publisher name and the date through which the ordinance is shown to be current in the source. Following the publication parenthetical, insert a comma and one space, followed by the phrase "*available at*" and the URL.

Examples

Official online source:	Fruita, Colo., City of Fruita Mun. Code § 610 (through Feb. 1, 2012), http://www.fruita.org/documents/admin/2012-03.ord.pdf.
Unofficial online source:	Carnation, Wash., Code of Ordinances § 3.24.020 (Municode through Ordinance No. 814, enacted May 1, 2012), *available at* http://library.municode.com/HTML/16777/book.html.

▉17.2▉ Full Citation Format for Uncodified Ordinances

A full citation to an uncodified ordinance contains four components.

Name of political subdivision, | State abbreviation, | Ordinance No. [number] *or* **Ordinance name | (Month Day, Year).**

Example

Name of political subdivision   Ordinance number

Garden City, Fla., Ordinance No. 5 (Sept. 21, 2009).

State abbreviation   Month Day, Year

17.2(a) Name of political subdivision and state

Begin with the name of the political subdivision and state, in ordinary type. Follow **Rule 17.1(a)** for spacing and abbreviations.

17.2(b) Number or name of uncodified ordinance

Following the code name, insert the phrase "Ordinance No." followed by a space and the ordinance number, or if the ordinance is not numbered, the name of the ordinance, in ordinary type. Capitalize words in the name of an ordinance according to **Rule 3**.

Examples

Moreno Valley, Cal., Ordinance No. 556 (Dec. 14, 1999).

Campbell Cnty., Va., Airport Development Area Special Service District § 4 (Apr. 3, 2006).

17.2(c) Date of enactment of uncodified ordinance

In parentheses, set out the exact date (Month Day, Year) on which the uncodified ordinance was enacted. Abbreviate the month according to **Appendix 3(A)**. For ordinances published in online sources, follow **Rule 17.1(c)**.

▉17.3(FN)▉ Full Citation Format for Codified or Uncodified Ordinance in Academic Footnotes

⚠ ACADEMIC FORMATTING

To cite a codified or uncodified ordinance in an academic footnote, follow **Rule 17.1** or **Rule 17.2** for its components, but use large and small capital letters for the name of the political subdivision, the name of the code, or if uncodified, the name of the ordinance.

Examples

²⁶ ALLENTOWN, PA., CODIFIED ORDINANCES § 710.02 (2013).

⁴² FRUITA, COLO., CITY OF FRUITA MUN. CODE § 610 (through Feb. 1, 2012), http://www.fruita.org/documents/admin/2012-03.ord.pdf.

⁷¹ MORENO VALLEY, CAL., ORDINANCE NO. 556 (Dec. 14, 1999).

⁸⁵ CAMPBELL CNTY., VA., AIRPORT DEVELOPMENT AREA SPECIAL SERVICE DISTRICT § 4 (Apr. 3, 2006).

17.4 Short Citation Formats for Codified and Uncodified Ordinances

17.4(a) Appropriate use of *id.* as short citation for ordinance

If a citation refers to a codified ordinance *within the same title, chapter, or part* as an ordinance cited in the citation immediately previous, use *id.* as the preferred short citation format, changing the section number as needed (see **Rule 11.3**). If a citation refers to an uncodified ordinance, use *id.* only to refer to the same ordinance cited in the immediately previous citation.

17.4(b) Other short citation formats for ordinances

If *id.* is not appropriate, use one of the short citation formats illustrated below, selecting one with enough information for the reader to easily recognize the citation in the context of the discussion.

Examples

Full citation (codified ordinance):	Loudon Cnty., Va., Codified Ordinances § 684.03 (2009).
Short citation options:	Loudon Cnty., Va., Codified Ordinances § 684.03.
	§ 684.03.
Full citation (uncodified ordinance):	Moreno Valley, Cal., Ordinance No. 556 (Dec. 14, 1999).
Short citation options:	Moreno Valley, Cal., Ordinance No. 556.
	Ordinance No. 556.

17.4(c)(FN) Short citation formats for ordinance in academic footnotes

⚠ ACADEMIC FORMATTING

In documents with academic footnotes, if *id.* is not appropriate (see **Rules 11.1(c)**, **11.3(c)**, and **11.3(f)**), you may use all required components of the full citation, omitting the date, or you may use one of the formats illustrated in **Rule 17.4(b)**. However, if the ordinance has not previously been cited in the same footnote or in any of the five previous footnotes, do not use a short form. Repeat the full citation. Do not use *supra* as a short citation format for an ordinance.

Examples

[33] Loudon Cnty., Va., Codified Ordinances § 684.03 (2009).

[34] *Id.* § 684.02.

. . .

[37] Loudon Cnty., Va., Codified Ordinances § 684.02.

. . .

[51] Loudon Cnty., Va., Codified Ordinances § 684.03 (2009).

18 Administrative and Executive Materials

Fast Formats

Administrative and Executive Materials	
Code of Federal Regulations	31 C.F.R. § 515.329 (2014).
Federal Register	Importation of Wood Packaging Material, 69 Fed. Reg. 55,719, 55,720–21 (Sept. 16, 2004).
Federal agency decision	*Bath Iron Works Corp.*, 345 N.L.R.B. 499, 506 (2005).
	Limitation of Access to Through-Highways Crossing Public Lands, 62 Interior Dec. 158, 161 (1955).
Attorney General opinion	Constitutionality of Proposed Legislation Affecting Tax Refunds, 37 Op. Att'y Gen. 56, 64 (1936).
Office of Legal Counsel opinion	Lawfulness of Recess Appointments During a Recess of the Senate Notwithstanding Periodic Pro Forma Sessions, 36 Op. O.L.C. 9 n.13 (2012).
Federal executive order	Exec. Order No. 13,588, 3 C.F.R. 281 (2012).
State administrative code	312 Ind. Admin. Code 5-2-7 (2013). Utah Admin. Code r. 105-1-10 (2013).
State administrative register	Notice of Hearing on Proposed Administrative Regulations of State Corporation Commission, 32 Kan. Reg. 456 (May 2, 2013).
State attorney general opinion	Colo. Att'y Gen. Op. 09-03, 2009 Colo. AG LEXIS 3 (June 9, 2009).
State executive order	Cal. Exec. Order No. S-14-09 (July 17, 2009), *available at* http://gov.ca.gov/news.php?id=12868.

Citations in academic footnotes	[22] 31 C.F.R. § 515.329 (2014). [27] Importation of Wood Packaging Material, 69 Fed. Reg. 55,719, 55,720–21 (Sept. 16, 2004). [28] Bath Iron Works Corp., 345 N.L.R.B. 499, 506 (2005). [35] Exec. Order No. 13588, 3 C.F.R. 281 (2012).
Short citations	31 C.F.R. § 515.329. § 515.329. Fisheries of the Caribbean, Gulf of Mexico, and South Atlantic, 78 Fed. Reg. at 25,049–50. *Bath Iron Works Corp.*, 345 N.L.R.B. at 505. 37 Op. Att'y Gen. at 60.

CODE OF FEDERAL REGULATIONS

Title 12 — Title number (Rule 18.1(a))
Banks and Banking

Parts 300 to 499

Revised as of January 1, 2013 — Date using only the year (Rule 18.1(c))

Containing a codification of documents
of general applicability and future effect

As of January 1, 2013

Published by the Office of the Federal Register
National Archives and Records Administration
as Special Edition of the Federal Register

Cover

Snapshot

Pinpoint reference
(Rule 18.1(b))

§ 308.503   12 CFR Ch. III (1–1–13 Edition)

or provided services), an assessment may be imposed against any such person or jointly and severally against any combination of such persons.

§ 308.503 Investigations.

(a) If an investigating official concludes that a subpoena pursuant to the authority conferred by 31 U.S.C. 3804(a) is warranted:

(1) The subpoena will identify the person to whom it is addressed and the authority under which the subpoena is issued and will identify the records or documents sought;

(2) The investigating official may designate a person to act on his or her behalf to receive the documents sought; and

(3) The person receiving such subpoena will be required to provide the investigating official or the person designated to receive the documents a certification that the documents sought have been produced, or that such documents are not available, and the reasons therefor, or that such documents, suitably identified, have been withheld based upon the assertion of an identified privilege.

(b) If the investigating official concludes that an action under the PFCRA may be warranted, the investigating official will submit a report containing the findings and conclusions of such investigation to the reviewing official.

(c) Nothing in this section will preclude or limit an investigating official's discretion to refer allegations directly to the United States Department of Justice (DOJ) for suit under the False Claims Act (31 U.S.C. 3729 *et seq.*) or other civil relief, or to preclude or limit the investigating official's discretion to defer or postpone a report or referral to the reviewing official to avoid interference with a criminal investigation or prosecution.

(d) Nothing in this section modifies any responsibility of an investigating official to report violations of criminal law to the Attorney General.

§ 308.504 Review by the reviewing official.

(a) If, based on the report of the investigating official under § 308.503(b) of this subpart, the reviewing official determines that there is adequate evidence to believe that a person is liable under § 308.502 of this subpart, the reviewing official will transmit to the Attorney General a written notice of the reviewing official's intention to issue a complaint under § 308.506 of this subpart.

(b) Such notice will include:

(1) A statement of the reviewing official's reasons for issuing a complaint;

(2) A statement specifying the evidence that supports the allegations of liability;

(3) A description of the claims or statements upon which the allegations of liability are based;

(4) An estimate of the amount of money or the value of property, services, or other benefits requested or demanded in violation of § 308.502 of this subpart;

(5) A statement of any exculpatory or mitigating circumstances that may relate to the claims or statements known by the reviewing official or the investigating official; and

(6) A statement that there is a reasonable prospect of collecting an appropriate amount of penalties and assessments. Such a statement may be based upon information then known, or upon an absence of any information indicating that the person may be unable to pay such amount.

§ 308.505 Prerequisites for issuing a complaint.

(a) The reviewing official may issue a complaint under § 308.506 of this subpart only if:

(1) The DOJ approves the issuance of a complaint in a written statement described in 31 U.S.C. 3803(b)(1); and

(2) In the case of allegations of liability under § 308.502(a) of this subpart with respect to a claim (or a group of related claims submitted at the same time as defined in paragraph (b) of this section) the reviewing official determines that the amount of money or the value of property or services demanded or requested does not exceed $150,000.

(b) For the purposes of this section, a group of related claims submitted at the same time will include only those claims arising from the same transaction (e.g., grant, loan, application, or

Inside Page

172

18.1 Full Citation Format for the *Code of Federal Regulations*

The *Code of Federal Regulations* ("C.F.R.") codifies general and permanent rules and regulations of the departments and agencies of the federal government. A full citation to C.F.R. has four components.

Title number | C.F.R. | Pinpoint reference | (Publication date).

Example

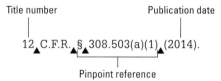

18.1(a) Title number

Begin with the title number of the C.F.R. volume containing the cited rule or regulation, followed by one space, the abbreviation "C.F.R." in ordinary type, and another space. For *Treasury Regulations* (Title 26) and *Federal Acquisition Regulations* (Title 48), see **Rule 18.1(d)**. For presidential orders and other executive documents (Title 3), see **Rule 18.9**.

18.1(b) Pinpoint references

While each C.F.R. title is divided into chapters and each chapter is further subdivided into parts covering specific regulatory areas, most of the titles are organized by sections. Cite the most specific section or other subdivision containing the referenced rules or regulations. For more information on subdivisions, see **Rules 5**, **6**, and **9**. Insert one space after the pinpoint reference.

Examples (spaces denoted by ▲)

6▲C.F.R.▲ch.▲1▲(2014).

12▲C.F.R.▲§▲1600.1▲(2014).

14▲C.F.R.▲pt.▲25,▲app.▲C▲(2014).

18.1(c) Publication date parenthetical

When citing material in the current official annual edition of C.F.R., whether in print or online, in the Federal Digital System (www.gpo.gov/fdsys/), set out the volume's year of publication in parentheses.

When citing a C.F.R. provision to an unofficial electronic database, such as GPO e-CFR (www.ecfr.gov), Lexis Advance, or WestlawNext, add the name of the database provider to the publication date parenthetical, and use the specific date (Month Day, Year) through which C.F.R. is current in that database. Use **Appendix 3(A)** to abbreviate the month.

In citations to historical versions of rules or regulations in C.F.R., the publication date parenthetical should indicate the relevant year of the cited material. See **Sidebar 18.1** for information regarding the publication dates for each title of C.F.R. and for information about C.F.R. provisions available on GPO e-CFR and commercial databases.

Examples

Current annual edition (print or official PDF on FDSys):	48 C.F.R. § 53.246 (2014).
Unofficial online version:	34 C.F.R. § 647.5(a)(2) (GPO e-CFR through Aug. 7, 2013).
	14 C.F.R. § 1201.102 (WestlawNext through Aug. 1, 2013).
	7 C.F.R. § 305.2 (Lexis Advance through Aug. 8, 2013).
Historical version:	20 C.F.R. § 404.140 (1998).

18.1(d) *Treasury Regulations; Federal Acquisition Regulations*

A small number of specialized federal regulations published in C.F.R. are not typically cited to their title number. These include the *Treasury Regulations* in Title 26 and the *Federal Acquisition Regulations* in Title 48. When citing these regulations, replace the title number and C.F.R. abbreviation with the abbreviations shown below, in ordinary type. Use a section symbol before the number of a treasury regulation, but omit it before a FAR regulation. In practice-based documents, you may omit the date parenthetical; do not omit it when citing these regulations in academic footnotes. For more information about citing treasury regulations, see **Appendix 6(C)(1)**.

Examples

Treasury Regulations	Treas. Reg.	Treas. Reg. § 1.921-2 (2013).
Federal Acquisition Regulations	FAR	FAR 9.403 (2012).

18.1(e) Name of rule or regulation

If it would assist readers in recognizing the cited rule or regulation, you may begin the citation with its name. Present the name in ordinary type, followed by a comma and one space. Use **Rule 3.2** for capitalization. If the name is extremely long, it may be shortened, so long as the reader can easily identify the cited material.

Example

Continental Shelf, 50 C.F.R. pt. 296 (2012).

The current *Code of Federal Regulations* is divided into 50 subject-matter titles representing broad areas under federal regulation, contained in more than 200 volumes. Although each volume is annually updated, the set is revised quarterly, as follows:

Title numbers	Revision date
1–16	January 1
17–27	April 1
28–41	July 1
42–50	October 1

The current official annual edition of C.F.R. is available in print and online in PDF format from the Government Printing Office's Federal Digital System, FDsys, http://www.gpo.gov/fdsys/search/home.action. The *Electronic Code of Federal Regulations* (e-CFR) is a currently updated online version of the C.F.R., but it is not official. The e-CFR compiles current C.F.R. sections and the latest *Federal Register* amendments; it is updated daily. The current update status appears at the top of all e-CFR web pages.

Unofficial electronic versions of C.F.R. are also available from commercial publishers such as LexisNexis and Westlaw. Because unofficial versions of C.F.R. may contain material not present in the current annual print or online edition, if you cite C.F.R. from one of these unofficial sources, it is important to convey that information parenthetically, as described in **Rule 18.1(c)**.

18.2   Short Citation Formats for the *Code of Federal Regulations*

18.2(a)   Short citation formats for C.F.R.

In practice-based documents, if *id.* is not appropriate (see **Rules 11.1(c)**, **11.3(c)**, and **11.3(f)**), use one of the short citation formats illustrated below, omitting the publication date parenthetical. If the reader could easily recognize the citation from the context of the discussion, you may omit the title number and C.F.R. abbreviation.

Examples

Full citation:	31 C.F.R. § 515.329 (2014).
Short citations:	31 C.F.R. § 515.329.
	§ 515.329.

18.2(b)(FN) Short citation formats for C.F.R. in academic footnotes

⚠ ACADEMIC
FORMATTING

In documents with academic footnotes, if *id.* is not appropriate, you may use one of the formats illustrated in **Rule 18.2(a)**. However, if the rule or regulation has not previously been cited in the same footnote or in any of the five previous footnotes, do not use a short form. Repeat the full citation. Do not use *supra* as a short citation.

18.3 Full Citation Format for the *Federal Register*

Cite the *Federal Register* for proposed rules and regulations, notices, and final regulations that are not yet printed in C.F.R. The *Federal Register* (abbreviated "Fed. Reg.") is published in print and in official and unofficial electronic formats, but its citation is the same regardless of the version used. A full citation to the *Federal Register* contains six components.

Title of rule or regulation | Volume number | Fed. Reg. | Initial page, | Pinpoint page(s) | (Month Day, Year).

Example

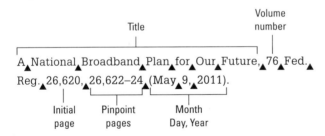

18.3(a) Title of rule or regulation

Begin the citation with the title of the notice, rule, or regulation, in ordinary type, followed by a comma and one space. Use **Rule 3.2** for capitalization. You may shorten lengthy titles as long as they remain descriptive. If the cited material does not have a formal title, you may provide your own description, in ordinary type.

Examples

> September 11th Victim Compensation Fund of 2001, 67 Fed. Reg. 11,233 (Mar. 13, 2002).
>
> Notice, 74 Fed. Reg. 28,877 (June 18, 2009).

18.3(b) Volume number and abbreviation

Following the title of the cited notice, rule, or regulation, set out the number of the *Federal Register* volume containing the cited material, followed by one space, the abbreviation "Fed. Reg." in ordinary type, and another space. Omit reference to the specific issue number.

18.3(c) Initial page and pinpoint references

Provide the initial page of the notice, rule, or regulation, and if citing only a portion of it, add the pinpoint page(s) of the more specific material. For five-digit (or larger) page numbers in the *Federal Register*, use a comma (*without* a following space) to separate the thousands from the hundreds. For the pinpoint page reference, separate the initial page from the pinpoint page with a comma and one space, as shown in the examples below. In this way, readers will not be confused about the page number references. See **Rule 5.2** for more information about pinpoint pages.

Examples

> Notice, 74 Fed. Reg. 14,790, 14,792 (Apr. 1, 2009).
>
> Certain Lined Paper Products from the People's Republic of China, 78 Fed. Reg. 34,640, 34,640–41 (June 10, 2013).

18.3(d) Exact date; indicating status of proposed rule or regulation

Because the *Federal Register* is published daily, the publication date parenthetical should refer to the exact date (Month Day, Year) of the cited volume. Abbreviate the month according to **Appendix 3(A)**.

If citing a proposed rule or regulation, indicate its proposed status in the publication date parenthetical.

Example

> Approval and Promulgation of Air Quality Implementation Plans, 74 Fed. Reg. 25,205 (proposed May 27, 2009).

18.3(e) Cross-reference to C.F.R.

When the *Federal Register* indicates that a rule or regulation will appear in or amend the *Code of Federal Regulations*, provide that information in a parenthetical following the exact date parenthetical, as illustrated below.

Examples

> Candidate Solicitation at State, District, and Local Party Fundraising Events, 70 Fed. Reg. 9013 (proposed Feb. 24, 2005) (to be codified at 11 C.F.R.§ 300.64(a)).

> Importation of Fresh Bananas, 78 Fed. Reg. 8957 (Mar. 25, 2009) (amending 7 C.F.R. pt. 319).

18.4 Short Citation Formats for the *Federal Register*

18.4(a) Short citation formats for the *Federal Register*

In practice-based documents, use *id.* as a short-form citation for the *Federal Register*. See **Rule 11.3** for more information on *id.* If *id.* is not appropriate (see **Rules 11.1(c)**, **11.3(c)**, and **11.3(f)**), omit the date parenthetical. Insert "at" before any pinpoint reference.

Example

Full citation:	Fisheries of the Caribbean, Gulf of Mexico, and South Atlantic, 78 Fed. Reg. 25,047, 25,047–48 (proposed Apr. 29, 2013) (amending 50 C.F.R. pt. 622).
Short citation:	Fisheries of the Caribbean, Gulf of Mexico, and South Atlantic, 78 Fed. Reg. at 25,049–50.

18.4(b)(FN) Short citation formats for the *Federal Register* in academic footnotes

⚠ ACADEMIC FORMATTING

In documents with academic footnotes, if *id.* is not appropriate, omit the date parenthetical, and insert "at" before any pinpoint reference. However, if the material from the *Federal Register* has not previously been cited in the same footnote or in any of the five previous footnotes, do not use a short form. Repeat the full citation. Do not use *supra* as a short citation.

18.5 Full Citation Format for Federal Agency Decisions

A full citation to an administrative decision such as an adjudication or arbitration typically contains six components.

Case name, | Volume number | Reporter abbreviation | Initial page, | Pinpoint page | (Date of decision).

Example

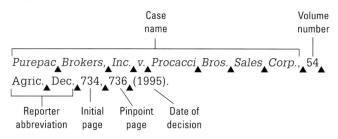

18.5(a) Case name

If the case involves adverse parties, follow **Rule 12.2**, indicating the first-listed party on each side. If the case involves an agency's application of rules or regulations to one or more parties, indicate solely the first-listed private party, omitting any procedural phrases that may be present. In either situation, abbreviate words in an organizational party's name according to **Appendix 3(E)**. Present the case name in italics.

18.5(b) Volume number and reporter abbreviation

There is no single publication source for federal agency decisions. If the decision is printed in an agency's official reporter, cite the volume number of that reporter, followed by one space and the abbreviation for the reporter. See **Appendix 7(A)** for abbreviations to many federal agencies' official reporters.

Many agency decisions are unofficially published in topical looseleaf services. If the decision is only available from a looseleaf service, follow **Rule 24**.

If the decision is only available from the agency's website, follow **Rule 31**. In any instance, you may add a parallel citation to the decision in a commercial database such as WestlawNext or Lexis Advance.

Examples

Official reporter:	*Clinton Milk Co.*, 31 Agric. Dec. 1231, 1238–40 (1972).
	Seattle Crescent Container Serv., Inc. v. Port of Seattle, 28 F.M.C. 336, 336 (1986).
Agency website:	*Pacific Rim Onion, Inc.*, Docket No. 13-0014 (U.S.D.A. Apr. 17, 2013), http://www.dm.usda.gov/oaljdecisions/130417_0014_DO_Pacific%20Rim%20Onion%20%20Inc.pdf.
Official reporter with parallel citation to commercial database:	*Cavazos v. Wanxiang Am. Corp.*, 10 OCAHO 1138, 2011 WL 1824675 (Apr. 27, 2011).

18.5(c) Subdivisions

After the reporter abbreviation, insert the initial subdivision. In bound reports, the initial subdivision will likely be a page number; however, in looseleaf services, the subdivision may be a paragraph or another division (see **Rule 24.1(e)**). Provide a pinpoint reference if possible. See **Rule 5.2** for more information on pinpoint references.

18.5(d) Date parenthetical

In a parenthetical, indicate the date of the decision. Follow **Rule 12.7**.

18.5(e) Agency abbreviation

If the agency who issued the decision cannot be determined from the name of the reporter or electronic database, add the agency's abbreviation to the date parenthetical, using abbreviations from **Appendix 7(B)**. Insert one space between the agency abbreviation and the date.

18.5(f) Arbitrator

When citing the decision of an arbitrator, provide the surname of the arbitrator, followed by a comma, one space, and the abbreviation "Arb." in a parenthetical following the date parenthetical.

Example (decision published in looseleaf service)

Am. Fed'n of Gov't Emps., Local 2270 v. Dep't of Veterans Affairs, 111 LRP 13,172 (2010) (Zeiser, Arb.).

> **SIDEBAR 18.2**   Citing Federal Tax Materials
>
> Citation information for commonly used federal tax materials is
> contained in **Appendix 6**. For tax materials not contained in **Appendix
> 6**, consult Joni Larson & Dan Sheaffer, *Federal Tax Research* (2d ed.
> 2011), or Gail Levin Richmond, *Federal Tax Research: Guide to Materi-
> als and Techniques* (8th ed. 2010).

18.5(g)(FN) **Full citation format for federal
agency decision in academic
footnotes**

Follow the relevant provisions of **Rule 18.5**, but use ordinary type for the case
name, analogizing to **Rule 12.2(a)(2)(FN)**.

18.6 Short Citation Formats for Federal Agency Decisions

Follow **Rule 12.19**.

18.7 Full Citation Format for Advisory Opinions

A full citation to an advisory opinion of the Attorney General of the United
States or the Justice Department's Office of Legal Counsel contains up to six
components.

Title, | Volume number | Source abbreviation | Initial page, | Pinpoint page(s) |
(Year of publication).

Examples

Attorney General opinion:

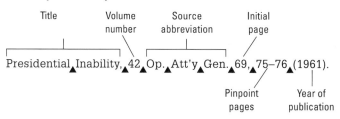

SIDEBAR 18.3   Purpose of Advisory Opinions

Advisory opinions are somewhat different from other agency decisions. They are written in response to inquiries from federal government officials, and rather than being binding, they are advisory in nature. Today, the Attorney General issues very few formal opinions. Instead, such opinions tend to come from the Justice Department's Office of Legal Counsel.

Office of Legal Counsel opinion:

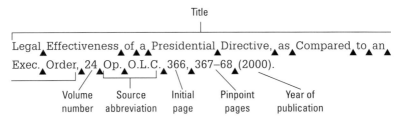

Legal Effectiveness of a Presidential Directive, as Compared to an Exec. Order, 24 Op. O.L.C. 366, 367–68 (2000).

Volume number — Source abbreviation — Initial page — Pinpoint pages — Year of publication

18.7(a) Title

Begin the citation with the title of the advisory opinion, if any, abbreviating words found in **Appendix 3(B)**, **(E)**, **(F)**, or **(G)**. Present the title in ordinary type. Insert a comma and one space after the title.

18.7(b) Volume number and source abbreviation

Following the title, set out the number of the volume containing the cited opinion, in ordinary type, followed by one space, an abbreviation for the publication source of the opinion, and another space. Abbreviate *Opinions of the Attorneys General of the United States* as "Op. Att'y Gen." Abbreviate *Opinions of the Office of Legal Counsel* as "Op. O.L.C."

18.7(c) Initial page and pinpoint references

Following the source abbreviation, indicate the initial page on which the cited material begins. To cite a particular part of the opinion, add a comma, one space, and a pinpoint page reference (**Rule 5.2**).

18.7(d) Publication date parenthetical

In parentheses, indicate the year in which the opinion was published.

Examples

> Relative Rank of Navy & Army Officers, 34 Op. Att'y Gen. 521, 523 (1925).
>
> Whether a Presidential Pardon Expunges Judicial & Exec. Branch Records of a Crime, 30 Op. O.L.C. 1 (2006).

18.8 Short Citation Formats for Advisory Opinions

When appropriate, use *id.* as a short-form citation. See **Rule 11.3** for more information on *id.* If *id.* is not appropriate, indicate the volume number and the source abbreviation. Insert "at" before a pinpoint page reference.

Example

Full citation: Review of Final Order in Alien Employer Sanctions Cases,13 Op. O.L.C. 370, 371 (1989).

Short citation: 13 Op. O.L.C. at 371.

18.9 Full Citation Format for Executive Documents

A full citation to a document such as an executive order, a proclamation, a determination, a finding, a memorandum, a notice, or a reorganization plan prepared by the President of the United States contains six or seven components.

Title | Document identification | No. | Document number, |
Source abbreviation | Initial subdivision, | Pinpoint subdivision | (Date).

Example

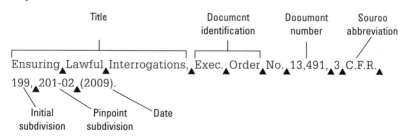

18.9(a) Document identification and document number

Begin by identifying the form of the executive document, whether it is an executive order, a proclamation, or some other executive document, and indicate its number, if any. For five-digit or larger numbers, use commas to separate the thousands from the hundreds (**Rule 4.1**). Abbreviate "Executive" as "Exec." and "Number" as "No.," but do not otherwise abbreviate words in the document identification. Use ordinary type, and capitalize words according to **Rule 3**. If the document has a title, you may elect to begin the citation with that title, in ordinary type.

Examples (spaces denoted by ▲)

> National▲Defense▲Resources▲Preparedness,▲Exec.▲Order▲No.▲13,603, ▲77▲Fed.▲Reg.▲16,651▲(Mar.▲22,▲2012).
>
> Presidential▲Notice▲of▲Mar.▲11,▲2009,▲74▲Fed.▲Reg.▲10,999▲ (Mar.▲13,▲2009).

18.9(b) Source abbreviation

Presidential orders, proclamations, and reorganization plans are printed in Title 3 of the *Code of Federal Regulations* ("3 C.F.R."). If the document is not in the *Code of Federal Regulations* or has not yet appeared there, cite its publication in the *Federal Register*, following **Rule 18.3**.

Cite executive documents not appearing in C.F.R. or the *Federal Register* to the sources in which they are published, such as *Public Papers of the Presidents* (abbreviated "Pub. Papers"), the *Weekly Compilation of Presidential Documents* ("Weekly Comp. Pres. Doc."), the *Daily Compilation of Presidential Documents* ("Daily Comp. Pres. Doc."), or the *U.S. Code Congressional and Administrative News* ("U.S.C.C.A.N."), in that order of preference. Use ordinary type for the source abbreviation.

Examples

> Exec. Order No. 12,834, 3 C.F.R. 580 (1993).
>
> Proclamation No. 8346, 74 Fed. Reg. 9735 (Feb. 27, 2009).

18.9(c) Subdivisions

Indicate the page or other subdivision on which the specific document begins. Unlike other titles of the C.F.R., most of the documents published in Title 3 use page numbers rather than section numbers, but you may encounter both. To refer to material within the document, insert a comma, one space, and the relevant pinpoint citation. See **Rules 5, 6**, and **9** for more information on subdivisions.

Examples

> Exec. Order No. 12,778, 3 C.F.R. 359, 360 (1992).
>
> Exec. Order No. 12,291, 3 C.F.R. 127, 128 § 2(c) (1981).

18.9(d) Publication date parenthetical

Because Title 3 of C.F.R. does not reprint past executive orders, when citing an executive order to C.F.R., use the publication year of the original volume containing the order. When citing an executive order or other executive document to the *Federal Register*, insert the exact date (Month Day, Year) of the cited issue. Abbreviate the month using **Appendix 3(A)**. Enclose the date in parentheses.

18.9(e) Parallel citation to document reprint

You may include a parallel citation to another source that reprints the cited document, such as the *United States Code, United States Code Congressional and Administrative News*, or *Statutes at Large*. Following the date parenthetical, insert the italicized phrase "*reprinted in*" followed by a full citation to the parallel source.

Examples

> Exec. Order No. 11,246, 3 C.F.R. 167 (1965), *reprinted in* 42 U.S.C. § 2000e app. 538–41 (2000).

> Exec. Order No. 11,785, 3 C.F.R. 874 (1974), *reprinted in* 1974 U.S.C.C.A.N. 8277.

18.9(f)(FN) Full citation format for executive document in academic footnotes

⚠ ACADEMIC FORMATTING

Follow the provisions of **Rule 18.9(a)** through **(e)**. Use ordinary type for abbreviated references to the *Code of Federal Regulations* or the *Federal Register,* but use large and small capital letters for abbreviations to other sources, such as *Public Papers of the Presidents* (addressed in **Rule 18.9(b)**).

Examples

> [78] Address to the Nation on the Terrorist Attacks, 1 PUB. PAPERS 1099 (Sept. 11, 2001).

> [128] Interagency Working Group on Coordination of Domestic Energy Development and Permitting in Alaska, Exec. Order No. 13,580, 76 Fed. Reg. 4198 (July 15, 2011).

18.10 Short Citation Formats for Executive Documents

When appropriate, use *id.* as a short-form citation. See **Rule 11.3** for more information on *id.* If *id.* is not appropriate, use the components of the full citation, omitting the initial page number and the date. Insert "at" before a pinpoint page.

Example

Full citation:	Exec. Order No. 12,778, 3 C.F.R. 359, 360 (1992).
Short citation:	Exec. Order No. 12,778, 3 C.F.R. at 360.

18.11 Citation Formats for Executive Agreements

Follow **Rule 19** for treaties, conventions, and agreements.

18.12 Citation Formats for Patents

Begin the citation with the abbreviation "U.S. Patent No." followed by the patent number (using commas as illustrated below), in ordinary type. In parentheses, insert the word "filed" followed by the exact date (Month Day, Year) on which the patent was filed, abbreviating the month (**Appendix 3(A)**). If relevant, you may begin the citation with the name of the patent (in ordinary type) or append a second parenthetical indicating the date on which the patent was issued. Use the same format for citations to patents in academic footnotes.

To cite a specific portion of the patent, insert an appropriate pinpoint reference immediately following the patent number. See **Appendix 3(C)** and **Rule 9** for more information on subdivisions.

For short citations, use the full citation format, but delete the date parenthetical. In textual-sentence references to a patent, you may use an apostrophe followed by the last three digits of the patent number, as shown below. Do not use this shortened reference if more than one patent would have the same designation.

Examples

Full citation:	U.S. Patent No. 4,396,601 (filed Sept. 3, 1982).
	U.S. Patent No. 6,918,136 fig.2 (filed Feb. 1, 2001).
	U.S. Patent No. 4,396,601 (filed Sept. 3, 1982) (issued Apr. 24, 1984).
	Service Operations on a Computer System, U.S. Patent No. 6,918,055 (filed Mar. 20,2002).
Short citations:	U.S. Patent No. 4,396,601.
	U.S. Patent No. 4,396,601 fig.1.
Short form in text:	In challenging the '601 Patent, Jones argued that . . .

18.13 Citation Formats for State Administrative Codes

Each state has its own administrative code, the state's equivalent of the *Code of Federal Regulations*. The citation typically includes a title number, the abbreviated name of the code, a pinpoint subdivision, and the year. The format for each state's code is listed under its entry in **Appendix 1(B)**.

When citing an official state administrative code from an electronic source, indicate the year of publication in parentheses (analogizing to **Rule 18.1(c)**), followed by a comma, one space, and the URL, as illustrated by the New Mexico example below.

For short citations, analogize to **Rule 18.2.**

Examples

Full citation:	Ohio Admin. Code 1501:9-1-08 (2012).
	N.M. Code R. § 14.5.1.8 (2013), http://www.nmcpr. state.nm.us/ nmac/parts/title14/14.005.0001.htm.
Short citation:	Ohio Admin. Code 1501:9-1-08.
	N.M. Code R. § 14.5.1.8.

18.14 Citation Formats for State Administrative Registers

Many, but not all, states have administrative registers, similar to the *Federal Register*. Consult **Appendix 1** to determine whether a particular state has an administrative register and, if so, the citation format to follow. As with the *Federal Register*, refer to the exact date listed on the front cover. See **Rule 18.3** for more guidance. For short citations, analogize to **Rule 18.4.**

Examples

Full citation:	56 D.C. Reg. 5875 (July 31, 2009).
	640 Wis. Admin. Reg. 22 (Apr. 14, 2009).
Short citation:	56 D.C. Reg.at 5875.
	640 Wis. Admin. Reg. at 22.

18.15 Citation Formats for State Agency Decisions

Analogize to **Rule 18.5** and **Rule 12**. If the identity of the agency issuing the decision cannot be determined from the name of the reporter or electronic database, add the agency's abbreviation to the date parenthetical, preceded by the state's abbreviation (**App. 3(B)(1)**). Because these materials are often most easily located in an online or electronic database, you may include that information using the rules in **Part 4** of the *ALWD Guide*. For short citations, follow **Rule 12.20.**

Examples

In re Avista Corp., Order No. 11080, at 13–14 (Or. Pub. Util. Comm'n Mar. 10, 2011), http://apps.puc.state.or.us/orders/2011ords/11-080.pdf.

L.B. v. Dep't of Children & Fam. Servs., 2008 Fla. Div. Adm. Hear. LEXIS 232, at *3 (Apr. 30, 2008).

18.16 Citation Formats for State Advisory Opinions

Cite analogously to **Rule 18.7**, but add the state's abbreviation (**Appendix 3(B) (1)**) to the beginning of the opinion abbreviation. Because these materials are often most easily located in an online or electronic database, you may include that information using the rules in **Part 4**. If desired, you may include a parallel citation to a state administrative code or register. For short citations, analogize to **Rule 18.8**.

Examples

Full citations:	Tex. Att'y Gen. Op. GA-0734, 34 Tex. Reg. 5621 (Aug. 21, 2009).
	Colo. Att'y Gen. Op. 09-03, 2009 Colo. AG LEXIS 3, at *5 (June 9, 2009).
Short citations:	Tex. Att'y Gen. Op. GA-0734, 34 Tex. Reg. at 5621.
	Colo. Att'y Gen. Op. 09-03, 2009 Colo. AG LEXIS 3, at *5.

18.17 Citation Formats for State Executive Materials

Cite analogously to **Rule 18.9**, but insert the state abbreviation at the beginning of the document abbreviation if the source abbreviation does not unambiguously indicate the state. Because these materials are often most easily located in an online or electronic database, you may include that information using the rules in **Part 4**. If desired, add a parallel citation to a state administrative code or register.

Examples

Statewide Language Access Policy, N.Y. Exec. Order No. 26 (Oct. 6, 2011), *available at* http://www.governor.ny.gov/executiveorder/26.

N.J. Exec. Order No. 68 (June 22, 2011), *available at* 2010 NJ EO 68 (WestlawNext).

18.18 Other Administrative and Executive Materials

To cite other federal or state administrative and executive materials not specifically addressed above, analogize to the closest rule above or use the following format. If the suggested format does not work exactly for your source, include as much of the information called for below as possible.

Title, | Document abbreviation | No. | Document number | Source abbreviation | Pinpoint reference | (Agency abbreviation | Date).

19 Treaties, Conventions, and Agreements; International and Foreign Law Sources

Fast Formats

Treaties, Conventions, and Agreements	
Bilateral treaty	Treaty on Measures for the Further Reduction and Limitation of Strategic Offensive Arms, U.S.-Russ., Apr. 8, 2010, S. Treaty Doc. No. 111-5 [hereinafter New START Treaty].
Multilateral treaty	Inter-American Treaty of Reciprocal Assistance, Sept. 2, 1947, 62 Stat. 1681, 21 U.N.T.S. 77.
Convention	Council of Europe, Convention on Cybercrime, Nov. 23, 2001, C.E.T.S. No. 185, *available at* http://conventions.coe.int/Treaty/en/Treaties/Html/185.htm.
Agreement	North American Free Trade Agreement, U.S.-Can.-Mex., art. 1120, Dec. 17, 1992, 32 I.L.M. 289 (1993) [hereinafter NAFTA].

19.1 Full Citation Format for Treaties, Conventions, and Agreements Currently in Force

A full citation to a treaty, a convention, or an executive agreement to which a nation or an international organization (such as the United Nations) is a party and that is currently in force varies slightly depending on whether it is a bilateral or multilateral agreement. If bilateral, it establishes legal rights and obligations between two nations or a nation and an international organization; if multilateral, it does so among three or more nations or organizations.

19.1(a) Bilateral treaty, convention, or agreement

A citation to a bilateral treaty, convention, or agreement has up to five components.

Title | Signatory parties, | Pinpoint reference (if any), | Exact date, | Treaty source.

Example

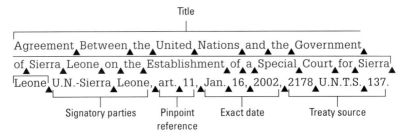

Title

Agreement Between the United Nations and the Government of Sierra Leone on the Establishment of a Special Court for Sierra Leone, U.N.-Sierra Leone, art. 11, Jan. 16, 2002, 2178 U.N.T.S. 137.

| Signatory parties | Pinpoint reference | Exact date | Treaty source |

19.1(b) Multilateral treaty, convention, or agreement

A citation to a multilateral treaty, convention, or agreement has up to four components.

Title | Pinpoint reference (if any), | Exact date, | Treaty source(s).

Example

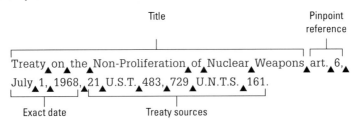

Title   Pinpoint reference

Treaty on the Non-Proliferation of Nuclear Weapons art. 6, July 1, 1968, 21 U.S.T. 483, 729 U.N.T.S. 161.

Exact date   Treaty sources

19.1(c) Title of treaty, convention, or agreement

For the title of a treaty, convention, or agreement, combine the term for the form of agreement (e.g., "Treaty," "Convention," "Protocol," "Agreement") and the subject-matter description shown on the document's title page. If the document displays more than one term for the form of agreement, use only the first shown. Present the title in ordinary type, and capitalize words according to **Rule 3**. Insert one space after the title.

If the title is lengthy or if the document is commonly referenced by a popular name, insert a bracketed "hereinafter" designation of a shorter name or the popular name at the end of the full citation. For guidance on using the "hereinafter" designation, see **Rule 11.5**.

Example

Treaty on Principles Governing the Activities of States in the Exploration and Use of Outer Space, Including the Moon and Other Celestial Bodies art. III, Jan. 27, 1967, 18 U.S.T. 2410, 610 U.N.T.S. 205 [hereinafter Outer Space Treaty].

19.1(d) Pinpoint references

When citing only part of an agreement, set out the appropriate subdivision immediately following the title, using the abbreviations listed in **Appendix 3(C)**. Insert a comma and one space after the subdivision. See **Rules 5, 6,** and **9** for more information on subdivisions.

Example

Convention for the Protection of Individuals with Regard to Automatic Processing of Personal Data pmbl., Jan. 28, 1981, 20 I.L.M. 317.

19.1(e) Signatory parties

If one of the signatory parties to a bilateral agreement is the United States or the United Nations, list it first. Otherwise, list the parties in alphabetical order, abbreviating their names according to **Appendix 3(B)**, and joining the abbreviations with hyphens (-). Following the last abbreviation, insert a comma and one space.

For multilateral agreements, the parties' names are typically omitted. If you wish to identify them, however, list their abbreviations after the name of the agreement, in alphabetical order, joined by hyphens.

Examples

Mutual Defense Treaty, U.S.-Phil., Aug. 30, 1951, 3 U.S.T. 3947.

North American Free Trade Agreement, U.S.-Can.-Mex., art. 1120, Dec. 17, 1992, 32 I.L.M. 289 (1993) [hereinafter NAFTA].

19.1(f) Date of signing

If possible, provide the exact date of signing, followed by a comma and one space. See **Appendix 3(A)** for abbreviations of months.

If the parties signed on different dates, use the date on which the last party signed. If the date of signing is not available, use one of the following dates, in the following order of preference:

▪ the effective date;

▪ the date on which ratifications were exchanged between or among the signatories;

▪ the date of ratification by the President of the United States;

▪ the date of ratification by the Senate; or

▪ any other date of significance.

When the date of signing is not used, parenthetically indicate the significance of the date being used.

Examples

Date of signing: Convention for the Unification of Certain Rules
Relating to International Transportation by Air, Oct.
12, 1929, 49 Stat. 3000.

Other date: Convention for the Unification of Certain Rules with
Respect to Assistance and Salvage at Sea art. 14, Sept.
23, 1910, 37 Stat. 1658 (entered into force Mar. 1, 1913).

19.1(g) Document sources

Following the date, cite a source in which the treaty, convention, or agreement
appears. For bilateral documents between the United States and another party,
cite an official source, if available. For multilateral documents to which the
United States is a party, cite an official source; if desired, you may add a parallel
citation to a source published by an international organization. For agreements
to which the United States is *not* a party, cite a source published by an international organization. If a treaty or agreement is not available in an official source
or a source published by an international organization, cite it to International
Legal Materials (I.L.M.), if therein; if not, cite to another unofficial source.

  See **Chart 19.1** for a list of document sources, their abbreviations and citation format, and for official sources, the order of preference for citation. For
documents that can be easily located on a reliable site on the World Wide Web,
such as a governmental website or the website of an international organization,
the citation may append the URL of the source.

Examples

Treaty Relating to the Uses of the Waters of the Niagara River art. IV,
U.S.-Can., Feb. 27, 1950, 1 U.S.T. 694.

Inter-American Convention on the Taking of Evidence Abroad art. 4, Jan.
30, 1975, 1438 U.N.T.S. 389, O.A.S. T.S. No. 44, *available at* http://www.
oas.org/juridico/english/treaties/b-37.html.

19.2 Full Citation Format for Treaties, Conventions, and Agreements No Longer in Force

When citing an agreement (or part of an agreement) that is no longer in force,
use the citation format for current agreements, but append a parenthetical indicating why and when the agreement was terminated or otherwise lost effect.

Example

Mutual Defense Treaty Between the United States of America and the
Republic of China art. 10, Dec. 2, 1954, 6 U.S.T. 433 (terminated on Jan.
1, 1980).

CHART 19.1	**Document Sources for Treaties, Conventions, and Agreements**

Official sources (in order of citation preference):	Abbreviation and format (spaces denoted by ▲):
United States Treaties and Other International Agreements	[Volume number]▲U.S.T.▲[Page number]
Statutes at Large	[Volume number]▲Stat.▲[Page number]
Treaties and Other International Acts Series	T.I.A.S.▲No.▲[Treaty number]
Treaty Series	T.S.▲No.▲[Treaty number]
Executive Agreement Series	E.A.S.▲No.▲[Treaty number]
United Nations Treaty Series	[Volume number]▲U.N.T.S.▲[Page number]
Senate Treaty Documents	S.▲Treaty▲Doc.▲No.▲[Treaty number]
Senate Executive Documents	S.▲Exec.▲Doc.▲No.▲[Document number]

Sources from international organizations:	Abbreviation and format:
Council of Europe Treaty Series	C.E.T.S.▲No.▲[Treaty number]
European Treaty Series	E.T.S.▲No.▲[Treaty number]
International Legal Materials	[Volume number]▲I.L.M.▲[Page number]
League of Nations Treaty Series	[Volume number]▲L.N.T.S.▲[Page number]
Organization of American States Treaty Series	O.A.S.▲T.S.▲No.▲[Treaty number]
Pan-American Treaty Series	[Volume number]▲Pan-Am.▲T.S.▲[Page number]

Unofficial sources (cite I.L.M., if therein; otherwise no citation preference):	Abbreviation and format:
International Legal Materials	[Volume number]▲I.L.M.▲[Page number]
Hein's United States Treaties and Other International Agreements	Hein's▲No.▲KAV▲[Treaty number]
Parry's Consolidated Treaty Series	[Volume number]▲Consol.▲T.S.▲[Page number]
Treaties and Other International Agreements of the United States of America(Charles I. Bevans comp.)	[Volume number]▲Bevans▲[Page number]

19.3 Short Citation Format for Treaties, Conventions, and Agreements

19.3(a) Short citation formats for treaty, convention, or agreement

When appropriate, use *id.* as the preferred short citation. See **Rule 11.3** for more information on *id.*

In practice-based documents, when *id.* is not appropriate, omit the title but keep the treaty source component, changing the pinpoint reference as needed. Analogize to short citations for statutes (**Rule 14.5**) or session laws (**Rule 14.9**).

Example

Full citation: Treaty on the Protection of Artistic and Scientific
Institutions and Historic Monuments, Apr. 13, 1935, 49
Stat. 3267.

Short citation: 49 Stat. at 3268.

19.3(b)(FN) Short citation formats for treaty, convention, or agreement in academic footnotes

⚠ ACADEMIC
FORMATTING

In documents with academic footnotes, do not use *id.* if the treaty, convention, or agreement has not previously been cited in the same footnote or in one of the previous five footnotes. Instead, use the *supra* format illustrated below, cross-referencing the footnote in which the document's full citation is first set out. If the full citation provided a "hereinafter" designation for the document, begin the short citation with that designation, followed by a comma, one space, and the *supra* cross-reference.

Example

Full citation: [32] Treaty on the Protection of Artistic and Scientific
Institutions and Historic Monuments, Apr. 13, 1935, 49
Stat. 3267 [hereinafter Roerich Pact].

Short citation: [44] Roerich Pact, *supra* note 32, at 3268.

19.4 International and Foreign Law Sources

For citations to foreign and international law sources, consult the *Guide to Foreign and International Legal Citations* (2d ed. 2009), prepared by the editors of New York University School of Law's *Journal of International Law and Politics*. Another useful guide for international law sources is Part IV of the Oxford University Standard for Citation of Legal Authorities (OSCOLA), http://www.law.ox.ac.uk/published/OSCOLA_2006_citing_international_law.pdf.

20 Books, Treatises, and Other Nonperiodic Materials

Fast Formats

Books, Treatises, and Other Nonperiodic Materials	
Single author	Martha C. Nussbaum, *Sex and Social Justice* 265–66 (1999).
Two authors	Mark Herrmann & David B. Alden, *Drug and Device Product Liability Litigation Strategy* 262–63 (2012).
Multi-volume treatise with multiple authors	7A Charles Alan Wright, Arthur R. Miller & Mary Kay Kane, *Federal Practice and Procedure* § 1758, 114–15 (3d ed. 2005).
	7A Charles Alan Wright et al., *Federal Practice and Procedure* § 1758, 114–15 (3d ed. 2005).
Work cited in academic footnote	44 RODNEY A. SMOLLA, FREE SPEECH IN AN OPEN SOCIETY 136–37 (1992).
Editor, but no listed author	*International Family Law Desk Book* ch. 8 (Ann Laquer Estin ed., 2012).
Author and editor	1 Arthur Linton Corbin, *Corbin on Contracts* § 4.14 (Joseph M. Perillo ed., rev. ed. 1993).
	Jeremy Bentham, *Of the Limits of the Penal Branch of Jurisprudence* § 4, 42–44 (Philip Schofield ed., Clarendon Press 2010).
Translator	Aldo Schiavone, *The Invention of Law in the West* 170–74 (Jeremy Carden & Antony Shugaar trans., Belknap Press of Harvard Univ. Press 2012).
Collected works of one author	Oliver Wendell Holmes, *Primitive Notions in Modern Law No. II, in* 3 The Collected Works of Justice Holmes 21, 30–31 (Sheldon M. Novick ed., 1995).
Collected works of multiple authors	Oliver Quick, *Medical Manslaughter and Expert Evidence: The Roles of Context and Character, in* 2 Bioethics, Medicine and the Criminal Law 101 (Danielle Griffiths & Andrew Sanders eds., 2013).
Short forms	Nussbaum, *supra*, at 267.
	86 SMOLLA, *supra* note 44, at 135.

20.1 Full Citation Format for Books, Treatises, and Other Nonperiodic Materials

A full citation to a treatise, book, or other nonperiodic work in print contains up to ten components.

[Volume number (if multi-volume work)] | Author, | *Title* | [at] | Pinpoint reference | ([Editor name] ed., | [Translator name] trans., | [Publisher (other than original)] | [Edition number (other than 1st)] ed. | Year of publication).

Example (spaces denoted by ▲)

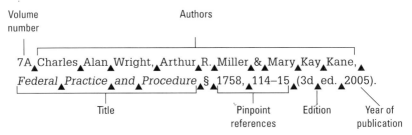

Volume number

Authors

7A▲Charles▲Alan▲Wright,▲Arthur▲R.▲Miller▲&▲Mary▲Kay▲Kane,▲
Federal▲Practice▲and▲Procedure▲§▲1758,▲114–15▲(3d▲ed.▲2005).

Title   Pinpoint   Edition   Year of
             references   publication

20.1(a) Volume number

If the cited work is from a multi-volume set, begin the citation with the volume number, set out as an arabic numeral in ordinary type, preceding the name of the author(s). If the volume number also includes a letter, capitalize the letter.

Examples

6A Stuart M. Speiser et al., *The American Law of Torts* § 18:199 (Monique C.M. Leahy ed., 2010 & Cum. Supp. 2012).

3 *State Constitutions for the Twenty-First Century* 149–54 (G. Alan Tarr & Robert F. Williams eds., 2006).

20.1(b) Author

20.1(b)(1) Single author of work

Set out the author's full name, in ordinary type, as represented on the cover or title page of the work, followed by a comma and one space. A full name includes designations such as Jr. (set off from the author's surname with a comma) and III (roman numerals not set off with a comma), but does not include degree information, such as J.D., Ph.D., or M.D., or titles of respect, such as "Hon.," "Dr.," or "Prof."

Example

Correct:	Arthur L. Rizer III,
Incorrect:	Arthur L. Rizer, III, J.D.,

⊛ 20.1(b)(2) Multiple authors of work

Set out the full names of multiple authors, in ordinary type, as represented and in the order in which they appear on the cover or title page of the work. When citing a single volume of a multi-volume work, set out only those authors whose names are attributed to that particular volume.

If the work has *two* authors, join their names with an ampersand (&). If the work has *three or more* authors, separate each name from the next with a comma and one space, except for the last two names, which are joined with an ampersand. Alternatively, you may use the phrase "et al." after the first author's name to indicate that the work has three or more authors, and omit the other names. Insert a comma and one space after the last author's name or the phrase "et al." There is no comma *before* "et al."

Examples

Anne Enquist & Laurel Currie Oates,

Ruth Anne Robbins, Steve Johansen & Ken Chestek,

Ruth Anne Robbins et al.,

20.1(b)(3) Institutional author of work

If an institution or organization is listed as author, give its full name as it appears on the cover or title page. However, if the author's name has two business designations (see **Rule 12.2(e)(1)** and **Chart 12.1**), omit the second. To save space, you may abbreviate any words appearing in **Appendix 3(B)** or **Appendix 3(E)**, as long as the author's name remains clearly identifiable. If the listed authors are both a person and an institution or organization, treat them as multiple authors, following **Rule 20.1(b)(2).**

Examples

2 ABA Bus. Law Section, *Annual Review of Developments in Business and Corporate Litigation* § 15.10.6 (Bradford K. Newman ed., 2012).

Meghan Spillane & Int'l Bar Ass'n, *International Moot Court: An Introduction* 54 (2008).

20.1(b)(4) Unlisted or unknown author of work

If a work does not have a listed author, or if the author is unknown, begin the citation with the title.

Example

> *Sir Gawain and the Green Knight* 34 n.3 (Paul Battles ed., 2012).

20.1(c) Title of work

20.1(c)(1) Words in title; subtitles

Present the title and subtitle, if any, in italics, but *do not* italicize information that would be italicized in text, such as case names (see **Rule 1.3** and **Chart 1.1**); present such information in ordinary type. Spell words in titles and subtitles exactly as they appear on the cover or title page. Capitalize the work's title and subtitle (if any) in accordance with **Rule 3**. Do not abbreviate any word in a title unless the word is so abbreviated on the work's cover or title page. Do not omit prepositions or other words from a title or subtitle.

Subtitles are optional; include them if desired. If the cover or title page of the book shows no punctuation between the main title and the subtitle, insert a colon and one space between them. If the main title ends with a question mark, exclamation point, or dash, do not change it, and do not insert a colon.

Examples

> Linda H. Edwards, *Estates in Land & Future Interests: A Step by Step Guide* ch. 13 (3d ed. 2009).

> James T. Patterson, Brown v. Board of Education*: A Civil Rights Milestone and Its Troubled History* 109–10 (2001).

> Eric Foner, *Who Owns History? Rethinking the Past in a Changing World* 144–45 (2002).

20.1(c)(2) Titles in foreign languages

Represent the title of a work published in a language other than English just as the title of any other book. If desired, you may provide a translation of the title, in square brackets, immediately following the title in the foreign language. For guidance on capitalization of words in foreign titles, consult the most recent edition of the *United States Government Printing Office Style Manual* or *The Chicago Manual of Style*.

Examples

> *Tratado Teórico, Práctico y Crítico de Derecho Privado Puertorriqueño*

> *Le Droit à la Santé en tant que Droit de l'Homme* [*The Right to Health as a Human Right*]

20.1(d) Pinpoint references

Following the last word of the title or subtitle, insert a space and a pinpoint reference that directs readers to the portion of the work that relates to the cited proposition or quotation. In most instances, works will use arabic page numbers for pinpoint references; pagination to front matter may use lowercase roman numerals. Treat roman numerals as you would any other page numbers. Insert one space after the pinpoint reference. Do not treat a volume number as a pinpoint reference; the volume number is the first component of the citation. See **Rule 20.1(a)** and its examples.

If the title of the work ends in a numeral, you may insert the preposition "at" before the pinpoint page (**Rule 5.2(c)**). For works divided both by pages and by sections or paragraphs, see **Rule 6.1(b)**. In general, see **Rules 5** through **9** for pinpoint references to pages, sections, chapters, notes, and other subdivisions.

Examples

> Michael J. Gerhardt, *The Federal Impeachment Process: A Constitutional and Historical Analysis* 208 n.50 (2d ed. 2000).
>
> Linda A. Pollock, *Forgotten Children: Parent-Child Relations from 1500 to 1900*, at 30 (1983).

20.1(e) Publication parenthetical

The final component of a citation to a book, treatise, or nonperiodic work in print is a parenthetical that identifies, at a minimum, the year of publication. Many works, however, have additional features that should be indicated in this parenthetical, such as the names of editors or translators, the numbers of later editions or printings, the names of later publishers, or the fact that the work is part of a larger series.

20.1(e)(1) Editor or translator of work

If the work lists one or more editors on the cover or title page, begin the publication parenthetical with the full name(s) of the editor(s), in ordinary type. Immediately after the name, with no intervening punctuation, insert the abbreviation "ed." (plural, "eds."), followed by a comma and one space.

Example

> *Antitrust Goes Global: What Future for Transatlantic Cooperation?* 117–18 (Simon J. Evenett, Alexander Lehmann & Benn Steil eds., 2000).

If the work is a translation, add the translator's name(s), in ordinary type, to the publication parenthetical. If the work has both an editor and a translator, identify the editor first. Present the translator's full name, followed immediately by the abbreviation "trans.," a comma, and one space.

Example

> Jean-François Lyotard, *The Postmodern Condition: A Report on Knowledge* 53–60 (Geoff Bennington & Brian Massum trans., Univ. Minn. Press 1984).

20.1(e)(2) Publisher of work

Add a publisher to the publication parenthetical only when citing a work published by someone *other than* the *original* publisher. Abbreviate words in the publisher name listed in **Appendices 3(A)**, **3(D)**, or **3(E)**, and omit prepositions and articles not needed for clarity.

Example

H.G. Wells, *The Time Machine* (Dover Publ'ns, Inc. 1995).

20.1(e)(3) Edition and printing

If possible, cite the most current edition of the work that relates to the cited passage or proposition. If the cited work is an edition other than the original or first edition, indicate the edition number in the publication parenthetical. For later numbered editions, use an ordinal contraction (**Rule 4.3(b)**) and the abbreviation "ed." followed by one space. Include all pertinent information about the edition, abbreviating any words listed in **Appendix 3(D)** (e.g., "rev. ed." for revised edition).

Example

Cynthia R. Mabry & Lisa Kelly, *Adoption Law: Theory, Policy, and Practice* 208 (2d ed. 2010).

If a specific printing of a work differs from other printings in a way that affects the substance of the cited material, set out the ordinal contraction (**Rule 4.3(b)**) for the number of the printing, a space, the abbreviation "prtg.," another space, and the year of the printing.

Example

Karl N. Llewellyn, *The Bramble Bush: On Our Law and Its Study* 70–72 (Oceana Publ'ns 9th prtg. 1991).

20.1(e)(4) Works in a series

When citing a work that is part of a series *issued by a specific author*, include the series number in the *title* of the work, using **Appendix 3(C)** to abbreviate any words relating to the series. Insert a comma and one space after the series information.

Example

U.S. Gov't Accountability Office, *No. GAO-09-251R, GAO Bid Protest Annual Report to the Congress for Fiscal Year 2008*, at 2 (2008).

If someone other than the author issues the series, however, put information about the series in the *publication parenthetical*, abbreviating any words found in **Appendices 3(B)**, **3(C)**, or **3(E)**. Insert a comma and one space after the series information.

Example

> Arend Lijphart, *Power-Sharing in South Africa* 6 (Inst. of Int'l Studies, Policy Papers in Int'l Affairs Ser. No. 24, 1985).

20.1(e)(5) Year of publication

The year of publication is the final component of the publication parenthetical. Set out the year shown on the title page or copyright page of the work, followed by a closing parenthesis. When citing a single volume of a multi-volume work, use the publication year of the cited volume. If citing a work that has supplements, follow **Rule 8**.

Examples

Supplement only:	1 Harvey L. McCormick, *Medicare and Medicaid Claims and Procedures* § 6.7 (4th ed. Supp. 2011).
Main volume and supplement:	Carolyn R. Carter et al., *Repossessions* § 4.1.6 (7th ed. 2010 & Supp. 2012).

For works published before 1900, you may cite either the original or a modern edition. If citing the original edition, insert the place of publication, a comma, one space, and the abbreviated name of the original publisher before the year of publication. If citing a modern edition of the work, add a second parenthetical containing the date of original publication. If citing a well-known work that has been republished, also provide the original date of publication in a second parenthetical. If the date of publication is not available, use the abbreviation "n.d." (no date).

Examples

> Hinton Rowan Helper, *The Impending Crisis of the South* 123–25 (N.Y., A.B. Bourdick 1859).

> Charles Dickens, *Bleak House* (Bantam Classics 1983) (1853).

20.1(f)(FN) Full citation format for books, treatises, and other nonperiodic materials in academic footnotes

⚠ ACADEMIC FORMATTING

To cite a book, treatise, or other nonperiodic document in an academic footnote, follow **Rule 20.1(a)** through **(e)**, but use large and small capital letters for both the author's name and the title and subtitle, if any. If the title contains words that would be italicized in text (e.g., a case name), present them in italicized large and small capital letters.

Examples

[51] LINDA H. EDWARDS, ESTATES IN LAND & FUTURE INTERESTS: A STEP BY STEP GUIDE ch. 13 (3d ed. 2009).

[59] JAMES T. PATTERSON, *BROWN V. BOARD OF EDUCATION*: A CIVIL RIGHTS MILESTONE AND ITS TROUBLED HISTORY 109–10, 208 (2001).

[85] JOSHUA DRESSLER, UNDERSTANDING CRIMINAL LAW § 10.04[A][1] (3d ed. 2001).

[93] 1 ARTHUR LINTON CORBIN, CORBIN ON CONTRACTS § 4.14 (Joseph M. Perillo ed., rev. ed. 1993).

[98] THE COMPLETE LETTERS OF SIGMUND FREUD TO WILHELM FLIESS, 1887–1904, at 264 (Jeffrey Moussaieff Masson ed. & trans., Belknap Press 1985).

[157] THE CHANGING CONSTITUTION 79–81 (Jeffrey Jowell & Dawn Oliver eds., 7th ed. 2011).

[168] HEINRICH RICKERT, THE LIMITS OF CONCEPT FORMATION IN NATURAL SCIENCE: A LOGICAL INTRODUCTION TO THE HISTORICAL SCIENCES ch. 4, 140–45 (Guy Oakes trans., Cambridge Univ. Press abr. ed. 1986) (1902).

20.2 Star Editions

In modern reprints of well-known and historic works, such as William Blackstone's *Commentaries* or Greek and Latin classics, the page number of the original work is indicated by an asterisk (*) in the margin or in the text, a practice known as "star pagination" (**Rule 5.5**). In citing a star-paginated work, you may ignore the pagination in the modern edition, and you may omit the publication parenthetical. Indicate a pinpoint reference by inserting a single asterisk (*) immediately before the page number(s), with no intervening space.

Example

4 William Blackstone, *Commentaries* *292–93.

20.3 Collected Works

20.3(a) Collected works of a single author

To cite a shorter work by one author that appears in a collection of that author's own works, use the following format.

Author, | *Title of shorter work,* | *in* | [Volume number of larger work (if any)] | *Title of larger work* | Initial page or subdivision of shorter work, | Pinpoint reference | ([Editor name] ed., | [Translator name] trans. | [Publisher (if not original)] | [Edition number (other than first or original)] ed. | Year of publication).

Use ordinary type for the author's name and italics for the two titles and the preposition "*in*." Omit components such as editors or translators if they are not relevant to the cited shorter work.

Example

Oliver Wendell Holmes, *Primitive Notions in Modern Law No. II, in* 3 *The Collected Works of Justice Holmes* 21, 22 (Sheldon M. Novick ed., 1995).

20.3(b) Collected works of multiple authors

To cite a shorter work within a collection of works by several authors, use the following format.

Author of shorter work, | *Title of shorter work,* | *in* | Author of larger work, | *Title of larger work* | Initial page or subdivision of shorter work, | Pinpoint reference | ([Editor name] ed., | [Translator name] trans., | [Publisher (if not original)] | [Edition number (other than first or original)] ed. | Year of publication).

Also use this rule to cite introductions, forewords, prefaces, and similar sections written by persons *other than* the author of the larger work. (For shorter works written by an author who also wrote the larger work in which they are contained, see **Rule 20.3(a)**.)

Use ordinary type for the names of the authors of both the shorter work and the larger work, and use italics for the two titles and the preposition "*in*." Omit components such as editors or translators if they are not relevant to the cited shorter work.

Examples

Francis C. Mezzadri, *Perinatal Abuse, in Child Abuse: A Medical Reference* 333, 338–39 (Stephen Ludwig & Allan E. Kornberg eds., 2d ed. 1992).

John Foster Dulles, *Introduction, in* Arthur H. Dean, *William Nelson Cromwell 1854–1948: An American Pioneer* i, iii (1957).

20.3(c) Reprint collections of previously published works

To cite reprint collections of works that were previously published elsewhere, follow the format set out in **Rule 20.3(a)** (collected works of single author) or **20.3(b)** (collected works of multiple authors) to cite the original source (if available), followed by the italicized phrase "*reprinted in*" and a full citation to the work containing the reprint.

Example

> William Faulkner, *The Bear, in Go Down, Moses and Other Stories* (1942), *reprinted in The Portable Faulkner* 177, 183–84 (Malcolm Cowley ed., Penguin Books rev. & expanded ed. 2003).

20.3(d) Collections of previously unpublished works

To cite works such as letters, memoranda, and reports that were not originally written for publication but that have subsequently been published in a collection, set out the name of the author (if available) or a description of the work in ordinary type, followed by the italicized preposition "*in*" and a full citation to the collection in which the work appears, following the format set out in **Rule 20.3(a)** (works of single author) or **20.3(b)** (works of multiple authors). If the original date of the work is available, you may append it in a parenthetical following the publication parenthetical, analogizing to the examples shown in **Rule 20.1(e)(5)**.

Example

> Letter from Louis Brandeis to Mrs. F.W. Wile, *in* 3 *Letters of Louis D. Brandeis* 535, 535–36 (Melvin I. Urofsky & David W. Levy eds., 1973) (June 19, 1915).

20.3(e)(FN) Full citation formats for collected works in academic footnotes

⚠ ACADEMIC FORMATTING

To cite the collected works of a single author in a document with academic footnotes, use large and small capital letters for the author's name, italics for the title of the shorter work and the preposition "*in*," and large and small capital letters for the title of the larger work.

Example

> [93] OLIVER WENDELL HOLMES, *Primitive Notions in Modern Law No. II, in* 3 THE COLLECTED WORKS OF JUSTICE HOLMES 21, 22 (Sheldon M. Novick ed., 1995).

To cite a shorter work within a collection of works by several authors, use ordinary type for the author of the shorter work and italics for its title; use large and small capital letters for the author of the larger work and its title.

Examples

> [67] Francis C. Mezzadri, *Perinatal Abuse, in* CHILD ABUSE: A MEDICAL REFERENCE 333, 338–39 (Stephen Ludwig & Allan E. Kornberg eds., 2d ed. 1992).

> [101] John Foster Dulles, *Introduction, in* ARTHUR H. DEAN, WILLIAM NELSON CROMWELL 1854–1948: AN AMERICAN PIONEER i, iii (1957).

20.4 Books, Treatises, and Other Nonperiodic Materials in Electronic Media

If a work is readily available in print, cite the print source in preference to any publication of the work in an electronic medium. If the work is solely available in an electronic medium, or if it is not readily available in print, provide a full citation in accordance with applicable sections of **Rule 20**, and add a reference to its location in a commercial database using the database's unique identifier, or to a reliable location on the World Wide Web, using its Uniform Resource Locator (URL). For more information about online and electronic citation formats, see **Rules 30** through **34**.

Examples

Thomas R. Young, *North Carolina Juvenile Code: Practice & Procedure* § 6.4 (2012), *available at* Westlaw NCJUVCODE.

Michael Hatfield, *The Ethics of Tax Lawyering* 50–51 (2011), *available at* http://elangdell.cali.org/sites/elangdell.cali.org/files/elangdell/ Hatfield-Ethics-of-Tax-Lawyering.pdf.

20.5 Full Citation Formats for Religious Works: The Bible, the Koran, and the Talmud

To cite a passage from the Bible, use the following format.

[Volume number (if any)] | *Book name* | Chapter number:Verse number | [(Version)].

Omit spaces before and after the colon joining the chapter number and verse number. Within the version component, you may abbreviate any word that appears in **Appendix 3**.

Examples

Matthew 5:17.   1 *Corinthians* 10.0 (New Am. Standard).

John 3:16 (King James).   *Psalms* 147:8–9 (New Int'l).

To cite a passage from the Koran, use the spelling "Koran" or "Qur'an" in ordinary type, followed immediately by the chapter and verse numbers, joined with a colon and no spaces. If relevant, you may indicate a particular translation in the publication parenthetical.

Examples

Koran 2:256.

Qur'an 51:1–10 (Abdullah Yusuf Ali trans.).

The Talmud consists of the Mishnah and Gemara. The Mishnah is divided into six orders. The Gemara provides a commentary on these codified laws. The Babylonian Talmud and the Jerusalem Talmud use different Gemara. The Babylonian Talmud takes precedence. Begin with the name of the version, in ordinary type, followed by the order and tractate numbers.

Examples

Babylonian Talmud, Eruvin 13b.

Jerusalem Talmud, Bava Metzia 27b.

20.6 Short Citation Formats for Books, Treatises, and Other Nonperiodic Materials

The form of the short citation to a book, treatise, or other nonperiodic work will vary depending on whether the citation refers to a single work or to a work within a larger collection, whether it refers to a religious text, and whether it is used in an academic footnote.

20.6(a) Short citation formats for single work

Use *id.* (if appropriate) as the short citation to a single work (i.e., one that is not published in a larger collection), changing the pinpoint reference if needed. *Id.* tells the reader that you are the citing the same work just cited in the immediately preceding citation. Do not use *id.* if the preceding citation contains references to two or more sources. For more information on the use of *id.*, see **Rule 11.3**. If *id.* is not appropriate, use one of the following short citation formats.

Author's surname, | *supra*, | [at] | Pinpoint reference.

or

Title, | *supra*, | [at] | Pinpoint reference.

If the work has one or more named authors, begin the short form with their surnames, followed by a comma and one space. If the work does not have a named author, begin the short form with the italicized title of the work, or if the full citation to a work with no author provided a "hereinafter" reference (see **Rule 11.5**), use its shortened name, followed by a comma and one space.

Use the preposition "at" only before pinpoint *page* references (**Rule 5.0**). If the work uses another form of subdivision, omit "at" and simply insert the specific pinpoint reference, consulting **Rules 6.0** (sections and paragraphs), **7.0** (footnotes), **8.0** (supplements), or **9.0** (graphical material and appendices), as needed.

Examples

Full citations:	Martha C. Nussbaum, *Sex and Social Justice* 265–66 (1999).
	Mark Herrmann & David B. Alden, *Drug and Device Product Liability Litigation Strategy* 262–63 (2012).
	Christopher C. Whitney et al., *Sticks & Bricks: A Practical Guide to Construction Systems and Technology* § 2.5, 72–74 (2001).
Short citations:	Nussbaum, *supra*, at 267.
	Herrmann & Alden, *supra*, at 280.
	Whitney et al., *supra*, § 2.8, at 77–81.

20.6(b) Short citation formats for collected works

For items cited under **Rule 20.3(a)** (collected works of single author) or **20.3(b)** (collected works of multiple authors), use the following short citation formats.

Use *id.* to refer to an immediately preceding citation that references the shorter work within the collection. If *id.* is not appropriate for the short form, set out the author's surname, *supra* (in italics), a comma and one space, the word "at," and a pinpoint reference.

However, for a new citation to a shorter work within a larger work that has previously been cited, do not use *id.* to refer to the larger work. Instead, use the following format:

> Full name(s) of shorter work's author(s) | *Title of shorter work,* | *in* | *Title of larger work,* | *supra,* | at | Pinpoint reference.

Examples

Full citation:	Margaret Vandiver, *Capital Punishment and the Families of Victims and Defendants, in The Future of America's Death Penalty: An Agenda for the Next Generation of Capital Punishment Research* 379, 387–89 (Charles S. Lanier, William J. Bowers & James R. Acker eds., 2009).
Short citation referring to Vandiver:	*Id.* at 388.
	or if *id.* is not appropriate,
	Vandiver, *supra*, at 388.
New citation to shorter work in larger work previously cited:	Richard C. Dieter, *The Future of Innocence, in The Future of America's Death Penalty, supra*, at 225.

20.6(c) Short citation format for religious works

For a short citation to the Bible, the Koran, or the Talmud, if *id.* is not appropriate, repeat the full citation.

20.6(d)(FN) Short citation formats for books, treatises, and other nonperiodic materials in academic footnotes

⚠ ACADEMIC
FORMATTING

20.6(d)(1)(FN) Short citation formats for single work in academic footnotes

In documents with academic footnotes, use *id.* (if appropriate) as the short citation for a single work (i.e., one that is not published in a larger collection), changing the pinpoint reference if needed. Do not use *id.* if the preceding footnote contains references to two or more sources. For more information on the use of *id.*, see **Rule 11.3**. If *id.* is not appropriate, use one of the *supra* formats that follow, cross-referencing the footnote in which the work's full citation is set out.

Author's Surname, | *supra* | note | [Note number], | [at] | Pinpoint reference.

or

Title, | *supra* | note | [Note number], | [at] | Pinpoint reference.

Begin the short form with the author surname(s) in large and small capital letters, followed by a comma and one space. If the work does not have an author, begin the short form with the title of the work, or if the full citation provided a "hereinafter" reference for the work, its shortened name. Present the title or "hereinafter" reference in large and small capital letters, followed by a comma and one space.

Add a *supra* reference to the earlier footnote containing the work's full citation (**Rule 11.4**), followed by a comma, a space, and a pinpoint reference.

Use the preposition "at" only before pinpoint *page* references (**Rule 5.0**). If the work uses another form of subdivision, omit "at" and simply insert the specific pinpoint reference, consulting **Rules 6.0** (sections and paragraphs), **7.0** (footnotes), **8.0** (supplements), or **9.0** (graphical material and appendices), as needed.

Example

[19] Larry W. Koch et al., The Death of the American Death Penalty 121–22 (2012).

· · ·

[25] Koch et al., *supra* note 19, at 122.

20.6(d)(2)(FN) Short citation formats for collected works in academic footnotes

In documents with academic footnotes, do not use *id.* to refer to a shorter work in a collection cited in the immediately preceding footnote. Instead, use the *supra* format (**Rule 11.4**), as shown below.

> Surname of shorter work's author, | *supra* | note | [Note number], | at | Pinpoint reference.

For a new citation to a shorter work within a larger work that has previously been cited, use the following format.

> Full name of shorter work's author, | *Title of Shorter Work,* | *in* | Main Title of Larger Work, | *supra* | note | [Number of note containing first full citation to larger work], | at | Initial page of shorter work, | Pinpoint reference.

Examples

Full citation:	[32] Margaret Vandiver, *Capital Punishment and the Families of Victims and Defendants, in* The Future of America's Death Penalty: An Agenda for the Next Generation of Capital Punishment Research 379, 387–89 (Charles S. Lanier, William J. Bowers & James R. Acker eds., 2009).
Short citation referring to Vandiver:	[33] Vandiver, *supra* note 32, at 388.
New citation to shorter work in larger work previously cited:	[34] Richard C. Dieter, *The Future of Innocence, in* The Future of America's Death Penalty, *supra* note 32, at 225, 225–26.

21 Legal and Other Periodicals

Fast Formats

Snapshot
STUDENT-AUTHORED LAW REVIEW ARTICLE

Periodical name (Rule 21.2(e));
abbreviate per Appendix 5

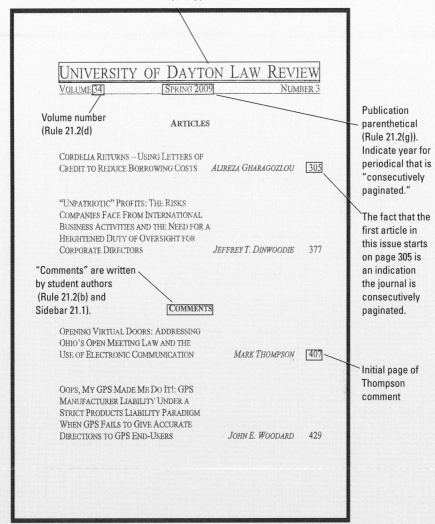

UNIVERSITY OF DAYTON LAW REVIEW

VOLUME 34   SPRING 2009   NUMBER 3

Volume number
(Rule 21.2(d)

ARTICLES

Publication
parenthetical
(Rule 21.2(g)).
Indicate year for
periodical that is
"consecutively
paginated."

CORDELIA RETURNS -- USING LETTERS OF
CREDIT TO REDUCE BORROWING COSTS   ALIREZA GHARAGOZLOU   305

"UNPATRIOTIC" PROFITS: THE RISKS
COMPANIES FACE FROM INTERNATIONAL
BUSINESS ACTIVITIES AND THE NEED FOR A
HEIGHTENED DUTY OF OVERSIGHT FOR
CORPORATE DIRECTORS   JEFFREY T. DINWOODIE   377

The fact that the
first article in
this issue starts
on page 305 is
an indication
the journal is
consecutively
paginated.

"Comments" are written
by student authors
(Rule 21.2(b) and
Sidebar 21.1).

COMMENTS

OPENING VIRTUAL DOORS: ADDRESSING
OHIO'S OPEN MEETING LAW AND THE
USE OF ELECTRONIC COMMUNICATION   MARK THOMPSON   407

Initial page of
Thompson
comment

OOPS, MY GPS MADE ME DO IT!: GPS
MANUFACTURER LIABILITY UNDER A
STRICT PRODUCTS LIABILITY PARADIGM
WHEN GPS FAILS TO GIVE ACCURATE
DIRECTIONS TO GPS END-USERS   JOHN E. WOODARD   429

Cover of law review

Reprinted, by permission, from University of *Dayton Law Review,* Vol. 34.

Snapshot

I. INTRODUCTION

Public trust is as critical to the success of American democracy today as it was when this country was founded. Open meeting laws, commonly referred to as "Sunshine Laws," have been in place since our nation's inception in order to ensure a transparent and accountable government. A government that is not accountable to its people would be a "prologue to a farce or a tragedy, or perhaps both."[1] However, the public's need to have access to the government's decision making machine, which is a principle as old as this nation itself, has clashed with one of the world's newest innovations: the Internet. In particular, government collaborations via on-line bulletin boards and e-mail have come under fire for violating open meeting laws.

Addressing the issue of virtual meetings requires an in-depth understanding of open meeting laws, as well as the various modes of communication available in the virtual world that have the potential of leading to open meeting law violations. Thus, Section II examines open meeting laws, why they are in place, and to what government operations they do and do not apply. In addition, Section II examines what constitutes a "meeting" and when a group covered under the Ohio OML[2] is required to meet publicly.

Section III examines approaches taken by a limited number of states to address virtual meeting issues. Using this comparative analysis in conjunction with an examination of the OML and current case law, this comment explores possible solutions to the on-line meeting dilemma. It

Indications that author is a stud (Sidebar 21.1)

---

[*] Mark Thompson is a student at the University of Dayton School of Law. He is expected to receive his Juris Doctorate in December of 2009. The author would like to thank his mother, Chris, as well as Stephanie and Rupert for their support and infinite patience over the past few years - it hasn't been easy on any of us and I couldn't have succeeded in law school without your help. I would also like to thank John Chambers for giving me the idea for this Comment, and for his advice and counsel about what it takes to succeed in law school and in the legal profession. Thank you all.

[1] Mary Taylor & Nancy H. Rogers, *Ohio Sunshine Laws 2008: An Open Government Resource Manual* 1 (Off. of the Ohio Atty. Gen. 2008). The Open Meeting Laws Manual gives a thorough description of Ohio's open meeting law including: definitions; interpretations; foundation; and research annotations. *See id.*

[2] Throughout this document, "OML" will be used when referring specifically to the Ohio Open Meeting Law. The phrase "open meeting law" will be used when referring to open meeting laws in general.

Initial page of article

Citation: Mark Thompson, Comment, *Opening Virtual Doors, Addressing Ohio's Open Meeting Law and the Use of Electronic Communication*, 34 U. Dayton L. Rev. 407 (2009).

Reprinted, by permission, from University of Dayton Law Review, Vol. 34.

21.1 Consecutive and Nonconsecutive Pagination

Citations to works published in periodicals distinguish between those published in a periodical whose page numbering continues from issue to issue ("**consecutive pagination**") and one whose page numbering starts over in each new issue ("**nonconsecutive pagination**"). This distinction affects the citation's required components, their order, and their format. Therefore, always make this initial determination before constructing the citation. A star (★) beside a periodical's entry in **Appendix 5** indicates that the periodical is nonconsecutively paginated. For periodicals not listed in **Appendix 5**, you may need to examine the issues preceding and following that in which the work appears to determine whether the page numbering continues or starts over.

21.2 Full Citation Format for Consecutively Paginated Periodicals

A full citation to a work published in a consecutively paginated periodical (e.g., a law review) may contain as many as eight components.

> Author, | [Designation of student-written work,] | *Title,* | Volume number | Periodical abbreviation | Initial page, | Pinpoint page | (Date).

Examples (consecutively paginated law review articles)

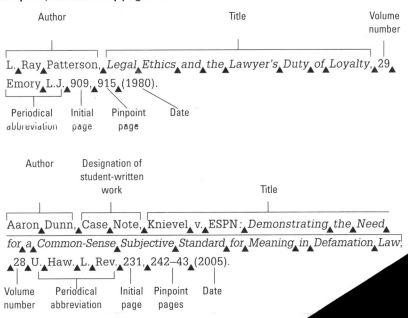

21.2(a) Author's name

Set out the author's full name as displayed in the work, in ordinary type, followed by a comma and one space. For a single author, follow **Rule 20.1(b)(1)**. For multiple authors, follow **Rule 20.1(b)(2)**. For institutional authors, follow **Rule 20.1(b)(3)**. If the author is not identified, follow **Rule 20.1(b)(4)**. If the author is a student, follow **Rule 21.2(b)**.

Example

Troy A. McKenzie, *Toward a Bankruptcy Model for Nonclass Aggregate Litigation*, 87 N.Y.U. L. Rev. 960, 965–66 (2012).

21.2(b) Student author

If the work was written by an identifiable student author (see **Sidebar 21.1**), immediately after the name, insert a comma, one space, and the designation of the work used by the periodical (e.g., "Note," "Legislative Note," "Recent Development," "Comment"). Identify any student-written book review, however, with the designation "Book Note." If the student author's name is not indicated, begin with the work's designation. In all cases, present the designation in ordinary type, followed by a comma and one space.

Examples

Nicholas H. Meza, Comment, *A New Approach for Clarity in the Determination of Protected Concerted Activity Online*, 45 Ariz. St. L.J. 329, 339–40 (2013).

Note, *Enabling Television Competition in a Converged Market*, 126 Harv. L. Rev. 2083, 2089–90 (2013).

21.2(c) Title and subtitle of work

Present the title, including any subtitle, as it appears on the first page of the work. Do not abbreviate or omit any words in a title or subtitle. Follow **Rule 3.2**

SIDE .1   Identifying Student Authors

guidelines to determine whether an author is
dent-written articles are often printed toward
. Second, student-written articles are typically
," "Comments," "Case Comments," or "Recent
in many law reviews, the names of student
e end—not the beginning—of the article.
e describing the author's background; an
candidate is a student.

for capitalization. For title of works written in a language other than English, follow **Rule 20.1(c)(2)**.

If the title and subtitle are joined with a dash, retain the subtitle, and do not alter the existing capitalization of the first word following the dash. If no punctuation is shown between a title and subtitle, join them with a colon followed by one space. Capitalize the first word following the colon, no matter what it is.

Examples

John G. Browning, *Keep Your Hands off My Nuts—Airlines, Peanut Allergies, and the Law*, 77 J. Air L. & Com. 3, 8 n.32 (2012).

Marc L. Roark, *"Opening the Barbarians' Gate" or Watching the Barbarians from the Coliseum: A Requiem on the Nomos of the Louisiana Civil Law*, 67 La. L. Rev. 451, 462–63 (2007).

Italicize the title and the subtitle, if any, but use ordinary type for words that would be italicized in text, such as case names (**Rule 1.6**).

Example

Clay Calvert, *Defining Public Concern after* Snyder v. Phelps*: A Pliable Standard Mingles with News Media Complicity*, 19 Vill. Sports & Ent. L.J. 39, 41 (2012).

If the full title ends with a question mark or exclamation mark, follow it with a comma and one space. If the full title ends with a quotation, place the comma inside the closing quotation mark.

Examples

Assaf Hamdani, *Who's Liable for Cyberwrongs?*, 87 Cornell L. Rev. 901, 940–45 (2002).

Neil Gotanda, *A Critique of "Our Constitution Is Color-Blind,"* 44 Stan. L. Rev. 1, 6 (1991).

If the work does not have a title, use the designation given to it by the periodical (e.g., "Case Note").

21.2(d) Volume number

Indicate the volume number of the periodical with an arabic numeral, followed by one space. If the periodical does not have a volume number, substitute its year of publication in place of the volume number and omit the publication parenthetical described in **Rule 21.2(g)**.

Examples

Benjamin P. Cooper, *The Lawyer's Duty to Inform His Client of His Own Malpractice*, 61 Baylor L. Rev. 174, 181–82 (2009).

Brandice Canes-Wrone & Tom S. Clark, *Judicial Independence and Nonpartisan Elections*, 2009 Wis. L. Rev. 21, 30–31.

21.2(e) Abbreviation of periodical name

Following the volume number, set out the **Appendix 5** abbreviation of the periodical, in ordinary type, inserting spaces where indicated by the triangles (▲). If the periodical is not listed in **Appendix 5**, search the appendix for abbreviations for individual words from the periodical's name. For geographic terms, use abbreviations from **Appendix 3(B)**. Otherwise, spell out the word. Do not use an abbreviation from another appendix, as it may be a word that should not be abbreviated in a periodical name, or it may be abbreviated differently.

Follow **Rule 2.2** for spacing. Omit the words "a," "at," "in," "of," and "the." Omit commas. Unless the periodical's abbreviation in **Appendix 5** indicates otherwise, omit colons and anything following them. Insert one space after the periodical abbreviation.

21.2(f) Initial page and pinpoint references

Following the periodical abbreviation, set out the initial page number. To refer to specific pages or other subdivisions within the work, add a comma, one space, and the relevant pinpoint reference. See **Rules 5** through **9** for more information on pinpoint references.

21.2(g) Publication parenthetical

Indicate the year of publication in parentheses. In citations to consecutively paginated periodicals, do not provide a more specific date or season, even if displayed in the publication.

Example

> Barbara B. Aldave, *Misappropriation: A General Theory of Liability for Trading on Nonpublic Information*, 13 Hofstra L. Rev. 101, 122 (1984).

If the periodical uses the year as the volume number, omit the publication parenthetical. See the examples in **Rules 21.2(d)** and **21.2(h)**.

21.2(h) Special issues, symposia, colloquia, surveys

A special issue is one in which all the major articles deal with a single topic or theme. In legal periodicals, this type of special issue may be referred to as a symposium, colloquium, or survey. When citing an *entire* special issue, as opposed to a single article within it, in place of author names, set out the descriptive term used by the periodical, as shown in the examples below, and for the initial page reference, use the opening page of the special issue.

Cite a single article in a special issue just as you would any other work in a consecutively paginated periodical. If it is important to let readers know that the single article is part of a special issue, you may identify the special issue in a parenthetical immediately following the periodical's abbreviated name.

Examples (citing entire issue)

Symposium, *An Ocean Apart? Freedom of Expression in Europe and the United States*, 84 Ind. L.J. 803 (2009).

Symposium, *Innovative Models of Lawyering*, 2008 J. Disp. Resol. 1.

Example (indicating single article in special issue)

Richard H. Pildes, *Free Enterprise Fund, Boundary-Enforcing Decisions, and the Unitary Executive Branch Theory of Government Administration*, 6 Duke J. Const. L. & Pub. Pol'y (Special Issue) 1 (2010).

21.2(i) Multi-part works

To cite a work published in multiple parts in *different volumes* of a consecutively paginated periodical, add a parenthetical after the title that identifies the numbers of the parts, followed by the volume number, periodical abbreviation, initial page, and publication parenthetical for each volume, as shown below.

If all parts appear in a *single volume* of the periodical, indicate the part numbers in a parenthetical after the title, and provide the initial page for each part.

To cite a *single part* of a work published in multiple parts, indicate the single part number in parentheses, and cite only the issue in which the part is published.

Examples

Citing all parts in multiple issues:	Vern Countryman, *Executory Contracts in Bankruptcy* (pts. 1 & 2), 57 Minn. L. Rev. 439 (1973), 58 Minn. L. Rev. 479 (1974).
Citing all parts in single issue:	John P. Dawson, *Negotiorum Gestio: The Altruistic Intermeddler* (pts. 1 & 2), 74 Harv. L. Rev. 817, 1073 (1961).
Citing one part in single issue:	Vern Countryman, *Executory Contracts in Bankruptcy* (pt. 2), 58 Minn. L. Rev. 479 (1974).

21.3 Full Citation Format for Nonconsecutively Paginated Periodicals

Nonconsecutively paginated periodicals include publications such as bar association journals, magazines, newspapers, and newsletters. Periodicals that are nonconsecutively paginated are indicated with a star (★) in **Appendix 5**. The format of a citation to a nonconsecutively paginated journal typically contains the following components.

Author, | *Title*, | Periodical abbreviation, | Publication date, | at | Initial
page, | Pinpoint page.

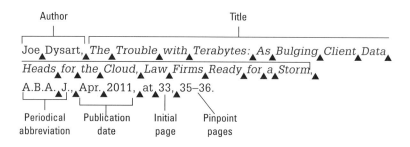

21.3(a) Author's name

Follow **Rule 21.2(a), (b)** and the rules that it cross-references.

21.3(b) Title of work

Follow **Rule 21.2(c)** and the rules that it cross-references.

21.3(c) Periodical abbreviation; volume number, if any

Follow **Rule 21.2(e)** and the rules that it cross-references. Immediately following the periodical abbreviation, insert a comma followed by a space. If the periodical displays a volume number, set it out *before* the periodical abbreviation.

Examples

> Jeffrey R. Young, *Journal Boycott over Online Access Is a Bust*, Chron.
> Higher Educ., May 31, 2002, at A34.

> Diane S. Kaplan, *The Baby Richard Amendments and the Law of
> Unintended Consequences*, 22 Child. Legal Rts. J., Winter 2002–2003, at 2.

> Andrew E. Taslitz, *The Cold Nose Might Actually Know? Science & Scent
> Lineups*, 28 Crim. Just., Summer 2013, at 4.

21.3(d) Publication date

Indicate the publication date as shown on the first page or cover of the issue. If
the publication date is a month, day, and year, abbreviate the month as shown
in **Appendix 3(A)**. If the date refers to a season, capitalize the season and insert
the year with no comma between them. If the periodical does not indicate a
more specific publication date, but shows an issue number, use the abbreviation "no." and the issue number shown on the first page, followed by a comma
and the year. Whatever the form of the date reference, follow it with a comma
and one space.

Examples

> Sally H. Scherer, *Our Children—The Legal System's Forgotten Ones*, N.C. St. B.J., Winter 2011, at 16, 18.
>
> Kevin M. Forde, *What Can a Court Do with Leftover Class Action Funds? Almost Anything!*, 35 Judge's J., no. 3, 1996, at 19.

21.3(e) Initial page and pinpoint references

Following the date of publication, insert a comma and one space, followed by the preposition "at" and the initial page number. If a pinpoint page reference is available, add a comma, one space, and the pinpoint page number(s).

21.3(f) Newspapers

In general, cite newspapers as nonconsecutively paginated periodicals, treating an article's headline as its title, and making the following modifications, as appropriate.

21.3(f)(1) Editorials, op-eds, and letters to the editor

To cite an editorial, op-ed, or letter to the editor, set out the author's name, if shown (following **Rule 21.2(a)**), followed by a comma, one space, and the designation "Editorial," "Letter to the Editor," or the abbreviation "Op-Ed. "(ending in a period). Use ordinary type for the designation.

If the piece displays a title, present it in italics, followed by a comma, one space, the volume number of the newspaper, if any, and the newspaper's abbreviation.

Examples

> Nancy A. Ransom, Letter to the Editor, *Better Eating, Through Home Ec?*, N.Y. Times, Sept. 8, 2003, at A22.
>
> Editorial, *An Endangered Act*, Wash. Post, Dec. 29, 2003, at A16.

21.3(f)(2) Place of publication

If the newspaper's place of publication is not evident from its name, add a parenthetical setting out the place of publication, in ordinary type, immediately after the periodical abbreviation. Use city and state abbreviations from **Appendix 3(B)**. Insert a comma and one space after the parenthetical information.

Example

> *Bush to Campaign for Bush*, Post & Courier (Charleston, S.C.), Jan. 15, 2000, at B4.

21.3(f)(3) Section and initial page

If the newspaper has multiple sections, preface the initial page reference with the letter of the section in which it appears (e.g., A2, B6). Cite only the initial page; omit subsequent pinpoint references.

21.3(g) Newsletters

Following the periodical abbreviation, add a parenthetical with the abbreviated name of the newsletter's issuing organization and its geographical location. Use abbreviations in **Appendices 3(B)** and **5**, and omit articles and prepositions not needed for clarity.

Example

> Gina Bongiovi, *Flying Solo: Marketing*, YLS Newsl. (State Bar Nev. Young Lawyers Section, Las Vegas, Nev.), July 2013, at 1.

21.4 Full Citation Format for Cartoons or Comic Strips

To cite a cartoon or comic strip, set out the artist's name, if available (following **Rule 21.2(a)**), the designation "Cartoon" or "Comic Strip" in ordinary type, the italicized title (if any) of the cartoon or comic strip, and information about the periodical in which the cartoon or comic strip appears, including the volume (if available), periodical abbreviation, publication date, and page reference. For cartoons or comic strips published in multi-section newspapers, preface the page number with the letter of the section in which it appears (e.g., A2, B6).

Examples

> Peter Steiner, Cartoon, *On the Internet, Nobody Knows You're a Dog*, 69 New Yorker, July 5, 1993, at 61.

> Scott Adams, Comic Strip, *Dilbert*, Bos. Globe, Aug. 15, 2002, at D16.

21.5 Full Citation Format for Electronic Periodicals

When citing an article from an electronic periodical published *only* on the World Wide Web, determine its form of pagination. If it resembles a consecutively paginated journal, follow **Rule 21.2**, and after the publication parenthetical, add a comma, one space, and the URL.

Example

> On Amir & Orly Lobel, *Driving Performance: A Growth Theory of Noncompete Law*, 16 Stan. Tech. L. Rev. 833, 841 (2013), http://stlr.stanford.edu/pdf/drivingperformance.pdf.

If the electronic periodical resembles a nonconsecutively paginated journal, follow **Rule 21.3**, and after the pinpoint page reference, add a comma, one space, and the URL.

Example

> Denise Amran, *Homosexuality and Child Custody Through the Lenses of Law: Between Tradition and Fundamental Rights*, 15.1 Electronic J. Comp. L., Dec. 2011, at 1, 5–7, http://www.ejcl.org/151/art151-1.pdf.

If the cited work is available in both a print and electronic version of the periodical, cite the print version if at all possible. You may add a parallel reference, however, to the electronic version by appending the italicized phrase "*available at*" and the URL.

21.6(FN) Full Citation Formats for Legal and Other Periodicals in Academic Footnotes

⚠ ACADEMIC FORMATTING

In academic footnotes, follow the provisions of **Rules 21.2**, **21.3**, **21.4**, or **21.5**, as appropriate, but use large and small capital letters for the periodical's abbreviation.

Examples

[33] Patricia M. Wald, *Selecting Law Clerks*, 89 MICH. L. REV. 152, 153 (1990).

[37] Kathryn J. Ball, Comment, *Horizontal Equity and the Tax Consequences of Attorney-Client Fee Agreements*, 74 TEMP. L. REV. 387, 407–08 (2001).

[30] Lewis H. Lazarus & Katherine J. Neikirk, *Litigating in the Court of Chancery*, 31 DEL. LAW., Summer 2013, at 16.

[45] Noel Yahanpath & SzeKee Koh, *Strength of Bond Covenants and Bond Assessment Framework*, 6 AUSTRALASIAN ACCT. BUS. & FIN. J., no. 2, 2012, at 71, 81–86.

[58] Adam Liptak, *Bucking a Trend, Supreme Court Justices Reject Video Coverage*, N.Y. TIMES, Feb. 18, 2013, at A15.

[64] Scott Adams, Comic Strip, *Dilbert*, BOS. GLOBE, Aug. 15, 2002, at D16.

[78] Denise Amran, *Homosexuality and Child Custody Through the Lenses of Law: Between Tradition and Fundamental Rights*, 15.1 ELECTRONIC J. COMP. L., Dec. 2011, at 1, 5–7, http://www.ejcl.org/151/art151-1.pdf.

21.7 Short Citation Formats for Legal and Other Periodicals

The form of the short citation to a periodical will vary depending on whether the citation is used in a practice-based document or in a document with academic footnotes.

21.7(a) Short citation formats for periodicals

In practice-based documents, use *id.* (if appropriate) as the short citation to a work published in any type of periodical, changing the pinpoint reference if needed. *Id.* tells the reader that you are citing the same work just cited in the immediately preceding citation. Do not use *id.* if the preceding citation contains references to two or more sources. For more information on the use of *id.*, see **Rule 11.3**. If *id.* is not appropriate, use one of the following formats:

Author's surname, | *supra*, | [at] | Pinpoint reference.

or

Title, | *supra*, | [at] | Pinpoint reference.

If the work has one or more named authors, begin the short form with the surnames, followed by a comma and one space. If the work does not have a named author, begin the short form with the italicized title of the work, or if the full citation to a work with no author provided a "hereinafter" reference for the work (see **Rule 11.5**), use its shortened name, followed by a comma and one space.

Use the preposition "at" only before pinpoint *page* references (**Rule 5.0**). If the work uses another form of subdivision, omit "at" and simply insert the specific pinpoint reference, consulting **Rules 6.0** (sections and paragraphs), **7.0** (footnotes), **8.0** (supplements), or **9.0** (graphical material and appendices), as needed.

Examples

Full citation:	L. Ray Patterson, *Legal Ethics and the Lawyer's Duty of Loyalty*, 29 Emory L.J. 909, 915 (1980).
Short citation:	Patterson, *supra*, at 919–20.
Full citation:	Sally H. Scherer, *Our Children—The Legal System's Forgotten Ones*, N.C. St. B.J., Winter 2011, at 16, 18.
Short citation:	Scherer, *supra*, at 17.

21.7(b)(FN) Short citation formats for periodicals in academic footnotes

In documents with academic footnotes, use *id.* (if appropriate) as the short citation to a work published in any type of periodical, changing the pinpoint reference if needed. *Id.* tells the reader that you are citing the same work just cited in the immediately preceding citation. Do not use *id.* if the preceding citation contains references to two or more sources. For more information on the use of *id.*, see **Rule 11.3**.

If *id.* is not appropriate, use one of the *supra* formats that follow, cross-referencing the previous footnote in which the work's full citation is set out.

Author's surname, | *supra* | note | [Note number], | [at] | Pinpoint reference.

or

Title [or Designation or *Hereinafter Reference*], | *supra* | note | [Note number], | [at] | Pinpoint reference.

If the work has one or more named authors, begin the short form with the author surname(s) in ordinary type, followed by a comma and one space. If the work does not have an author, begin the short form with the italicized title of the work, or if the full citation to a work with no author provided a "hereinafter" reference for the work, use its shortened name, as indicated in the full citation, followed by a comma and one space.

The *supra* reference should indicate the number of the earlier footnote containing the work's full citation (**Rule 11.4**), followed by a comma, a space, and a pinpoint reference. Use the preposition "at" only before pinpoint *page* references (**Rule 5.0**). If the work uses another form of subdivision, omit "at" and simply insert the specific pinpoint reference, consulting **Rules 6.0** (sections and paragraphs), **7.0** (footnotes), **8.0** (supplements), or **9.0** (graphical material and appendices), as needed.

Examples

² L. Ray Patterson, *Legal Ethics and the Lawyer's Duty of Loyalty*, 29 EMORY L.J. 909, 915 (1980).

. . .

⁴ Patterson, *supra* note 2, at 919–20.

⁵² Sally H. Scherer, *Our Children—The Legal System's Forgotten Ones*, N.C. ST. B.J., Winter 2011, at 16, 18.

. . .

⁶¹ Scherer, *supra* note 52, at 17.

22 Dictionaries, Encyclopedias, and A.L.R. Annotations

Fast Formats

Dictionaries, Encyclopedias, and A.L.R. Annotations	
Dictionary	James R. Fox, *Dictionary of International and Comparative Law* 56 (2003).
American Jurisprudence 2d	67 Am. Jur. 2d *Robbery* § 96 (2003).
Corpus Juris Secundum	30A C.J.S. *Entertainment and Amusement* § 65 (2007).
Single-volume encyclopedia with named author	John R. Vile, *Encyclopedia of Constitutional Amendments, Proposed Amendments, and Amending Issues, 1789–2002*, at 133–34 (2d ed. 2003).
Multi-volume encyclopedia with named editor	3 *Oxford International Encyclopedia of Legal History* 120–23 (Stanley N. Katz ed., 2009).
A.L.R. First Series	P.H. Vartanian, Annotation, *"Res Ipsa Loquitur" as a Presumption or a Mere Permissible Inference*, 167 A.L.R. 658, 660 (1947).
A.L.R. Federal Series	Marjorie A. Shields, Annotation, *Admissibility of Evidence Discovered in Search of Defendant's Property or Residence Authorized by Defendant's Spouse*, 154 A.L.R. Fed. 579, § 2(a) (1999).
Citations in academic footnotes	[54] JAMES R. FOX, DICTIONARY OF INTERNATIONAL AND COMPARATIVE LAW 56 (2003).
	[90] JOHN R. VILE, ENCYCLOPEDIA OF CONSTITUTIONAL AMENDMENTS, PROPOSED AMENDMENTS, AND AMENDING ISSUES, 1789–2002, at 133–34 (2d ed. 2003).
	[102] Edward K. Esping, Annotation, *Liability in Admiralty for Collision Between Vessel and Drawbridge Structure*, 134 A.L.R. FED. 537, § 2(a) (1996).
Short citations	30A C.J.S. *Entertainment and Amusement* § 65, *supra*, at 82.
	Shields, *supra*, § 2(b).
	[124] VILE, *supra* note 90, at 499.

22.1 Full Citation Format for Dictionaries

22.1(a) Full citation format for dictionary

Cite a dictionary like a book under **Rule 20.1**. For multi-volume dictionaries, follow **Rule 20.2**.

> [Author (if named)], | *Title* | Pinpoint reference | ([Editor name] ed., | [Edition number (other than first)] ed. | Year of publication).

Example (spaces denoted by ▲)

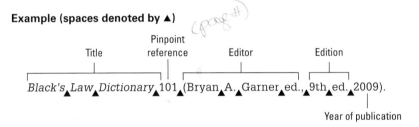

Black's▲Law▲Dictionary▲101▲(Bryan▲A.▲Garner▲ed.,▲9th▲ed.,▲2009).

If the dictionary indicates an author, begin the citation with the author's name, in ordinary type. Present the title in italics. If the dictionary has an editor, the editor's name is the first component of the publication parenthetical, followed by the abbreviation "ed." (plural "eds."), then a comma. Indicate editions other than the first, using an ordinal contraction (**Rule 4.3(b)**) and the abbreviation "ed."

Examples

Eric Partridge, *A Dictionary of Slang and Unconventional English* 111 (8th ed. 1984).

1 *Oxford English Dictionary* 207 (J.A. Simpson & E.S.C. Weiner eds., 1989).

22.1(b)(FN) Full citation format for dictionary in academic footnotes

⚠ ACADEMIC FORMATTING

In academic footnotes, follow **Rule 22.1(a)** for the citation components, but use large and small capital letters for the author's name (if any) and the title, with the remainder of the citation in ordinary type.

Examples

[15] ERIC PARTRIDGE, A DICTIONARY OF SLANG AND UNCONVENTIONAL ENGLISH 111 (8th ed. 1984).

[231] OXFORD ENGLISH DICTIONARY 207 (J.A. Simpson & E.S.C. Weiner eds., 1989).

▋22.2▋ Short Citation Formats for Dictionaries

22.2(a) Short citation formats for dictionary

Follow Rule **20.6(a)** for books.

Example

Full citation:	*Merriam-Webster's Collegiate Dictionary* 1547 (11th ed. 2003).
Short citations:	*Id.* at 1112.
	Merriam-Webster's Collegiate Dictionary, supra, at 348.

22.2(b)(FN) Short citation formats for dictionary in academic footnotes

⚠ ACADEMIC FORMATTING

Follow **Rule 20.6(b)** for books.

Example

[45] ALAN GILPIN, DICTIONARY OF ENVIRONMENTAL LAW 42 (2001).

[46] *Id.* at 68.

. . .

[93] GILPIN, *supra* note 45, at 60.

▋22.3▋ Full Citation Format for Multi-Volume Encyclopedias

Legal encyclopedias address a variety of legal topics and consequently are published in multiple volumes. Use this rule to cite multi-volume legal encyclopedias such as *American Jurisprudence, Second Series* ("Am. Jur. 2d"), *Corpus Juris Secundum* ("C.J.S."), the encyclopedias listed in **Chart 22.1**, and similar multi-volume encyclopedias. If the encyclopedia has a named author or editor, or if it is a single-volume encyclopedia, follow **Rule 22.4**. A full citation to an entry in a multi-volume legal encyclopedia has the following components.

Volume number | Encyclopedia abbreviation | *Title* or *Topic* | § | Section number | (Year of publication).

Example (spaces denoted by ▲)

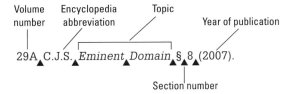

Volume number
Encyclopedia abbreviation
Topic
Year of publication

29A▲C.J.S.▲*Eminent*▲*Domain*▲§▲8▲(2007).

Section number

22.3(a) Volume number

Begin the citation with the volume number, set out as an arabic numeral in ordinary type, followed by a space. If the volume number also includes a letter, capitalize the letter.

Example (spaces denoted by ▲)

60A▲Am.▲Jur.▲2d▲*Pensions*▲§▲1098▲(2003▲&▲Supp.▲2012).

22.3(b) Encyclopedia abbreviation

Following the volume number, set out the abbreviation for the name of the encyclopedia, in ordinary type, followed by one space. **Chart 22.1** displays abbreviations for representative legal encyclopedias. To cite an entry in a multi-volume encyclopedia not shown in the chart, abbreviate any words in its name that appear in **Chart 22.1** or **Appendix 3(B)**. For an encyclopedia series after the first, use the appropriate ordinal contraction (**Rule 4.3(b)**).

22.3(c) Title or topic name

Following the encyclopedia abbreviation, set out the full main title or topic name of the cited entry, in italics. Capitalize words in the title or topic name according to **Rule 3.2**. Do not omit or abbreviate any words in the title or topic name. However, omit names of subsections or other subdivisions of the entry.

Example

Main title:	*Robbery*
Subsection:	§ 91 Unlawful Entry
Correct:	67 Am. Jur. 2d *Robbery* § 91 (2003).
Incorrect:	67 Am. Jur. 2d *Unlawful Entry* § 91 (2003).

22.3(d) Pinpoint references

Following the title or topic name, insert one or more section symbols, followed by one space and the number(s) of the cited section(s) and subsection(s), if any. See **Rule 6** for more guidance on citing sections and subdivisions.

CHART 22.1	Representative Encyclopedia Abbreviations

Encyclopedia name:	Abbreviation (spaces denoted by ▲):
American Jurisprudence	Am.▲Jur.
American Jurisprudence, Second Series	Am.▲Jur.▲2d
Corpus Juris	C.J.
Corpus Juris Secundum	C.J.S.
California Jurisprudence, Third Series	Cal.▲Jur.▲3d
Georgia Jurisprudence	Ga.▲Jur.
Illinois Law & Practice	Ill.▲L.▲&▲Prac.
Indiana Law Encyclopedia	Ind.▲L.▲Encyclopedia
Michigan Civil Jurisprudence	Mich.▲Civ.▲Jur.
New York Jurisprudence, Second Series	N.Y.▲Jur.▲2d

22.3(e) Publication parenthetical

Following the section number(s), add a parenthetical to indicate the year of publication of the cited volume and its supplement, if any. See **Rule 8** for guidance on citing a main volume, a supplement, or both. When citing an encyclopedia entry in a commercial database, add the name of the database provider, and provide the date through which the database is current.

Examples

Cited material only in main volume:	79A C.J.S. *Securities Regulation* § 4 (2009).
Cited material only in supplement:	79A C.J.S. *Securities Regulation* § 37 (Supp. 2012).
Cited material in both main volume and supplement:	76 Am. Jur. 2d *Trusts* § 1 (2005 & Supp. 2012).
Cited material in commercial database:	5 Am. Jur. 2d *Arrest* § 104 (WestlawNext through Aug. 2013).

22.3(f)(FN) Full citation format for multi-volume encyclopedia in academic footnotes

⚠ ACADEMIC FORMATTING

To cite a multi-volume encyclopedia in a document with academic footnotes, follow **Rule 22.3(a)** through **(d)**, but present the abbreviated name of the encyclopedia in large and small capital letters.

Example

> ⁶² 13A CAL. JUR. 3D *Consumer and Borrower Protection Law* §§ 156–157 (2004).

22.4 Full Citation Format for Encyclopedias with Named Authors or Editors

22.4(a) Full citation format for encyclopedia with named author or editor

To cite a single-volume encyclopedia or an entry in a multi-volume encyclopedia that has a named author or editor, follow **Rule 20.1**. To cite a specific author's article within an encyclopedia, follow **Rule 20.3(b)**.

Examples

> J.O. Urmson & Jonathan Rée, *The Concise Encyclopedia of Western Philosophy & Philosophers* 272 (3d ed. 2004).
>
> *Encyclopedia of Animal Rights and Animal Welfare* 34 (Marc Bekoff ed., 2d ed. 2010).
>
> Gerhard Casper, *Constitutionalism, in* 2 *Encyclopedia of the American Constitution* 633 (Leonard W. Levy & Kenneth L. Karst eds., 2d ed. 2000).

22.4(b)(FN) Full citation format for encyclopedia with named author or editor in academic footnotes

⚠ ACADEMIC FORMATTING

To cite a single-volume encyclopedia or an entry in a multi-volume encyclopedia that has a named author or editor, follow **Rule 20.1(f)(FN)**. To cite a specific author's article within an encyclopedia, follow **Rule 20.3(e)(FN)**.

Examples

> ⁶¹ J.O. URMSON & JONATHAN RÉE, THE CONCISE ENCYCLOPEDIA OF WESTERN PHILOSOPHY & PHILOSOPHERS 272 (3d ed. 2004).
>
> ⁷⁹ ENCYCLOPEDIA OF ANIMAL RIGHTS AND ANIMAL WELFARE 34 (Marc Bekoff ed., 2d ed. 2010).
>
> ¹³⁵ GERHARD CASPER, *Constitutionalism, in* 2 ENCYCLOPEDIA OF THE AMERICAN CONSTITUTION 633 (Leonard W. Levy & Kenneth L. Karst eds., 2d ed. 2000).

▌**22.5** Short Citation Formats for Encyclopedias

22.5(a) Short citation format using *id.*

When appropriate, use *id.* as a short-form citation to any form of legal encyclopedia. For more information on *id.*, see **Rule 11.3**. If possible, indicate a pinpoint reference. Use the preposition "at" only before pinpoint *page* references (**Rule 5.0**). If the work uses another form of subdivision, omit "at" and simply insert the specific pinpoint reference, consulting **Rules 6.0** (sections and paragraphs), **7.0** (footnotes), **8.0** (supplements), or **9.0** (graphical material and appendices), as needed.

22.5(b) Short citation format for multi-volume encyclopedia

In practice-based documents, if *id.* is not appropriate, use the full citation of the multi-volume encyclopedia, but omit the publication parenthetical.

Example

Full citation: 45C Am. Jur. 2d *Job Discrimination* § 2219 (2012).

Short citation: 45C Am. Jur. 2d *Job Discrimination* § 2219.

22.5(c) Short citation format for single-volume encyclopedia or encyclopedia with named author or editor

In practice-based documents, if *id.* is not appropriate, analogize to **Rules 20.6(a)** and **20.6(c)**. Begin the short citation with the author's surname, or if the encyclopedia does not display an author name, its title, followed by a comma and one space, the italicized word *supra*, and a new pinpoint reference.

Examples

Urmson & Rée, *supra,* at 273.

Encyclopedia of Animal Rights and Animal Welfare, supra, at 37.

Casper, *supra,* at 634.

22.5(d)(FN) Short citation formats for encyclopedias in academic footnotes   ⚠ ACADEMIC FORMATTING

For short citations to multi-volume encyclopedias in documents with academic footnotes, when *id.* is not appropriate, omit the date parenthetical and append a *supra* reference to the earlier footnote containing the full citation, followed by a pinpoint reference.

Example

> [6] 45C AM. JUR. 2D *Job Discrimination* § 2219 (2012).
>
> [7] *Id.* § 2220.
>
> . . .
>
> [13] 45C AM. JUR. 2D *Job Discrimination, supra* note 6, § 2223.

For short citations to single-volume encyclopedias or encyclopedias with a named author or editor, keep the author name(s), or if no author, the title, followed by a *supra* reference to the earlier footnote containing the full citation, followed by a pinpoint reference.

Examples

> [61] J.O. URMSON & JONATHAN RÉE, THE CONCISE ENCYCLOPEDIA OF WESTERN PHILOSOPHY & PHILOSOPHERS 272 (3d ed. 2004).
>
> [62] *Id.*
>
> . . .
>
> [69] URMSON & RÉE, *supra* note 61, at 273.
>
> [79] ENCYCLOPEDIA OF ANIMAL RIGHTS AND ANIMAL WELFARE 34 (Marc Bekoff ed., 2d ed. 2010).
>
> [80] *Id.* at 36.
>
> . . .
>
> [112] ENCYCLOPEDIA OF ANIMAL RIGHTS AND ANIMAL WELFARE, *supra* note 79, at 33.

For short citations to a specific author's article within an encyclopedia, do not use *id.*, even to refer to the immediately preceding footnote. Instead, set out the author's surname, followed by a *supra* reference to the earlier footnote containing the full citation, followed by a pinpoint reference.

Examples

> [135] GERHARD CASPER, *Constitutionalism*, in 2 ENCYCLOPEDIA OF THE AMERICAN CONSTITUTION 633 (Leonard W. Levy & Kenneth L. Karst eds., 2d ed. 2000).
>
> [136] CASPER, *supra* note 135, at 634.
>
> . . .
>
> [156] CASPER, *supra* note 135, at 636.

■22.6■ Full Citation Format for A.L.R. Annotations

An annotation is a detailed article on a narrow topic of the law, containing extensive references to judicial opinions and other sources dealing with that topic. Annotations are collected and published in volumes of the *American Law Reports* series ("A.L.R.") addressing state or federal law. A full citation to an annotation contains eight components. (Also follow this format to cite the predecessor of A.L.R., *Lawyer's Reports Annotated* (substituting the abbreviation "L.R.A.")).

Author, | Annotation, | *Title,* | Volume number | A.L.R. series abbreviation | Initial page, | Pinpoint reference | (Year of publication).

Example (spaces denoted by ▲)

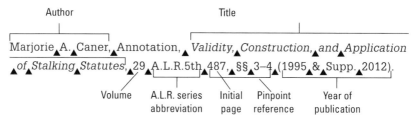

Author   Title

Marjorie▲A.▲Caner,▲Annotation,▲ *Validity,▲Construction,▲and▲Application* ▲*of*▲*Stalking*▲*Statutes,*▲29▲A.L.R.5th▲487,▲§§▲3–4▲(1995▲&▲Supp.▲2012).

Volume   A.L.R. series   Initial   Pinpoint   Year of
          abbreviation   page   reference   publication

22.6(a) Author's name; annotation designation

Begin with the author's name, following **Rule 20.1(b)** for books. After the author's name, add a comma, one space, and the word "Annotation," in ordinary type, also followed by a comma and one space. If the annotation does not show an author, begin the citation with the designation "Annotation."

Examples

Kristine Cordier Karnezis, Annotation, *Validity of State Statutory Cap on Punitive Damages,* 103 A.L.R.5th 379, § 2(b) (2002).

Annotation, *Per Diem Compensation of Public Officer,* 1 A.L.R. 276, 279 (1919).

22.6(b) Annotation title

Present the title exactly as it appears on the first page of the annotation, without omitting any words. Follow **Rule 3.2** for capitalization. Italicize the title and subtitle, if any, but use ordinary type for words that would be italicized in text, such as case names (**Rule 1.6**). Insert a comma and one space after the title.

Examples

Ann K. Wooster, Annotation, *Issues Concerning Bankruptcy Proceedings of Limited Liability Companies*, 37 A.L.R. Fed. 2d 129, § 11 (2009).

Eric C. Surette, Annotation, *Propriety of Federal Court's Abstention, Under Younger v. Harris, 401 U.S. 37, 91 S. Ct. 746, 27 L. Ed. 2d 669 (1971), to Avoid Interference in Ongoing State Proceedings Involving Licensing and Regulation of Occupations*, 57 A.L.R. Fed. 2d 355 (2011).

22.6(c) Volume number and A.L.R. series

Following the title, set out the volume number of the series in which the annotation appears. Insert one space after the volume number.

Immediately following the volume number, indicate the abbreviation for the A.L.R. series in which the work is published, in ordinary type. The A.L.R. series consists of the abbreviation "A.L.R." followed by an ordinal contraction (for the second and later series) or another designation (for the first or later federal series), followed by one space. Abbreviations for the A.L.R. series are shown in **Chart 22.2.**

Examples

Cara Yates, Annotation, *Application of State Law to Age Discrimination in Employment*, 51 A.L.R.5th 1, § 1(a) n.3 (1997).

Marjorie A. Shields, Annotation, *Admissibility of Evidence Discovered in Search of Defendant's Property or Residence Authorized by Defendant's Spouse*, 154 A.L.R. Fed. 579, § 3(a) (1999) (collecting cases holding that spouse may consent to warrantless search of property).

CHART 22.2	**Abbreviations for A.L.R. Series**

(The symbol ▲ denotes a space.)

First Series (1919–1948)	A.L.R.
Second Series (1948–1965)	A.L.R.2d
Third Series (1965–1980)	A.L.R.3d
Fourth Series (1980–1992)	A.L.R.4th
Fifth Series (1992–2005)	A.L.R.5th
Sixth Series (2005–present)	A.L.R.6th
Federal Series (1969–2005)	A.L.R.▲Fed.
Federal Series, Second (2005–present)	A.L.R.▲Fed.▲2d

22.6(d) Initial page and pinpoint references

Following the series abbreviation, set out the initial page number of the annotation. If the citation will include a pinpoint reference, add a comma and one space, followed by a section number (preferred), a page number, a footnote number, or a combination of these references. See **Rules 5** through **9** for more guidance on pinpoint references.

Example

> William H. Danne, Jr., Annotation, *"Palimony" Actions for Support Following Termination of Nonmarital Relationships*, 21 A.L.R.6th 351, § 13 cmt. (2007).

22.6(e) Year of publication

End the citation with a publication parenthetical setting out the year in which the A.L.R. volume containing the cited annotation was published, or if the cited portion of the annotation appears in a supplement to that volume, the year the supplement was published, or both. Annotations are frequently supplemented; see **Rule 8** for more information on citing supplements.

Example

> Gregory G. Sarno, Annotation, *Legal Malpractice in Handling or Defending Medical Malpractice Claim*, 78 A.L.R.4th 725, § 4(b) (1990 & Supp. 2012).

22.6(f) E-annotations

The A.L.R. databases on commercial databases such as WestlawNext and Lexis Advance also include electronic annotations, which have no print counterpart. To cite an e-annotation, follow **Rule 22.6(a)** through **(e)**, but substitute the year of publication for the volume number, and substitute the annotation number for the initial page. Add a parenthetical with the name of the commercial database. E-annotations can be superseded by a printed A.L.R. annotation; when this occurs, cite the superseding print source instead.

Example

Annotation, *Evidence Considered in Tracing Currency, Bank Account, or Cash Equivalent to Illegal Drug Trafficking so as to Permit Forfeiture, or Declaration as Contraband, under State Law—Factors Other Than Proximity, Explanation, Amount, Packaging, and Odor*, 2005 A.L.R.6th 1, § 2 (WestlawNext).

22.6(g)(FN) Full citation format for annotation in academic footnotes   ⚠ ACADEMIC FORMATTING

In documents with academic footnotes, cite annotations following **Rule 22.6(a)** through **(f)**, but use large and small capital letters for the series abbreviation.

Examples

[78] Cara Yates, Annotation, *Application of State Law to Age Discrimination in Employment*, 51 A.L.R.5TH 1, § 1(a) n.3 (1997).

[82] Marjorie A. Shields, Annotation, *Admissibility of Evidence Discovered in Search of Defendant's Property or Residence Authorized by Defendant's Spouse*, 154 A.L.R. FED. 579, § 3(a) (1999) (collecting cases holding that spouse may consent to warrantless search of property).

22.7 Short Citation Formats for A.L.R. Annotations

22.7(a) Short citation formats for annotation

Follow **Rule 21.7(a)** for legal periodicals.

Examples

Full citation: Deborah F. Buckman, Annotation, *Reverse Confusion Doctrine under State Trademark Law*, 114 A.L.R.5th 129, § 1(a) (2003).

Short citations: *Id.* § 4.

Buckman, *supra*, § 6.

22.7(b)(FN) Short citation formats for annotation in academic footnotes

⚠ ACADEMIC FORMATTING

Follow **Rule 21.7(b)** for legal periodicals.

Example

[2] Deborah F. Buckman, Annotation, *Reverse Confusion Doctrine under State Trademark Law*, 114 A.L.R.5TH 129, § 1(a) (2003).

[3] *Id.* § 4.

.   .   .

[27] Buckman, *supra* note 2, § 6.

23 Restatements, Model Codes, Uniform Laws, and Sentencing Guidelines

Fast Formats

Restatements, Model Codes, Uniform Laws, and Sentencing Guidelines	
Restatement (first series)	Restatement of Sec. § 141 (1941).
Restatement (later series)	Restatement (Second) of Agency § 27 (1958).
Restatement (draft)	Restatement (Third) of Suretyship § 31 (Tentative Draft No. 4, 1995).
Model code	Model Penal Code § 2.02(2)(a)(i) (1985).
ABA model rules and ethics codes	Model Rules of Prof'l Conduct R. 2.1 (2004).
	Model Code of Prof'l Responsibility DR 5-105(B) (1978).
Uniform law	Unif. Trade Secrets Act § 1(4), 14 U.L.A. 438 (1990).
Sentencing guidelines	U.S. Sentencing Guidelines Manual § 4B1.2(a) (2012).
Citations in academic footnotes	[33] RESTATEMENT (THIRD) OF PROP.: MORTGS. § 3.1 (1997).
	[34] MODEL CODE OF PROF'L RESPONSIBILITY EC 7-1 (1981).
	[35] UNIF. ELEC. TRANSACTIONS ACT § 3(b) (1999).
	[36] U.S. SENTENCING GUIDELINES MANUAL § 4A1.1 (2012).
Short citations	Restatement (Second) of Contracts § 90.
	§ 90.

RESTATEMENT OF THE LAW THIRD

THE AMERICAN LAW INSTITUTE

RESTATEMENT OF THE LAW
THE
FOREIGN RELATIONS LAW
OF THE
UNITED STATES

Volume 2

§§ 501–End

TABLES and INDEX

As Adopted and Promulgated

BY

THE AMERICAN LAW INSTITUTE

AT WASHINGTON, D.C.

May 14, 1986

·A·L·I· ®

ST. PAUL, MINN.
AMERICAN LAW INSTITUTE PUBLISHERS
1987

Title, subject matter, and series (Rule 23.1(a)). Because this is the first Restatement on the topic, do not include a series.

Year of publication (Rule 23.1(c)).

Title page

napshot

Chapter Three

HIGH SEAS

Section
521. Freedom of High Seas
522. Enforcement Jurisdiction over Foreign Ships on High Seas
523. Exploitation of Mineral Resources of Deep Sea-Bed

§ 521. Freedom of High Seas

Pinpoint refere
(Rule 23.1(b))

(1) The high seas are open and free to all states, whether coastal or land-locked.

(2) Freedom of the high seas comprises, *inter alia*:

(a) freedom of navigation;

(b) freedom of overflight;

(c) freedom of fishing;

(d) freedom to lay submarine cables and pipelines;

(e) freedom to construct artificial islands, installations, and structures; and

(f) freedom of scientific research.

(3) These freedoms must be exercised by all states with reasonable regard to the interests of other states in their exercise of the freedom of the high seas.

Source Note:

This section is based on Article 2 of the 1958 Convention on the High Seas, and Articles 87 and 89 of the LOS Convention.

Comment:

a. *Area in which high seas freedoms can be exercised.* This section applies to all parts of the sea that are not included in the internal waters, the territorial sea, or the exclusive economic zone of any state, or in the archipelagic waters of an archipelagic state. Certain of these freedoms may be exercised also in the exclusive economic zone of other states, as specified in § 514. See LOS Convention, Article 86; compare 1958 Convention on the High Seas, Article 1.

No state may appropriate any part of the high seas or otherwise subject the high seas to its sovereignty. See LOS Convention,

78

Inside page

23.1 Full Citation Format for Restatements

A full citation to a Restatement (published by the American Law Institute) has the following components, which vary depending on whether the Restatement is in its first or a later series and whether it is in final or draft form.

Restatement | [(Series, if not the first)] | of | [Subject matter] | Pinpoint reference | ([Draft information] | Year of publication).

Example (spaces denoted by ▲)

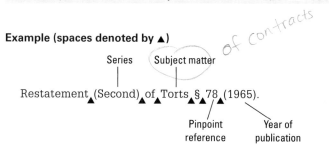

23.1(a) Title, subject matter, and series

If the Restatement is the first series, begin with the title "Restatement" followed by the preposition "of" and its subject matter, abbreviating any words that appear in **Appendix 3(E)**. If the Restatement has a subtitle, insert it following a colon. If the Restatement is from a second or later series, indicate the series in a parenthetical after the title "Restatement," spelling out the ordinal number. Capitalize according to **Rule 3.2**, and use ordinary type for the title, subject matter, and series.

Examples

Restatement (Second) of Contracts § 90 (1981).

Restatement (Third) of Torts: Prods. Liab. § 2 cmt. d (1998).

23.1(b) Pinpoint references

Following the title, provide a pinpoint reference, indicating sections, subsections, or relevant subdivisions such as comments and illustrations. Abbreviate subdivisions as indicated in **Appendix 3(C)**.

Examples

Restatement (Second) of Conflict of Laws § 291 cmt. g (1971).

Restatement of Prop.: Servitudes § 453 illus. 1 (1944).

23.1(c) Year of publication

In a parenthetical, indicate the cited Restatement's year of publication. Do not use the date of the Restatement's adoption.

SIDEBAR 23.1   Subject Matters of Restatements

Current subject matters of the Restatements include the following. Abbreviate words appearing in **Appendix 3(E)**:

- Agency
- Conflict of Laws
- Contracts
- Employment Law
- Foreign Relations Law of the United States
- International Commercial Arbitration
- Judgments
- Law Governing Lawyers
- Property: Landlord & Tenant
- Property: Mortgages
- Property: Servitudes
- Property: Wills & Other Donative Transfers

- Restitution & Unjust Enrichment
- Security
- Suretyship & Guaranty
- Torts
- Torts: Apportionment of Liability
- Torts: Liability for Economic Harm
- Torts: Liability for Physical & Emotional Harm
- Torts: Products Liability
- Trusts
- Unfair Competition

23.1(d) Draft information

When citing a draft Restatement, indicate the type of draft within the publication parenthetical, preceding the year of publication. Present the information about the draft in ordinary type, capitalized and without abbreviation. If the draft is numbered, insert the abbreviation "No." before its number, and place a comma between the number and the year of publication.

Examples

Numbered official draft:	Restatement of Contracts § 111 (Official Draft No. 1, 1928).
Numbered tentative draft:	Restatement (Third) of Suretyship § 31 (Tentative Draft No. 4, 1995).
Numbered proposed draft:	Restatement (Third) of Restitution & Unjust Enrichment (Proposed Draft No. 6, 2004).
Unnumbered discussion draft:	Restatement (Third) of Torts §§ 3–4 (Discussion Draft 1999).

23.1(e)(FN) Full citation format for Restatement in academic footnotes

⚠ ACADEMIC FORMATTING

To cite a Restatement in a document using academic footnotes, follow **Rule 23.1(a)** through **(d)**, but use large and small capital letters for the title, subject matter, and series.

Examples

> [21] RESTATEMENT OF PROP.: SERVITUDES § 453 illus. 1 (1944).

> [64] RESTATEMENT (THIRD) OF TORTS: PRODS. LIAB. § 2 cmt. d (1998).

> [76] RESTATEMENT (THIRD) OF TORTS §§ 3–4 (Discussion Draft 1999).

23.2   Short Citation Formats for Restatements

23.2(a) Short citation formats for Restatement

If *id.* is appropriate, use *id.* as the preferred short citation format. See **Rule 11.3** for more information on *id.* If *id.* is not appropriate, keep all components except the publication parenthetical.

Example

Full citation: Restatement (Second) of Contracts § 90 (1979).

Short citation: Restatement (Second) of Contracts § 90.

23.2(b)(FN) Short citation formats for Restatement in academic footnotes

⚠ ACADEMIC FORMATTING

If *id.* is appropriate, use *id.* as the preferred short citation format (**Rule 11.3**). Otherwise, keep all components except the publication parenthetical. Repeat the full citation if the Restatement has not been cited, in full or in short form (including *id.*), in the same footnote or one of the previous five footnotes.

Examples

> [51] RESTATEMENT OF PROP.: SERVITUDES § 451 (1944).

> [52] *Id.*

> . . .

> [55] RESTATEMENT OF PROP.: SERVITUDES § 451.

> . . .

> [64] RESTATEMENT OF PROP.: SERVITUDES § 451 (1944).

23.3   Full Citation Format for Model Codes and Acts

23.3(a)   Full citation format for model code or act

Cite model codes and acts analogously to federal statutes under **Rules 14.2** and **14.6**, using ordinary type and abbreviating words in the title of the code or act using **Appendix 3(E)**. You may omit articles and prepositions not needed for clarity.

The date parenthetical should indicate the year the cited version was adopted, unless the version indicates that it was subsequently amended. In that case, use the year of its most recent amendment.

If the model code or act was promulgated by an organization *other than* the American Bar Association, American Law Institute, or National Conference of Commissioners on Uniform State Laws, indicate the organization's name in the date parenthetical immediately before the year. Abbreviate any words appearing in **Appendix 3(B)** or **Appendix 3(E)**.

If citing a tentative or proposed draft, follow **Rule 23.1(d)**.

Examples

Model Penal Code § 2.05 cmt. 1 (1985).

Model Land Dev. Code app. A (Tentative Draft No. 3, 1971).

Model Relocation Act § 10 (Am. Acad. Matrimonial Lawyers Tentative Draft 1996).

23.3(b)(FN)   Full citation format for model code or act in academic footnotes

⚠ ACADEMIC FORMATTING

To cite a model code or act in a document with academic footnotes, follow **Rule 23.3(a)**, but use large and small capital letters for its title.

Examples

[35] MODEL PENAL CODE § 2.05 cmt. 1 (1985).

[43] *See* MODEL RULES OF PROF'L CONDUCT R. 3.1, 3.3(a)(1) (2009).

23.4   Short Citation Formats for Model Codes and Acts

Follow **Rule 14.5**.

Examples

Full citation:	Model Penal Code § 2.02(2)(a)(i) (1985).
Short citation options:	Model Penal Code § 2.02(2)(a)(i).
	§ 2.02(2)(a)(i).
	Id. § 2.02(2)(a)(ii).

23.5   Full Citation Format for Uniform Laws

23.5(a)   Full citation format for uniform law

Cite uniform laws analogously to federal statutes under **Rule 14.2**. Abbreviate words in the law's title using **Appendix 3(E)**, and provide a pinpoint reference to the cited section(s). You may omit articles and prepositions not needed for clarity. Indicate the year of publication in a date parenthetical.

Example

> Unif. Common Interest Ownership Act § 4-113 (1994).

If a uniform act has been withdrawn, superseded, or amended, indicate that status and the year it took place in a second parenthetical.

Example

> Unif. Sales Act § 17, 1 U.L.A. 309 (1950) (withdrawn 1962).

If citing a uniform law as adopted by a particular state, cite it as a statute from that state, using **Rule 14.4** and the components of the state's statutory code (consult **Appendix 1**).

Example (Delaware version of U.C.C. § 2-206)

> Del. Stat. Ann. tit. 6, § 2-206 (2009).

23.5(b)   Publication in *Uniform Laws Annotated*

If citing a uniform law to its publication in *Uniform Laws Annotated* (abbreviated as "U.L.A."), insert a comma after the title and section number, followed by the volume number or supplement number of the U.L.A. and the page number on which the cited section begins.

Example

> Unif. Parentage Act § 803(b)(2), 9B U.L.A. 364 (2001).

23.5(c)(FN) Full citation format for uniform law in academic footnotes

ACADEMIC FORMATTING

Follow **Rule 23.5(a)** and **(b)**, but use large and small capital letters for the title of the uniform law and, if applicable, the abbreviation U.L.A.

Examples

> [80] Unif. Common Interest Ownership Act § 4-113 (1994).

> [87] Unif. Sales Act § 17, 1 U.L.A. 309 (1950) (withdrawn 1962).

23.6 Short Citation Formats for Uniform Laws

Follow **Rule 14.5**.

Example

Full citation:	Unif. P'ship Act § 202(c) (1997).
Short citation options:	Unif. P'ship Act § 202(c).
	§ 202(c).
	Id. § 202(c).

23.7 Full Citation Format for Sentencing Guidelines

23.7(a) Full citation format for sentencing guidelines

Begin with the title of the guidelines, presented in ordinary type. For federal sentencing guidelines, abbreviate "United States" as "U.S." For state guidelines, use the state's abbreviation from **Appendix 3(B)**.

Following the title, provide a pinpoint reference, indicating sections, sub-sections, or relevant subdivisions such as comments and illustrations. Abbreviate subdivisions as indicated in **Appendix 3(C)**.

In the date parenthetical, indicate the year the cited guidelines manual was *adopted*, unless the cited version indicates subsequent amendment. In that case, use the year of the guidelines' most recent amendment.

Examples

U.S. Sentencing Guidelines Manual § 2D1.1 (2013).

U.S. Sentencing Guidelines Manual § 1B1.3 cmt. background (2010).

23.7(b)(FN) Full citation format for sentencing guidelines in academic footnotes

⚠ ACADEMIC FORMATTING

To cite sentencing guidelines in academic footnotes, follow **Rule 23.7(a)**, but use large and small capital letters for the title.

Example

> [57] U.S. SENTENCING GUIDELINES MANUAL § 1B1.3 cmt. background (2010).

23.8 Short Citation Formats for Sentencing Guidelines

23.8(a) Short citation formats for sentencing guidelines

If *id.* is appropriate, use *id.* as the preferred short citation format. See **Rule 11.3** for more information on *id.* If *id.* is not appropriate, keep all components except the date parenthetical.

Examples

Full citation: U.S. Sentencing Guidelines Manual § 4B1.2(a) (2009).

Short citation: U.S. Sentencing Guidelines Manual § 4B1.2(a).

23.8(b)(FN) Short citation formats for sentencing guidelines in academic footnotes

⚠ ACADEMIC FORMATTING

If *id.* is appropriate, use *id.* as the preferred short citation format. See **Rule 11.3** for more information on *id.* Otherwise, keep all components except the date parenthetical. Repeat the full citation if the sentencing guidelines have not been cited, in full or in short form (including *id.*), in the same footnote or one of the previous five footnotes.

Examples

> [57] U.S. SENTENCING GUIDELINES MANUAL § 1B1.3 cmt. background (2010).

> [58] *Id.*

> . . .

> [60] U.S. SENTENCING GUIDELINES MANUAL § 1B1.3 cmt. background.

> . . .

> [71] U.S. SENTENCING GUIDELINES MANUAL § 1B1.3 cmt. background (2010).

Fast Formats

Looseleaf Services and Reporters

Case in looseleaf reporter	*Glasow v. DuPont de Nemours & Co.*, 7 Trade Reg. Rep. (CCH) ¶ 74,791, at 101,998 (N.D. May 17, 2005).
Material in transfer binder	*Copyright.Net Music Publ'g v. MP3.Com*, [2002–2003 Transfer Binder] Copyright L. Dec. (CCH) ¶ 28,613, at 35,941 (S.D.N.Y. 2003).
Non-case material in looseleaf service	*Environmental Groups Appeal BLM Decision to Allow Coal Mine to Expand in Colorado*, 44 Env't Rep. 292 (BNA) (Feb. 1, 2013).

24.1 Full Citation Format for Case Materials in Looseleaf Services

A full citation to a case or administrative decision printed in a looseleaf service or topical reporter is similar to a full citation to a case under **Rule 12**, and it uses the following components.

Case name, | Looseleaf volume | Looseleaf name or abbreviation | (Publisher abbreviation) | Initial subdivision | Pinpoint reference | (Court abbreviation | Date), | [Subsequent history].

Example (spaces denoted by ▲)

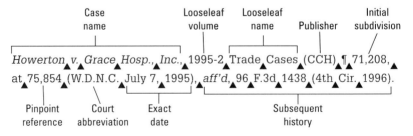

24.1(a) Case name

Present case names in italics, following **Rule 12.2** for components and abbreviating words that appear in **Appendix 3(E)**.

24.1(b) Looseleaf volume designation

Following the case name, designate the volume of the looseleaf service in which the case appears, followed by one space. The looseleaf service may designate a volume by a number, a year, a descriptive subtitle from the volume's spine, or a combination of these. If the volume designation, or part thereof, might be confused with the looseleaf service's abbreviation, enclose the volume designation in square brackets. If the volume is a transfer binder, the volume designation should also indicate the years covered by that binder.

Examples (volume designation in red)

United States v. Med. Mut. of Ohio, **1998-1** Trade Cases (CCH) ¶ 50,846, at 51,942 (N.D. Ohio Sept. 30, 1998).

Bradley v. United States, **91-2** U.S. Tax Cases (CCH) ¶ 50,332 (2d Cir. June 24, 1991).

Black & Decker Corp. v. United States, **[2004]** 2 Stand. Fed. Tax Rep. (CCH) ¶ 50,359 (D. Md. Aug. 3, 2004).

Taft v. Ackermans, **[Current Transfer Binder]** Fed. Sec. L. Rep. (CCH) ¶ 93,245, at 96,224 (S.D.N.Y. Apr. 13, 2005).

Bishop v. PCS Admin., **[2006 Transfer Binder]** Fed. Sec. L. Rep. (CCH) ¶ 93,882 (N.D. Ill. May 23, 2006).

24.1(c) Looseleaf service abbreviation

Treat looseleaf service abbreviations analogously to reporter abbreviations in **Rule 12.4**, and present them in ordinary type. Abbreviate any words appearing in **Appendix 5**. Abbreviate ordinal numerals as shown in **Rule 4.3**. Insert one space after the looseleaf abbreviation.

Examples (spaces denoted by ▲)

Full name of looseleaf:	Abbreviation:
Congressional Index	Cong.▲Index▲
Employment Safety and Health Guide	Emp.▲Safety▲&▲Health▲Guide▲

| Federal Tax Coordinator Second | Fed. ▲ Tax ▲ Coord. ▲ 2d ▲ |
| Media Law Reporter | Media ▲ L. ▲ Rep. ▲ |

24.1(d) Publisher

Immediately following the looseleaf service abbreviation, indicate the name of the looseleaf publisher, in parentheses, using the abbreviations shown below in **Chart 24.1**. If the publisher is not listed in **Chart 24.1**, abbreviate any words in its name appearing in **Appendices 3(B)** or **3(E)**. Insert one space after the closing parenthesis.

24.1(e) Initial subdivision and pinpoint references

A looseleaf that is updated by interfiling new material is typically organized by paragraph or section numbers. For looseleafs organized that way, indicate the initial subdivision with a paragraph (¶) or section (§) symbol, followed by one space and the paragraph or section number. To assist a reader in more quickly locating specific material, you may add the preposition "at" and a pinpoint reference to a page number.

Newsletter-style looseleafs are typically organized in a binder by report number. For looseleafs organized that way, use the abbreviation "No." followed by the report number. If possible, add a pinpoint reference to a paragraph, section, or page number within the report.

If a looseleaf uses another form of subdivision, analogize to the rules above to the extent possible, providing enough information for readers to locate the cited material. See **Rules 5** through **9** for more information on subdivisions.

Examples

In re Silicon Graphics, Inc. Sec. Litig., [1997 Transfer Binder] Fed. Sec. L. Rep. (CCH) ¶ 99,468 (N.D. Cal. May 23, 1997).

SEC v. Eskind, 29 Sec. Rep. & L. Reg. (BNA) No. 27, at 934 (N.D. Cal. June 26, 1997).

EEOC v. Golden St. Glass Co., Equal Emp. Compl. Man. (CCH) § 615.1, at 3202 (C.D. Cal. Mar. 6, 1980).

24.1(f) Court abbreviation

Follow **Rule 12.6** for cases. Abbreviations for court names are in **Appendices 1** and **4**.

CHART 24.1	Abbreviations for Names of Looseleaf Publishers

Publisher name:	Abbreviation (spaces denoted by ▲):
American Bar Association	ABA
Bureau of National Affairs, Inc. or BNA Books	BNA
Clark Boardman Callaghan	CBC
Commerce Clearing House, Inc. or CCH	CCH
LexisNexis	LexisNexis
LRP Publications	LRP
Matthew Bender	MB
National Association of College and University Attorneys	NACUA
Pike & Fischer	P▲&▲F
Practising Law Institute	PLI
Prentice-Hall	PH
Research Institute of America, Inc.	RIA
University Publishing Group	Univ.▲Pub.▲Group
West, a Thomson Reuters Co.	West
William S. Hein & Co.	Hein
Wolters Kluwer Law & Business-Aspen Publishers	Aspen▲Publishers

24.1(g) Date of decision

Follow **Rule 12.7** for cases, providing the exact date (Month Day, Year) of the decision.

24.1(h) Subsequent history

Present subsequent history information in accordance with **Rule 12.8**.

24.1(i) Prior history and other information

Follow **Rules 12.9** (prior history) and **12.10** (parenthetical information).

24.1(j)(FN) Full citation format for looseleaf service case materials in academic footnotes

⚠ ACADEMIC FORMATTING

In full citations to looseleaf service case materials in academic footnotes, follow **Rule 24.1(a)** through **(i)**, but present case names in ordinary type, as shown in **Rule 12.2(a)(2)**.

24.2 Short Citation Formats for Case Materials in Looseleaf Services

Follow **Rule 12.19** for cases.

Example

Full citation: *Howerton v. Grace Hosp., Inc.*, 1995-2 Trade Cases (CCH) ¶ 71,208 (W.D.N.C. July 7, 1995), *aff'd*, 96 F.3d 1438 (4th Cir. 1996).

Short citation: *Howerton*, 1995-2 Trade Cases ¶ 71,208, at 75,856.

24.3 Full Citation Format for Non-Case Materials in Looseleaf Services

For non-case materials published by a looseleaf service, follow the rule that covers an analogous source (e.g., **Rule 23** for periodicals), and substitute the looseleaf service citation components as shown in **Rule 24.1**.

SIDEBAR 24.1   **Understanding Paragraphs in Looseleaf Services**

A "paragraph" in looseleaf terminology is a term of art and usually does not refer to a single block of type. Instead, it can designate any quantity of material and typically spans several pages. In looseleaf services organized by paragraphs, each case is typically assigned a single paragraph number. The process of determining the paragraph number to cite can sometimes be confusing, as some pages within the source may contain both a paragraph number and a page number. When a service contains both paragraph and page numbers, the paragraph number is preceded by the paragraph symbol (¶).

Examples

> *Internet Service Provider Not Liable for User's Infringement*, 2 Copy. L. (CCH) No. 290, at 4 (May 24, 2002).

> *Industry Canada Issues Final Rules Defining "Secure Electronic Signatures,"* 10 Elec. Com. & L. Rep. (BNA) No. 9, at 194 (Mar. 2, 2005).

24.4 Short Citation Formats for Non-Case Materials in Looseleaf Services

For short citations to non-case materials in a looseleaf service, follow the rules for short citations to an analogous source.

25 Practitioner and Court Documents, Transcripts, and Appellate Records

Fast Formats

Practitioner and Court Documents, Transcripts, and Appellate Records	
Affidavit	Aff. Bert Corcoran ¶¶ 1–3, Oct. 19, 2013.
Brief	Pet'r's Br. Supp. Mot. Reh'g 19.
Court order	Order Granting Defs.' Mot. Summ. J. 3–4.
Discovery document	Pl.'s 1st Set Interrogs. Nos. 3, 6, & 9.
Pleading	Def.'s 2d Am. Answer ¶¶ 5–12.
Hearing transcript	TRO Hr'g Tr. 45:3, Jan. 15, 2014.
Appellate record (options)	R. at 4.
	(R. at 4.)

25.1 Scope of Rule

Rule 25 applies to practitioner and court documents in a case being litigated. Practitioner and court documents include, but are not limited to, pleadings, motions and responses, briefs, memoranda of law, discovery and disclosure material, affidavits, declarations, evidence, notices, stipulations, orders, and judgments. See **Rule 12.18** to cite court documents, transcripts, and records in other cases.

25.2 Full Citation Format for Practitioner and Court Documents

Unless a local court rule requires otherwise (consult the jurisdiction's entry in **Appendix 2**), there typically are three to five components in a full citation to a document in a case being litigated. If desired, you may enclose the entire citation in parentheses.

Document name | Pinpoint reference, | Exact date[,] | [CM/ECF No. | Case number].

Example (spaces denoted by ▲)

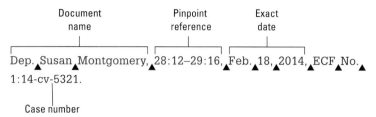

25.2(a) Document name

Present the document name as it appears on the document's face, set out in ordinary type. Unless local court rules provide otherwise (consult **Appendix 2**), you may abbreviate any word that appears in **Appendix 3(G)** or any word of six letters or more, so long as the result is unambiguous. Eliminate articles and prepositions not needed for clarity.

Some attorneys prefer to spell out the document name completely the first time it is cited and to use the abbreviated name in subsequent citations. This practice is acceptable.

Examples

Document name:	Abbreviation:
Plaintiff's Complaint	Pl.'s Compl.
Affidavit of Joshua Allen	Aff. Joshua Allen
Defendants' Response to Motion in Limine	Defs.' Resp. Mot. Limine

25.2(b) Pinpoint references

Following the document name, provide the most specific pinpoint reference possible, according to the document's subdivisions. Litigation documents commonly use paragraph numbers, page numbers, or page and line numbers.

If there is a possibility of confusion between a number used in the document's name and the pinpoint reference, you may insert the preposition "at" before a pinpoint *page* number. See also **Sidebar 5.2** for guidance on presenting a span of pinpoint references.

Examples

Defs.' 1st Am. Answer ¶¶ 1–5, Aug. 5, 2013, No. 2013-675.

Pet'rs' Mot. for Recons. Under Rule 71.2, at 3–4, Feb. 17, 2014.

25.2(c) Date of filing, service, or preparation

While dates are typically omitted from citations to court documents, if the presiding court's rules require supplying a date, or if a date will help identify a particular document filed with the court, following the pinpoint reference, set out the month, day, and year, preferably the date on which the document was filed.

For material served on opposing counsel but not filed with the court, use the date shown in the certificate of service. If the document was neither filed nor served, use its date of preparation (e.g., the date a deposition was taken). In any of these situations, abbreviate the month according to **Appendix 3(A)**.

Example

Pl.'s Mot. Limine 3, May 26, 2012, No. 2014-RGT-1:4568.

25.2(d) Case number

Every litigated case is assigned a unique identification number that links all documents connected to that case. For state cases, check local court rules (consult **Appendix 2**) to determine whether they require a case number in citations to documents filed in a particular case.

For cases being litigated in the federal courts, citations to court documents should indicate their assigned case management/electronic case file (CM/ECF) numbers. In *federal district courts*, these typically are four-part numbers beginning with the number of the divisional office, followed by a colon and the year, a hyphen and the case type abbreviation, followed by a second hyphen and the case number. Case type abbreviations include adversary proceeding ("ap"), bankruptcy ("br"), civil ("cv"), criminal ("cr"), or miscellaneous proceeding ("mp"). Some district courts also add the initials of the judge presiding over the case. In *federal appellate courts*, the CM/ECF numbers typically consist of two-part numbers representing the last two digits of the year and the four- or five-digit case number (e.g., 13-2453).

Example (federal district court CM/ECF number)

25.3 Full Citation Format for Transcripts

Unless a local court rule requires otherwise (consult **Appendix 2**), a full citation to the transcript of a trial, hearing, or deposition contains three components.

Transcript abbreviation | Pinpoint reference, | Exact date.

Example

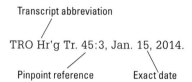

Transcript abbreviation

TRO Hr'g Tr. 45:3, Jan. 15, 2014.

Pinpoint reference   Exact date

25.3(a) Transcript abbreviation

Begin the citation with the name of the transcribed proceeding, following **Rule 25.2(a)** and abbreviating any word that appears in **Appendix 3(G)**.

25.3(b) Pinpoint references

Follow **Rule 25.2(b)**. To denote a line number within the transcript, use the page number, a colon (with no space on either side), and the line number(s) on which the cited material appears. For example, 12:3 means that the cited material falls on line 3 of page 12. If there is a possibility of confusion between a number used in the document's name and the pinpoint reference, you may insert the preposition "at" before a pinpoint page number. See also **Sidebar 5.2** for guidance on presenting a span of references.

Examples

Document and pinpoint reference:	Citation:
Hearing Transcript page 4, lines 10 through 12	Hr'g Tr. 4:10–12, Feb. 5, 2014.
Trial Transcript volume 2, pages 47 through 49	Trial Tr. vol. 2, at 47–49, Mar. 21, 2013.
Deposition of Marie Ducote at page 120, line 17, through page 122, line 3	Dep. Marie Ducote 120:17–122:3, Oct. 4, 2013.
	or
	Dep. Marie Ducote 120:17 to 122:3, Oct. 4, 2013.

25.3(c) Date of proceeding

Following the pinpoint reference, provide the exact date of the transcribed proceeding, abbreviating the month according to **Appendix 3(A)**.

Example

> Trial Tr. vol. 1, at 6–8, Feb. 4–5, 2013.

25.4 Short Citation Formats for Practitioner and Court Documents and Transcripts

In general, do not use *id.* as a short citation unless the name of the document or transcript is extremely long. Instead, use all required components, but refer to individuals by their surnames and omit the date, if any. For more information on surnames, see **Rule 12.2(d)**.

Example

Document:	Deposition of Carlton Rhys-Smith, May 22, 2014.
Full citation:	Dep. Carlton Rhys-Smith 1:1–5:17, May 22, 2014.
Short citation:	Dep. Rhys-Smith 4:13.

25.5 Full Citation Format for Appellate Records

25.5(a) Full citation options

Unless a local court rule requires otherwise (see **Appendix 2**), a full citation to an appellate record consists of two components: the abbreviation "R." for "record" and a pinpoint page reference following the preposition "at." The entire citation may be enclosed in parentheses if desired. Acceptable formats are illustrated below. Once you select a format, use it consistently throughout the document.

Examples

Formats:	R. at 4. (R. at 4.)

25.5(b) Pinpoint references to line numbers

To denote a line number within a specific page of the record, use the page number, a colon (with no space on either side), and the line number. Thus, 12:3 means that the cited material falls on line 3 of page 12.

Example

> The Petitioner, Monique Vasquez, worked as a bank teller for seventeen years. (R. at 6:21.) Her primary job duty was to complete customer transactions. (R. at 7:12–15.)

25.6 Short Citation Format for Appellate Records

Do not use *id.* as a short form for record citations. Instead, repeat the full citation, as reflected in **Rule 25.5** and its examples.

26 Speeches, Addresses, and Oral Presentations

Fast Formats

Speeches, Addresses, and Oral Presentations	
Unpublished speech	Luis A. Aguilar, Comm'r, SEC, Reducing the Temptation of Advisers to Misuse Political Contributions (July 22, 2009), *available at* http://www.sec.gov/news/speech/2009/spch072209laa.htm.
Published speech	Stephen Breyer, *Our Democratic Constitution* (Oct. 22, 2001), *in* 77 N.Y.U. L. Rev. 245 (2002).
Citation in academic footnote	[62] Luis A. Aguilar, Comm'r, SEC, Reducing the Temptation of Advisers to Misuse Political Contributions (July 22, 2009), *available at* http://www.sec.gov/news/speech/2009/spch072209laa.htm.
Short citations	Aguilar, Reducing the Temptation of Advisers to Misuse Political Contributions. [73] Aguilar, *supra* note 62.

26.1 Full Citation Format for Unpublished Speeches, Addresses, and Other Oral Presentations

A full citation to an unpublished speech, address, or other oral presentation may contain as many as seven components.

Speaker's name, | Speaker's title, if available | Speaker's institutional affiliation, if available | Title or subject of presentation | Pinpoint reference | (Exact date of presentation) | (Location of transcript or recording) [or], *available at* [URL].

Example (spaces denoted by ▲)

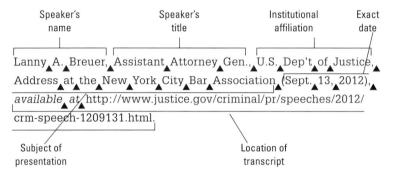

26.1(a) Speaker's name, title, and institutional affiliation

Give the speaker's full name, followed by a comma and one space. Analogize to **Rule 20.1(a)** for book authors. If the speaker is not generally known, or if the information would be helpful to the reader, you may set out the speaker's title and/or institutional affiliation after his or her name, set off by a comma. You may abbreviate words in the title or affiliation that appear in **Appendices 3(B)** and **3(E)**, and you may eliminate articles and prepositions not needed for clarity.

26.1(b) Subject or title of presentation

If the presentation has a formal title, set it out in full. If it does not have a formal title, provide a concise description of the subject matter. Present the title or subject in ordinary type, following **Rule 3.2** on capitalization. Insert one space after the subject or title.

Example

Barack Obama, Inaugural Address (Jan. 20, 2009), *video recording available at* http://www.whitehouse.gov/the_press_office/ President_Barack_Obamas_Inaugural_Address.

26.1(c) Pinpoint references

When possible, provide a pinpoint reference to the location of specific material within the presentation, such as a page, paragraph, or section number. See **Rule 5.2** for guidance.

Example

Deborah Platt Majoras, Chairman, Fed. Trade Comm'n, Finding the Solutions to Fight Spyware: The FTC's Three Enforcement Principles 7 (Feb. 9, 2006), *available at* http://www.ftc.gov/speeches/ majoras/060209cdtspyware.pdf.

26.1(d) Date of presentation

Following the title or subject, in parentheses, indicate its exact date, if available. Abbreviate the month according to **Appendix 3(A)**. At a minimum, provide the year. If no date is available, use "n.d." (abbreviation for "no date") in place of the year.

Example

> Tom Vilsack, Sec'y, U.S. Dep't Agric., Keynote Address at 2013 USDA Ag Outlook Conference (Feb. 21, 2013).

26.1(e) Information for locating source of transcript or recording

If the speech was transcribed or recorded, indicate its availability in a private or publicly accessible location. If the transcript or recording is privately maintained (e.g., in the files of a law review), indicate in a parenthetical where or how readers might obtain a copy. You may abbreviate the name of an organization that maintains the source using **Appendix 3(E)** or **Appendix 5**. If the transcript or recording is available on the World Wide Web, insert a comma, followed by the italicized phrase *"available at"* and the URL.

Examples

> Oprah Winfrey, Harvard University Commencement Address (May 30, 2013), *available at* http://news.harvard.edu/gazette/story/2013/05/winfreys-commencement-address/.
>
> Joshua Cohen, Martha Sutton Weeks Professor of Ethics in Soc'y, Stanford Univ., Address at the Edmond J. Safra Center for Ethics at Harvard University 7–8 (Mar. 11, 2011) (transcript on file with author).

26.1(f)(FN) Full citation to unpublished speech, address, or other oral presentation in academic footnotes

⚠ ACADEMIC FORMATTING

Follow **Rule 26.1(a)** through **(e)**. There is no difference in the full citation format used in academic footnotes.

26.2 Published Presentations

If the presentation has been published, analogize to **Rule 20.3** (collected works), **Rule 21.2** (consecutively paginated periodical), **Rule 21.3** (nonconsecutively paginated periodical), or other relevant rules, depending on the nature of the publication source and whether the citation will be used in a practice-based document or in a document with academic footnotes.

26.3 Short Citation Formats for Speeches, Addresses, and Oral Presentations

26.3(a) Short citation formats for speeches, addresses, and oral presentations

If appropriate, use *id.* as the short citation. For more information on *id.*, see **Rule 11.3.** If *id.* is not appropriate, use the last name of the speaker, the title of the presentation, and a pinpoint reference (e.g., "at" before a pinpoint page number), if available.

Example

    Full citation: Deborah Platt Majoras, Chairman, Fed. Trade Comm'n, Finding the Solutions to Fight Spyware: The FTC's Three Enforcement Principles 7 (Feb. 9, 2006), *available at* http://www.ftc.gov/speeches/majoras/060209cdtspyware.pdf.

    Short citation: Majoras, Finding the Solutions to Fight Spyware: The FTC's Three Enforcement Principles at 5.

26.3(b)(FN) Short citation formats for speeches, addresses, and oral presentations in academic footnotes

⚠ ACADEMIC FORMATTING

In documents with academic footnotes, if *id.* is not appropriate, use the *supra* format that follows, cross-referencing the footnote containing the full citation, and providing a pinpoint reference, if available. See **Rule 11.4** for additional information on *supra*.

    Speaker's last name, | *supra* | note | [Note number], | at | Pinpoint reference.

Example

    [148] Deborah Platt Majoras, Chairman, Fed. Trade Comm'n, Finding the Solutions to Fight Spyware: The FTC's Three Enforcement Principles 7 (Feb. 9, 2006), *available at* http://www.ftc.gov/speeches/majoras/060209cdtspyware.pdf.

    . . .

    [157] Majoras, *supra* note 148, at 6.

27 Interviews, Letters, and Memoranda

Fast Formats

Interviews, Letters, and Memoranda	
In-person interview	Interview with John Paul Stevens, Assoc. Justice, U.S. Supreme Court, in Washington, D.C. (Apr. 21, 2011) (on file with author).
Telephone interview	Telephone Interview with Melissa Mikesell, Attorney, Alliance for Justice (July 18, 2012).
Anonymous or confidential source	Interview with anonymous canine officer (June 19, 2012).
Interview conducted by another	Telephone Interview by Coleman Gerber with Sofia Dominik, Chief Exec. Officer, Naperville Ltd. (Aug. 24, 2013).
Unpublished memorandum	Memorandum from Jonathan B. Perlin, Undersec'y for Health, Dep't of Veterans' Affairs, to Dep't of Veterans' Affairs Primary Care Clinicians, *Screening and Clinical Management of Traumatic Brain Injury* 1 (Jan. 25, 2006) (on file with Fordham Law Review).
Published letter	Letter from William Lloyd Garrison to Reverend Samuel J. May (July 17, 1845), *in* 3 *The Letters of William Lloyd Garrison* 303 (Walter M. Merrill ed., 1974).
Citations in academic footnotes	[52] Interview with John Paul Stevens, Assoc. Justice, U.S. Supreme Court, in Washington, D.C. (Apr. 21, 2011) (on file with author).
	[78] Memorandum from Jonathan B. Perlin, Undersec'y for Health, Dep't of Veterans' Affairs, to Dep't of Veterans' Affairs Primary Care Clinicians, *Screening and Clinical Management of Traumatic Brain Injury* 1 (Jan. 25, 2006) (on file with Fordham Law Review).
	[135] Letter from William Lloyd Garrison to Reverend Samuel J. May (July 17, 1845), *in* 3 THE LETTERS OF WILLIAM LLOYD GARRISON 303 (Walter M. Merrill ed., 1974).
Short citations	Telephone interview with Melissa Mikesell.
	Memorandum from Jonathan B. Perlin at 1.
	[148] Letter from William Lloyd Garrison, *supra* note 135, at 303.

27.1 Full Citation Format for Interviews Conducted by the Author

A full citation to an interview you conducted may contain as many as six components.

Designation | Interviewee's name, | Interviewee's title | Institutional affiliation | Location of interview | (Exact date).

Example (spaces denoted by ▲)

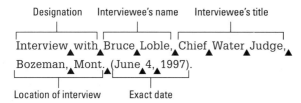

27.1(a) Designation of interview

Depending on the type of interview conducted, the citation begins with a designation such as "Interview with" (for in-person interviews), "Telephone Interview with," or "Written Interview with."

Examples

> Interview with James Jordan, Exec. Dir., Alaska State Med. Ass'n (May 18, 2007).

> Telephone Interview with Leo Katz, Frank Carano Professor of Law, Univ. Pa. Law Sch. (Sept. 18, 2008).

> Written Interview with Juan Tokatlian, Dir., Dep't Political Sci. & Int'l Relations, Univ. San Andrés, Buenos Aires, Arg. (May 16, 2004).

27.1(b) Interviewee's name, title, and institutional affiliation

Following the designation, set out the interviewee's full name, analogizing to **Rule 20.1(a)** for book authors, but using ordinary type. Following the name of the interviewee, add a comma and one space, followed by the interviewee's official title and institutional affiliation, if any. Abbreviate words found in **Chart 12.1**, **Appendices 3(B)**, and **3(E)**, and capitalize according to **Rule 3.2** You may delete articles and prepositions not needed for clarity.

Example

> Written Interview with Jean-Paul Triallie, Partner, De Wolf & Partners, Brussels, Belg. (Dec. 10, 2008).

27.1(c) Anonymous interviewee

Although it is preferable to identify the interviewee, if that is not possible due to privacy or related concerns, indicate that the source is anonymous or confidential, and, to the extent possible, provide a description of the interviewee.

Example

> Interview with anonymous canine officer (June 19, 2012).

27.1(d) Location of interview

If the location of an in-person interview is relevant or would be meaningful to readers, following the identification of the interviewee, you may indicate that location in a prepositional phrase, abbreviating words found in **Appendix 3(B)**.

Example

> Interview with Gordon Matthew Sumner, Musician, in Newcastle, Eng. (Oct. 2, 2013).

27.1(e) Date parenthetical

In parentheses, set out the exact date(s) (Month Day, Year) of the interview. For a written interview, use the date on which the written answers were provided by the interviewee. Abbreviate the month using **Appendix 3(A)**.

27.2 Full Citation Format for Interviews Conducted by Another

If you did not personally conduct the interview, use the format described in **Rule 27.1**, but change the designation (**Rule 27.1(a)**) to add the interviewer's full name, as shown in the example below.

Example

> Telephone Interview by Razvan Axente with Thomas J. Miner, Assistant Dist. Attorney, 31st Judicial Dist. (June 20, 2012).

27.3 Full Citation Format for Unpublished Letters and Memoranda

A full citation to an unpublished letter or memorandum has as many as nine components. As used in this context, "unpublished" means that the letter or memorandum is not available in another publication, such as a newspaper or book; it may nevertheless be available online or may be on file with the author or publisher.

> Designation | Author's name | Author's title and affiliation | to | Recipient's name, | Recipient's title and affiliation | *Title* or *Subject*, | Pinpoint reference | (Exact date) | (Document's location) [or] , *available at* [URL].

Example (unpublished memorandum) (spaces denoted by ▲)

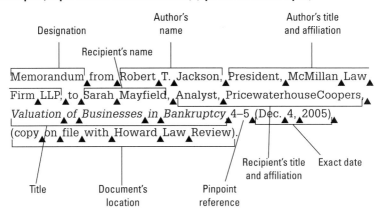

27.3(a) Designation of unpublished letter or memorandum

Begin the citation with the phrase "Letter from," "Memorandum from," or a similar description, in ordinary type, followed by one space.

27.3(b) Author's name, title, and affiliation

Set out the author's full name as shown in the source, analogizing to **Rule 20.1(a)**. Following the surname, add a comma, one space, and the author's title and affiliation, if any, as shown in **Rule 27.1(b)**.

27.3(c) Recipient's name, title, and affiliation

Following the author's name, title, and affiliation, insert a comma, one space, the word "to," another space, and the full name of the recipient, as shown in the source. Follow **Rule 27.1(b)** to indicate the recipient's title and affiliation, if any. For "open letters" and other letters without a named recipient, follow the third example shown below.

Examples

> Memorandum from Robert E. Fabricant, Gen. Counsel, EPA, to Marianne L. Horinko, Acting Adm'r, EPA, *EPA's Authority to Impose Mandatory Controls to Address Global Climate Change Under the Clean Air Act* 4–5 (Aug. 28, 2003) (copy on file with Columbia Law Review).

> Letter from Thomas E. Perez, Assistant Attorney Gen., U.S. Dep't of Justice, to Kamala D. Harris, Cal. Attorney Gen. & George H. Brown, Gibson, Dunn & Crutcher, *2011 Redistricting Plans for California Congressional Delegation* (Jan. 17, 2012), *available at* http://redistricting.lls.edu/files/CA%20preclearance%2020120117.pdf.

> Open Letter from Gregory L. Parham, Adm'r, Animal & Plant Health Inspection Serv., U.S. Dep't of Agric., to Stakeholders, *Reducing Backlog of Investigations* (Jan. 11, 2012), *available at* http://www.aphis.usda.gov/ies/pdf/ies_stakeholders_letter.pdf.

27.3(d) Title or subject of letter or memorandum

Provide the title or concisely describe the subject of the letter or memorandum. Present the title or subject in italics. Use **Rule 3.2** for capitalization. Do not abbreviate words unless they are abbreviated in the source.

27.3(e) Pinpoint references

Indicate, if possible, the page or other subdivision on which the cited material appears, followed by one space. See **Rule 5.2** for more information about pinpoint citations.

27.3(f) Date parenthetical

In parentheses, set out the exact date (Month Day, Year) shown on the letter or memorandum. Abbreviate the month using **Appendix 3(A)**. If no date is displayed, use the abbreviation "n.d." in the parenthetical.

27.3(g) Information for locating copy of letter or memorandum

If possible, indicate a private or publicly accessible location for the letter or memorandum. If it is privately maintained (e.g., in the files of a law review or in the author's own files), describe in a parenthetical where or how readers might obtain a copy (e.g., "copy on file with . . . "). You may abbreviate words in the name of an organization that maintains the source using **Chart 12.1**, **Appendices 3(B)**, and **3(E)**, and you may omit prepositions and articles not needed for clarity. If the letter or memorandum is publicly available on the World Wide Web, insert a comma, then the italicized phrase *"available at"* followed by the URL.

Examples

Letter from Henry L. Stimson, Sec'y of War, to Earl Warren, Governor of Cal. (Jan. 8, 1943) (on file with Army Corps of Eng'rs, L.A. Dist., and copy on file with author).

Letter from Thomas O. Barnett, Assistant Attorney Gen., Dep't of Justice, to Robert A. Skitol, Drinker, Biddle & Reath, LLP, *Business Review Letter re Proposed Patent Policy* 4 (Oct. 30, 2006), *available at* http://www.justice.gov/atr/public/busreview/219380.pdf.

27.4 Citation Formats for Published Letters and Memoranda

Cite published letters and memoranda—such as letters to the editor or historical letters collected in other publications—according to **Rule 20.3**.

27.5 Short Citation Formats for Interviews, Letters, and Memoranda

27.5(a) Short citation formats for interviews, letters, and memoranda

If appropriate, use *id.* as the short citation. For more information on *id.*, see **Rule 11.3**. If *id.* is not appropriate, use the following format:

Designation | Interviewee's or Author's full name | at | Pinpoint reference.

Examples

Full citations: Interview with James Jordan, Exec. Dir., Alaska State Med. Ass'n (May 18, 2007).

Telephone Interview by Razvan Axente with Thomas J. Miner, Assistant Dist. Attorney, 31st Judicial Dist. (June 20, 2012).

Letter from Thomas O. Barnett, Assistant Attorney Gen., Dep't of Justice, to Robert A. Skitol, Drinker, Biddle & Reath, LLP, *Business Review Letter re Proposed Patent Policy* 4 (Oct. 30, 2006), *available at* http://www.justice. gov/ atr/public/busreview/219380.pdf.

Short citations: Interview with James Jordan.

Telephone Interview with Thomas J. Miner.

Letter from Thomas O. Barnett at 3.

27.5(b)(FN) Short citation formats for interviews, letters, and memoranda in academic footnotes

⚠ ACADEMIC FORMATTING

In documents with academic footnotes, if *id.* is not appropriate, use the *supra* format that follows, cross-referencing the earlier footnote containing the full citation. See **Rule 11.4** for additional information on *supra*.

> Designation, | Interviewee's or Author's full name | *supra* | note | [Note number], | at | Pinpoint reference.

Examples

[65] Interview with James Jordan, Exec. Dir., Alaska State Med. Ass'n (May 18, 2007).

[66] *Id.*

· · ·

[112] Interview with James Jordan, *supra* note 65.

· · ·

[178] Letter from Thomas O. Barnett, Assistant Attorney Gen., Dep't of Justice, to Robert A. Skitol, Drinker, Biddle & Reath, LLP, *Business Review Letter re Proposed Patent Policy* 4 (Oct. 30, 2006), *available at* http://www.justice.gov/atr/public/busreview/219380.pdf.

[179] *Id.*

· · ·

[191] Letter from Thomas O. Barnett, *supra* note 178, at 3.

28 Video and Visual Programs; Radio; Audio Recordings; Microformed Sources

Fast Formats

	Video and Visual Programs; Radio; Audio Recordings; Microformed Sources
Movie	*To Kill a Mockingbird* (United Artists 1962).
Television broadcast (episode)	*Boston Legal: Made in China* (NBC television broadcast Dec. 8, 2008).
Radio broadcast	*All Things Considered: Critics Question Reporter's Airing of Personal Views* (Nat'l Pub. Radio broadcast Sept. 26, 2006).
Audio recording	Nirvana, *Nevermind* (Geffen Records 1991).
Audio recording in larger collection	Bob Marley & the Wailers, *I Shot the Sheriff, on Burnin'* (Harry J. Studios 1973).
Microformed source	Rex A. Martin, Cardboard Warriors: The Rise and Fall of an American Wargaming Subculture, 1958–1998, at 202 (Aug. 2001) (unpublished Ph.D. dissertation, Penn State University), *microformed on* UMI Microform 3020503 (Univ. Microforms Int'l).
Citations in academic footnotes	[23] TO KILL A MOCKINGBIRD (United Artists 1962). [37] *Boston Legal: Made in China* (NBC television broadcast Dec. 8, 2008). [51] BOB MARLEY & THE WAILERS, *I Shot the Sheriff, on* BURNIN' (Harry J. Studios 1973). [83] Rex A. Martin, Cardboard Warriors: The Rise and Fall of an American Wargaming Subculture, 1958–1998, at 202 (Aug. 2001) (unpublished Ph.D. dissertation, Penn State University), *microformed on* UMI Microform 3020503 (Univ. Microforms Int'l).
Short citations	*Boston Legal: Made in China.* Nirvana. [64] BOB MARLEY & THE WAILERS, *supra* note 51. [97] Martin, *supra* note 83, at 199.

28.1 Full Citation Format for Video and Visual Programs

Citations to video or visual programs—including movies, television shows, and other visual recordings and broadcasts—consider the nature of the program (e.g., a movie or a television broadcast) and whether the program is nonepisodic (e.g., a television special) or episodic (e.g., a television series). If the program is episodic, the citation varies depending on whether it refers to a particular episode or to the series as a whole. For video and visual recordings originally broadcast on the World Wide Web, see **Rules 31.2** and **33.4**.

A full citation to a movie has three components.

Title | (Producer or broadcaster name | Year).

Example (movie)

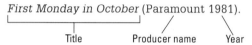

A full citation to a *nonepisodic* program has four or five components.

Title | Pinpoint reference, if available | (Producer or broadcaster name | Type of program | Exact date).

Example (nonepisodic program)

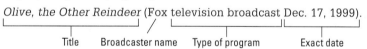

A full citation to an *episodic* program typically has five or six components.

Title: Name of Episode | Pinpoint reference, if available | (Producer or broadcaster name | Type of program | Exact date).

Example (episodic program—single episode)

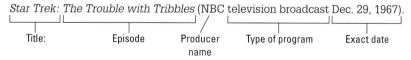

28.1(a) Title of program

Begin the citation with the title of the program, in italics. Follow **Rule 3.2** for capitalization. If the program is episodic, such as a weekly television series or a daily news broadcast, begin with the name of the program, not the name of the episode, even if you will also cite an episode by its title (see **Rule 28.1(b)**).

28.1(b) Title of episode

When citing a specific episode of a program, following the program title, insert a colon and one space, followed by the episode title.

Example

> *Game of Thrones: Mhysa* (HBO television broadcast June 9, 2013).

28.1(c) Pinpoint references

If the cited program makes use of pinpoint references such as scene numbers or timestamps, you may provide that information following the program title or episode title.

28.1(d) Producer, broadcaster, and program/date parenthetical

Following the title and pinpoint reference, if any, insert a parenthetical identifying the person or company that produced, broadcast, or recorded the program, followed by one space. If the program was not commercially made, use the name of the individual or organization that made it. Use any appropriate abbreviations listed in **Appendices 3(B)** and **3(E)** or common acronyms, such as ABC, CBS, CNN, CSPAN, ESPN, and HBO.

Following the name of the producer or broadcaster, set out the date of the program. For a movie, use the year in which it was released. For other programs, indicate their type (e.g., television broadcast), followed by the exact date (Month Day, Year) of the broadcast, if it is available. Abbreviate months as shown in **Appendix 3(A)**.

To cite an entire series, use the span of years during which the program originally aired. If the series is still running, use the word "present" after the hyphen or en dash that indicates the span.

Examples

> *The Paper Chase* (Twentieth Century Fox Film Corp. 1973).
>
> *12 Angry Men* (Orion Nova Prods. 1957).
>
> *Mad Men: Nixon vs. Kennedy* (AMC television broadcast Oct. 11, 2007).
>
> *The West Wing* (NBC television series 1999–2006).
>
> *Good Morning, America* (ABC television series 1975–present).

28.1(e) Transcripts and parallel citations to online versions of programs

If a transcript of the program is available, following the producer, broadcaster, and program/date parenthetical, you may add a parenthetical reference to the transcript's location.

Similarly, if a program is also available online, following the producer/date parenthetical, you may add an *"available at"* citation to the URL of the online version. For programs originally broadcast online, follow **Rules 31.2** and **33.4**.

Examples

> *Face the Nation* (CBS television broadcast July 26, 2009) (host Bob Schieffer interviews White House adviser David Axelrod), *transcript available in* LEXIS, News library, CBS News Transcripts file.
>
> *Tiny Telescope Implant Helps Restore Age-Related Vision Loss* (NBC television broadcast June 27, 2013), *available at* http://www.nbcnews.com/health/tiny-telescope-implant-helps-restore-age-related-vision-loss-6C10474402.

28.1(f)(FN) Full citation format for video or visual program in academic footnotes

⚠ ACADEMIC FORMATTING

In academic footnotes, use large and small capital letters for a movie title, but use italics for titles of television programs and other video or visual sources.

Examples

> [165] 12 ANGRY MEN (Orion Nova Prods. 1957).
>
> [177] *Mad Men: Nixon vs. Kennedy* (AMC television broadcast Oct. 11, 2007).

28.2 Full Citation Format for Radio Broadcasts and Series

Follow **Rule 28.1** for video and visual programs.

Examples

> *The Joe Scarborough Show* (WABC radio broadcast July 27, 2009) (AM channel 77, N.Y.C.).
>
> *All Things Considered: Critics Question Reporter's Airing of Personal Views* (Nat'l Pub. Radio broadcast Sept. 26, 2006), *transcript and audio available at* http://www.npr.org/templates/story/story.php?storyId_6146693.
>
> *The Hitchhiker's Guide to the Galaxy* (BBC radio series 4 1978–2005).

28.3 Full Citation Format for Audio Recordings

A full citation to an audio recording— such as an LP record, tape recording, compact disc, MP3 download—contains four or five components. To cite a single audio recording in a collection, follow **Rule 28.4**.

Performer or composer name, | *Title* | (Recording entity | Year).

Example

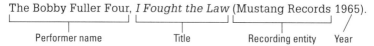

The Bobby Fuller Four, *I Fought the Law* (Mustang Records 1965).

      Performer name   Title   Recording entity   Year

28.3(a) Performer or composer name

Begin the citation with the performer's or composer's full name in ordinary type, followed by a comma and one space. Analogize to **Rule 20.1(b)** for authors of books.

28.3(b) Title of audio recording

Present the title of the recording, including any subtitle, in italics, analogizing to **Rule 20.1(c)** (book titles). Capitalize according to **Rule 3.2**.

28.3(c) Pinpoint references

If the recording makes use of pinpoint references such as timestamps, you may provide that information following the title.

28.3(d) Recording parenthetical

In parentheses, set out the name of the recording entity (e.g., a record company) in ordinary type, followed by the year of the recording's release or broadcast. Analogize to **Rule 28.1(d)** for video and visual programs.

Example

Joseph Silverstein, *Vivaldi: The Four Seasons* (Telarc 1990).

28.4 Full Citation Format for Single Audio Recording in a Collection

A full citation to a single audio recording in a collection (e.g., a single track on an album) contains six components. Analogize to **Rule 20.3** for collected works in print. Follow **Rule 28.3(d)** for the recording parenthetical.

Performer or composer name, | *Title of shorter work,* | on | *Title of collection* | (Recording entity | Year).

Example

> Ray Charles, *Here We Go Again, on Genius Loves Company* (Concord Records 2004).

28.5(FN) Full Citation Formats for Audio Recordings in Academic Footnotes

⚠ ACADEMIC FORMATTING

In citations to audio recordings in academic footnotes, present both the name of the performer or composer and the title of the recording in large and small capital letters. To cite a single recording in a collection, italicize the title of the shorter work, but use large and small capital letters for the title of the larger work.

Examples

> [50] THE POLICE, SYNCHRONICITY (A & M Records 1983).

> [72] RAY CHARLES, *Here We Go Again, on* GENIUS LOVES COMPANY (Concord Records 2004).

28.6 Full Citation Format for Microformed Sources

28.6(a) When to cite a microformed source

If a source is readily available in print, cite its print version. Provide a parallel citation to a microformed version of the source only if it would be helpful for readers to locate or obtain the original source. Prepare the primary citation by following the relevant rules for the particular type of source. For example, if citing a letter, follow **Rule 27**; if citing an unpublished work, follow **Rule 29.2**. Add a parallel citation to the microformed source following **Rule 28.6(b)**.

28.6(b) Parallel citation to microformed source

Create a parallel citation to a microformed version of a source by appending to its full citation a comma, one space, the phrase "*microformed on,*" and the name of the collection, in ordinary type. You may abbreviate any words in the collection name that appear in **Appendices 3(B)** and **3(E)**, and you may omit articles and prepositions not needed for clarity.

If the microformed document bears a unique identifier number or code, indicate that identifier after the name of the collection. If the publisher uses its own system for identifying documents within a collection, follow that system.

Conclude the citation with a parenthetical identifying the publisher of the microform collection. Abbreviate words in the publisher name as shown in **Appendices 3(B)** and **3(E)**.

Examples

H.R. Rep. No. 52-1290, at 3 (1892), *microformed on* CIS No. 3045-H.r.p. 1290 (Cong. Info. Serv.).

Letter from E. Polk Johnson to John Marshall Harlan (Apr. 24, 1911), *microformed on* John Marshall Harlan Papers, Reel 8 (Library of Cong.).

Rex A. Martin, Cardboard Warriors: The Rise and Fall of an American Wargaming Subculture, 1958–1998, at 202 (Aug. 2001) (unpublished Ph.D. dissertation, Penn State University), *microformed on* UMI Microform 3020503 (Univ. Microforms Int'l).

28.6(c)(FN) Full citation format for microformed source in academic footnotes

⚠ ACADEMIC FORMATTING

In citations to microformed sources in academic footnotes, follow **Rule 28.6(a)** and **(b)**, but also consult the academic footnote rules for the original source (e.g., **Rule 20.1(f)(FN)**). For example, if the original source is a book, both the author name and the book title will be presented in large and small capital letters.

Examples

[112] FRANCIS BACON, NOVUM ORGANUM 4 (London, Thomas Lee 1676), *microformed on* Ann Arbor, Mich. Early English Books, 1641–1700, 1115:7 (Univ. Microfilms Int'l).

[194] S. REP. No. 93-690, at 43 (1974), *microformed on* CIS No. 74-S543-3 (Cong. Info. Serv.).

28.7   Short Citation Formats for Video and Visual Programs, Radio, Audio Recordings, and Microformed Sources

28.7(a) Short citation formats for programs, recordings, and microformed sources

If appropriate, use *id.* as the short citation. For more information on *id.*, see **Rule 11.3**. If *id.* is not appropriate, the form of the short citation will vary depending on the type of source being cited. For video and visual programs, radio, and audio recordings, use the title of the program or recording or the name of the performer or composer, followed by a pinpoint reference, if available. For microformed documents, use the short form for the original source, and omit reference to the microformed version.

Examples

Full citation:	Short citation:
Trial by Jury (Warner Bros. DVD 2000).	*Trial by Jury* sc. 10.
Grateful Dead, *Casey Jones, on* *Workingman's Dead* (Warner Bros. 1970).	Grateful Dead.
Letter from E. Polk Johnson to John Marshall Harlan (Apr. 24, 1911), *microformed on* John Marshall Harlan Papers, Reel 8 (Library of Cong.).	Letter from E. Polk Johnson.

28.7(b)(FN) Short citation format for video and visual programs, audio recordings, and microformed sources in academic footnotes

⚠ ACADEMIC FORMATTING

If appropriate, use *id.* as the short citation. For more information on *id.*, see **Rule 11.3**. If *id.* is not appropriate, the form of the short citation will vary depending on the type of source being cited.

For video and visual programs and audio recordings, use the *supra* format that follows, referring to the earlier note containing the full citation. See **Rule 11.4** for more information on *supra*. You may use "hereinafter" to shorten a title.

AUTHOR, PERFORMER, COMPOSER, OR TITLE, | *supra* | note | [Note number].

Examples

[38] REVERSAL OF FORTUNE (Sovereign Pictures 1990).

[39] *Id.*

. . .

[47] REVERSAL OF FORTUNE, *supra* note 38.

. . .

[61] *World News with Charles Gibson* (ABC television broadcast Aug. 22, 2009) [hereinafter *World News*].

. . .

[75] *World News, supra* note 61.

. . .

[109] GRATEFUL DEAD, *Casey Jones, on* WORKINGMAN'S DEAD (Warner Bros. 1970).

. . .

[120] GRATEFUL DEAD, *supra* note 109.

For microformed sources, use the appropriate type of short form for the original source, and omit reference to the microformed version.

Examples

[112] FRANCIS BACON, NOVUM ORGANUM 4 (London, Thomas Lee 1676), *microformed on* Ann Arbor, Mich. Early English Books, 1641–1700, 1115:7 (Univ. Microfilms Int'l).

[113] *Id.*

. . .

[141] BACON, *supra* note 112, at 10.

29 Forthcoming Works, Unpublished Works, and Working Papers

Fast Formats

Forthcoming Works, Unpublished Works, and Working Papers	
Forthcoming works	Steven M. Sheffrin, *Tax Fairness and Folk Justice* (forthcoming Oct. 2013).
	Michael M. O'Hear, *Mass Incarceration in Three Midwestern States: Origins and Trends*, 47 Val. U. L. Rev. (forthcoming 2013) (manuscript at 19–22), *available at* http://papers.ssrn.com/sol3/ papers.cfm?abstract_id=2197342.
Unpublished manuscript	John Asker, Joan Farre-Mensa & Alexander Ljungqvist, Comparing the Investment Behavior of Public and Private Firms 12–13 (July 29, 2011) (unpublished manuscript), *available at* http://pages.stern.nyu.edu/ ~jasker/AFML.pdf.
	T.B. McCord, Jr., John Page of Rosewell: Reason, Religion, and Republican Government from the Perspective of a Virginia Planter, 1743–1808, at 605 (1990) (unpublished Ph.D. dissertation, American University) (on file with American University).
Working paper	Allen N. Berger, Leora F. Klapper & Rima Turk-Ariss, *Bank Competition and Financial Stability* 14 (World Bank, Working Paper No. 4696, 2008), *available at* http://ssrn.com/ abstract=1243102.
Academic footnotes	[17] STEVEN M. SHEFFRIN, TAX FAIRNESS AND FOLK JUSTICE (forthcoming Oct. 2013).
	[28] Michael M. O'Hear, *Mass Incarceration in Three Midwestern States: Origins and Trends*, 47 VAL. U. L. REV. (forthcoming 2013) (manuscript at 19–22), *available at* http://papers.ssrn.com/sol3/ papers.cfm?abstract_id=2197342.
Short citations	Asker et al., *supra*, at 15.
	[38] O'Hear, *supra* note 28, at 20.

29.1 Full Citation Format for Forthcoming Works

If a work has not yet been published but is scheduled for publication, cite the work using the rules that will apply to the work when published, with the modifications described below. Do not use **Rule 29** to cite cases that have not yet been published in a reporter; for such cases, follow **Rule 12.12**.

29.1(a) Omission of initial page reference

For works whose full citation format requires reference to an initial page (e.g., a law review article), when it is not yet available, omit the initial page reference without comment. Do not insert underlined spaces to indicate the missing page number.

29.1(b) Forthcoming publication date

In the citation's date parenthetical, use the term "forthcoming" if the date of publication is unknown. If the date of publication is known, insert "forthcoming" before the intended month, if available, and intended year of publication. Abbreviate the month as shown in **Appendix 3(A)**.

29.1(c) Parentheticals for pinpoint reference and location of manuscript

If it is available, indicate a pinpoint reference in a second parenthetical, using page numbers or other subdivisions from the unpublished manuscript itself.

In a third parenthetical, you may describe the location of the forthcoming work (e.g., "on file with [law review name]"). Alternatively, for a forthcoming work available online, you may indicate its location with the phrase "*available at*" followed by its URL.

Examples

> Steven M. Sheffrin, *Tax Fairness and Folk Justice* (forthcoming Oct. 2013).
>
> Michael M. O'Hear, *Mass Incarceration in Three Midwestern States: Origins and Trends*, 47 Val. U. L. Rev. (forthcoming 2013) (manuscript at 19–22), *available at* http://papers.ssrn.com/sol3/papers.cfm?abstract_id=2197342.

29.2 Full Citation Format for Unpublished Works

Use this rule for sources (other than cases) that are unpublished and not scheduled for publication. Use **Rule 12.13** for unpublished cases. Use **Rule 29.1** for works that presently are unpublished but are forthcoming publications. A full citation to an unpublished work, such as an unpublished manuscript, thesis, or dissertation, contains up to six components.

Author's name, | Title | Pinpoint reference | (Exact date) |
(Descriptive parenthetical) | (Location).

Example (spaces denoted by ▲)

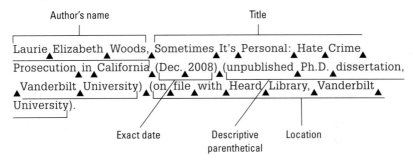

29.2(a) Author's name

Begin the citation with the author's full name, in ordinary type, followed by a comma and one space.

29.2(b) Title

Set out the title as it appears on the cover page of the manuscript. Omit any subtitle unless it is particularly relevant. Present the title in ordinary type.

29.2(c) Pinpoint references

Insert the relevant pinpoint reference, if any, following **Rules 5.2** through **5.4** and **20.1(d)**.

29.2(d) Date parenthetical

Following the title and pinpoint reference, if any, insert a parenthetical setting out the manuscript's exact date (Month Day, Year), abbreviating months using **Appendix 3(A)**. If the day is not available, use the month and year. If the month and day are not available, use the year.

29.2(e) Descriptive parenthetical

Following the date parenthetical, insert a second parenthetical describing the cited work (e.g., "unpublished manuscript"). Describe a student thesis or dissertation with the adjective "unpublished" followed by the abbreviation for the degree for which the paper was written and an identification of the type of work (e.g., thesis, dissertation), followed by a comma, one space, and the full name of the school.

Examples

> Andrew Theodore Urban, An Intimate World: Race, Migration, and Chinese and Irish Domestic Servants in the United States, 1850–1920, at 233–84 (June 2009) (unpublished Ph.D. dissertation, University of Minnesota) (on file with author).

> Christopher W. Bordeaux, Optimizing Nutrient Management and Vegetative Ground Cover on Pastured-Pig Operations 7–10 (Oct. 28, 2010) (unpublished M.S. thesis, North Carolina State University), *available at* http://repository.lib.ncsu.edu/ir/bitstream/1840.16/6532/1/etd.pdf.

29.2(f) Location of manuscript

In a third parenthetical, describe where or how readers can obtain a copy of the unpublished work. Alternatively, for unpublished manuscripts available online, you may add a parallel citation to its URL introduced by the phrase "*available at.*"

Example

> Charlene Y. Taylor, Girls and Boys, Apples and Oranges? A Theoretically Informed Analysis of Gender-Specific Predictors of Delinquency 105–07 (July 21, 2009) (unpublished Ph.D. dissertation, University of Cincinnati), *available at* http://cech.uc.edu/criminaljustice/ dissertations.html.

29.3 Full Citation Format for Working Papers

To cite an unpublished manuscript designated as a working paper, analogize to **Rules 29.1** and **29.2** for other unpublished works, but with the following two modifications. First, place the title of the working paper in italics. Second, in the date parenthetical, precede the date with the name of the sponsoring organization, followed by the term "Working Paper," and, if available, any number assigned to the paper, preceded by the abbreviation "No." Abbreviate words in the sponsoring organization's name that are in **Appendices 3(B)** and **3(E)**, or **Chart 12.1**, and omit prepositions and articles not needed for clarity.

Example

> Frederic S. Mishkin & Eugene N. White, *U.S. Stock Market Crashes and Their Aftermath: Implications for Monetary Policy* 50 fig.8 (Nat'l Bureau Econ. Research, Working Paper No. 8892, 2002), *available at* http://www.nber.org/papers/w8992.pdf.

29.4(FN) Full Citation Formats for
Forthcoming Works, Unpublished
Works, and Working Papers in
Academic Footnotes

⚠ ACADEMIC
FORMATTING

To cite forthcoming works in academic footnotes, follow **Rule 29.1**, but also consult the academic footnote rules for the analogous source in publication (e.g., **Rule 20.1(f)(FN)**). For example, if the analogous source is a book, both the author name and the title will be presented in large and small capital letters.

To cite unpublished works in academic footnotes, follow **Rule 29.2**. To cite working papers in academic footnotes, follow **Rule 29.3**. There are no typeface modifications.

29.5 Short Citation Formats for Forthcoming Works,
Unpublished Works, and Working Papers

If *id.* is appropriate, use it as the preferred short citation. See **Rule 11.3** for more information on *id.* Otherwise, use the short form for the analogous published version of the cited authority. For example, use **Rule 20.6** for short forms of works analogous to books, or use **Rule 21.7** for short forms of works analogous to articles in legal periodicals.

Part 4
Electronic Sources

30 Electronic Sources in General

30.1 General Information About Citations to Sources in Print and Electronic Versions

30.1(a) Sources available both in print and electronic versions

In general, if a source appears both in print and electronic versions, cite the print version if it is readily available to most readers. Types of material that are readily available in print include most cases, constitutions, statutes, federal administrative materials, and law review articles.

While not always convenient to access, print has the advantage of permanence, and that is why it is favored in legal citations. No one can deny the convenience of accessing sources online, but it often can be difficult to find a cited online source, particularly given that web pages are constantly being redesigned, moved, or deleted. Moreover, just because information is online does not mean that it is accurate, up to date, or trustworthy.

Increasingly, electronic versions of sources are exact reproductions of their print counterparts (e.g., the *Code of Federal Regulations* in FDsys, the Government Printing Office's website containing authenticated online versions of many federal sources). But often, an electronic version of a source provides the researcher with a somewhat different format (or even content) than what appears in the print version, and therefore, citations to print and electronic

---

SIDEBAR 30.1   Types of Websites and Indicia of Reliability

Not all websites are created equal. Thus, before you rely on or cite a particular website, consider the following factors, which can help you assess the "cite-worthiness" of a particular source:

- **authority of the author or creator** (e.g., the author's qualifications, the type of organization that created the site);
- **currency** (e.g., whether the site is up to date, whether hyperlinks function);
- **accuracy** (e.g., whether the site contains obvious errors);
- **objectivity and fairness** (e.g., whether the site is biased, the site's purpose (does it advocate a particular position, sell a product, or inform readers?)); and
- **coverage** (e.g., detail, breadth, depth of coverage).

versions will differ in specific ways. For example, a citation to a statute in a commercial electronic database refers to the date through which the database is current, whereas a citation to the same statute in print will refer to the print version's date of publication.

30.1(b) Authenticated, official, and exact reproduction sources

If a print source is available in an authenticated or official electronic version, or if the electronic version is an exact reproduction of the print source (e.g., an online PDF displaying the page numbers shown in the print version), cite it the same way you would cite its print counterpart. Prefer authenticated, official, or exact reproductions of print sources over other electronic versions that may be available.

30.2 Citing Sources in Electronic Format

If a source is available or readily accessible only in electronic format, determine whether there is an electronic format rule for the specific type of source you are citing. **Chart 30.1** provides cross-references to rules for several primary and secondary sources in electronic formats, as well as rules for adding parallel electronic source citations to print source citations.

See **Rule 31** for citations to other sources on the World Wide Web and **Rule 32** for citations to other sources in commercial databases.

SIDEBAR 30.2   **Choosing Which Electronic Version of a Source to Cite**

A source may appear online as a PDF file (portable document format) or as an HTML file (text file). A PDF file reproduces the pages of the source as they appear in print, and it usually displays the page numbers that correspond to the print version. A source that appears on a website as an HTML document typically is not paginated.

If an electronic source is available in both formats, use PDF because it lets you cite specific page numbers. When you print an HTML document, page numbers may be visible, but page breaks may differ depending on the printer used; therefore, do not refer to those page numbers in your citation.

Select sources that have high indicia of trustworthiness. Prefer content on a government-sponsored website (.gov) over the same content on a commercial website (.com).

CHART 30.1	Rules for Electronic Formats and Parallel Electronic Source Citations
Cases not yet available in print reporter	**Rule 12.12**
Unpublished cases available in commercial databases	**Rule 12.13(b)**
Cases on the World Wide Web	**Rule 12.16**
Constitutions published in commercial databases or official websites	**Rule 13.2(d)**
Statutes in commercial databases	**Rule 14.2(f)**
Session laws in authenticated online sources and commercial databases	**Rule 14.6(d)**
Federal legislative measures	**Rule 15.1(g)**
Congressional reports, documents, and prints	**Rule 15.7(f)**
State legislative measures	**Rule 15.13(f)**
Ordinances	**Rule 17.1(c)**
Code of Federal Regulations	**Rule 18.1(c)**
Federal agency decisions	**Rule 18.5(b)**
State administrative codes	**Rule 18.13**
Treaties, conventions, and agreements	**Rule 19.1(g)**
Books, treatises, and other nonperiodic materials	**Rule 20.4**
Electronic journals	**Rule 21.5**
Encyclopedias	**Rule 22.3(e)**
A.L.R. e-annotations	**Rule 22.6(f)**
Forthcoming works	**Rule 29.1(c)**
E-books	**Rule 33.5**

31 World Wide Web Sites

Fast Formats

World Wide Web Sites

Owner identified in website title, specific date	*American Memory: A Century of Lawmaking for a New Nation*, Library of Congress (May 1, 2003), http://memory.loc.gov/ammem/amlaw/.
Author, title, website, specific date and time	Ben Brumfield, *U.S. Military Jettisons Bombs near Australia's Great Barrier Reef*, CNN (July 21, 2013, 12:02 PM EDT), http://www.cnn.com/2013/07/21/world/asia/ australia-reef-u-s-bombs/index.html?hpt=hp_t2.
Blog	Kay Bauer, *Ten Practical Tips for Effectively Using Retained Expert Witnesses*, Lawyerist (July 5, 2013), http://lawyerist.com/ ten-practical-tips-for-effectively-using-retained-expert-witnesses/.
Web source cited in academic footnote	[103] Jeffrey Passel & Mark Hugo Lopez, *Up to 1.7 Million Unauthorized Immigrant Youth May Benefit from New Deportation Rules*, PEW RES. HISP. CTR. (Aug. 14, 2012), http://www.pewhispanic.org/2012/08/14/up-to-1-7-million-unauthorized-immigrant-youth-may-benefit-from-new-deportation-rules.
Short citations	Bauer, *supra*.
	[115] Passel & Lopez, *supra* note 103.

31.1 When to Cite a Source on the World Wide Web

Cite a source on the World Wide Web in two instances: when the source is only available on the World Wide Web or when providing a parallel citation to a source also cited in print.

31.2 Full Citation Format for Sources Only Available on the World Wide Web

A full citation to a source only available on the World Wide Web varies depending on (a) whether the author or owner is specifically identified; (b) whether the website's homepage title indicates the owner; (c) whether the writer is citing the entire website or a specific page therein; and (d) whether the cited source is specifically dated or whether the only available date is that of the writer's access to the website.

Example (spaces denoted by ▲)

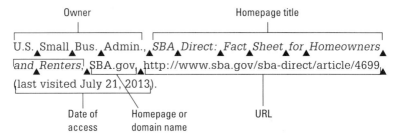

31.2(a) Author's or owner's name

Begin the citation with the full name of its author, or if no author is shown, the name of the entity that owns the website. Before concluding that a website does not have a named author or owner, take time to navigate around the site. You may find the author's name at the end of the cited source, or on another page of the site. If the name of the owner is evident from the website's title, however, you may omit the owner's name.

Present the name in ordinary type. Follow **Rule 20.1(b)** in presenting an author or owner name. For institutions or organizations, you may abbreviate any words appearing in **Chart 12.1**, **Appendix 3(B)**, or **Appendix 3(E)**, as long as the name remains clearly identifiable.

Examples

Name of website's owner	Ass'n of Legal Writing Dirs., *ALWD Comments to the Standards Review Committee*, ALWD, http://www.alwd.org/resources/alwd-comments/ (last visited Aug. 25, 2013).
Name of owner evident from title of website	*Attorney Friends Catch Up While Briskly Walking Down Courthouse Steps*, The Onion (Mar. 15, 2013), http://www.theonion.com/articles/attorney-friends-catch-up-while-briskly-walking-do,31677/.

31.2(b) Title of cited page and homepage or domain name

Following the author or owner name, if any, provide the title as shown on the cited page, in italics, and capitalized according to **Rule 3.2**. To find the title, look for a heading at the top of the page or in the page's title bar.

Following the page title, insert a comma, one space, and the name of the homepage, in ordinary type. The homepage is a website's opening page or main page; it typically provides an overview of the site and it may contain links to internal pages. Abbreviate words in the homepage name found in **Appendix 5**.

If you cannot determine the site's homepage name, use its domain name, in ordinary type. The domain name of every website appears in the address bar of the web browser. While many domain names are preceded by "www" (which is not part of the domain name), others omit the "www" prefix. All domain names have a domain suffix, such as ".com" or ".edu," indicating the type of website. Some domain names end with a country code, such as ".ca" (Canada) or ".se" (Sweden), identifying the location and audience of the website. See **Chart 31.1**, Common Domain Name Suffixes.

31.2(c) Pinpoint references

Indicate a pinpoint reference, such as a page number or a section or paragraph number, if it is a fixed feature of the document. A "fixed feature" is one

CHART 31.1	Common Domain Name Suffixes		
.aero	air-transport industry	.mobi	mobile devices
.asia	Asia-Pacific region	.museum	museums
.biz	business	.name	individuals, by name
.com	commercial	.net	network
.coop	cooperatives	.org	organization
.edu	educational	.post	postal services
.gov	governmental	.pro	professions
.info	information	.tel	Internet communication services
.int	international organizations	.travel	travel and tourism industry related sites
.jobs	companies	.xxx	adult entertainment
.mil	U.S. military		

that does not change when printed on different machines. Do not make up a "screen number," as screen sizes vary from computer to computer. Documents in PDF format appear in the same format as the original print format (see **Sidebar 30.2**). Therefore, page numbers presented in PDF documents may be used as pinpoint references. Insert the pinpoint reference immediately after the homepage or domain name.

Examples

> *Guide to Simplified Proceedings*, Occupational Safety & Health Rev. Commission § 2 (Mar. 2010), http://www.oshrc.gov/publications/proceedings.html.

> Thomas D. Barton & James M. Cooper, *Preventive Law and Creative Problem Solving: Multi-Dimensional Lawyering*, Nat'l Center for Preventive Law 8-9, http://www.preventivelawyer.org/content/pdfs/Multi_Dimensional_Lawyer.pdf (last visited Oct. 22, 2013).

31.2(d) URL

The Uniform Resource Locator (URL) is the electronic address for the source being cited. A URL typically consists of the protocol, domain name, directory, and file, separated by slashes (/).

Set out the entire URL if the address links directly to the cited material. Because URLs often are case sensitive, cite characters as they are presented without changing capitalization, punctuation, or spacing. The safest way to transcribe a URL correctly is to copy it from the browser window and paste it into the citation.

Typically do *not* underline the URL; underlining signifies an active hyperlink. In documents that will be published electronically, however, you may want to keep hyperlinks. Do *not* enclose the URL in angle brackets (< >).

Because URLs can be long, they may not fit onto a single line of text. Break a long URL at a logical point, preferably after a slash. If necessary, you also may break the URL *before* a period; breaking after a period may cause the reader to mistakenly assume the citation has ended. Occasionally you will need to determine another logical break point, such as after an existing hyphen or underscore in the original URL. Never insert your own hyphen into the URL, because the hyphen will look like part of the address.

Examples

Preferred breaking point: http://yosemite.epa.gov/opa/admpress.nsf/
names/ hq_2011-5-16_sdwaecho

Alternative breaking point: http://yosemite.epa.gov/opa/admpress
.nsf/names/hq_2011-5-16_sdwaecho

Incorrect breaking points: http://yosemite.epa.gov/opa/admpress.
nsf/names/hq_2011-5-16_sdwaecho

http://yosemite.epa.gov/opa/adm-
press.nsf/names/hq_2011-5-16_sdwaecho

31.2(e) Keystroke identifier alternative to URL

If the URL is very lengthy, or if it will not lead the reader directly to the cited material, set out just the protocol, domain name, and directory name (**Rule 32.1(d)**), and identify in a parenthetical the keystroke identifiers (e.g., "click," "select," "follow," "path," "search," "scroll down") that will lead the user to the particular page being cited. Place search terms in quotation marks.

Examples using keystroke identifiers

Andrew J. McClurg, *McClurg's Legal Humor*, Lawhaha.com, http://
lawhaha.com/ (from menu bar, select "Law School Stories," then select "Exam Madness") (last visited Oct. 23, 2013).

Karen Sloan, *ABA Seeks Obama's Help in Fight for Reciprocity with India*, Nat'l L.J. (Nov. 11, 2010), http://www.law.com/jsp/law/index.jsp (search website for "ABA Seeks Obama's Help"; scroll down results window to Nov. 11, 2010; follow hyperlink with the article's title).

31.2(f) Date parenthetical

The location and content of the date parenthetical will vary depending whether the website itself sets out a date or whether the only ascertainable date is that of the writer's visit to the site. Provide as specific a date as possible, in the following order of preference.

(1) Exact date of the document being cited

Use this option for dated reports, articles, and other information that will not change once posted. In parentheses, set out the exact date (Month Day, Year) immediately after the homepage or domain name. Abbreviate months according to **Appendix 3(A).**

Example

> Karl M. Manheim, *J'Accuse Twitter*, JURIST Forum (Apr. 8, 2013),
> http://jurist.org/forum/2013/03/karl-manheim-twitter-france.php.

(2) Exact date plus specific time of posting

Web pages that indicate a specific time of posting are often seen with news articles and similar items that are updated over a period of time. In parentheses, set out the exact date and time of the posting immediately after the homepage or domain name. Use the abbreviations "AM" or "PM" to differentiate morning and evening. If the time of the posting includes a reference to a time zone (e.g., EST (Eastern Standard Time), CDT (Central Daylight Time)), use it as well.

Example

> Ben Brumfield, *U.S. Military Jettisons Bombs near Australia's Great Barrier Reef*, CNN (July 21, 2013, 12:02 PM EDT), http://www.cnn.com/2013/ 07/21/world/asia/ australia-reef-u-s-bombs/index.html?hpt=hp_t2.

(3) Date of site's last update or modification

When the cited page is not specifically dated, but the website indicates when it was last updated or modified, provide that information in a parenthetical following the URL.

Example

> *50 State Surveys of Law*, Seattle U. Sch. L. Libr., http://lawlibguides .seattleu.edu/50state (last updated May 6, 2013).

(4) Date on which writer last visited the source.

When no date can be ascertained from the cited page or the website itself, indicate the writer's date of access. In a parenthetical following the URL, insert the phrase "last visited" before the date of access.

Example

> *CODIS Brochure*, Fed. Bureau Investigation, http://www.fbi.gov/ about-us/lab/biometric-analysis/codis/codis-brochure-2010 (last visited Mar. 31, 2013).

31.2(g)(FN) Full citation format for World Wide Web sources in academic footnotes

In documents with academic footnotes, follow **Rule 31.2(a)** through **(f)**, but present the homepage name in large and small capital letters.

Examples

[23] *Report on Nuclear Employment Strategy of the United States,* U.S. DEP'T OF DEF. 3–5 (June 12, 2013), http://www.defense.gov/pubs/ ReporttoCongressonUSNuclearEmploymentStrategy_Section491.pdf.

[55] Nat'l Highway Traffic Safety Admin., *Did You Know Archive,* FATALITY ANALYSIS REPORTING SYSTEM (FARS) ENCYCLOPEDIA, http://www-fars.nhtsa.dot .gov/Main/DidYouKnow.aspx (follow "Trends" hyperlink) (last visited July 8, 2012).

[82] *CODIS Brochure,* FED. BUREAU INVESTIGATION, http://www.fbi.gov/about-us/ lab/biometric-analysis/codis/codis-brochure-2010 (last visited Mar. 31, 2013).

31.3 Blogs, Microblogs, and Wikis

To cite a posting on a blog, a microblog (e.g., Twitter), or a wiki, analogize to sites on the World Wide Web in **Rule 31.2**. For the author, provide the user-name shown for the person who posted the entry, followed by the italicized title of the posting (if any), and the site name (in ordinary type). Add a date parenthetical showing the exact date the cited entry was posted (Month Day, Year) and, if available, the time of the posting (including a time zone reference, if shown), followed by the URL.

To cite a comment to a post, insert the phrase "Comment to" in ordinary type before the title of the post; you may omit the name of the author of the original post. The date parenthetical should reflect the date and time of the comment, including a time zone reference, if shown.

Examples

Lyle Denniston, *The President's Powers Case, Made Simple*, SCOTUSblog (July 11, 2013, 12:29 PM), http://www.scotusblog.com/2013/07/ the-presidents-powers-case-made-simple/.

Anne Lamott, Twitter (July 17, 2013, 12:16 PM), https://twitter.com/ ANNELAMOTT.

Legal Citation, Wikipedia (last modified Sept. 24, 2013, 1:43 PM), http:// en.wikipedia.org/wiki/Legal_citation.

Steve Hubbard, Comment to *Lighting the Fuse: It Is Time to Get Rid of Court Reporters in the Federal Courts*, Hercules and the Umpire (Sept. 16, 2013, 12:36 PM), http://herculesandtheumpire.com/2013/07/19/lighting- the-fuse-it-is-time-to-get-rid-of-court-reporters-in-the-federal-courts/.

31.4 Parallel Citations to Sources on the World Wide Web

To any print source's citation, you may add a parallel citation indicating where a version on the World Wide Web is also available. This type of information is particularly helpful to readers when you are citing hard-to-locate sources. Examples of hard-to-locate sources include wire service reports, certain government reports, state administrative materials, out-of-state newspapers, and foreign sources.

Append the parallel citation to the full citation with a comma, one space, and the italicized phrase *available at* followed by the URL for the online version.

Examples

Frederic Kidder, *History of the Boston Massacre, March 5, 1770*, at 116–17 (Albany, N.Y., Joel Munsell 1870), *available at* http://www.loc.gov/law/help/rare-books/pdf/ john_adams_1870_history.pdf.

Sheryl Gay Stolberg, *In Speech to N.A.A.C.P., Bush Offers Reconciliation*, N.Y. Times, July 21, 2006, at A16, *available at* http://www.nytimes.com/2006/07/21/washington/ 21bush.html.

Letter from Cass R. Sunstein, Adm'r, Office of Info. & Regulatory Affairs, to Lisa P. Jackson, Adm'r, EPA (Sept. 2, 2011), *available at* http://www.whitehouse.gov/sites/default/files/ ozone_national_ambient_air_ quality_standards_letter.pdf.

For additional guidance on providing parallel electronic citations to specific sources, see **Chart 30.1**.

31.5 Short Citation Format for Sources on the World Wide Web

31.5(a) Short citation formats for World Wide Web sources

In practice-based documents, use *id.* (if appropriate) as the short citation (see **Rule 11.3**). If *id.* is not appropriate, analogize to **Rule 21.7(a)**, setting out the author's last name or the owner's name, or if neither is available, the name of the website, followed by the italicized word *supra*.

Example

Full citation:	Ben Brumfield, *U.S. Military Jettisons Bombs near Australia's Great Barrier Reef*, CNN (July 21, 2013, 12:02 PM EDT), http://www.cnn.com/2013/07/ 21/world/asia/australia-reef-u-s-bombs/index.html?hpt=hp_t2.
Short citation:	Brumfield, *supra*.

31.5(b)(FN) Short citation formats for World Wide Web sources in academic footnotes

⚠ ACADEMIC FORMATTING

If *id.* is not appropriate, use a *supra* reference as described in **Rule 11.4.**

Example

---

263 Eric Posner, *The Imperial President of Arizona*, SLATE (June 26, 2012, 12:04 PM), http://www.slate.com/articles/news_and_ politics/ jurisprudence/2012/06/ the_supreme_court_s_arizona_immigration_ruling_ and_the_imperial_presidency_.single .html.

264 132 S. Ct. 2492 (2012).

265 *Id.* at 2501.

266 Posner, *supra* note 263.

Fast Formats

	Commercial Databases
Database citation using unique identifier	William W. Bassett, *Supreme Court Splits on Same-Sex Marriage—Striking DOMA, Shelving Prop. 8*, 2013 WL 3244866 (June 28, 2013).
	H.R. 4310, 112th Cong. § 537 (2012), 2011 CONG US HR 4310 (Westlaw).
Database citation without unique identifier	Sheryl Stratton, *Black & Decker to Settle; Bigger Case on Horizon*, Tax Notes Today, Mar. 5, 2007, *available at* LEXIS, 2007 TNT 43-1.
Database citation in academic footnote	[63] Greg Berman & Emily Gold, *Procedural Justice from the Bench*, JUDGES' J., Spring 2012, at *20, *available at* WL, JUDGEJ database.
Short citations	Fla. Att'y Gen. Op. 2013-14, 2013 WL 3388124, at *3.
	Stratton, *supra*.
	[81] Berman & Gold, *supra* note 63, at *22.

32.1 When to Cite Commercial Databases

You may cite a source to a commercial database when the source is not available in print, or you may provide the commercial database information in a parallel citation appended to the source's standard citation when the source will be more readily and easily accessed in the database. (See **Chart 30.1** for rules for citing specific sources to a commercial database or providing parallel citations.)

The best-known commercial databases include Bloomberg BNA, Lexis Advance, and WestlawNext, but many lawyers also use smaller commercial databases such as Fastcase and Loislaw, and many law libraries provide their users with access to database collections such as HeinOnline.

While the majority of legal sources may be retrieved from these databases by entering their print-version citations into a search box, other sources—particularly those that have no print counterparts—are assigned unique identifiers by the databases, and these identifiers are an integral part of the sources' citations. See **Rule 32.2** for more information about unique database identifiers.

32.2 Full Citation Format When a Unique Identifier Is Available

A unique identifier is a code assigned to a document that will retrieve the document from a specific commercial database. The identifier typically consists of a year, the database abbreviation (e.g., BL, WL), and a document number. In Lexis Advance, you may see a more specific database indicator along with the main database abbreviation (e.g., U.S. Dist. LEXIS, indicating a subdirectory of case law from United States district courts).

If the commercial database cannot easily be ascertained from the unique identifier, identify the database in a parenthetical appended to the full citation. See the second example (administrative regulation) in **Rule 32.2(b)**.

32.2(a) Direct citation to source with unique identifier

Depending on the nature of the source, follow the basic citation rule for the print version of the source, but in place of the print publication component of the citation (e.g., volume/periodical abbreviation/initial page), substitute the unique identifier from the commercial database.

Examples

Article	William W. Bassett, *Supreme Court Splits on Same-Sex Marriage— Striking DOMA, Shelving Prop. 8*, 2013 WL 3244866 (June 28, 2013).
Court document	Complaint, *I Am Other Entertainment, LLC v. Adams*, No. 13 CV 4547, 2013 WL 3297482, at *1 (S.D.N.Y. July 1, 2013).
Administrative decision	*Hispanics United of Buffalo, Inc.*, 2012 NLRB LEXIS 852 (NLRB Dec. 14, 2012).

32.2(b) Parallel citation to source with unique identifier

To provide a parallel citation to a source that has a unique identifier, following the full citation to the source in print, add a comma, one space, the italicized phrase "*available at*" and the unique identifier.

Examples

Newspaper	Robert Dodge, *Bush Learning His Economics from Experts,* Dallas Morn. News, June 28, 1999, at 1D, *available at* 1999 WL 4131653.
Administrative regulation	Nev. Admin. Code § 432B.135 (Supp. 2012), *available at* NV ADC 432B.135 (Westlaw).

32.3 Full Citation Format When a Unique Identifier Is Not Available

To cite a source to a commercial database when a unique identifier is not available, use the following format.

Regular citation for print source, | *available at* | Commercial database publisher, | Database name.

Examples

10 Ind. Admin. Code 1.5-4-4 (2009), *available at* WL, IN-ADC database.

2 J.I. Clark Hare, *American Constitutional Law* 823 (1889), *available at* HeinOnline, Legal Classics Library.

32.4 Short Citation Formats for Commercial Databases

32.4(a) Short citation formats for commercial databases

If *id.* is appropriate, use *id.* as the preferred short citation format. See **Rule 11.3** for more information on *id.* If *id.* is not appropriate, locate the rule for short citations to the analogous print source and adapt it as needed. If the full citation contains a unique identifier, retain it in the short citation, and if needed, change the pinpoint reference.

Example

Full citation: Fla. Att'y Gen. Op. 2013-14, 2013 WL 3388124, at *2 (July 2, 2013).

Short citation: Fla. Att'y Gen. Op. 2013-14, 2013 WL 3388124, at *3.

32.4(b)(FN) Short citation formats for commercial databases in academic footnotes

⚠ ACADEMIC FORMATTING

If *id.* is appropriate, use *id.* as the preferred short citation format. See **Rule 11.3** for more information on *id.* If *id.* is not appropriate, use a *supra* reference to the footnote containing the full citation and change only the pinpoint reference, if necessary. See **Rule 11.4** for more information about using *supra*.

Example

Full citation: [63] Greg Berman & Emily Gold, *Procedural Justice from the Bench*, JUDGES' J., Spring 2012, at *20, *available at* WL, JUDGEJ database.

Short citation: [81] Berman & Gold, *supra* note 63, at *22.

33 Electronic Mail and Postings; New Media Sources; E-Readers; CD-ROMs

Fast Formats

Electronic Mail and Postings; New Media Sources; E-Readers; CD-ROMs	
Private email	Email from Jan M. Levine, Assoc. Professor & Dir. Legal Research & Writing, Duquesne Univ. Sch. Law, to Richard K. Neumann, Jr., Professor, Hofstra Law Sch., *ALWD Conference* (June 28, 2009, 3:20 PM EDT) (copy on file with Professor Levine).
Posting to listserv	Posting of Carole G. Bremen, cgbremen@ gmail.com, to lawclinic@lists.washlaw.edu, *First Arguments in New Term* (Oct. 22, 2013, 13:45 EDT) (on file with author).
E-book	Daniel Kahneman, *Thinking, Fast and Slow* 323–24 (Kindle ed. 2011).
CD-ROM	*Intuitive Estate Planner* (Thomson Reuters CD-ROM, Version 16.2, 2013).

33.1 Full Citation Format for Electronic Mail

33.1(a) Designation of email

Follow **Rule 27.3** for unpublished letters and memoranda, but use "Email from" as the designation. Email addresses of the author or recipient are permissible, but not required. If included, insert the email address after the person's title and affiliation. For the title and affiliation, abbreviate words found in **Appendix 3(B)** and **Appendix 3(E)**. If you must break an email address, do so at a logical place, such as after a backslash (/) or before a period; do not insert a hyphen, as it may be read as part of the address. You may include the exact time of the email (including a reference to the time zone, if available) after the date.

33.1(b) Subject of email

In place of a title, use the words in the "Subject" line of the email message. But as email messages are exchanged, people often forget to change the subject line. Therefore, if the subject line does not describe the content of the email, use a general description instead. If the subject line of the email is blank, insert a general description in place of the title. Present the title or description in italics and capitalize according to **Rule 3.**

33.1(c) Location of copy

Because email messages are not generally available for others to view, in a separate parenthetical, describe where or how readers might obtain a copy of the email.

Examples

> Email from Jan M. Levine, Assoc. Professor & Dir. Legal Research & Writing, Duquesne Univ. Sch. Law, to Richard K. Neumann, Jr., Professor, Hofstra Law Sch., *ALWD Conference* (June 28, 2009, 3:20 PM EDT) (copy on file with Professor Levine).

> [49] Email from Michael Smith to Author, *Background on* Jones v. Smith *Case* (Dec. 14,2008, 7:35 AM EST) (copy on file with Villanova Law Review).

■ 33.2 ■ Full Citation Format for Listserv Postings

A posting sent to a listserv is automatically sent to all of the listserv's subscribers. Follow **Rule 33.1,** but following the name, title, and affiliation, if any, of the person who made the posting, add that person's email address, and in place of a recipient's name, provide the email address of the listserv.

Example

> Posting from Coleen Barger, Professor of Law, cmbarger@ualr.edu, to LAWFAC-L@ualr.edu, *New Scholarly Journal* (Sept. 3, 2013, 3:30 PM CDT) (copy on file with author).

■ 33.3 ■ Postings to Discussion Groups and Forums

Postings made to discussion groups and forums will typically display the username of the person making the post but not the person's email address. Cite analogously to blogs and blog comments (**Rule 31.3**).

■ 33.4 ■ Full Citation Format for New Media Sources

The term "new media" refers to a variety of digital, computerized, or networked information and communication technologies. New media sources constantly evolve; you may need to cite a program in a source that has only recently been developed. If a source you wish to cite is not illustrated in this rule, analogize to the closest rule possible. For direct citations to websites, see **Rule 31.0**. If the suggested full citation format below does not completely work for the source, include as much of the information as possible.

Presenter, Author, or Host, | *Title* | Pinpoint reference | (Owner, Sponsor, or Recorder | Type of source | Exact date), | URL [or] other location information.

33.4(a) Presenter, author, or host

Begin with the name of the presenter, author, or host of the source, if any, analogizing to the author of a book under **Rule 20.1(b)**. You may use a screen name or other pseudonym for the presenter, author, or host, if that is the form of identification shown in the source. Represent the spelling and capitalization of a screen name or other pseudonym exactly as it is rendered in the source. Insert a comma and one space after the name.

33.4(b) Title of source

Present the title of the source in italics or underlining, following **Rule 3.2** on capitalization. For additional guidance, analogize to **Rules 20.1(c)** (books) and **28.1(a)** (video and visual programs). Insert a comma and one space after the title.

33.4(c) Pinpoint references

If you are not citing the entire source, provide a time stamp or other specific reference, if it is available, after the title.

33.4(d) Owner, sponsor, or recorder and date parenthetical

In a parenthetical following the title and pinpoint reference, if any, identify the person or organization that owns, sponsors, or recorded the source. Analogize to **Rule 28.1(d)**. For individuals, use the person's full name. For organizations, abbreviate any words appearing in **Chart 12.1** and **Appendices 3(B)** and **3(E)**.

Immediately after the name of the owner, sponsor, or recorder, add a descriptive term or phrase for the type of source, followed by the exact date (Month Day, Year) of the source's creation or posting. Abbreviate the month as shown in **Appendix 3(A)**. If you do not have an exact date, provide the year, if available. If no date is available, indicate your date of access in a separate parenthetical, analogizing to the last option in **Rule 31.2(f)**, the date on which the writer last visited the source.

33.4(e) URL or other location information; transcript availability

Following the date parenthetical, provide the reader with information for locating the new media source, such as its Uniform Resource Locator (URL) address. For guidance, see **Rule 31.2(d)**.

Examples

David Steinberg, *Surviving Law School* 0:28–1:15 (Thomas Jefferson Sch. Law video Feb. 12, 2008), http://www.youtube.com/watch?v=00tIbgOCYY4.

Emory Law Follies 2013, *Laws Misérables: I Dreamed a Dream*, at 02:56–04:39 (Apr. 12, 2013), http://www.youtube.com/watch?v=IxMxDFbgFzo.

CNN iReport, *New Colorado Gambling Law* (CNN video July 3, 2009), http://www.ireport.com/docs/DOC-290812.

American Experience: The Panama Canal ch. 4 (PBS vodcast Apr. 3, 2012), http://video.pbs.org/video/1747929120.

Martin Sullivan, *Remarks at DePaul University College of Law Symposium on Acquiring and Maintaining Collections of Cultural Objects: Challenges Confronting American Museums in the 21st Century* (DePaul Univ. Coll. Law podcast Oct. 16, 2008), http://www.law.depaul.edu/centers_institutes/ciplit/museum/symposium_program.asp.

If a transcript of the source is available, following the producer/date parenthetical, you may add a reference to the transcript's location, analogizing to **Rule 26.1(e)**.

Example

Ira Glass, *This American Life: Fine Print* (Chi. Pub. Radio podcast July 27, 2009), *transcript available at* http://www.thisamericanlife.org/radio-archives/episode/386/fine-print.

33.5 Citation Formats for E-Readers and E-Books

33.5(a) Availability in conventional media as well as e-reader

Before citing a source in an e-reader format, determine whether your audience will accept and can access that version. If not, the better practice is to cite a more accessible version: one in print, on a commercial database, or on the World Wide Web.

33.5(b) Modified citation components for e-books

To cite an e-book, follow **Rule 20**, with the following modifications. First, refer to a fixed feature when providing a pinpoint reference. A "fixed feature" is one that does not change when the font size changes. In many e-readers, page numbers are not fixed features. Some older generation e-readers have only two font selections. With those, you may use a page number if it is the best way to designate a pinpoint, but parenthetically note whether you used the smaller or larger font size. Some e-readers—like the current versions of Kindle—use location numbers as a fixed feature. You may use the various conventions for page numbers in **Rule 5**—such as citing consecutive or scattered pages—to cite location numbers. Another fixed feature is a chapter number; however, a chapter number may not serve as an adequate pinpoint reference because it may contain more material than you are actually citing.

Second, provide the date of the e-book edition, which may not be the same as the print edition. Because e-books can change more rapidly than books in print, use the most specific date available for the edition, which may be more than the year. In some e-books, it is difficult to discern the publication date from the actual source; in this case, consult the website from which you ordered the source.

Example

Daniel Kahneman, *Thinking, Fast and Slow* 323–24 (Kindle ed. 2011).

33.5(c) Other e-reader sources

For other sources accessed on an e-reader, use the ALWD rule that pertains to an analogous source. Follow that rule as closely as possible, but note in an appropriate place—using the examples above as guides—either that you used an e-reader or cited an electronic edition.

33.6 Full Citation Format for Material on CD-ROM

33.6(a) Availability in conventional media as well as CD-ROM

If the source is available in print or on a commercial database, cite the print or commercial database version, in that order of preference, rather than citing a CD-ROM version of the source.

33.6(b) Citing source on commercially published CD-ROM

To the extent possible, follow the rule for an analogous source in print, with the following modifications. To the date parenthetical, add the name of the publisher and the notation "CD-ROM." Publishers typically update CD-ROMs by sending replacement disks at regular intervals, such as monthly or quarterly. This means that the material is only as current as the update. Indicate the date shown on the actual disk, and, if relevant to the publication, include the version or release. You may represent the date as "current through" a specific date.

Examples

Intuitive Estate Planner (Thomson Reuters CD-ROM, Version 16.2, 2013).

Anderson's Ohio Annotated Bankruptcy Handbook § 107 (LexisNexis CD-ROM current through Sept. 6, 2012).

33.7 Short Citation Formats for Email and Other Electronic Media

For email, analogize to **Rule 27.5** for short citations to unpublished letters and memoranda. For sources in other electronic media, analogize to rules for making short citations in print. For example, if citing a book on CD-ROM, follow **Rule 20.6**.

Part 5
Incorporating Citations into Documents

34 Citation Placement and Use

34.1 Placement Options

Legal citations are used in a variety of types of writing, including practice-based documents—such as office memoranda, pleadings, motions, and briefs—or documents of an academic nature, including books, treatises, and law review articles.

Depending on the type of work, citations may be placed within a document's text or in its footnotes. In general, practice-based documents place citations within the text, although some courts have adopted rules permitting writers to place citations in footnotes.

Academic works, on the other hand, almost always relegate citations to footnotes or endnotes. (Depending on the nature of the cited source, citations in academic footnotes may need a different typeface than would be used in practice-based documents, as explained in the (FN)-marked rules in Parts 3 and 4 of the *ALWD Guide*.) Therefore, the first decision for citation placement is whether your document calls for citations in its text (**Rule 34.2**) or in academic footnotes or endnotes (**Rule 34.3**).

In legal writing, the placement of a citation also depends on whether the cited source provides support for an entire sentence (**Rule 34.1(a)**) or support for only a portion of a sentence (**Rule 34.1(b)**). In addition, legal writers must consider how often to cite sources (**Rule 34.2**). That frequency depends in large part on the nature of the document and the expectations of its readers.

For guidance on ways to indicate the nature and degree of support a citation provides for a stated proposition, see **Rule 35** (Signals). For guidance on using citations to multiple sources in support of a single proposition, see **Rule 36** (Order of Authorities).

34.1(a) Citation sentences

When a cited source relates to the proposition of an entire textual sentence, place its citation immediately afterward in a separate citation sentence. Like a textual sentence, a citation sentence begins with a capital letter and ends with a period.

Examples (citation sentences in red)

"[S]tudents do not shed their rights to freedom of speech or expression at the school house gate." *Tinker v. Des Moines Indep. Cmty. Sch. Dist.,* 393 U.S. 503, 506 (1969).

The federal judicial power extends to certain categories of cases or controversies. *See* U.S. Const. art. III, § 2, cl. 1.

34.1(b) Citation clauses

When a cited source relates to only part of a textual sentence, place its citation in a clause within the textual sentence, immediately following the proposition it concerns, set off with commas. If the citation clause concludes the textual sentence, use a period as the final punctuation.

Examples (citation clauses in red)

Although the Fourth Amendment prohibits unreasonable searches, *Elkins v. United States*, 364 U.S. 206, 222 (1960), each case must be decided on its own facts and circumstances, *Harris v. United States*, 331 U.S. 145, 150 (1947).

Courts have defined the viewpoint variously as that of "an ordinary reader of a particular race," *e.g., Ragin v. N.Y. Times Co.*, 923 F.2d 995, 1000 (2d Cir. 1991), and that of "a reasonable black person," *e.g., Harris v. Int'l Paper Co.*, 765 F. Supp. 1509, 1516 n.12 (D. Me. 1991).

34.1(c) Embedded citations

A citation may be used as a grammatical element of a textual sentence, such as a direct object or an object of a preposition. Such citations are called "embedded citations." When using an embedded citation, do not use an introductory signal. Do not repeat the citation at the end of the sentence.

Examples (embedded citations in red)

In *International Shoe Co. v. Washington*, 326 U.S. 310, 316 (1945), the Court held that if the defendant was not present in the forum, due process required that he have certain minimum contacts with that forum.

The statute of limitations for such actions is one year as provided by 49 U.S.C. § 16(3)(f).

34.1(d) Textual references

You may refer to an authority in text without using a full or short-form citation. A textual reference can be an appropriate way to refer to an authority when it has already been cited once in full citation format nearby or when all the information that typically would be conveyed in a citation is already included in the text.

Example (textual reference in red)

Federal Rule of Civil Procedure 30(a)(2)(A) presumptively limits each party to ten depositions.

34.1(e)(FN) Placement of citations in academic footnotes and endnotes

⚠ ACADEMIC
FORMATTING

In documents using academic footnotes or endnotes, all citations should be placed in the notes. Do not use citation sentences, citation clauses, or embedded citations in the text. Instead, "note reference" numbers inserted in the text direct readers to the corresponding footnotes or endnotes containing the citations.

34.1(e)(1)(FN) Note reference numbers

⚠ ACADEMIC
FORMATTING

A note reference number is a superscript numeral, set slightly above the regular text (**example:** [75]). Each note reference number corresponds to a footnote or endnote containing a citation to a source relating to the textual proposition. Notes are typically numbered consecutively, beginning with the number 1.

34.1(e)(2)(FN) Placement of note references

⚠ ACADEMIC
FORMATTING

In general, insert a note reference for each citation to the source of a proposition in the main text. If a single source relates to the entire sentence, place its note reference at the end of the sentence. If the source concerns only a portion of the sentence, however, place the note reference within the sentence, immediately following the portion to which it relates. When a case is referenced in the text for the first time, insert a note reference immediately after its name. A note reference *follows* most marks of punctuation; however, it should *precede* a dash.

Examples (note reference numbers in red)

Source relates to entire sentence	The Family and Medical Leave Act grants twelve weeks of leave during a twelve-month period to any eligible employee who, because of a serious health condition, cannot perform the functions of the position she holds.[11]
	 —————— [11] 29 U.S.C. § 2612 (2012).
Sources relate to portions of sentence	Although one court held that an interrogatory with multiple related subparts constituted a single interrogatory,[42] another court ruled that these subparts amounted to multiple interrogatories.[43]
	 —————— [42] *Am. Chiropractic Ass'n v. Trigon Healthcare, Inc.*, 2002 WL 1792062, at *2 (W.D. Va. Aug. 5, 2002). [43] *Valdez v. Ford Motor Co.*, 143 F.R.D. 296, 298 (D. Nev. 1991).

First textual reference to case	In *International Shoe Co. v. Washington*,[104] the Court held that if the defendant was not present in the forum, due process required that he have certain minimum contacts with that forum.

---

[104] 326 U.S. 310, 316 (1945).

34.1(e)(3)(FN) Multiple note references within a single textual sentence

⚠ ACADEMIC FORMATTING

Although a document may have more than one note reference within a single sentence, it should not display two consecutive note reference numbers without any intervening text. When two or more citations relate to the same proposition, put them in a string citation (see **Rule 34.3**).

Incorrect example (error marked in red)

In federal cases, all phases of civil deposition are subject to court control;[61] the court has discretion to issue orders designed to prevent abusive tactics during depositions.[62] [63]

34.1(e)(4)(FN) Note reference numbers within quoted material

⚠ ACADEMIC FORMATTING

A note reference number generally should not appear within quoted material because it is not part of the quoted text. If it is necessary to place a note reference number within a quotation, use square brackets around the note reference number (**example:** [[17]]). **Rule 40.3(c)** addresses the *omission* of note reference numbers within the original quoted material.

SIDEBAR 34.1	**Using Your Word Processor to Format Footnotes**

Most word-processing programs have a footnote and endnote function. If you insert note numbers using this function, the program automatically will superscript the note reference numbers, place the notes on the appropriate pages with corresponding text, number and renumber notes if other notes are added or deleted, insert separator lines, and adjust the main text. However, when notes are added or deleted, the program may not automatically renumber cross-references (see **Rule 10** regarding cross-references).

Therefore, if a note reference number changes, be sure always to check the document's cross-references to that note. As a practical matter, it may be best to draft the paper using only full citations in the notes—or short citations other than *id.*—and then substitute appropriate short forms and cross-references for them in the final editing stages.

34.2 Frequency of Citation

Legal writing requires appropriate attribution. Place a citation immediately after each sentence—or if applicable, part of a sentence—that contains a statement of legal principle, a reference to or a description of a legal authority, or an idea, thought, or expression borrowed from another source.

When you refer to material from the *same* page, section, or other subdivision of the same source within a single paragraph of a practice-based document, you may place a single citation to the source at the end of the material. Do not use this convention if the pinpoint reference to the cited material changes. In that situation, use an appropriate short form with a new pinpoint reference.

Example

> An Illinois court has discussed whether a covenant not to compete prohibits a seller from engaging in "any conceivable business activity." *Smith v. Burkitt*, 795 N.E.2d 385, 392 (Ill. App. Ct. 2003). In September 1999, Billy and Brenda Smith entered into a contract with Fred and Dorothy Burkitt to purchase the Burkitts' business. The contract included a noncompetition agreement. In November 2001, the Smiths sued the Burkitts for conducting business in violation of the noncompetition agreement. *Id.* at 387.

34.3 Number of Sources to Cite

The number of sources cited for a single proposition depends on several factors: the type of document you are writing, the audience for whom you are writing, the type and number of sources relevant to the proposition, and the status of those sources in terms of their primacy, acceptance, or influence. A citation sentence or citation clause that contains citations to multiple authorities for a single proposition is called a "string citation." (For guidance on selecting the order of authorities in a string citation, see **Rule 36**.)

34.3(a) Type of document and audience

Academic writing features more string citations than practice-based documents such as office memoranda or briefs. Judges and practitioners who read court documents and legal memoranda typically want to see only those authorities that provide the best and strongest support for a stated proposition. Because these readers are busy, with limited time to read, most do not like to see string citations throughout a document. In contrast, scholars and others who read law review articles and other scholarly materials expect many more citations relative to the stated propositions because the citations provide the depth of reference necessary to understand and master the selected topic.

34.3(b) Number of relevant authorities

The more authorities that are relevant to a proposition, the more from which you have to choose, and the greater the likelihood that you will want to cite more than one to support or contradict the proposition. In such a case, the "*e.g.,*" introductory signal, which can be used alone or combined with another signal, should prove helpful. See **Rule 35** for more information on signals.

34.3(c) Whether the proposition is established, contested, or novel

If a particular proposition is well established, it may be sufficient to cite fewer supporting sources, particularly if they are mandatory primary authorities. (For more information about primary authorities, see **Part 1, section A.**) In contrast, if a proposition is novel or contested, it may be necessary to cite more sources in order to persuade the reader.

34.4 Guidelines for Determining Which Authorities to Cite

The following guidelines will help you determine which and how many authorities to cite to show readers that you have conducted thorough research, while not overwhelming them with too many citations. Begin by predicting the amount of citation and explanation that interested, but busy, readers would want to see. Put yourself in the reader's position. Ask which authorities would be most likely to affect your decision in the matter—whether favorably or unfavorably for your client. Alternatively, ask how you would feel if you made a decision without knowing about a particular authority. Cite and discuss those authorities. Discard other peripheral sources unless you need them to fill gaps in your argument or analysis.

A primary source is more persuasive than a secondary source. In addition, mandatory authority from the jurisdiction is preferable to persuasive authority from other jurisdictions. Remember that primary authority includes more than just case law. Consider whether statutes or regulations, for example, may apply to the issues.

As for case law, particularly if you have limited space, select the case that not only addresses the same legal issue but also is most factually on point. If two or more cases are equally good, typically select the case from the highest court. If the cases are from the same court, select either the most recent case or the landmark case—the case to which all later cases tend to refer.

35 Signals

35.1 Function of Signals

A signal prefaces a citation to indicate the type and degree of support or contradiction a cited authority provides for a proposition in text. Use signals not only before full citations but also before short citations.

35.2 Significance of No Signal

The absence of a signal before a citation is itself a signal, signifying one of three things:

(1) the cited authority provides **direct support for a stated proposition;**

(2) the cited authority is the **source of a quotation;** or

(3) the cited authority is the **source of a general reference in text.**

Examples (no signal)

Direct support for proposition	The Family and Medical Leave Act grants twelve work weeks of leave during any twelve-month period to any eligible employee who, because of a serious health condition, cannot perform the functions of the position she holds. 29 U.S.C. § 2612 (2006).
Source of quotation	Summary judgment is appropriate "if the pleadings, the discovery and disclosure materials on file, and any affidavits show that there is no genuine issue as to any material fact and that the movant is entitled to judgment as a matter of law." Fed. R. Civ. P. 56(c)(2).
Source of general reference in text	The Supreme Court faced the issue surrounding Title II in *Tennessee v. Lane*.[21]

---

[21]541 U.S. 509 (2004).

If an authority is cited for a reason other than one of those listed above, the citation must be preceded by one of the *other* signals listed below in **Chart 35.1**.

35.3 Categories of Signals

Unless an authority is cited for a reason identified in the "no-signal" group (**Rule 35.2**), use one of the other signals listed below in **Chart 35.1**, as appropriate to the type and degree of support (or contradiction) the authority provides for the text.

CHART 35.1	Categories of Signals: Types and Degrees of Support

A signal is a shortcut indicator of a cited source's relationship to a stated proposition. Signals are categorized by four general *types*:

▪ indicating the source's *support* for the proposition;

▪ inviting *comparison* between the cited sources' treatment or conclusions about the proposition;

▪ demonstrating the source's *contradiction* to the proposition; and

▪ providing *general background* relevant to the proposition.

As the chart shows, some categories contain multiple signals. While the signals within that category offer the same *type* of support, the signals' *degree* of support within that category differs. The chart arranges signals from strongest to weakest in terms of their relationship to the proposition and their degree of support.

Signals that indicate support:	
[no signal]	Use when the cited authority provides direct support for a proposition or is the source of a quotation; use when making a general reference in text to the existence of a particular authority.
E.g.,	Use when the cited authority is representative of, or merely an example of, many authorities that stand for the same proposition but are not cited. Although the two periods in the signal are italicized, the comma that *follows* the signal is not italicized. The signal may be combined with another appropriate signal, preceded by an *italicized* comma. Thus: *See, e.g., . . .* *Compare, e.g., . . . with, e.g., . . .* *See generally, e.g., . . .*
Accord	Use when two or more authorities state or support the proposition but the text quotes or refers to only one; the others are then preceded by "*accord.*" Also use to show that the law of one jurisdiction is essentially similar to that of another jurisdiction.

(Continued)

CHART 35.1	Categories of Signals: Types and Degrees of Support CONTINUED
See	Use when the cited authority only implicitly supports the stated proposition.
See also	Use to cite authority, *in addition to that previously cited*, that supports the proposition. This signal's support for a proposition is not as strong or direct as [no signal] or *see*. In addition, *see also* may be used when the cited authority supports a point, but is in some respect distinguishable from previously cited authorities. Consider adding an explanatory parenthetical to the citation, as discussed in **Rule 37**.
Cf.	Use when the cited authority supports the stated proposition only by analogy. Consider adding an explanatory parenthetical to the citation (**Rule 37**).
Signal that draws a comparison:	
Compare . . . [, and . . .] , with . . . [, and . . .]	Use to compare authorities or groups of authorities that reach different results concerning the stated proposition. Separate references to authorities using a non-italicized comma and one space. Consider adding an explanatory parenthetical to the citation (**Rule 37**).
Signals that indicate contradiction:	
Contra	Use when the cited authority directly contradicts the stated proposition.
But see	Use when the cited authority implicitly contradicts the stated proposition. Omit "*but*" when the signal follows another citation using the *contra* signal.
But cf.	Use when the cited authority contradicts the stated proposition by analogy. Omit "*but*" when the signal follows another citation using the *contra* or *but see* signal. Consider adding an explanatory parenthetical to the citation (**Rule 37**).
Signal that indicates background material:	
See generally	Use when the cited authority provides helpful background information related to the stated proposition. Consider adding an explanatory parenthetical to the citation (**Rule 37**).

35.4 Formatting Signals

Capitalize the first letter of a signal that begins a citation sentence. Use lower-case for the first letter of a signal beginning a citation clause. Insert one space between the signal and the citation(s) it precedes.

Ordinarily, italicize signals (**Rule 1**). Do not, however, italicize a signal word that functions as the verb of a textual sentence.

Examples (signals marked in red)

Capitalizing first letter of signal beginning a citation sentence	*See* Ellie Margolis, *Authority Without Borders: The World Wide Web and the Delegalization of Law*, 41 Seton Hall L. Rev. 909 (2011); Jeremy Patrick, *Beyond Case Reporters: Using Newspapers to Supplement the Legal-Historical Record (a Case Study of Blasphemous Libel)*, 3 Drexel L. Rev. 539 (2011); Frederick Schauer & Virginia J. Wise, *Nonlegal Information and the Delegalization of Law*, 29 J. Legal Stud. 495 (2000).
Not capitalizing first letter of signal appearing at beginning of a citation clause	Where courts have been willing to accord judicial notice to facts in Wikipedia articles, they typically justify their actions by stating that the noticed facts are not subject to dispute, *e.g.*, *First Nat'l Bank in Sioux Falls v. First Nat'l Bank S.D., SPC*, 655 F. Supp. 2d 979, 992 n.6 (D.S.D. 2009) (geography and population statistics); *Io Group, Inc. v. Veoh Networks, Inc.*, 586 F. Supp. 2d 1132, 1145 n.8 (N.D. Cal. 2008) (ability of multiple users to share an IP address), or by stressing Wikipedia's value in addressing topics unlikely to be found in traditional scholarly works, *see AVS Found. v. Eugene Berry Enter., LLC*, No. 11 CV 01084, 2011 WL 6056903, at *6 (W.D. Pa. Dec. 6, 2011) (in trademark action, as source for judicial notice of a trademark's fame, citing Wikipedia's coverage of a sports towel).
Signal used as verb	For examples of unprofessionalism in documents filed with courts, see Judith D. Fischer, *Bareheaded and Barefaced Counsel: Courts React to Unprofessionalism*, 31 Suffolk U. L. Rev. 1 (1997).

35.5 Signals for Multiple Authorities; Changing Signals

35.5(a) Same type and degree of support

When more than one authority provides the *same type and degree* of support for a single proposition, use the appropriate signal (as shown in **Chart 35.1**) at the *beginning* of a string citation to those authorities; do not repeat the signal before each citation in the string. Think of the signal as "carrying through" to the end of the string. (For the order of authorities *within* a single signal, see **Rule 36**.)

Example (in practice-based document)

The proposition in this example is supported by a string citation with four authorities, all providing direct support, as indicated by [no signal].	Whenever it has been asked to examine Congress's enforcement of the Fifteenth Amendment's voting rights guarantees, the Supreme Court has approved the use of any rational means to prevent racial discrimination. *Lopez v. Monterey Cnty.*, 525 U.S. 266, 282–85 (1999); *City of Rome v. United States*, 446 U.S. 156, 175–78 (1980); *Georgia v. United States*, 411 U.S. 526, 535 (1973); *South Carolina v. Katzenbach*, 383 U.S. 301, 325–27 (1966).

35.5(b) Different types or degrees of support

When authorities cited for a single proposition provide *different types* or *different degrees* of support, arrange them by signal *in the order shown* in **Chart 35.1**. If the signal "*e.g.,*" is combined with another signal (for example, "*see, e.g.,*" "*but see, e.g.,*"), use the order of the other signal.

In practice-based documents, when the citations for a single proposition appear in a *citation clause* (relating to only a portion of the textual sentence, as described in **Rule 34.1(b)**), separate them with semicolons, even when the signal changes to a different type of support.

When the cited authorities relate to the entire textual sentence, group those of the *same type* in a single *citation sentence*, separating the citations with semicolons, even if the *degree* of support changes. When the *type* of support changes, however, begin a new citation sentence.

Examples (in practice-based documents)

These citations show different types and degrees of support for the single proposition set out in text. The group in the first citation sentence provides the same *type* of support: direct support for the quotations, indicated by the citations introduced with [no signal], and implicit support, indicated by the two citations introduced with	The crime-fraud exception to the attorney-client privilege "is not without its costs." *United States v. Zolin*, 491 U.S. 554, 563 (1989); *see Clark v. United States*, 289 U.S. 1, 15 (1933) (explaining that "[t]he privilege takes flight if the relation is abused"); *In re Grand Jury Matter 91-01386*, 969 F.2d 995, 997 (11th Cir. 1992) (stating that the attorney-client privilege is, as a matter of

the *see* signal. When the type of support changes to background material, however, a second citation sentence is needed, prefaced by the *see generally* signal.

law, construed narrowly so as not to exceed means necessary to support the policy it promotes). *See generally* Edna Selan Epstein, *The Attorney-Client Privilege and the Work-Product Doctrine* 251 (3d ed. 1997) (commenting that "[s]ociety . . . has no interest in facilitating the commission of contemplated but not yet committed crimes, torts, or frauds").

These citations demonstrate different types and degrees of support for two propositions in text, each supported by its own citation clause. The first clause cites authority giving direct support for the first proposition, indicated by a citation introduced with [no signal]. The second proposition is supported by the second citation clause, which contains both direct support and a contradictory authority, prefaced with the *but cf.* signal. Because both citations relate to the second proposition, they are joined with a semicolon. If they were not joined, it would not be clear that the *Nooner* case related only to the second proposition.

A witness's opinion is not objectionable solely because his opinion embraces an issue that the trier of fact will decide, Ark. R. Evid. 704, but in order for such evidence to be admissible, its probative value cannot be substantially outweighed by the likelihood of misleading the jury, Ark. R. Evid. 403; *but cf. Nooner v. State*, 907 S.W.2d 677, 685 (Ark. 1995) (permitting any lay witness testimony that is reasonably based and helpful).

35.5(c)(FN) Changing signals in documents with academic footnotes

In documents with academic footnotes, when citing multiple authorities that provide the *same type and degree* of support for a proposition, follow **Rule 35.5(a)** and place all the citations after the appropriate signal in a single string citation.

When citing multiple authorities for a single proposition from the *same type* category in **Chart 35.1**, but differing in their *degree* of support, follow the order of signals shown in the chart, inserting a semicolon between each group. If the signal "*e.g.,*" is combined with another signal (for example, "*see, e.g.,*" "*but see, e.g.,*"), use the order of the other signal.

However, if the additional citations related to a proposition provide a *different type* of support (i.e., from a different category in **Chart 35.1**), use the appropriate signal to begin a new citation sentence.

Examples (in academic footnotes)

The proposition in this example is supported by a string citation with four authorities, all providing direct support, as indicated by [no signal].

Whenever it has been asked to examine Congress's enforcement of the Fifteenth Amendment's voting rights guarantees, the Supreme Court has approved the use of any rational means to prevent racial discrimination.[23]

---

[23] Lopez v. Monterey Cnty., 525 U.S. 266, 282–85 (1999); City of Rome v. United States, 446 U.S. 156, 175–78 (1980); Georgia v. United States, 411 U.S. 526, 535 (1973); South Carolina v. Katzenbach, 383 U.S. 301, 325–27 (1966).

These citations show different types and degrees of support for the single proposition set out in text. The group in the first citation sentence provides the same *type* of support: direct support for the quotations, indicated by the citations introduced with [no signal], and implicit support, indicated by the two citations introduced with the see signal. When the type of support changes to background material, however, a second citation sentence is needed, prefaced by the see generally signal.

The crime-fraud exception to the attorney-client privilege "is not without its costs."[35]

---

[35] United States v. Zolin, 491 U.S. 554, 563 (1989; *see* Clark v. United States, 289 U.S. 1, 15 (1933) (explaining that "[t]he privilege takes flight if the relation is abused"); *In re* Grand Jury Matter 91-01386, 969 F.2d 995, 997 (11th Cir. 1992) (stating that the attorney-client privilege is, as a matter of law, construed narrowly so as not to exceed means necessary to support the policy it promotes). *See generally* EDNA SELAN EPSTEIN, THE ATTORNEY-CLIENT PRIVILEGE AND THE WORK-PRODUCT DOCTRINE 251 (3d ed. 1997) (commenting that "[s]ociety . . . has no interest in facilitating the commission of contemplated but not yet committed crimes, torts, or frauds").

These citations demonstrate different types and degrees of support for two propositions in text. The citation in footnote 57 cites authority giving direct support for the first proposition, indicated by a citation introduced with [no signal]. Footnote 58 relates to the second proposition. Its first citation sentence provides direct support. The second citation sentence refers to a contradictory authority, whose citation is prefaced with the *but cf.* signal. Because the *Nooner* case is cited in footnote 58, it is clear that it relates only to the second proposition.

A witness's opinion is not objectionable solely because his opinion embraces an issue that the trier of fact will decide,[57] but in order for such evidence to be admissible, its probative value cannot be substantially outweighed by the likelihood of misleading the jury.[58]

---

[57] Ark. R. Evid. 704.

[58] Ark. R. Evid. 403. *But cf.* Nooner v. State, 907 S.W.2d 677, 685 (Ark. 1995) (permitting any lay witness testimony that is reasonably based and helpful).

36 Order of Cited Authorities

36.1 Ordering Multiple Authorities

Use this rule to determine the order of multiple authorities in a single citation following the same signal (also known as a "string citation"). For example, use this rule when citing three cases that all require the "*see*" signal because they implicitly support a textual proposition. Start the ordering process over when the signal changes. (For more information on the order of signals themselves, see **Rule 35.5(b)** and **Chart 35.1**.)

Example

Order signals according to their position in Chart 35.1. Order authorities following each signal according to Rule 36.3. **Begin ordering anew when the signal changes.**	Even if the high-ranking official has personal knowledge, courts will examine whether the party seeking the deposition can obtain the same information through another form of discovery, such as interrogatories. *E.g., Stone City Music v. Thunderbird, Inc.*, 116 F.R.D. 473, 474 (N.D. Miss. 1987); *Mulvey v. Chrysler Corp.*, 106 F.R.D. 364 (D.R.I. 1985); *Buryan v. Max Factor & Co.*, 41 F.R.D. 330, 332 (S.D.N.Y. 1967). *But see Scotch Whiskey Ass'n v. Majestic Distilling Co.*, 1988 U.S. Dist. LEXIS 16531, at *15 (D. Md. Nov. 30, 1988) (denying request that interrogatories be served before top official was deposed); *Matarazzi v. H.J. Williams Co.*, 1988 U.S. Dist. LEXIS 8706, at *2 (E.D. Pa. Aug. 10, 1988) (denying request for protective order that discovering party had to submit interrogatories before deposing defendant's CEO).

36.2 General Guidelines for Ordering Authorities

If a particular authority is more significant than others within the same signal, cite it first, regardless of its type, origin, or age. Otherwise, determine its order in a string citation according to the general guidelines set out below, and more precisely, by the order of specific authorities shown in **Rule 36.3**. Separate the citations following a signal with a semicolon and one space.

36.2(a) Primary authority before secondary authority

Cite primary authority (such as statutes or cases) before secondary authority (such as treatises or legal periodicals).

36.2(b) Federal authority before state authority

Within a specific category (e.g., statutes, cases), cite a federal authority before a state authority.

36.2(c) Cases from the same jurisdiction

For cases from the same jurisdiction, cite those decided by higher courts before those decided by lower courts. Thus, cite a case from the United States Supreme Court before a case from the United States Court of Appeals for the Seventh Circuit. Cite a Seventh Circuit case before a case from the United States District Court for the Northern District of Illinois. Cite a case from the Alabama Supreme Court before a case from the Alabama Court of Civil Appeals.

36.2(d) Cases from the same court

For cases from the same court, cite in reverse chronological order. For example, cite a 2010 case from the United States Supreme Court before a 2007 case from the United States Supreme Court; cite a 2009 case from the Kentucky Court of Appeals before a 2003 case from the Kentucky Court of Appeals.

For purposes of this rule, treat all United States Circuit Courts of Appeal as a single court; similarly, treat all United States District Courts as a single court. For example, cite a 2013 case from the Ninth Circuit before a 2011 case from the Third Circuit; cite a 1985 case from the United States District Court for the Southern District of New York before a 1962 case from the United States District Court for the Northern District of Alabama. A case decided by the Third Circuit on October 2, 2009, comes before a case that court decided on October 1, 2009.

If cases from the same court in the same reporter display the same date of decision, put the case with the highest initial page number first.

36.2(e) Position of case unaffected by subsequent or prior history

When ordering cases, ignore subsequent and prior histories. Histories merely "tag along" with a case's full citation.

Example (subsequent history marked in red)

Dravo Corp. v. Liberty Mut. Ins. Co., 164 F.R.D. 70, 75 (D. Neb. 1995); *Frazier v. Se. Pa. Transp. Auth.*, 161 F.R.D. 309, 316 (E.D. Pa. 1995), *aff'd,*

91 F.3d 123 (3d Cir. 1996); *Ethicon Endo-Surgery v. U.S. Surgical Corp.*, 160 F.R.D. 98, 99 (S.D. Ohio 1995).

36.2(f) Position of case unaffected by publication status

When ordering cases, ignore a case's publication status (published, unpublished, slip opinion, not designated for publication).

36.2(g) Authored materials

In general, order authored material alphabetically by the author's last name. Law review pieces written by other authors should precede all student-written pieces.

When citing multiple pieces by a single author, order them in reverse chronological order. When citing a document written by more than one author, order by the last name of the first-listed author.

When citing material attributed to an organization as author, order alphabetically by the first word of the organization's name.

If no author's name is shown, order alphabetically by the first word of the work's title, but for purposes of this rule, disregard any initial article ("A," "An," or "The") in the title.

36.2(h) Forthcoming works

Place forthcoming works where they would fall if published. For example, put a forthcoming book in position by the author's last name.

36.2(i) Material available in electronic format

If material is available in *both* print and electronic formats, follow the specific ordering rule for the print source (as shown in **Rule 36.3**). If the material is available only in electronic format, follow **Rule 36.3(i)(13)**.

36.2(j) Position of short citation

Position a short citation in the same place that the authority's full citation would fall.

36.3 Order of Specific Sources

Cite specific sources in the order shown below. If a source is not listed in this rule, position it according to its closest analog on the list.

36.3(a) **Constitutions (within each category, cite constitutions from the same jurisdiction in reverse chronological order; cite constitutions in force before repealed versions):**

(1) Federal constitution;

(2) State constitutions (alphabetically by state);

(3) Foreign constitutions (alphabetically by country); and

(4) Foundational documents of the United Nations, the League of Nations, and the European Union, in that order.

36.3(b) **Statutes; rules of evidence and procedure (within each category, cite statutes or rules in force before repealed or superseded versions):**

(1) Codified federal statutes (sequentially by title number, then sequentially by section number);

(2) Uncodified federal statutes (in reverse chronological order of enactment);

(3) Federal rules of evidence and procedure (alphabetically by code name; within a code, sequentially by rule number);

(4) Repealed federal statutes (in reverse chronological order of enactment);

(5) Codified state statutes (alphabetically by state; within a state, sequentially by title number, then sequentially by section number);

(6) Uncodified state statutes (alphabetically by state; within a state, in reverse chronological order of enactment);

(7) State rules of evidence and procedure (alphabetically by state; within a state, alphabetically by code name; within a code, sequentially by rule number);

(8) Repealed state statutes (alphabetically by state; within a state, in reverse chronological order of enactment);

(9) Codified foreign statutes (alphabetically by country; within a country, sequentially by title number, then sequentially by section number);

(10) Uncodified foreign statutes (in reverse chronological order of enactment);

(11) Foreign rules (alphabetically by country; within a country, alphabetically by code name; within a code, sequentially by rule number); and

(12) Repealed foreign statutes (in reverse chronological order of enactment).

36.3(c) Treaties, international rules, and international agreements (in reverse chronological order). Follow Rule 36.3(a) for ordering foundational documents of the United Nations, the League of Nations, and the European Union.

36.3(d) Cases (within each category, in reverse chronological order):

(1) Federal cases (for cases from the same court, see **Rule 36.2(d)**):

— United States Supreme Court;

— United States Courts of Appeals;

— Emergency Court of Appeals;

— Temporary Emergency Court of Appeals;

— Court of Claims;

— Court of Customs and Patent Appeals;

— Bankruptcy Appellate Panels;

— United States District Courts;

— Judicial Panel on Multidistrict Litigation;

— Court of International Trade (formerly Customs Court);

— District Bankruptcy Courts;

— Railroad Reorganization Court;

— Court of Federal Claims (formerly the trial division for the Court of Claims);

— Court of Appeals for the Armed Forces (formerly the Court of Military Appeals);

— Court of Appeals for Veterans Claims;

— Tax Court (formerly the Board of Tax Appeals); and

— Agencies (alphabetically by agency; within an agency, in reverse chronological order);

(2) State cases (for cases from the same court, see **Rule 36.2(d)**):

— Courts (alphabetically by state; within a state, by rank of court; within a court, in reverse chronological order); and

— Agencies (alphabetically by state; within a state, alphabetically by agency name; within an agency, in reverse chronological order);

(3) Foreign cases:

— Courts (alphabetically by country; within a country, by rank of court; within a court, in reverse chronological order); and

— Agencies (alphabetically by country; within a country, alphabetically by name of agency; within an agency, in reverse chronological order);

(4) International cases:

— International Court of Justice;

— Permanent Court of International Justice; and

— Other international tribunals and arbitral panels (alphabetically by name); and

(5) Any other cases, followed by any other agency decisions.

36.3(e) Legislative materials (within each category, in reverse chronological order):

(1) Federal legislative material:

— Bills and resolutions;

— Committee hearings (alphabetically by committee or subcommittee name);

— Reports, documents, and committee prints;

— Floor debates; and

— Any other legislative material;

(2) State legislative material (alphabetically by state):

— Bills and resolutions;

— Committee hearings (alphabetically by committee or subcommittee name);

— Reports, documents, and committee prints;

— Floor debates; and

— Any other state legislative material.

36.3(f) Executive and administrative materials (within each category, in reverse chronological order; material currently in force before repealed or superseded material):

(1) Federal administrative and executive materials:

— Executive orders and presidential proclamations;

— Current Treasury regulations;

— Proposed Treasury regulations;

— Regulations (sequentially by title in *Code of Federal Regulations*, then sequentially by chapter, part, or section number);

— Proposed regulations or rules (sequentially by proposed title in *Code of Federal Regulations*; otherwise, in reverse chronological order of proposal);

— *Federal Register*; and

— Other administrative or material (alphabetically by source);

(2) State executive and administrative material (alphabetically by state);

(3) Foreign administrative and executive material (alphabetically by country); and

(4) Other executive and administrative materials.

36.3(g) Materials from intergovernmental organizations (within each category, in reverse chronological order):

(1) Resolutions, decisions, and regulations from the United Nations and League of Nations (General Assembly, then Security Council, then other organs in alphabetical order); and

(2) Resolutions, decisions, and regulations from other organizations (alphabetically by name of organization).

36.3(h) Case-related materials (records, pleadings, briefs, petitions, in that order; within each category, by rank of court in which material was filed; see Rule 36.3(d)):

(1) Records or petitions in the same case, in reverse chronological order; and

(2) Briefs in same case and court, by party, in the following order: plaintiff, appellant, or petitioner; defendant, appellee, or respondent; amicus curiae (if more than one, alphabetically by first word of amicus party's name).

36.3(i) Secondary sources (unless otherwise noted, alphabetically by author's last name):

(1) Uniform laws, model codes, and restatements (in that order; within each category, in reverse chronological order);

(2) Books, treatises, and shorter works in a collection of a single author's works (see **Rule 36.2(g)**);

(3) Works in consecutively paginated law reviews and journals;

(4) Shorter works in a collection of multiple authors' works (see **Rule 36.2(g)**);

(5) Book reviews not written by students (alphabetically by last name of reviewer);

(6) Student-written works in consecutively paginated law reviews and journals, including student-written book reviews; if no author shown, by first word of title (see **Rule 36.2(g)**);

(7) A.L.R. annotations (in reverse chronological order);

(8) Works in non-consecutively paginated sources, including magazines and newspapers; if no author shown, by first word of title (see **Rule 36.2(g)**);

(9) Legal encyclopedias (alphabetically by encyclopedia name; then alphabetically by topic or title name);

(10) Legal dictionaries;

(11) Working papers;

(12) Unpublished material not forthcoming; if no author shown, by first word of title (see **Rule 36.2(g)**);

(13) Works available only in electronic sources, including the World Wide Web; and

(14) Any other secondary source.

36.3(j) **Internal cross-references (see Rule 10 for more information on internal cross-references):**

(1) *Supra* references (lower numbers before higher numbers); and

(2) *Infra* references (lower numbers before higher numbers).

37 Explanatory Parentheticals, Commentary, and Treatment

37.1 Using Explanatory Parentheticals

An explanatory parenthetical is appended to an authority's citation; it typically uses a participial phrase, a quotation, or a short description to help readers understand the authority's significance.

An explanatory parenthetical is appropriate for use when the information to be conveyed is relatively short and uncomplicated. Explanatory parentheticals can also be useful in providing a set of brief examples to illustrate a rule's meaning or operation. The more significant or complex the ideas represented by the source, the more the writer should consider dealing with them in the text. Too much information—or too many words—in an explanatory parenthetical will destroy its effectiveness.

Examples

Using participial phrases	Very few cases actually proceed to trial. Harry T. Edwards, *Alternative Dispute Resolution: Panacea or Anathema?*, 99 Harv. L. Rev. 668, 670 (1986) (reporting that about ninety percent of state and federal cases settle or are dismissed before trial); Marc Galanter & Mia Cahill, *"Most Cases Settle": Judicial Promotion and Regulation of Settlements*, 46 Stan. L. Rev. 1339, 1340 (1994) (noting that approximately two-thirds of federal cases settle before trial).
Using brief illustrations	A qualifying expense under the Illinois Family Expense Act includes both household goods and services. *E.g., Carter v. Romano*, 662 N.E.2d 883, 884 (Ill. 2007) (doctor and hospital bills); *Armani v. Gucci*, 893 N.E.2d 99, 101 (Ill. App. Ct. 2009) (clothing); *Crocker v. Hines*, 645 N.E.2d 583, 587 (Ill. App. Ct. 1998) (food); *Broyhill v. Lane*, 559 N.E.2d 32, 33 (Ill. App. Ct. 1992) (furniture).

37.2 Placement of Explanatory Parentheticals

37.2(a) Placement in general

In general, an explanatory parenthetical immediately follows the citation to the source to which it relates. In full citations to cases, place the explanatory parenthetical immediately after the court/date parenthetical, preceding subsequent history (if any).

Examples

> *See, e.g.*, 29 C.F.R. § 1910.6 (2012) (identifying various standards incorporated by reference into OSHA regulations).
>
> *Bensusan Rest. Corp. v. King*, 937 F. Supp. 295 (S.D.N.Y. 1996) (refusing to exercise personal jurisdiction when defendant limited its advertising to local audience), *aff'd*, 126 F.3d 25 (2d Cir. 1997).

37.2(b) Placement with other parentheticals

Place an explanatory parenthetical *after* any parenthetical that must be included as part of a citation. For more information, see **Sidebar 37.1, Order of Parentheticals**.

Example

> The court stressed that the Rehabilitation Act "addresses the confidentiality of medical records only in the *limited context* of pre-employment examinations." *Lee v. City of Columbus, Ohio*, 636 F.3d 245, 252 (6th Cir. 2011) (emphasis added) (agreeing with district court that ADA limitations on disclosure of medical information are incorporated by reference into the Rehabilitation Act).

SIDEBAR 37.1   Order of Parentheticals

Parentheticals are common elements in legal citations. For example, most source citations contain a date parenthetical; citations to non-majority opinions parenthetically indicate their authors; omissions to quotations are often noted parenthetically.

When explanatory parentheticals are also added to citations, it can be confusing to determine the order in which to present them. Use the following guide to order multiple parentheticals within a citation:

- court/date and other date/publication parentheticals (see, e.g., **Rules 12.6, 12.7, 14.2(g), 20.1(e), 21.2(g), 22.3(e), 29.1(b)**);
- dissenting, concurring, and plurality opinions (**Rule 12.10(a)**);
- weight of authority (**Rule 12.10(b)**);
- table cases (**Rule 12.11**);
- alterations, including added emphasis (**Rule 39.4(a)**); and
- omission of footnote or citation (**Rule 40.3(c)**).

A case's subsequent or prior history always *follows* any explanatory parenthetical. See **Rules 12.8** and **12.9** and their examples.

37.2(c) Parenthetical requiring its own parenthetical

Follow the examples below if an explanatory parenthetical itself requires a parenthetical.

Examples

> Byron C. Keeling, *A Prescription for Healing the Crisis in Professionalism: Shifting the Burden of Enforcing Professional Standards of Conduct*, 25 Tex. Tech L. Rev. 31, 38 (1993) (warning that "[u]ntil the profession takes active steps to eliminate [discovery] abuses, the public will continue to hold the legal profession in the same moral contempt that it reserves for used car salesmen" (footnote omitted)).

> [362] Inker, *supra* note 350, at 27 (explaining that "[d]omestic relations litigants may be particularly vulnerable because *a spouse* or former spouse can reveal confidential information that will embarrass or otherwise harm the other spouse" (emphasis added)).

37.3 Constructing Explanatory Parentheticals

Unless the explanatory parenthetical consists of a quoted sentence or short descriptive phrase, begin with a verb's present participle ("–ing" form) in lower case and in ordinary type. Because the participial phrase is not a complete sentence, do not end it with a period.

Examples

> *In re Kerr*, 548 P.2d 297, 302 (Wash. 1976) (en banc) (ruling that attorney who knowingly participates in subornation of perjury should be disbarred).

> *Turman-Kent v. Merit Sys. Prot. Bd.*, 657 F.3d 1280, 1290 n.5 (Fed. Cir. 2011) (citing three medical dictionaries for proposition that "brain damage resulting from a stroke is irreversible").

> *See, e.g., Winzler v. Toyota Motor Sales U.S.A., Inc.*, 681 F.3d 1208, 1213 (10th Cir. 2012) (taking notice of the existence, although not the truthfulness, of vehicle defect documents in administrative agency's files).

> *See also* John J. Hasko, *Persuasion in the Court: Nonlegal Materials in U.S. Supreme Court Opinions*, 94 Law Libr. J. 427 (2002) (finding a broad pattern of use of nonlegal materials in the justices' opinions).

When the explanatory parenthetical contains a quotation that is a grammatically complete sentence, however, the sentence should begin with a capital letter, and final punctuation is required.

Examples

> *Clark v. United States*, 289 U.S. 1, 15 (1933) ("The privilege takes flight if the relation is abused.").

> [92] Quan v. Gonzales, 428 F.3d 883, 891 n.1 (9th Cir. 2005) (O'Scannlain, J., dissenting) (citation omitted) ("The majority's reliance on a website of unknown reliability to establish that 'banks in China are *typically* open on Sundays,' is a novel—and, I would respectfully suggest, misguided—application of the doctrine of judicial notice.").

37.4 Commentary About Source or Treatment of Source

A source's citation can refer to another source in two general ways: (1) The citation may provide some sort of *commentary or information about the other source*, such as citing it, quoting it, or otherwise discussing it; or (2) the citation may provide information about *the way another source treats the subject of the citation*, such as indicating its reprint in that other source, its quotation in that other source, its citation in that other source, and so forth. The distinction is important, as the *commentary or information* will be presented in a parenthetical appended to the citation, while the source's *treatment* will be introduced with an italicized descriptive phrase.

37.4(a) Parenthetical commentary about external source

When indicating a source's commentary on or additional information about an external source, place the reference to the external source in a parenthetical appended to the original source's citation, as shown in the examples below. Such parenthetical commentary commonly uses a participial phrase to indicate the nature of the commentary or information (e.g., "citing," "quoting," "reviewing").

Examples

> *Martinos v. Drotko*, 404 F.3d 878, 884 (5th Cir. 2005) (citing 28 U.S.C. § 2254(d)(1)).

> *Tellabs, Inc. v. Makor Issues & Rights, Ltd.*, 551 U.S. 308, 314 (2007) (construing 15 U.S.C. § 78u-4(b)(2) (2006)).

> *Qualley v. Clo-Tex, Int'l, Inc.*, 212 F.3d 1123, 1128 (8th Cir. 2000) (quoting Fed. R. Evid. 201(a) advisory committee's note).

> [61] Larry Alexander & Lawrence B. Solum, *Popular? Constitutionalism?*, 118 HARV. L. REV. 1594, 1640 (2005) (reviewing LARRY D. KRAMER, THE PEOPLE THEMSELVES: POPULAR CONSTITUTIONALISM AND JUDICIAL REVIEW (2004)).

37.4(b) Treatment introduced with descriptive phrase

When a cited source has been treated in some way by another source, do not use a parenthetical. Instead, following the citation to the cited source, insert a comma, one space, and an italicized phrase describing the treatment, followed by a citation to the external source. Such phrases commonly use a descriptive verb and a preposition (e.g., *"cited in," "quoted in," "construed in," "reprinted in," "repealed by"*).

Examples

Kan. Stat. Ann. § 21-3502(1)(d) (1969), *quoted in State v. Chaney*, 5 P.3d 492, 495 (Kan. 2000).

Robert H. Bork, *The Antitrust Paradox* 81–89 (1978), *cited with approval in Aspen Skiing Co. v. Aspen Highlands Skiing Corp.*, 472 U.S. 585, 603 n.29 (1985).

U.S. Const. amend. XVIII, *repealed by* U.S. Const. amend. XXI.

N.C. Gen. Stat. § 75-16, *as construed in Hyde v. Abbott Labs., Inc.*, 473 S.E.2d 680, 686–87 (N.C. Ct. App. 1996).

[81] Gregory P. Joseph, *Internet and Email Evidence*, 13 Prac. Litigator, Mar. 2002, at 21, *reprinted in* 5 Stephen A. Saltzburg et al., Federal Rules of Evidence Manual, pt. 4, at 21 (9th ed. 2006).

[97] St. Clair v. Johnny's Oyster & Shrimp, Inc., 76 F. Supp. 2d 773, 774–75 (S.D. Tex. 1999), *cited in* Crochet v. Wal-Mart Stores, Inc., No. 6:11–01404, 2012 WL 489204, at *4 (W.D. La. Feb. 13, 2012).

[113] Larry D. Kramer, The People Themselves: Popular Constitutionalism and Judicial Review (2004), *reviewed in* Larry Alexander & Lawrence B. Solum, *Popular? Constitutionalism?*, 118 Harv. L. Rev. 1594, 1640 (2005).

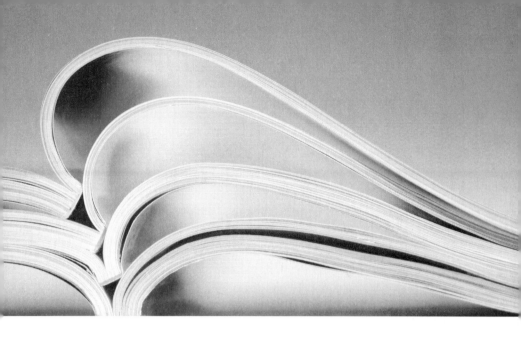

Part 6
Quotations

38 Quotations

38.1 When to Quote

Use quotations sparingly. Reserve their use for statutory language, for language that must be presented precisely, and for particularly famous, unique, or vivid language. Resist the temptation to quote rather than explain in your own words. When readers encounter writing that contains a lot of quotations, they may skip sections or read less attentively. They may also conclude that the writer did not understand the material well enough to paraphrase it.

38.2 Quoting Accurately

It is essential to present quotations accurately. When you quote, reproduce the words exactly as they appear in the original source. Never misrepresent the original meaning of a quotation by altering or omitting words. Do not make any changes to the original without indicating what you have altered or omitted, as shown in **Rules 39** and **40**. To indicate an error in the original quotation, see **Rule 39.6**.

38.3 Quotation Formats

The format of a quotation generally depends on its length. Short quotations (49 or fewer words) are surrounded by double quotation marks (" "), and they typically are run into the text. **Rule 38.4** covers short quotations. Longer quotations of 50 words or more (or quotations of verse or poetry of any length) are typically set off from the text as indented blocks. Use **Rule 38.5** for longer quotations.

38.4 Short Quotations

38.4(a) Enclosure with double quotation marks

If a quotation is 49 or fewer words and is not an epigraph or a quotation of verse or poetry (addressed in **Rule 38.6**), enclose it in double quotation marks, but do not otherwise set it off from the surrounding text.

Example

> The Eighth Amendment's prohibition of cruel and unusual punishment "guarantees individuals the right not to be subjected to excessive sanctions." *Roper v. Simmons*, 543 U.S. 551, 560 (2005).

38.4(b) Punctuation of short quotations

38.4(b)(1) Quotation of whole sentence

When you quote an entire sentence of 49 or fewer words without alteration, simply enclose it in quotation marks, and keep its original punctuation. (For alterations to quoted language, see **Rule 39.0**.)

Examples

> Explaining why juveniles should not be treated as adults for sentencing purposes, Justice Kagan wrote, "Mandatory life without parole for a juvenile precludes consideration of his chronological age and its hallmark features—among them, immaturity, impetuosity, and failure to appreciate risks and consequences." *Miller v. Alabama*, ___ U.S. ___, 132 S. Ct. 2455, 2468 (2012).

> "The Federal district courts shall have exclusive original jurisdiction of all suits to which a China Trade Act corporation, or a stockholder, director, or officer thereof in his capacity as such, is a party." 15 U.S.C. § 146a (2012).

38.4(b)(2) Commas and periods

When integrating a short quotation into text, set it off with a comma only when the quotation is used in conjunction with a speaker identification tag (e.g., she said, the court stated) or when the sentence would need a comma even if there were no quotation.

Examples

Comma follows speaker identification tag	The Iowa Supreme Court stated, "Our rule is that words in a criminal statute are to be interpreted strictly."
Comma required by sentence structure	Under the jurisprudence of the Iowa Supreme Court, "words in a criminal statute are to be interpreted strictly."
No comma needed	The Iowa Supreme Court has held that "words in a criminal statute are to be interpreted strictly."

When concluding a short quotation in text, place necessary periods and commas *inside* the closing quotation marks, regardless of whether they are part of the original quotation.

Examples

Original [material to be quoted in gray]	Every patent shall contain a short title of the invention and a grant to the patentee, his heirs or assigns, of the right to exclude others from making, using, offering for sale, or selling the invention throughout the United States or importing the invention into the United States, and, if the invention is a process, of the right to exclude others from using, offering for sale or selling throughout the United States, or importing into the United States, products made by that process, referring to the specification for the particulars thereof.
Quotation with period	The Patent Act grants a patentee "the right to exclude others from making, using, offering for sale, or selling the invention." 35 U.S.C. § 154(a)(1) (2006).
Quotation with comma	Although patentees have "the right to exclude others from making, using, offering for sale, or selling the invention," 35 U.S.C. § 154(a)(1) (2006), that right is limited by the doctrine of patent exhaustion.

38.4(b)(3) Colons and semicolons

Place a textual sentence's necessary colons or semicolons *outside* the closing quotation marks, even if the language in the original uses that punctuation. In selecting the words to quote, stop short of the colon or semicolon.

Examples

Original [material to be quoted in gray]	Except as authorized by this subchapter, it shall be unlawful for any person knowingly or intentionally—
	(1) to manufacture, distribute, or dispense, or possess with intent to manufacture, distribute, or dispense, a controlled substance; or
	(2) to create, distribute, or dispense, or possess with intent to distribute or dispense, a counterfeit substance.
Quotation	The defendants say that it was impossible for them to "possess with intent to manufacture, distribute, or dispense, a controlled substance"; therefore, they argue, they did not violate the statute.

38.4(b)(4) Question marks and exclamation marks

Put question marks and exclamation marks either inside or outside the closing quotation marks according to whether the writer is using the original punctuation of the quoted passage.

Examples

Original [material to be quoted in gray]	(4) "Deadly weapon" means:
	(A) A firearm or anything manifestly designed, made, or adapted for the purpose of inflicting death or serious physical injury; or
	(B) Anything that in the manner of its use or intended use is capable of causing death or serious physical injury;
Quotation	Why did the State fail to argue that the antique rifle was "manifestly designed, made, or adapted for the purpose of inflicting death"?
Original [material to be quoted in gray]	Having started with "was there clear error," the court then finds itself in the unpleasant circumstance of later lamenting the pointlessness of sending this case back to be inevitably reversed. Surely Congress wouldn't have wanted to prevent an interlocutory challenge to an incorrect ruling!
Quotation	The article describes the court's reluctance to remand the case: "Surely Congress wouldn't have wanted to prevent an interlocutory challenge to an incorrect ruling!"

38.4(c) Quotation within a short quotation

To punctuate a short quotation that itself contains a quotation from another authority, use double quotation marks around the primary quotation and single quotation marks around the internal quotation. If possible, the citation should indicate both sources, as shown in the example below.

Example (quotation marks in red)

The Supreme Court explains that the "enquiry focuses on whether the new work merely supersedes the objects of the original creation, or whether and to what extent it is 'transformative,' altering the original with new expression, meaning, or message." *Campbell*, 510 U.S. at 579 (quoting Pierre N. Leval, *Toward a Fair Use Standard*, 103 Harv. L. Rev. 1105, 1111 (1990)).

38.4(d) Placement of citation to source of short quotation

In practice-based documents, place the citation to the source of a short quotation immediately following the sentence that contains the quoted material. If the sentence contains quotations from two or more sources, however, place each source's citation in a citation clause that immediately follows its quotation. For more information about citation clauses, see **Rule 34.1(b)**.

Examples

> Under the common-fund doctrine in equity, "a litigant or a lawyer who recovers a common fund for the benefit of persons other than himself or his client is entitled to a reasonable attorney's fee from the fund as a whole." *Boeing Co. v. Van Gemert*, 444 U.S. 472, 478 (1980).

> Courts may vacate an arbitrator's decision "only in very unusual circumstances," *First Options of Chi., Inc. v. Kaplan*, 514 U.S. 938, 942 (1995), in a limited judicial review that "maintain[s] arbitration's essential virtue of resolving disputes straightaway," *Hall St. Assocs., L.L.C. v. Mattel, Inc.*, 552 U.S. 576, 588 (2008).

38.4(e)(FN) Placement of citation to source of short quotation in academic footnotes

⚠ ACADEMIC FORMATTING

In documents with academic footnotes, place the note reference number for the citation to the source of a short quotation immediately after its closing quotation marks. If a sentence contains quotations from different sources, place the note reference number for each cited source immediately following its quotation's closing quotation marks.

Examples

> Under the common-fund doctrine in equity, "a litigant or a lawyer who recovers a common fund for the benefit of persons other than himself or his client is entitled to a reasonable attorney's fee from the fund as a whole."[17]

> ---
>
> [17] Boeing Co. v. Van Gemert, 444 U.S. 472, 478 (1980).

> Courts may vacate an arbitrator's decision "only in very unusual circumstances,"[32] in a limited judicial review that "maintain[s] arbitration's essential virtue of resolving disputes straightaway."[33]

> ---
>
> [32] First Options of Chi., Inc. v. Kaplan, 514 U.S. 938, 942 (1995).

> [33] Hall St. Assocs., L.L.C. v. Mattel, Inc., 552 U.S. 576, 588 (2008).

38.4(f) Source of quotation identified in sentence

If the quotation's source can be identified from material within the sentence in which the quotation is placed, a duplicative citation to the source following the sentence is not needed.

Example

> Under Federal Rule of Evidence 803(2), an out-of-court statement is admissible as an excited utterance if the statement "relat[es] to a startling event or condition made while the declarant was under the stress of excitement caused by the event or condition."

38.5 Long Quotations

38.5(a) Block format

If a quotation contains at least fifty words, or if the material quoted is a verse, poem, or epigraph (**Rule 38.6**), present the quotation in a single-spaced block indented by one tab on both the right and the left. Do not use quotation marks around a block quotation. Separate the block quotation from the text above and below it with a blank line, creating a frame of white space around the block.

Example

> In fact, the Court recognized that freedom of speech
>
>> may indeed best serve its high purpose when it induces a condition of unrest, creates dissatisfaction with conditions as they are, or even stirs people to anger. Speech is often provocative and challenging. It may strike at prejudices and preconceptions and have profound unsettling effects as it presses for acceptance of an idea. That is why freedom of speech, though not absolute, is nevertheless protected against censorship or punishment, unless shown likely to produce a clear and present danger of a serious substantive evil that rises far above public inconvenience, annoyance, or unrest. There is no room under our Constitution for a more restrictive view.
>
> *Terminiello v. City of Chi.*, 337 U.S. 1, 4–5 (1949) (internal citations omitted).

38.5(b) Quotation within a block-format quotation

If a block-format quotation contains a quotation from another authority, punctuate it exactly as it appears in the original, enclosing the internal quotation in double quotation marks. Enclose quotations within these quotations (sometimes described as "nested quotations") in single quotation marks. Follow punctuation conventions described in **Rule 38.4(b)**. If possible, the citation should indicate both sources, as shown in the examples below.

Examples

> Not all agree on the constitutionality of incitement-to-riot statutes:
>
>> It may seem entirely reasonable to have a law against inciting a riot. The Supreme Court itself said in dicta that "[n]o one would have the hardihood to suggest that the principle of freedom of speech sanctions incitement to riot . . . ." But that comment depends on a limited understanding of incitement, and a limited understanding of riot. If "riot" is defined broadly—which it often is—and "incitement" is not defined at all—which it often is not—then incitement to riot can sweep in innocuous or even socially beneficial activity.
>
> Margot E. Kaminski, *Incitement to Riot in the Age of Flash Mobs*, 81 U. Cin. L. Rev. 1, 8 (2012) (quoting *Cantwell v. Connecticut*, 310 U.S. 296, 308 (1940)).

> When Roger Taney was Attorney General of the United States, he was asked whether the president could lawfully direct federal prosecutors to discontinue an action involving stolen jewels.
>
>> According to Taney, presidential direction of prosecutions occurred with some regularity in the early years of our Constitution. But Taney's reasoning went beyond the context of a criminal prosecution. The President's authority did not derive from the pardon power; rather, his authority was "embraced by that clause of the constitution which makes it his duty 'to [sic] take care that the laws be faithfully executed.' "
>
> Kate Andrias, *The President's Enforcement Power*, 88 N.Y.U. L. Rev. 1031, 1053 (2013) (quoting 2 Op. Att'y Gen. at 486 (quoting U.S. Const. art. II, § 3)).

38.5(c) Long quotations in parentheticals

When presenting a long quotation in a parenthetical, do not use block formatting. Instead, prevent reader confusion by enclosing the quotation in double quotation marks. For more information on using parentheticals, see **Rule 37**.

Example

> 4 U.S.C. § 110 (2012) (defining "Federal area" as "any lands or premises held or acquired by or for the use of the United States or any department, establishment, or agency, of the United States; and any Federal area, or any part thereof, which is located within the exterior boundaries of any State").

38.5(d) Paragraphing within block-format quotations

In long quotations, retain the original source's paragraphing. If a long quotation comes from the beginning of a paragraph, block indent the whole paragraph, but further indent the first line. If a long quotation spans multiple paragraphs, reflect the original paragraph breaks by indenting the first line of each quoted paragraph.

Example

There is reason to question that approach:

> The categorical approach to admitting hearsay relies on the
> use of external generalizations. The categorical exceptions are
> substantive generalizations not formulated by the trier of fact,
> but drafted by judges and legislators to represent their collective
> beliefs about what kinds of hearsay statements are more
> likely to be reliable. All hearsay that does not conform to these
> generalizations about reliability is excluded from the trier of fact.
>
> However, there is little support for the claim that the
> categorical approach admits individual items of hearsay that are
> more reliable than the items it excludes. First, the categorical
> generalizations about what enhances the reliability of hearsay
> are unvalidated. We lack systematic empirical research about
> how the testimonial circumstances of declarants actually affect
> reliability. The research conducted on a few exceptions flatly
> contradicts their underlying assumptions about enhanced
> reliability of perception, memory, and sincerity.

Eleanor Swift, *A Foundation Fact Approach to Hearsay*, 75 Cal. L. Rev.
1339, 1351 (1987).

38.5(e) Placement of citation to source of quotation

The citation to the source of a long quotation is not part of the quoted material; therefore, do not place the source's citation within the block. In practice-
based documents, return to regular margins and line spacing, and place the
citation at the left margin on the first line of text beneath the block. If you do
not want to start a new paragraph after the citation, simply continue the text
on the same line as the citation.

Example

Some crimes must be charged with greater specificity. As the Supreme
Court has explained,

> [T]he very core of criminality under 2 U.S.C. § 192 is pertinency to
> the subject under inquiry of the questions which the defendant
> refused to answer. What the subject actually was, therefore,
> is central to every prosecution under the statute. Where guilt
> depends so crucially upon such a specific identification of fact,
> our cases have uniformly held that an indictment must do more
> than simply repeat the language of the criminal statute.

Russell v. United States, 369 U.S. 749, 764 (1962).

When a block quotation itself contains a quotation, you may place the
internal quotation source's citation in a parenthetical following the citation for
the main quotation.

Example

> These days, "friends" do not necessarily live in the same locale:
>
>> It is not that communities are disappearing; they are simply
>> transforming—traditional neighborhood and small-community
>> groups giving way to social networks that defy location, but
>> include vigorous, nourishing, deeply personal relationships.
>> These networks are thriving as a result of the human need to
>> "preserve the benefits of community in a more splintered world:
>> remaining connected in our relationships, creating and retaining
>> common experience, engaging peer opinion, and building
>> reputation."
>
> Kristin R. Brown, Comment, *Somebody Poisoned the Jury Pool: Social
> Media's Effect on Jury Impartiality*, 19 Tex. Wesleyan L. Rev. 809, 814–15
> (2013) (quoting H. Brian Holland, *Privacy Paradox 2.0*, 19 Widener L.J.
> 893, 918 (2010)).

However, if the source of an internal quotation is cited within the larger
quotation, retain the citation within the quotation, and do not repeat it in a
parenthetical to the citation for the main quotation.

Example

> Although the Court rejected the position cited in *Hildwin*, it
> characterized the nature of capital sentencing by quoting *Poland
> v. Arizona*, 476 U.S. 147, 156 (1986). In that case, the Court
> described statutory specifications or aggravating circumstances
> in capital sentences as "standards to guide the . . . choice
> between the alternative verdicts of death and life imprisonment."
> *Id.* The Court thus characterized the finding of aggravating facts
> as a choice between a greater and lesser penalty, not a process of
> raising the ceiling of the sentencing range available.
>
> *Jones v. United States*, 526 U.S. 227, 251 (1999).

38.5(f)(FN) Placement of citation to source of quotation in academic footnotes

⚠ ACADEMIC FORMATTING

In documents with academic footnotes, place the note reference number at the
end of the block quotation.

If a block quotation contains an internal quotation, place the citation to the
source of the internal quotation in a parenthetical appended to the citation for
the block quotation.

Examples

> Some crimes must be charged with greater specificity. As the Supreme
> Court has explained,
>
>> [T]he very core of criminality under 2 U.S.C. § 192 is pertinency
>> to the subject under inquiry of the questions which the

defendant refused to answer. What the subject actually was, therefore, is central to every prosecution under the statute. Where guilt depends so crucially upon such a specific identification of fact, our cases have uniformly held that an indictment must do more than simply repeat the language of the criminal statute.[18]

Indictments that fail to specifically identify the facts upon . . .

---

[18] Russell v. United States, 369 U.S. 749, 764 (1962).

These days, "friends" do not necessarily live in the same locale:

It is not that communities are disappearing; they are simply transforming—traditional neighborhood and small-community groups giving way to social networks that defy location, but include vigorous, nourishing, deeply personal relationships. These networks are thriving as a result of the human need to "preserve the benefits of community in a more splintered world: remaining connected in our relationships, creating and retaining common experience, engaging peer opinion, and building reputation."[27]

More important than locale are our networks, and therefore, . . .

---

[27] Kristin R. Brown, Comment, *Somebody Poisoned the Jury Pool: Social Media's Effect on Jury Impartiality*, 19 TEX. WESLEYAN L. REV. 809, 814–15 (2013) (quoting H. Brian Holland, *Privacy Paradox 2.0*, 19 WIDENER L.J. 893, 918 (2010)).

38.6 Epigraphs

An epigraph is a quotation set at the beginning of a work or chapter. Do not place an epigraph in quotation marks, regardless of its length. Format an epigraph as a block quotation under **Rule 38.5(a).**

38.6(a) Placement of citation to source of epigraph

In practice-based documents, place the citation to the source of the epigraph underneath the quotation, flush right. Skip one line between the epigraph and the citation. Single-space the citation if it does not fit on a single line. You may place an em dash (—) before the citation.

Example

This scarecrow of a suit has, in course of time, become so complicated, that no man alive knows what it means.

—Charles Dickens, *Bleak House* 14 (Stephen Gill ed., Oxford Univ. Press 2008) (1853).

38.6(b)(FN) Placement of citation to source of epigraph in academic footnotes

⚠ ACADEMIC FORMATTING

In documents with academic footnotes, place the note reference number after the epigraph, and set out the source's citation in the corresponding footnote.

Example

> This scarecrow of a suit has, in course of time, become so complicated, that no man alive knows what it means.[1]

---

[1] CHARLES DICKENS, BLEAK HOUSE 14 (Stephen Gill ed., Oxford Univ. Press 2008) (1853).

39 Altering Quotations

39.1 Altering the Case of a Single Letter in a Word

Within a quotation, when changing a letter from uppercase to lowercase, or vice versa, enclose the altered letter in square brackets.

Examples

Original:	Alteration:
"The court held . . . ."	Moreover, "[t]he court held . . . ."
"In the latter event, the court shall permit the parties or their attorneys to supplement the examination by such further inquiry as it deems appropriate . . . ."	"[T]he court shall permit the parties or their attorneys to supplement the examination by such further inquiry as it deems appropriate . . . ."

39.2 Adding, Changing, or Omitting One or More Letters in a Word

When adding, changing, or deleting one or more letters in a quoted word, enclose the added, changed, or deleted letters in square brackets. Alternatively, replace the entire word, as described in **Rule 39.3**. Indicate the omission of one or more letters with empty brackets.

Examples

Original:	Alterations:
state	state[d], stat[ing], state[s] **or** [stated], [stating], [states]
held	h[o]ld **or** [hold]
the employee was	the employee[s were] **or** the [employees were]
the courts indicated	the court[ ] indicated **or** the [court] indicated

39.3 Substituting or Adding Words to a Quotation

When substituting or adding words to a quotation, enclose the substituted or new words in square brackets. For example, you may add material to clarify an ambiguity, to supply a missing word, or to provide necessary explanations or translations.

Examples

Original:	**Alteration:**
"The court ruled for Mr. Jamison."	"The court ruled for [the defendant]."
"He found it there."	"He found it [by the door]."

39.4   Altering Typeface in a Quotation

Sometimes your only change to a quotation is an alteration of its typeface, such as italicizing certain words, or putting certain language in bold. Or you may desire to substitute ordinary type for words that appeared in another typeface in the original. Do not use brackets around words that have merely undergone a typeface change, but rather, indicate the changes parenthetically, as described below.

39.4(a)   Parenthetical description of alteration

When altering the typeface of quoted material, such as creating emphasis by italicizing certain words, simply describe the alteration in a parenthetical that follows the citation (e.g., "emphasis added") rather than enclose the changed words in brackets. It is not necessary to parenthetically indicate emphasis in the original (but see **Rule 39.4(b)** for handling original and added emphasis in a single quotation).

Example

Original:

> We think a "permanent physical occupation" has occurred, for purposes of this rule, where individuals are given a permanent and continuous right to pass to and fro, so that the real property may continuously be traversed, even though no particular individual is permitted to station himself permanently upon the premises.

Nollan v. Cal. Coastal Comm'n, 483 U.S. 825, 832 (1987).

Alteration:

> We think a "permanent physical occupation" has occurred, for purposes of this rule, where individuals are given a *permanent and continuous right to pass to and fro*, so that the real property may continuously be traversed, even though no particular individual is permitted to station himself permanently upon the premises.

Nollan v. Cal. Coastal Comm'n, 483 U.S. 825, 832 (1987) (emphasis added).

39.4(b)   Distinguishing original and added emphasis

When a quotation contains two or more instances of emphasis, some of which was in the original and some of which was added, parenthetically indicate which emphasis was added. If it would be helpful to readers, you may also indicate which emphasis was in the original.

Example

> In *Shaw v. Reno,* 509 U.S. 630 (1993), Justice O'Connor, writing for the majority, described the relationship between race and redistricting:
>
>> [R]edistricting differs from other kinds of state decisionmaking in that the legislature always is aware of race when it draws district lines, just as it is *aware* of age, economic status, religious and political persuasion, and a variety of other demographic factors. That sort of race consciousness does not lead *inevitably* to impermissible race discrimination.
>
> *Id.* at 646 (first emphasis in original, second emphasis added).

39.5(FN) Adding a Footnote Within a Block Quotation

⚠ ACADEMIC FORMATTING

As explained in **Rule 38.5(f)(FN)**, in documents with academic footnotes, typically insert a note reference number *at the end* of a block quotation. Although unusual, it is on occasion necessary or desirable to add a note reference number *within* a block quotation. When this situation occurs, enclose the superscripted note reference number in square brackets.

Example

> We recognize, as does *Clayton,* that absent a constitutional basis for a challenge,[3] the . . . standing rule, applied to cases of this type,[4] creates a rare situation [where] there is a wrong without a remedy. That is because even though the citizen taxpayer, who is also a voter, may "throw the rascals out" at the next election, even if such action exacts a measure of retribution it will not restore the looted treasury nor undo the illegally increased tax obligation.[5]

39.6 Indicating Mistakes Within Original Source

An original source may contain mistakes, such as spelling, typographical, or grammatical errors. In quoting such a source, it is your choice whether to correct the mistake or to indicate that the mistake appeared in the original.

If you wish to correct the mistake, enclose your correction in square brackets as described in **Rules 39.2** and **39.3.** If you wish to retain the mistake but indicate that it appeared in the original (and is thus not attributable to you), insert the bracketed term "[sic]" immediately after the word containing the mistake. When quoting obviously archaic or nonstandard writing, you may dispense with inserting [sic] or making other alterations.

Examples

Alternative 1: Correcting the mistake

Original:	Alteration:
"The court dismissed there motion."	"The court dismissed [their] motion."
"The court hold that"	"The court h[e]ld that" or "The court[s] hold that"

Alternative 2: Using [sic]

Original:	Alteration:
"The court dismissed there motion."	"The court dismissed there [sic] motion."
"The court hold that"	"The court hold [sic] that"

40 Indicating Omissions in Quotations

40.1 Indicating Omissions with an Ellipsis

An ellipsis in a quotation alerts readers that one or more words—and perhaps even several sentences or paragraphs—have been omitted from the original. To indicate an omitted *letter* within a single word, use empty square brackets (**Rule 39.2**).

Type an ellipsis as three spaced points (periods), as shown in the examples below. Insert spaces between the ellipsis points; to do so, you may need to override your word processor's default settings. Do not allow ellipsis points to break across a line; think of the spaces between them as the glue that holds them together. Use your word processor to insert a nonbreaking space (also referred to as a "hard space") between the points.

A space always precedes an ellipsis. In most instances, a space follows an ellipsis. However, when quotation marks immediately follow an ellipsis, omit the space between the last ellipsis point and the closing quotation mark (▲·▲·▲.").

Examples (spaces denoted by ▲)

Correct uses of ellipsis	"The Federal Rules of Evidence explicitly recognize ▲·▲·▲·▲that treatises can be established as reliable authority▲·▲·▲·▲by judicial notice." *United States v. Norman*, 415 F.3d 466, 473 (5th Cir. 2005) (citing Fed. R. Evid. 803(18)).
Incorrect uses of ellipsis	"The Federal Rules of Evidence explicitly recognize▲·▲·. ▲·▲that treatises can be established as reliable authority▲. ▲·▲·▲by judicial notice." United *States v. Norman*, 415 F.3d 466, 473 (5th Cir. 2005) (citing Fed. R. Evid. 803(18)).

40.2 When to Use an Ellipsis

40.2(a) Omission of words within a quoted sentence

When you omit one word or a group of words from a quoted passage, insert an ellipsis to indicate the omission. For omissions of internal citations or footnotes from a quoted passage, see **Rule 40.3(c)**.

Example (spaces denoted by ▲)

Original passage	This implicit license typically permits the visitor to approach the home by the front path, knock promptly, wait briefly to be received, and then (absent invitation to linger longer) leave. *Florida v. Jardines*, ___ U.S. ___, 133 S. Ct. 1409, 1416 (2013).
Quotation	While custom and tradition invite "the visitor to approach the home by the front path, knock promptly, wait briefly to be received, and then▲.▲.▲.▲leave," *Florida v. Jardines*, ___ U.S. ___, 133 S. Ct. 1409, 1416 (2013), they do not permit greater intrusion without a warrant.

40.2(b) Omission of words from end of quoted sentence

When omitting one or more words from the end of a quoted sentence, insert an ellipsis, followed by the sentence's final punctuation. Do not end the sentence with only the ellipsis; an ellipsis does not also work as a period.

Example (spaces denoted by ▲)

Original	We hold today that the Sixth Amendment's right of an accused to confront the witnesses against him is likewise a fundamental right and is made obligatory on the States by the Fourteenth Amendment.
Correct use of ellipsis	"[T]he Sixth Amendment's right of an accused to confront the witnesses against him . . . is . . . a fundamental right▲.▲.▲.▲."
Incorrect use of ellipsis	"[T]he Sixth Amendment's right of an accused to confront the witnesses against him . . . is . . . a fundamental right▲.▲.▲."

40.2(c) Omission of full sentence from quoted passage

When quoting a passage of three or more sentences, indicate the omission of an internal sentence with an ellipsis.

Example (spaces denoted by ▲)

"Certainly the presence of reporters inside the home was not related to the objectives of the authorized intrusion.▲.▲.▲.▲The reporters therefore were not present for any reason related to the justification for police entry into the home—the apprehension of Dominic Wilson." *Wilson v. Layne*, 526 U.S. 603, 611 (1999).

40.2(d) Omission of one or more paragraphs from quoted passage

When omitting one or more paragraphs from a quoted passage, indicate that omission by placing the ellipsis on its own line, centered, with five to seven spaces between each ellipsis point.

Example (spaces denoted by ▲)

> The Congress shall have Power To lay and collect Taxes, Duties, Imposts and Excises, to pay the Debts and provide for the common Defence and general Welfare of the United States; but all Duties, Imposts and Excises shall be uniform throughout the United States;
>
> To borrow Money on the credit of the United States;
>
> To regulate Commerce with foreign Nations, and among the several States, and with the Indian Tribes;
>
> ▴▲▲▲▲▲ ▲▲▲▲▲ ▴
>
> To make all Laws which shall be necessary and proper for carrying into
>
> Execution the foregoing Powers, and all other Powers vested by this Constitution in the Government of the United States, or in any Department or Officer thereof.

U.S. Const. art. I, § 8.

40.3 When Not to Use an Ellipsis

40.3(a) Before or after words and phrases incorporated into writer's sentence

Do not use an ellipsis to denote an omission before or after a single word, phrase, or fragment of a sentence that is incorporated into the writer's own sentence structure.

Examples

Original [material to be quoted in gray]	But introducing a trained police dog to explore the area around the home in hopes of discovering incriminating evidence is something else. There is no customary invitation to do *that*. An invitation to engage in canine forensic investigation assuredly does not inhere in the very act of hanging a knocker.

Quotation incorporated into writer's sentence	While the presence of a door knocker is an implied invitation to enter a home, it does not invite "a trained police dog to explore the area around the home in hopes of discovering incriminating evidence." *Florida v. Jardines,* ___ U.S. ___, 133 S. Ct. 1409, 1416 (2013).
Incorrect use of ellipsis	While the presence of a door knocker is an implied invitation to enter a home, it does not invite ". . . a trained police dog to explore the area around the home in hopes of discovering incriminating evidence . . . ." *Florida v. Jardines,* ___ U.S. ___, 133 S. Ct. 1409, 1416 (2013).

40.3(b) At the beginning of a quotation

Do not use an ellipsis to denote an omission at the beginning of a quotation. Instead, capitalize the first letter of the word beginning the sentence, using square brackets as shown in **Rule 39.2**.

Examples

Original [material to be quoted in gray]	"But, in our system, undifferentiated fear or apprehension of disturbance is not enough to overcome the right to freedom of expression." *Tinker v. Des Moines Indep. Cmty. Sch. Dist.,* 393 U.S. 503, 508 (1969).
Correct omission	"[I]n our system, undifferentiated fear or apprehension of disturbance is not enough to overcome the right to freedom of expression." *Tinker v. Des Moines Indep. Cmty. Sch. Dist.,* 393 U.S. 503, 508 (1969).
Incorrect omission	". . . [I]n our system, undifferentiated fear or apprehension of disturbance is not enough to overcome the right to freedom of expression." *Tinker v. Des Moines Indep. Cmty. Sch. Dist.,* 393 U.S. 503, 508 (1969).

40.3(c) To indicate omission of material following a complete sentence

Do not use an ellipsis to indicate an omission following a complete sentence or at the end of a block quotation that concludes with a complete sentence.

However, to indicate a sentence that the writer deliberately wants to leave incomplete, use three ellipsis points and no final punctuation:

Example

The First Amendment begins, "Congress shall make no law . . ."

40.3(d) To indicate omission of footnotes or citations

Do not use an ellipsis to indicate the omission of a footnote or a citation from a quoted passage. Indicate the omission in a parenthetical after the citation.

Example

> The First Amendment begins, "Congress shall make no law . . ."

Examples

Original [footnote to be omitted in gray]	"Even electronic surveillance substantially contemporaneous with an individual's arrest could hardly be deemed an 'incident' of that arrest.[20]" *Katz v. United States*, 389 U.S. 347, 357 (1967).
Correct omission	"Even electronic surveillance substantially contemporaneous with an individual's arrest could hardly be deemed an 'incident' of that arrest." *Katz v. United States*, 389 U.S. 347, 357 (1967) (footnote omitted).
Incorrect omission	"Even electronic surveillance substantially contemporaneous with an individual's arrest could hardly be deemed an 'incident' of that arrest . . . ." *Katz v. United States*, 389 U.S. 347, 357 (1967) (footnote omitted).
Original [citations to be omitted in gray]	The Supreme Court has articulated four factors to determine whether an area is within the curtilage: (1) the proximity of the area to the house; (2) whether the area is included within an enclosure surrounding the home; (3) the nature of the use to which the area is put; and (4) the steps taken by the resident to protect the area from observation. *United States v. Dunn*, 480 U.S. 294, 301, 107 S. Ct. 1134, 94 L. Ed. 2d 326 (1987). The central inquiry is "whether the area in question is so intimately tied to the home itself that it should be placed under the home's 'umbrella' of Fourth Amendment protection." *Id.*
	United States v. McDowell, 713 F.3d 571, 574 (10th Cir. 2013).

Correct omissions

The Supreme Court has articulated four factors to determine whether an area is within the curtilage: (1) the proximity of the area to the house; (2) whether the area is included within an enclosure surrounding the home; (3) the nature of the use to which the area is put; and (4) the steps taken by the resident to protect the area from observation. The central inquiry is "whether the area in question is so intimately tied to the home itself that it should be placed under the home's 'umbrella' of Fourth Amendment protection."

United States v. McDowell, 713 F.3d 571, 574 (10th Cir. 2013) (citations omitted).

Incorrect omissions

The Supreme Court has articulated four factors to determine whether an area is within the curtilage: (1) the proximity of the area to the house; (2) whether the area is included within an enclosure surrounding the home; (3) the nature of the use to which the area is put; and (4) the steps taken by the resident to protect the area from observation. . . . The central inquiry is "whether the area in question is so intimately tied to the home itself that it should be placed under the home's 'umbrella' of Fourth Amendment protection." . . .

United States v. McDowell, 713 F.3d 571, 574 (10th Cir. 2013).

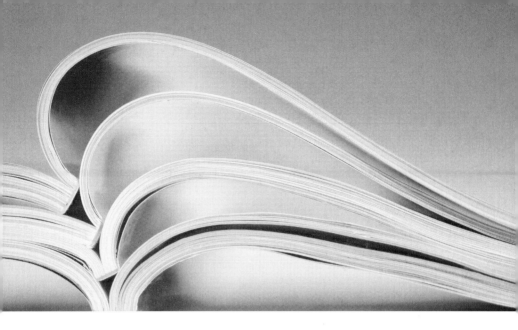

Part 7
Appendices

**Primary Sources by
Jurisdiction**

This appendix contains citation information about reporters, constitutions, statutory compilations, session laws, administrative compilations and registers, and court websites for state, territorial, and federal jurisdictions, current through August 2013. Federal primary sources are listed first, followed by the states (along with the District of Columbia) and then by Native American and territorial sources.

At the beginning of each jurisdiction's entry, its courts are listed in hierarchical order. Beside each court's name, in parentheses, is its abbreviation. For more information about court names and their abbreviations, see **Rule 12.6**. Beneath each court's name, the table lists the most common case reporters in which the court's opinions are published, the abbreviations for those reporters, and their coverage dates. Official reporters are designated with a star (★). Official reporters are those published by a government or by government authority; unofficial reporters are published by commercial entities. Unofficial reporters contain the same cases as official reporters but may also include editorial enhancements such as headnotes or star pagination. To determine which reporter to use, see **Rule 12.4**. This appendix does not list older, named reporters (for information, see **Rule 12.4(b)(4)** and **Sidebar 12.4**).

The statutory compilation table for each jurisdiction lists each current code, along with its citation format. Official codes are designated with a star (★). Code publishers occasionally change, so it is wise to check the publisher noted on the actual source, as opposed simply to copying the publisher listed in the table. When citing statutes, follow the numbering system shown in the source itself (e.g., numbers connected by hyphens or periods, subsection letters in parentheses).

If the jurisdiction's session laws are published, the table provides the names of those sources and their citation formats, designating official sources with a star (★).

If an administrative compilation or an administrative register is available for the jurisdiction, the table displays the name of the source and its citation format and marks any preferred sources with a star (★).

This appendix shows formats and abbreviations for citing primary sources under the rules of the *ALWD Guide to Legal Citation*. Required spaces are indicated by triangles (▲). The citation formats shown in the tables are those used in practice-based documents. A citation component **printed in red** will vary depending on what is being cited from the source. Use the abbreviations shown even if they differ from abbreviations indicated for other types of sources in another appendix in the *ALWD Guide*.

For citations in academic footnotes, the typeface for some components may need to change to large and small capital letters; check the rules corresponding to the specific source to be cited.

If the jurisdiction has local citation rules or neutral citation rules that must be followed when submitting a document to its courts, the appendix cross-references **Appendix 2**, which contains website URLs and citations to local rules addressing those requirements.

Finally, each jurisdiction's table contains URLs, if available, to official websites corresponding to the courts, the legislature, and the administrative branch of government.

1(A) Federal Primary Sources

Court system and reporters:		
United States Supreme Court (U.S.) *Note:* For information on citing U.S. Supreme Court cases decided between 1789 and 1874, see **Sidebar 12.3**.		
Reporter	*Abbreviation*	*Dates*
★United States Reports	U.S.	1790–present
Supreme Court Reporter	S.▲Ct.	1882–present
United States Supreme Court Reports, Lawyers' Edition	L.▲Ed.	1790–1956
Second Series	L.▲Ed.▲2d	1956–present
United States Law Week	U.S.L.W.	1933–present
United States Circuit Courts of Appeals (e.g., **1st▲Cir., 2d▲Cir., D.C.▲Cir.**) *Note:* For more federal court abbreviations, see **Appendix 4(A)**; for information on citing cases from the old federal circuits (abolished in 1912), see **Rule 12.6(c)(4)**.		
Reporter	*Abbreviation*	*Dates*
Federal Reporter	F.	1880–1924
Second Series	F.2d	1924–1993
Third Series	F.3d	1993–present
Federal Appendix	Fed.▲App'x	2001–present
Temporary Emergency Court of Appeals (Temp.▲Emer.▲Ct.▲App.) **(1971–1993),** **Emergency Court of Appeals (Emer.▲Ct.▲App.) (1942–1961),** **Commerce Court (Com.▲Ct.) (1910–1913)**		
Reporter	*Abbreviation*	*Dates*
Federal Reporter	F.	1880–1924
Second Series	F.2d	1924–1993

United States Court of Appeals for the Federal Circuit (Fed. ▲ Cir.) (created 1982), **United States Court of Customs and Patent Appeals (C.C.P.A.), Court of Customs Appeals (Ct. ▲ Cust. ▲ App.), Court of Claims (Ct. ▲ Cl.)**		
Reporter	*Abbreviation*	*Dates*
★Court of Customs Appeals Reports	Ct. ▲ Cust.	1910–1929
★Court of Customs and Patent Appeals Reports	C.C.P.A.	1929–1982
★Court of Claims Reports	Ct. ▲ Cl.	1956–1982
Federal Reporter	F.	1880–1924
Second Series	F.2d	1924–1993
Third Series	F.3d	1993–present
United States Court of Federal Claims (Fed. ▲ Cl.) (created 1992), United States Claims Court (Cl. ▲ Ct.) (created 1982), Court of Claims (Ct. ▲ Cl.)		
Reporter	*Abbreviation*	*Dates*
★Court of Claims Reports	Ct. ▲ Cl.	1863–1982
Federal Supplement	F. ▲ Supp.	1932–1960
Federal Reporter Second Series	F.2d	1930–1932, 1960–1982
United States Claims Court Reporter	Cl. ▲ Ct.	1983–1992
Federal Claims Reporter	Fed. ▲ Cl.	1992–present
United States Court of International Trade (Ct. ▲ Int'l ▲ Trade) (created 1980), United States Customs Court (Cust. ▲ Ct.) (created 1926)		
Reporter	*Abbreviation*	*Dates*
★Customs Court Reports	Cust. ▲ Ct.	1938–1980
★Customs Bulletin and Decisions	Cust. ▲ B. ▲ & ▲ Dec.	1967–present
★Court of International Trade Reports	Ct. ▲ Int'l ▲ Trade	1980–present
Federal Supplement	F. ▲ Supp.	1980–1998
Second Series	F. ▲ Supp. ▲ 2d	1998–present
International Trade Reporter Decisions	I.T.R.D. ▲ (BNA)	1980–present

United States District Courts (e.g., S.D. Cal., W.D.N.Y., D. Mass.)		
Reporter	*Abbreviation*	*Dates*
Federal Supplement	F. Supp.	1932–1998
Second Series	F. Supp. 2d	1998–present
Federal Rules Decisions	F.R.D.	1938–present
Bankruptcy Reporter	B.R.	1979–present
Federal Reporter	F.	1880–1924
Second Series	F.2d	1924–1932

United States Bankruptcy Courts (e.g., Bankr. S.D.N.Y.), Bankruptcy Appellate Panels (e.g., Bankr. App. 1st Cir.)		
Reporter	*Abbreviation*	*Dates*
Bankruptcy Reporter	B.R.	1979–present

Judicial Panel on Multidistrict Litigation (J.P.M.L.) (created 1968), Special Court, Regional Rail Reorganization Act (Reg'l Rail Reorg. Ct.) (created 1973)		
Reporter	*Abbreviation*	*Dates*
Federal Supplement	F. Supp.	1968–1998
Second Series	F. Supp. 2d	1998–present

Tax Court (T.C.): *See* **Appendix 6**		

United States Court of Appeals for Veterans Claims (Vet. App.), United States Court of Veteran Appeals (Vet. App.) (1988–1999)		
West's Veterans Appeals Reporter	Vet. App.	1900–present

United States Court of Appeals for the Armed Forces (C.A.A.F.), United States Court of Military Appeals (C.M.A.)		
Court Martial Reports	C.M.R.	1951–1975
Decisions of the United States Court of Military Appeals	C.M.A.	1951–1975
West's Military Justice Reporter	M.J.	1978–present

Military Service Courts of Criminal Appeals (A. Ct. Crim. App., A.F. Ct. Crim. App., C.G. Ct. Crim. App., N-M. Ct. Crim. App.), Courts of Military Review (e.g., A.C.M.R.), Boards of Review (e.g., A.B.R.)		
Court Martial Reports	C.M.R.	1951–1975
West's Military Justice Reporter	M.J.	1978–present

Constitution:	
United States Constitution	U.S. ▲ Const. ▲ [art. *or* amend.] ▲ number, ▲ § ▲ section number.
Statutory compilations:	
★United States Code	Title number ▲ U.S.C. ▲ § ▲ section number ▲ (Year).
United States Code Annotated	Title number ▲ U.S.C.A. ▲ § ▲ section number ▲ (West ▲ Year).
United States Code Service	Title number ▲ U.S.C.S. ▲ § ▲ section number ▲ (LexisNexis ▲ Year).
Session laws:	
★United States Statutes at Large	Pub. ▲ L. ▲ No. ▲ public law number, ▲ volume number ▲ Stat. ▲ page number ▲ (enactment or effective date).
	Priv. ▲ L. ▲ No. ▲ private law number, ▲ volume number ▲ Stat. ▲ page number ▲ (enactment or effective date).
★Federal Digital System (FDsys) (online)	Pub. ▲ L. ▲ No. ▲ public law number, ▲ volume number ▲ Stat. ▲ page number ▲ (enactment or effective date).
	Priv. ▲ L. ▲ No. ▲ private law number, ▲ volume number ▲ Stat. ▲ page number ▲ (enactment or effective date).
Administrative compilation:	
★Code of Federal Regulations	Title number ▲ C.F.R. ▲ Pinpoint reference ▲ (Year).
Administrative register:	
★Federal Register	Volume number ▲ Fed. ▲ Reg. ▲ page number ▲ (Month ▲ Day, ▲ Year).
Local citation rules?	See **Appendix 2(A)**.
Neutral citation rules?	No.
Court website:	http://www.supremecourt.gov/
Legislative websites:	http://www.senate.gov/
	http://www.house.gov/
	http://thomas.loc.gov/home/thomas.php
	http://beta.congress.gov/
Administrative websites:	http://www.gpo.gov/fdsys/
	http://www.ecfr.gov/

1(B) States' and District of Columbia's Primary Sources

Alabama

Court system and reporters:		
Alabama Supreme Court (Ala.)		
Reporter	*Abbreviation*	*Dates*
★Alabama Reports	Ala.	1840–1976
Southern Reporter	So.	1886–1941
★Second Series (official since 1976)	So.▲2d	1941–2008
★Third Series	So.▲3d	2008–present
Alabama Court of Civil Appeals (Ala.▲Civ.▲App.) and Alabama Court of Criminal Appeals (Ala.▲Crim.▲App.) *Note:* Before 1969, Alabama Court of Appeals (Ala.▲Ct.▲App.).		
Reporter	*Abbreviation*	*Dates*
★Alabama Appellate Court Reports	Ala.▲App.	1911–1976
Southern Reporter	So.	1911–1941
★Second Series (official since 1976)	So.▲2d	1941–2008
★Third Series	So.▲3d	2008–present
Constitution:		
Alabama Constitution of 1901	Ala.▲Const.▲[art. *or* amend.]▲number, ▲§▲section number.	
Statutory compilations:		
★Code of Alabama, 1975	Ala.▲Code▲§▲section number▲(Year).	
Michie's Alabama Code	Ala.▲Code▲§▲section number▲(LexisNexis▲Year).	
Session laws:		
★Acts of Alabama	Year▲Ala.▲Acts▲page number.	
West's Alabama Legislative Service	Year▲Ala.▲Legis.▲Serv.▲page number ▲(West).	
Michie's Alabama Code Advance Legislative Service	Year–Pamphlet number▲Ala.▲Adv.▲Legis. ▲Serv.▲page number▲(LexisNexis).	
Administrative compilation:		
Alabama Administrative Code	Ala.▲Admin.▲Code▲r.▲rule number ▲(Year).	

Administrative register:	
Alabama Administrative Monthly	Volume number▲Ala.▲Admin.▲Monthly ▲page number▲(Month▲Day,▲Year).
Local citation rules?	Yes. See **Appendix 2**.
Neutral citation rules?	No.
Court website:	http://judicial.alabama.gov/
Legislative website:	http://alisondb.legislature.state.al.us/ACAS/ acaslOGINflRE.ASP
Administrative website:	http://www.alabamaadministrativecode .state.al.us/

Alaska

Court system and reporters:		
Alaska Supreme Court (Alaska)		
Reporter	*Abbreviation*	*Dates*
★Pacific Reporter Second Series	P.2d	1959–2000
★Third Series	P.3d	2000–present
Alaska Court of Appeals (Alaska▲Ct.▲App.)		
Reporter	*Abbreviation*	*Dates*
★Pacific Reporter Second Series	P.2d	1980–2000
★Third Series	P.3d	2000–present
Constitution:		
Alaska Constitution	Alaska▲Const.▲[art. *or* amend.]▲number, ▲§▲section number.	
Statutory compilations:		
★Alaska Statutes	Alaska▲Stat.▲§▲section number▲(Year).	
West's Alaska Statutes Annotated	Alaska▲Stat.▲Ann.▲§▲section number ▲(West▲Year).	
Session laws:		
★Session Laws of Alaska	Year▲Alaska▲Sess.▲Laws▲page number.	
Alaska Statutes Advance Legislative Service	Year–Pamphlet number▲Alaska▲Adv.▲ Legis.▲Serv.▲page number▲(LexisNexis).	

West's Alaska Legislative Service	Year▲Alaska▲Legis.▲Serv.▲page number▲(West).
Administrative compilation:	
Alaska Administrative Code	Alaska▲Admin.▲Code▲tit.▲title number, ▲§▲section number▲(Year).
Administrative register:	
Alaska Administrative Journal	Issue number▲Alaska▲Admin.▲J.▲page number▲(Month▲Day,▲Year).
Local citation rules?	No.
Neutral citation rules?	No.
Court website:	http://courts.alaska.gov/
Legislative websites:	http://w3.legis.state.ak.us/index.php
	http://www.legis.state.ak.us/basis/folio.asp
Administrative website:	http://w3.legis.state.ak.us/index.php (select "Publications"; select "The Alaska Administrative Code")

Arizona

Court system and reporters:		
Arizona Supreme Court (Ariz.)		
Reporter	*Abbreviation*	*Dates*
★Arizona Reports	Ariz.	1866–present
Pacific Reporter	P.	1883–1931
Second Series	P.2d	1931–2000
Third Series	P.3d	2000–present
Arizona Court of Appeals (Ariz.▲Ct.▲App.)		
Reporter	*Abbreviation*	*Dates*
★Arizona Appeals Reports	Ariz.▲App.	1965–1976
★Arizona Reports	Ariz.	1976–present
Pacific Reporter Second Series	P.2d	1965–2000
Third Series	P.3d	2000–present

Arizona Tax Court (Ariz.▲T.C.)		
Reporter	*Abbreviation*	*Dates*
Pacific Reporter Second Series	P.2d	1989–2000
Third Series	P.3d	2000–present
Constitution:		
Arizona Constitution	Ariz.▲Const.▲[art. *or* amend.]▲number, ▲§▲section number.	
Statutory compilations:		
★Arizona Revised Statutes Annotated	Ariz.▲Rev.▲Stat.▲Ann.▲§▲section number ▲(Year).	
Arizona Revised Statutes	Ariz.▲Rev.▲Stat.▲§▲section number ▲(LexisNexis▲Year).	
Session laws:		
★Session Laws of Arizona	Ariz.▲Sess.▲Laws▲page number▲(Year).	
West's Arizona Legislative Service	Year▲Ariz.▲Legis.▲Serv.▲page number ▲(West).	
Arizona Advance Legislative Service	Year–Pamphlet number▲Ariz.▲Adv.▲Legis. ▲Serv.▲page number▲(LexisNexis).	
Administrative compilation:		
Arizona Administrative Code	Ariz.▲Admin.▲Code▲§▲section number ▲(Year).	
Administrative register:		
Arizona Administrative Register	Volume number▲Ariz.▲Admin.▲Reg.▲ page number▲(Month▲Day,▲Year).	
Local citation rules?	Yes. See **Appendix 2**.	
Neutral citation rules?	No.	
Court website:	http://www.azcourts.gov/	
Legislative website:	http://www.azleg.gov/	
Administrative website:	http://www.azsos.gov/public_services/Table_ of_Contents.htm	

Arkansas

Court system and reporters:		
Arkansas Supreme Court (Ark.)		
Reporter	*Abbreviation*	*Dates*
★Arkansas Reports	Ark.	1837–2009
★Official Opinions of the Arkansas Supreme Court (online)	Ark.	2009–present
South Western Reporter	S.W.	1886–1928
Second Series	S.W.2d	1928–1999
Third Series	S.W.3d	1999–present
Arkansas Court of Appeals (Ark.▲ Ct.▲ App.)		
Reporter	*Abbreviation*	*Dates*
★Arkansas Appellate Reports	Ark.▲App. *(bound with Ark.)*	1981–2009
★Official Opinions of the Arkansas Court of Appeals (online)	Ark.▲App.	2009–present
★Arkansas Reports	Ark.	1979–1981
South Western Reporter Second Series	S.W.2d	1979–1999
Third Series	S.W.3d	1999–present
Constitution:		
Arkansas Constitution of 1874	Ark.▲Const.▲[art. *or* amend.]▲number, ▲§▲section number.	
Statutory compilations:		
★Arkansas Code of 1987 Annotated	Ark.▲Code▲Ann.▲§▲section number▲(Year).	
West's Arkansas Code Annotated	Ark.▲Code▲Ann.▲§▲section number▲(West▲Year).	
Session laws:		
★Arkansas Acts	Year▲Ark.▲Acts▲page number.	
West's Arkansas Legislative Service	Year▲Ark.▲Legis.▲Serv.▲page number ▲(West).	
Arkansas Code of 1987 Annotated Advance Legislative Service	Year–Pamphlet number▲Ark.▲Adv.▲Legis. ▲Serv.▲page number▲(LexisNexis).	

Administrative compilation:	
Weil's Code of Arkansas Rules	Agency number–Sub–agency number–Chapter number▲Code▲Ark.▲R.▲§ ▲section number▲(LexisNexis▲Year).
Administrative register:	
★Arkansas Register	Volume number▲Ark.▲Reg.▲ page number▲(Month▲Year).
Arkansas Government Register	Issue number▲Ark.▲Gov't▲Reg.▲page number▲(LexisNexis▲Month▲Year).
Local citation rules?	Yes. See **Appendix 2.**
Neutral citation rules?	Yes. See **Appendix 2.**
Court website:	https://courts.arkansas.gov/
Legislative website:	http://www.arkleg.state.ar.us/
Administrative website:	http://www.sos.arkansas.gov/ rules_and_regs/

California

Court system and reporters:		
California Supreme Court (Cal.)		
Reporter	*Abbreviation*	*Dates*
★California Reports	Cal.	1850–1934
★Second Series	Cal.▲2d	1934–1969
★Third Series	Cal.▲3d	1969–1991
★Fourth Series	Cal.▲4th	1991–present
Pacific Reporter	P.	1883–1931
Second Series	P.2d	1931–2000
Third Series	P.3d	2000–present
West's California Reporter	Cal.▲Rptr.	1959–1991
Second Series	Cal.▲Rptr.▲2d	1991–2003
Third Series	Cal.▲Rptr.▲3d	2003–present

California Court of Appeal (Cal. Ct. App.)		
Note: Before 1966, the California District Court of Appeal (Cal. Dist. Ct. App.).		
Reporter	*Abbreviation*	*Dates*
★California Appellate Reports	Cal. App.	1905–1934
★Second Series	Cal. App. 2d	1934–1969
★Third Series	Cal. App. 3d	1969–1991
★Fourth Series	Cal. App. 4th	1991–present
Pacific Reporter	P.	1905–1931
Second Series	P.2d	1931–1959
West's California Reporter	Cal. Rptr.	1959–1991
Second Series	Cal. Rptr. 2d	1991–2003
Third Series	Cal. Rptr. 3d	2003–present
Appellate Divisions of California Superior Court (Cal. App. Dep't Super. Ct.)		
Reporter	*Abbreviation*	*Dates*
★California Appellate Reports Supplement	Cal. App. Supp.	1929–1934
★Second Series	Cal. App. Supp. 2d	1934–1969
★Third Series	Cal. App. Supp. 3d *(bound with Cal. App. 3d)*	1969–1991
★Fourth Series	Cal. App. Supp. 4th *(bound with Cal. App. 4th)*	1991–present
Pacific Reporter	P.	1929–1931
Second Series	P.2d	1931–1959
West's California Reporter	Cal. Rptr.	1959–1991
Second Series	Cal. Rptr. 2d	1991–2003
Third Series	Cal. Rptr. 3d	2003–present
Constitution:		
California Constitution of 1879	Cal. Const. [art. *or* amend.] number, § section number.	

Statutory compilations:	
West's Annotated California Codes	Cal. ▲ Subject Abbreviation ▲ Code ▲ § ▲ section number ▲ (West ▲ Year).
Deering's California Codes Annotated	Cal. ▲ Subject Abbreviation ▲ Code ▲ § ▲ section number ▲ (LexisNexis ▲ Year).

Subject abbreviations for statutory compilations:

Agricultural	Agric.		Insurance	Ins.
Business and Professions	Bus. ▲ & ▲ Prof.		Labor	Lab.
Civil	Civ.		Military and Veterans	Mil. ▲ & ▲ Vet.
Civil Procedure	Civ. ▲ Proc.		Penal	Penal
Commercial	Com.		Probate	Prob.
Corporations	Corps.		Public Contract	Pub. ▲ Cont.
Education	Educ.		Public Resources	Pub. ▲ Res.
Elections	Elec.			
Evidence	Evid.		Public Utilities	Pub. ▲ Util.
Family	Fam.		Revenue and Taxation	Rev. ▲ & ▲ Tax.
Financial	Fin.			
Fish and Game	Fish ▲ & ▲ Game		Streets and Highways	Sts. ▲ & ▲ High.
Food and Agricultural	Food ▲ & ▲ Agric.		Unemployment Insurance	Unemp. ▲ Ins.
Government	Gov't		Vehicle	Veh.
Harbors and Navigation	Harb. ▲ & ▲ Nav.		Water	Water
Health and Safety	Health ▲ & ▲ Safety		Welfare and Institutions	Welf. ▲ & ▲ Inst.

Session laws:	
★Statutes of California	Year ▲ Cal. ▲ Stat. ▲ page number.
West's California Legislative Service	Year ▲ Cal. ▲ Legis. ▲ Serv. ▲ page number ▲ (West).
Deering's California Advance Legislative Service	Year–Pamphlet number ▲ Cal. ▲ Adv. ▲ Legis. ▲ Serv. ▲ page number ▲ (LexisNexis).

Administrative compilation:	
★Barclay's Official Code of California Regulations	Cal. ▲ Code ▲ Regs. ▲ tit. ▲ title number, ▲ § ▲ section number ▲ (Year).
Administrative register:	
California Regulatory Notice Register	Issue number ▲ Cal. ▲ Regulatory ▲ Notice ▲ Reg. ▲ page number ▲ (Month ▲ Day, ▲ Year).
Local citation rules?	Yes. See **Appendix 2.**
Neutral citation rules?	No.
Court website:	http://www.courts.ca.gov/
Legislative website:	http://leginfo.legislature.ca.gov/
Administrative website:	http://ccr.oal.ca.gov/

Colorado

Court system and reporters:		
Colorado Supreme Court (Colo.)		
Reporter	*Abbreviation*	*Dates*
★Colorado Reports	Colo.	1864–1980
Pacific Reporter	P.	1883–1931
★Second Series (official since 1980)	P.2d	1931–2000
★Third Series	P.3d	2000–present
Colorado Court of Appeals (Colo. ▲ Ct. ▲ App.)		
Reporter	*Abbreviation*	*Dates*
★Colorado Court of Appeals Reports	Colo. ▲ App.	1891–1980
Pacific Reporter	P.	1891–1931
★Second Series (official since 1980)	P.2d	1970–2000
★Third Series	P.3d	2000–present
Constitution:		
Colorado Constitution	Colo. ▲ Const. ▲ [art. *or* amend.] ▲ number, ▲ § ▲ section number.	

Statutory compilations:	
★Colorado Revised Statutes	Colo.▲Rev.▲Stat.▲§▲section number▲(Year).
West's Colorado Revised Statutes Annotated	Colo.▲Rev.▲Stat.▲Ann.▲§▲section number ▲(West▲Year).
Session laws:	
★Session Laws of Colorado	Year▲Colo.▲Sess.▲Laws▲page number.
West's Colorado Legislative Service	Year▲Colo.▲Legis.▲Serv.▲page number▲(West).
Colorado Advance Legislative Service	Year–Pamphlet number▲Colo.▲Adv.▲Legis.▲Serv.▲page number▲(LexisNexis).
Administrative compilations:	
★Colorado Code of Regulations (online)	Volume number▲Colo.▲Code▲Regs.▲§▲section number▲(Year).
Code of Colorado Regulations	Volume number▲Colo.▲Code▲Regs.▲§▲section number▲(LexisNexis▲Year).
Administrative register:	
★Colorado Register (online; official as of July 1, 2007)	Volume number▲Issue number ▲Colo.▲Reg.▲(Month▲Year).
Colorado Register	Volume number▲Issue number ▲Colo.▲Reg.▲page number▲(Month▲Year).
Local citation rules?	Yes. See **Appendix 2**.
Neutral citation rules?	Yes. See **Appendix 2**.
Court website:	http://www.courts.state.co.us/
Legislative website:	http://www.leg.state.co.us/
Administrative websites:	http://www.sos.state.co.us/CCR/Welcome.do
	http://www.sos.state.co.us/CCR/RegisterHome.do

Connecticut

Court system and reporters:		
Connecticut Supreme Court (Conn.)		
Note: Before 1966, Connecticut Supreme Court of Errors (Conn.).		
Reporter	*Abbreviation*	*Dates*
★Connecticut Reports	Conn.	1814–present

Atlantic Reporter	A.	1885–1938
Second Series	A.2d	1938–2010
Third Series	A.3d	2010–present

Connecticut Appellate Court (Conn. ▲App. ▲Ct.)		
Reporter	*Abbreviation*	*Dates*
★Connecticut Appellate Reports	Conn. ▲App.	1983–present
Atlantic Reporter Second Series	A.2d	1983–2010
Third Series	A.3d	2010–present

Connecticut Superior Court (Conn. ▲Super. ▲Ct.) and Court of Common Pleas (Conn. ▲C.P.)		
Reporter	*Abbreviation*	*Dates*
★Connecticut Supplement	Conn. ▲Supp.	1935–present
Connecticut Law Reporter	Conn. ▲L. ▲Rptr.	1990–present
Connecticut Superior Court Reports	Conn. ▲Super. ▲Ct.	1986–1994
Atlantic Reporter Second Series	A.2d	1954–2010
Third Series	A.3d	2010–present

Connecticut Circuit Court (Conn. ▲Cir. ▲Ct.)		
Reporter	*Abbreviation*	*Dates*
★Connecticut Circuit Court Reports	Conn. ▲Cir.	1961–1974
Atlantic Reporter Second Series	A.2d	1961–1974

Constitution:	
Connecticut Constitution of 1965	Conn. ▲Const. ▲[art. *or* amend.] ▲number, ▲§ ▲section number.

Statutory compilations:	
★General Statutes of Connecticut	Conn. ▲Gen. ▲Stat. ▲§ ▲section number ▲(Year).
West's Connecticut General Statutes Annotated	Conn. ▲Gen. ▲Stat. ▲Ann. ▲§ ▲section number ▲(West ▲Year).

Session laws:	
★Connecticut Public and Special Acts, 1972–present	Year▲Conn.▲Acts▲page number▲([Reg. *or* Spec.]▲Sess.).
★Connecticut Public Acts, 1650–1971	Year▲Conn.▲Pub.▲Acts▲page number.
★Connecticut Special Acts, 1789–1971	Year▲Conn.▲Spec.▲Acts▲page number.
Connecticut Advance Legislative Service	Year–Pamphlet number▲Conn.▲Adv.▲Legis.▲Serv.▲page number▲(LexisNexis).
West's Connecticut Legislative Service	Year▲Conn.▲Legis.▲Serv.▲page number▲(West).
Administrative compilation:	
Regulations of Connecticut State Agencies	Conn.▲Agencies▲Regs.▲§▲section number▲(Year).
Administrative register:	
★Connecticut Law Journal	Volume number▲Conn.▲L.J.▲page number▲(Month▲Day,▲Year).
Connecticut Government Register	Issue number▲Conn.▲Gov't▲Reg.▲page number▲(LexisNexis▲Month▲Year).
Local citation rules?	Yes. See **Appendix 2**.
Neutral citation rules?	No.
Court website:	http://www.jud.ct.gov/
Legislative website:	http://www.cga.ct.gov/
Administrative website:	http://www.sots.ct.gov/sots/cwp/view.asp?a=4431&q=520270

Delaware

Court system and reporters:		
Delaware Supreme Court (Del.) *Note:* Before 1897, Delaware High Court of Errors and Appeals (Del.).		
Reporter	*Abbreviation*	*Dates*
★Delaware Reports	Del.	1832–1965
Atlantic Reporter	A.	1885–1938

★Second Series (official since 1966)	A.2d	1938–2010
★Third Series	A.3d	2010–present

Delaware Court of Chancery (Del. ▲ Ch.)		
Reporter	*Abbreviation*	*Dates*
★Delaware Chancery Reports	Del. ▲ Ch.	1814–1967
Atlantic Reporter	A.	1885–1938
★Second Series (official since 1966)	A.2d	1938–2010
★Third Series	A.3d	2010–present

Delaware Superior Court (Del. ▲ Super. ▲ Ct.)		
Note: Before 1897, Delaware Superior Court and Orphans' Court (Del. ▲ Super. ▲ Ct. ▲ & ▲ Orphans' ▲ Ct.).		
Reporter	*Abbreviation*	*Dates*
Atlantic Reporter Second Series	A.2d	1951–2010
Third Series	A.3d	2010–present

Delaware Family Court (Del. ▲ Fam. ▲ Ct.)		
Reporter	*Abbreviation*	*Dates*
★Atlantic Reporter Second Series	A.2d	1977–2010
★Third Series	A.3d	2010–present

Constitution:	
Delaware Constitution of 1897	Del. ▲ Const. ▲ [art. *or* amend.] ▲ number, ▲§▲ section number.

Statutory compilations:	
★Delaware Code Annotated	Del. ▲ Code ▲ Ann. ▲ tit. ▲ title number, ▲§▲ section number ▲ (Year).
West's Delaware Code Annotated	Del. ▲ Code ▲ Ann. ▲ tit. ▲ title number, ▲§▲ section number ▲ (West ▲ Year).

Session laws:	
★Laws of Delaware	Volume number ▲ Del. ▲ Laws ▲ page number ▲ (Year).

Delaware Code Annotated Advance Legislative Service	Year–Pamphlet number▲ Del.▲ Code▲ Ann.▲ Adv. ▲Legis.▲ Serv.▲ page number▲ (LexisNexis).
West's Delaware Legislative Service	Year▲ Del.▲ Legis.▲ Serv.▲ page number▲ (West).
Administrative compilation:	
★Delaware Administrative Code	Title number▲ Del.▲ Admin.▲ Code▲ regulation number–section number▲ (Year).
Administrative register:	
★Delaware Register of Regulations	Volume number▲ Del.▲ Reg.▲ Regs.▲ page number▲ (Month▲ Day,▲ Year).
Delaware Government Register	Issue number▲ Del.▲ Gov't▲ Reg.▲ page number ▲(LexisNexis▲ Month▲ Year).
Local citation rules?	Yes. See **Appendix 2**.
Neutral citation rules?	No.
Court website:	http://courts.delaware.gov/
Legislative website:	http://legis.delaware.gov/
Administrative website:	http://regulations.delaware.gov/AdminCode/

District of Columbia

Court system and reporters:		
District of Columbia Court of Appeals (D.C.) *Note:* Before 1970, Municipal Court of Appeals (D.C.).		
Reporter	*Abbreviation*	*Dates*
★Atlantic Reporter Second Series	A.2d	1943 2010
★Third Series	A.3d	2010–present
Statutory compilations:		
★District of Columbia Official Code	D.C.▲ Code▲ §▲ section number▲ (Year).	
District of Columbia Code	D.C.▲ Code▲ §▲ section number▲ (LexisNexis▲ Year).	
Session laws:		
★United States Statutes at Large	Volume number▲ Stat.▲ page number▲ (Year).	

★District of Columbia Statutes at Large (1976–1986)	Year▲D.C.▲Stat.▲law number.
District of Columbia Session Law Service	D.C.▲Sess.▲L.▲Serv.▲page number▲(West▲Year).
District of Columbia Code Advance Legislative Service	Year–Pamphlet number▲D.C.▲Code▲Adv.▲Legis.▲Serv.▲page number▲(LexisNexis).
Municipal regulations:	
★District of Columbia Municipal Regulations	D.C.▲Mun.▲Regs.▲tit.▲title number,▲§▲section number▲(Year).
Code of District of Columbia Municipal Regulations	D.C.▲Code▲Mun.▲Regs.▲§▲section number▲(LexisNexis▲Year).
Administrative register:	
District of Columbia Register	Volume number▲D.C.▲Reg.▲page number▲(Month▲Day,▲Year).
Local citation rules?	Yes. See **Appendix 2.**
Neutral citation rules?	No.
Court website:	http://www.dccourts.gov/internet/welcome.jsf
Legislative website:	http://www.dccouncil.washington.dc.us/
Administrative website:	http://www.dcregs.org/

Florida

Court system and reporters:		
Florida Supreme Court (Fla.)		
Reporter	*Abbreviation*	*Dates*
★Florida Reports	Fla.	1846–1948
Florida Law Weekly	Fla.▲L.▲Weekly	1978–present
Southern Reporter	So.	1887–1941
★Second Series (official since 1948)	So.▲2d	1941–2008
★Third Series	So.▲3d	2008–present

Florida District Court of Appeal (Fla. ▲ Dist. ▲ Ct. ▲ App.)		
Reporter	*Abbreviation*	*Dates*
★Southern Reporter Second Series	So. ▲ 2d	1957–2008
★Third Series	So. ▲ 3d	2008–present
Florida Law Weekly	Fla. ▲ L. ▲ Weekly	1978–present
Florida Circuit Court (Fla. ▲ Cir. ▲ Ct.), Florida County Court (Fla. ▲ Name of County ▲ County ▲ Ct.), Florida Public Service Commission (Fla. ▲ P.S.C.), and other Florida lower courts		
Reporter	*Abbreviation*	*Dates*
★Florida Supplement	Fla. ▲ Supp.	1948–1980
★Second Series	Fla. ▲ Supp. ▲ 2d	1980–1992
Florida Law Weekly Supplement	Fla. ▲ L. ▲ Weekly ▲ Supp.	1992–present
Constitution:		
Florida Constitution of 1968	Fla. ▲ Const. ▲ [art. *or* amend.] ▲ number, ▲ § ▲ section number.	
Statutory compilations:		
★Florida Statutes	Fla. ▲ Stat. ▲ § ▲ section number ▲ (Year).	
West's Florida Statutes Annotated	Fla. ▲ Stat. ▲ Ann. ▲ § ▲ section number ▲ (West ▲ Year).	
Session laws:		
★Laws of Florida	Year ▲ Fla. ▲ Laws ▲ page number.	
West's Florida Session Law Service	Year ▲ Fla. ▲ Sess. ▲ L. ▲ Serv. ▲ page number ▲ (West).	
Administrative compilation:		
Florida Administrative Code Annotated	Fla. ▲ Admin. ▲ Code ▲ Ann. ▲ r. ▲ rule number ▲ (Year).	
Administrative register:		
Florida Administrative Law Weekly	Volume number ▲ Fla. ▲ Admin. ▲ Weekly ▲ page number ▲ (Month ▲ Day, ▲ Year).	
Local citation rules?	Yes. See **Appendix 2**.	
Neutral citation rules?	No.	
Court website:	http://flcourts.org/	

Legislative website:	http://www.leg.state.fl.us/
Administrative website:	https://www.flrules.org/Default.asp

Georgia

Court system and reporters:		
Georgia Supreme Court (Ga.)		
Reporter	*Abbreviation*	*Dates*
★Georgia Reports	Ga.	1846–present
South Eastern Reporter	S.E.	1886–1939
Second Series	S.E.2d	1939–present
Georgia Court of Appeals (Ga. ▲ Ct. ▲ App.)		
Reporter	*Abbreviation*	*Dates*
★Georgia Appeals Reports	Ga. ▲ App.	1906–present
South Eastern Reporter	S.E.	1906–1939
Second Series	S.E.2d	1939–present
Constitution:		
Georgia Constitution of 1983	Ga. ▲ Const. ▲ [art. *or* amend.] ▲ number, ▲ § ▲ section number.	
Statutory compilations:		
★Official Code of Georgia Annotated	Ga. ▲ Code ▲ Ann. ▲ § ▲ section number ▲ (Year).	
West's Georgia Code Annotated	Ga. ▲ Code ▲ Ann. ▲ § ▲ section number ▲ (West ▲ Year).	
Session laws:		
★Georgia Laws	Year ▲ Ga. ▲ Laws ▲ page number.	
Georgia Advance Legislative Service	Year–Pamphlet number ▲ Ga. ▲ Code ▲ Ann. ▲ Adv. ▲ Legis. ▲ Serv. ▲ page number ▲ (LexisNexis).	
West's Georgia Legislative Service	Year ▲ Ga. ▲ Code ▲ Ann. ▲ Adv. ▲ Legis. ▲ Serv. ▲ page number ▲ (West).	
Administrative compilation:		
★Official Compilation of the Rules and Regulations of the State of Georgia	Ga. ▲ Comp. ▲ R. ▲ & ▲ Regs. ▲ § ▲ title number–chapter number–section number ▲ (Year).	

Administrative register:	
Georgia Government Register	Issue number▲ Ga.▲ Gov't▲ Reg.▲ page number▲ (LexisNexis▲ Month▲ Year).
Local citation rules?	Yes. See **Appendix 2**.
Neutral citation rules?	No.
Court websites:	http://www.gasupreme.us/index.php
	http://www.gaappeals.us/
Legislative website:	http://www.legis.ga.gov/en-US/default.aspx
Administrative website:	http://sos.georgia.gov/rules_regs.htm

Hawaii

Court system and reporters:		
Hawaii Supreme Court (Haw.)		
Reporter	*Abbreviation*	*Dates*
★Hawaii Reports	Haw.	1847–1994
★West's Hawaii Reports	Haw.	1994–present
★Pacific Reporter Second Series	P.2d	1959–2000
★Third Series	P.3d	2000–present
Hawaii Intermediate Court of Appeals (Haw.▲ Ct.▲ App.)		
Reporter	*Abbreviation*	*Dates*
★Hawaii Appellate Reports	Haw.▲ App.	1980–1994
★West's Hawaii Reports	Haw.	1994–present
★Pacific Reporter Second Series	P.2d	1980–present
★Third Series	P.3d	2000–present
Constitution:		
Hawaii Constitution	Haw.▲ Const.▲ [art. *or* amend.]▲ number, ▲§▲ section number.	
Statutory compilations:		
★Hawaii Revised Statutes	Haw.▲ Rev.▲ Stat.▲§▲ section number ▲(Year).	

Michie's Hawaii Revised Statutes Annotated	Haw. ▲ Rev. ▲ Stat. ▲ Ann. ▲ § ▲ section number ▲ (LexisNexis ▲ Year).
West's Hawaii Revised Statutes	Haw. ▲ Rev. ▲ Stat. ▲ § ▲ section number ▲ (West ▲ Year).
Session laws:	
★Session Laws of Hawaii	Year ▲ Haw. ▲ Sess. ▲ Laws ▲ page number.
Michie's Hawaii Revised Statutes Annotated Advance Legislative Service	Year–Pamphlet number ▲ Haw. ▲ Rev. ▲ Stat. ▲ Ann. ▲ Adv. ▲ Legis. ▲ Serv. ▲ page number ▲ (LexisNexis).
West's Hawaii Legislative Service	Year ▲ Haw. ▲ Legis. ▲ Serv. ▲ page number ▲ (West).
Administrative compilation:	
Code of Hawaii Rules	Haw. ▲ Code ▲ R. ▲ § ▲ section number ▲ (LexisNexis ▲ Year).
Administrative register:	
Hawaii Government Register	Haw. ▲ Gov't ▲ Reg. ▲ page number ▲ (LexisNexis ▲ Month ▲ Year).
Local citation rules?	Yes. See **Appendix 2**.
Neutral citation rules?	No.
Court website:	http://www.courts.state.hi.us/
Legislative website:	http://www.capitol.hawaii.gov/
Administrative website:	http://ltgov.hawaii.gov/the-office/administrative-rules/

Idaho

Court system and reporters:		
Idaho Supreme Court (Idaho)		
Reporter	*Abbreviation*	*Dates*
★Idaho Reports	Idaho	1866–present
Pacific Reporter	P.	1883–1931
Second Series	P.2d	1931–2000
Third Series	P.3d	2000–present
Idaho Court of Appeals (Idaho ▲ Ct. ▲ App.)		
Reporter	*Abbreviation*	*Dates*
★Idaho Reports	Idaho	1982–present

Pacific Reporter		
Second Series	P.2d	1982–2000
Third Series	P.3d	2000–present
Constitution:		
Idaho Constitution of 1890	Idaho ▲ Const. ▲ [art. *or* amend.] ▲ number, ▲§▲ section number.	
Statutory compilations:		
★Idaho Code Annotated	Idaho ▲ Code ▲ Ann. ▲§▲ section number ▲ (Year).	
West's Idaho Code Annotated	Idaho ▲ Code ▲ Ann. ▲§▲ section number ▲ (West ▲ Year).	
Session laws:		
★Session Laws of Idaho	Year ▲ Idaho ▲ Sess. ▲ Laws ▲ page number.	
Idaho Code Annotated Advance Legislative Service	Year–Pamphlet number ▲ Idaho ▲ Code ▲ Ann. ▲ Adv. ▲ Legis. ▲ Serv. ▲ page number ▲ (LexisNexis).	
West's Idaho Legislative Service	Year ▲ Idaho ▲ Legis. ▲ Serv. ▲ page number ▲ (West).	
Administrative compilation:		
★Idaho Administrative Code (online)	Idaho ▲ Admin. ▲ Code ▲ r. ▲ title number. chapter number.section number ▲ (Year).	
Idaho Administrative Code (through 2004)	Idaho ▲ Admin. ▲ Code ▲ r. ▲ rule number ▲ (Year).	
Administrative register:		
Idaho Administrative Bulletin	Volume number ▲ Idaho ▲ Admin. ▲ Bull. ▲ page number ▲ (Month ▲ Day, ▲ Year).	
Local citation rules?	Yes. See **Appendix 2.**	
Neutral citation rules?	No.	
Court website:	http://www.isc.idaho.gov/	
Legislative website:	http://legislature.idaho.gov/index.htm	
Administrative website:	http://adminrules.idaho.gov/	

Illinois

Court system and reporters:		
Illinois Supreme Court (Ill.)		
Reporter	*Abbreviation*	*Dates*
★Illinois Reports	Ill.	1819–1954
★Second Series	Ill.▲2d	1954–2011
★Illinois Official Reports (online)	Ill.	2011–present
North Eastern Reporter	N.E.	1885–1936
Second Series	N.E.2d	1936–present
Illinois Appellate Court (Ill.▲App.▲Ct.)		
Reporter	*Abbreviation*	*Dates*
★Illinois Appellate Court Reports	Ill.▲App.	1877–1954
★Second Series	Ill.▲App.▲2d	1954–1972
★Third Series	Ill.▲App.▲3d	1972–2011
★Illinois Official Reports (online)	Ill.▲App.	2011–present
North Eastern Reporter, Second Series	N.E.2d	1936–present
Illinois Court of Claims (Ill.▲Ct.▲Cl.)		
Reporter	*Abbreviation*	*Dates*
★Illinois Court of Claims Reports	Ill.▲Ct.▲Cl.	1889–present
Constitution:		
Illinois Constitution of 1970	Ill.▲Const.▲[art. *or* amend.]▲number,▲ §▲section number.	
Statutory compilations:		
★Illinois Compiled Statutes	Chapter number▲Ill.▲Comp.▲Stat.▲ act number/section number▲(Year).	
West's Smith–Hurd Illinois Compiled Statutes Annotated	Chapter number▲Ill.▲Comp.▲Stat.▲ Ann.▲act number/section number▲ (West▲Year).	
Illinois Compiled Statutes Annotated	Chapter number▲Ill.▲Comp.▲Stat.▲Ann. ▲act number/section number▲ (LexisNexis▲Year).	
Session laws:		
★Laws of Illinois	Year▲Ill.▲Laws▲page number.	

Illinois Legislative Service (West)	Year▲ Ill.▲ Legis.▲ Serv.▲ page number ▲(West).
Illinois Compiled Statutes Annotated Advance Legislative Service	Year–Pamphlet number▲ Ill.▲ Comp.▲ Stat. ▲Ann.▲ Adv.▲ Legis.▲ Serv.▲ page number ▲(LexisNexis).
Administrative compilations:	
★Illinois Administrative Code	Ill.▲ Admin.▲ Code▲ tit.▲ title number, ▲§▲ section number▲ (Year).
Code of Illinois Rules	Volume number▲ Ill.▲ Code▲ R.▲ rule number▲ (LexisNexis▲ Year).
Administrative register:	
Illinois Register	Volume number▲ Ill.▲ Reg.▲ page number ▲(Month▲ Day,▲ Year).
Local citation rules?	Yes. See **Appendix 2**.
Neutral citation rules?	Yes. See **Appendix 2**.
Court website:	http://www.state.il.us/court/
Legislative website:	http://www.ilga.gov/
Administrative websites:	http://www.ilga.gov/commission/jcar/ admincode/titles.html
	http://www.cyberdriveillinois.com/ departments/index/register/home.html

Indiana

Court system and reporters:		
Indiana Supreme Court (Ind.)		
Reporter	*Abbreviation*	*Dates*
★Indiana Reports	Ind.	1848–1981
North Eastern Reporter	N.E.	1885–1936
★Second Series (official since 1981)	N.E.2d	1936–present
Indiana Court of Appeals (Ind.▲ Ct.▲ App.) *Note:* Before 1972, Indiana Appellate Court (Ind.▲ App.▲ Ct.)		
Reporter	*Abbreviation*	*Dates*
★Indiana Court of Appeals Reports	Ind.▲ App.	1891–1979

North Eastern Reporter	N.E.	1891–1936
★Second Series (official since 1979)	N.E.2d	1936–present
Indiana Tax Court (Ind. ▲ T.C.)		
Reporter	*Abbreviation*	*Dates*
North Eastern Reporter	N.E.	1885–1936
Constitution:		
Indiana Constitution of 1851	Ind. ▲ Const. ▲ [art. *or* amend.] ▲ number, ▲ § ▲ section number.	
Statutory compilations:		
★Indiana Code	Ind. ▲ Code ▲ § ▲ section number ▲ (Year).	
Burns Indiana Statutes Annotated	Ind. ▲ Code ▲ Ann. ▲ § ▲ section number ▲ (LexisNexis ▲ Year).	
West's Annotated Indiana Code	Ind. ▲ Code ▲ Ann. ▲ § ▲ section number ▲ (West ▲ Year).	
Session laws:		
★Acts of Indiana	Year ▲ Ind. ▲ Acts ▲ page number.	
West's Indiana Legislative Service	Year ▲ Ind. ▲ Legis. ▲ Serv. ▲ page number ▲ (West).	
Burns Indiana Statutes Annotated Advance Legislative Service	Year–Pamphlet number ▲ Ind. ▲ Stat. ▲ Ann. ▲ Adv. ▲ Legis. ▲ Serv. ▲ page number ▲ (LexisNexis).	
Administrative compilations:		
★Indiana Administrative Code	Title number ▲ Ind. ▲ Admin. ▲ Code ▲ rule number ▲ (Year).	
West's Indiana Administrative Code	Title number ▲ Ind. ▲ Admin. ▲ Code ▲ rule number ▲ (West ▲ Year).	
Administrative register:		
Indiana Register	Format for pre–July 2, 2006, documents: Volume number ▲ Ind. ▲ Reg. ▲ page number ▲ (Month ▲ Day, ▲ Year).	
	Format for post–July 2, 2006, documents (online): Volume number ▲ Ind. ▲ Reg. ▲ document identification number. (See **Note** below.)	

Note: A document identification number has eight components, e.g., in 20090726–IR–317050065FRA: (1) Year of posting on database website (2009); (2) month of posting (07); (3) day of posting (26); (4) "IR" for database identifier; (5) entity identifier, either Indiana Administrative Code title number or three–letter designation (here, title number 317); (6) six-digit LSA document number (050065); (7) type of document (here, FR for final rule); and (8) a wildcard (most will end in "A").

Local citation rules?	Yes. See **Appendix 2**.
Neutral citation rules?	No.
Court website:	http://www.in.gov/judiciary/
Legislative website:	http://www.ai.org/legislative/
Administrative websites:	http://www.ai.org/legislative/iac/
	http://www.ai.org/legislative/iac/irtoc.htm

Iowa

Court system and reporters:		
Iowa Supreme Court (Iowa)		
Reporter	*Abbreviation*	*Dates*
★Iowa Reports	Iowa	1855–1968
North Western Reporter	N.W.	1879–1941
★Second Series (official since 1968)	N.W.2d	1941–present
Iowa Court of Appeals (Iowa ▲ Ct. ▲ App.)		
Reporter	*Abbreviation*	*Dates*
★North Western Reporter Second Series	N W 2d	1977–present
Constitution:		
Iowa Constitution of 1857	Iowa ▲ Const. ▲ [art. *or* amend.] ▲ number, ▲ § ▲ section number.	
Statutory compilations:		
★Code of Iowa	Iowa ▲ Code ▲ § ▲ section number ▲ (Year).	
West's Iowa Code Annotated	Iowa ▲ Code ▲ Ann. ▲ § ▲ section number ▲ (West ▲ Year).	

Session laws:	
★Iowa Acts	Year▲Iowa▲Acts▲page number.
West's Iowa Legislative Service	Year▲Iowa▲Legis.▲Serv.▲page number▲(West).
Administrative compilation:	
Iowa Administrative Code	Iowa▲Admin.▲Code▲r.▲rule number▲(Year).
Administrative register:	
Iowa Administrative Bulletin	Volume number▲Iowa▲Admin.▲Bull.▲page number▲(Month▲Day,▲Year).
Local citation rules?	Yes. See **Appendix 2**.
Neutral citation rules?	No.
Court website:	http://www.iowacourts.gov/
Legislative website:	https://www.legis.iowa.gov/index.aspx
Administrative website:	https://www.legis.iowa.gov/IowaLaw/AdminCode/adminLaw.aspx

Kansas

Court system and reporters:		
Kansas Supreme Court (Kan.)		
Reporter	*Abbreviation*	*Dates*
★Kansas Reports	Kan.	1862–present
Pacific Reporter	P.	1883–1931
Second Series	P.2d	1931–2000
Third Series	P.3d	2000–present
Kansas Court of Appeals (Kan.▲Ct.▲App.)		
Reporter	*Abbreviation*	*Dates*
★Kansas Court of Appeals Reports	Kan.▲App.	1895–1901
★Second Series	Kan.▲App.▲2d	1977–present
Pacific Reporter	P.	1895–1931
Second Series	P.2d	1977–2000
Third Series	P.3d	2000–present
Constitution:		
Kansas Constitution	Kan.▲Const.▲[art. *or* amend.]▲number,▲§▲section number.	

Statutory compilations:	
★Kansas Statutes Annotated	Kan.▲Stat.▲Ann.▲§▲section number▲(Year).
West's Kansas Statutes Annotated	Kan.▲Stat.▲Ann.▲§▲section number▲(West▲Year).
Session laws:	
★Session Laws of Kansas	Year▲Kan.▲Sess.▲Laws▲page number.
West's Kansas Legislative Service	Year▲Kan.▲Legis.▲Serv.▲page number▲(West).
Administrative compilation:	
Kansas Administrative Regulations	Kan.▲Admin.▲Regs.▲§▲section number▲(Year).
Administrative register:	
Kansas Register	Volume number▲Kan.▲Reg.▲page number▲(Month▲Day,▲Year).
Local citation rules?	Yes. See **Appendix 2.**
Neutral citation rules?	No.
Court website:	http://www.kscourts.org/
Legislative website:	http://kslegislature.org/
Administrative website:	http://www.kssos.org/Pubs/pubs_kar.aspx

Kentucky

Court system and reporters:		
Kentucky Supreme Court (Ky.)		
Note: Before 1976, Kentucky Court of Appeals (Ky.).		
Reporter	*Abbreviation*	*Dates*
★Kentucky Reports	Ky.	1785–1951
South Western Reporter	S.W.	1886–1928
★Second Series (official since 1973)	S.W.2d	1928–1999
★Third Series	S.W.3d	1999–present

Kentucky Court of Appeals (Ky. ▲ Ct. ▲ App.)		
Reporter	*Abbreviation*	*Dates*
★South Western Reporter Second Series	S.W.2d	1976–1999
★Third Series	S.W.3d	1999–present
Constitution:		
Kentucky Constitution of 1891	Ky. ▲ Const. ▲ [art. *or* amend.] ▲ number, ▲ § ▲ section number.	
Statutory compilations:		
Baldwin's Kentucky Revised Statutes Annotated	Ky. ▲ Rev. ▲ Stat. ▲ Ann. ▲ § ▲ section number ▲ (West ▲ Year).	
Michie's Kentucky Revised Statutes Annotated	Ky. ▲ Rev. ▲ Stat. ▲ Ann. ▲ § ▲ section number ▲ (LexisNexis ▲ Year).	
Session laws:		
★Kentucky Acts	Year ▲ Ky. ▲ Acts ▲ page number.	
Kentucky Revised Statutes and Rules Service (West)	Year ▲ Ky. ▲ Rev. ▲ Stat. ▲ & ▲ R. ▲ Serv. ▲ page number ▲ (West).	
Kentucky Revised Statutes Advance Legislative Service	Year–Pamphlet number ▲ Ky. ▲ Rev. ▲ Stat. ▲ Adv. ▲ Legis. ▲ Serv. ▲ page number ▲ (LexisNexis).	
Administrative compilation:		
Kentucky Administrative Regulations Service	Title number ▲ Ky. ▲ Admin. ▲ Regs. ▲ rule number ▲ (Year).	
Administrative register:		
Administrative Register of Kentucky	Volume number ▲ Ky. ▲ Reg. ▲ page number ▲ (Month ▲ Year).	
Local citation rules?	Yes. See **Appendix 2**.	
Neutral citation rules?	No.	
Court website:	http://courts.ky.gov/	
Legislative website:	http://www.lrc.state.ky.us/legislation.htm	
Administrative websites:	http://www.lrc.state.ky.us/kar/frntpage.htm	
	http://www.lrc.ky.gov/kar/contents/ 2010/06register.htm	

Louisiana

Court system and reporters:		
Louisiana Supreme Court (La.) *Note:* Before 1813, the Superior Court of Louisiana (La.), and the Superior Court of the Territory of Orleans (Orleans).		
Reporter	*Abbreviation*	*Dates*
★Louisiana Reports	La.	1900–1972
Southern Reporter	So.	1887–1941
Second Series	So.▲2d	1941–2008
Third Series	So.▲3d	2008–present
Louisiana Court of Appeal (La.▲Ct.▲App.)		
Reporter	*Abbreviation*	*Dates*
Southern Reporter	So.	1928–1941
Second Series	So.▲2d	1941–2008
Third Series	So.▲3d	2008–present
Constitution:		
Louisiana Constitution of 1974	La.▲Const.▲[art. *or* amend.]▲number,▲§▲section number.	
Statutory compilations:		
West's Louisiana Children's Code Annotated	La.▲Child.▲Code▲Ann.▲art.▲article number▲(Year).	
West's Louisiana Civil Code Annotated	La.▲Civ.▲Code▲Ann.▲art.▲article number▲(Year).	
West's Louisiana Code of Civil Procedure Annotated	La.▲Code▲Civ.▲Proc.▲Ann.▲art.▲article number▲(Year).	
West's Louisiana Code of Criminal Procedure Annotated	La.▲Code▲Crim.▲Proc.▲Ann.▲art.▲article number▲(Year).	
West's Louisiana Code of Evidence Annotated	La.▲Code▲Evid.▲Ann.▲art.▲article number▲(Year).	
West's Louisiana Revised Statutes Annotated	La.▲Rev.▲Stat.▲Ann.▲§▲section number▲(Year).	
LexisNexis Louisiana Revised Annotated Statutes	La.▲Rev.▲Stat.▲Ann.▲§▲section number▲(LexisNexis▲Year).	
Session laws:		
★State of Louisiana: Acts of the Legislature	Year▲La.▲Acts▲page number.	

West's Louisiana Session Law Service	Year▲La.▲Sess.▲L.▲Serv.▲page number.
Louisiana Annotated Statutes Advance Legislative Service	Year–Pamphlet number▲La.▲Ann.▲Stat.▲Adv.▲Legis.▲Serv.▲page number▲(LexisNexis).
Administrative compilation:	
★Louisiana Administrative Code	La.▲Admin.▲Code▲tit.▲title number, ▲§▲section number▲(Year).
Administrative register:	
Louisiana Register	Volume number▲La.▲Reg.▲page number ▲(Month▲Year).
Local citation rules?	Yes. See **Appendix 2.**
Neutral citation rules?	Yes. See **Appendix 2.**
Court website:	http://louisiana.gov/Government/Judicial_Branch/
Legislative website:	http://www.legis.la.gov/
Administrative websites:	http://www.doa.louisiana.gov/osr/lac/lac.htm
	http://www.doa.louisiana.gov/osr/reg/register.htm

Maine

Court system and reporters:		
Maine Supreme Judicial Court (Me.)		
Reporter	*Abbreviation*	*Dates*
★Maine Reports	Me.	1820–1965
Atlantic Reporter	A.	1885–1938
★Second Series (official since 1966)	A.2d	1938–2010
★Third Series	A.3d	2010–present
Constitution:		
Maine Constitution	Me.▲Const.▲[art. *or* amend.]▲number,▲ §▲section number.	

Statutory compilation:	
★Maine Revised Statutes	Me.▲ Rev.▲ Stat.▲ tit.▲ title number,▲ §▲ section number▲ (Year).
Maine Revised Statutes Annotated	Me.▲ Rev.▲ Stat.▲ Ann.▲ tit.▲ title number,▲ §▲ section number▲ West▲ Year).
Session laws:	
★Laws of the State of Maine	Year▲ Me.▲ Laws▲ page number.
Maine Legislative Service (West)	Year▲ Me.▲ Legis.▲ Serv.▲ page number▲ (West).
Administrative compilation:	
Code of Maine Rules	Volume number▲ Code▲ Me.▲ R.▲ §▲ section number▲ (LexisNexis▲ Year).
Administrative register:	
Maine Government Register	Issue number▲ Me.▲ Gov't▲ Reg.▲ page number ▲ (LexisNexis▲ Month▲ Year).
Local citation rules?	No.
Neutral citation rules?	Yes. See **Appendix 2**.
Court website:	http://www.courts.state.me.us/
Legislative website:	http://www.maine.gov/legis/
Administrative website:	http://www.maine.gov/sos/cec/rules/rules.html

Maryland

Court system and reporters:		
Maryland Court of Appeals (Md.)		
Reporter	*Abbreviation*	*Dates*
★Maryland Reports	Md.	1851–present
Atlantic Reporter	A.	1885–1938
Second Series	A.2d	1938–2010
Third Series	A.3d	2010–present
Maryland Court of Special Appeals (Md.▲ Ct.▲ Spec.▲ App.)		
Reporter	*Abbreviation*	*Dates*
★Maryland Appellate Reports	Md.▲ App.	1967–present

Atlantic Reporter		
Second Series	A.2d	1967–2010
Third Series	A.3d	2010–present

Constitution:		
Maryland Constitution of 1867	Md. Const. [art. *or* amend.] number, § section number.	

Statutory compilations:		
Michie's Annotated Code of Maryland	Md. Code Ann., Subject Abbreviation § section number (LexisNexis Year).	
West's Annotated Code of Maryland	Md. Code Ann., Subject Abbreviation § section number (West Year).	

Subject abbreviations for statutory compilations:

Agriculture	Agric.		Environment	Env't
Business Occupations and Professions	Bus. Occ. & Prof.		Estates and Trusts	Est. & Trusts
			Family Law	Fam. Law
Business Regulation	Bus. Reg.		Financial Institutions	Fin. Inst.
Commercial Law	Com. Law		Health–General	Health–Gen.
Corporations and Associations	Corps. & Ass'ns		Health Occupations	Health Occ.
Correctional Services	Corr. Servs.		Housing and Community Development	Hous. & Cmty. Dev.
Courts and Judicial Proceedings	Cts. & Jud. Proc.		Human Services	Hum. Servs.
			Insurance	Ins.
Criminal Law	Crim. Law		Labor and Employment	Lab. & Empl.
Criminal Procedure	Crim. Proc.		Natural Resources	Nat. Res.
Economic Development	Econ. Dev.			
			Public Safety	Pub. Safety
Education	Educ.		Public Utility Companies	Pub. Util. Cos.
Election Law	Elec. Law			

Real Property	Real␣Prop.
State Finance and Procurement	State␣Fin.␣&␣Proc.
State Government	State␣Gov't

State Personnel and Pensions	State␣Pers.␣&␣Pens.
Tax–General	Tax–Gen.
Tax–Property	Tax–Prop.
Transportation	Transp.

Session laws:	
★Laws of Maryland	Year␣Md.␣Laws␣page number.
Michie's Annotated Code of Maryland Advance Legislative Service	Year–Pamphlet number␣Md.␣Code␣Ann.␣Adv.␣Legis.␣Serv.␣page number␣(LexisNexis).
West's Maryland Legislative Service	Year␣Md.␣Legis.␣Serv.␣page number␣(West).
Administrative compilation:	
Code of Maryland Regulations	Md.␣Code␣Regs.␣regulation number␣(Year).
Administrative register:	
Maryland Register	Volume␣Md.␣Reg.␣page number␣(Month␣Day,␣Year).
Local citation rules?	Yes. See **Appendix 2**.
Neutral citation rules?	No.
Court website:	http://www.courts.state.md.us/
Legislative website:	http://mgaleg.maryland.gov/
Administrative website:	http://www.dsd.state.md.us/comar/

Massachusetts

Court system and reporters:		
Massachusetts Supreme Judicial Court (Mass.)		
Reporter	*Abbreviation*	*Dates*
★Massachusetts Reports	Mass.	1804–present
North Eastern Reporter	N.E.	1885–1936
Second Series	N.E.2d	1936–present

Massachusetts Appeals Court (Mass. ▲App. ▲Ct.)		
Reporter	*Abbreviation*	*Dates*
★Massachusetts Appeals Court Reports	Mass. ▲App. ▲Ct.	1972–present
North Eastern Reporter Second Series	N.E.2d	1972–present

Massachusetts District Court, Appellate Division (Mass. ▲Dist. ▲Ct.), Boston Municipal Court, Appellate Division (Bos. ▲Mun. ▲Ct.)		
Reporter	*Abbreviation*	*Dates*
★Massachusetts Appellate Division Reports (official since 1980)	Mass. ▲App. ▲Div.	1936–1950 1980-present
Massachusetts Appellate Decisions	Mass. ▲App. ▲Dec.	1941–1977
Massachusetts Reports Supplement	Mass. ▲Supp.	1980–1983

Massachusetts Superior Court (Mass. ▲Super. ▲Ct.)		
Reporter	*Abbreviation*	*Dates*
Massachusetts Law Reporter	Mass. ▲L. ▲Rptr.	1993–present

Constitution:	
Massachusetts Constitution	Mass. ▲Const. ▲[art. *or* amend.] ▲number, ▲§ ▲section number.

Statutory compilations:	
★General Laws of Massachusetts	Mass. ▲Gen. ▲Laws ▲ch. ▲chapter number, ▲§ ▲section number▲ (Year).
Massachusetts General Laws Annotated	Mass. ▲Gen. ▲Laws ▲Ann. ▲ch. ▲chapter number, ▲§ ▲section number▲ (West ▲Year).
Annotated Laws of Massachusetts	Mass. ▲Ann. ▲Laws ▲ch. ▲chapter number,▲ § ▲section number▲ (LexisNexis ▲Year).

Session laws:	
★Acts and Resolves of Massachusetts	Year▲Mass. ▲Acts ▲page number.
Massachusetts Legislative Service	Year▲Mass. ▲Legis. ▲Serv. ▲page number ▲(West).

Massachusetts Advance Legislative Service	Year–Pamphlet number▲ Mass. ▲Adv. ▲Legis.▲ Serv.▲ page number▲ (LexisNexis).
Administrative compilation:	
★Code of Massachusetts Regulations	Title number▲ Mass. ▲Code▲ Regs. ▲§▲ section number▲ (Year).
Administrative register:	
Massachusetts Register	Issue number▲ Mass. ▲Reg. ▲page number ▲(Month▲ Day,▲ Year).
Local citation rules?	Yes. See **Appendix 2**.
Neutral citation rules?	No.
Court website:	http://www.mass.gov/courts/
Legislative website:	https://malegislature.gov/
Administrative website:	http://www.lawlib.state.ma.us/source/mass/cmr/

Michigan

Court system and reporters:		
Michigan Supreme Court (Mich.)		
Reporter	*Abbreviation*	*Dates*
★Michigan Reports	Mich.	1847–present
North Western Reporter	N.W.	1879–1941
Second Series	N.W.2d	1941–present
Michigan Court of Appeals (Mich. ▲Ct. ▲App.)		
Reporter	*Abbreviation*	*Dates*
★Michigan Appeals Reports	Mich. ▲App.	1965–present
North Western Reporter Second Series	N.W.2d	1965–present
Constitution:		
Michigan Constitution of 1963	Mich. ▲Const. ▲[art. *or* amend.]▲ number, ▲§▲ section number.	
Statutory compilations:		
★Michigan Compiled Laws (1979)	Mich. ▲Comp. ▲Laws ▲§▲ section number ▲(Year).	
Michigan Compiled Laws Annotated	Mich. ▲Comp. ▲Laws ▲Ann. ▲§▲ section number▲ (West▲ Year).	

Michigan Compiled Laws Service	Mich. ▲ Comp. ▲ Laws ▲ Serv. ▲ § ▲ section number ▲ (LexisNexis ▲ Year).
Session laws:	
★Public and Local Acts of the Legislature of the State of Michigan	Year ▲ Mich. ▲ Pub. ▲ Acts ▲ page number.
Michigan Legislative Service	Year ▲ Mich. ▲ Legis. ▲ Serv. ▲ page number ▲ (West).
Michigan Advance Legislative Service	Year–Pamphlet number ▲ Mich. ▲ Adv. ▲ Legis. ▲ Serv. ▲ page number ▲ (LexisNexis).
Administrative compilation:	
Michigan Administrative Code	Mich. ▲ Admin. ▲ Code ▲ r. ▲ rule number ▲ (Year).
Administrative register:	
Michigan Register	Issue number ▲ Mich. ▲ Reg. ▲ page number ▲ (Month ▲ Day, ▲ Year).
Local citation rules?	Yes. See **Appendix 2**.
Neutral citation rules?	No.
Court website:	http://courts.michigan.gov/
Legislative website:	http://www.legislature.mi.gov/
Administrative website:	http://www.michigan.gov/lara/

Minnesota

Court system and reporters:		
Minnesota Supreme Court (Minn.)		
Reporter	*Abbreviation*	*Dates*
★Minnesota Reports	Minn.	1851–1977
North Western Reporter	N.W.	1879–1941
★Second Series (official since 1978)	N.W.2d	1941–present
Minnesota Court of Appeals (Minn. ▲ Ct. ▲ App.)		
Reporter	*Abbreviation*	*Dates*
★North Western Reporter Second Series	N.W.2d	1983–present

Constitution:	
Minnesota Constitution	Minn.▲Const.▲[art. *or* amend.]▲number,▲§▲section number.
Statutory compilations:	
★Minnesota Statutes	Minn.▲Stat.▲§▲section number▲(Year).
Minnesota Statutes Annotated	Minn.▲Stat.▲Ann.▲§▲section number▲(West▲Year).
Session laws:	
★Laws of Minnesota	Year▲Minn.▲Laws▲page number.
Minnesota Session Law Service	Year▲Minn.▲Sess.▲L.▲Serv.▲page number▲(West).
Administrative compilation:	
Minnesota Rules	Minn.▲R.▲rule number▲(Year).
Administrative register:	
Minnesota State Register	Volume number▲Minn.▲Reg.▲page number▲(Month▲Day,▲Year).
Local citation rules?	No.
Neutral citation rules?	No.
Court website:	http://www.mncourts.gov/default.aspx
Legislative website:	http://www.leg.state.mn.us/
Administrative website:	https://www.revisor.mn.gov/rules/

Mississippi

Court system and reporters:		
Mississippi Supreme Court (Miss.) *Note:* Between 1832–1868, High Court of Errors and Appeals (Miss.).		
Reporter	*Abbreviation*	*Dates*
★Mississippi Reports	Miss.	1818–1966
Southern Reporter	So.	1887–1941
★Second Series (official since 1966)	So.▲2d	1941–2008
★Third Series	So.▲3d	2008–present

Mississippi Court of Appeals (Miss. Ct. App.)		
Reporter	*Abbreviation*	*Dates*
★Southern Reporter Second Series	So. 2d	1995–2008
★Third Series	So. 3d	2008–present
Constitution:		
Mississippi Constitution of 1890	Miss. Const. [art. *or* amend.] number, § section number.	
Statutory compilations:		
★Mississippi Code of 1972 Annotated	Miss. Code Ann. § section number (Year).	
West's Annotated Mississippi Code	Miss. Code Ann. § section number (West Year).	
Session laws:		
★General Laws of Mississippi	Year Miss. Laws page number.	
Mississippi General Laws Advance Sheets	Year–Pamphlet number Miss. Laws Adv. Sh. page number (LexisNexis).	
West's Mississippi Legislative Service	Year Miss. Legis. Serv. page number (West).	
Administrative compilation:		
Code of Mississippi Rules	Title number–chapter number Code Miss. R. § section number (LexisNexis Year).	
Administrative register:		
Mississippi Government Register	Issue number Miss. Gov't Reg. page number (LexisNexis Month Year).	
Local citation rules?	Yes. See **Appendix 2.**	
Neutral citation rules?	Yes. See **Appendix 2.**	
Court website:	http://courts.ms.gov/	
Legislative website:	http://www.legislature.ms.gov/	
Administrative website:	http://www.sos.ms.gov/ regulation_and_enforcement_admin_ procedures3.aspx	

Missouri

<table>
<tr><td colspan="3">Court system and reporters:</td></tr>
<tr><td colspan="3" align="center">Missouri Supreme Court (Mo.)</td></tr>
<tr><td>Reporter</td><td>Abbreviation</td><td>Dates</td></tr>
<tr><td>★Missouri Reports</td><td>Mo.</td><td>1821–1956</td></tr>
<tr><td>South Western Reporter</td><td>S.W.</td><td>1887–1928</td></tr>
<tr><td>★Second Series (official since 1956)</td><td>S.W.2d</td><td>1928–1999</td></tr>
<tr><td>★Third Series</td><td>S.W.3d</td><td>1999–present</td></tr>
<tr><td colspan="3" align="center">Missouri Court of Appeals (Mo. ▲ Ct. ▲ App.)</td></tr>
<tr><td>Reporter</td><td>Abbreviation</td><td>Dates</td></tr>
<tr><td>★Missouri Appeals Reports</td><td>Mo. ▲ App.</td><td>1876–1952</td></tr>
<tr><td>South Western Reporter</td><td>S.W.</td><td>1902–1928</td></tr>
<tr><td>★Second Series (official since 1954)</td><td>S.W.2d</td><td>1928–1999</td></tr>
<tr><td>★Third Series</td><td>S.W.3d</td><td>1999–present</td></tr>
<tr><td colspan="3">Constitution:</td></tr>
<tr><td>Missouri Constitution of 1945</td><td colspan="2">Mo. ▲ Const. ▲ [art. or amend.] ▲ number, ▲ § ▲ section number.</td></tr>
<tr><td colspan="3">Statutory compilations:</td></tr>
<tr><td>★Missouri Revised Statutes</td><td colspan="2">Mo. ▲ Rev. ▲ Stat. ▲ § ▲ section number ▲ (Year).</td></tr>
<tr><td>Vernon's Annotated Missouri Statutes</td><td colspan="2">Mo. ▲ Rev. ▲ Stat. ▲ Ann. ▲ § ▲ section number (West ▲ Year).</td></tr>
<tr><td colspan="3">Session laws:</td></tr>
<tr><td>★Laws of Missouri</td><td colspan="2">Year ▲ Mo. ▲ Laws ▲ page number.</td></tr>
<tr><td>Missouri Legislative Service</td><td colspan="2">Year ▲ Mo. ▲ Legis. ▲ Serv. ▲ page number ▲ (West).</td></tr>
<tr><td colspan="3">Administrative compilation:</td></tr>
<tr><td>Missouri Code of State Regulations Annotated</td><td colspan="2">Mo. ▲ Code ▲ Regs. ▲ Ann. ▲ tit. ▲ title number, ▲ § ▲ section number ▲ (Year).</td></tr>
<tr><td colspan="3">Administrative register:</td></tr>
<tr><td>Missouri Register</td><td colspan="2">Volume number ▲ Mo. ▲ Reg. ▲ page number ▲ (Month ▲ Day, ▲ Year).</td></tr>
</table>

Local citation rules?	No.
Neutral citation rules?	No.
Court website:	http://www.courts.mo.gov/
Legislative website:	http://www.moga.mo.gov/
Administrative website:	http://www.sos.mo.gov/adrules/csr/csr.asp

Montana

Court system and reporters:		
Montana Supreme Court (Mont.)		
Reporter	*Abbreviation*	*Dates*
★Montana Reports	Mont.	1868–present
Pacific Reporter	P.	1883–1931
Second Series	P.2d	1931–2000
Third Series	P.3d	2000–present
Constitution:		
Montana Constitution of 1972	Mont.▲Const.▲[art. *or* amend.]▲number, ▲§▲section number.	
Statutory compilations:		
★Montana Code Annotated	Mont.▲Code▲Ann.▲§▲section number▲ (Year).	
West's Montana Code Annotated	Mont.▲Code▲Ann.▲§▲section number▲ (West▲Year).	
Session laws:		
Laws of Montana	Year▲Mont.▲Laws▲page number.	
Administrative compilation:		
Administrative Rules of Montana	Mont.▲Admin.▲R.▲rule number▲(Year).	
Administrative register:		
Montana Administrative Register	Issue number▲Mont.▲Admin.▲Reg.▲ page number▲(Month▲Day,▲Year).	
Local citation rules?	Yes. See **Appendix 2**.	
Neutral citation rules?	Yes. See **Appendix 2**.	

Court website:	http://courts.mt.gov/default.mcpx
Legislative website:	http://leg.mt.gov/css/default.asp
Administrative website:	http://www.mtrules.org/

Nebraska

Court system and reporters:		
Nebraska Supreme Court (Neb.)		
Reporter	*Abbreviation*	*Dates*
★Nebraska Reports	Neb.	1871–present
North Western Reporter	N.W.	1879–1941
Second Series	N.W.2d	1941–present
Nebraska Court of Appeals (Neb.▲Ct.▲App.)		
Reporter	*Abbreviation*	*Dates*
★Nebraska Appellate Reports	Neb.▲App.	1992–present
North Western Reporter Second Series	N.W.2d	1992–present

Constitution:	
Nebraska Constitution of 1875	Neb.▲Const.▲[art. *or* amend.]▲number,▲§▲section number.

Statutory compilations:	
★Revised Statutes of Nebraska	Neb.▲Rev.▲Stat.▲§▲section number▲(Year).
Revised Statutes of Nebraska Annotated	Neb.▲Rev.▲Stat.▲Ann.▲§▲section number ▲(LexisNexis▲Year).
West's Revised Statutes of Nebraska Annotated	Neb.▲Rev.▲Stat.▲Ann.▲§▲section number ▲(West▲Year).

Session laws:	
★Laws of Nebraska	Year▲Neb.▲Laws▲page number.

Administrative compilation:	
Nebraska Administrative Code	Title number▲Neb.▲Admin.▲Code▲§▲section number▲(Year).

Local citation rules?	Yes. See **Appendix 2**.
Neutral citation rules?	No.

Court website:	http://www.supremecourt.ne.gov/
Legislative website:	http://nebraskalegislature.gov/
Administrative website:	http://www.sos.state.ne.us/rules-and-regs/regsearch/

Nevada

Court system and reporters:		
Nevada Supreme Court (Nev.)		
Reporter	*Abbreviation*	*Dates*
★Nevada Reports	Nev.	1865–present
Pacific Reporter	P.	1883–1931
Second Series	P.2d	1931–2000
Third Series	P.3d	2000–present
Constitution:		
Nevada Constitution	Nev. Const. [art. *or* amend.] number, § section number.	
Statutory compilations:		
★Nevada Revised Statutes	Nev. Rev. Stat. § section number (Year).	
Michie's Nevada Revised Statutes Annotated	Nev. Rev. Stat. Ann. § section number (LexisNexis Year).	
West's Nevada Revised Statutes Annotated	Nev. Rev. Stat. Ann. § section number (West Year).	
Session laws:		
★Statutes of Nevada	Year Nev. Stat. page number.	
West's Nevada Legislative Service	Year Nev. Legis. Serv. page number (West).	
Administrative compilation:		
Nevada Administrative Code	Nev. Admin. Code § section number (Year).	
Administrative register:		
Nevada Register of Administrative Regulations	Volume number Nev. Reg. Admin. Regs. regulation number (Month Day, Year).	
Local citation rules?	Yes. See **Appendix 2**.	
Neutral citation rules?	No.	

Court website:	http://www.nevadajudiciary.us/
Legislative website:	http://www.leg.state.nv.us/
Administrative website:	http://www.leg.state.nv.us/law1.cfm

New Hampshire

Court system and reporters:		
New Hampshire Supreme Court (N.H.)		
Reporter	*Abbreviation*	*Dates*
★New Hampshire Reports	N.H.	1816–present
Atlantic Reporter	A.	1885–1938
Second Series	A.2d	1938–2010
Third Series	A.3d	2010–present
Constitution:		
New Hampshire Constitution of 1784	N.H. ▲ Const. ▲ [art. *or* amend.] ▲ number, ▲ § ▲ section number.	
Statutory compilations:		
★New Hampshire Revised Statutes Annotated	N.H. ▲ Rev. ▲ Stat. ▲ Ann. ▲ § ▲ section number ▲ (Year).	
Lexis New Hampshire Revised Statutes Annotated	N.H. ▲ Rev. ▲ Stat. ▲ Ann. ▲ § ▲ section number ▲ (LexisNexis ▲ Year).	
Session laws:		
★Laws of the State of New Hampshire	Year ▲ N.H. ▲ Laws ▲ page number.	
New Hampshire Revised Statutes Annotated Advance Legislative Service	Year–Pamphlet number ▲ N.H. ▲ Rev. ▲ Stat. ▲ Ann. ▲ Adv. ▲ Legis ▲ Serv ▲ page number ▲ (LexisNexis).	
Administrative compilations:		
★New Hampshire Code of Administrative Rules Annotated	N.H. ▲ Code ▲ Admin. ▲ R. ▲ Ann. ▲ Abbreviated department name ▲ rule number ▲ (Year).	
Code of New Hampshire Rules	N.H. ▲ Code ▲ R. ▲ Abbreviated department name ▲ rule number ▲ (LexisNexis ▲ Year).	
Administrative registers:		
★New Hampshire Rulemaking Register	Volume number ▲ N.H. ▲ Rulemaking ▲ Reg. ▲ page number ▲ (Month ▲ Day, ▲ Year).	

New Hampshire Government Register	Issue number▲N.H.▲Gov't▲Reg.▲ page number▲(LexisNexis▲Month▲Year).
Local citation rules?	Yes. See **Appendix 2.**
Neutral citation rules?	No.
Court website:	http://www.courts.state.nh.us/
Legislative website:	http://gencourt.state.nh.us/
Administrative websites:	http://gencourt.state.nh.us/rules/index.html
	http://www.gencourt.state.nh.us/rules/register/default.htm

New Jersey

Court system and reporters:		
New Jersey Supreme Court (N.J.) *Note:* Before 1948, New Jersey Court of Errors and Appeals (N.J.).		
Reporter	*Abbreviation*	*Dates*
★New Jersey Reports	N.J.	1948–present
★New Jersey Law Reports	N.J.L.	1790–1948
★New Jersey Equity Reports	N.J.▲Eq.	1830–1948
New Jersey Miscellaneous Reports	N.J.▲Misc.	1923–1948
Atlantic Reporter	A.	1885–1938
Second Series	A.2d	1938–2010
Third Series	A.3d	2010–present
New Jersey Superior Court Appellate Division (N.J.▲Super.▲Ct.▲App.▲Div.), New Jersey Superior Court Chancery Division (N.J.▲Super.▲Ct.▲Ch.▲Div.), New Jersey Superior Court Law Division (N.J.▲Super.▲Ct.▲L.▲Div.), New Jersey County Courts (N.J.▲Name of County▲County▲Ct.), and other New Jersey lower courts *Note:* Before 1947, New Jersey Superior Court was New Jersey Supreme Court (N.J.▲Sup.▲Ct.), New Jersey Court of Chancery (N.J.▲Ch.), and New Jersey Prerogative Court (N.J.▲Prerog.▲Ct.).		
Reporter	*Abbreviation*	*Dates*
★New Jersey Superior Court Reports	N.J.▲Super.	1948–present
★New Jersey Law Reports	N.J.L.	1790–1948

★New Jersey Equity Reports	N.J. ▲ Eq.	1830–1948
New Jersey Miscellaneous Reports	N.J. ▲ Misc.	1923–1948
Atlantic Reporter	A.	1885–1938
Second Series	A.2d	1938–2010
Third Series	A.3d	2010–present
New Jersey Tax Court (N.J.T.C.)		
Reporter	*Abbreviation*	*Dates*
New Jersey Tax Court Reports	N.J. ▲ Tax	1979–present
Constitution:		
New Jersey Constitution of 1947	N.J. ▲ Const. ▲ [art. *or* amend.] ▲ number, ▲ § ▲ section number.	
Statutory compilations:		
★New Jersey Statutes Annotated	N.J. ▲ Stat. ▲ Ann. ▲ § ▲ section number ▲ (Year).	
New Jersey Revised Statutes (1937)	N.J. ▲ Rev. ▲ Stat. ▲ § ▲ section number ▲ (Year).	
Session laws:		
★Laws of New Jersey	Year ▲ N.J. ▲ Laws ▲ page number.	
New Jersey Session Law Service	Year ▲ N.J. ▲ Sess. ▲ L. ▲ Serv. ▲ page number ▲ (West).	
Administrative compilation:		
New Jersey Administrative Code	N.J. ▲ Admin. ▲ Code ▲ § ▲ title:chapter–subchapter.section number ▲ (Year).	
Administrative register:		
New Jersey Register	Volume number ▲ N.J. ▲ Reg. ▲ page number ▲ (Month ▲ Day, ▲ Year).	
Local citation rules?	Yes. See **Appendix 2**.	
Neutral citation rules?	No.	
Court website:	http://www.judiciary.state.nj.us/	
Legislative website:	http://www.njleg.state.nj.us/	
Administrative website:	http://www.state.nj.us/oal/rules.html	

New Mexico

Court system and reporters:		
New Mexico Supreme Court (N.M.)		
Reporter	*Abbreviation*	*Dates*
★New Mexico Reports	N.M.	1852–present
Pacific Reporter	P.	1883–1931
Second Series	P.2d	1931–2000
Third Series	P.3d	2000–present
New Mexico Court of Appeals (N.M.▲Ct.▲App.)		
Reporter	*Abbreviation*	*Dates*
★New Mexico Reports	N.M.	1966–present
Pacific Reporter Second Series	P.2d	1966–2000
Third Series	P.3d	2000–present
Constitution:		
New Mexico Constitution	N.M.▲Const.▲[art. *or* amend.]▲number, ▲§▲section number.	
Statutory compilations:		
★New Mexico Statutes Annotated 1978 (Conway Rede)	N.M.▲Stat.▲Ann.▲§▲section number ▲(Year).	
West's New Mexico Statutes Annotated	N.M.▲Stat.▲Ann.▲§▲section number ▲(West▲Year).	
Michie's Annotated Statutes of New Mexico	N.M.▲Stat.▲Ann.▲§▲section number ▲(LexisNexis▲Year).	
Session laws:		
★Laws of the State of New Mexico	Year▲N.M.▲Laws▲page number.	
New Mexico Advance Legislative Service	Year▲N.M.▲Adv.▲Legis.▲Serv.▲ page number.	
West's New Mexico Legislative Service	Year▲N.M.▲Legis.▲Serv.▲page number ▲(West).	
Administrative compilation:		
Code of New Mexico Rules	N.M.▲Code▲R.▲§▲section number (LexisNexis▲Year).	

Administrative register:	
New Mexico Register	Volume number ▲ N.M. ▲ Reg. ▲ page number ▲ (Month ▲ Day, ▲ Year).
Local citation rules?	Yes. See **Appendix 2.**
Neutral citation rules?	Yes. See **Appendix 2.**
Court website:	http://www.nmcourts.gov/
Legislative website:	http://www.nmlegis.gov/lcs/
Administrative websites:	http://www.nmcpr.state.nm.us/nmac/
	http://www.nmcpr.state.nm.us/nmregister/

New York

Court system and reporters:		
New York Court of Appeals (N.Y.) *Note:* Before 1846, the highest state courts were the New York Court for the Correction of Errors (N.Y. ▲ Errors) and the New York Supreme Court of Judicature (N.Y.). The highest court of equity was the New York Court of Chancery (N.Y. ▲ Ch.). Each court had its own reporters, which are not included below.		
Reporter	*Abbreviation*	*Dates*
★New York Reports	N.Y.	1847–1956
★Second Series	N.Y.2d	1956–2003
★Third Series	N.Y.3d	2004–present
North Eastern Reporter	N.E.	1885–1936
Second Series	N.E.2d	1936–present
West's New York Supplement Second Series	N.Y.S.2d	1956–present
New York Supreme Court, Appellate Division (N.Y. ▲ App. ▲ Div.), previously Supreme Court, General Term (N.Y. ▲ Gen. ▲ Term)		
Reporter	*Abbreviation*	*Dates*
★New York Appellate Division Reports	A.D.	1896–1955
★Second Series	A.D.2d	1956–2003
★Third Series	A.D.3d	2004–present

West's New York Supplement	N.Y.S.	1888–1937
Second Series	N.Y.S.2d	1937–present

Other New York lower courts (e.g., N.Y.▲App.▲Term, N.Y.▲Sup.▲Ct., N.Y.▲Ct.▲Cl., N.Y.▲Civ.▲Ct., N.Y.▲Crim.▲Ct., N.Y.▲Fam.▲Ct.)		
Reporter	*Abbreviation*	*Dates*
★New York Miscellaneous Reports	Misc.	1892–1955
★Second Series	Misc.▲2d	1956–2003
★Third Series	Misc.▲3d	2003–present
West's New York Supplement	N.Y.S.	1888–1937
Second Series	N.Y.S.2d	1937–present

Constitution:

New York Constitution of 1938	N.Y.▲Const.▲[art. *or* amend.]▲number,▲ §▲section number.

Statutory compilations:

McKinney's Consolidated Laws of New York Annotated	N.Y.▲Subject Abbreviation▲Law▲§▲section number▲(McKinney▲Year).
New York Consolidated Laws Service	N.Y.▲Subject Abbreviation▲Law▲§▲section number▲(Consol.▲Year).
Gould's Consolidated Laws of New York	N.Y.▲Subject Abbreviation▲Law▲§▲section number▲(Gould▲Year).

Subject abbreviations for statutory compilations:

Abandoned Property	Aband.▲Prop.	Benevolent Orders	Ben.▲Ord.
Agriculture and Markets	Agric.▲&▲Mkts.	Business Corporation	Bus.▲Corp.
Alcoholic Beverage Control	Alco.▲Bev.▲Cont.	Canal	Canal
		Civil Practice Law and Rules	N.Y.▲C.P.L.R.▲rule number
Alternative County Government	Alt.▲Cnty.▲Gov't	Civil Rights	Civ.▲Rights
		Civil Service	Civ.▲Serv.
Arts and Cultural Affairs	Arts▲&▲Cult.▲Aff.	Commerce	Com.
Banking	Banking	Cooperative Corporations	Coop.▲Corps.

Correction	Correct.		Highway	High.
County	County		Indian	Indian
Criminal Procedure	Crim. Proc.		Insurance	Ins.
Debtor and Creditor	Debt. & Cred.		Judiciary Court Acts	Jud. Ct. Acts
Domestic Relations	Dom. Rel.		Labor	Lab.
Economic Development	Econ. Dev.		Legislative	Legis.
Education	Educ.		Lien	Lien
Elder	Elder		Limited Liability Company	Ltd. Liab. Co.
Election	Elec.		Local Finance	Local Fin.
Eminent Domain Procedure	Em. Dom. Proc.		Mental Hygiene	Mental Hyg.
Employers' Liability	Empl'rs Liab.		Military	Mil.
Energy	Energy		Multiple Dwelling	Mult. Dwell.
Environmental Conservation	Envtl. Conserv.		Multiple Residence	Mult. Resid.
Estates, Powers and Trusts	Est. Powers & Trusts		Municipal Home Rule and Statute of Local Governments	Mun. Home Rule
Executive	Exec.		Navigation	Nav.
General Associations	Gen. Ass'ns		Not–for–Profit Corporation	Not–for–Profit Corp.
General Business	Gen. Bus.		Optional County Government	Opt. Cnty. Gov't
General City	Gen. City		Parks, Recreation and Historic Preservation	Parks Rec. & Hist. Preserv.
General Construction	Gen. Constr.		Partnership	P'ship
General Municipal	Gen. Mun.		Penal	Penal
General Obligations	Gen. Oblig.		Personal Property	Pers. Prop.

Private Housing Finance	Priv. Hous. Fin.	State	State
Public Authorities	Pub. Auth.	State Administrative Procedure Act	A.P.A.
Public Buildings	Pub. Bldgs.	State Finance	State Fin.
Public Health	Pub. Health	State Printing and Public Documents	State Print. & Pub. Docs.
Public Housing	Pub. Hous.	State Technology	State Tech.
Public Lands	Pub. Lands	Statutes	Stat.
Public Officers	Pub. Off.	Surrogate's Court Procedure Act	Surr. Ct. Proc. Act
Public Service	Pub. Serv.	Tax	Tax
Racing, Pari–Mutuel Wagering and Breeding	Rac. Pari–Mut. Wag. & Breed.	Town	Town
Railroad	R.R.	Transportation	Transp.
Rapid Transit	Rapid Trans.	Transportation Corporations	Transp. Corps.
Real Property	Real Prop.	Unconsolidated	Unconsol.
Real Property Actions and Proceedings	Real Prop. Acts.	Uniform Commercial Code	U.C.C.
Real Property Tax	Real Prop. Tax	Vehicle and Traffic	Veh. & Traf.
Religious Corporations	Relig. Corps.	Village	Village
Retirement and Social Security	Retire. & Soc. Sec.	Volunteer Ambulance Workers' Benefit	Vol. Ambul. Workers' Ben.
Rural Electric Cooperative	Rural Elec. Coop.	Volunteer Firefighters' Benefit	Vol. Fire. Ben.
Second Class Cities	Second Class Cities	Workers' Compensation	Workers' Comp.
Social Services	Soc. Servs.		
Soil and Water Conservations Districts	Soil & Water Conserv. Dist.		

Subject abbreviations for uncompiled laws (use format for statutory compilation sources):			
Code of Criminal Procedure	Code ▲ Crim. ▲ Proc.	New York City Criminal Court Act	City ▲ Crim. ▲ Ct. ▲ Act
Court of Claims Act	Ct. ▲ Cl. ▲ Act	Uniform City Court Act	Uniform ▲ City ▲ Ct. ▲ Act
Family Court Act	Fam. ▲ Ct. ▲ Act	Uniform District Court Act	Uniform ▲ Dist. ▲ Ct. ▲ Act
New York City Civil Court Act	City ▲ Civ. ▲ Ct. ▲ Act	Uniform Justice Court Act	Uniform ▲ Just. ▲ Ct. ▲ Act

Session laws:	
★Laws of New York	Year ▲ N.Y. ▲ Laws ▲ page number.
McKinney's Session Laws of New York	Year ▲ N.Y. ▲ Sess. ▲ Laws ▲ page number ▲ (McKinney).
New York Consolidated Laws Service Advance Legislative Service	Year–Pamphlet number ▲ N.Y. ▲ Consol. ▲ Laws ▲ Adv. ▲ Legis. ▲ Serv. ▲ page number ▲ (LexisNexis).
Administrative compilation:	
★Official Compilation of Codes, Rules, and Regulations of the State of New York	N.Y. ▲ Comp. ▲ Codes ▲ R. ▲ & ▲ Regs. ▲ tit. ▲ title number, ▲ § ▲ section number ▲ (Year).
Administrative register:	
New York State Register	Volume number ▲ N.Y. ▲ Reg. ▲ page number ▲ (Month ▲ Day, ▲ Year).
Local citation rules?	Yes. See **Appendix 2**.
Neutral citation rules?	No.
Court website:	http://www.courts.state.ny.us/
Legislative website:	http://public.leginfo.state.ny.us/menuf.cgi
Administrative websites:	http://www.dos.ny.gov/info/nycrr.html
	http://www.dos.ny.gov/info/register.htm

North Carolina

Court system and reporters:		
North Carolina Supreme Court (N.C.)		
Reporter	*Abbreviation*	*Dates*
★North Carolina Reports	N.C.	1778–present
South Eastern Reporter	S.E.	1886–1939
Second Series	S.E.2d	1939–present
North Carolina Court of Appeals (N.C. ▲ Ct. ▲ App.)		
Reporter	*Abbreviation*	*Dates*
★North Carolina Court of Appeals Reports	N.C. ▲ App.	1968–present
South Eastern Reporter Second Series	S.E.2d	1968–present
Constitution:		
North Carolina Constitution of 1971	N.C. ▲ Const. ▲ [art. *or* amend.] ▲ number, ▲ § ▲ section number.	
Statutory compilations:		
★General Statutes of North Carolina	N.C. ▲ Gen. ▲ Stat. ▲ § ▲ section number ▲ (Year).	
West's North Carolina General Statutes Annotated	N.C. ▲ Gen. ▲ Stat. ▲ Ann. ▲ § ▲ section number ▲ (West ▲ Year).	
Session laws:		
★Session Laws of North Carolina	Year ▲ N.C. ▲ Sess. ▲ Laws ▲ page number.	
North Carolina Advance Legislative Service	Year–Pamphlet number ▲ N.C. ▲ Adv. ▲ Legis. ▲ Serv. ▲ page number ▲ (LexisNexis).	
North Carolina Legislative Service	Year ▲ N.C. ▲ Legis. ▲ Serv. ▲ page number ▲ (West).	
Administrative compilation:		
North Carolina Administrative Code	Title number ▲ N.C. ▲ Admin. ▲ Code ▲ rule number ▲ (Year).	
Administrative register:		
North Carolina Register	Volume number ▲ N.C. ▲ Reg. ▲ page number ▲ (Month ▲ Day, ▲ Year).	
Local citation rules?	Yes. See **Appendix 2**.	

Neutral citation rules?	No.
Court website:	http://www.nccourts.org/
Legislative website:	http://www.ncga.state.nc.us/
Administrative websites:	http://reports.oah.state.nc.us/ncac.asp
	http://www.oah.state.nc.us/rules/register/

North Dakota

Court system and reporters:		
North Dakota Supreme Court (N.D.)		
Reporter	*Abbreviation*	*Dates*
★North Dakota Reports	N.D.	1890–1953
North Western Reporter	N.W.	1890–1941
★Second Series (official since 1953)	N.W.2d	1941–present
North Dakota Court of Appeals (N.D. ▲ Ct. ▲ App.)		
Reporter	*Abbreviation*	*Dates*
★North Western Reporter Second Series	N.W.2d	1987–present
Constitution:		
North Dakota Constitution	N.D. ▲ Const. ▲ [art. *or* amend.] ▲ number, ▲ § ▲ section number.	
Statutory compilations:		
★North Dakota Century Code	N.D. ▲ Cent. ▲ Code ▲ § ▲ section number ▲ (Year).	
West's North Dakota Century Code Annotated	N.D. ▲ Cent. ▲ Code ▲ Ann. ▲ § ▲ section number ▲ (West ▲ Year).	
Session laws:		
★Laws of North Dakota	Year ▲ N.D. ▲ Laws ▲ page number.	
North Dakota Century Code Advance Legislative Service	Year–Pamphlet number ▲ N.D. ▲ Cent. ▲ Code ▲ Adv. ▲ Legis. ▲ Serv. ▲ page number ▲ (LexisNexis).	
West's North Dakota Legislative Service	Year ▲ N.D. ▲ Legis. ▲ Serv. ▲ page number ▲ (West).	

Administrative compilation:	
North Dakota Administrative Code	N.D.▲Admin.▲Code▲rule number▲(Year).
Local citation rules?	No.
Neutral citation rules?	Yes. See **Appendix 2**.
Court website:	http://www.ndcourts.gov/
Legislative website:	http://www.legis.nd.gov/
Administrative website:	http://www.legis.nd.gov/agency-rules/north-dakota-administrative-code

Ohio

Court system and reporters:		
Ohio Supreme Court (Ohio)		
Reporter	*Abbreviation*	*Dates*
★Ohio Reports	Ohio	1821–1851
★Ohio State Reports	Ohio▲St.	1852–1964
★Second Series	Ohio▲St.▲2d	1964–1982
★Third Series	Ohio▲St.▲3d	1982–present
North Eastern Reporter	N.E.	1885–1936
Second Series	N.E.2d	1936–present
Ohio Court of Appeals (Ohio▲Ct.▲App.)		
Reporter	*Abbreviation*	*Dates*
★Ohio Appellate Reports	Ohio▲App.	1913–1965
★Second Series	Ohio▲App.▲2d	1965–1982
★Third Series	Ohio▲App.▲3d	1982–present
North Eastern Reporter	N.E.	1923–1936
Second Series	N.E.2d	1936–present
Other Ohio lower courts (e.g., **Ohio Court of Common Pleas (Ohio▲C.P.)**)		
Reporter	*Abbreviation*	*Dates*
★Ohio Miscellaneous Reports	Ohio▲Misc.	1960–1982
★Second Series	Ohio▲Misc.▲2d	1982–present

★Ohio Opinions	Ohio ▲ Op.	1934–1957
★Second Series	Ohio ▲ Op. ▲ 2d	1957–1976
★Third Series	Ohio ▲ Op. ▲ 3d	1976–1982

Constitution:		
Ohio Constitution of 1912	Ohio ▲ Const. ▲ [art. *or* amend.] ▲ number, ▲ § ▲ section number.	

Statutory compilations:	
Page's Ohio Revised Code Annotated	Ohio ▲ Rev. ▲ Code ▲ Ann. ▲ § ▲ section number ▲ (LexisNexis ▲ Year).
Baldwin's Ohio Revised Code Annotated	Ohio ▲ Rev. ▲ Code ▲ Ann. ▲ § ▲ section number ▲ (West ▲ Year).

Session laws:	
★State of Ohio: Legislative Acts Passed and Joint Resolutions Adopted	Year ▲ Ohio ▲ Laws ▲ page number.
Page's Ohio Legislative Bulletin	Year ▲ Ohio ▲ Legis. ▲ Bull. ▲ page number ▲ (LexisNexis).
Baldwin's Ohio Legislative Service Annotated	Year ▲ Ohio ▲ Legis. ▲ Serv. ▲ Ann. ▲ page number ▲ (West).

Administrative compilation:	
Baldwin's Ohio Administrative Code	Ohio ▲ Admin. ▲ Code ▲ rule number ▲ (Year).

Administrative register:	
Baldwin's Ohio Monthly Record	Ohio ▲ Monthly ▲ Rec. ▲ page number ▲ (Month ▲ Year).

Local citation rules?	Yes. See **Appendix 2**.
Neutral citation rules?	Yes. See **Appendix 2**.
Court website:	http://www.sconet.state.oh.us/
Legislative website:	http://www.legislature.state.oh.us/
Administrative websites:	http://codes.ohio.gov/oac/
	http://www.registerofohio.state.oh.us/

Oklahoma

Court system and reporters:		
Oklahoma Supreme Court (Okla.)		
Reporter	*Abbreviation*	*Dates*
★Oklahoma Reports	Okla.	1893–1953
Pacific Reporter	P.	1890–1931
★Second Series (official since 1953)	P.2d	1931–2000
★Third Series	P.3d	2000–present
Oklahoma Court of Criminal Appeals (Okla.▲Crim.▲App.) *Note:* Before 1959, the Oklahoma Criminal Court of Appeals (Okla.▲Crim.▲App.).		
Reporter	*Abbreviation*	*Dates*
★Oklahoma Criminal Reports	Okla.▲Crim.	1908–1955
Pacific Reporter	P.	1908–1931
★Second Series (official since 1953)	P.2d	1931–2000
★Third Series	P.3d	2000–present
Oklahoma Court of Civil Appeals (Okla.▲Civ.▲App.)		
Reporter	*Abbreviation*	*Dates*
★Pacific Reporter Second Series	P.2d	1967–2000
★Third Series	P.3d	2000–present
Oklahoma Court of Appeals of the Indian Territory (Indian▲Terr.)		
Reporter	*Abbreviation*	*Dates*
★Indian Territory Reports	Indian▲Terr.	1896–1907
South Western Reporter	S.W.	1896–1907
Constitution:		
Oklahoma Constitution	Okla.▲Const.▲[art. *or* amend.]▲number, ▲§▲section number.	
Statutory compilations:		
★Oklahoma Statutes	Okla.▲Stat.▲tit.▲title number,▲§▲ section number▲(Year).	
Oklahoma Statutes Annotated	Okla.▲Stat.▲Ann.▲tit.▲title number, ▲§▲section number▲(West▲Year).	

Session laws:	
Oklahoma Session Laws	Year▲Okla.▲Sess.▲Laws▲page number.
Oklahoma Session Law Service	Year▲Okla.▲Sess.▲Law▲Serv.▲ page number▲(West).
Administrative compilation:	
Oklahoma Administrative Code	Okla.▲Admin.▲Code▲§▲section number ▲(Year).
Administrative registers:	
Oklahoma Register	Volume number▲Okla.▲Reg.▲page number ▲(Month▲Day,▲Year).
Oklahoma Gazette (1962–1983)	Volume number▲Okla.▲Gaz.▲page number ▲(Month▲Day,▲Year).
Local citation rules?	Yes. See **Appendix 2**.
Neutral citation rules?	Yes. See **Appendix 2**.
Court website:	www.oscn.net
Legislative website:	http://www.oklegislature.gov/
Administrative website:	http://www.oar.state.ok.us/

Oregon

Court system and reporters:		
Oregon Supreme Court (Or.)		
Reporter	*Abbreviation*	*Dates*
★Oregon Reports	Or.	1853–present
Pacific Reporter	P.	1883–1931
Second Series	P.2d	1931–2000
Third Series	P.3d	2000–present
Oregon Court of Appeals (Or.▲Ct.▲App.)		
Reporter	*Abbreviation*	*Dates*
★Oregon Reports, Court of Appeals	Or.▲App.	1969–present
Pacific Reporter Second Series	P.2d	1969–2000
Third Series	P.3d	2000–present

Oregon Tax Court (Or. ▲ T.C.)		
Reporter	*Abbreviation*	*Dates*
★Oregon Tax Court Reports	Or. ▲ Tax	1962–present
Constitution:		
Oregon Constitution	Or. ▲ Const. ▲ [art. *or* amend.] ▲ number, ▲ § ▲ section number.	
Statutory compilations:		
★Oregon Revised Statutes	Or. ▲ Rev. ▲ Stat. ▲ § ▲ section number ▲ (Year).	
West's Oregon Revised Statutes Annotated	Or. ▲ Rev. ▲ Stat. ▲ Ann. ▲ § ▲ section number ▲ (West ▲ Year).	
Session laws:		
★Oregon Laws	Year ▲ Or. ▲ Laws ▲ page number.	
West's Oregon Legislative Service	Year ▲ Or. ▲ Legis. ▲ Serv. ▲ page number ▲ (West).	
Administrative compilation:		
Oregon Administrative Rules	Or. ▲ Admin. ▲ R. ▲ rule number ▲ (Year).	
Administrative register:		
Oregon Bulletin	Volume number ▲ Or. ▲ Bull. ▲ page number ▲ (Month ▲ Day, ▲ Year).	
Local citation rules?	Yes. See **Appendix 2**.	
Neutral citation rules?	No.	
Court website:	http://courts.oregon.gov/OJD/	
Legislative website:	http://www.leg.state.or.us/index.html	
Administrative website:	http://arcweb.sos.state.or.us/pages/rules/index.html	

Pennsylvania

Court system and reporters:		
Pennsylvania Supreme Court (Pa.) *Note:* Before 1804, High Court of Errors and Appeals (Pa.).		
Reporter	*Abbreviation*	*Dates*
★Pennsylvania State Reports	Pa.	1845–present
Atlantic Reporter	A.	1885–1938

Second Series	A.2d	1938–2010
Third Series	A.3d	2010–present

Pennsylvania Superior Court (Pa.▲Super.▲Ct.)		
Reporter	*Abbreviation*	*Dates*
★Pennsylvania Superior Court Reports	Pa.▲Super.	1895–1997
Atlantic Reporter	A.	1930–1938
★Second Series (official since 1997)	A.2d	1938–2010
★Third Series	A.3d	2010–present

Pennsylvania Commonwealth Court (Pa.▲Commw.▲Ct.)		
Reporter	*Abbreviation*	*Dates*
★Pennsylvania Commonwealth Court Reports	Pa.▲Commw.	1970–1994
★Atlantic Reporter Second Series (official since 1995)	A.2d	1970–2010
★Third Series	A.3d	2010–present

Pennsylvania District and County Courts (Pa.▲Name of County or District▲Ct.)		
Reporter	*Abbreviation*	*Dates*
★Pennsylvania District and County Reports	Pa.▲D.▲&▲C.	1922–1954
★Second Series	Pa.▲D.▲&▲C.2d	1955–1977
★Third Series	Pa.▲D.▲&▲C.3d	1977–1989
★Fourth Series	Pa.▲D.▲&▲C.4th	1989–2007
★Fifth Series	Pa.▲D.▲&▲C.5th	2007–present

Constitution:		
Pennsylvania Constitution of 1968	Pa.▲Const.▲[art. *or* amend.]▲number, ▲§▲section number.	

Statutory compilations:		
★Pennsylvania Consolidated Statutes	Title number▲Pa.▲Cons.▲Stat.▲§▲ section number▲(Year).	

Purdon's Pennsylvania Statutes and Consolidated Statutes Annotated	Title number▲Pa.▲Cons.▲Stat.▲Ann.▲§▲ section number▲(West▲Year).
Purdon's Pennsylvania Statutes Annotated (for titles not yet consolidated in official compilation)	Pa.▲Stat.▲Ann.▲tit.▲title number, ▲§▲section number▲(West▲Year).
Session laws:	
★Laws of Pennsylvania	Year▲Pa.▲Laws▲page number.
Purdon's Pennsylvania Legislative Service	Year▲Pa.▲Legis.▲Serv.▲page number ▲(West).
Administrative compilation:	
Pennsylvania Code	Title number▲Pa.▲Code▲§▲section number ▲(Year).
Administrative register:	
Pennsylvania Bulletin	Volume number▲Pa.▲Bull.▲page number ▲(Month▲Day,▲Year).
Local citation rules?	Yes. See **Appendix 2**.
Neutral citation rules?	Yes. See **Appendix 2**.
Court website:	http://ujsportal.pacourts.us/
Legislative website:	http://www.legis.state.pa.us/
Administrative website:	http://www.pacode.com/

Rhode Island   *Check dates* ✱

Court system and reporters:		
✱ **Rhode Island Supreme Court (R.I.)**		
Reporter	*Abbreviation*	*Dates*
★Rhode Island Reports	R.I.	1828–1980
Atlantic Reporter	A.	1885–1938
★Second Series (official since 1980)	A.2d	1938–2010
★Third Series	A.3d	2010–present
Constitution:		
Rhode Island Constitution of 1986	R.I.▲Const.▲[art. *or* amend.]▲number, ▲§▲section number.	

Statutory compilations:	
★General Laws of Rhode Island	R.I. ▲ Gen. ▲ Laws ▲ § ▲ section number ▲ (Year).
West's General Laws of Rhode Island Annotated	R.I. ▲ Gen. ▲ Laws ▲ Ann. ▲ § ▲ section number ▲ (West ▲ Year).
Session laws:	
★Public Laws of Rhode Island and Providence Plantations	Year ▲ R.I. ▲ Pub. ▲ Laws ▲ page number.
Acts and Resolves of Rhode Island and Providence Plantations	Year ▲ R.I. ▲ Acts ▲ & ▲ Resolves ▲ page number.
West's Rhode Island Legislative Service	Year ▲ R.I. ▲ Legis. ▲ Serv. ▲ page number ▲ (West).
Rhode Island Advance Legislative Service	Year–Pamphlet number ▲ R.I. ▲ Adv. ▲ Legis. ▲ Serv. ▲ page number ▲ (LexisNexis).
Administrative compilation:	
Code of Rhode Island Rules	Title number–Chapter number ▲ R.I. ▲ Code R. ▲ § ▲ section number ▲ (LexisNexis ▲ Year).
Administrative register:	
Rhode Island Government Register	Issue number ▲ R.I. ▲ Gov't ▲ Reg. ▲ page number ▲ (LexisNexis ▲ Month ▲ Year).
Local citation rules?	No.
Neutral citation rules?	No.
Court website:	http://www.courts.ri.gov/default.aspx
Legislative website:	http://www.rilin.state.ri.us/
Administrative website:	http://sos.ri.gov/rules/

South Carolina

Court system and reporters:		
South Carolina Supreme Court (S.C.)		
Reporter	*Abbreviation*	*Dates*
★South Carolina Reports	S.C.	1868–present
South Eastern Reporter	S.E.	1887–1939
Second Series	S.E.2d	1939–present

South Carolina Court of Appeals (S.C. ▲ Ct. ▲ App.)		
Reporter	*Abbreviation*	*Dates*
★South Carolina Reports	S.C.	1983–present
South Eastern Reporter Second Series	S.E.2d	1983–present
Constitution:		
South Carolina Constitution of 1895	S.C. ▲ Const. ▲ [art. *or* amend.] ▲ number, ▲ § ▲ section number.	
Statutory compilation:		
★Code of Laws of South Carolina 1976 Annotated	S.C. ▲ Code ▲ Ann. ▲ § ▲ section number ▲ (Year).	
Session laws:		
★Acts and Joint Resolutions of South Carolina	Year ▲ S.C. ▲ Acts ▲ page number.	
Administrative compilation:		
Code of Laws of South Carolina 1976 Annotated: Code of Regulations	S.C. ▲ Code ▲ Ann. ▲ Regs. ▲ regulation number ▲ (Year).	
Administrative register:		
South Carolina State Register	Volume number ▲ S.C. ▲ Reg. ▲ page number ▲ (Month ▲ Day, ▲ Year).	
Local citation rules?	Yes. See **Appendix 2**.	
Neutral citation rules?	No.	
Court website:	http://www.judicial.state.sc.us/	
Legislative website:	http://www.scstatehouse.gov/	
Administrative website:	http://www.scstatehouse.gov/coderegs/statmast.php	

South Dakota

Court system and reporters:		
South Dakota Supreme Court (S.D.)		
Reporter	*Abbreviation*	*Dates*
★South Dakota Reports	S.D.	1890–1976
North Western Reporter	N.W.	1890–1941

★Second Series (official since 1976)	N.W.2d	1941–present
Constitution:		
South Dakota Constitution	S.D.▲Const.▲[art. *or* amend.]▲number,▲ §▲section number.	
Statutory compilation:		
★South Dakota Codified Laws	S.D.▲Codified▲Laws▲§▲section number ▲(Year).	
Session laws:		
★Session Laws of South Dakota	Year▲S.D.▲Sess.▲Laws▲page number.	
Administrative compilation:		
Administrative Rules of South Dakota	S.D.▲Admin.▲R.▲rule number▲(Year).	
Administrative register:		
South Dakota Register	Volume number▲S.D.▲Reg.▲page number ▲(Month▲Day,▲Year).	
Local citation rules?	Yes. See **Appendix 2**.	
Neutral citation rules?	Yes. See **Appendix 2**.	
Court website:	http://www.sdjudicial.com/	
Legislative website:	http://legis.state.sd.us/index.aspx	
Administrative website:	http://legis.state.sd.us/rules/index.aspx	

Tennessee

Court system and reporters:		
Tennessee Supreme Court (Tenn.)		
Reporter	*Abbreviation*	*Dates*
★Tennessee Reports	Tenn.	1791–1972
South Western Reporter	S.W.	1886–1928
★Second Series (official since 1972)	S.W.2d	1928–1999
★Third Series	S.W.3d	1999–present

Tennessee Court of Appeals (Tenn.▲Ct.▲App.▲)		
Reporter	*Abbreviation*	*Dates*
★Tennessee Appeals Reports	Tenn.▲App.	1925–1971
★South Western Reporter Second Series (official since 1972)	S.W.2d	1932–1999
★Third Series	S.W.3d	1999–present
Tennessee Court of Criminal Appeals (Tenn.▲Crim.▲App.)		
Reporter	*Abbreviation*	*Dates*
★Tennessee Criminal Appeals Reports	Tenn.▲Crim.▲App.	1967–1971
★South Western Reporter Second Series (official since 1972)	S.W.2d	1967–1999
★Third Series	S.W.3d	1999–present
Constitution:		
Tennessee Constitution of 1870	Tenn.▲Const.▲[art. *or* amend.]▲number, ▲§▲section number.	
Statutory compilations:		
★Tennessee Code Annotated	Tenn.▲Code▲Ann.▲§▲section number ▲(Year).	
West's Tennessee Code Annotated	Tenn.▲Code▲Ann.▲§▲section number ▲(West▲Year).	
Session laws:		
★Public Acts of the State of Tennessee	Year▲Tenn.▲Pub.▲Acts▲ch.▲chapter number.	
★Private Acts of the State of Tennessee	Year▲Tenn.▲Priv.▲Acts▲ch.▲chapter number.	
Tennessee Code Annotated Advance Legislative Service	Year–Pamphlet number▲Tenn.▲Code▲Ann.▲Adv.▲Legis.▲Serv.▲page number ▲(LexisNexis).	
West's Tennessee Legislative Service	Year▲Tenn.▲Legis.▲Serv.▲page number ▲(West).	
Administrative compilation:		
Official Compilation—Rules and Regulations of the State of Tennessee	Tenn.▲Comp.▲R.▲&▲Regs.▲agency control number–division number–chapter number–rule number▲(Year).	

Administrative register:	
Tennessee Administrative Register	Volume number ▲ Tenn. ▲ Admin. ▲ Reg. ▲page number ▲ (Month ▲ Year).
Local citation rules?	Yes. See **Appendix 2**.
Neutral citation rules?	No.
Court website:	http://www.tsc.state.tn.us/
Legislative website:	http://www.legislature.state.tn.us/
Administrative website:	http://state.tn.us/sos/rules/index.htm

Texas

Court system and reporters:		
Texas Supreme Court (Tex.)		
Reporter	*Abbreviation*	*Dates*
★Texas Reports	Tex.	1846–1962
South Western Reporter	S.W.	1886–1928
★Second Series (official since 1962)	S.W.2d	1928–1999
★Third Series	S.W.3d	1999–present
Texas Court of Criminal Appeals (Tex. ▲ Crim. ▲ App.) *Note:* Before 1891, the Texas Court of Appeals (Tex. ▲ App.).		
Reporter	*Abbreviation*	*Dates*
★Texas Criminal Reports	Tex. ▲ Crim.	1892–1962
South Western Reporter	S.W.	1892–1928
★Second Series (official since 1962)	S.W.2d	1928–1999
★Third Series	S.W.3d	1999–present
Texas Court of Appeals (Tex. ▲ App.) *Note:* Before 1891, the Texas Court of Civil Appeals (Tex. ▲ Civ. ▲ App.).		
Reporter	*Abbreviation*	*Dates*
★Texas Civil Appeals Reports	Tex. ▲ Civ. ▲ App.	1892–1911
★South Western Reporter (official since 1911)	S.W.	1892–1928
★Second Series	S.W.2d	1928–1999
★Third Series	S.W.3d	1999–present

Constitution:	
Texas Constitution of 1876	Tex. Const. [art. *or* amend.] number, § section number.
Statutory compilations:	
★Vernon's Texas Codes Annotated	Tex. Subject Abbreviation Code Ann. § section number (West Year).
Vernon's Texas Business Corporation Act Annotated	Tex. Bus. Corp. Act Ann. art. article number (West Year).
Vernon's Texas Code of Criminal Procedure Annotated	Tex. Code Crim. Proc. Ann. art. article number (West Year).
Vernon's Texas Insurance Code Annotated	Tex. Ins. Code Ann. art. article number (West Year).
Vernon's Texas Probate Code Annotated	Tex. Prob. Code Ann. § section number (West Year).
Vernon's Texas Revised Civil Statutes Annotated	Tex. Rev. Civ. Stat. Ann. art. article number, § section number (West Year).

Note: When it enacts the Code of Criminal Procedure, Texas will complete a codification project begun in 1963, superseding the Revised Texas Statutes of 1925 with twenty-seven subject-matter codes. Researchers should note that it still may be necessary to refer to both the newer subject–matter codes and the older codes. *See* Legis. Ref. Lib. of Tex., *Statutory Revision*, http://www.lrl. state.tx.us/legis/revisorsNotes.cfm (last visited Aug. 30, 2013).

Subject abbreviations for statutory compilations:

Agriculture	Agric.	Criminal Procedure (not enacted as of Aug. 2013; when enacted, will replace Vernon's Texas Code of Criminal Procedure Annotated)	Crim. Proc.
Alcoholic Beverage	Alco. Bev.		
Business and Commerce	Bus. & Com.		
Business Organizations	Bus. Orgs.		
Civil Practice and Remedies	Civ. Prac. & Rem.		

Education	Educ.		Natural Resources	Nat. ▲ Res.
Election	Elec.		Occupations	Occ.
Estates	Est.		Parks and Wildlife	Parks ▲ & ▲ Wild.
Family	Fam.			
Finance	Fin.		Penal	Penal
Government	Gov't		Property	Prop.
Health and Safety	Health ▲ & ▲ Safety		Special District Local Laws	Spec. ▲ Dists.
Human Resources	Hum. ▲ Res.		Tax	Tax
Insurance	Ins.		Transportation	Transp.
Labor	Lab.		Utilities	Util.
Local Government	Loc. ▲ Gov't		Water	Water

Session laws:	
★General and Special Laws of the State of Texas	Year ▲ Tex. ▲ Gen. ▲ Laws ▲ page number.
Vernon's Texas Session Law Service	Year ▲ Tex. ▲ Sess. ▲ Law ▲ Serv. ▲ page number ▲ (West).
Administrative compilation:	
Texas Administrative Code	Title number ▲ Tex. ▲ Admin. ▲ Code ▲ § ▲ section number ▲ (Year).
Administrative register:	
Texas Register	Volume number ▲ Tex. ▲ Reg. ▲ page number ▲ (Month ▲ Day, ▲ Year).
Local citation rules?	Yes. See **Appendix 2**.
Neutral citation rules?	No.
Court website:	http://www.courts.state.tx.us/
Legislative website:	http://www.legis.state.tx.us/
Administrative websites:	http://www.sos.state.tx.us/tac/
	http://www.sos.state.tx.us/texreg/index.shtml

Utah

Court system and reporters:		
Utah Supreme Court (Utah)		
Reporter	*Abbreviation*	*Dates*
★Utah Reports	Utah	1855–1952
★Second Series	Utah ▲2d	1953–1974
Pacific Reporter	P.	1881–1931
★Second Series (official since 1974)	P.2d	1931–2000
★Third Series	P.3d	2000–present
Utah Court of Appeals (Utah ▲Ct. ▲App.)		
Reporter	*Abbreviation*	*Dates*
★Pacific Reporter Second Series	P.2d	1974–2000
★Third Series	P.3d	2000–present
Constitution:		
Utah Constitution of 1895	Utah ▲Const. ▲[art. *or* amend.] ▲number, ▲§ ▲section number.	
Statutory compilations:		
★Utah Code (online)	Utah ▲Code ▲§ ▲section number ▲(Year).	
Utah Code Annotated (LexisNexis)	Utah ▲Code ▲Ann. ▲§ ▲section number ▲(LexisNexis ▲Year).	
West's Utah Code Annotated	Utah ▲Code ▲Ann. ▲§ ▲section number ▲(West ▲Year).	
Session laws:		
★Laws of Utah	Year ▲Utah ▲Laws ▲page number.	
Utah Legislative Service	Year ▲Utah ▲Legis. ▲Serv. ▲page number ▲(West).	
Utah Code Advance Legislative Service	Year–Pamphlet number ▲Utah ▲Adv. ▲Legis. ▲Serv. ▲page number ▲(LexisNexis).	
Administrative compilation:		
Utah Administrative Code	Utah ▲Admin. ▲Code ▲r. ▲rule number ▲(Year).	

Administrative register:	
Utah State Bulletin	Issue number ▲ Utah ▲ Bull. ▲ page number ▲(Month ▲ Day, ▲ Year).
Local citation rules?	Yes. See **Appendix 2**.
Neutral citation rules?	Yes. See **Appendix 2**.
Court website:	http://www.utcourts.gov/
Legislative website:	http://le.utah.gov/
Administrative website:	http://www.rules.utah.gov/publicat/code.htm

Vermont

Court system and reporters:		
Vermont Supreme Court (Vt.)		
Reporter	*Abbreviation*	*Dates*
★Vermont Reports	Vt.	1826–present
Atlantic Reporter	A.	1885–1938
Second Series	A.2d	1938–2010
Third Series	A.3d	2010–present
Constitution:		
Vermont Constitution of 1793	Vt. ▲ Const. ▲ [art. *or* amend.] ▲ number, ▲ § ▲ section number.	
Statutory compilations:		
★Vermont Statutes Annotated	Vt. ▲ Stat. ▲ Ann. ▲ tit. ▲ title number, ▲ § ▲ section number (Year).	
West's Vermont Statutes Annotated	Vt. ▲ Stat. ▲ Ann. ▲ tit. ▲ title number, ▲ § ▲ section number ▲ (West ▲ Year).	
Session laws:		
★Acts and Resolves of Vermont	Year ▲ Vt. ▲ Acts ▲ & ▲ Resolves ▲ page number.	
West's Vermont Legislative Service	Year ▲ Vt. ▲ Legis. ▲ Serv. ▲ page number ▲(West).	
Vermont Advance Legislative Service	Year–Pamphlet number ▲ Vt. ▲ Adv. ▲ Legis. ▲ Serv. ▲ page number ▲(LexisNexis).	

Administrative compilation:	
Code of Vermont Rules	Title number–chapter number ▲ Code ▲ Vt. ▲ R. ▲ § ▲ section number ▲ (Year).
Administrative register:	
Vermont Government Register	Issue number ▲ Vt. ▲ Gov't ▲ Reg. ▲ page number ▲ (LexisNexis ▲ Month ▲ Year).
Local citation rules?	Yes. See **Appendix 2**.
Neutral citation rules?	Yes. See **Appendix 2**.
Court website:	http://www.vermontjudiciary.org/
Legislative website:	http://www.leg.state.vt.us/
Administrative website:	http://vermont-archives.org/aparules/

Virginia

Court system and reporters:		
Virginia Supreme Court (Va.) *Note:* Before 1971, the Virginia Supreme Court was the Virginia Supreme Court of Appeals (Va.).		
Reporter	*Abbreviation*	*Dates*
★Virginia Reports	Va.	1790–present
South Eastern Reporter	S.E.	1887–1939
Second Series	S.E.2d	1939–present
Virginia Court of Appeals (Va. ▲ Ct. ▲ App.)		
Reporter	*Abbreviation*	*Dates*
★Virginia Court of Appeals Reports	Va. ▲ App.	1985–present
South Eastern Reporter Second Series	S.E.2d	1985–present
Virginia Circuit Court (Va. ▲ Cir. ▲ Ct.)		
Reporter	*Abbreviation*	*Dates*
★Virginia Circuit Court Opinions	Va. ▲ Cir.	1985–present

Constitution:	
Virginia Constitution of 1776	Va.▲Const.▲[art. *or* amend.]▲number,▲ §▲section number.
Statutory compilations:	
★Code of Virginia 1950 Annotated	Va.▲Code▲Ann.▲§▲section number ▲(Year).
West's Annotated Code of Virginia	Va.▲Code▲Ann.▲§▲section number ▲(West▲Year).
Session laws:	
★Acts of the General Assembly of the Commonwealth of Virginia	Year▲Va.▲Acts▲page number.
West's Virginia Legislative Service	Year▲Va.▲Legis.▲Serv.▲page number ▲(West).
Virginia Advance Legislative Service	Year–Pamphlet number▲Va.▲Adv.▲Legis.▲ Serv.▲page number▲(LexisNexis).
Administrative compilation:	
Virginia Administrative Code (West)	Title number▲Va.▲Admin.▲Code▲§▲ section number (Year).
Administrative register:	
Virginia Register of Regulations	Volume number▲Va.▲Reg.▲Regs.▲ page number▲(Month▲Day,▲Year).
Local citation rules?	Yes. See **Appendix 2**.
Neutral citation rules?	No.
Court website:	http://www.courts.state.va.us/
Legislative website:	http://virginiageneralassembly.gov/
Administrative websites:	http://leg1.state.va.us/cgi-bin/legp504 .exe?000+men+SRR
	http://register.dls.virginia.gov/

Washington

Court system and reporters:		
Washington Supreme Court (Wash.)		
Reporter	*Abbreviation*	*Dates*
★Washington Territory Reports	Wash.▲Terr.	1854–1888

★Washington Reports	Wash.	1889–1939
★Second Series	Wash.▲2d	1939–present
Pacific Reporter	P.	1880–1931
Second Series	P.2d	1931–2000
Third Series	P.3d	2000–present

Washington Court of Appeals (Wash.▲Ct.▲App.)

Reporter	Abbreviation	Dates
★Washington Appellate Reports	Wash.▲App.	1969–present
Pacific Reporter Second Series	P.2d	1969–2000
Third Series	P.3d	2000–present

Constitution:

Washington Constitution of 1889	Wash.▲Const.▲[art. *or* amend.]▲number, ▲§▲section number.

Statutory compilations:

★Revised Code of Washington	Wash.▲Rev.▲Code▲§▲section number ▲(Year).
Revised Code of Washington Annotated	Wash.▲Rev.▲Code▲Ann.▲§▲section number ▲(West▲Year).
Annotated Revised Code of Washington	Wash.▲Rev.▲Code▲Ann.▲§▲section number ▲(LexisNexis▲Year).

Session laws:

★Session Laws of the State of Washington	Year▲Wash.▲Sess.▲Laws▲page number.
West's Washington Legislative Service	Year▲Wash.▲Legis.▲Serv.▲page number ▲(West).

Administrative compilation:

Washington Administrative Code	Wash.▲Admin.▲Code▲title number– chapter number–section number▲(Year).

Administrative register:

Washington State Register	Format for Issues 08-08 and earlier (2008): Issue number▲Wash.▲Reg.▲ page number▲(Month▲Day,▲Year).
	Format for Issue 08-09 and subsequent: Wash.▲Reg.▲Issue number–rule filing number▲(Month▲Day,▲Year).

Note: Since the publication of Issue 08-09 in 2008, the official publication of the Washington State Register is on the Code Reviser's web site, http://www.leg.wa.gov/codereviser/pages/washington_state_register.aspx.

Local citation rules?	Yes. See **Appendix 2.**
Neutral citation rules?	No.
Court website:	http://www.courts.wa.gov/
Legislative website:	http://www.leg.wa.gov/pages/home.aspx
Administrative websites:	http://apps.leg.wa.gov/WAC/
	http://www.leg.wa.gov/codereviser/pages/washington_state_register.aspx

West Virginia

Court system and reporters:		
West Virginia Supreme Court of Appeals (W. ▲ Va.)		
Reporter	*Abbreviation*	*Dates*
★West Virginia Reports	W. ▲ Va.	1864–present
South Eastern Reporter	S.E.	1886–1939
Second Series	S.E.2d	1939–present
West Virginia Court of Claims (W. ▲ Va. ▲ Ct. ▲ Cl.)		
Reporter	*Abbreviation*	*Dates*
★West Virginia Court of Claims Reports	W. ▲ Va. ▲ Ct. ▲ Cl.	1942–present
Constitution:		
West Virginia Constitution of 1872	W. ▲ Va. ▲ Const. ▲ [art. *or* amend.] ▲ number, ▲ § ▲ section number.	
Statutory compilations:		
★West Virginia Code	W. ▲ Va. ▲ Code ▲ § ▲ section number ▲ (Year).	
Michie's West Virginia Code Annotated	W. ▲ Va. ▲ Code ▲ Ann. ▲ § ▲ section number ▲ (LexisNexis ▲ Year).	
West's Annotated Code of West Virginia	W. ▲ Va. ▲ Code ▲ Ann. ▲ § ▲ section number ▲ (West ▲ Year).	
Session laws:		
★Acts of the Legislature of West Virginia	Year ▲ W. ▲ Va. ▲ Acts ▲ page number.	

West's West Virginia Legislative Service	Year▲ W.▲ Va.▲ Legis.▲ Serv.▲ page number.
West Virginia Advance Legislative Service	Year–Pamphlet number▲ W.▲ Va.▲ Adv.▲ Legis.▲ Serv.▲ page number▲ (LexisNexis).
Administrative compilation:	
West Virginia Code of State Rules	W.▲ Va.▲ Code▲ R.▲ §▲ section number ▲(Year).
Administrative register:	
West Virginia State Register	Volume number▲ W.▲ Va.▲ Reg.▲ page number▲ (Month▲ Day,▲ Year).
Local citation rules?	Yes. See **Appendix 2**.
Neutral citation rules?	No.
Court website:	http://www.courtswv.gov/
Legislative website:	http://www.legis.state.wv.us/
Administrative website:	http://www.sos.wv.gov/administrative-law/Pages/default.aspx

Wisconsin

Court system and reporters:		
Wisconsin Supreme Court (Wis.)		
Reporter	*Abbreviation*	*Dates*
★Wisconsin Reports	Wis.	1853–1957
★Second Series	Wis.▲ 2d	1957–present
North Western Reporter	N.W.	1879–1941
Second Series	N.W.2d	1941–present
Wisconsin Court of Appeals (Wis.▲ Ct.▲ App.)		
Reporter	*Abbreviation*	*Dates*
★Wisconsin Reports Second Series	Wis.▲ 2d	1978–present
North Western Reporter Second Series	N.W.2d	1978–present
Constitution:		
Wisconsin Constitution of 1848	Wis.▲ Const.▲ [art. *or* amend.]▲ number, ▲§▲ section number.	

Statutory compilations:	
★Wisconsin Statutes	Wis.▲Stat.▲§▲section number▲(Year).
Wisconsin Statutes Annotated	Wis.▲Stat.▲Ann.▲§▲section number ▲(West▲Year).
Session laws:	
★Wisconsin Session Laws	Year▲Wis.▲Sess.▲Laws▲page number.
West's Wisconsin Legislative Service	Year▲Wis.▲Legis.▲Serv.▲page number ▲(West).
Administrative compilation:	
Wisconsin Administrative Code Note: Use **Appendix 3** for agency abbreviations.	Wis.▲Admin.▲Code▲Agency Abbreviation▲§▲section number▲(Year).
Administrative register:	
Wisconsin Administrative Register	Issue number▲Wis.▲Admin.▲Reg.▲ page number▲(Month▲Day,▲Year).
Local citation rules?	Yes. See **Appendix 2**.
Neutral citation rules?	Yes. See **Appendix 2**.
Court website:	http://www.wicourts.gov/
Legislative website:	http://legis.wisconsin.gov/
Administrative website:	http://legis.wisconsin.gov/rsb/code.htm

Wyoming

Court system and reporters:		
Wyoming Supreme Court (Wyo.)		
Reporter	*Abbreviation*	*Dates*
★Wyoming Reports	Wyo.	1870–1959
Pacific Reporter	P.	1883–1931
★Second Series (official since 1959)	P.2d	1931–2000
★Third Series	P.3d	2000–present
Constitution:		
Wyoming Constitution	Wyo.▲Const.▲[art. *or* amend.]▲number,▲ §▲section number.	

Statutory compilations:	
★Wyoming Statutes Annotated	Wyo.▲Stat.▲Ann.▲§▲section number▲(Year).
West's Wyoming Statutes Annotated	Wyo.▲Stat.▲Ann.▲§▲section number ▲(West▲Year).
Session laws:	
★Session Laws of Wyoming	Year▲Wyo.▲Sess.▲Laws▲page number.
West's Wyoming Legislative Service	Year▲Wyo.▲Legis.▲Serv.▲page number ▲(West).
Administrative compilation:	
Code of Wyoming Rules	Title number–chapter number▲Wyo.▲Code▲R.▲§▲section number▲(LexisNexis▲Year).
Administrative register:	
Wyoming Government Register	Issue number▲Wyo.▲Gov't▲Reg.▲page number▲(LexisNexis▲Month▲Year).
Local citation rules?	No.
Neutral citation rules?	Yes. See **Appendix 2**.
Court website:	http://courts.state.wy.us/
Legislative website:	http://legisweb.state.wy.us/
Administrative website:	http://soswy.state.wy.us/Rules/default.aspx

1(C) Territories' and Tribal Courts' Primary Sources

American Samoa

Court system and reporters:		
High Court of American Samoa (Am.▲Samoa)		
Reporter	*Abbreviation*	*Dates*
★American Samoa Reports	Am.▲Samoa	1900–1975
★Second Series	Am.▲Samoa▲2d	1983–1997
★Third Series	Am.▲Samoa▲3d	1997–present
Constitution:		
Revised Constitution of American Samoa	Am.▲Samoa▲Const.▲[art. *or* amend.]▲number,▲§▲section number.	

Statutory compilation:	
★American Samoa Code Annotated	Am.▲Samoa▲Code▲Ann.▲§▲ section number▲(Year).
Administrative compilation:	
American Samoa Administrative Code	Am.▲Samoa▲Admin.▲Code▲§▲ section number▲(Year).
Local citation rules?	No.
Neutral citation rules?	No.

Guam

Court system and reporters:		
Supreme Court of Guam (Guam)		
Reporter	*Abbreviation*	*Dates*
★Guam Reports	Guam	1955–1987
Superior Court of Guam (Guam▲Super.▲Ct.)		
Reporter	*Abbreviation*	*Dates*
★Guam Reports	Guam	1955–1987
Constitution:		
Organic Act of Guam, 64 Stat. 384 (1950), *codified as amended in* 48 U.S.C. §§ 1421–1428e (2006).		
Statutory compilation:		
Guam Code Annotated	Title number▲Guam▲Code▲Ann.▲ §▲section number▲(Year).	
Session laws:		
Guam Session Laws	Guam▲Pub.▲L.▲number▲(Year).	
Administrative compilation:		
Administrative Rules and Regulations of the Government of Guam	Title number▲Guam▲Admin.▲R.▲&▲Regs. ▲§▲section number▲(Year).	
Local citation rules?	No.	
Neutral citation rules?	No.	
Court websites:	http://www.guamcourts.org/supreme.html	
	http://www.guamsupremecourt.com/ superior.html	

Legislative websites:	http://www.guamlegislature.com/
	http://www.justice.gov.gu/CompilerofLaws/
Administrative websites:	http://www.guamcourts.org/AdmRules/admrules.html
	http://www.guamcourts.org/compileroflaws/gar.html

Navajo Nation

Court system and reporters:		
Supreme Court of the Navajo Nation (Navajo) *Note:* The Supreme Court of the Navajo Nation was previously known as the Navajo Court of Appeals (Navajo).		
Reporter	*Abbreviation*	*Dates*
★Navajo Reporter	Navajo▲Rptr.	1969–present
Navajo District Court (Navajo▲D.▲Ct.)		
Reporter	*Abbreviation*	*Dates*
★Navajo Reporter	Navajo▲Rptr.	1969–present
Statutory compilations:		
★Navajo Nation Code	Navajo▲Nation▲Code▲tit.▲title number, ▲§▲section number▲(Equity▲Year).	
Navajo Nation Code Annotated (West)	Navajo▲Nation▲Code▲Ann.▲tit.▲ Title number, ▲§▲section number▲(Year).	
Local citation rules?	No.	
Neutral citation rules?	No.	
Court website:	http://www.navajocourts.org/	

Northern Mariana Islands

Court system and reporters:		
Commonwealth Supreme Court of the Northern Mariana Islands (N.▲Mar.▲I.)		
Reporter	*Abbreviation*	*Dates*
★Northern Mariana Islands Reporter	N.▲Mar.▲I.	1990–present

Commonwealth Superior Court of the Northern Mariana Islands (N.▲Mar.▲I.▲Commw.▲Super.▲Ct.)		
Note: Before 1989, the Commonwealth Trial Court of the Northern Mariana Islands (N.▲Mar.▲I.▲Commw.▲Trial▲Ct.)		
Reporter	*Abbreviation*	*Dates*
★Northern Mariana Islands Commonwealth Reporter	N.▲Mar.▲I.▲Commw.	1978–present
Constitution:		
Constitution of the Commonwealth of the Northern Mariana Islands	N.▲Mar.▲I.▲Const.▲[art. *or* amend.]▲number,▲§▲section number.	
Statutory compilation:		
★Northern Mariana Islands Commonwealth Code	Title number▲N.▲Mar.▲I.▲Code▲§▲section number▲(Year).	
Session laws:		
Northern Mariana Islands Session Laws	Year▲N.▲Mar.▲I.▲Pub.▲L.▲number.	
Administrative compilation:		
Northern Mariana Islands Administrative Code	Title number▲N.▲Mar.▲I.▲Admin.▲Code▲§▲section number▲(Year).	
Administrative register:		
Northern Mariana Islands Commonwealth Register	Volume number▲N.▲Mar.▲I.▲Reg.▲page number▲(Month▲Day,▲Year).	
Local citation rules?	No.	
Neutral citation rules?	Yes. See **Appendix 2**.	
Court website:	http://www.justice.gov.mp/	
Legislative website:	http://cnmilaw.org/legislativebranch.html	

Puerto Rico

Court system and reporters:		
Puerto Rico Supreme Court (P.R.) (Tribunal Supremo de Puerto Rico)		
Reporter	*Abbreviation*	*Dates*
★Puerto Rico Reports	P.R.	1899–1978
★Decisiones de Puerto Rico	P.R.▲Dec.	1899–present

★Official Translations of the Supreme Court of Puerto Rico	P.R. ▲ Offic. ▲ Trans.	1978–present
Jurisprudencia del Tribunal Supremo de Puerto Rico	J.T.S.	1973–present

Puerto Rico Circuit Court of Appeals (P.R. ▲ Cir.) (Tribunal de Circuito de Apelaciones)		
Reporter	*Abbreviation*	*Dates*
Decisiones del Tribunal de Circuito de Apelaciones Puerto Rico	T.C.A.	1995–present

Constitution:		
Constitution of the Commonwealth of Puerto Rico	P.R. ▲ Const. ▲ [art. *or* amend.] ▲ number, ▲ § ▲ section number.	

Statutory compilation:	
Laws of Puerto Rico Annotated (Leyes de Puerto Rico Anotadas) (LexisNexis)	P.R. ▲ Laws ▲ Ann. ▲ title number, ▲ § ▲ section number ▲ (Year).

Session laws:	
Laws of Puerto Rico (Leyes de Puerto Rico)	Year ▲ P.R. ▲ Laws ▲ page number.

Administrative register:	
Puerto Rico Register of Regulations	Volume number ▲ P.R. ▲ Reg. ▲ Issue number ▲ (Month ▲ Day, ▲ Year).
Local citation rules?	Yes. See **Appendix 2.**
Neutral citation rules?	Yes. See **Appendix 2.**
Court website:	http://www.ramajudicial.pr/comienzo.htm (in Spanish)
Legislative websites:	http://senado.pr.gov/
	http://www.camaraderepresentantes.org/

Virgin Islands

Court system and reporters:		
Supreme Court of the United States Virgin Islands (V.I.)		
Reporter	*Abbreviation*	*Dates*
★Virgin Islands Reports	V.I.	1917–present

Superior Court of the Virgin Islands (V.I. ▲ Super. ▲ Ct.) Note: Before 2004, the Territorial Court of the Virgin Islands.		
Reporter	*Abbreviation*	*Dates*
★Virgin Islands Reports	V.I.	1917–present
Statutory compilation:		
★Virgin Islands Code Annotated	V.I. ▲ Code ▲ Ann. ▲ tit. ▲ title number, ▲ § ▲ section number ▲ (Year).	
Session laws:		
Session Laws of the Virgin Islands	Year ▲ V.I. ▲ Sess. ▲ Laws ▲ page number.	
Virgin Islands Code Annotated Advance Legislative Service	Year–Pamphlet number ▲ V.I. ▲ Code ▲ Ann. ▲ Adv. ▲ Legis. ▲ Serv. ▲ page number ▲ (LexisNexis).	
Administrative compilation:		
Code of U.S. Virgin Islands Rules	Title number–chapter number ▲ V.I. ▲ Code ▲ R. ▲ § ▲ section number ▲ (LexisNexis ▲ Year).	
Administrative register:		
Virgin Islands Government Register	Issue number ▲ V.I. ▲ Gov't ▲ Reg. ▲ page number ▲ (LexisNexis ▲ Month ▲ Year).	
Local citation rules?	Yes. See **Appendix 2.**	
Neutral citation rules?	No.	
Court websites:	http://www.visupremecourt.org/	
	http://www.visuperiorcourt.org/	
Legislative website:	http://www.legvi.org/	

Appendix 2   Local Court Citation Rules

Appendix 2 contains information concerning local citation rules promulgated by federal and state courts, citing court rules or administrative orders, where available, and providing URLs to court websites and court rules, and citations to local rules and other information relevant to legal citation in those jurisdictions.

The information in **Appendix 2** is current as of September 2013. Always consult the most current version of a court's rules before submitting a document to it. Note that court rules often change and that information online changes as well. If the URL does not take you to the desired information, look at the website's structure and design, including search boxes and tables of contents to find where the information you seek has moved. Not all jurisdictions have published local rules concerning citation; they may, however, have preferences or practices that are not listed here.

Appendix 2 contains local court rule information arranged as follows, with individual jurisdictions in alphabetical or numerical order:

   A.   Federal Courts
   1. United States Supreme Court
   2. United States Circuit Courts of Appeal
   3. United States District Courts (States and Territories)
   B.   State Courts

2(A)   Federal Courts

(1) United States Supreme Court

United States Supreme Court	
Court website:	http://www.supremecourt.gov/
Court rules online:	http://www.supremecourt.gov/ctrules/ 2013RulesoftheCourt.pdf
Neutral citation rule:	No.
Other local rules affecting citation:	U.S. Sup. Ct. R. 34.5 (statutory citations to U.S.C. or Stat.)

(2) United States Circuit Courts of Appeal

The Federal Rules of Appellate Procedure apply to all federal circuit courts of appeal, who also may promulgate their own local rules affecting procedure and briefs. Although the tables below reflect local rules affecting citation, all federal circuit courts of appeal will also follow Federal Rule of Appellate Procedure 32.1, Citing Judicial Dispositions.

United States Court of Appeals for the First Circuit	
Court website:	http://www.ca1.uscourts.gov/
Court rules online:	http://www.ca1.uscourts.gov/sites/ca1/files/rulebook.pdf
Neutral citation rule:	No.
Other local rules affecting citation:	1st Cir. R. 32.2 (citing state decisions and law review articles); 1st Cir. R. 32.1.0 (citing unpublished decisions).

United States Court of Appeals for the Second Circuit	
Court website:	http://www.ca2.uscourts.gov/
Court rules online:	http://www.ca2.uscourts.gov/clerk/Rules/Rules_home.htm
Neutral citation rule:	No.
Other local rules affecting citation:	2d Cir. Local R. 25.1(i) (ECF hyperlink no substitute for citation); 2d Cir. Local R. 32.1.1 (citation of summary order).

United States Court of Appeals for the Third Circuit	
Court website:	http://www.ca3.uscourts.gov/
Court rules online:	http://www2.ca3.uscourts.gov/legacyfiles/2011_LAR_Final.pdf
Neutral citation rule:	No.
Other local rules affecting citation:	3d Cir. R. 28.3(a) (citation form; hyperlinks accompanied by parallel citation to print source).

United States Court of Appeals for the Fourth Circuit	
Court website:	http://www.ca4.uscourts.gov/
Court rules online:	http://www.ca4.uscourts.gov/pdf/RULES.pdf
Neutral citation rule:	No.
Other local rules affecting citation:	4th Cir. R. 25(a)(12) (ECF hyperlink no substitute for citation); 4th Cir. R. 32.1 (citing unpublished decisions).

United States Court of Appeals for the Fifth Circuit	
Court website:	http://www.ca5.uscourts.gov/
Court rules online:	http://www.ca5.uscourts.gov/clerk/docs/5thCir-IOP.pdf
Neutral citation rule:	No.

Other local rules affecting citation:	5th Cir. R. 25.2.14 (ECF hyperlink no substitute for citation); 5th Cir. R. 28.7 (citing unpublished decisions); 5th Cir. R. 47.5.3 (citing unpublished decisions).
Other resources:	*Practitioner's Guide to the U.S. Court of Appeals for the 5th Circuit* 57–59, http://www.ca5 .uscourts.gov/clerk/docs/pracguide.pdf.

United States Court of Appeals for the Sixth Circuit	
Court website:	http://www.ca6.uscourts.gov/
Court rules online:	http://www.ca6.uscourts.gov/internet/rules_and_ procedures/pdf/rules2004.pdf
Neutral citation rule:	No.
Other local rules affecting citation:	6th Cir. R. 28(a)(2) (citing record); 6th Cir. R. 32.1(a) (citing unpublished decisions).

United States Court of Appeals for the Seventh Circuit	
Court website:	http://www.ca7.uscourts.gov/
Court rules online:	http://www.ca7.uscourts.gov/Rules/rules.htm
Neutral citation rule:	No.
Other local rules affecting citation:	7th Cir. R. 28(f) (citing cases from U.S. Supreme Court); 7th Cir. R. 32.1(d) (citing orders pre-dating Jan. 1, 2007).
Other resources:	*Painting with Print*, http://www.ca7.uscourts.gov/ Rules/Painting_with_Print.pdf (reproducing Ruth Anne Robbins, *Painting with Print*, 2 J. ALWD 108 (2004)).

United States Court of Appeals for the Eighth Circuit	
Court website:	http://www.ca8.uscourts.gov/
Court rules online:	http://media.ca8.uscourts.gov/newrules/coa/ localrules.pdf
Neutral citation rule:	No.
Other local rules affecting citation:	8th Cir. R. 32.1A (citing unpublished decisions).

United States Court of Appeals for the Ninth Circuit	
Court website:	http://www.ca9.uscourts.gov/
Court rules online:	http://cdn.ca9.uscourts.gov/datastore/ cmecf/2013/06/29/help.pdf
Neutral citation rule:	No.
Other local rules affecting citation:	9th Cir. R. 36-3 (citing unpublished decisions); 9th Cir. BAP R. 8018-2 (citing Local Rules of Bankruptcy Appeal Procedure).

United States Court of Appeals for the Tenth Circuit	
Court website:	http://www.ca10.uscourts.gov/
Court rules online:	http://www.ca10.uscourts.gov/downloads/ 2013-rules.pdf
Neutral citation rule:	No.
Other local rules affecting citation:	10th Cir. R. 28.1 (citation of references to appendix and record); 10th Cir. R. 32.1 (citing unpublished decisions).
Other resources:	*Practitioners' Guide to the United States Court of Appeals for the Tenth Circuit* 41 (9th rev. ed. Feb. 2013), http://www.ca10.uscourts.gov/downloads/ pracguide_web.pdf (form of citation).

United States Court of Appeals for the Eleventh Circuit	
Court website:	http://www.ca11.uscourts.gov/
Court rules online:	http://www.ca11.uscourts.gov/documents/pdfs/ BlueAUG13.pdf
Neutral citation rule:	No.
Other local rules affecting citation:	11th Cir. R. 28-1(k) (form of citation, parallel citations); 11th Cir. R. 36-2 (citing unpublished decisions).

United States Court of Appeals for the District of Columbia	
Court website:	http://www.cadc.uscourts.gov/
Court rules online:	http://www.cadc.uscourts.gov/internet/home.nsf/ Content/VL%20-%20RPP%20-%20Circuit% 20Rules/$FILE/RulesDecember2011LINKSand BOOKMARKScj2013.pdf
Neutral citation rule:	No.
Other local rules affecting citation:	D.C. Cir. R. 28(a)(2), (b) (prohibiting use of *passim*); D.C. Cir. R. 32.1 (citing published opinions and statutes; citing unpublished decisions);
Other resources:	*Handbook of Practice and Local Procedures* (2011), *available at* http://www .cadc.uscourts.gov/internet/home.nsf/ Content/VL%20-%20RPP%20% 20Handbook%202006%20Rev%202007/$FILE/ HandbookDecember2011WITHTOCLINKS22.pdf.

United States Court of Appeals for the Federal Circuit	
Court website:	http://www.cafc.uscourts.gov/
Court rules online:	http://www.cafc.uscourts.gov/rules-of-practice/rules.html
Neutral citation rule:	No.
Other local rules affecting citation:	Fed. Cir. R. 28(e) (citation form); Fed. Cir. R. 32.1(c) (citing unpublished decisions).

(3) United States District Courts (States and Territories)

Middle District of Alabama	
Court website:	http://www.almd.uscourts.gov/
Court rules online:	http://www.almd.uscourts.gov/rulesproc/localrules.htm
Neutral citation rule:	No.

Northern District of Alabama	
Court website:	http://www.alnd.uscourts.gov/
Court rules online:	http://www.alnd.uscourts.gov/Local/local_rules.htm
Neutral citation rule:	No.

Southern District of Alabama	
Court website:	http://www.als.uscourts.gov/
Court rules online:	http://www.als.uscourts.gov/documents/forms/local-rules.pdf
Neutral citation rule:	No.

District of Alaska	
Court website:	http://www.akd.uscourts.gov/
Court rules online:	http://www.akd.uscourts.gov/ref_rules.htm
Neutral citation rule:	No.

District of Arizona	
Court website:	http://www.azd.uscourts.gov/
Court rules online:	http://www.azd.uscourts.gov/local-rules
Neutral citation rule:	No.

Eastern District of Arkansas	
Court website:	http://www.are.uscourts.gov/
Court rules online:	http://www.are.uscourts.gov/ default.cfm?content=LocalRules
Neutral citation rule:	No.

Western District of Arkansas	
Court website:	http://www.arwd.uscourts.gov/
Court rules online:	http://www.arwd.uscourts.gov/ index.php?page=local-rules
Neutral citation rule:	No.

Central District of California	
Court website:	http://www.cacd.uscourts.gov/
Court rules online:	http://www.cacd.uscourts.gov/court-procedures/ local-rules
Neutral citation rule:	No.
Other local rules affecting citation:	C.D. Cal. Loc. R. 5-4.3.3 (prohibiting hyperlinks); C.D. Cal. Loc. R. 11–3.9 (citations to Acts of Congress, regulations, cases; parallel citations); Bankr. C.D. Cal. Loc. R. 9013-2(c) (citations to Acts of Congress, regulations, cases, pinpoint references).

Eastern District of California	
Court website:	http://www.caed.uscourts.gov/
Court rules online:	http://www.caed.uscourts.gov/caednew/ index.cfm/rules/local-rules/
Neutral citation rule:	No.
Other local rules affecting citation:	E.D. Cal. Loc. R. 133(i) (form of citations to federal and state decisions, official California Reports)

Northern District of California	
Court website:	http://www.cand.uscourts.gov/home
Court rules online:	http://www.cand.uscourts.gov/localrules
Neutral citation rule:	No.
Other local rules affecting citation:	N.D. Cal. Civ. Loc. R. 3–4(d) (form of citations); N.D. Cal. Civ. Loc. R. 3–4(e) (citing unpublished decisions).

Southern District of California	
Court website:	http://www.casd.uscourts.gov/
Court rules online:	http://www.casd.uscourts.gov/Rules/ LocalRules.aspx
Neutral citation rule:	No.
Other local rules affecting citation:	S.D. Cal. Civ. R. 5.1(*l*) (citations to Acts of Congress, *Code of Federal Regulations*).

District of Colorado	
Court website:	http://www.cod.uscourts.gov/
Court rules online:	http://www.cod.uscourts.gov/CourtOperations/ RulesProcedures/LocalRules.aspx
Neutral citation rule:	No.
Other local rules affecting citation:	D. Colo. Civ. Loc. R. 7.1(D) (requiring pinpoint references).

District of Connecticut	
Court website:	http://www.ctd.uscourts.gov/
Court rules online:	http://www.ctd.uscourts.gov/sites/default/files/ forms/Revised%20Local%20Rules%20%208-8-13 .pdf
Neutral citation rule:	No.

District of Delaware	
Court website:	http://www.ded.uscourts.gov/
Court rules online:	http://www.ded.uscourts.gov/court-info/ local-rules-and-orders
Neutral citation rule:	No.
Other local rules affecting citation:	D. Del. Civ. Loc. R. 7.1.3(a)(5) (form of citations); D. Del. Civ. Loc. R. 7.1.3(a)(6) (citing earlier-filed documents in case); Bankr. D. Del. R. 7007-2(a)(v) (form of citations); Bankr. D. Del. R. 7007-2(a)(vi) (citing earlier-filed documents in case).

District of District of Columbia	
Court website:	http://www.dcd.uscourts.gov/dcd/
Court rules online:	http://www.dcd.uscourts.gov/dcd/rules-forms
Neutral citation rule:	No.

Middle District of Florida	
Court website:	http://www.flmd.uscourts.gov/
Court rules online:	http://www.flmd.uscourts.gov/LocalRules.htm
Neutral citation rule:	No.
Other local rules affecting citation:	M.D. Fla. Loc. R. 7.01(b) (citation formats for admiralty, maritime, and local rules).

Northern District of Florida	
Court website:	http://www.flnd.uscourts.gov/
Court rules online:	http://www.flnd.uscourts.gov/forms/Court%20Rules/local_rules.pdf
Neutral citation rule:	No.
Other local rules affecting citation:	N.D. Fla. Adm. & Mar. R. A(2) (citation formats for admiralty, maritime, and local rules).

Southern District of Florida	
Court website:	http://www.flsd.uscourts.gov/
Court rules online:	http://www.flsd.uscourts.gov/wp-content/uploads/2012/12/December-2012-Local-Rules.pdf
Neutral citation rule:	No.
Other local rules affecting citation:	S.D. Fla. Adm. & Mar. R. A(2) (citation formats for admiralty and maritime rules).

Middle District of Georgia	
Court website:	http://www.gamd.uscourts.gov/
Court rules online:	http://www.gamd.uscourts.gov/localrulesorders.htm
Neutral citation rule:	No.

Northern District of Georgia	
Court website:	http://www.gand.uscourts.gov/home/
Court rules online:	http://www.gand.uscourts.gov/pdf/NDGARulesCV.pdf
Neutral citation rule:	No.
Other local rules affecting citation:	N.D. Ga. Loc. R. 5.1(F) (citations to Acts of Congress, *Code of Federal Regulations*; pinpoint references).

Southern District of Georgia	
Court website:	http://www.gasd.uscourts.gov/
Court rules online:	http://www.gasd.uscourts.gov/lr/usdcLocalRules.htm
Neutral citation rule:	No.

District of Guam	
Court website:	http://www.gud.uscourts.gov/
Court rules online:	http://www.justice.gov.gu/Rules/rules.html
Neutral citation rule:	No.
Other local rules affecting citation:	D. Guam Gen. R. 1.1(a) (abbreviations for local rules of practice); D. Guam Adm. Loc. R. A(3) (abbreviation "ADLR"); Guam Code Ann. tit. 1, § 101(b) (abbreviation "GCA").
Other resources:	*How to Cite Guam Law* (Sandra E. Cruz, comp., 3d ed. 2002), *available at* http://www.jurispacific .com/public/guam_law_citation_guide_09-02.pdf.

District of Hawaii	
Court website:	http://www.hid.uscourts.gov/
Court rules online:	http://www.hid.uscourts.gov/docs%5Clocalrules/ Civil_Local_Rules_08_13.pdf?PID=11&MID=47
Neutral citation rule:	No.
Other local rules affecting citation:	D. Haw. Loc. R. 7.6 (citations to United States Code).
Other resources:	Am. Gen. Order Adopting Electronic Case Filing Procedures § 12 (D. Haw. Feb. 1, 2006) (ECF hyperlink no substitute for citation).

District of Idaho	
Court website:	http://www.id.uscourts.gov/default.cfm
Court rules online:	http://www.id.uscourts.gov/docs/LocalRules-DC-Clean.pdf
Neutral citation rule:	No.

Central District of Illinois	
Court website:	http://www.ilcd.uscourts.gov/
Court rules online:	http://www.ilcd.uscourts.gov/court-info/ local-rules-and-orders/local-rules
Neutral citation rule:	No.

Northern District of Illinois	
Court website:	http://www.ilnd.uscourts.gov/
Court rules online:	http://www.ilnd.uscourts.gov/ LocalRules.aspx?rtab=localrule
Neutral citation rule:	No.

Southern District of Illinois	
Court website:	http://www.ilsd.uscourts.gov/
Court rules online:	http://www.ilsd.uscourts.gov/LocalCourtRules.aspx
Neutral citation rule:	No.

Northern District of Indiana	
Court website:	http://www.innd.uscourts.gov/
Court rules online:	http://www.innd.uscourts.gov/docs/localrules/lr.pdf
Neutral citation rule:	No.

Southern District of Indiana	
Court website:	http://www.insd.uscourts.gov/
Court rules online:	http://www.insd.uscourts.gov/Publications/Local%20Rules%201-1-12.pdf
Neutral citation rule:	No.

Northern District of Iowa	
Court website:	http://www.iand.uscourts.gov/
Court rules online:	http://www.iand.uscourts.gov/e-web/documents.nsf/0/58BE642F7E9E99E2862573C00000E093/$File/2009+Local+Rules.pdf
Neutral citation rule:	No.
Other local rules affecting citation:	N.D. & S.D. Iowa Loc. R. 10(e) (citation to statutes).

Southern District of Iowa	
Court website:	http://www.iasd.uscourts.gov/
Court rules online:	http://www.iasd.uscourts.gov/index.php?option=com_content&view=article&id=154&Itemid=91
Neutral citation rule:	No.
Other local rules affecting citation:	N.D. & S.D. Iowa Loc. R. 10(e) (citation to statutes).

District of Kansas	
Court website:	http://www.ksd.uscourts.gov/
Court rules online:	http://www.ksd.uscourts.gov/flex/?fc=1
Neutral citation rule:	No.
Other local rules affecting citation:	D. Kan. Loc. R. 7.6(c) (citing unpublished decisions); Bankr. D. Kan. Loc. R. 9013.1(d) (citing unpublished decisions).

Eastern District of Kentucky	
Court website:	http://www.kyed.uscourts.gov/
Court rules online:	http://www.kyed.uscourts.gov/kyed_lrf/CIVIL_ RULES.pdf
Neutral citation rule:	No.

Western District of Kentucky	
Court website:	http://www.kywd.uscourts.gov/
Court rules online:	http://www.kywd.uscourts.gov/sites/kywd/files/ local_rules/Joint_Civil_Local_Rules.pdf
Neutral citation rule:	No.

Eastern District of Louisiana	
Court website:	http://www.laed.uscourts.gov/
Court rules online:	http://www.laed.uscourts.gov/LocalRules/ LocalRules.htm
Neutral citation rule:	No.

Middle District of Louisiana	
Court website:	http://www.lamd.uscourts.gov/
Court rules online:	http://www.lamd.uscourts.gov/localrules/local_ rules_3-11-11.pdf
Neutral citation rule:	No.

Western District of Louisiana	
Court website:	http://www.lawd.uscourts.gov/
Court rules online:	http://www.lawd.uscourts.gov/local-rules
Neutral citation rule:	No.

District of Maine	
Court website:	http://www.med.uscourts.gov/
Court rules online:	http://www.med.uscourts.gov/pdf/Local_Rules .pdf
Neutral citation rule:	No.

District of Maryland	
Court website:	https://www.mdd.uscourts.gov/
Court rules online:	https://www.mdd.uscourts.gov/localrules/ LocalRules.pdf
Neutral citation rule:	No.

District of Massachusetts	
Court website:	http://www.mad.uscourts.gov/
Court rules online:	http://www.mad.uscourts.gov/general/pdf/LC/ LOCALRULEScombined.pdf
Neutral citation rule:	No.

Eastern District of Michigan	
Court website:	http://www.mied.uscourts.gov/
Court rules online:	http://www.mied.uscourts.gov/Rules/LocalRules/ civilRules.cfm
Neutral citation rule:	No.
Other local rules affecting citation:	E.D. Mich. Electronic Filing Policies & Procedures R. 5(d) (ECF hyperlink no substitute for citation); Bankr. E.D. Mich. ECF Procedure 8(b) (ECF hyperlink no substitute for citation).

Western District of Michigan	
Court website:	http://www.miwd.uscourts.gov/
Court rules online:	http://www.miwd.uscourts.gov/RULES %20OPINIONS/Local%20Civil%20Rules.pdf
Neutral citation rule:	No.

District of Minnesota	
Court website:	http://www.mnd.uscourts.gov/
Court rules online:	http://www.mnd.uscourts.gov/local_rules/Local-Rules-Master.pdf
Neutral citation rule:	No.
Other resources:	*Electronic Case Filing Procedures Guide: Civil Cases* 21 (Dec. 2012) (ECF hyperlink no substitute for citation); *Electronic Case Filing Procedures Guide: Criminal Cases* 17 (Dec. 2012) (ECF hyperlink no substitute for citation).

Northern District of Mississippi	
Court website:	http://www.msnd.uscourts.gov/
Court rules online:	http://www.msnd.uscourts.gov/sites/msnd/files/ forms/2013_LOCAL_UNIFORM_CV_RULES_4-30-13.pdf
Neutral citation rule:	No.

Southern District of Mississippi	
Court website:	http://www.mssd.uscourts.gov/
Court rules online:	http://www.mssd.uscourts.gov/sites/mssd/files/2013MASTERCOPYCIVIL_NEW.pdf
Neutral citation rule:	No.

Eastern District of Missouri	
Court website:	http://www.moed.uscourts.gov/
Court rules online:	http://www.moed.uscourts.gov/sites/default/files/CMECF_loclrule.pdf
Neutral citation rule:	No.
Other local rules affecting citation:	E.D. Mo. Loc. R. 7-2.16 (ECF hyperlink no substitute for citation).

Western District of Missouri	
Court website:	http://www.mow.uscourts.gov/
Court rules online:	http://www.mow.uscourts.gov/district/rules/dc_rules.pdf
Neutral citation rule:	No.

District of Montana	
Court website:	http://www.mtd.uscourts.gov/
Court rules online:	http://www.mtd.uscourts.gov/pdf/rulesorders/Local%20Rules.pdf
Neutral citation rule:	No.
Other local rules affecting citation:	D. Mont. Loc. R. 1.5(d) (form of citations; pinpoint references; permitted hyperlinking); Bankr. D. Mont. Loc. R. 5005-2(a)(7) (form of citations).

District of Nebraska	
Court website:	http://www.ned.uscourts.gov/
Court rules online:	http://www.ned.uscourts.gov/attorney/local-rules
Neutral citation rule:	No.
Other local rules affecting citation:	D. Neb. Loc. Civ. R. 10.1(a)(4) (ECF hyperlink no substitute for citation); D. Neb. Loc. Crim. R. 49.2(a)(4) (ECF hyperlink no substitute for citation).

District of Nevada	
Court website:	http://www.nvd.uscourts.gov/
Court rules online:	http://www.nvd.uscourts.gov/Files/ LOCAL%20RULES%20OF%20PRACTICE% 20August%202011.pdf
Neutral citation rule:	No.
Other local rules affecting citation:	D. Nev. Loc. Civ. R. 7-3 (citations to Acts of Congress, *Code of Federal Regulations*, case reporters; pinpoint references; ECF hyperlink no substitute for citation); D. Nev. Loc. Crim. R. 47-8 (citations to Acts of Congress, *Code of Federal Regulations*, case reporters; pinpoint references).

District of New Hampshire	
Court website:	http://www.nhd.uscourts.gov/
Court rules online:	http://www.nhd.uscourts.gov/ru/
Neutral citation rule:	Yes. D.N.H. Loc. R. 5.3(b) (format for unreported opinions published on the court's website and issued after Jan. 1, 2000).
Other local rules affecting citation:	D.N.H. Loc. R. 5.3 (citation format); D.N.H. Loc. R. App. A, Supp. R. for Electronic Case Filing 2.3(i) (ECF hyperlink no substitute for citation); Bankr. D.N.H. Loc. R. 1050-1 (citation format; unpublished decisions); Bankr. D.N.H. Loc. R. 5072-1(e) (prohibiting citation to commercial works written or edited by judge).

District of New Jersey	
Court website:	http://www.njd.uscourts.gov/
Court rules online:	http://www.njd.uscourts.gov/sites/njd/files/ completelocalRules.pdf
Neutral citation rule:	No.

District of New Mexico	
Court website:	http://www.nmcourt.fed.us/web/DCDOCS/ dcindex.html
Court rules online:	http://www.nmcourt.fed.us/web/DCDOCS/files/ LocalCivilRulesAmended%201-1-2012.pdf
	http://www.nmcourt.fed.us/web/DCDOCS/ dcindex.html
Neutral citation rule:	No.

Eastern District of New York	
Court website:	https://www.nyed.uscourts.gov/
Court rules online:	https://www.nyed.uscourts.gov/sites/default/files/local_rules/localrules.pdf
Neutral citation rule:	No.

Northern District of New York	
Court website:	http://www.nynd.uscourts.gov/
Court rules online:	http://www.nynd.uscourts.gov/sites/nynd/files/local_rules/2013_LOCAL_RULES.pdf
Neutral citation rule:	No.
Other local rules affecting citation:	N.D.N.Y. Loc. R. 7.1(a)(1) (requiring parallel citations in memoranda of law in civil cases); N.D.N.Y. Loc. R. 12.1(a) (requiring parallel citations in memoranda of law in criminal cases).

Southern District of New York	
Court website:	http://www.nysd.uscourts.gov/
Court rules online:	http://www.nysd.uscourts.gov/rules/rules.pdf
Neutral citation rule:	No.

Western District of New York	
Court website:	http://www.nywd.uscourts.gov/
Court rules online:	http://www.nywd.uscourts.gov/sites/default/files/civil%20-%202013.pdf
	http://www.nywd.uscourts.gov/sites/default/files/criminal%20-%202013.pdf
Neutral citation rule:	No.

Eastern District of North Carolina	
Court website:	http://www.nced.uscourts.gov/
Court rules online:	http://www.nced.uscourts.gov/pdfs/localRules/CivilLocalRules.pdf
	http://www.nced.uscourts.gov/pdfs/localRules/CriminalLocalRules.pdf
Neutral citation rule:	No.
Other local rules affecting citation:	E.D.N.C. Loc. Civ. R. 7.2(b) (parallel citations); E.D.N.C. Loc. Civ. R. 7.2(d) (citing unpublished decisions); E.D.N.C. Loc. Crim. R. 47.2(b) (parallel citations); E.D.N.C. Loc. Crim. R. 47.2(d) (citing unpublished decisions).

Middle District of North Carolina	
Court website:	http://www.ncmd.uscourts.gov/
Court rules online:	http://www.ncmd.uscourts.gov/sites/default/files/CIV_LR.pdf
Neutral citation rule:	No.
Other local rules affecting citation:	M.D.N.C. Loc. Civ. R. 7.2(b) (form of citation); M.D.N.C. Loc. Civ. R. 7.2(c) (citing unpublished decisions).

Western District of North Carolina	
Court website:	http://www.ncwd.uscourts.gov/
Court rules online:	http://www.ncwd.uscourts.gov/sites/default/files/local_rules/LocalRulesMaster2011.Final_.pdf
Neutral citation rule:	No.

District of North Dakota	
Court website:	http://www.ndd.uscourts.gov/
Court rules online:	http://www.ndd.uscourts.gov/lci/2009_Local_Rules.pdf
Neutral citation rule:	No.
Other resources:	*Administrative Policy Governing Electronic Filing and Service* XVIII(B), at 10 (July 16, 2012) (ECF hyperlink no substitute for citation).

District of Northern Mariana Islands	
Court website:	http://www.nmid.uscourts.gov/
	http://www.justice.gov.mp/
Court rules online:	http://www.nmid.uscourts.gov/localrules.php
	http://www.cnmilaw.org/pdf/court_rules/R01.pdf
Neutral citation rule:	No, for U.S. District Court.
	In re Adoption of Universal Citations for Appellate Opinions Without Such Citations, N. Mar. I. Sup. Ct. Gen. Order No. 2004-100 (assigning neutral citations to cases decided issued subsequent to publication of N.M.I. Reporter, Vol. 5, but prior to effective date of 2001 neutral citation order), *available at* http://www.cnmilaw.org/pdf/new/04-100.pdf.

	In re Adoption of Universal Citations for Appellate Opinions, N. Mar. I. Sup. Ct. Gen. Order No. 2001-100 (applying to cases published after June 12, 1996, and opinions published in N.M.I. Reporter, Vol. 5 and subsequent volumes), *available at* http://cnmilaw.org/pdf/general_order/01-100.pdf.
Other local rules affecting citation:	D. N. Mar. I. Civ. Loc. R. 1.1(a) (abbreviation "LR"); D. N. Mar. I. Civ. Loc. R. app. A, R. 15 (hyperlink no substitute for citation); *In re Citation to Local Case Law*, N. Mar. I. Sup. Ct. Gen. Order No. 2000-200 (requiring citations to local cases where relevant); N. Mar. I. Sup. Ct. R. 32.1(a) (citing unpublished decisions); N. Mar. I. Sup. Ct. Admin. Order No. 2007-ADM-0013-MSC (citation of slip opinion).
Other resources:	*Northern Mariana Islands Supreme Court Style Manual* (rev. ed. 2010), *available at* http://www.cnmilaw.org/pdf/style_manual/style_manual.pdf.

Northern District of Ohio	
Court website:	http://www.ohnd.uscourts.gov/
Court rules online:	http://www.ohnd.uscourts.gov/home/rules-and-orders/local-civil-rules/
	http://www.ohnd.uscourts.gov/home/rules-and-orders/local-bankruptcy-rules/
Neutral citation rule:	No.
Other local rules affecting citation:	Bankr. N.D. Ohio Loc. R. 9013-2(c) (citations to statutes and regulations).

Southern District of Ohio	
Court website:	http://www.ohsd.uscourts.gov/
Court rules online:	http://www.ohsd.uscourts.gov/localrules/Local%20Rules%2012-15-2011-revised%20table%20of%20contents.pdf
Neutral citation rule:	No.
Other local rules affecting citation:	S.D. Ohio Loc. R. 7.2(b) (citations to statutes and regulations, Supreme Court citations).

Eastern District of Oklahoma	
Court website:	http://www.oked.uscourts.gov/
Court rules online:	http://www.oked.uscourts.gov/ (scroll to "Rules & Procedures")
Neutral citation rule:	No.

Northern District of Oklahoma	
Court website:	http://www.oknd.uscourts.gov/
Court rules online:	http://www.oknd.uscourts.gov/docs/ 69a019fb-2e0b-4897-be40-b16c876b9429/local_ rules_civil.pdf
	http://www.oknd.uscourts.gov/docs/ ab6f41e8-c0c2-4a4c-9b70-1778561b23be/ local_rules_criminal.pdf
Neutral citation rule:	No.

Western District of Oklahoma	
Court website:	http://www.okwd.uscourts.gov/
Court rules online:	http://www.okwd.uscourts.gov/files/ local_rules_5_1_2013.pdf
Neutral citation rule:	No.

District of Oregon	
Court website:	http://www.ord.uscourts.gov/
Court rules online:	http://www.ord.uscourts.gov/index.php/ attorneys/local-rules/local-rules-of-civil-procedure
Neutral citation rule:	No.
Other local rules affecting citation:	D. Or. Loc. Civ. R. 100-9(b) (ECF hyperlink no substitute for citation).

Eastern District of Pennsylvania	
Court website:	http://www.paed.uscourts.gov/
Court rules online:	http://www.paed.uscourts.gov/documents/ locrules/civil/cvrules.pdf
Neutral citation rule:	No.

Middle District of Pennsylvania	
Court website:	http://www.pamd.uscourts.gov/
Court rules online:	http://www.pamd.uscourts.gov/sites/default/ files/local_rules/LR120112.pdf
Neutral citation rule:	No.
Other local rules affecting citation:	M.D. Pa. Loc. R. 7.8(a) (parallel citations); M.D. Pa. Loc. R. 51.1 (pinpoint references to citations in jury instructions).

Western District of Pennsylvania	
Court website:	http://www.pawd.uscourts.gov/
Court rules online:	http://www.pawd.uscourts.gov/Documents/Forms/lrmanual.pdf
Neutral citation rule:	No.

District of Puerto Rico	
Court website:	http://www.prd.uscourts.gov/
	http://www.ramajudicial.pr/ (in Spanish)
Court rules online:	http://www.prd.uscourts.gov/sites/default/files/documents/94/Local_Rules_amended_as_of_Sept_2_2010_with_TOC.pdf
	http://www.ramajudicial.pr/leyes/index.htm (in Spanish)
Neutral citation rule:	P.R. Sup. Ct. Resolution (June 11, 1999) (applying to cases beginning Jan. 1998).
Other local rules affecting citation:	D.P.R. Loc. R. 1(d) (citation of local rules); D.P.R. Loc. R. 101(d) (citation of local rules of criminal practice); P.R. Sup. Ct. R. 44(d) (citing unpublished decisions).

District of Rhode Island	
Court website:	http://www.rid.uscourts.gov/
Court rules online:	http://www.rid.uscourts.gov/menu/generalinformation/rulesandprocedures/localrulesandprocedures/Local_Rules-011513.pdf
Neutral citation rule:	No.

District of South Carolina	
Court website:	http://www.scd.uscourts.gov/
Court rules online:	http://www.scd.uscourts.gov/Rules/2012/CivRules_Jan12.pdf
	http://www.scd.uscourts.gov/Rules/2012/CrRules_Jan12.pdf
Neutral citation rule:	No.

District of South Dakota	
Court website:	https://www.sdd.uscourts.gov/
Court rules online:	https://www.sdd.uscourts.gov/sites/default/files/localrules/SOUTH_DAKOTA_CIVIL_LOCAL_RULES_5_16_11_FINAL.pdf
	https://www.sdd.uscourts.gov/sites/default/files/localrules/2011SDcrimrules20120514.pdf
Neutral citation rule:	No.

Eastern District of Tennessee	
Court website:	http://www.tned.uscourts.gov/
Court rules online:	http://www.tned.uscourts.gov/docs/localrules.pdf
	http://www.tned.uscourts.gov/docs/ecf_rules_procedures.pdf
Neutral citation rule:	No.
Other local rules affecting citation:	E.D. Tenn. Loc. R. 7.4 (form of citation); E.D. Tenn. Electronic Case Filing R. 16 (ECF hyperlink no substitute for citation).

Middle District of Tennessee	
Court website:	http://www.tnmd.uscourts.gov/
Court rules online:	http://www.tnmd.uscourts.gov/files/LocalRules-20120425.pdf
Neutral citation rule:	No.
Other local rules affecting citation:	M.D. Tenn. Loc. R. 7.01(e)(2)-(5) (form of citation).

Western District of Tennessee	
Court website:	http://www.tnwd.uscourts.gov/
Court rules online:	http://www.tnwd.uscourts.gov/pdf/content/LocalRules.pdf
Neutral citation rule:	No.

Eastern District of Texas	
Court website:	http://www.txed.uscourts.gov/
Court rules online:	http://www.txed.uscourts.gov/page1.shtml?location=rules
Neutral citation rule:	No.

Northern District of Texas	
Court website:	http://www.txnd.uscourts.gov/
Court rules online:	http://www.txnd.uscourts.gov/pdf/CIVRULES.pdf
Neutral citation rule:	No.
Other local rules affecting citation:	Bankr. N.D. Tex. R. 8010.2 (citations to record).

Southern District of Texas	
Court website:	http://www.txs.uscourts.gov/
Court rules online:	http://www.txs.uscourts.gov/district/rulesproc/dclclrl2012.pdf
Neutral citation rule:	No.

Western District of Texas	
Court website:	http://www.txwd.uscourts.gov/
Court rules online:	http://www.txwd.uscourts.gov/Rules/Documents/txwd-rules.pdf
Neutral citation rule:	No.

District of Utah	
Court website:	http://www.utd.uscourts.gov/
Court rules online:	http://www.utd.uscourts.gov/forms/rules.pdf
Neutral citation rule:	No.
Other local rules affecting citation:	D. Utah Loc. Civ. R. 7-2 (citing unpublished decisions).
Other resources:	*District of Utah CM/ECF and E-filing Administrative Procedures Manual* 5 (Jan. 2, 2013) (ECF hyperlink no substitute for citation), *available at* http://www.utd.uscourts.gov/documents/utahadminproc.pdf.

District of Vermont	
Court website:	http://www.vtd.uscourts.gov/
Court rules online:	http://www.vtd.uscourts.gov/sites/vtd/files/LocalRules.pdf
Neutral citation rule:	No.

District of Virgin Islands	
Court website:	http://www.vid.uscourts.gov/
Court rules online:	http://www.vid.uscourts.gov/court-info/ local-rules-and-orders/local-rules
	http://www.visupremecourt.org/Court_Rules/
Neutral citation rule:	No.
Other local rules affecting citation:	D.V.I. Civ. R. 5.4(m)(2) (hyperlinks no substitute for citations); D.V.I. R. App. P. 1(a) (abbreviation "VIRAP"); D.V.I. R. App. P. 15(b) (form of citation; indication of Appellate Division cases); D.V.I. R. App. P. 22(i) (form of citations; parallel citation to V.I. Reports; ; citation of unpublished federal decisions; prohibition of citation to services, looseleafs, electronic databases when case published in U.S., F., F. Supp., or F.R.D. reporters; citation to regional reporters); V.I. Code Ann. tit. 1, § 1(b) (abbreviation "[title number] V.I.C. [section, chapter, part number]").
Other resources:	D.V.I. App. Div. I.O.P. app., *Style Guide, available at* http://www.vid.uscourts.gov/sites/vid/files/local_rules/Guide.pdf (last visited Sept. 13, 2013).

Eastern District of Virginia	
Court website:	http://www.vaed.uscourts.gov/
Court rules online:	http://www.vaed.uscourts.gov/localrules/ LocalRulesEDVA.pdf
Neutral citation rule:	No.

Western District of Virginia	
Court website:	http://www.vawd.uscourts.gov/
Court rules online:	http://www.vawd.uscourts.gov/media/519/ local_rules.pdf
Neutral citation rule:	No.

Eastern District of Washington	
Court website:	http://www.waed.uscourts.gov/
Court rules online:	http://www.waed.uscourts.gov/sites/default/ files/local_rules/Local_Rules-20130901.pdf
Neutral citation rule:	No.
Other local rules affecting citation:	E.D. Wash. Loc. R. 7.1(f) (form of citation; citing unpublished decisions); E.D. Wash. Loc. R. 10-1(a)(4) (citing earlier-filed ECF documents in same case).

Western District of Washington	
Court website:	http://www.wawd.uscourts.gov/
Court rules online:	http://www.wawd.uscourts.gov/sites/wawd/files/LocalCivilRules_Dec17_2012.pdf
	http://www.wawd.uscourts.gov/sites/wawd/files/ECFFilingProceduresAmended12.20.12.pdf
Neutral citation rule:	No.
Other local rules affecting citation:	W.D. Wash. Loc. Civ. R. 10(e)(6) (citations to documents already in record; pinpoint references).
Other resources:	W.D. Wash. Electronic Filing Procedures for Civ. & Crim. Cases R. III(F) (ECF hyperlink no substitute for citation).

Northern District of West Virginia	
Court website:	http://www.wvnd.uscourts.gov/
Court rules online:	http://www.wvnd.uscourts.gov/sites/wvnd/files/Local%20Rules%20-%20Final%20July%202020 10%20JPB_1.pdf
Neutral citation rule:	No.
Other local rules affecting citation:	N.D. W. Va. Admin. Proc. for Electronic Case Filing R. 22 (ECF hyperlink no substitute for citation).

Southern District of West Virginia	
Court website:	http://www.wvsd.uscourts.gov/
Court rules online:	http://www.wvsd.uscourts.gov/sites/default/files/local_rules/LocalRules_4.pdf
Neutral citation rule:	No.
Other local rules affecting citation:	S.D. W. Va. Admin. Proc. for Electronic Case Filing R. 22 (ECF hyperlink no substitute for citation).

Eastern District of Wisconsin	
Court website:	http://www.wied.uscourts.gov/
Court rules online:	http://www.wied.uscourts.gov/index.php?option=com_content&task=view&id=12&Itemid=39
Neutral citation rule:	No.
Other local rules affecting citation:	E.D. Wis. Loc. Civ. R. 7(j) (citing unpublished decisions).

Western District of Wisconsin	
Court website:	http://www.wiwd.uscourts.gov/
Court rules online:	http://www.wiwd.uscourts.gov/sites/default/files/Local_Rules.pdf
	http://www.wiwd.uscourts.gov/sites/default/files/AdminProcedures.pdf
Neutral citation rule:	No.
Other local rules affecting citation:	W.D. Wis. Electronic Filing Procedures R. IV(H) (ECF hyperlink no substitute for citation).

District of Wyoming	
Court website:	http://www.wyd.uscourts.gov/
Court rules online:	http://www.wyd.uscourts.gov/pdfforms/localrules-cv.pdf
Neutral citation rule:	No.

2(B) State Courts

This section of **Appendix 2** provides URLs to state supreme court or judiciary websites, and where available, to court rules online. It cites and briefly summarizes statutes and court rules affecting citation. Note, however, that citation practices in many jurisdictions are not governed by statute or rule, but rather reflect the custom of the courts and practitioners there. Therefore, not all local formats are reflected in this appendix. Good sources for determining alternative citation formats used in a particular jurisdiction are the official reports of the state's appellate courts.

Alabama	
Court website:	http://judicial.alabama.gov/
Court rules online:	http://judicial.alabama.gov/library/rules_of_court.cfm
Neutral citation rule:	No.
Other local rules affecting citation:	Ala. R. App. P. 28(g) (form of citations, pinpoint references); Ala. R. App. P. 53(d) (prohibiting citation to "no-opinion" affirmance by Alabama Supreme Court or Court of Civil Appeals); Ala. R. App. P. 54(d) (prohibiting citation to "no-opinion" affirmance by Alabama Court of Criminal Appeals).

Alaska	
Court website:	http://courts.alaska.gov/
Court rules online:	http://www.courts.alaska.gov/rules.htm
Neutral citation rule:	No.
Other local rules affecting citation:	Alaska R. App. P. 214(d) (citing unpublished decisions); Alaska R. App. P. app., Clerk's Instructions for Preparation of Excerpts, *available at* http://www.courts.alaska.gov/rules/excerpt .pdf.

Arizona	
Court website:	http://www.azcourts.gov/
Court rules online:	http://www.azcourts.gov/rules/Home.aspx
Neutral citation rule:	No.
Other local rules affecting citation:	Ariz. R. Civ. App. P. 13(a)(6) (parallel citations); Ariz. R. Civ. App. P. 28(c) (limitations on citation of memorandum decisions); Ariz. Sup. Ct. R. 111(c) (limitations on citation of memorandum decisions); Ariz. Sup. Ct. Admin. Order No. 97-67 (for cases decided after Jan. 1, 1998, requiring pinpoint references to paragraph numbers); Ariz. Rev. Stat. § 1-101 (abbreviation "A.R.S.").

Arkansas	
Court website:	https://courts.arkansas.gov/
Court rules online:	https://courts.arkansas.gov/ rules-and-administrative-orders/court-rules
Neutral citation rule:	Ark. R. Sup. Ct. & Ct. App. 5-2(d) (for published decisions between Feb. 14, 2009, and July 1, 2009, and all decisions issued after July 1, 2009, and available on the Arkansas Judiciary website).
Other local rules affecting citation:	Ark. Code Ann. § 1-2-113(c) (abbreviation "A.C.A."); Ark. R. Civ. P. 85 (abbreviation "ARCP"); Ark. R. Evid. 1102 (abbreviation "A.R.E. Rule _"); Ark. R. Sup. Ct. & Ct. App. 4-2(a)(7) (parallel citations; neutral citations).
Other resources:	Arkansas Supreme Court and Arkansas Court of Appeals, *House Style Guide, available at* https:// courts.arkansas.gov/sites/default/files/ House%20Style%20Guide%20September2010.pdf.

California	
Court website:	http://www.courts.ca.gov/
Court rules online:	http://www.courts.ca.gov/rules.htm
Neutral citation rule:	No.
Other local rules affecting citation:	Cal. R. Ct. 1.200 (form of citation); Cal. R. Ct. 3.1113(c) (requiring citation to official reporter, page number, and year of decision); Cal. R. Ct. 8.204 (citation to record).
Other resources:	*California Style Manual* (4th ed. 2001); *Citing Your Sources of Information, available at* http://www.courts.ca.gov/documents/Appendix4.pdf.

Colorado	
Court website:	http://www.courts.state.co.us/
Neutral citation rule:	Colo. C.J. Directive 12-01, *available at* http://www.courts.state.co.us/Courts/Supreme_Court/Directives/CJD%2012-01.pdf (effective Jan. 1, 2012) (neutral citation format; numbered paragraphs; no public domain format for opinions not designated for publication).
Other local rules affecting citation:	*Policies of the Court of Appeals*, http://www.courts.state.co.us/Courts/Court_Of_Appeals/Forms_Policies.cfm (citing unpublished decisions); Colo. App. R. 58 (abbreviation "C.A.R."); Colo. App. R. 58 (abbreviation "C.A.R."); Colo. R. Civ. P. 1(c) (abbreviation "C.R.C.P."); Colo. R. Prof'l Conduct 9 (abbreviation "Colo. RPC").

Connecticut	
Court website:	http://jud.state.ct.us/
Court rules online:	http://www.jud.ct.gov/PB.htm
Neutral citation rule:	No.
Other local rules affecting citation:	Conn. R. App. P. § 67-11(a) (form of citations to cases; parallel citations; required citation to official reporter).
Other resources:	*The Manual of Style for Connecticut Courts* (3d ed. 2013), *available at* http://www.jud.ct.gov/Publications/Manual_of_style.pdf.

Delaware	
Court website:	http://courts.delaware.gov/
Court rules online:	http://courts.delaware.gov/Rules/
Neutral citation rule:	No.
Other local rules affecting citation:	Del. Code Ann. tit. 1, § 101(b) (abbreviation "Del. C."); Del. Sup. Ct. R. 14(g) (citing unpublished decisions; form of citations); Del. Sup. Ct. R. 93(d) (form of citations); Del. Super. Ct. Crim. R. 60 (abbreviation "Super. Ct. Crim. R."). *See also* Del. Super. Ct. R. 107(c)(4); Del. Ch. Ct. R. 171(g); Del. Ct. Civ. Pleas R. 107(c)(4).
Other resources:	Del. St. Bar Ass'n, *Delaware Uniform Citation* (2008), *available at* http://courts.delaware.gov/ Superior/pdf/de_uniform_citation_2008.pdf.
	Guide to the Delaware Rules of Legal Citation in the Superior Court of Delaware (2d ed. 2004), *available at* http://courts.delaware.gov/Superior/ pdf/citation_guide.pdf.

District of Columbia	
Court website:	http://www.dccourts.gov/internet/welcome.jsf
Court rules online:	http://www.dccourts.gov/internet/appellate/ dccarules.jsf
Neutral citation rule:	No.
Other local rules affecting citation:	D.C. Super. Ct. Civ. P.R. 12-I(e) (parallel citations to D.C. Cir. cases); *see also* D.C. Super. Ct. Small Claims & Conciliation R. 13(a); D.C. Super. Ct. Crim. P.R. 47-I(b); D.C. Super. Ct. Domestic Relations Proceedings R. 7(b)(1); D.C. Super. Ct. Juv. P.R. 47-I(b); D.C. Super. Ct. Neglect & Abuse Proceedings R. 43(a); D.C. Super. Ct. R. Crim. P. 60 (abbreviation "SCR-Criminal").
Other resources:	*District of Columbia Court of Appeals Citation and Style Guide* (Sept. 2009), *available at* http:// www.dcappeals.gov/internet/documents/ RevisedCitationGuide2009.pdf.

Florida	
Court website:	http://flcourts.org/
Court rules online:	http://www.floridasupremecourt.org/decisions/barrules.shtml
Neutral citation rule:	No.
Other local rules affecting citation:	Fla. R. App. P. 9.010 (abbreviation "Fla. R. App. P."); Fla. R. App. P. 9.800 (uniform citation system for cases, statutes, rules, attorney general opinions; form of citation for other authorities).
Other resources:	Fla. St. Univ. L. Rev., *Florida Style Manual* (7th ed. 2010), *available at* http://www.law.fsu.edu/journals/lawreview/downloads/floridastylemanual.pdf; Edward M. Mullins & Annette C. Escobar, *Florida Bar Legal Citations* (May 2008), *available at* https://www.floridabar.org (select "News & Events"; then "Media Resources"; then "Reporter's Handbook"; then "Florida Bar Legal Citations").

Georgia	
Court website:	http://www.gasupreme.us/index.php
Court rules online:	http://www.gasupreme.us/rules/
Neutral citation rule:	No.
Other local rules affecting citation:	Ga. Code Ann. § 1-1-8(e) (abbreviation "O.C.G.A."); Ga. Ct. App. R. 24(d) (form of citation); Ga. Sup. Ct. R. 22 (requiring citation to official reporter).
Other resources:	*Georgia Bar Journal:Manuscript Format and Citation Guidelines*, *available at* http://www.gabar.org/newsandpublications/georgiabarjournal/upload/manuscript.pdf (last visited Sept. 10, 2013).

Hawaii	
Court website:	http://www.courts.state.hi.us/
Court rules online:	http://www.courts.state.hi.us/legal_references/rules/rulesOfCourt.html
Neutral citation rule:	No.
Other local rules affecting citation:	Haw. R. App. P. 1(c) (abbreviation "HRAP"); Haw. R. App. P. 28(b)(1) (parallel citations; form of citation; citation to cases in online databases).
Other resources:	*A Handbook of Citation Form for Law Clerks at the Appellate Courts of the State of Hawaii* (2008), *available at* https://www.law.hawaii.edu/sites/www.law.hawaii.edu/files/content/library/HandbookofCitationForm.pdf.

Idaho	
Court website:	http://www.isc.idaho.gov/
Court rules online:	http://www.isc.idaho.gov/iar
Neutral citation rule:	No.
Other local rules affecting citation:	Idaho App. R. 1 (abbreviation "I.A.R."); Idaho App. R. 35(e) (citation to record); Idaho Crim. R. 2(b) (abbreviation "I.C.R."); Idaho R. Civ. P. 87 (abbreviation "I.R.C.P."); Idaho R. Evid. 101(a) (abbreviation "I.R.E."); Idaho Sup. Ct. Internal R. 15(e) (form of citation).

Illinois	
Court website:	http://www.state.il.us/court/
Court rules online:	http://www.state.il.us/court/SupremeCourt/ Rules/default.asp
	http://www.state.il.us/court/AppellateCourt/ RulesDefault.asp
Neutral citation rule:	Ill. Sup. Ct. R. 6 (for Illinois cases filed on or after July 11, 2011).
Other local rules affecting citation:	Ill. Sup. Ct. R. 6 (form of citation for statutes, session laws, secondary sources; pinpoint references).
Other resources:	*Style Manual for the Supreme and Appellate Courts of Illinois* (4th rev. ed. 2012), *available at* http://www.state.il.us/court/StyleManual/SupCrt_ StyleManual.pdf.

Indiana	
Court website:	http://www.in.gov/judiciary/
Court rules online:	http://www.in.gov/judiciary/2695.htm
Neutral citation rule:	No.
Other local rules affecting citation:	Ind. Code § 1-1-1-1 (abbreviation "IC"); Ind. R. App. P. 22 (form of citation for cases, statutes, regulations, court rules; abbreviations for court documents).

Iowa	
Court website:	http://www.iowacourts.gov/
Court rules online:	http://www.iowacourts.gov/Court_Rules_and_Forms/
Neutral citation rule:	No.
Other local rules affecting citation:	Iowa R. App. P. 6.904(2) (form of citation to cases, court rules; citing unpublished decisions; pinpoint references); Iowa R. App. P. 6.904(4) (citations to record); Iowa R. Evid. 5.1103 (abbreviation "Iowa R. Evid.").

Kansas	
Court website:	http://www.kscourts.org/
Court rules online:	http://www.kscourts.org/rules/default.asp
Neutral citation rule:	No.
Other local rules affecting citation:	Kan. Sup. Ct. R. 6.08 (parallel citations).

Kentucky	
Court website:	http://courts.ky.gov/
Court rules online:	http://courts.ky.gov/courts/supreme/Pages/rulesprocedures.aspx
Neutral citation rule:	No.
Other local rules affecting citation:	Ky. R. Civ. P. 1(1) (abbreviation "CR"); Ky. R. Civ. P. 76.12(4)(g) (form of citations to statutes, cases; parallel citations); Ky. R. Crim. P. 1.02(1) (abbreviation "RCr"); Ky. R. Evid. 101 (abbreviation "KRE"); Ky. Sup. Ct. R. 1.000 (abbreviation "SCR").

Louisiana	
Court website:	http://louisiana.gov/Government/Judicial_Branch/
Court rules online:	http://www.lasc.org/rules/
	http://www.la-fcca.org/index.php/clerks-office/uniform-rules
Neutral citation rule:	La. Sup. Ct. Gen. Admin. R. 8(A)(1).
Other local rules affecting citation:	La. Admin. Code tit. 1, § 103 (citation of Louisiana Administrative Code); La. Admin. Code tit. 1, § 305 (citation of *Louisiana Register*); La. Sup. Ct. Gen. Admin. R. 8(A)(3) (Jan. 14, 2013) (parallel citations); La. Unif. R. Ct. App. 2-12.4 (parallel citations).

Maine	
Court website:	http://www.courts.state.me.us/
Court rules online:	http://www.courts.state.me.us/rules_adminorders/index.html
Neutral citation rule:	Although the 1996 administrative order authorizing neutral citations, Me. Admin. Order No. SJC-216 (Aug. 20, 1996), was withdrawn in 2005, Me. Admin. Order No. JB-05-01 (Aug. 1, 2005) (withdrawing all administrative orders issued prior to 2005), local practice continues to use neutral citations; *see also* Me. Admin. Order No. JB-05-01 (A.9-11) (Sept. 19, 2011). For more information on neutral citation formats used in Maine, see *Uniform Maine Citations*, described below.
Other resources:	Me. L. Rev., *Uniform Maine Citations* (2012), *available at* http://mainelaw.maine.edu/academics/pdf/UMC2012.pdf (endorsed by Maine Supreme Court, contains local citation formats for all primary and secondary sources).

Maryland	
Court website:	http://www.courts.state.md.us/
Court rules online:	http://www.courts.state.md.us/rules/index.html
Neutral citation rule:	No.
Other local rules affecting citation:	Md. R. 1-104 (citing unpublished decisions); Md. R. 8-504(a)(1) (citation to official reports).

Massachusetts	
Court website:	http://www.mass.gov/courts/
Court rules online:	http://www.mass.gov/courts/sjc/rules.html
Neutral citation rule:	No.
Other local rules affecting citation:	Mass. R. App. P. 16(g) (form of citation to cases and statutes; pinpoint references); see also Mass. Dist. & Mun. App. Div. R. 16(g).
Other resources:	C. Clifford Allen, Official Reports Style Manual (2012), available at http://massreports.com/style2012jan.pdf.

Michigan	
Court website:	http://courts.mi..gov/
Court rules online:	http://courts.mi.gov/courts/ michigansupremecourt/rules/pages/current-court-rules.aspx
Neutral citation rule:	No.
Other local rules affecting citation:	*Uniform System of Citation*, Mich. Sup. Ct. Admin. Order No. 2006-3 (establishing citation form for all authorities cited in opinions of Michigan courts), *available at* http://courts.mi.gov/Courts/ MichiganSupremeCourt/CurrentCourtRules/ 9MichiganUniformSystemOfCitation.pdf (updated Sept. 4, 2013); Mich. Ct. R. 1.101 (abbreviation "MCR"); Mich. R. Evid. 1102 (abbreviation "MRE"); Mich. R. Prof'l Conduct 1.0(a) (abbreviation "MRPC").
Other resources:	Michigan State Law Library, *Common Legal Citations and Where to Find Them*, http:// michigan.gov/documents/mde/ ATJ_Common_Legal_Citations_and_Where_to_ Find_Them_335880_7.pdf (July 2012).

Minnesota	
Court website:	http://www.mncourts.gov/default.aspx
Court rules online:	http://www.mncourts.gov/default.aspx?page=511
Neutral citation rule:	No.
Other resources:	Minn. St. Legis., *Citing Minnesota Legal Sources*, http://www.leg.state.mn.us/leg/leghist/citations .aspx (form of citations to constitution, statutes, session laws, court rules, legislative materials).

Mississippi	
Court website:	http://courts.ms.gov/
Court rules online:	http://courts.ms.gov/rules/msrules.html
Neutral citation rule:	Miss. R. App. P. 28(f) (for cases decided from and after July 1, 1997).
Other local rules affecting citation:	Miss. R. App. P. 28(f)(2)(i) (parallel citations for cases decided prior to 1967); Miss. R. App. P. 49 (abbreviation "M.R.A.P."); Miss. R. Civ. P. 85 (abbreviation "M.R.C.P."); Miss. R. Evid. 1102 (abbreviation "M.R.E."); Miss. Unif. Cir. & Cnty. Ct. R. 1.01 (abbreviation "URCCC").

Missouri	
Court website:	http://www.courts.mo.gov/
Court rules online:	http://www.courts.mo.gov/page.jsp?id=46
Neutral citation rule:	No.
Other resources:	Journal of the Missouri Bar, *Conventions for Citations*, http://www.mobar.org/ uploadedFiles/Home/Publications/Journal/ citations-conventions.pdf (last visited Sept. 11, 2013); Patrick Deaton, *Show Me Citations*, http:// www.thomaspatrickdeaton.com/ ShowMeCitations2011-0205.pdf (2010).

Montana	
Court website:	http://courts.mt.gov/default.mcpx
Court rules online:	http://courts.mt.gov/library/montana_laws .mcpx#sup_court_rules
Neutral citation rules:	*In re Amending Citation Standards for the Mont. Sup. Ct.* (Jan. 22, 2009) (revising 1997 order with regard to pinpoint paragraph references), *available at* http://courts.mt.gov/supreme/ new_rules/default.mcpx (scroll to "AF 07-0064 (01-22-09) Matter of Amending Citation Standards for MT Supreme Court"); *In re Opinion Forms & Citation Standards of Mont. Sup. Ct.; & Adoption of Form of Pub. Domain & Neutral-Format Citation* (Mont. Dec. 16, 1997), *available at* http:// courts.mt.gov/content/library/docs/cite_cases.pdf.
Other local rules affecting citation:	Mont. R. App. P. 1 (abbreviation "M. R. App. P.").

Nebraska	
Court website:	http://www.supremecourt.ne.gov/
Court rules online:	http://www.supremecourt.ne.gov/rules/index .shtml?sub3
Neutral citation rule:	No.
Other local rules affecting citation:	Neb. Ct. R. § 6-1505(C) (parallel citation); Neb. Sup. Ct. R. 2-109(C) (form of citation; citation to record, official reports, statutes, session laws, secondary sources; pinpoint reference).

Nevada	
Court website:	http://www.nevadajudiciary.us/
Court rules online:	http://www.leg.state.nv.us/CourtRules/index .html
Neutral citation rule:	No.
Other local rules affecting citation:	Nev. Rev. Stat. § 220.170(4) (abbreviation "NRS"); Nev. Dist. Ct. R. 12.5 (citation to Nevada official reports; parallel citations to U.S. Supreme Court cases); Nev. R. App. P. 48 (abbreviation "N.R.A.P."); Nev. R. Civ. P. 85 (abbreviation "N.R.C.P."); Nev. Sup. Ct. R. 1 (abbreviation "S.C.R.").

New Hampshire	
Court website:	http://www.courts.state.nh.us/
Court rules online:	http://www.courts.state.nh.us/rules/index.htm
Neutral citation rule:	No.
Other local rules affecting citation:	N.H. Sup. Ct. R. 16(9) (citations to record, to U.S. Supreme Court cases, to unpublished federal decisions, to official New Hampshire Reports, and for other states, to regional reporters).

New Jersey	
Court website:	http://www.judiciary.state.nj.us/
Court rules online:	http://www.judiciary.state.nj.us/rules/index.html
Neutral citation rule:	No.
Other local rules affecting citation:	N.J. R. App. Prac. 2:6-2(a)(5) (citations to official reports and regional reporters); N.J. R. Evid. 1103 (abbreviation "N.J.R.E.").
Other resources:	*New Jersey Manual on Style for Judicial Opinions* (N.J. Sup. Ct. 2004) (establishing citation form for all authorities cited in opinions of New Jersey courts), *available at* http://www.judiciary.state .nj.us/appdiv/manualonstyle.pdf.

New Mexico	
Court website:	http://www.nmcourts.gov/
Court rules online:	https://coa.nmcourts.gov/Forms/ appellateinstructions.php
Neutral citation rule:	N.M. R. Ann. 23-112 & Appendix (as amended by N.M. Sup. Ct. Order No. 13-8300-013, effective July 1, 2013, for papers to be filed on or after Aug. 1, 2013).

Other local rules affecting citation:	N.M. R. Ann. 1-001(D) (rules of civil procedure for district courts; abbreviation "Rule 1-__, NMRA"); N.M. R. Ann. 5-101(D) (rules of criminal procedure for district courts; abbreviation "NMRA, Rule 5-___"); N.M. R. Ann. 12-101(B) (rules of appellate procedure; abbreviation "NMRA, 12-__"); N.M. R. Ann. 12-213(E) (requiring citations in briefs to conform to N.M. R. Ann. 23-112).
Other resources:	N.M. Compilation Comm'n, *Citation Rule and Appendix, available at* http://www.nmcompcomm.us/CitationRule.htm.

New York	
Court website:	http://www.courts.state.ny.us/
Court rules online:	http://www.courts.state.ny.us/rules/index.shtml
Neutral citation rule:	No.
Other local rules affecting citation:	N.Y. C.P.L.R. 5529(e) (citation of New York cases to official reports; parallel citations for cases from other jurisdictions); N.Y. Ct. App. R. 500.1(g) (parallel citations); N.Y. App. Div. R. 600.10(a)(11) (parallel citations).
Other resources:	*New York Official Reports Style Manual* (Kathleen B. Hughes et al., eds., 2012) (also known as the "Tan Book"), *available at* http://www.courts.state.ny.us/reporter/new_styman.htm.

North Carolina	
Court website:	http://www.nccourts.org/
Court rules online:	http://www.nccourts.org/Courts/CRS/Policies/Default.asp
Neutral citation rule:	No.
Other local rules affecting citation:	N.C. R. App. P. 30(e)(3) (citation of unpublished decisions); N.C. R. App. P. app. B (form of citation; parallel citations), *available at* http://www.aoc.state.nc.us/www/public/html/pdf/therules.pdf (last visited Sept. 12, 2013).
Other resources:	N.C. Bar Ass'n App. Rules Study Comm., *A Style Manual for the North Carolina Rules of Appellate Procedure* (2011), *available at* http://www.ncbar.org/media/17350356/appellatestylemanual_09202011.pdf; Susan Lyons Rowe, *Legal Citation in North Carolina and South Carolina, available at* http://www.charlottelaw.edu/downloads/lawlibrary/research/Citation%20in%20NCSC.pdf (last visited Sept. 12, 2013).

North Dakota	
Court website:	http://www.ndcourts.gov/
Court rules online:	http://www.ndcourts.gov/Court/Rules/Frameset.htm
Neutral citation rule:	N.D. R. Ct. 11.6 (for cases decided after Jan. 1, 1997).
Other resources:	*North Dakota Supreme Court Citation Manual, available at* http://www.ndcourts.gov/citation/ (last updated July 26, 2000).

Ohio	
Court website:	http://www.supremecourt.ohio.gov/
Court rules online:	http://www.supremecourt.ohio.gov/LegalResources/Rules/
	http://www.hamilton-co.org/appealscourt/forms/Local%20Rules.pdf (1st App. Dist.)
	http://www.mcohio.org/SecondDistrictAppeals/2012_Second_District_Local_Rules.pdf (2d App. Dist.)
	http://www.third.courts.state.oh.us/rulestoc.htm (3d App. Dist.)
	http://www.supremecourt.ohio.gov/JudSystem/districtCourts/district4/dist4rules.pdf (4th App. Dist.)
	http://www.fifthdist.org/rules.htm (5th App. Dist.)
	http://www.co.lucas.oh.us/documents/80/RULES%20COMPLETE%20UPDATED%20JULY%202013-hyperlinked_201309120955382653.pdf (6th App. Dist.)
	http://www.seventh.courts.state.oh.us/rules.html (7th App. Dist.)
	http://appeals.cuyahogacounty.us/PDF/Localrules.pdf (8th App. Dist.)
	http://www.ninth.courts.state.oh.us/Rules/2012%20Local%20Rules.pdf (9th App. Dist.)
	http://www.tenthdistrictcourt.org/formspdf/localrules2012a.pdf (10th App. Dist.)
	http://www.11thcourt.co.trumbull.oh.us/pdfs/LOCALRULES2013FINAL.pdf (11th App. Dist.)
	http://www.twelfth.courts.state.oh.us/default.asp?page=rules (12th App. Dist.)

Neutral citation rule:	Ohio Sup. Ct., *Writing Manual: A Guide to Citations, Style, and Judicial Opinion Writing* § 1.1 (2d ed. 2013) (for cases decided after May 1, 2002).
Other local rules affecting citation:	Ohio R. App. P. 42 (abbreviation "App.R. _"); Ohio R. Civ. P. 85 (abbreviation "Civ.R. _"); Ohio R. Crim. P. 60 (abbreviation "Crim.P. _"); Ohio R. Evid. 1103 (abbreviation "Evid.R. _"); Ohio R. Juv. P. 48 (abbreviation "Juv. R. _"); Ohio R. Prof'l Conduct Form of Citation (abbreviation "Prof. Cond. Rule _"); Ohio Sup. Ct. Prac. R. 1.05 (abbreviation "S.Ct.Prac.R."); Ohio Sup. Ct. Prac. R. 3.01 (referring practitioners to Ohio Sup. Ct. *Writing Manual*); Ohio 1st Dist. Ct. App. R. 16.1(F) (citations according to Ohio Sup. Ct. *Writing Manual*); Ohio 2d Dist. Ct. App. R. 9 (citations according to Ohio Sup. Ct. *Writing Manual*); Ohio 3d Dist. Ct. App. R. 7(C) (citations to record; prohibiting citations in footnotes; pinpoint references); Ohio 6th Dist. Ct. App. R. 10(C) (citations to record; prohibiting citations in footnotes; pinpoint references; citations according to Ohio Sup. Ct. *Writing Manual*); Ohio 8th Dist. Ct. App. R. 16(B) (prohibiting citations in footnotes; citations according to Ohio Sup. Ct. *Writing Manual*); Ohio 9th Dist. Ct. App. R. 7(G) (pinpoint references; citations according to Ohio Sup. Ct. *Writing Manual*); Ohio 10th Dist. Ct. App. R. 8(A)(3) (citations according to Ohio Sup. Ct. *Writing Manual*); Ohio 11th Dist. Ct. App. R. 16 (citations to record; citations according to Ohio Sup. Ct. *Writing Manual*); Ohio 12th Dist. Ct. App. R. 16(A)(1), (C) (citations to record; parallel citations).
Other resources:	Ohio Sup. Ct., *Writing Manual: A Guide to Citations, Style, and Judicial Opinion Writing* (2d ed. 2013), *available at* http://www.supremecourt.ohio.gov/ROD/manual.pdf. *Note:* Ohio Supreme Court also permits citations that "conform to another generally recognized and accepted style manual." Ohio Sup. Ct. Prac. R. app. prefatory note, at 115.

Oklahoma	
Court website:	http://www.oscn.net
Court rules online:	http://www.oscn.net/applications/oscn/index.asp?ftdb=STOKRU&level=1
	http://www.okcca.net/online/rules/rulesrvr.jsp
	http://www.oklahomacounty.org/Judges/page/Local-Court-Rules.aspx
Neutral citation rules:	Okla. Crim. App. R. 3.5(C); Okla. Sup. Ct. R. 1.200(E) (applying to Oklahoma cases decided after May 1, 1997).
Other local rules affecting citation:	Okla. Sup. Ct. R. 1.1(a) (abbreviation "Okla. Sup. Ct. R."); Okla. Sup. Ct. R. 1.11(*l*) (citations to National Reporter System; parallel citations to U.S. Supreme Court cases); Okla. Sup. Ct. R. 1.200(b)(5), (c), (d) (citation of unpublished decisions; citation prior to issuance of mandate); Okla. Sup. Ct. R. 1.200(e) (pinpoint references; parallel citations; citations of non-majority opinions; citation to jury instructions).
Other resources:	OKLaw.org, *Local Court Rules,* http://www.oklahomacounty.org/Judges/page/Local-Court-Rules.aspx.

Oregon	
Court website:	http://courts.oregon.gov/OJD/
Court rules online:	http://www.publications.ojd.state.or.us/docs/RULE211.pdf
	http://courts.oregon.gov/OJD/programs/utcr/utcrrules.page
Neutral citation rule:	No.
Other local rules affecting citation:	Or. R. App. P. 1(F) (abbreviation "ORAP"); Or. R. App. P. 5.20(3), (4) (citations to record; referring to *Oregon Appellate Courts Style Manual* for citation form); Or. R. App. P. 5.35(3) (discouraging use of *passim* and *et seq.*); Or. R. App. P. 16.50(2) (hyperlink no substitute for citation); Or. R. Civ. P. 1(F) (abbreviation "ORCP"); Or. Unif. Trial Ct. R. 1.070(1), (2) (abbreviations "UTCR," "SLR"); Or. Unif. Trial Ct. R. 2.010(13) (citation of Oregon cases).
Other resources:	*Oregon Appellate Courts Style Manual* (rev. ed. Sept. 2013), *available at* http://www.publications.ojd.state.or.us/docs/PrinterFriendlyWithoutHyperlinks.pdf.

Pennsylvania	
Court website:	http://www.pacourts.us/
Court rules online:	http://www.pacourts.us/courts/supreme-court/ committees/rules-committees/
Neutral citation rule:	No.
Other local rules affecting citation:	Pa. R. App. P. 101 (abbreviation "Pa.R.A.P."); Pa. R. App. P. 2119(b) (citation to statutes; parallel citations); Pa. R. Civ. P. 51 (abbreviation "Pa.R.C.P. No.").
Other resources:	Pa. Bar Inst., *PAstyle: A PA Stylebook and Citation Guide for Legal Writing* (4th ed. 2010).

Rhode Island	
Court website:	http://www.courts.ri.gov/default.aspx
Court rules online:	http://www.courts.ri.gov/Courts/SupremeCourt/ Pages/Supreme%20Court%20Rules.aspx
Neutral citation rule:	No.
Other local rules affecting citation:	R.I. Dist. Ct. Civ. R. (abbreviation "D.C.R."); R.I. Dist. Ct. R. Crim. P. (abbreviation "Dist. R. Crim. P."); R.I. R. Dom. Rel. P. 85 (abbreviation "R. Dom. Rel. P."); R.I. R. Prac. 1.1 (abbreviation "R.P."); R.I. Sup. Ct. R. 16(j) (prohibiting citation of unpublished orders); R.I. Super. Ct. R. Prac. 1.1 (abbreviation "R.P."); R.I. Super. Ct. R. Crim. P. 60 (abbreviation "Super. R. Crim. P.").

South Carolina	
Court website:	http://www.sccourts.org/
Court rules online:	http://www.judicial.state.sc.us/courtReg/index .cfm
Neutral citation rule:	No.
Other local rules affecting citation:	S.C. App. Ct. R. 101(b) (abbreviation "SCACR"); S.C. App. Ct. R. 268 (form of citation; abbreviations); S.C. R. Civ. P. 85(a) (abbreviation "SCRCP"); S.C. R. Crim. P. 38 (abbreviation "SCRCrimP"); S.C. R. Evid. 1103 (abbreviation "SCRE"); S.C. Fam. Ct. R. 1 (abbreviation "SCRFC").
Other resources:	Paula Gail Benson, *A Guide to South Carolina Legal Research and Citation* (2d ed. 2009).

South Dakota	
Court website:	http://ujs.sd.gov/Supreme_Court/
Court rules online:	http://ujs.sd.gov/Supreme_Court/rules.aspx
Neutral citation rule:	S.D. R. App. P. § 15-26A-69.1 (applying to South Dakota cases decided since Jan. 1, 1996).
Other local rules affecting citation:	S.D. R. App. P. § 15-26A-69.1 (pinpoint references; parallel citations); S.D. R. Civ. App. P. § 15-26A-93 (abbreviation "S.D.R.C. App.P."); S.D. R. Civ. P. § 15-6-85 (abbreviation "RCP"); S.D. Sup. Ct. R. 13-11 (effective Jan. 1, 2014) (format for electronic filing); S.D. Sup. Ct. R. 13-12(B)(8) (effective July 1, 2014, in circuit court electronic filing, pinpoint references to paragraph numbers).

Tennessee	
Court website:	http://www.tsc.state.tn.us/
Court rules online:	http://www.tsc.state.tn.us/courts/rules
Neutral citation rule:	No.
Other local rules affecting citation:	Tenn. Code Ann. § 1-2-101(a) (abbreviation "T.C.A."); Tenn. Ct. App. R. 12 (citing unpublished decisions); Tenn. Ct. Crim. App. R. 19.4 (citing unpublished decisions); Tenn. R. App. P. 27(h) (form of citation; pinpoint references); Tenn. Sup. Ct. R. 1 (abbreviations "T.R.A.P.," "Tenn.R.App.P."); Tenn. Sup. Ct. R. 4(E)(2) (citing unpublished decisions); Tenn. Sup. Ct. R. 8 Scope ¶ 24 (abbreviation for professional conduct rules as "Tenn. Sup. Ct. R. 8, RPC _"); Tenn. Sup. Ct. R. 28 § 11 (abbreviation for post-conviction rules as "Tenn. Sup. Ct. R. 28, § _").

Texas	
Court websites:	http://www.courts.state.tx.us/
	http://www.supreme.courts.state.tx.us/
	http://www.courts.state.tx.us/courts/coa.asp
	http://www.cca.courts.state.tx.us/
Court rules online:	http://www.supreme.courts.state.tx.us/rules/rules.asp
	http://www.supreme.courts.state.tx.us/rules/traphome.asp
	http://www.cca.courts.state.tx.us/rules/rules.asp
Neutral citation rule:	No.

Other local rules affecting citation:	Tex. R. App. P. 47.7 (citation of unpublished decisions); Tex. 4th Ct. App. R. 8 cmt. (form of citation; pinpoint references; citations to record); Tex. 10th Ct. App. R. 12(b), (c) (pinpoint references; citations to record).
Other resources:	Texas Law Review Ass'n, *The Greenbook: Texas Rules of Form* (12th ed. 2010).

Utah	
Court websites:	http://www.utcourts.gov/
	http://www.utcourts.gov/courts/sup/
Court rules online:	http://www.utcourts.gov/resources/rules/
Neutral citation rule:	Utah Sup. Ct. Standing Order No. 4, *available at* http://www.utcourts.gov/resources/rules/urap/ Supctso.htm#4 (applying to Utah cases decided on or after Jan. 1, 1999).
Other local rules affecting citation:	Utah R. App. P. 30(f) (citing unpublished decisions); Utah R. Civ. P. 85 (abbreviation "U.R.C.P."); Utah R. Crim. P. 37 (citing unpublished decisions); Utah R. Juv. P. 1(c) (abbreviation "Utah R. Juv. P.").
Other resources:	Kenneth A. Hanson, *Rulewriting Manual for Utah* (12th ed. 2013), *available at* http://www.rules .utah.gov/agencyresources/manual-rw/index.html.

Vermont	
Court website:	https://www.vermontjudiciary.org/default.aspx
Court rules online:	https://www.vermontjudiciary.org/LC/ statutesandrules.aspx
Neutral citation rules:	Vt. R. App. P. 28.2(a), (b) (applying to Vermont Supreme Court cases decided after Jan. 1, 2003); Vt. R. App. P. 28.2(c) (neutral citations to cases from other jurisdictions).
Other local rules affecting citation:	Vt. Stat. Ann. tit. 1, § 51 (abbreviation "_ V.S.A. § _"); Vt. R. App. P. 1(d) (abbreviation "V.R.A.P."); Vt. R. App. P. 28.2(d) (citing unpublished decisions); Vt. R. Civ. P. 85 (abbreviation "V.R.C.P."); Vt. R. Prob. P. 85 (abbreviation "V.R.P.P.").

Virginia	
Court website:	http://www.courts.state.va.us/
Court rules online:	http://www.courts.state.va.us/courts/scv/rulesofcourt.pdf
Neutral citation rule:	No.
Other local rules affecting citation:	Va. Sup. Ct. R. 5:1(f) (citing unpublished decisions); Va. Sup. Ct. R. 5:17.1(c)(3) (requiring inclusion of year in citations to authorities); *see also* Va. Sup. Ct. R. 5:27(a), 5:28(a), 5A:20(a), 5A:21(a).

Washington	
Court website:	http://www.courts.wa.gov/
Court rules online:	http://www.courts.wa.gov/court_rules/
Neutral citation rule:	No.
Other local rules affecting citation:	Wash. Rev. Code Ann. § 1.04.040 (abbreviation "RCW"); Wash. Gen. Application Ct. R. 14.1 (citing unpublished decisions); Wash. Infraction R. Ct. Ltd. J. 6.3 (abbreviation "IRLJ"); Wash. Juv. Ct. R. 11.21 (abbreviation "JuCR"); Wash. R. App. P. 18.1 (abbreviation "RAP"); Wash. R. App. Dec. Cts. Ltd. J. 11.9 (abbreviation "RALJ"); Wash. R. Evid. 1103 (abbreviation "ER"); Wash. Super. Ct. Civ. R. 85 (abbreviation "CR").
Other resources:	Wash. Office of Reporter of Decisions, *Style Sheet* (2010), *available at* http://www.courts.wa.gov/appellate_trial_courts/supreme/?fa=atc_supreme.style.

West Virginia	
Court website:	http://www.courtswv.gov/
Court rules online:	http://www.courtswv.gov/legal-community/court-rules.html
Neutral citation rule:	No.
Other local rules affecting citation:	W.V. R. App. P. 21(e) (citation of memorandum decisions); W.V. R. App. P. 38(d) (citations in footnotes; parallel citations; indication of *per curiam* decisions); W.V. R. Evid. 1102 (abbreviation "WVRE").

Wisconsin	
Court website:	http://www.wicourts.gov/
Court rules online:	http://www.wicourts.gov/scrules/index.htm
	http://www.wicourts.gov/supreme/sc_rules.jsp
Neutral citation rules:	Wis. R. App. P. 809.19(1)(e) (form of citation); Wis. Sup. Ct. R. 80.001 (defining "public domain citation"); Wis. Sup. Ct. R. 80.01 (designation of official publications); Wis. Sup. Ct. R. 80.02 (applying to Washington appellate cases following Jan. 1, 2000).
Other resources:	*Wisconsin Guide to Citation* (Melissa Greipp ed., 7th ed. 2012); *Legal Citation of Wisconsin Court Cases Guide*, http://law.marquette.edu/law-library/research-guides-legal-citation-wisconsin-court-cases (last visited Sept. 13, 2013).

Wyoming	
Court website:	http://courts.state.wy.us/
Court rules online:	http://courts.state.wy.us/CourtRules.aspx
Neutral citation rules:	Order Amending Citation Format (Wyo. Aug. 19, 2005), *available at* http://www.courts.state.wy.us/LawLibrary/univ_cit_amend.pdf; Order Adopting a Public Domain or Neutral-Format Citation (Wyo. Oct. 2, 2000), *available at* http://www.courts.state.wy.us/LawLibrary/univ_cit.pdf.
Other local rules affecting citation:	Wyo. R. Crim. P. 60 (abbreviation "W.R.Cr.P."); Wyo. R. Evid. 1103 (abbreviation "WRE").

Appendix 3   General Abbreviations

Appendix 3 contains general abbreviations for a variety of citation components, including those needed to indicate dates, locations, subdivisions, and abbreviations for words in primary authorities such as cases, statutes, legislation, and court documents.

In each section of **Appendix 3**, entries are arranged in alphabetical order. Required spaces are indicated by triangles (▲). Note that some abbreviations shown in **Appendix 3** are different from those shown in appendices relevant to other types of citation components. Therefore, place close attention to the nature of the source you are citing.

In addition, the citation formats shown in this appendix are those used in practice-based documents. For citations in academic footnotes, some abbreviations should be presented in large and small capital letters; check the rules corresponding to the specific source to be cited.

This appendix is divided into the following sections:

A. Calendar Divisions
B. United States and World Geography
   1. States and Territories of the United States
   2. Major United States Cities
   3. Countries and Regions
C. Subdivisions
D. Publishing Terms
E. Case Names and Statutes
F. Legislative Terms
G. Court Documents

3(A)   Calendar Divisions

Month	Abbreviation	Day of the Week	Abbreviation
January	Jan.	Monday	Mon.
February	Feb.	Tuesday	Tues.
March	Mar.	Wednesday	Wed.
April	Apr.	Thursday	Th.
May	May	Friday	Fri.
June	June	Saturday	Sat.
July	July	Sunday	Sun.
August	Aug.		
September	Sept.		
October	Oct.		
November	Nov.		
December	Dec.		

3(B) United States and World Geography

Use these abbreviations for case names and court names in case citations (**Rules 12.2** and **12.6**); for institutional authors of books (**Rule 20.1(b)(3)**); and for treaty citations (**Rule 19.1**).

1. States and Territories of the United States

State or Territory	Abbreviation	State or Territory	Abbreviation
Alabama	Ala.	Montana	Mont.
Alaska	Alaska	Nebraska	Neb.
American Samoa	Am. Sam.	Nevada	Nev.
Arizona	Ariz.	New Hampshire	N.H.
Arkansas	Ark.	New Jersey	N.J.
California	Cal.	New Mexico	N.M.
Colorado	Colo.	New York	N.Y.
Connecticut	Conn.	North Carolina	N.C.
Delaware	Del.	North Dakota	N.D.
District of Columbia	D.C.	Northern Mariana Islands	N. Mar. I.
Florida	Fla.	Ohio	Ohio
Georgia	Ga.	Oklahoma	Okla.
Guam	Guam	Oregon	Or.
Hawaii	Haw.	Pennsylvania	Pa.
Idaho	Idaho	Puerto Rico	P.R.
Illinois	Ill.	Rhode Island	R.I.
Indiana	Ind.	South Carolina	S.C.
Iowa	Iowa	South Dakota	S.D.
Kansas	Kan.	Tennessee	Tenn.
Kentucky	Ky.	Texas	Tex.
Louisiana	La.	Utah	Utah
Maine	Me.	Vermont	Vt.
Maryland	Md.	Virgin Islands	V.I.
Massachusetts	Mass.	Virginia	Va.
Michigan	Mich.	Washington	Wash.
Minnesota	Minn.	West Virginia	W. Va.
Mississippi	Miss.	Wisconsin	Wis.
Missouri	Mo.	Wyoming	Wyo.

2. Major United States Cities

City	Abbreviation	City	Abbreviation
Baltimore	Balt.	Los Angeles	L.A.
Boston	Bos.	New York	N.Y.
Chicago	Chi.	Philadelphia	Phila.
Dallas	Dall.	Phoenix	Phx.
District of Columbia	D.C.	San Francisco	S.F.
Houston	Hous.		

3. Countries and Regions

Province, Country, or Region	Abbreviation	Province, Country, or Region	Abbreviation
Afghanistan	Afg.	Channel Islands	Channel ▲ Is.
Africa	Afr.	Chile	Chile
Albania	Alb.	China, People's Republic of	China
Alberta	Alta.		
Algeria	Alg.	Colombia	Colom.
America	Am.	Comoros	Comoros
Andorra	Andorra	Congo, Democratic Republic of the	Dem. ▲ Rep. ▲ Congo
Angola	Angl.		
Anguilla	Anguilla	Congo, Republic of the	Congo
Antarctica	Antarctica	Costa Rica	Costa ▲ Rica
Antigua and Barbuda	Ant. ▲ & ▲ Barb.	Côte d'Ivoire	Côte ▲ d'Ivoire
Argentina	Arg.	Croatia	Croat.
Armenia	Arm.	Cuba	Cuba
Asia	Asia	Cyprus	Cyprus
Australia	Austl.	Czech Republic	Czech [Note: no period]
Australian Capital Territory	Austl. ▲ Cap. ▲ Terr.		
		Denmark	Den.
Austria	Austria	Djibouti	Djib.
Azerbaijan	Azer.	Dominica	Dominica
Bahamas	Bah.	Dominican Republic	Dom. ▲ Rep.
Bahrain	Bahr.	Ecuador	Ecuador
Bangladesh	Bangl.	Egypt	Egypt
Barbados	Barb.	El Salvador	El ▲ Sal.
Belarus	Belr.	England	Eng.
Belgium	Belg.	Equatorial Guinea	Eq. ▲ Guinea
Belize	Belize	Eritrea	Eri.
Benin	Benin	Estonia	Est.
Bermuda	Berm.	Ethiopia	Eth.
Bhutan	Bhutan	Europe	Eur.
Bolivia	Bol.	Falkland Islands	Falkland ▲ Is.
Bosnia and Herzegovina	Bosn. ▲ & ▲ Herz.	Fiji	Fiji
		Finland	Fin.
Botswana	Bots.	France	Fr.
Brazil	Braz.	Gabon	Gabon
British Columbia	B.C.	Gambia	Gam.
Brunei	Brunei	Georgia [for U.S. state, see **Appendix 3(B)(1)**]	Geor.
Bulgaria	Bulg.		
Burkina Faso	Burk. ▲ Faso	Germany	Ger.
Burundi	Burundi	Ghana	Ghana
Cambodia	Cambodia	Gibraltar	Gib.
Cameroon	Cameroon	Great Britain	Gr. ▲ Brit.
Canada	Can.	Greece	Greece
Cape Verde	Cape ▲ Verde	Greenland	Green.
Cayman Islands	Cayman ▲ Is.	Grenada	Gren.
Central African Republic	Cent. ▲ Afr. ▲ Rep.	Guadeloupe	Guad.
		Guatemala	Guat.
Chad	Chad	Guinea	Guinea

Province, Country, or Region	Abbreviation	Province, Country, or Region	Abbreviation
Guinea–Bissau	Guinea–Bissau	Moldova	Mold.
Guyana	Guy.	Monaco	Monaco
Haiti	Haiti	Mongolia	Mong.
Honduras	Hond.	Montenegro	Montenegro
Hong Kong	H.K.	Montserrat	Montserrat
Hungary	Hung.	Morocco	Morocco
Iceland	Ice.	Mozambique	Mozam.
India	India	Myanmar	Myan.
Indonesia	Indon.	Namibia	Namib.
Iran	Iran	Nauru	Nauru
Iraq	Iraq	Nepal	Nepal
Ireland	Ir.	Netherlands	Neth.
Israel	Isr.	New Brunswick	N.B.
Italy	It.	New South Wales	N.S.W.
Jamaica	Jam.	New Zealand	N.Z.
Japan	Jap.	Newfoundland & Labrador	Nfld.
Jordan	Jordan		
Kazakhstan	Kaz.	Nicaragua	Nicar.
Kenya	Kenya	Niger	Niger
Kiribati	Kiribati	Nigeria	Nigeria
Korea, North	N. Kor.	North America	N. Am.
Korea, South	S. Kor.	Northern Ireland	N. Ir.
Kosovo	Kos.	Northern Territory (Australia)	N. Terr.
Kuwait	Kuwait		
Kyrgyzstan	Kyrg.	Northwest Territories (Canada)	N.W.T.
Laos	Laos		
Latvia	Lat.	Norway	Nor.
Lebanon	Leb.	Nova Scotia	N.S.
Lesotho	Lesotho	Nunavut	Nun.
Liberia	Liber.	Oman	Oman
Libya	Libya	Ontario	Ont.
Liechtenstein	Liech.	Pakistan	Pak.
Lithuania	Lith.	Palau	Palau
Luxembourg	Lux.	Panama	Pan.
Macau	Mac.	Papua New Guinea	Papua N.G.
Macedonia	Maced.	Paraguay	Para.
Madagascar	Madag.	Peru	Peru
Malawi	Malawi	Philippines	Phil.
Malaysia	Malay.	Pitcairn Island	Pitcairn Is.
Maldives	Maldives	Poland	Pol.
Mali	Mali	Portugal	Port.
Malta	Malta	Prince Edward Island	P.E.I.
Manitoba	Man.	Qatar	Qatar
Marshall Islands	Marsh. Is.	Québec	Que.
Martinique	Mart.	Queensland	Queensl.
Mauritania	Mauritania	Réunion	Réunion
Mauritius	Mauritius	Romania	Rom.
Mexico	Mex.	Russia	Russ.
Micronesia	Micr.	Rwanda	Rwanda

Province, Country, or Region	Abbreviation	Province, Country, or Region	Abbreviation
Saint Helena	St. Helena	Tanzania	Tanz.
Saint Kitts and Nevis	St. Kitts & Nevis	Tasmania	Tas.
		Thailand	Thai.
Saint Lucia	St. Lucia	Timor–Leste	Timor–Leste
Saint Vincent and the Grenadines	St. Vincent	Togo	Togo
		Tonga	Tonga
Samoa	Samoa	Trinidad and Tobago	Trin. & Tobago
San Marino	San Marino		
São Tomé and Príncipe	São Tomé & Príncipe	Tunisia	Tunis.
		Turkey	Turk.
Saskatchewan	Sask.	Turkmenistan	Turkm.
Saudi Arabia	Saudi Arabia	Turks and Caicos Islands	Turks & Caicos Is.
Scotland	Scot.		
Senegal	Sen.	Tuvalu	Tuvalu
Serbia	Serb.	Uganda	Uganda
Seychelles	Sey.	Ukraine	Ukr.
Sierra Leone	Sierra Leone	United Arab Emirates	U.A.E.
Singapore	Sing.	United Kingdom	U.K.
Slovakia	Slovk.	United States of America	U.S.
Slovenia	Slovn.		
Solomon Islands	Solom. Is.	Uruguay	Uru.
Somalia	Som.	Uzbekistan	Uzb.
South Africa	S. Afr.	Vanuatu	Vanuatu
South America	S. Am.	Vatican City	Vatican
South Australia	S. Austl.	Venezuela	Venez.
Spain	Spain	Victoria	Vict.
Sri Lanka	Sri Lanka	Vietnam	Viet.
Suriname	Surin.	Virgin Islands, British	Virgin Is.
Swaziland	Swaz.	Wales	Wales
Sweden	Swed.	Western Australia	W. Austl.
Switzerland	Switz.	Yemen	Yemen
Syria	Syria	Yukon Territory	Yukon
Taiwan	Taiwan	Zambia	Zam.
Tajikistan	Taj.	Zimbabwe	Zim.

3(C) Subdivisions

Word/Term	Abbreviation
addendum	add.
amendment	amend.
annotation	annot.
appendices	apps.
appendix	app.
article	art.
bibliography	bibliog.
book	bk.
chapter	ch.

Word/Term	Abbreviation
clause	cl.
column	col.
comment(ary)	cmt.
decision	dec.
department	dept.
division	div.
endnote	n.[Note: no space before following number]
endnotes	nn.[Note: no space before following numbers]
example	ex.
figure	fig.[Note: no space before following number]
folio	fol.
footnote (in internal cross-reference)	note
footnote	n.[Note: no space before following number]
footnotes (in internal cross-reference)	notes
footnotes	nn.[Note: no space before following numbers]
historical note	hist. ▲ n.[Note: no space before following number]
historical notes	hist. ▲ nn.[Note: no space before following numbers]
hypothetical	hypo.
illustration(s)	illus.
introduction	intro.
line	l.
lines	ll.
note (in internal cross-reference)	note
note	n.[Note: no space before following number]
notes (in internal cross-reference)	notes
notes	nn.[Note: no space before following numbers]
number	no.
page (in internal cross-reference)	p.
pages (in internal cross-reference)	pp.
paragraph	¶ or para. [Note: Use symbol if shown in source]
paragraphs	¶¶ or paras. [Note: Use symbols if shown in source]
part	pt.
preamble	pmbl.
principle	princ.
publication	pub.
record	rec.
reference	ref.
reporter's note	rptr. ▲ n.[Note: no space before following number]
reporter's notes	rptr. ▲ nn.[Note: no space before following numbers]

Word/Term	Abbreviation
rule	r.
schedule	sched.
section	§ *or* sec. [Note: Use symbol if shown in source]
sections	§§ *or* secs. [Note: Use symbols if shown in source]
seri(al, es)	ser.
subdivision	subdiv.
subsection	subsec.
subpart	subpt.
supplement	supp.
table	tbl.[Note: no space before following number]
title	tit.
volume	vol.

3(D) Publishing Terms

Word/Term	Abbreviation	Word/Term	Abbreviation
abridge(d, ment)	abr.	old series	o.s.
annotated	ann.	permanent	perm.
anonymous	anon.	photoduplicated reprint	photo. ▲ reprt.
circa	ca.	printing	prtg.
compil(ation, ed, er)	comp.	replacement	repl.
copyright	copy.	reprint(ed)	reprt.
draft	drft.	revis(ed, ion)	rev.
edit(ion, or)	ed.	seri(al, es)	ser.
editors	eds.	special	spec.
manuscript	ms.	temporary	temp.
mimeograph	mimeo.	tentative	tent.
new series	n.s.	translat(ed, ion, or)	trans.
no date	n.d.	unabridged	unabr.
no place	n.p.	volume	vol.
no publisher	n. ▲ pub.		

3(E) Case Names and Statutes

Use the abbreviations in **Appendix 3(E)** and **Chart 12.1** (common business designations) for case names and names of statutes, and elsewhere indicated by specific citation rules. While most abbreviations end in a period, several in this appendix are contractions formed with apostrophes; such contractions do not end with a period. For abbreviations of names of case reporters, see **Chart 12.2** or a jurisdiction's entry in **Appendix 1**. For abbreviations of statutory compilations, see a jurisdiction's entry in **Appendix 1**.

The abbreviations shown are formatted for practice-based documents. Depending on the context in which you will use an abbreviation, it may not need to be capitalized. In citations in academic footnotes, depending on the nature of the source to be cited, the typeface for some abbreviations may change to large and small capital letters or italics.

No matter the type of document in which the abbreviation is used, to form a plural, add "s" to the end of the abbreviation unless the word listed indicates otherwise or the abbreviation would awkwardly end with "ss." For example, the "(s)" in "Resource(s)" means that the listed abbreviation is the same for the singular and plural.

In a few instances, an abbreviation will differ depending on the source to which it refers; such differences are noted in the table below in bracketed notes. In addition, some abbreviations refer to more than one word or to related forms of a word (indicated in parentheses).

You may abbreviate a word of eight or more letters that is not listed in **Appendix 3(E)** if doing so will not only considerably shorten the word but also produce an abbreviation that is recognizable. Finally, note that in order to prevent reader confusion, you sometimes may find it advisable to spell out a word instead of abbreviating it.

Word/Term	Abbreviation	Word/Term	Abbreviation
Abandoned	Aband.	Bankruptcy [Note: *not* for reporter; see **Chart 12.2**]	Bankr.
Academy	Acad.		
Administrat(ion, ive)	Admin.	Board	Bd.
Administrator	Adm'r	Broadcast(ing)	Broad.
Administratrix	Adm'x	Brotherhood	Bhd.
Advertising	Adver.	Brothers	Bros.
Affair(s) [Note: for statutory subject-matter code]	Aff.	Building	Bldg.
		Business	Bus.
		Casualty	Cas.
Agricultur(al, e)	Agric.	Cent(er, re)	Ctr.
Alcoholic Beverage Control [Note: for statutory subject-matter code]	Alco. ▲ Bev. ▲ Cont.	Central	Cent.
		Chemical	Chem.
		Coalition	Coal.
		College	Coll.
Alternative	Alt.	Commission	Comm'n
America(n)	Am.	Commissioner	Comm'r
and	&	Committee	Comm.
Associate	Assoc.	Communication	Commc'n
Association	Ass'n	Community	Cmty.
Atlantic [Note: *not* for reporter; see **Chart 12.2**]	Atl.	Company	Co.
		Compensation	Comp.
Authority	Auth.	Condominium	Condo.
Automo(bile, tive)	Auto.	Congress(ional)	Cong.
Avenue	Ave.	Consolidated	Consol.

Word/Term	Abbreviation	Word/Term	Abbreviation
Construction	Constr.	Federal [Note: *not* for	Fed.
Continental	Cont'l	reporter; see **Chart**	
Cooperative	Coop.	**12.2**]	
Corporation	Corp.	Federation	Fed'n
Correction(al, s)	Corr.	Fidelity	Fid.
County [Note: *not* for	Cnty.	Financ(e, ial, ing)	Fin.
subject-matter code]		Foundation	Found.
Criminal [Note: for	Crim.	General	Gen.
statutory subject-		Gender	Gend.
matter code]		Government	Gov't
Defense	Def.	Group	Grp.
Department	Dep't	Guaranty	Guar.
Detention	Det.	Harbor(s) [Note: for	Harb.
Development	Dev.	statutory subject-	
Director	Dir.	matter code]	
Discount	Disc.		
Distribut(ing, or)	Distrib.	Hospital	Hosp.
District	Dist.	Housing	Hous.
Division	Div.	Import(ation, er)	Imp.
East(ern)	E.	Incorporated	Inc.
Econom(ic, ical, ics, y)	Econ.	Indemnity	Indem.
Education(al)	Educ.	Independent	Indep.
Elections [Note: for	Elec.	Industr(ial, ies, y)	Indus.
statutory subject-		Information	Info.
matter code]		Institut(e, ion)	Inst.
		Insurance	Ins.
Electr(ic, ical, icity)	Elec.	International	Int'l
Electronic	Elec.	Investment	Inv.
Employee	Emp.	Laboratory	Lab.
Employer	Emp'r	Liability	Liab.
Employment	Emp't	Limited	Ltd.
Engineer	Eng'r	Litigation	Litig.
Engineering	Eng'g	Machine(ry)	Mach.
Enterprise	Enter.	Maintenance	Maint.
Entertainment	Entm't	Management	Mgmt.
Evidence [Note: for	Evid.	Manufacturer	Mfr.
statutory subject-		Manufacturing	Mfg.
matter code]		Maritime	Mar.
Environment	Env't	Market	Mkt.
Environmental	Envtl.	Marketing	Mktg.
Equality	Equal.	Mechanic(al)	Mech.
Equipment	Equip.	Medic(al, ine)	Med.
Examiner	Exam'r	Memorial	Mem'l
Exchange	Exch.	Merchan(dise, dising, t)	Merch.
Executive	Exec.	Metropolitan	Metro.
Executor	Ex'r	Mortgage	Mortg.
Executrix	Ex'x	Municipal	Mun.
Export(ation, er)	Exp.	Mutual	Mut.
Family	Fam.	National	Nat'l

Word/Term	Abbreviation	Word/Term	Abbreviation
North(ern)	N.	Secretary	Sec'y
Northeast(ern) [Note: *not* for reporter; see **Chart 12.2**]	Ne.	Securit(ies, y)	Sec.
		Service	Serv.
		Shareholder	S'holder
Northwest(ern) [Note: *not* for reporter; see **Chart 12.2**]	Nw.	Social	Soc.
		Society	Soc'y
Number	No.	South(ern) [Note: *not* for reporter; see **Chart 12.2**]	S.
Opinion	Op.		
Organiz(ation, ing)	Org.	Southeast(ern) [Note: *not* for reporter; see **Chart 12.2**]	Se.
Pacific [Note: *not* for reporter; see **Chart 12.2**]	Pac.		
		Southwest(ern) [Note: *not* for reporter; see **Chart 12.2**]	Sw.
Partnership	P'ship		
Person(al, nel)	Pers.	Steamship(s)	S.S.
Pharmaceutic(al, als, s)	Pharm.	Street	St.
Preserv(ation, e)	Pres.	Subcommittee	Subcomm.
Probate [Note: for statutory subject-matter code]	Prob.	Superior	Super.
		Supreme [Note: *not* for reporter; see **Chart 12.2**]	Sup.
Probation	Prob.	Surety	Sur.
Product(ion)	Prod.	System(s)	Sys.
Professional	Prof'l	Technology	Tech.
Property	Prop.	Telecommunication(s)	Telecomm.
Protection	Prot.	Telegraph	Tel.
Public	Pub.	Telephone	Tel.
Publication	Publ'n	Temporary	Temp.
Publishing	Publ'g	Township	Twp.
Railroad	R.R.	Transcontinental	Transcon.
Railway	Ry.	Transport(ation)	Transp.
Refining	Ref.	Trustee	Tr.
Regional	Reg'l	Turnpike	Tpk.
Rehabilitation	Rehab.	Uniform	Unif.
Reproduct(ion, ive)	Reprod.	Uniform Commercial Code	U.C.C.
Resource(s)	Res.		
Restaurant	Rest.	University [Note: *not* for periodical title; see **Appendix 5**]	Univ.
Retirement	Ret.		
Road	Rd.	Utility	Util.
Savings	Sav.	Village	Vill.
School(s)	Sch.	West(ern)	W.
Science	Sci.		

3(F) Legislative Terms

Use these abbreviations in citations to legislative measures and related documents. To form the plural, add "s" to the end of the abbreviation unless the word listed indicates otherwise or the abbreviation would awkwardly end with "ss." Note that some words in this appendix are **not** abbreviated. You may, however, abbreviate other words of more than six letters not appearing in this appendix if the resulting abbreviation is unambiguous. Omit articles and prepositions from titles of documents if not needed for clarity.

Word/Term	Abbreviation	Word/Term	Abbreviation
Annals	Annals	House of Representatives	H.R.
Annual	Ann.	Joint	J.
Assembly(man, woman, member)	Assemb.	Legislat(ion, ive)	Legis.
		Legislature	Leg.
Attorney General	Att'y▲Gen.	Miscellaneous	Misc.
Bill	B.	Number	No.
Commissioner	Comm'r	Order	Order
Committee	Comm.	Record	Rec.
Concurrent	Con.	Register	Reg.
Conference	Conf.	Regular	Reg.
Congress(ional)	Cong.	Report	Rep.
Debate	Deb.	Representative	Rep.
Delegate	Del.	Resolution(s)	Res.
Document(s)	Doc.	Senate	S.
Executive	Exec.	Senator	Sen.
Federal	Fed.	Service	Serv.
General	Gen.	Session(s)	Sess.
House	H.	Special	Spec.
House of Delegates	H.D.	Subcommittee	Subcomm.

3(G) Court Documents

Use these abbreviations in citations to legal documents in a case being litigated. Note that some words in **Appendix 3(G)** are **not** abbreviated. You may, however, abbreviate other words of more than six letters not appearing in this appendix if the resulting abbreviation is unambiguous. Omit articles and prepositions from titles of documents if not needed for clarity.

Word/Term	Abbreviation	Word/Term	Abbreviation
Administrative	Admin.	Application	Appl.
Administrative Law Judge	A.L.J.	Arbitrat(ion, or)	Arb.
		Argument	Arg.
Admiralty	Adm.	Attachment	Attach.
Admission(s)	Admis.	Attorney	Att'y
Affidavit	Aff.	Attorney General	Att'y▲Gen.
Affirm	Affirm	Brief	Br.
Amended	Am.	Certiorari	Cert.
and	&	Chancellor	C.
Answer	Answer	Chancery	Ch.
Appeal	Appeal	Chief Justice, Chief Judge	C.J.
Appellant	Appellant	Circuit	Cir.
Appellate Court	App.▲Ct.	Civil	Civ.
Appellee	Appellee	Compel	Compel
Appendix [Note: *not* when citing Joint Appendix]	App.	Complaint	Compl.
		Consolidated	Consol.
		Counterclaim	Countercl.

Word/Term	Abbreviation	Word/Term	Abbreviation
County	Cnty.	Opposition	Opp'n
Court	Ct.	Order	Order
Criminal	Crim.	Permanent	Perm.
Cross-claim	Cross-cl.	Petition	Pet.
Decision	Dec.	Petitioner	Pet'r
Declaration	Decl.	Petitioner's	Pet'r's
Defendant	Def.	Petitioners	Pet'rs
Defendant's	Def.'s	Petitioners'	Pet'rs'
Defendants	Defs.	Plaintiff	Pl.
Defendants'	Defs.'	Plaintiff's	Pl.'s
Defense	Def.	Plaintiffs	Pls.
Demurrer	Dem.	Plaintiffs'	Pls.'
Deny[ing]	Den.	Points and Authorities	P. & A.
Deposition	Dep.	Preliminary	Prelim.
Discovery	Disc.	Probat(e, ion)	Prob.
Dismiss	Dismiss	Produc(e, tion)	Prod.
District [federal]	D.	Quash	Quash
District [state]	Dist.	Reconsideration	Recons.
District Attorney	D.A.	Record	R.
Division	Div.	Referee	Ref.
Docket	Dkt.	Rehearing	Reh'g
Document	Doc.	Reply	Reply
Evidence	Evid.	Reporter	Rep.
Examination	Exam.	Request	Req.
Exhibit	Ex.	Respondent	Resp't
General	Gen.	Respondent's	Resp't's
Grant	Grant	Respondents	Resp'ts
Hearing	Hr'g	Respondents'	Resp'ts'
Independent	Indep.	Response	Resp.
Information	Info.	Review	Rev.
Injunction	Inj.	Rule(s)	R.
Instruction(s)	Instr.	Session(s)	Sess.
Interrogatory	Interrog.	Solicitor	Sol.
Joint Appendix	J.A.	Special	Spec.
Judge	J.	State	St.
Judges	JJ.	Stay	Stay
Judgment	J.	Subpoena	Subpoena
Justice	J.	Summary	Summ.
Justices	JJ.	Supplement(al)	Supp.
Juvenile	Juv.	Suppress	Suppress
Letter	Ltr.	Surroga(cy, te)	Surrog.
Litigation	Litig.	Temporary	Temp.
Magistrate	Mag.	Temporary Restraining	TRO
Mediat(ion, or)	Med.	Order	
Memorandum	Mem.	Testimony	Test.
Minutes	Mins.	Transcript	Tr.
Motion	Mot.	Trial	Trial
Number	No.	Verified Statement	V.S.
Numbers	Nos.	Versus	v.
Opinion	Op.		

Appendix 4   Court Abbreviations

Appendix 4 contains abbreviations for federal and state courts, at both the appellate and trial levels. Required spaces are indicated by triangles (▲). If you cannot find an entry for the court you wish to cite, consult **Appendix 1** and **Appendix 3(B)** to construct an abbreviation for the court.

This appendix is divided into the following sections:

A.   Federal Court Abbreviations
B.   State Court Abbreviations

4(A)   Federal Courts

The listed federal courts include the Supreme Court, circuit courts of appeal, trial courts of general jurisdiction, military courts, and specialty courts.

Court Name	Abbreviation
United States Supreme Court	U.S.
United States Courts of Appeals	
First Circuit	1st ▲ Cir.
Second Circuit	2d ▲ Cir.
Third Circuit	3d ▲ Cir.
Fourth Circuit	4th ▲ Cir.
Fifth Circuit	5th ▲ Cir.
Sixth Circuit	6th ▲ Cir.
Seventh Circuit	7th ▲ Cir.
Eighth Circuit	8th ▲ Cir.
Ninth Circuit	9th ▲ Cir.
Tenth Circuit	10th ▲ Cir.
Eleventh Circuit	11th ▲ Cir.
District of Columbia Circuit	D.C. ▲ Cir.
Federal Circuit	Fed. ▲ Cir.
United States District Courts	
Middle District of Alabama	M.D. ▲ Ala.
Northern District of Alabama	N.D. ▲ Ala.
Southern District of Alabama	S.D. ▲ Ala.
District of Alaska	D. ▲ Alaska
District of Arizona	D. ▲ Ariz.
Eastern District of Arkansas	E.D. ▲ Ark.
Western District of Arkansas	W.D. ▲ Ark.
Central District of California	C.D. ▲ Cal.
Eastern District of California	E.D. ▲ Cal.
Northern District of California	N.D. ▲ Cal.
Southern District of California	S.D. ▲ Cal.
District of the Canal Zone	D.C.Z.
District of Colorado	D. ▲ Colo.
District of Connecticut	D. ▲ Conn.

Court Name	Abbreviation
District of Delaware	D. Del.
District of the District of Columbia	D.D.C.
Middle District of Florida	M.D. Fla.
Northern District of Florida	N.D. Fla.
Southern District of Florida	S.D. Fla.
Middle District of Georgia	M.D. Ga.
Northern District of Georgia	N.D. Ga.
Southern District of Georgia	S.D. Ga.
District of Guam	D. Guam
District of Hawaii	D. Haw.
District of Idaho	D. Idaho
Central District of Illinois	C.D. Ill.
Northern District of Illinois	N.D. Ill.
Southern District of Illinois	S.D. Ill.
Northern District of Indiana	N.D. Ind.
Southern District of Indiana	S.D. Ind.
Northern District of Iowa	N.D. Iowa
Southern District of Iowa	S.D. Iowa
District of Kansas	D. Kan.
Eastern District of Kentucky	E.D. Ky.
Western District of Kentucky	W.D. Ky.
Eastern District of Louisiana	E.D. La.
Middle District of Louisiana	M.D. La.
Western District of Louisiana	W.D. La.
District of Maine	D. Me.
District of Maryland	D. Md.
District of Massachusetts	D. Mass.
Eastern District of Michigan	E.D. Mich.
Western District of Michigan	W.D. Mich.
District of Minnesota	D. Minn.
Northern District of Mississippi	N.D. Miss.
Southern District of Mississippi	S.D. Miss.
Eastern District of Missouri	E.D. Mo.
Western District of Missouri	W.D. Mo.
District of Montana	D. Mont.
District of Nebraska	D. Neb.
District of Nevada	D. Nev.
District of New Hampshire	D.N.H.
District of New Jersey	D.N.J.
District of New Mexico	D.N.M.

Court Name	Abbreviation
Eastern District of New York	E.D.N.Y.
Northern District of New York	N.D.N.Y.
Southern District of New York	S.D.N.Y.
Western District of New York	W.D.N.Y.
Eastern District of North Carolina	E.D.N.C.
Middle District of North Carolina	M.D.N.C.
Western District of North Carolina	W.D.N.C.
District of North Dakota	D.N.D.
District of the Northern Mariana Islands	D. N. Mar. I.
Northern District of Ohio	N.D. Ohio
Southern District of Ohio	S.D. Ohio
Eastern District of Oklahoma	E.D. Okla.
Northern District of Oklahoma	N.D. Okla.
Western District of Oklahoma	W.D. Okla.
District of Oregon	D. Or.
Eastern District of Pennsylvania	E.D. Pa.
Middle District of Pennsylvania	M.D. Pa.
Western District of Pennsylvania	W.D. Pa.
District of Puerto Rico	D.P.R.
District of Rhode Island	D.R.I.
District of South Carolina	D.S.C.
District of South Dakota	D.S.D.
Eastern District of Tennessee	E.D. Tenn.
Middle District of Tennessee	M.D. Tenn.
Western District of Tennessee	W.D. Tenn.
Eastern District of Texas	E.D. Tex.
Northern District of Texas	N.D. Tex.
Southern District of Texas	S.D. Tex.
Western District of Texas	W.D. Tex.
District of Utah	D. Utah
District of Vermont	D. Vt.
Eastern District of Virginia	E.D. Va.
Western District of Virginia	W.D. Va.
District of the Virgin Islands	D.V.I.
Eastern District of Washington	E.D. Wash.
Western District of Washington	W.D. Wash.
Northern District of West Virginia	N.D. W. Va.
Southern District of West Virginia	S.D. W. Va.
Eastern District of Wisconsin	E.D. Wis.
Western District of Wisconsin	W.D. Wis.
District of Wyoming	D. Wyo.

Court Name	Abbreviation
Military Courts	
United States Air Force Court of Criminal Appeals	A.F.▲Ct.▲Crim.▲App.
United States Army Court of Criminal Appeals	A.▲Ct.▲Crim.▲App.
United States Coast Guard Court of Criminal Appeals	C.G.▲Ct.▲Crim.▲App.
United States Court of Appeals for the Armed Forces	C.A.A.F.
United States Court of Appeals for Veterans Claims	Vet.▲App.
United States Court of Military Appeals	C.M.A.
United States Navy–Marine Court of Criminal Appeals	N.–M.▲Ct.▲Crim.▲App.

Bankruptcy Courts

Bankruptcy Appellate Panels
Each United States Circuit Court of Appeals has a corresponding bankruptcy appellate panel. Add the abbreviation "B.A.P." before the circuit court abbreviation.

B.A.P.▲5th▲Cir.
B.A.P.▲8th▲Cir.

Bankruptcy Courts
Each United States District Court has a corresponding bankruptcy court. Add the abbreviation "Bankr." before the district court abbreviation.

Bankr.▲N.D.▲Ala.
Bankr.▲D.▲Mass.

Other Federal Courts	
United States Court of Federal Claims	Fed.▲Cl.
United States Claims Court	Cl.▲Ct.
Court of Claims	Ct.▲Cl.
United States Court of Customs and Patent Appeals	C.C.P.A.
United States Court of International Trade	Ct.▲Int'l▲Trade
Tax Court	T.C.
United States Customs Court	Cust.▲Ct.
Board of Tax Appeals	B.T.A.
Judicial Panel on Multidistrict Litigation	J.P.M.L.
Special Court, Regional Rail Reorganization Act	Reg'l▲Rail▲Reorg.▲Ct.
Foreign Intelligence Surveillance Court	FISC
Foreign Intelligence Surveillance Court of Review	FISA▲Ct.▲Rev.

4(B) State Court Abbreviations

Appendix 4(B) lists abbreviations for each state's court of last resort, any intermediate appellate court, and trial courts of general jurisdiction. Courts are listed hierarchically, with the highest court in the state appearing first. Note that some intermediate-level appellate courts deal solely with civil or criminal matters. Required spaces are indicated by triangles (▲).

Court Name	Abbreviation
Alabama Supreme Court	Ala.
Alabama Court of Civil Appeals	Ala. Civ. App.
Alabama Court of Criminal Appeals	Ala. Crim. App.
Alabama Court of Appeals (before 1969)	Ala. Ct. App.
Alabama Circuit Court	Ala. Cir. Ct.
Alaska Supreme Court	Alaska
Alaska Court of Appeals	Alaska Ct. App.
Alaska Superior Court	Alaska Super. Ct.
Arizona Supreme Court	Ariz.
Arizona Court of Appeals	Ariz. Ct. App.
Arizona Tax Court	Ariz. T.C.
Arizona Superior Court	Ariz. Super. Ct.
Arkansas Supreme Court	Ark.
Arkansas Court of Appeals	Ark. Ct. App.
Arkansas Circuit Court	Ark. Cir. Ct.
Arkansas Chancery Court (before 2001)	Ark. Ch. Ct.
California Supreme Court	Cal.
California Court of Appeal	Cal. Ct. App.
California District Court of Appeal	Cal. Dist. Ct. App.
California Superior Court Appellate Department	Cal. App. Dep't Super. Ct.
California Superior Court	Cal. Super. Ct.
Colorado Supreme Court	Colo.
Colorado Court of Appeals	Colo. Ct. App.
Colorado District Court	Colo. Dist. Ct.
Connecticut Supreme Court	Conn.
Connecticut Appellate Court	Conn. App. Ct.
Connecticut Superior Court	Conn. Super. Ct.
Connecticut District Court	Conn. Dist. Ct.
Delaware Supreme Court	Del.
Delaware Court of Chancery	Del. Ch.
Delaware Superior Court	Del. Super. Ct.
Delaware Superior Court and Orphans' Court	Del. Super. Ct. & Orphans' Ct.
Delaware Family Court	Del. Fam. Ct.
District of Columbia Court of Appeals	D.C.
District of Columbia Superior Court	D.C. Super. Ct.
Florida Supreme Court	Fla.
Florida District Court of Appeal	Fla. Dist. Ct. App.
Florida Circuit Court	Fla. Cir. Ct.
Georgia Supreme Court	Ga.
Georgia Court of Appeals	Ga. Ct. App.
Georgia Superior Court	Ga. Super. Ct.
Hawaii Supreme Court	Haw.
Hawaii Intermediate Court of Appeals	Haw. Ct. App.
Hawaii Circuit Court	Haw. Cir. Ct.

Court Name	Abbreviation
Idaho Supreme Court	Idaho
Idaho Court of Appeals	Idaho Ct. App.
Idaho District Court	Idaho Dist. Ct.
Illinois Supreme Court	Ill.
Illinois Appellate Court	Ill. App. Ct.
Illinois Court of Claims	Ill. Ct. Cl.
Illinois Circuit Court	Ill. Cir. Ct.
Indiana Supreme Court	Ind.
Indiana Court of Appeals	Ind. Ct. App.
Indiana Tax Court	Ind. T.C.
Indiana Superior Court	Ind. Super. Ct.
Iowa Supreme Court	Iowa
Iowa Court of Appeals	Iowa Ct. App.
Iowa District Court	Iowa Dist. Ct.
Kansas Supreme Court	Kan.
Kansas Court of Appeals	Kan. Ct. App.
Kansas District Court	Kan. Dist. Ct.
Kentucky Supreme Court	Ky.
Kentucky Court of Appeals	Ky. Ct. App.
Kentucky Circuit Court	Ky. Cir. Ct.
Louisiana Supreme Court	La.
Louisiana Court of Appeal	La. Ct. App.
Louisiana District Court	La. Dist. Ct.
Maine Supreme Judicial Court	Me.
Maine Superior Court	Me. Super. Ct.
Maryland Court of Appeals	Md.
Maryland Court of Special Appeals	Md. Ct. Spec. App.
Maryland Circuit Court	Md. Cir. Ct.
Massachusetts Supreme Judicial Court	Mass.
Massachusetts Appeals Court	Mass. App. Ct.
Trial Court of the Commonwealth	Mass. Commw. Ct.
Massachusetts District Court	Mass. Dist. Ct.
Michigan Supreme Court	Mich.
Michigan Court of Appeals	Mich. Ct. App.
Michigan Court of Claims	Mich. Ct. Cl.
Michigan Circuit Court	Mich. Cir. Ct.
Minnesota Supreme Court	Minn.
Minnesota Court of Appeals	Minn. Ct. App.
Minnesota District Court	Minn. Dist. Ct.
Mississippi Supreme Court	Miss.
Mississippi Court of Appeals	Miss. Ct. App.
Mississippi Circuit Court	Miss. Cir. Ct.
Mississippi Chancery Court	Miss. Ch. Ct.

Court Name	Abbreviation
Missouri Supreme Court	Mo.
Missouri Court of Appeals	Mo. Ct. App.
Missouri Circuit Court	Mo. Cir. Ct.
Montana Supreme Court	Mont.
Montana District Court	Mont. Dist. Ct.
Nebraska Supreme Court	Neb.
Nebraska Court of Appeals	Neb. Ct. App.
Nebraska District Court	Neb. Dist. Ct.
Nevada Supreme Court	Nev.
Nevada District Court	Nev. Dist. Ct.
New Hampshire Supreme Court	N.H.
New Hampshire Superior Court	N.H. Super. Ct.
New Jersey Supreme Court	N.J.
New Jersey Superior Court, Appellate Division	N.J. Super. Ct. App. Div.
New Jersey Superior Court, Chancery Division	N.J. Super. Ct. Ch. Div.
New Jersey Superior Court, Law Division	N.J. Super. Ct. Law Div.
New Jersey Tax Court	N.J.T.C.
New Jersey Court of Chancery	N.J. Ch.
New Jersey Prerogative Court	N.J. Prerog. Ct.
New Mexico Supreme Court	N.M.
New Mexico Court of Appeals	N.M. Ct. App.
New Mexico District Court	N.M. Dist. Ct.
New York Court of Appeals	N.Y.
New York Supreme Court, Appellate Division	N.Y. App. Div.
New York Supreme Court	N.Y. Sup. Ct.
New York Court of Claims	N.Y. Ct. Cl.
New York Civil Court	N.Y. Civ. Ct.
New York Criminal Court	N.Y. Crim. Ct.
New York Family Court	N.Y. Fam. Ct.
North Carolina Supreme Court	N.C.
North Carolina Court of Appeals	N.C. Ct. App.
North Carolina Superior Court	N.C. Super. Ct.
North Dakota Supreme Court	N.D.
North Dakota Court of Appeals	N.D. Ct. App.
North Dakota District Court	N.D. Dist. Ct.
Ohio Supreme Court	Ohio
Ohio Court of Appeals	Ohio Ct. App.
Ohio Court of Common Pleas	Ohio Ct. Com. Pl.
Oklahoma Supreme Court	Okla.
Oklahoma Court of Criminal Appeals	Okla. Crim. App.
Oklahoma Court of Civil Appeals	Okla. Civ. App.
Oklahoma District Court	Okla. Dist. Ct.
Oregon Supreme Court	Or.
Oregon Court of Appeals	Or. Ct. App.
Oregon Tax Court	Or. T.C.
Oregon Circuit Court	Or. Cir. Ct.

Court Name	Abbreviation
Pennsylvania Supreme Court	Pa.
Pennsylvania Superior Court	Pa. Super. Ct.
Pennsylvania Commonwealth Court	Pa. Commw. Ct.
Pennsylvania District and County Court	Pa. Dist. & Cnty. Ct.
Rhode Island Supreme Court	R.I.
Rhode Island Superior Court	R.I. Super. Ct.
South Carolina Supreme Court	S.C.
South Carolina Court of Appeals	S.C. Ct. App.
South Carolina Circuit Court	S.C. Cir. Ct.
South Dakota Supreme Court	S.D.
South Dakota Circuit Court	S.D. Cir. Ct.
Tennessee Supreme Court	Tenn.
Tennessee Court of Appeals	Tenn. Ct. App.
Tennessee Court of Criminal Appeals	Tenn. Crim. App.
Tennessee Circuit Court	Tenn. Cir. Ct.
Tennessee Criminal Court	Tenn. Crim. Ct.
Tennessee Chancery Court	Tenn. Ch. Ct.
Texas Supreme Court	Tex.
Texas Court of Criminal Appeals (previously named Texas Court of Appeals; see Texas entry in **Appendix 1**)	Tex. Crim. App. (Tex. Ct. App.)
Texas Commission of Appeals	Tex. Comm'n App.
Texas Court of Appeals (previously named Texas Court of Civil Appeals; see Texas entry in **Appendix 1**)	Tex. App. (Tex. Civ. App.)
Texas District Court	Tex. Dist. Ct.
Texas Criminal District Court	Tex. Crim. Dist. Ct.
Utah Supreme Court	Utah
Utah Court of Appeals	Utah Ct. App.
Utah District Court	Utah Dist. Ct.
Vermont Supreme Court	Vt.
Vermont Superior Court	Vt. Super. Ct.
Vermont District Court	Vt. Dist. Ct.
Virginia Supreme Court	Va.
Virginia Court of Appeals	Va. Ct. App.
Virginia Circuit Court	Va. Cir. Ct.
Washington Supreme Court	Wash.
Washington Court of Appeals	Wash. Ct. App.
Washington Superior Court	Wash. Super. Ct.
West Virginia Supreme Court of Appeals	W. Va.
West Virginia Circuit Court	W. Va. Cir. Ct.
Wisconsin Supreme Court	Wis.
Wisconsin Court of Appeals	Wis. Ct. App.
Wisconsin Circuit Court	Wis. Cir. Ct.
Wyoming Supreme Court	Wyo.
Wyoming District Court	Wyo. Dist. Ct.

Appendix 5   Periodical Abbreviations

Use **Appendix 5** to abbreviate the names of legal and other periodicals. The citation form for periodicals is addressed in **Rule 21**. Selected periodicals are listed in alphabetical order by the periodical's current name. Prior names of a periodical are listed immediately below its current name. Use the abbreviation that corresponds to the volume you are citing; do not use the current abbreviation if citing older volumes. You may also use these abbreviations for names of looseleaf services and for the homepage name of sources on the World Wide Web.

To help you determine spacing in each abbreviation, the appendix uses the symbol ▲ to designate a required space. Omit this symbol when you type the abbreviation. Follow **Rule 2** to properly space abbreviations.

The appendix uses the symbol ★ to indicate periodicals that are nonconsecutively paginated; see **Rules 21.1** and **21.3** for additional information about citing nonconsecutively paginated periodicals.

Although this appendix contains abbreviations for many periodicals, it is not exhaustive. If the name of the periodical you wish to cite is not here, look for individual words from its title. If you do not find an individual word listed, you may use an abbreviation that appears in another title in this appendix, and for geographic references, you may use **Appendix 3(B)**. If you cannot find any abbreviation for the word in **Appendix 5** or **Appendix 3(B)**, however, spell it out. Do not use an abbreviation from any other appendix, as it may be a word that should not be abbreviated in a periodical name, or it may be abbreviated differently in another context.

Omit the articles "a," "an," and "the," as well as the prepositions "at," "in," and "of," unless a reader would otherwise not be able to discern the publication name. Omit commas in periodical abbreviations. Unless shown otherwise for a specific periodical title in this appendix, omit colons, and everything following them, appearing within a title. If the periodical title itself contains an abbreviation, use it in the abbreviated name (e.g., BYU J. Pub. L.).

Periodical Name	Abbreviation
★ABA Journal	A.B.A. ▲J.
Was: American Bar Association Journal (Vol. 1–Vol. 69)	ABA▲J.
Academ(ic, y)	Acad.
Account(ancy, ant, ants, ing)	Acct.
Adelaide Law Review	Adel. ▲L. ▲Rev.
Administrat(ion, ive, or)	Admin.
Administrative Law Review of the American University	Admin. ▲L. ▲Rev. ▲Am. ▲U.
Was: Administrative Law Journal (Vol. 1–Vol. 5)	Admin. ▲L.J.
Administrative Law Review	Admin. ▲L. ▲Rev.
Was: Administrative Law Bulletin (Vol. 1–Vol. 12)	Admin. ▲L. ▲Bull.
Advertising	Advert.

507

Periodical Name	Abbreviation
Advoca(cy, te)	Advoc.
★Advocate	Advoc.
Absorbed: Idaho State Bar News Bulletin (Mar. 1958)	Idaho▲St.▲B.▲News▲Bull.
Affairs	Aff.
Affirmative	Aff.
Afric(a, an)	Afr.
Agricultur(al, e)	Agric.
Air	Air
★Air and Space Lawyer, The	Air▲&▲Space▲Law.
Air Force Law Review	A.F.▲L.▲Rev.
Was: United States Air Force JAG Law Review (Vol. 6, no. 6–Vol. 15, no. 2)	U.S.A.F.▲JAG▲L.▲Rev.
Was: United States Air Force JAG Bulletin (Vol. 1, no. 1–Vol. 6, no. 5)	U.S.A.F.▲JAG▲Bull.
Akron Intellectual Property Journal	Akron▲Intell.▲Prop.▲J.
Akron Law Review	Akron▲L.▲Rev.
Akron Tax Journal	Akron▲Tax▲J.
Alabama Law Review	Ala.▲L.▲Rev.
★Alabama Lawyer, The	Ala.▲Law.
Alaska Law Review	Alaska▲L.▲Rev.
Was: UCLA–Alaska Law Review (Vol. 1–Vol. 12)	UCLA–Alaska▲L.▲Rev.
Was: Alaska Law Journal	Alaska▲L.J.
Albany Government Law Review	Alb.▲Gov't▲L.▲Rev.
Was: Albany Law Environmental Outlook Journal (Vol. 1–Vol. 12)	Alb.▲L.▲Envtl.▲Outlook▲J.
Albany Law Journal of Science & Technology	Alb.▲L.J.▲Sci.▲&▲Tech.
Albany Law Review	Alb.▲L.▲Rev.
★ALI–ABA Business Law Course Materials Journal	ALI–ABA▲Bus.▲L.▲Course▲Materials▲J.
Was: ★ALI–ABA Course Materials Journal (Vol. 1–Vol. 24, no. 2)	ALI–ABA▲Course▲Materials▲J.
America(n)	Am.
American Bankruptcy Institute Law Review	Am.▲Bankr.▲Inst.▲L.▲Rev.
American Bankruptcy Law Journal, The	Am.▲Bankr.▲L.J.
Was: Journal of the National Conference of Referees in Bankruptcy (Vol. 40–Vol. 44)	J.▲Nat'l▲Conf.▲Referees▲Bankr.
Was: Journal of the National Association of Referees in Bankruptcy (Vol. 1–Vol. 39; Vol. 45–Vol. 65)	J.▲Nat'l▲Ass'n▲Referees▲Bankr.
American Bar Association Journal—*see* ABA Journal	
American Bar Foundation Research Journal—*see* Law & Social Inquiry: Journal of American Bar Foundation	
American Business Law Journal	Am.▲Bus.▲L.J.
Supersedes: American Business Law Bulletin, The	Am.▲Bus.▲L.▲Bull.
American Criminal Law Review	Am.▲Crim.▲L.▲Rev.
Was: American Criminal Law Quarterly (Vol. 1–Vol. 9, no. 1)	Am.▲Crim.▲L.Q.
American Indian Law Review	Am.▲Indian▲L.▲Rev.

Periodical Name	Abbreviation
American Intellectual Property Law Association Quarterly Journal	AIPLA Q.J.
American Journal of Comparative Law	Am. J. Comp. L.
American Journal of Criminal Law	Am. J. Crim. L.
American Journal of Family Law	Am. J. Fam. L.
American Journal of International Law	Am. J. Int'l L.
American Journal of Jurisprudence	Am. J. Juris.
Was: Natural Law Forum (Vol. 1–Vol. 13)	Nat. L.F.
American Journal of Law & Medicine	Am. J.L. & Med.
American Journal of Legal History	Am. J. Legal Hist.
American Journal of Mediation	Am. J. Mediation
American Journal of Tax Policy	Am. J. Tax Pol'y
American Journal of Trial Advocacy	Am. J. Trial Advoc.
American Law Institute	A.L.I.
American Law Register, The—*see* University of Pennsylvania Law Review	
American Law Reports	A.L.R.
American Lawyer	Am. Law.
American Review of International Arbitration, The	Am. Rev. Int'l Arb.
American Society of International Law Proceedings	Am. Soc'y Int'l L. Proc.
American University International Law Review	Am. U. Int'l L. Rev.
Was: American University Journal of International Law and Policy (Vol. 1–Vol. 12, no. 6)	Am. U. J. Int'l L. & Pol'y
American University Journal of Gender, Social Policy & the Law	Am. U. J. Gender Soc. Pol'y & L.
Was: American University Journal of Gender and the Law (Vol. 1–Vol. 6, no. 3)	Am. U. J. Gender & L.
American University Law Review	Am. U. L. Rev.
Was: American University Intramural Law Review (Vol. 1–Vol. 5)	Am. U. Intramural L. Rev.
★AmLaw Tech	AmLaw Tech
and	&
Anglo–American Law Review—*see* Common Law World Review	
Animal Law	Animal L.
Annals	Annals
Annals of the American Academy of Political and Social Science	Annals Am. Acad. Pol. & Soc. Sci.
Annals of Health Law	Annals Health L.
Annual	Ann.
Annual Institute on Securities Regulation	Ann. Inst. Sec. Reg.
Annual Review of Banking and Financial Law—*see* Review of Banking and Financial Law	
Annual Review of Banking Law	Ann. Rev. Banking L.
Annual Survey of American Law—*see* New York University Annual Survey of American Law	
Annual Survey of International & Comparative Law	Ann. Surv. Int'l & Comp. L.
Antitrust	Antitrust

Periodical Name	Abbreviation
Antitrust Bulletin	Antitrust Bull.
★Antitrust Law and Economics Review	Antitrust L. & Econ. Rev.
Antitrust Law Journal	Antitrust L.J.
Appalachian Journal of Law	Appalachian J.L.
App(eal, eals, ellate)	App.
Arbitrat(ion, or, ors)	Arb.
★Arizona Attorney	Ariz. Att'y
Was: Arizona Bar Journal (June 1965–July 1998)	Ariz. B.J.
Was: Arizona Bar Briefs	Ariz. B. Briefs
Arizona Journal of International and Comparative Law	Ariz. J. Int'l & Comp. L.
Arizona Law Review	Ariz. L. Rev.
Arizona Republic	Ariz. Republic
Arizona State Law Journal	Ariz. St. L.J.
Was: Law and the Social Order (1969–1973)	L. & Soc. Ord.
★Arkansas Law Notes	Ark. L. Notes
Arkansas Law Review	Ark. L. Rev.
Was: Arkansas Law Review and Bar Association Journal (Vol. 1–Vol. 21)	Ark. L. Rev. & B. Ass'n J.
★Arkansas Lawyer	Ark. Law.
★Army Lawyer	Army Law.
Art	Art
Art and Museum Law Journal	Art & Museum L.J.
Art & the Law—*see* Columbia Journal of Law & the Arts, The	
Asian	Asian
Asian American Law Journal	Asian Am. L.J.
Was: Asian Law Journal (Vol. 1–Vol. 12)	Asian L.J.
Asian Business Lawyer	Asian Bus. Law.
Asian Law Journal	Asian L.J.
Asian Pacific American Law Journal: UCLA School of Law	Asian Pac. Am. L.J.
Asian–Pacific Law and Policy Journal	Asian–Pac. L. & Pol'y J.
Was: Asian American Pacific Islands Law Journal	Asian Am. Pac. Is. L.J.
Association	Ass'n
★Atlanta Journal & Constitution	Atl. J. & Const.
Atomic Energy Law Journal	Atomic Energy L.J.
Attorney	Att'y
Auckland University Law Review	Auckland U. L. Rev.
Australian Dispute Resolution Journal	Austl. Disp. Res. J.
Australian Law Journal	Austl. L.J.
Ave Maria Law Review	Ave Maria L. Rev.
Aviation	Av.
★Baltimore Sun	Balt. Sun
Banking Law Journal	Banking L.J.
Absorbed: Business Law Journal (1932)	Bus. L.J.
Absorbed: Bankers Magazine	Bankers Mag.
Bankruptcy	Bankr.

Periodical Name	Abbreviation
Bankruptcy Developments Journal—*see* Emory Bankruptcy Developments Journal	
Bar	B.
★Bar Examiner, The	B. ▲ Examiner
★Bar Leader	B. ▲ Leader
Was: ★Bar Activities (Vol. 1–Vol. 7, no. 2)	B. ▲ Activities
Was: ★Bar Keys	B. ▲ Keys
Barrister—*see* Young Lawyer	
Barry Law Review	Barry ▲ L. ▲ Rev.
Baylor Law Review	Baylor ▲ L. ▲ Rev.
Behavior(al)	Behav.
Behavioral Sciences & the Law	Behav. ▲ Sci. ▲ & ▲ L.
Belmont Law Review	Belmont ▲ L. ▲ Rev.
★Bench & Bar	Bench ▲ & ▲ B.
Was: Kentucky Bench & Bar	Ky. ▲ Bench ▲ & ▲ B.
★Bench & Bar of Minnesota	Bench ▲ & ▲ B. ▲ Minn.
Benchmark	Benchmark
Benefits Law Journal	Benefits ▲ L.J.
Berkeley Journal of African–American Law & Policy	Berkeley ▲ J. ▲ Afr.–Am. ▲ L. ▲ & ▲ Pol'y
Was: African–American Law & Policy Report (Vol. 1–Vol. 7)	Afr.–Am. ▲ L. ▲ & ▲ Pol'y ▲ Rep.
Berkeley Journal of Employment and Labor Law	Berkeley ▲ J. ▲ Emp. ▲ & ▲ Lab. ▲ L.
Was: Industrial Relations Law Journal (Vol. 1–Vol. 13)	Indus. ▲ Rel. ▲ L.J.
Berkeley Journal of Gender, Law, and Justice	Berkeley ▲ J. ▲ Gender ▲ L. ▲ & ▲ Just.
Berkeley Journal of Health Care Law	Berkeley ▲ J. ▲ Health ▲ Care ▲ L.
Berkeley Journal of International Law	Berkeley ▲ J. ▲ Int'l ▲ L.
Was: International Tax & Business Lawyer (Vol. 1–Vol. 13, no. 2)	Int'l ▲ Tax ▲ & ▲ Bus. ▲ Law.
Berkeley La Raza Law Journal	Berkeley ▲ La ▲ Raza ▲ L.J.
Was: La Raza Law Journal (Vol. 1–Vol. 12)	La ▲ Raza ▲ L.J.
Berkeley Technology Law Journal	Berkeley ▲ Tech. ▲ L.J.
Was: High Technology Law Journal (Vol. 1–Vol. 10)	High ▲ Tech. ▲ L.J.
Berkeley Women's Law Journal	Berkeley ▲ Women's ▲ L.J.
★Beverly Hills Bar Association Journal	Beverly ▲ Hills ▲ B. ▲ Ass'n ▲ J.
Was: ★Journal of the Beverly Hills Bar Association (Vol. 1–Vol. 11, no. 3)	J. ▲ Beverly ▲ Hills ▲ B. ▲ Ass'n
Black Law Journal—*see* National Black Law Journal	
Bloomberg Corporate Law Journal	Bloomberg ▲ Corp. ▲ L.J.
Boalt Journal of Criminal Law	Boalt ▲ J. ▲ Crim. ▲ L.
Was: California Journal of Criminal Law (2000–2004)	Cal. ▲ J. ▲ Crim. ▲ L.
★Boston Bar Journal	Boston ▲ B.J.
Was: ★Bar Bulletin (Jan. 1924–Dec. 1956)	B. ▲ Bull.
Boston College Environmental Affairs Law Review	B.C. ▲ Envtl. ▲ Aff. ▲ L. ▲ Rev.
Was: Environmental Affairs (Vol. 1–Vol. 6)	Envtl. ▲ Aff.

Periodical Name	Abbreviation
Boston College International and Comparative Law Review	B.C. Int'l & Comp. L. Rev.
Was: Boston College International and Comparative Law Journal (Vol. 1–Vol. 2, no. 1)	B.C. Int'l & Comp. L.J.
Boston College Law Review	B.C. L. Rev.
Was: Boston College Industrial and Commercial Law Review (Vol. 1–Vol. 18)	B.C. Indus. & Com. L. Rev.
Boston College Third World Law Journal	B.C. Third World L.J.
★Boston Globe	Bos. Globe
★Boston Herald	Bos. Herald
Boston University International Law Journal	B.U. Int'l L.J.
Boston University Journal of Science & Technology Law	B.U. J. Sci. & Tech. L.
Was: Journal of Science & Technology Law (Vol. 1–Vol. 6)	J. Sci. & Tech. L.
Boston University Journal of Tax Law	B.U. J. Tax L.
Boston University Law Review	B.U. L. Rev.
Boston University Public Interest Law Journal	B.U. Pub. Int. L.J.

Brandeis Law Journal—*see* University of Louisville Law Review

Bridgeport Law Review—*see* QLR

Briefcase	Briefcase
Brigham Young University Education and Law Journal	BYU Educ. & L.J.
Was: Brigham Young University Journal of Law and Education (Vol. 1)	BYU J.L. & Educ.
Brigham Young University Journal of Public Law	BYU J. Pub. L.
Brigham Young University Law Review	BYU L. Rev.
British	Brit.
Brooklyn Journal of Corporate, Financial & Commercial Law	Brook. J. Corp. Fin. & Com. L.
Brooklyn Journal of International Law	Brook. J. Int'l L.
Brooklyn Law Review	Brook. L. Rev.

Buffalo Criminal Law Review—*see* New Criminal Law Review

Buffalo Environmental Law Journal	Buff. Envtl. L.J.
Buffalo Human Rights Law Review	Buff. Hum. Rts. L. Rev.
Was: Buffalo Journal of International Law (Vol. 1, no. 1–Vol. 3, no. 2)	Buff. J. Int'l L.
Buffalo Law Review	Buff. L. Rev.
★Buffalo News	Buff. News
Buffalo Public Interest Law Journal: In the Public Interest	Buff. Pub. Int. L.J.
Was: Buffalo Journal of Public Interest Law	Buff. J. Pub. Int. L.
Buffalo Women's Law Journal	Buff. Women's L.J.
Was: CIRCLES: The Buffalo Women's Journal of Law and Social Policy (Vol. 1–Vol. 6)	CIRCLES
Bulletin	Bull.

Periodical Name	Abbreviation
Bulletin of the Copyright Society of the U.S.A.—*see* Journal of the Copyright Society of the U.S.A.	
Business	Bus.
Business Law Journal	Bus.▲L.J.
Business Law Review—*see* Florida State University Business Law Review	
Business Law Review (UK)	Bus.▲L.▲Rev.▲(UK)
Business Lawyer	Bus.▲Law.
★Business Week	Bus.▲Wk.
California Bankruptcy Journal	Cal.▲Bankr.▲J.
California Criminal Law Review	Cal.▲Crim.▲L.▲Rev.
California International Practitioner, The	Cal.▲Int'l▲Pract.
California Law Review	Cal.▲L.▲Rev.
★California Lawyer	Cal.▲Law.
Was: ★California State Bar Journal (Vol. 47–Vol. 56)	Cal.▲St.▲B.J.
Was: ★Journal–State Bar of California (Vol. 17, no. 3–Vol. 46)	J.–St.▲B.▲Cal.
Was: ★State Bar Journal of the State Bar of California (Vol. 1–Vol. 17, no. 2)	St.▲B.J.▲St.▲B.▲Cal.
California Regulatory Law Reporter	Cal.▲Reg.▲L.▲Rep.
California State Bar Journal	Cal.▲St.▲B.J.
California Western International Law Journal	Cal.▲W.▲Int'l▲L.J.
California Western Law Review	Cal.▲W.▲L.▲Rev.
Cambridge Law Journal	Cambridge▲L.J.
Campaign	Camp.
Campbell Law Review	Campbell▲L.▲Rev.
Canada–United States Law Journal	Can.–U.S.▲L.J.
Canadian–American Law Journal	Can.–Am.▲L.J.
Canadian Journal of Law and Jurisprudence	Can.▲J.L.▲&▲Jur.
Canadian Labour & Employment Law Journal	Can.▲Lab.▲&▲Emp.▲L.J.
Canterbury Law Review	Canterbury▲L.▲Rev.
Capital Defense Digest	Cap.▲Def.▲Dig.
Capital Defense Journal	Cap.▲Def.▲J.
Capital University Law Review	Cap.▲U.▲L.▲Rev.
Cardozo Arts and Entertainment Law Journal	Cardozo▲Arts▲&▲Ent.▲L.J.
Cardozo Journal of International and Comparative Law	Cardozo▲J.▲Int'l▲&▲Comp.▲L.
Was: New Europe Law Review (Vol. 1–Vol. 2, no.1)	New▲Eur.▲L.▲Rev.
Cardozo Journal of Conflict Resolution	Cardozo▲J.▲Conflict▲Resol.
Cardozo Journal of Law & Gender	Cardozo▲J.L.▲&▲Gender
Was: Cardozo Women's Law Journal (Vol. 1–Vol. 11)	Cardozo▲Women's▲L.J.
Absorbed: Women's Annotated Legal Bibliography	Women's▲Annotated▲Legal▲Bibliog.
Cardozo Law Review	Cardozo▲L.▲Rev.
Cardozo Online Journal of Conflict Resolution	Cardozo▲Online▲J.▲Conflict▲Resol.
Cardozo Studies in Law and Literature—*see* Law & Literature	

Periodical Name	Abbreviation
★Case & Comment	Case ▲ & ▲ Comment
Case Western Reserve Journal of International Law	Case ▲ W. ▲ Res. ▲ J. ▲ Int'l ▲ L.
Case Western Reserve Law Review	Case ▲ W. ▲ Res. ▲ L. ▲ Rev.
Was: Western Reserve Law Review (Vol. 1–Vol. 18)	W. ▲ Res. ▲ L. ▲ Rev.
Catholic	Cath.
Cases	Cas.
Catholic Lawyer—*see* Journal of Catholic Legal Studies	
Catholic University Law Review	Cath. ▲ U. ▲ L. ▲ Rev.
Was: Catholic University of America Law Review, The (Vol. 22–Vol. 23)	Cath. ▲ U. ▲ Am. ▲ L. ▲ Rev.
Was: Catholic University Law Review, The (Vol. 20–Vol. 21)	Cath. ▲ U. ▲ L. ▲ Rev.
Was: Catholic University of America Law Review, The (Vol. 1–Vol. 19)	Cath. ▲ U. ▲ Am. ▲ L. ▲ Rev.
★CBA Record	CBA ▲ Rec.
Was: ★Chicago Bar Record (Vol. 16–Vol. 67, no. 2)	Chi. ▲ B. ▲ Rec.
Was: ★Chicago Bar Association Record, The (Vol. 1–Vol. 15)	Chi. ▲ B. ▲ Ass'n ▲ Rec.
Central	Cent.
Chapman Law Review	Chap. ▲ L. ▲ Rev.
Charleston Law Review	Charleston ▲ L. ▲ Rev.
Charlotte Law Review	Charlotte ▲ L. ▲ Rev.
Chartered Life Underwriters	C.L.U.
Chicago Journal of International Law	Chi. ▲ J. ▲ Int'l ▲ L.
Chicago–Kent Journal of Intellectual Property	Chi.–Kent ▲ J. ▲ Intell. ▲ Prop.
Chicago–Kent Law Review	Chi.–Kent ▲ L. ▲ Rev.
Was: Chicago–Kent Review, The (Vol. 1–Vol. 16)	Chi.–Kent ▲ Rev.
★Chicago Sun Times	Chi. ▲ Sun ▲ Times
★Chicago Tribune	Chi. ▲ Trib.
Chicano–Latino Law Review	Chicano–Latino ▲ L. ▲ Rev.
Was: Chicano Law Review (Vol. 1–Vol. 10)	Chicano ▲ L. ▲ Rev.
Child(ren, ren's)	Child.
★Children's Legal Rights Journal	Child. ▲ Legal ▲ Rts. ▲ J.
China Law Reporter	China ▲ L. ▲ Rep.
★Chronicle of Higher Education	Chron. ▲ Higher ▲ Educ.
Chronicle	Chron.
CIRCLES—*see* Buffalo Women's Law Journal	
Civil	Civ.
Civil Liberties	C.L.
Civil Rights	C.R.
Clearinghouse Review	Clearinghouse ▲ Rev.
Cleveland State Law Review	Clev. ▲ St. ▲ L. ▲ Rev.
Was: Cleveland–Marshall Law Review (Vol. 1–Vol. 18, no. 2)	Clev.–Marshall ▲ L. ▲ Rev.

Periodical Name	Abbreviation
Clinical Law Review: A Journal of Lawyering and Legal Education	Clinical L. Rev.
Colorado Journal of International Environmental Law and Policy	Colo. J. Int'l Envtl. L. & Pol'y
★Colorado Lawyer	Colo. Law.
College	C.
Columbia Business Law Review	Colum. Bus. L. Rev.
Columbia Human Rights Law Review	Colum. Hum. Rts. L. Rev.
Was: Columbia Survey of Human Rights Law Review (Vol. 1–Vol. 3)	Colum. Surv. Hum. Rights L. Rev.
Columbia Journal of Asian Law	Colum. J. Asian L.
Was: Journal of Chinese Law (Vol. 1–Vol. 9)	J. Chinese L.
Columbia Journal of East European Law	Colum. J. E. Eur. L.
Was: Journal of East European Law (Vol. 6–Vol. 11)	J. E. Eur. L.
Columbia Journal of Environmental Law	Colum. J. Envtl. L.
Columbia Journal of European Law	Colum. J. Eur. L.
Columbia Journal of Gender and Law	Colum. J. Gender & L.
Columbia Journal of Law & the Arts	Colum. J.L. & Arts
Was: Columbia–VLA Journal of Law & the Arts (Vol. 1–Vol. 24)	Colum.–VLA J.L. & Arts
Was: Art & the Law (Dec. 1974–1985)	Art & L.
Columbia Journal of Law and Social Problems	Colum. J.L. & Soc. Probs.
Columbia Journal of Transnational Law	Colum. J. Transnat'l L.
Columbia Law Review	Colum. L. Rev.
Columbia Science and Technology Law Review	Colum. Sci. & Tech. L. Rev.

Columbia–VLA Journal of Law & the Arts—*see* Columbia Journal of Law & the Arts

Commentary	Comment.
Commerc(e, ial)	Com.
Commercial Law Journal	Com. L.J.
Was: Commercial Law League Journal (Vol. 28, no. 9–Vol. 35, no. 7)	Com. L. League J.
Was: Commercial Law League Bulletin (Vol. 27, no. 9–Vol. 28, no. 8)	Com. L. League Bull.
Was: Bulletin of the Commercial Law League of America, The (Vol. 6–Vol. 27, no. 8)	Bull. Com. L. League Am.
Was: League Bulletin (Vol. 1–Vol. 5)	League Bull.
CommLaw Conspectus: Journal of Communications Law and Policy	CommLaw Conspectus
Common	Common
Common Law World Review	Common L. World Rev.
Was: Anglo–American Law Review (Vol. 1–Vol. 29, no. 4)	Anglo–Am. L. Rev.
Common Market Law Review	Common Mkt. L. Rev.
Communication(s)	Comm.
Comparative	Comp.
Comparative Juridical Review	Comp. Juridical Rev.
Comparative Labor Law & Policy Journal	Comp. Lab. L. & Pol'y J.

Periodical Name	Abbreviation
Was: Comparative Labor Law Journal (Vol. 8–Vol. 18, no. 3)	Comp. Lab. L.J.
Was: Comparative Labor Law (Vol. 1–Vol. 7)	Comp. Lab. L.
Compleat Lawyer—*see* General Practice, Solo & Small Firm Lawyer	
Compliance	Compl.
Computer	Computer
Computer/Law Journal—*see* John Marshall Journal of Computer & Information Law, The	
Computer Law Review & Technology Journal	Computer L. Rev. & Tech. J.
Computer Lawyer, The	Computer Law.
Conference	Conf.
Congressional	Cong.
Congressional Digest	Cong. Dig.
★Connecticut Bar Journal	Conn. B.J.
Connecticut Insurance Law Journal	Conn. Ins. L.J.
Connecticut Journal of International Law	Conn. J. Int'l L.
Connecticut Law Review	Conn. L. Rev.
Connecticut Probate Law Journal—*see* Quinnipiac Probate Law Journal	
Connecticut Public Interest Law Journal	Conn. Pub. Int. L.J.
Constitution(al)	Const.
Constitutional Commentary	Const. Comment.
★Construction Lawyer	Constr. Law.
Consumer	Consumer
Consumer Finance Law Quarterly Report	Consumer Fin. L.Q. Rep.
Was: Personal Finance Law Quarterly Report (Vol. 9, no. 2–Vol. 38, no. 2)	Personal Fin. L.Q. Rep.
Was: Quarterly Report: Conference on Personal Finance Law (Vol. 1, no. 1–Vol. 9, no. 1)	Q. Rep.
Contemporary	Contemp.
Contemporary Drug Problems	Contemp. Drug Probs.
Contract(s)	Cont.
Control	Cont.
Conveyancer and Property Lawyer (new series)	Conv. & Prop. Law. (n.s.)
Cooley Law Review—*see* Thomas M. Cooley Law Review	
Coordinator	Coord.
Copyright	Copyright
Copyright Law Symposium (American Society of Composers, Authors, & Publishers)	Copyright L. Symp. (ASCAP)
Cornell International Law Journal	Cornell Int'l L.J.
Cornell Journal of Law and Public Policy	Cornell J.L. & Pub. Pol'y
Cornell Law Review	Cornell L. Rev.
Was: Cornell Law Quarterly (Vol. 1–Vol. 52)	Cornell L.Q.
Corporat(e, ion)	Corp.
★Corporate Counsel	Corp. Couns.
Corporate Counsel Review	Corp. Couns. Rev.
★Corporate Counsel's Quarterly	Corp. Couns.'s Q.
Corporate Governance	Corp. Governance
Corporate Taxation	Corp. Tax'n

Periodical Name	Abbreviation
Was: Journal of Corporate Taxation, The (Vol. 1–Vol. 27)	J.▲Corp.▲Tax'n
Counsel(or, or's, ors, ors')	Couns.
★Courier–Journal (Louisville, Ky.)	Courier–J. (Louisville, Ky.)
Court	Ct.
Court Review	Ct.▲Rev.
Was: Municipal Court Review (Vol. 1–Vol. 9, no. 1)	Mun.▲Ct.▲Rev.
Credit	Cred.
Creighton Law Review	Creighton▲L.▲Rev.
Crime	Crime
Crime and Justice: Review of Research	Crime▲&▲Just.
Criminal	Crim.
★Criminal Justice	Crim.▲Just.
Criminal Justice and Behavior	Crim.▲Just.▲&▲Behav.
Supersedes: Correctional Psychologist (Vol. 1–Vol. 9)	Correctional▲Psychol.
★Criminal Justice Ethics	Crim.▲Just.▲Ethics

Criminal Justice Journal—*see* Thomas Jefferson Law Review

Criminal Law Brief	Crim.▲L.▲Brief
Criminal Law Bulletin	Crim.▲L.▲Bull.
Criminal Law Forum	Crim.▲L.F.
Criminal Law Review	Crim.▲L.▲Rev.
Criminology	Criminology
Was: ★Criminologica (Vol. 1–Vol. 7)	Criminologica
Cumberland Law Review	Cumb.▲L.▲Rev.
Was: Cumberland–Samford Law Review (Vol. 1–Vol. 5)	Cumb.–Samford▲L.▲Rev.
Current Issues in Criminal Justice	Current▲Issues▲Crim.▲Just.
Current Medicine for Attorneys	Current▲Med.▲for▲Att'ys
★Currents: International Trade Law Journal	Currents:▲Int'l▲Trade▲L.J.
Dalhousie Law Journal	Dalhousie▲L.J.
★Dallas Morning News	Dallas▲Morn.▲News

D.C. Bar Journal—*see* Washington Lawyer, The

Decisions	Dec.
Defense	Def.
Defense Counsel Journal	Def.▲Couns.▲J.
Was: Insurance Counsel Journal (Vol. 1–Vol. 53)	Ins.▲Couns.▲J.
Defense Law Journal	Def.▲L.J.
Delaware Journal of Corporate Law	Del.▲J.▲Corp.▲L.
Delaware Law Review	Del.▲L.▲Rev.
★Delaware Lawyer	Del.▲Law.
Delinquency	Delinq.
Denver Journal of International Law and Policy	Denv.▲J.▲Int'l▲L.▲&▲Pol'y
★Denver Post	Denv.▲Post
Denver University Law Review	Denv.▲U.▲L.▲Rev.
Was: Denver Law Journal (Vol. 43–Vol. 61)	Denv.▲L.J.

Periodical Name	Abbreviation
Was: Denver Law Center Journal (Vol. 40– Vol. 42)	Denv. L. Ctr. J.
Was: Dicta (Vol. 6–Vol. 39)	Dicta
Was: Denver Bar Association Record, The (Vol. 1–Vol. 5)	Denv. B. Ass'n Rec.
Department	Dep't
Department of State Bulletin	Dep't St. Bull.
DePaul Business & Commercial Law Journal	DePaul Bus. & Com. L.J.
DePaul Business Law Journal	DePaul Bus. L.J.
DePaul Journal for Social Justice	DePaul J. Soc. Just.
DePaul Journal of Health Care Law	DePaul J. Health Care L.
DePaul Law Review	DePaul L. Rev.
DePaul–LCA Journal of Art and Entertainment Law and Policy	DePaul–LCA J. Art & Ent. L. & Pol'y

Detroit College of Law at Michigan State University Entertainment & Sports Law Journal— *see* Entertainment and Sports Lawyer

Detroit College of Law at Michigan State University Law Review—*see* Michigan State Law Review

Detroit College of Law Entertainment & Sports Law Forum—*see* Entertainment and Sports Lawyer

Detroit College of Law Journal of International Law and Practice—*see* Michigan State University DCL Journal of International Law

★Detroit News	Det. News
Development(s)	Dev.
Dickinson International Law Annual	Dick. Int'l L. Ann.
Dickinson Journal of Environmental Law & Policy	Dick. J. Envtl. L. & Pol'y

Dickinson Journal of International Law—*see* Penn State International Law Review

Dickinson Law Review—*see* Penn State Law Review

Digest	Dig.
The Digest: The National Italian American Bar Association Law Journal	Digest
Diplomacy	Dipl.
Dispute	Disp.
★Dispute Resolution Journal	Disp. Res. J.
Was: ★Arbitration Journal (Vol. 1–Vol. 6; n.s. Vol. 1–Vol. 48)	Arb. J.

District Lawyer—*see* Washington Lawyer, The

District of Columbia Law Review—*see* University of the District of Columbia Law Review, The

Divorce Litigation	Divorce Litig.
Drake Journal of Agricultural Law	Drake J. Agric. L.
Drake Law Review	Drake L. Rev.
Drexel Law Review	Drexel L. Rev.
Dublin University Law Journal	Dublin U. L.J.
Duke Environmental Law & Policy Forum	Duke Envtl. L. & Pol'y F.
Duke Forum for Law & Social Change	Duke F.L. & Soc. Change
Duke Journal of Comparative & International Law	Duke J. Comp. & Int'l L.

Periodical Name	Abbreviation
Was: Duke International and Comparative Law Annual (until 1990)	Duke Int'l & Comp. L. Ann.
Duke Journal of Constitutional Law & Public Policy	Duke J. Const. L. & Pub. Pol'y
Duke Journal of Gender Law & Policy	Duke J. Gender L. & Pol'y
Duke Law Journal	Duke L.J.
Was: Duke Bar Journal (Vol. 1–Vol. 6, no. 2)	Duke B.J.
Duquesne Business Law Journal	Duq. Bus. L.J.
Duquesne Law Review	Duq. L. Rev.
Was: Duquesne University Law Review (Vol. 1–Vol. 6)	Duq. U. L. Rev.
East(ern)	E.
★East European Constitutional Review	E. Eur. Const. Rev.
Ecology Law Currents	Ecology L. Currents
Ecology Law Quarterly	Ecology L.Q.
Econom(ic, ics, y)	Econ.
The Economist	Economist
Edinburgh Law Review	Edinburgh L. Rev.
Education(al)	Educ.
Education and Law Journal	Educ. & L.J.
Elder Law Journal	Elder L.J.

Elder's Advisor: The Journal of Elder Law and PostRetirement Planning—*see* Marquette Elder's Advisors

Election Law Journal	Election L.J.
Elon Law Review	Elon L. Rev.
Emory Bankruptcy Developments Journal	Emory Bankr. Dev. J.
Was: Bankruptcy Developments Journal (Vol. 1–Vol. 20)	Bankr. Dev. J.
Emory International Law Review	Emory Int'l L. Rev.
Was: Emory Journal of International Dispute Resolution (Vol. 1–Vol. 3)	Emory J. Int'l Disp. Res.
Emory Law Journal	Emory L.J.
Was: Journal of Public Law (Vol. 1–Vol. 22)	J. Pub. L.
Employ(ee, ment)	Emp.
Employee Relations Law Journal	Emp. Rel. L.J.
Employee Rights and Employment Policy Journal	Emp. Rts. & Emp. Pol'y J.
Energy	Energy
Energy Law Journal	Energy L.J.
Engl(and, ish)	Eng.
Entertainment	Ent.

Entertainment & Sports Law Journal—*see* University of Miami Entertainment & Sports Law Review

Entertainment and Sports Lawyer	Ent. & Sports Law.
Was: Detroit College of Law at Michigan State University Entertainment & Sports Law Journal (Vol. 2–Vol. 3)	Det. C.L. Mich. St. U. Ent. & Sports L.J.
Was: Detroit College of Law Entertainment & Sports Law Forum (Vol. 1)	Det. C.L. Ent. & Sports L.F.

Periodical Name	Abbreviation
Entertainment Law Journal—*see* Loyola of Los Angeles Entertainment Law Journal	
Entertainment Law Review	Ent. ▲ L. ▲ Rev.
Entrepreneurial Business Law Journal	Entrepreneurial ▲ Bus. ▲ L.J.
Environment	Env't
Environmental	Envtl.

Environmental Affairs—*see* Boston College Environmental Affairs Law Review

Environmental and Energy Law and Policy Journal	Envtl. ▲ & ▲ Energy ▲ L. ▲ & ▲ Pol'y ▲ J.
Environmental Claims Journal	Envtl. ▲ Claims ▲ J.
Environmental Forum, The	Envtl. ▲ F.
Environmental Justice	Envtl. ▲ Just.
Environmental Law	Envtl. ▲ L.
Environmental Law Quarterly	Envtl. ▲ L.Q.
Environmental Lawyer, The	Envtl. ▲ Law.

Environmental Perspectives—*see* University of Baltimore Journal of Environmental Law
Environmental Practice News—*see* William and Mary Environmental Law and Policy Review

Estate(s)	Est.
★Estate Planning	Est. ▲ Plan.
Estate Planning Institute	Est. ▲ Plan. ▲ Inst.
Ethics	Ethics
Europe(an)	Eur.
Exchange	Ex.
Faculty	Fac.
Family	Fam.
★Family Advocate	Fam. ▲ Advoc.
Was: ★Family Law Newsletter, The (Vol. 11–Vol. 18)	Fam. ▲ L. ▲ Newsl.
Was: ★Family Lawyer, The (Vol. 1–Vol. 10)	Fam. ▲ Law.
★Family Court Review: An Interdisciplinary Journal	Fam. ▲ Ct. ▲ Rev.
Was: ★Family and Conciliation Courts Review (Vol. 27, no. 1–Vol. 38, no. 4)	Fam. ▲ & ▲ Conciliation ▲ Cts. ▲ Rev.
Family Law Quarterly	Fam. ▲ L.Q.
Was: ABA Section of Family Law (1964–1965)	ABA ▲ Sec. ▲ Fam. ▲ L.
FAMU Law Review	FAMU ▲ L. ▲ Rev.
Faulkner Law Review	Faulkner ▲ L. ▲ Rev.
Was: Jones Law Review (Vol. 1, 1997–Vol. 13, 2008)	Jones ▲ L. ▲ Rev.
FDCC Quarterly	FDCC ▲ Q.
Was: FICC Quarterly (Vol. 50–Vol. 52)	FICC ▲ Q.
Federal	Fed.
Federal Circuit Bar Journal	Fed. ▲ Cir. ▲ B.J.
Federal Communications Law Journal	Fed. ▲ Comm. ▲ L.J.
Was: Federal Communications Bar Journal (Vol. 1–Vol. 29)	Fed. ▲ Comm. ▲ B.J.
Federal Courts Law Review	Fed. ▲ Cts. ▲ L. ▲ Rev.
Federal Law Review	Fed. ▲ L. ▲ Rev.

Periodical Name	Abbreviation
★Federal Lawyer, The	Fed. ▲ Law.
Was: ★Federal Bar & News Journal (Vol. 28–Vol. 41)	Fed. ▲ B. ▲ & ▲ News ▲ J.
Was: ★Federal Bar News (Vol. 1–Vol. 27)	Fed. ▲ B. ▲ News
★Federal Probation	Fed. ▲ Probation
Federal Sentencing Reporter	Fed. ▲ Sent'g ▲ Rep.
Federation	Fed'n
FICC Quarterly—*see* FDCC Quarterly	
Financ(e, es, ial)	Fin.
First Amendment Law Review	First ▲ Amend. ▲ L. ▲ Rev.

FIU Law Review—*see* Florida International University Law Review

FJC Directions	FJC ▲ Directions
Fletcher Forum of World Affairs, The	Fletcher ▲ F. ▲ World ▲ Aff.
Was: Fletcher Forum, The (Vol. 1–Vol. 12)	Fletcher ▲ F.
★Florida Bar Journal	Fla. ▲ B.J.
Was: ★Florida Law Journal (Vol. 8–Vol. 27, no. 6)	Fla. ▲ L.J.
Was: ★Florida State Bar Association Law Journal (Vol. 1–Vol. 8)	Fla. ▲ St. ▲ B. ▲ Ass'n ▲ L.J.
Florida Coastal Law Review	Fla. ▲ Coastal ▲ L. ▲ Rev.
Florida Entertainment, Art & Sport Law Journal	Fla. ▲ Ent. ▲ Art ▲ & ▲ Sport ▲ L.J.
Florida International University Law Review	FIU ▲ L. ▲ Rev.
Florida Journal of International Law	Fla. ▲ J. ▲ Int'l ▲ L.
Was: Florida International Law Journal (Vol. 1–Vol. 5)	Fla. ▲ Int'l ▲ L.J.
Florida Law Review	Fla. ▲ L. ▲ Rev.
Was: University of Florida Law Review (Vol. 1–Vol. 40)	U. ▲ Fla. ▲ L. ▲ Rev.
Florida State Journal of Transnational Law & Policy	Fla. ▲ St. ▲ J. ▲ Transnat'l ▲ L. ▲ & ▲ Pol'y
Florida State University Business Review	Fla. ▲ St. ▲ U. ▲ Bus. ▲ Rev.
Was: Business Law Review (Vol. 1–Vol. 6, no. 1)	Bus. ▲ L. ▲ Rev.
Florida State University Journal of Land Use & Environmental Law	Fla. ▲ St. ▲ U. ▲ J. ▲ Land ▲ Use ▲ & ▲ Envtl. ▲ L.
Florida State University Law Review	Fla. ▲ St. ▲ U. ▲ L. ▲ Rev.
Florida Tax Review	Fla. ▲ Tax ▲ Rev.
Food and Drug Law Journal	Food ▲ & ▲ Drug ▲ L.J.
Was: Food Drug Cosmetic Law Journal (Vol. 5–Vol. 46)	Food ▲ Drug ▲ Cosm. ▲ L.J.
Was: Food Drug Cosmetic Law Quarterly (Vol. 1–Vol. 4)	Food ▲ Drug ▲ Cosm. ▲ L.Q.
★For the Defense	For ▲ Def.
Fordham Environmental Law Review	Fordham ▲ Envtl. ▲ L. ▲ Rev.
Was: Fordham Environmental Law Journal (Vol. 5–Vol. 14, no. 3)	Fordham ▲ Envtl. ▲ L.J.
Was: Fordham Environmental Law Report (Vol. 1–Vol. 4)	Fordham ▲ Envtl. ▲ L. ▲ Rep.
Fordham Intellectual Property, Media & Entertainment Law Journal	Fordham ▲ Intell. ▲ Prop. ▲ Media ▲ & ▲ Ent. ▲ L.J.

Periodical Name	Abbreviation
Was: Fordham Entertainment, Media & Intellectual Property Law Forum (Vol. 1–Vol. 3, no. 1)	Fordham Ent. Media & Intell. Prop. L.F.
Fordham International Law Journal	Fordham Int'l L.J.
Was: Fordham International Law Forum (Vol. 1–Vol. 3)	Fordham Int'l L.F.
Fordham Journal of Corporate and Financial Law	Fordham J. Corp. & Fin. L.
Was: Financial, Securities and Tax Law Forum (Vol. 1–Vol. 4)	Fin. Sec. & Tax L.F.
Fordham Law Review	Fordham L. Rev.
Fordham Urban Law Journal	Fordham Urb. L.J.
Foreign	Foreign
Foreign Broadcast Information Service	F.B.I.S.
Forensic	Forensic
Forensic Science International	Forensic Sci. Int'l
★Fort Worth Star–Telegram	Ft. Worth Star–Teleg.
Fortnightly	Fort.
Fortune	Fortune
Forum	F.
The Forum	Forum
Foundation(s)	Found.
Franchise	Franchise
★Franchise Law Journal	Franchise L.J.
Was: ★Journal of the Forum Committee on Franchising (Vol. 1, no. 4–Vol. 3)	J.F. Committee on Franchising
Was: ★Newsletter of the Forum Committee on Franchising (Vol. 1, nos. 1–3)	Newsl. F. Committee on Franchising
Futures	Fut.
Gaming Law Review	Gaming L. Rev.
Gender	Gender
General	Gen.
★General Practice, Solo & Small Firm Lawyer	Gen. Prac. Solo & Small Firm Law.
Was: ★Compleat Lawyer, The (Vol. 1–Vol. 15, no. 2)	Compleat Law.
George Mason Law Review	Geo. Mason L. Rev.
Was: George Mason Independent Law Review (1992–Summer 1995)	Geo. Mason Indep. L. Rev.
Was: George Mason University Law Review (1981–Summer 1992)	Geo. Mason U. L. Rev.
Was: GMU Law Review (Winter 1978–Spring 1980)	GMU L. Rev.
Was: ISL Law Review (Spring 1976–Winter 1977)	ISL L. Rev.
George Mason University Civil Rights Law Journal	Geo. Mason U. C.R. L.J.
George Washington International Law Review	Geo. Wash. Int'l L. Rev.

Periodical Name	Abbreviation
Was: George Washington Journal of International Law and Economics (Vol. 16–Vol. 32)	Geo.▲Wash.▲J.▲Int'l▲L.▲&▲Econ.
Was: Journal of International Law and Economics, The (Vol. 5, no. 2–Vol. 15, no. 3)	J.▲Int'l▲L.▲&▲Econ.
Was: Journal of Law and Economic Development, The (Vol. 2, no. 2–Vol. 5, no. 1)	J.L.▲&▲Econ.▲Dev.
Was: Studies in Law and Economic Development (Apr. 1966–1967)	Stud.▲L.▲&▲Econ.▲Dev.
George Washington Law Review	Geo.▲Wash.▲L.▲Rev.
Georgetown Immigration Law Journal	Geo.▲Immigr.▲L.J.
Was: ★Georgetown University Law Center Immigration Reporter (Fall 1983–Spring 1985)	Geo.▲U.▲L.▲Ctr.▲Immigr.▲Rep.
Was: ★Immigration Monitoring Report (1981–Spring 1983)	Immigr.▲Monitoring▲Rep.
Georgetown International Environmental Law Review	Geo.▲Int'l▲Envtl.▲L.▲Rev.
Georgetown Journal of Gender and the Law	Geo.▲J.▲Gender▲&▲L.
Georgetown Journal of International Law	Geo.▲J.▲Int'l▲L.
Was: Law and Policy in International Business (Winter 1969–Summer 2003)	L.▲&▲Pol'y▲Int'l▲Bus.
Georgetown Journal of Law and Public Policy	Geo.▲J.L.▲&▲Pub.▲Pol'y
Georgetown Journal of Legal Ethics	Geo.▲J.▲Legal▲Ethics
Georgetown Journal on Poverty Law and Policy	Geo.▲J.▲on▲Poverty▲L.▲&▲Pol'y
Was: Georgetown Journal on Fighting Poverty (Vol. 1–Vol. 5, no. 2)	Geo.▲J.▲on▲Fighting▲Poverty
Georgetown Law Journal	Geo.▲L.J.
Georgetown Law Journal Annual Review of Criminal Procedure	Geo.▲L.J.▲Ann.▲Rev.▲Crim.▲Proc.
Was part of the Georgetown Law Journal Before 32d edition	
★Georgia Bar Journal	Ga.▲B.J.
Was: Georgia State Bar Journal (Vol. 1–Vol. 31)	Ga.▲St.▲B.J.
Georgia Journal of International & Comparative Law	Ga.▲J.▲Int'l▲&▲Comp.▲L.

Georgia Journal of Southern Legal History—*see* Journal of Southern Legal History, The

Georgia Law Review	Ga.▲L.▲Rev.
Georgia State University Law Review	Ga.▲St.▲U.▲L.▲Rev.
Glendale Law Review	Glendale▲L.▲Rev.
Golden Gate University Environmental Law Journal	Golden▲Gate▲U.▲Envtl.▲L.J.
Golden Gate University Law Review	Golden▲Gate▲U.▲L.▲Rev.
Was: Golden Gate Law Review (Vol. 1–Vol. 5)	Golden▲Gate▲L.▲Rev.
Gonzaga Journal of International Law	Gonz.▲J.▲Int'l▲L.
Gonzaga Law Review	Gonz.▲L.▲Rev.

Periodical Name	Abbreviation
Government	Gov't
★Government Union Review and Public Policy Digest	Gov't▲Union▲Rev.▲&▲Pub.▲Pol'y▲Dig.
Graven Images: A Journal of Culture, Law and the Sacred	Graven▲Images
★Great Plains Natural Resources Journal	Great▲Plains▲Nat.▲Resources▲J.
Was: Greater North Central Natural Resources Journal	Greater▲N.▲Cent.▲Nat.▲Resources▲J.
Green Bag	Green▲Bag
Green Bag 2d	Green▲Bag▲2d
Guild Practitioner	Guild▲Pract.
Was: Law in Transition (Vol. 21–Vol. 23)	L.▲Transition
Was: ★Lawyers Guild Review (Vol. 1–Vol. 20)	Laws.▲Guild▲Rev.
Was: National Lawyer's Guild Quarterly (1937–1940)	Nat'l▲Law.'s▲Guild▲Q.
Hamline Journal of Public Law and Policy	Hamline▲J.▲Pub.▲L.▲&▲Pol'y
Was: Hamline Journal of Public Law (Vol. 3–Vol. 6)	Hamline▲J.▲Pub.▲L.
Was: Journal of Minnesota Public Law (Vol. 1–Vol. 2)	J.▲Minn.▲Pub.▲L.
Hamline Law Review	Hamline▲L.▲Rev.
Harvard Blackletter Law Journal	Harv.▲Blackltr.▲L.J.
Was: Harvard Blackletter Journal (Vol. 1–Vol. 10)	Harv.▲Blackltr.▲J.
Harvard Civil Rights–Civil Liberties Law Review	Harv.▲C.R.–C.L.▲L.▲Rev.
Harvard Environmental Law Review	Harv.▲Envtl.▲L.▲Rev.
Harvard Human Rights Journal	Harv.▲Hum.▲Rts.▲J.
Was: Harvard Human Rights Yearbook (Vol. 1–Vol. 2)	Harv.▲Hum.▲Rts.▲Y.B.
Harvard International Law Journal	Harv.▲Int'l▲L.J.
Was: Harvard International Law Club Journal (Vol. 4–Vol. 7, no. 2)	Harv.▲Int'l▲L.▲Club▲J.
Was: ★Harvard International Law Club Bulletin, The (Vol. 3)	Harv.▲Int'l▲L.▲Club▲Bull.
Was: Bulletin of the Harvard International Law Club (Vol. 1–Vol. 2)	Bull.▲Harv.▲Int'l▲L.▲Club
Harvard Journal of Law and Gender	Harv.▲J.L.▲&▲Gender
Was: Harvard Women's Law Journal (Vol. 1–Vol. 27)	Harv.▲Women's▲L.J.
Harvard Journal of Law and Public Policy	Harv.▲J.L.▲&▲Pub.▲Pol'y
Harvard Journal of Law and Technology	Harv.▲J.L.▲&▲Tech.
Harvard Journal on Legislation	Harv.▲J.▲on▲Legis.
Harvard Journal on Racial & Ethnic Justice	Harv.▲J.▲on▲Racial▲&▲Ethnic▲Just.
Harvard Latino Law Review	Harv.▲Latino▲L.▲Rev.
Harvard Law and Policy Review	Harv.▲L.▲&▲Pol'y▲Rev.
Harvard Law Review	Harv.▲L.▲Rev.
Harvard Negotiation Law Review	Harv.▲Negot.▲L.▲Rev.

Periodical Name	Abbreviation
Hastings Business Law Journal	Hastings▲Bus.▲L.J.
Hastings Communications and Entertainment Law Journal	Hastings▲Comm.▲&▲Ent.▲L.J.
Was: Comm/Ent (Vol. 1–Vol. 10)	Comm/Ent
Hastings Constitutional Law Quarterly	Hastings▲Const.▲L.Q.
Hastings International and Comparative Law Review	Hastings▲Int'l▲&▲Comp.▲L.▲Rev.
Hastings Law Journal	Hastings▲L.J.
Was: ★Hastings Journal, The (Vol. 1)	Hastings▲J.
Hastings Race and Poverty Law Journal	Hastings▲Race▲&▲Poverty▲L.J.
Hastings West–Northwest Journal of Environmental Law and Policy	Hastings▲W.–Nw.▲J.▲Envtl.▲L.▲&▲Pol'y
Hastings Women's Law Journal	Hastings▲Women's▲L.J.
★Hawaii Bar Journal	Haw.▲B.J.
Health	Health
Health Matrix: Journal of Law–Medicine	Health▲Matrix
Herald	Herald
High	High

High Technology Law Journal—*see* Berkeley Technology Law Journal

Hispanic	Hisp.

Hispanic Law Journal: The University of Texas School of Law—*see* Texas Hispanic Journal of Law & Policy: The University of Texas School of Law

Histor(ical, y)	Hist.
Hofstra Labor & Employment Law Journal	Hofstra▲Lab.▲&▲Emp.▲L.J.
Was: Hofstra Labor Law Journal (Vol. 2–Vol. 14)	Hofstra▲Lab.▲L.J.
Was: Hofstra Labor Law Forum (Vol. 1)	Hofstra▲Lab.▲L.F.
Hofstra Law & Policy Symposium	Hofstra▲L.▲&▲Pol'y▲Symp.
Hofstra Law Review	Hofstra▲L.▲Rev.
Hofstra Property Law Journal	Hofsta▲Prop.▲L.J.
Was: International Property Investment Journal	Int'l▲Prop.▲Inv.▲J.
Hospital	Hosp.

Hospital Law—*see* Journal of Health Law

Housing	Hous.
Houston Business and Tax Law Journal	Hous.▲Bus.▲&▲Tax▲L.J.
★Houston Chronicle	Hous.▲Chron.
Houston Journal of International Law	Hous.▲J.▲Int'l▲L.
Houston Law Review	Hous.▲L.▲Rev.
Howard Law Journal	How.▲L.J.
Howard Scroll: The Social Justice Law Review	How.▲Scroll
Human	Hum.
Human Rights and Globalization Law Review	Hum.▲Rts.▲&▲Global.▲L.▲Rev.
Human Rights Law Journal	Hum.▲Rts.▲L.J.
Absorbed: Human Rights Review (1976–1981)	Hum.▲Rts.▲Rev.
Human Rights Quarterly	Hum.▲Rts.▲Q.
Was: ★Universal Human Rights (Vol. 1–Vol. 2)	Universal▲Hum.▲Rts.
Humanit(ies, y)	Human.

Periodical Name	Abbreviation
Hybrid: Journal of Law and Social Change at the University of Pennsylvania—*see* Journal of Law and Social Change	
ICC Practitioner's Journal—*see* Journal of Transportation Law, Logistics, and Policy	
ICSID Review–Foreign Investment Law Journal	ICSID ▲ Rev.
Idaho Law Review	Idaho ▲ L. ▲ Rev.
IDEA: The Intellectual Property Law Review	IDEA
Was: IDEA: The Journal of Law and Technology (Vol. 19–Vol. 45)	IDEA
Was: IDEA: The PTC Journal of Research and Education (Vol. 16–Vol. 18, no. 1)	IDEA
Was: Patent, Trademark, and Copyright Journal of Research and Education, The (Vol. 1–Vol. 15)	Pat. ▲ Trademark ▲ & ▲ Copy. ▲ J. ▲ Res. ▲ & ▲ Educ.
★Illinois Bar Journal	Ill. ▲ B.J.
Was: ★Quarterly Bulletin (1912–1931)	Q. ▲ Bull.
ILSA Journal of International & Comparative Law	ILSA ▲ J. ▲ Int'l ▲ & ▲ Comp. ▲ L.
Was: ILSA Journal of International Law (Vol. 11–Vol. 16)	ILSA ▲ J. ▲ Int'l ▲ L.
Was: Association of Student International Law Societies/ASILS International Law Journal (Vol. 1–Vol. 10)	ASILS ▲ Int'l ▲ L.J.
Immigration	Immigr.
Immigration Journal	Immigr. ▲ J.
Immigration and Nationality Law Review	Immigr. ▲ & ▲ Nat'lity ▲ L. ▲ Rev.
In the Public Interest	In ▲ Pub. ▲ Int.
Independent	Indep.
Indian	Indian
Indiana International & Comparative Law Review	Ind. ▲ Int'l ▲ & ▲ Comp. ▲ L. ▲ Rev.
Indiana Journal of Global Legal Studies	Ind. ▲ J. ▲ Global ▲ Legal ▲ Stud.
Indiana Law Journal	Ind. ▲ L.J.
Indiana Law Review	Ind. ▲ L. ▲ Rev.
Was: Indiana Legal Forum (Vol. 1–Vol. 5)	Ind. ▲ Legal ▲ F.
Industr(ial, y)	Indus.
Industrial and Labor Relations Review	Indus. ▲ & ▲ Lab. ▲ Rel. ▲ Rev.
Industrial Law Journal	Indus. ▲ L.J.
Industrial Relations Law Journal—*see* Berkeley Journal of Employment and Labor Law	
Information	Info.
Injury	Inj.
Institute	Inst.
Institute on Federal Taxation	Inst. ▲ on ▲ Fed. ▲ Tax'n
Institute on Oil and Gas Law and Taxation	Inst. ▲ on ▲ Oil ▲ & ▲ Gas ▲ L. ▲ & ▲ Tax'n
Institute on Planning, Zoning, and Eminent Domain	Inst. ▲ on ▲ Plan. ▲ Zoning ▲ & ▲ Eminent ▲ Domain
Institute on Private Investments and Investors Abroad	Inst. ▲ on ▲ Priv. ▲ Inv. ▲ & ▲ Inv. ▲ Abroad
Institute on Securities Regulation	Inst. ▲ on ▲ Sec. ▲ Reg.

Periodical Name	Abbreviation
Insurance	Ins.
Insurance Counsel Journal—*see* Defense Counsel Journal	
Intellectual	Intell.
★Intellectual Property & Technology Law Journal	Intell. Prop. & Tech. L.J.
Was: Journal of Proprietary Rights (Vol. 1–Vol. 13)	J. Proprietary Rts.
Intellectual Property Law Bulletin	Intell. Prop. L. Bull.
Intellectual Property Law Review	Intell. Prop. L. Rev.
Was: Patent Law Review (Vol. 1–Vol. 9)	Pat. L. Rev.
Intercultural Human Rights Law Review	Intercultural Hum. Rts. L. Rev.
Interdisciplinary	Interdisc.
Interdisciplinary Journal of Human Rights Law	Interdisc. J. Hum. Rts. L.
Interest	Int.
International	Int'l
International and Comparative Law Quarterly	Int'l & Comp. L.Q.
International Herald Tribune	Int'l Herald Trib.
International Journal of Corporate Governance	Int'l J. Corp. Governance
International Journal of Law and Psychiatry	Int'l J.L. & Psychiatry
International Journal of Legal Information	Int'l J. Legal Info.
Was: International Journal of Law Libraries (Vol. 1–Vol. 9)	Int'l J.L. Libs.
International Journal of Marine and Coastal Law, The	Int'l J. Marine & Coastal L.
Was: International Journal of Estuarine and Coastal Law (Vol. 1–Vol. 7)	Int'l J. Estuarine & Coastal L.
International Journal of Refugee Law	Int'l J. Refugee L.
International Law and Management Review	Int'l L. & Mgmt. Rev.
International Lawyer	Int'l Law.
Was: ABA Section of International and Comparative Law Bulletin (1957–1966)	ABA Sec. Int'l & Comp. L. Bull.
International Legal Perspectives Nonconsecutively paginated in 2004	Int'l Legal Persps.
International Organization	Int'l Org.
International Organization Law Review	Int'l Org. L. Rev.
International Property Investment Journal—*see* Hofstra Property Law Journal	
International Quarterly	Int'l Q.
International Review of Law and Economics	Int'l Rev. L. & Econ.
International Review of Law, Computers & Technology	Int'l Rev. L. Computers & Tech.
★International Tax Journal, The	Int'l Tax J.
International Trade Law Journal, The—*see* Maryland Journal of International Law and Trade	
Invest(ment, ments, or, ors)	Inv.
Iowa Law Review	Iowa L. Rev.
Was: Iowa Law Bulletin (Vol. 1–Vol. 10)	Iowa L. Bull.
Irish Law Times	Irish L. Times

Periodical Name	Abbreviation
I/S: A Journal of Law and Policy for the Information Society	I/S
Issues in Law & Medicine	Issues L. & Med.
JAG Journal, The—*see* Naval Law Review	
Jewish Lawyer, The	Jewish Law.
John Marshall Journal of Computer & Information Law, The	J. Marshall J. Computer & Info. L.
Was: Computer/Law Journal (Vol. 1–Vol. 11)	Computer/L.J.
John Marshall Law Journal	J. Marshall L.J.
John Marshall Law Review, The	J. Marshall L. Rev.
Was: John Marshall Journal of Practice and Procedure, The (Vol. 1–Vol. 12)	J. Marshall J. Prac. & Proc.
Was: John Marshall Law Quarterly, The (Dec. 1935–June 1943)	J. Marshall L.Q.
Jones Law Review—*see* Faulkner Law Review	
Journal	J.
Journal of Accountancy	J. Acct.
Journal of Affordable Housing & Community Development Law	J. Affordable Hous. & Community Dev. L.
Was: ABA Journal of Affordable Housing & Community Development Law (Vol. 1–Vol. 3)	ABA J. Affordable Hous. & Community Dev. L.
Journal of Agricultural Law	J. Agric. L.
Journal of Animal Law	J. Animal L.
Journal of Animal Law and Ethics	J. Animal L. & Ethics
Journal of Air Law and Commerce	J. Air L. & Com.
Was: Journal of Air Law (Vol. 1–Vol. 9)	J. Air. L.
Journal of Appellate Practice and Process	J. App. Prac. & Process
Journal of Art, Technology and Intellectual Property Law	J. Art Tech. & Intell. Prop. L.
Was: Journal of Art and Entertainment Law (Vol. 1–Vol. 17, no. 2)	J. Art & Ent. L.
Journal of Arts Management, Law and Society	J. Arts Mgmt. L. & Soc'y
Was: ★Journal of Arts Management and Law (Vol. 12–Vol. 21)	J. Arts Mgmt. & L.
Was: Performing Arts Review (Vol. 1–Vol. 11)	Performing Arts Rev.
Journal of Bankruptcy Law and Practice—*see* Norton's Journal of Bankruptcy Law and Practice	
Journal of BioLaw and Business, The	J. BioLaw & Bus.
Journal of Business and Securities Law	J. Bus. & Sec. L.
Journal of Business and Technology Law	J. Bus. & Tech. L.
Journal of Business, Entrepreneurship and the Law	J. Bus. Entrepreneurship & L.
Journal of Business Law	J. Bus. L.
Journal of Catholic Legal Studies	J. Cath. Legal Stud.
Was: Catholic Lawyer (Vol. 1–Vol. 43, no. 2)	Cath. Law.
Journal of Chinese Law—*see* Columbia Journal of Asian Law	
Journal of Church and State	J. Church & St.
Journal of Collective Negotiations	J. Collective Negots.

Periodical Name	Abbreviation
Was: Journal of Collective Negotiations in the Public Sector (Vol. 1–Vol. 30)	J.▲Collective▲Negots.▲Pub.▲Sector
Journal of College and University Law, The	J.C.▲&▲U.L.
Supersedes: College Counsel (Vol. 1–Vol. 6)	C.▲Couns.
Journal of Conflict and Security Law	J.▲Conflict▲&▲Sec.▲L.
Was: Journal of Armed Conflict Law (Vol. 1–Vol. 4)	J.▲Armed▲Conflict▲L.
Journal of Constitutional Law	J.▲Const.▲L.
Journal of Contemporary Health Law and Policy	J.▲Contemp.▲Health▲L.▲&▲Pol'y
Journal of Contemporary Law	J.▲Contemp.▲L.
Journal of Contemporary Legal Issues, The	J.▲Contemp.▲Legal▲Issues
Journal of Contract Law	J.▲Contract▲L.
Journal of Corporate Taxation, The—*see* Corporate Taxation	
Journal of Corporation Law	J.▲Corp.▲L.
Journal of Criminal Justice	J.▲Crim.▲Just.
Journal of Criminal Law	J.▲Crim.▲L.
Journal of Criminal Law and Criminology, The	J.▲Crim.▲L.▲&▲Criminology
Was: Journal of Criminal Law, Criminology & Police Science (Vol. 42–Vol. 63)	J.▲Crim.▲L.▲Criminology▲&▲Police▲Sci.
Was: Journal of Criminal Law and Criminology (Vol. 22–Vol. 41)	J.▲Crim.▲L.▲&▲Criminology
Was: Journal of the American Institute of Criminal Law and Criminology (Vol. 1–Vol. 21)	J.▲Am.▲Inst.▲Crim.▲L.▲&▲Criminology
Absorbed: American Journal of Police Science	Am.▲J.▲Police▲Sci.
Journal of Digital Forensics, Security and Law	J.▲Digital▲Forensics▲Sec.▲&▲L.
Journal of Dispute Resolution	J.▲Disp.▲Resol.
Was: Missouri Journal of Dispute Resolution (1984–1987)	Mo.▲J.▲Disp.▲Resol.
Journal of Empirical Legal Studies	J.▲Empirical▲Legal▲Stud.
Journal of Energy Law & Policy—*see* Journal of Land, Resources, & Environmental Law	
Journal of Energy, Natural Resources & Environmental Law—*see* Journal of Land, Resources, & Environmental Law	
Journal of Environmental Law	J.▲Envtl.▲L.
Journal of Environmental Law and Litigation	J.▲Envtl.▲L.▲&▲Litig.
Journal of Eurasian Law	J.▲Eurasian▲L.
Was: Columbia Journal of East European Law (Vol. 1–2007)	Colum.▲J.▲E.▲Eur.▲L.
Was: Journal of East European Law (Vol. 6–Vol. 11)	J.▲E.▲Eur.▲L.
Was: Parker School Journal of East European Law (Vol. 1–Vol. 5)	Parker▲Sch.▲J.▲E.▲Eur.▲L.
Journal of Family Law—*see* Brandeis Law Journal	
Journal of Forensic and Legal Medicine	J.▲Forensic▲&▲Legal▲Med.
Was: Journal of Clinical Forensic Medicine (Vol. 1–Vol. 13)	J.▲Clinical▲Forensic▲Med.
Journal of Gender, Race and Justice	J.▲Gender▲Race▲&▲Just.
Journal of Health and Biomedical Law	J.▲Health▲&▲Biomedical▲L.

Periodical Name	Abbreviation
Was: Journal of Health and Hospital Law (Vol. 21–Vol. 31, no. 2)	J. Health & Hosp. L.
Was: Hospital Law (Vol. 1–Vol. 20)	Hosp. L.
Journal of Health Care Law & Policy, The	J. Health Care L. & Pol'y
Was: Maryland Journal of Contemporary Legal Issues (1990–1997)	Md. J. Contemp. Legal Issues
Was: Maryland Law Forum (1978–1989)	Md. L.F.
Was: University of Maryland Law Forum, The (1970–1978)	U. Md. L.F.
Journal of Health and Life Sciences Law	J. Health & Life Sci. L.
Journal of Health, Politics, Policy and Law	J. Health Pol. Pol'y & L.
Journal of High Technology Law	J. High Tech. L.
Journal of Individual Employment Rights	J. Individual Emp. Rts.
Journal of Information, Law and Technology	J. Info. L. & Tech.
Was: Law Technology Journal (Vol. 1–Vol. 15)	L. Tech. J.
Journal of Intellectual Property, The	J. Intell. Prop.
Journal of Intellectual Property Law, The	J. Intell. Prop. L.
Journal of International Aging Law and Policy	J. Int'l Aging L. & Pol'y
Journal of International Arbitration	J. Int'l Arb.
Journal of International Banking Law and Regulation	J. Int'l Banking L. & Reg.
Was: Journal of International Banking Law (Vol. 1–Vol. 18)	J. Int'l Banking L.
Journal of International Economic Law	J. Int'l Econ. L.
Journal of International Legal Studies	J. Int'l Legal Stud.
Journal of International Wildlife Law & Policy	J. Int'l Wildlife L. & Pol'y
★Journal of Internet Law	J. Internet L.

Journal of Juvenile & Family Courts—*see* Juvenile & Family Court Journal
Journal of Juvenile Law—*see* University of La Verne Law Review

Periodical Name	Abbreviation
Journal of Land, Resources & Environmental Law	J. Land Resources & Envtl. L.
Was: Journal of Energy, Natural Resources & Environmental Law (Vol. 11–Vol. 16)	J. Energy Nat. Resources & Envtl. L.
Was: Journal of Energy Law & Policy, The (Vol. 1–Vol. 10)	J. Energy L. & Pol'y
Journal of Land Use and Environmental Law	J. Land Use & Envtl. L.
Journal of Law and Commerce	J.L. & Com.
Journal of Law and Economics	J.L. & Econ.
Journal of Law & Education	J.L. & Educ.
Journal of Law and Family Studies	J.L. & Fam. Stud.
Journal of Law and Health	J.L. & Health
Journal of Law and Medicine	J.L. & Med.
Journal of Law and Policy	J.L. & Pol'y
Journal of Law and Politics	J.L. & Pol.
Journal of Law and Religion, The	J.L. & Religion
Journal of Law and Social Change	J.L. & Soc. Change
Was: Hybrid: Journal of Law and Social Change at the University of Pennsylvania (Vol. 1–Vol. 5)	Hybrid

Periodical Name	Abbreviation
Journal of Law and Society	J.L. & Soc'y
Journal of Law, Economics & Organization, The	J.L. Econ. & Org.
Journal of Law, Economics and Policy	J.L. Econ. & Pol'y
Journal of Law in Society	J.L. Soc'y
Journal of Law, Information & Science	J.L. Info. & Sci.
Was: Journal of Information Science (Vol. 1–Vol. 15)	J. Info. Sci.
Journal of Law, Medicine & Ethics, The	J.L. Med. & Ethics
Was: ★Law, Medicine & Health Care (Vol. 9, no. 4–Vol. 20)	L. Med. & Health Care
Was: ★Medicolegal News (Vol. 1–Vol. 9, no. 3)	Medicolegal News
Absorbed: ★Nursing Law & Ethics	Nursing L. & Ethics

Journal of Law Reform—*see* University of Michigan Journal of Law Reform

Journal of Legal Economics	J. Legal Econ.
Journal of Legal Education	J. Legal Educ.
Journal of Legal Medicine, The	J. Legal Med.
Journal of Legal Scholarship	J. Legal Scholarship
Journal of Legal Studies	J. Legal Stud.
Journal of Legal Studies Education	J. Legal Stud. Educ.
Journal of Legal Studies/The United States Air Force Academy	J. Legal Stud./U.S. A.F. Acad.
Journal of Legislation	J. Legis.
Was: Notre Dame Journal of Legislation (Vol. 1–Vol. 2)	Notre Dame J. Legis.
Journal of Maritime Law and Commerce	J. Mar. L. & Com.
Journal of Media Law & Ethics	J. Media L. & Ethics
Journal of Medical Law	J. Med. L.
Journal of Medicine and Law	J. Med. & L.

Journal of Mineral Law & Policy—*see* Journal of Natural Resources & Environmental Law

Journal of National Security Law, The	J. Nat'l Sec. L.
Journal of National Security Law and Policy	J. Nat'l Sec. L. & Pol'y
Journal of Natural Resources & Environmental Law	J. Nat. Resources & Envtl. L.
Was: Journal of Mineral Law & Policy (Vol. 1–Vol. 7)	J. Mineral L. & Pol'y
Journal of Online Law	J. Online L.
Journal of Pension Planning & Compliance	J. Pension Plan. & Compl.
Was: Pension and Profit–Sharing Tax Journal (Vol. 1–Vol. 3)	Pension & Profit–Sharing Tax J.
Journal of Pharmacy & Law	J. Pharm. & L.
Journal of Products and Toxics Liability	J. Prods. & Toxics Liab.
Was: Journal of Products Liability (Vol. 1–Vol. 14)	J. Prods. Liab.
Journal of Psychiatry & Law, The	J. Psych. & L.

Journal of Public Law—*see* Emory Law Journal

Journal of Real Estate Taxation	J. Real Est. Tax'n
Journal of S Corporation Taxation, The	J. S Corp. Tax'n

Periodical Name	Abbreviation
Journal of Science & Technology Law—*see* Boston University Journal of Science & Technology Law	
Journal of Small and Emerging Business Law, The—*see* Lewis & Clark Law Review	
Journal of Southern Legal History, The	J.S. Legal Hist.
Was: Georgia Journal of Southern Legal History (Vol. 1–Vol. 2)	Ga. J.S. Legal Hist.
Journal of Space Law	J. Space L.
★Journal of State Taxation	J. St. Tax'n
Journal of Supreme Court History	J. S. Ct. Hist.
Was: Supreme Court Historical Society Yearbook—Supreme Court Historical Society (1976–1989)	S. Ct. Hist. Socy. Y.B.
Journal of Taxation	J. Tax'n
Journal of Taxation of Investments	J. Tax'n Inv.
Journal of Technology Law & Policy	J. Tech. L. & Pol'y
Journal of the American Academy of Matrimonial Lawyers	J. Am. Acad. Matrim. Law.
Journal of the American Academy of Psychiatry and the Law, The	J. Am. Acad. Psych. & L.
Was: Bulletin of the American Academy of Psychiatry and the Law, The (Vol. 1–Vol. 25)	Bull. Am. Acad. Psych. & L.
Journal of the American Judicature Society—*see* Judicature	
Journal of the American Medical Association	JAMA
Journal of the Association of Legal Writing Directors—*see* Legal Communication & Rhetoric	
Journal of the Copyright Society of the U.S.A.	J. Copy. Soc'y U.S.A.
Was: Bulletin of the Copyright Society of the U.S.A. (Vol. 1–Vol. 29, no. 1)	Bull. Copy. Soc'y U.S.A.
★Journal of the Kansas Bar Association, The	J. Kan. B. Ass'n
Was: ★Journal of the Bar Association of the State of Kansas, The (Vol. 1–Vol. 32)	J.B. Ass'n St. Kan.
Absorbed: ★Kansas Barletter	Kan. Barltr.
Journal of the Legal Profession, The	J. Legal Prof.
Journal of the Missouri Bar	J. Mo. B.
Was: Missouri Bar Journal (1930–1944)	Mo. B.J.
Journal of the National Association of Administrative Law Judiciary	J. Nat'l Ass'n Admin. L. Jud.
Was: Journal of the National Association of Administrative Law Judges (Vol. 1–Vol. 26, no. 1)	J. Nat'l Ass'n Admin. L. Judges
Journal of the National Association of Referees in Bankruptcy—*see* American Bankruptcy Law Journal	
Journal of the National Conference of Referees in Bankruptcy—*see* American Bankruptcy Law Journal	
Journal of the Patent and Trademark Office Society	J. Pat. & Trademark Off. Soc'y
Was: Journal of the Patent Office Society (Vol. 1–Vol. 66)	J. Pat. Off. Soc'y

Periodical Name	Abbreviation
Journal of the Suffolk Academy of Law	J. Suffolk Acad. L.
Journal of Transnational Law and Policy	J. Transnat'l L. & Pol'y
Journal of Transportation Law, Logistics, and Policy	J. Transp. L. Logistics & Pol'y
Was: Transportation Practitioners Journal (Vol. 52–Vol. 61)	Transp. Prac. J.
Was: ICC's Practitioner's Journal (Vol. 1–Vol. 51)	ICC's Prac.'s J.
Was: Bulletin of the Association of Practitioners Before the Interstate Commerce Commission (1931–1933)	Bull. Ass'n Prac. Before ICC
Journal of Urban Law—*see* University of Detroit Mercy Law Review	
Journal on Telecommunications and High Technology Law	J. Telecomm. & High Tech. L.
Journal of World Trade	J. World Trade
Judge	Judge
★Judges Journal	Judges J.
Was: ★Trial Judges' Journal (Vol. 1–Vol. 10, no. 1)	Trial Judges' J.
★Judicature	Judicature
Was: ★Journal of the American Judicature Society (Vol. 1–Vol. 49)	J. Am. Judicature Soc'y
Judicial	Jud.
Juridical Review	Jurid. Rev.
Jurimetrics	Jurimetrics
Was: Jurimetrics Journal (Vol. 8–Vol. 36)	Jurimetrics J.
Was: Modern Uses of Logic in Law (Vol. 1–Vol. 7)	M.U.L.L.
Juris Doctor	Juris Dr.
Juris Magazine	Juris Mag.
Jurist: Studies in Church Law and Ministry, The	Jurist
Justice	Just.
★Justice System Journal, The	Just. Sys. J.
Juvenile	Juv.
★Juvenile & Family Court Journal	Juv. & Fam. Ct. J.
Was: ★Journal of Juvenile & Family Courts (Vol. 1–Vol. 29, no. 1)	J. Juv. & Fam. Cts.
Journal of Products Liability	J. Prod. Liab.
★Kansas City Star	Kan. City Star
★Kansas Journal of Law and Public Policy	Kan. J.L. & Pub. Pol'y
Kentucky Bench & Bar—*see* Bench & Bar	
Kentucky Law Journal	Ky. L.J.
La Raza Law Journal—*see* Berkeley La Raza Law Journal	
Labor	Lab.
Labor Law Journal	Lab. L.J.
Labor Lawyer, The	Lab. Law.
Land	Land

Periodical Name	Abbreviation
Land and Water Law Review—*see* Wyoming Law Review	
Law (when first word in periodical name)	Law
Law (when second or later word in periodical name)	L.
Law & Business Review of the Americas	Law▲&▲Bus.▲Rev.▲Ams.
Was: NAFTA, Law & Business Review of the Americas (Vol. 1–Vol. 6)	NAFTA▲L.▲&▲Bus.▲Rev.▲Ams.
Law and Contemporary Problems	Law▲&▲Contemp.▲Probs.
Law and History Review	Law▲&▲Hist.▲Rev.
Law and Human Behavior	Law▲&▲Hum.▲Behav.
Law and Inequality: A Journal of Theory and Practice	Law▲&▲Ineq.
Law & Literature	Law▲&▲Lit.
Was: Cardozo Studies in Law and Literature (Vol. 1–Vol. 13)	Cardozo▲Stud.▲L.▲&▲Lit.
Law and Philosophy	Law▲&▲Phil.
Law and Policy	Law▲&▲Pol'y
Was: Law and Policy Quarterly (Vol. 1–Vol. 5)	Law▲&▲Pol'y▲Q.

Law and Policy in International Business—*see* Georgetown Journal of International Law

Law & Psychology Review	Law▲&▲Psychol.▲Rev.
Law and Sexuality	Law▲&▲Sexuality
Law & Social Inquiry: Journal of American Bar Foundation	Law▲&▲Soc.▲Inquiry
Was: American Bar Foundation Research Journal (Vol. 1–Vol. 12)	Am.▲B.▲Found.▲Res.▲J.
Law and Society Review	Law▲&▲Soc'y▲Rev.
Supersedes: Law & Society Association Newsletter	Law▲&▲Soc'y▲Ass'n▲Newsl.
Law Library Journal	Law▲Lib.▲J.
Absorbed: Law Library News (Sept. 1937)	Law▲Lib.▲News

Law, Medicine & Health Care—*see* Journal of Law, Medicine & Ethics, The

★Law Office and Computing	Law▲Off.▲&▲Computing
★Law Practice	Law▲Prac.
Was: ★Law Practice Management (Vol. 16–Vol. 29)	Law▲Prac.▲Mgmt.
Was: ★Legal Economics (Vol. 1–Vol. 15)	Legal▲Econ.
★Law School Record, The	Law▲Sch.▲Rec.
Law, Social Justice & Global Development Journal	Law▲Soc.▲Just.▲&▲Global▲Dev.▲J.
★Law/Technology	Law/Tech.
Was: Law and Computer Technology (Vol. 1–Vol. 13, no. 1/2)	Law▲&▲Computer▲Tech.
Lawyer('s, s, s')	Law.

Lawyer of the Americas—*see* University of Miami Inter-American Law Review, The

★Lawyers USA	Law.▲USA
Was: ★Lawyers Weekly USA (Issue 93-1 through Issue 2006-8)	Law.▲Wkly.▲USA

Periodical Name	Abbreviation
Lawyer's Reports Annotated	L.R.A.
Legal	Legal
Legal Communication & Rhetoric	Legal▲Comm.▲&▲Rhetoric
Was: Journal of the Association of Legal Writing Directors (Vol. 1–Vol. 7)	J.▲ALWD
★Legal Management	Legal▲Mgmt.
Was: ★Legal Administrator (Vol. 1–Vol. 7)	Legal▲Admin.
Legal Medicine	Legal▲Med.
Was: Legal Medicine Annual (1972–1975)	Legal▲Med.▲Ann.
★Legal Reference Services Quarterly	Legal▲Ref.▲Servs.▲Q.
Legal Studies	Legal▲Stud.
Was: Journal of the Society of Public Teachers of Law (1924–1938; n.s. Vol. 1 (1947–1951)–Vol. 15 (Mar. 1980))	J.▲Soc'y▲Pub.▲Teachers▲L.
Legal Studies Forum	Legal▲Stud.▲F.
Was: American Legal Studies Association: ALSA Forum (Vol. 2–Vol. 8)	ALSA▲F.
Was: ★Newsletter (American Legal Studies Association) (Vol. 1)	ALSA▲Newsl.
Legal Theory	Legal▲Theory
Legal Writing: The Journal of the Legal Writing Institute	Legal▲Writing
Legislati(on, ve)	Legis.
Legislative Studies Quarterly	Legis.▲Stud.▲Q.
Lewis & Clark Law Review	Lewis▲&▲Clark▲L.▲Rev.
Was: Journal of Small & Emerging Business Law (Vol. 1–Vol. 8)	J.▲Small▲&▲Emerging▲Bus.▲L.
Liberty, Life and Family: An Interdisciplinary Journal of Common Concerns	Liberty▲Life▲&▲Fam.
Liberty University Law Review	Liberty▲U.▲L.▲Rev.
Librar(ian, ies, y)	Libr.
★Lincoln Law Review	Lincoln▲L.▲Rev.
★Litigation	Litig.
Local	Loc.
★Los Angeles Lawyer	L.A.▲Law.
★Los Angeles Times	L.A.▲Times
Louisiana Bar Journal	La.▲B.J.
Louisiana Law Review	La.▲L.▲Rev.
Loyola Consumer Law Review	Loy.▲Consumer▲L.▲Rev.
Was: Loyola Consumer Law Reporter (Vol. 1–Vol. 9)	Loy.▲Consumer▲L.▲Rep.
Loyola Journal of Public Interest Law	Loyola▲J.▲Pub.▲Int.▲L.
Loyola Law & Technology Annual	Loyola▲L.▲&▲Tech.▲Ann.

Periodical Name	Abbreviation
Was: Loyola University New Orleans School of Law Intellectual Property & High Technology Journal (Vol. 3–2001, combined issue with previous title)	Loyola U. New Orleans Sch. L. Intell. Prop. & High Tech. J.
Was: Loyola Intellectual Property & High Technology Law Quarterly (Vol. 1, no. 4–Vol. 3, no. 1/2)	Loyola Intell. Prop. & High Tech. L.Q.
Loyola Law Review (New Orleans)	Loy. L. Rev.
Loyola of Los Angeles Entertainment Law Journal	Loy. L.A. Ent. L.J.
Was: Loyola Entertainment Law Journal (Vol. 2–Vol. 11)	Loy. Ent. L.J.
Was: Entertainment Law Journal (Vol. 1)	Ent. L.J.
Loyola of Los Angeles Entertainment Law Review	Loy. L.A. Ent. L. Rev.
Loyola of Los Angeles International and Comparative Law Review	Loy. L.A. Int'l & Comp. L. Rev.
Was: Loyola of Los Angeles International and Comparative Law Journal (Vol. 4–Vol. 21, no. 4)	Loy. L.A. Int'l & Comp. L.J.
Loyola of Los Angeles Law Review	Loy. L.A. L. Rev.
Was: Loyola University of Los Angeles Law Review (Vol. 1–Vol. 4)	Loy. U. L.A. L. Rev.
Loyola Poverty Law Journal	Loy. Poverty L.J.
Loyola University of Chicago Law Journal	Loy. U. Chi. L.J.
Magazine	Mag.
Maine Bar Journal	Me. B.J.
Was: Bar Bulletin (1983–1985)	B. Bull.
Was: ★Maine Bar Bulletin (1967–1982)	Me. B. Bull.
Maine Law Review	Me. L. Rev.
Absorbed: Portland University Law Review	Portland U. L. Rev.
Major Tax Planning	Major Tax Plan.
Management	Mgmt.
Manitoba Law Journal	Man. L.J.
Manual	Man.

Margins: Maryland's Interdisciplinary Publication on Race, Religion, Gender and Class—*see* University of Maryland Law Journal of Race, Religion, Gender and Class

Maritime	Mar.
Marquette Elder's Advisor	Marq. Elder's Advisor
Was: Elder's Advisor: The Journal of Elder Law and Post Retirement Planning (Vol. 1–Vol. 4)	Elder's Advisor
Marquette Intellectual Property Law Review	Marq. Intell. Prop. L. Rev.
Marquette Law Review	Marq. L. Rev.
Marquette Sports Law Review	Marq. Sports L. Rev.
Was: Marquette Sports Law Journal (Vol. 1, no. 1–Vol. 10, no. 2)	Marq. Sports L.J.
★Maryland Bar Journal	Md. B.J.

Periodical Name	Abbreviation
Maryland Journal of Contemporary Legal Issues—*see* Journal of Health Care Law & Policy, The	
Maryland Journal of International Law and Trade	Md. J. Int'l L. & Trade
Was: International Trade Law Journal, The (Vol. 1–Vol. 7)	Int'l Trade L.J.
Maryland Law Forum—*see* Journal of Health Care Law & Policy, The	
Maryland Law Review	Md. L. Rev.
Massachusetts Law Review	Mass. L. Rev.
Was: Massachusetts Law Quarterly (Vol. 1–Vol. 62)	Mass. L.Q.
McGeorge Law Review	McGeorge L. Rev.
Was: Pacific Law Journal (Vol. 1–Vol. 28)	Pac. L.J.
McGill International Journal of Sustainable Development Law & Policy	McGill Int'l J. Sust. Dev. L. & Pol'y
McGill Law Journal	McGill L.J.
Media	Media
Media Law & Policy	Media L. & Pol'y
Mediation	Mediation
Medic(al, ine)	Med.
Medical Trial Technique Quarterly Annual	Med. Trial Technique Q. Ann.
Medicolegal News—*see* Journal of Law, Medicine & Ethics, The	
Melbourne University Law Review	Melb. U. L. Rev.
Memphis State University Law Review—*see* University of Memphis Law Review	
Mental & Physical Disability Law Reporter	Mental & Physical Disability L. Rep.
Mercer Law Review	Mercer L. Rev.
Miami Law Quarterly—*see* University of Miami Law Review	
★Michigan Bar Journal	Mich. B.J.
Was: ★Journal/State Bar of Michigan (Vol. 55, no. 3–Vol. 57)	J./St. B. Mich.
Was: ★Michigan State Bar Journal (Vol. 1–Vol. 55, no. 2)	Mich. St. B.J.
Michigan Business Law Journal	Mich. Bus. L.J.
Michigan Journal of Gender & Law	Mich. J. Gender & L.
Michigan Journal of International Law	Mich. J. Int'l L.
Was: Michigan Yearbook of International Legal Studies (Vol. 1–Vol. 9)	Mich. Y.B. Int'l Legal Stud.
Michigan Journal of Race & Law	Mich. J. Race & L.
Michigan Law & Policy Review	Mich. L. & Pol'y Rev.
Michigan Law Journal	Mich. L.J.
Michigan Law Review	Mich. L. Rev.
Michigan State Law Review	Mich. St. L. Rev.
Was: Michigan State DCL Law Review (Summer 2003–Fall 2003)	Mich. St. DCL L. Rev.
Was: Law Review of Michigan State University Detroit College of Law, The (Spring 1999–Spring 2003)	L. Rev. Mich. St. U. Det. C.L.

Periodical Name	Abbreviation
Was: Detroit College of Law at Michigan State University Law Review (1995, no. 3–1998)	Det. C.L. Mich. St. U. L. Rev.
Was: Detroit College of Law Review (1975–1995)	Det. C.L. Rev.
Michigan State University–DCL Journal of International Law	Mich. St. U. DCL J. Int'l L.
Was: Detroit College of Law Journal of International Law and Practice (Vol. 1–Vol. 7)	Det. C.L. J. Int'l L. & Prac.
Michigan Tax Lawyer	Mich. Tax Law.
Michigan Telecommunications & Technology Law Review	Mich. Telecomm. & Tech. L. Rev.
Military Law Review	Mil. L. Rev.
★Milwaukee Journal & Sentinel	Milw. J. & Sent.
Mineral	Min.
Minnesota Journal of Global Trade	Minn. J. Global Trade
Was: Minnesota Journal of International Law (Vol. 1–Vol. 14)	Minn. J. Int'l L.
Minnesota Journal of Law, Science & Technology	Minn. J.L. Sci. & Tech.
Was: Minnesota Intellectual Property Review (Vol. 1–Vol. 5)	Minn. Intell. Prop. Rev.
Minnesota Law Review	Minn. L. Rev.
Mississippi College Law Review	Miss. C. L. Rev.
Mississippi Law Journal	Miss. L.J.
Missouri Environmental Law and Policy Review	Mo. Envtl. L. & Pol'y Rev.

Missouri Journal of Dispute Resolution—*see* Journal of Dispute Resolution

Missouri Law Review	Mo. L. Rev.
Modern	Mod.
Modern Law Review	Mod. L. Rev.
Monash University Law Review	Monash U. L. Rev.
Montana Law Review	Mont. L. Rev.
Monthly	Monthly
★Monthly Labor Review	Monthly Lab. Rev.
MSL Law Review: A Journal for Practitioners and Judges	MSL L. Rev.
Municipal	Mun.
Mutual	Mut.
NAELA Journal	NAELA J.
National	Nat'l
National Black Law Journal	Nat'l Black L.J.
Was: Black Law Journal (Vol. 1–Vol. 9)	Black L.J.
★National Law Journal	Nat'l L.J.
National Tax Journal	Nat'l Tax J.

Natural Law Forum—*see* American Journal of Jurisprudence

Natural	Nat.
★Natural Resources & Environment	Nat. Resources & Env't
Was: Natural Resources Lawyer (1968–1985)	Nat. Resources Law.

Periodical Name	Abbreviation
Natural Resources Journal	Nat. Resources J.
Naval Law Review	Naval L. Rev.
Was: JAG Journal, The (Vol. 1–Vol. 33)	JAG J.
Nebraska Law Review	Neb. L. Rev.
Was: Nebraska Law Bulletin (Vol. 1–Vol. 19)	Neb. L. Bull.
Negligence	Negl.
Negotiation(s)	Negot.
Nevada Law Journal	Nev. L.J.
★Nevada Lawyer	Nev. Law.
Was: ★Inter Alia Journal of the State Bar of Nevada (Apr. 1973–Oct. 1992)	Inter Alia J. St. B. Nev.
Was: ★Nevada State Bar Journal (Jan. 1936–Jan. 1973)	Nev. St. B.J.
New Criminal Law Review	New Crim. L. Rev.
Was: Buffalo Criminal Law Review (Vol. 1–Vol. 9)	Buff. Crim. L. Rev.
New England Journal of International and Comparative Law	New Eng. J. Int'l & Comp. L.
Was: New England International and Comparative Law Annual (Vol. 1–Vol. 7)	New Eng. Int'l & Comp. L. Ann.
New England Journal of Medicine	New Eng. J. Med.
New England Journal on Criminal and Civil Confinement	New Eng. J. on Crim. & Civ. Confinement
Was: New England Journal on Prison Law (Vol. 1–Vol. 8)	New Eng. J. on Prison L.
New England Law Review	New Eng. L. Rev.
Was: Portia Law Journal (Vol. 1–Vol. 4, no. 1)	Portia L.J.
★New Hampshire Bar Journal	N.H. B.J.
★New Jersey Lawyer	N.J. Law.
New Law Journal	New L.J.
New Mexico Law Review	N.M. L. Rev.
★New Orleans Times–Picayune	N.O. Times–Picayune
New York City Law Review	N.Y. City L. Rev.
New York International Law Review	N.Y. Int'l L. Rev.
New York Law Journal	N.Y. L.J.
New York Law School Journal of Human Rights	N.Y.L. Sch. J. Hum. Rts.
Was: New York Law School Human Rights Annual (Vol. 1–Vol. 4)	N.Y.L. Sch. Hum. Rts. Ann.
New York Law School Journal of International and Comparative Law	N.Y.L. Sch. J. Int'l & Comp. L.
Absorbed: New York Law School Law Review	N.Y.L. Sch. L. Rev.
Was: Journal of International and Comparative Law/New York Law School (Vol. 3)	J. Int'l & Comp. L.
Was: New York Law School Journal of International and Comparative Law (Vol. 1–Vol. 2)	N.Y.L. Sch. J. Int'l & Comp. L.
New York Law School Law Review	N.Y.L. Sch. L. Rev.
Was: New York Law Forum (Vol. 1–Vol. 21)	N.Y. L.F.

Periodical Name	Abbreviation
New York State Bar Association Antitrust Law Symposium	N.Y. ▲ St. ▲ B. ▲ Ass'n ▲ Antitrust ▲ L. ▲ Symp.
New York State Bar Association Journal	N.Y. ▲ St. ▲ B. ▲ Ass'n ▲ J.
Was: New York State Bar Journal (Vol. 1–Vol. 71)	N.Y. ▲ St. ▲ B.J.
★New York Times	N.Y. ▲ Times
New York University Annual Institute on Federal Taxation	N.Y.U. ▲ Ann. ▲ Inst. ▲ on ▲ Fed. ▲ Tax'n
New York University Annual Survey of American Law	N.Y.U. ▲ Ann. ▲ Surv. ▲ Am. ▲ L.
Was: Annual Survey of American Law (Vol. 1–Vol. 21)	Ann. ▲ Surv. ▲ Am. ▲ L.
New York University Environmental Law Journal	N.Y.U. ▲ Envtl. ▲ L.J.
New York University Journal of International Law and Politics	N.Y.U. ▲ J. ▲ Int'l ▲ L. ▲ & ▲ Pol.
New York University Journal of Law & Business	N.Y.U. ▲ J.L. ▲ & ▲ Bus.
New York University Journal of Legislation and Public Policy	N.Y.U. ▲ J. ▲ Legis. ▲ & ▲ Pub. ▲ Pol'y
New York University Law Review	N.Y.U. ▲ L. ▲ Rev.
Was: New York University Law Quarterly Review (Vol. 7–Vol. 24)	N.Y.U. ▲ L.Q. ▲ Rev.
Was: New York University Law Review (Vol. 2–Vol. 6)	N.Y.U. ▲ L. ▲ Rev.
Was: Annual Review of the Law School of New York University (Vol. 1)	Ann. ▲ Rev. ▲ L. ▲ Sch. ▲ N.Y.U.
New York University Review of Law and Social Change	N.Y.U. ▲ Rev. ▲ L. ▲ & ▲ Soc. ▲ Change
New York University School of Law Moot Court Casebook	N.Y.U. ▲ Moot ▲ Ct. ▲ Casebook
New Zealand Journal of Public and International Law	NZJPIL
New Zealand Universities Law Review	N.Z. ▲ U. ▲ L. ▲ Rev.
News Media and the Law, The	News ▲ Media ▲ & ▲ L.
Supersedes: Press Censorship Newsletter (1973–1976)	Press ▲ Censorship ▲ Newsl.
Newsletter	Newsl.
NEXUS: Chapman's Journal of Law and Public Policy	NEXUS
Was: NEXUS: A Journal of Opinion (Vol. 1–Vol. 13)	NEXUS
North(ern)	N.
North Carolina Banking Institute	N.C. ▲ Banking ▲ Inst.
North Carolina Central Law Review	N.C. ▲ Cent. ▲ L. ▲ Rev.
Was: North Carolina Central Law Journal (Vol. 1–Vol. 29)	N.C. ▲ Cent. ▲ L.J.
North Carolina Journal of International Law and Commercial Regulation	N.C. ▲ J. ▲ Int'l ▲ L. ▲ & ▲ Com. ▲ Reg.
Was: Journal of International Law and Commercial Regulation (Vol. 1)	J. ▲ Int'l ▲ L. ▲ & ▲ Com. ▲ Reg.
North Carolina Law Review	N.C. ▲ L. ▲ Rev.

Periodical Name	Abbreviation
North Dakota Law Review	N.D. ▲ L. ▲ Rev.
Was: North Dakota Bar Briefs: Journal of the State Bar Association (Vol. 24, issue 2–Vol. 26)	N.D. ▲ B. ▲ Briefs
Was: Bar Briefs (Vol. 1–Vol. 24, issue 1)	B. ▲ Briefs
Northern Illinois University Law Review	N. ▲ Ill. ▲ U. ▲ L. ▲ Rev.
Was: Lewis University Law Review	Lewis ▲ U. ▲ L. ▲ Rev.
Northern Kentucky Law Review	N. ▲ Ky. ▲ L. ▲ Rev.
Was: Northern Kentucky State Law Forum (Vol. 1–Vol. 3, no. 1)	N. ▲ Ky. ▲ St. ▲ L.F.
Northwestern Journal of International Law and Business	Nw. ▲ J. ▲ Int'l ▲ L. ▲ & ▲ Bus.
Northwestern University Law Review	Nw. ▲ U. ▲ L. ▲ Rev.
Was: Illinois Law Review/Northwestern University (Vol. 33, no. 5–Vol. 46)	Ill. ▲ L. ▲ Rev./Nw. ▲ U.
Was: Illinois Law Review of Northwestern University (Vol. 31, no. 8–Vol. 33, no. 4)	Ill. ▲ L. ▲ Rev. ▲ Nw. ▲ U.
Was: Illinois Law Review/Northwestern University (Vol. 1–Vol. 31, no. 7)	Ill. ▲ L. ▲ Rev./Nw. ▲ U.
Absorbed: Illinois Law Quarterly (Dec. 1921– June 1924)	Ill. ▲ L.Q.
Norton Journal of Bankruptcy Law & Practice	Norton ▲ J. ▲ Bankr. ▲ L. ▲ & ▲ Prac.
Was: Journal of Bankruptcy Law & Practice (Vol. 1–Vol. 15)	J. ▲ Bankr. ▲ L. ▲ & ▲ Prac.
Nota Bene	Nota ▲ Bene
Notre Dame Journal of Law, Ethics & Public Policy	Notre ▲ Dame ▲ J.L. ▲ Ethics ▲ & ▲ Pub. ▲ Pol'y
Notre Dame Journal of Legislation—see Journal of Legislation	
Notre Dame Law Review	Notre ▲ Dame ▲ L. ▲ Rev.
Was: Notre Dame Lawyer (Vol. 1–Vol. 57)	Notre ▲ Dame ▲ Law.
Nova Law Review	Nova ▲ L. ▲ Rev.
Was: Nova Law Journal (Vol. 1–Vol. 10)	Nova ▲ L.J.
NU Forum: A Cooperative Law Journal of Northeastern University School of Law	NU ▲ F.
Nursing Law & Ethics—see Journal of Law, Medicine & Ethics, The	
Ocean and Coastal Law Journal	Ocean ▲ & ▲ Coastal ▲ L.J.
Was: Territorial Sea Journal	Territorial ▲ Sea ▲ J.
Ocean Development and International Law	Ocean ▲ Dev. ▲ & ▲ Int'l ▲ L.
Was: ★Ocean Development and International Law Journal (Vol. 1, nos. 1–2)	Ocean ▲ Dev. ▲ & ▲ Int'l ▲ L.J.
Office	Off.
Ohio Northern University Law Review	Ohio ▲ N.U. ▲ L. ▲ Rev.
Ohio State Journal on Dispute Resolution	Ohio ▲ St. ▲ J. ▲ on ▲ Disp. ▲ Resol.
Ohio State Law Journal	Ohio ▲ St. ▲ L.J.
Oil, Gas & Energy Quarterly	Oil ▲ Gas ▲ & ▲ Energy ▲ Q.
Was: Oil & Gas Tax Quarterly (Vol. 1–Vol. 45)	Oil ▲ & ▲ Gas ▲ Tax ▲ Q.
Oklahoma City University Law Review	Okla. ▲ City ▲ U. ▲ L. ▲ Rev.

Periodical Name	Abbreviation
Oklahoma Law Review	Okla. L. Rev.
★Orange County Register	Orange County Reg.
Order	Ord.
Oregon Law Review	Or. L. Rev.
Oregon Review of International Law	Or. Rev. Int'l L.
Organization	Org.
★Orlando Sentinel	Orlando Sent.
Otago Law Review	Otago L. Rev.
Ottawa Law Review	Ottawa L. Rev.
Oxford Journal of Legal Studies	Oxford J. Legal Stud.
Oxford University Commonwealth Law Journal	Oxford U. Commonwealth L.J.
Pace Environmental Law Review	Pace Envtl. L. Rev.
Pace International Law Review	Pace Int'l L. Rev.
Was: Pace Yearbook of International Law	Pace Y.B. Int'l L.
(Vol. 1–Vol. 4)	
Pace Law Review	Pace L. Rev.
Pacific	Pac.
Pacific Law Journal	Pac. L.J.
Pacific McGeorge Global Business and	Pac. McGeorge Global
Development Law Journal	Bus. & Dev. L.J.
Was: Transnational Lawyer, The	Transnat'l Law.
(Vol. 1–Vol. 18)	
Pacific Rim Law & Policy Journal	Pac. Rim L. & Pol'y J.
PAR: Public Administration Review	PAR
Parker School Journal of East European Law	Parker Sch. J. E. Eur. L.
Patent	Pat.
Patent Law Annual	Pat. L. Ann.
Was: Patent Law Developments (1964–1965)	Pat. L. Dev.
Was: Patent Procurement and Exploitation	Pat. Procurement &
(1963)	Exploitation
Patent Law Review—*see* Intellectual Property Law Review	
Patent, Trademark, and Copyright Journal of Research and Education—*see* IDEA: The Journal of Law and Technology	
Penn State Environmental Law Review	Penn St. Envtl. L. Rev.
Penn State International Law Review	Penn St. Int'l L. Rev.
Was: Dickinson Journal of International Law	Dick. J. Int'l L.
(Vol. 2, no. 2–Vol. 19)	
Was: Dickinson International Law Annual	Dick. Int'l L. Ann.
(Vol. 1–Vol. 2, no. 1)	
Penn State Law Review	Penn St. L. Rev.
Was: Dickinson Law Review (Vol. 13–Vol. 107)	Dick. L. Rev.
Was: Forum (Vol. 1–Vol. 12)	Forum
Pennsylvania Bar Association Quarterly	Pa. B. Ass'n Q.
Pension and Profit–Sharing Tax Journal—*see* Journal of Pension Planning & Compliance	
Pepperdine Dispute Resolution Law Journal	Pepp. Disp. Resol. L.J.
Pepperdine Law Review	Pepp. L. Rev.
Performing Arts Review—*see* Journal of Arts Management, Law and Society	
Personal	Pers.

Periodical Name	Abbreviation
Personal Finance Law Quarterly Report—*see* Consumer Finance Law Quarterly Report	
Perspectives	Persps.
★Philadelphia Inquirer	Phila. Inquirer
Philosoph(ical, y)	Phil.
Phoenix Law Review	Phoenix L. Rev.
Pierce Law Review	Pierce L. Rev.
Pittsburgh Journal of Environmental and Public Health Law	Pitt. J. Envtl. & Pub. Health L.
★Pittsburgh Post–Gazette	Pitt. Post–Gaz.
Planning	Plan.
Police	Police
Policy	Pol'y
Politic(al, s)	Pol.
★Portland Oregonian	Port. Oregonian
Potomac Law Review	Potomac L. Rev.
Practi(cal, ce, tioners)	Prac.
★Practical Lawyer	Prac. Law.
★Practical Litigator, The	Prac. Litigator
★Practical Real Estate Lawyer, The	Prac. Real Est. Law.
★Practical Tax Lawyer, The	Prac. Tax Law.
Practical Tax Strategies	Prac. Tax Strategies
Was: Taxation for Lawyers (Vol. 1–Vol. 27, no.2)	Tax'n for Law.
★Preventive Law Reporter	Preventive L. Rep.
Was: ★Preventive Law Newsletter	Preventive L. Newsl.
Preview of United States Supreme Court Cases	Preview U.S. Sup. Ct. Cases
Probate	Prob.
★Probate & Property	Prob. & Prop.
Probate Law Journal (National College of Probate Judges and Boston University School of Law)	Prob. L.J.
Problems	Probs.
Proce(dure, edings)	Proc.
Profession(al)	Prof.
★Professional Lawyer, The	Prof. Law.
Property	Prop.
★Prosecutor, Journal of the National District Attorneys Association, The Nonconsecutively paginated starting with Vol. 16	Prosecutor
Was: NDAA: Journal of the National District Attorneys Association (Vol. 1–Vol. 3, no. 3)	NDAA
Prospectus—*see* University of Michigan Journal of Law Reform	
Psychiatry	Psychiatry
Psycholog(ical, y)	Psychol.
Psychology, Public Policy, and Law	Psychol. Pub. Pol'y & L.
Publi(c, shing)	Pub.
Public Contract Law Journal	Pub. Cont. L.J.

Periodical Name	Abbreviation
★Public Interest Law Reporter	Pub. Int. L. Rep.
Public Interest Law Review, The	Pub. Int. L. Rev.
Public Land & Resources Law Review	Pub. Land & Resources L. Rev.
Was: Public Land Law Review (Vol. 1–Vol. 16)	Pub. Land L. Rev.
Publishing, Entertainment, Advertising and Allied Fields Law Quarterly	Pub. Ent. Advert. & Allied Fields L.Q.
QLR	QLR
Was: Bridgeport Law Review (Vol. 12, no. 2–Vol. 13)	Bridgeport L. Rev.
Was: University of Bridgeport Law Review (Vol. 1–Vol. 12, no. 1)	U. Bridgeport L. Rev.
Quarterly	Q.
★Quarterly/Christian Legal Society	Q./CLS
Was: ★Christian Legal Society Quarterly (Vol. 1)	Christian Legal Soc'y Q.
Queensland University of Technology Law and Justice Journal	Queensland U. Tech. L. & Just. J.
Quinnipiac Health Law Journal	Quinnipiac Health L.J.
Quinnipiac Law Review	Quinnipiac L. Rev.
Quinnipiac Probate Law Journal	Quinnipiac Prob. L.J.
Was: Connecticut Probate Law Journal (Vol. 1–Vol. 10)	Conn. Prob. L.J.

Race and Ethnic Ancestry Law Journal—*see* Washington and Lee Journal of Civil Rights and Social Justice

Real	Real
Real Estate Law Journal	Real Est. L.J.
Real Property, Trust and Estate Law Journal	Real Prop. Tr. & Est. L.J.
Was: Real Property, Probate and Trust Journal (Vol. 1–Vol. 41)	Real Prop. Prob. & Tr. J.
Record	Rec.
Referee(s)	Ref.
Reform	Reform
Regent University Law Review	Regent U. L. Rev.
Register	Reg.
Regulat(ion, ory)	Reg.
Relations	Rel.
Report(ed, er, s)	Rep.
Reproduct(ion, ive)	Reprod.
★Res Gestae	Res Gestae
Research	Res.
Research in Law and Economics	Res. L. & Econ.
Reserve	Res.
Resolution	Resol.
Resources	Resources
Restitution Law Review	Restitution L. Rev.
Review	Rev.
Review of Banking and Financial Law	Rev. Banking & Fin. L.

Periodical Name	Abbreviation
Was: Annual Review of Banking and Financial Law (Vol. 22–Vol. 26)	Ann.▲Rev.▲Banking▲&▲Fin.▲L.
Was: Annual Review of Banking (Vol. 1–Vol. 21)	Ann.▲Rev.▲Banking
Review of Litigation	Rev.▲Litig.
Review of Securities & Commodities Regulation	Rev.▲Sec.▲&▲Commodities▲Reg.
Revista de Derecho Puertorriqueño	Rev.▲Der.▲P.R.
Revista Juridica de la Universidad de Puerto Rico	Rev.▲Jur.▲U.P.R.
★Rhode Island Bar Journal	R.I.▲B.J.
Richmond Journal of Global Law and Business	Rich.▲J.▲Global▲L.▲&▲Bus.
Richmond Journal of Law and the Public Interest	Rich.▲J.L.▲&▲Pub.▲Int.
Richmond Journal of Law & Technology	Rich.▲J.L.▲&▲Tech.
Rights	Rts.
Risk	Risk
RISK: Health, Safety, & Environment	RISK
Was: RISK: Issues in Health & Safety (Vol. 1–Vol. 4)	RISK

Rocky Mountain Law Review/University of Colorado—*see* University of Colorado Law Review

Rocky Mountain Mineral Law Institute	Rocky▲Mtn.▲Min.▲L.▲Inst.
★Rocky Mountain News	Rocky▲Mtn.▲News
Roger Williams University Law Review	Roger▲Williams▲U.▲L.▲Rev.
Rutgers Computer and Technology Law Journal	Rutgers▲Computer▲&▲Tech.▲L.J.
Was: Rutgers Journal of Computers, Technology, and the Law (Vol. 7–Vol. 8, no. 1)	Rutgers▲J.▲Computers▲Tech.▲&▲L.
Was: Rutgers Journal of Computers and the Law (Vol. 1–Vol. 6)	Rutgers▲J.▲Computers▲&▲L.
Rutgers Conflict Resolution Law Journal	Rutgers▲Conflict▲Resol.▲L.J.
Rutgers Law Journal	Rutgers▲L.J.
Was: Rutgers–Camden Law Journal (Vol. 1–Vol. 11)	Rutgers–Camden▲L.J.
Rutgers Law Record	Rutgers▲L.▲Rec.
Rutgers Law Review	Rutgers▲L.▲Rev.
Was: Rutgers University Law Review (Vol. 1–Vol. 2)	Rutgers▲U.▲L.▲Rev.
Rutgers Race & the Law Review	Rutgers▲Race▲&▲L.▲Rev.
Saint (*see also* listings under "St." for "Saint")	St.
Saint Louis University Law Journal	St.▲Louis▲U.▲L.J.
Saint Louis University Public Law Review	St.▲Louis▲U.▲Pub.▲L.▲Rev.
Was: Public Law Forum (Vol. 1–Vol. 5)	Pub.▲L.F.
Saint Louis–Warsaw Transatlantic Law Journal	St.▲Louis–Warsaw▲Transatlantic▲L.J.
★San Antonio Express–News	San▲Antonio▲Express–News
San Diego Law Review	San▲Diego▲L.▲Rev.
★San Diego Union–Tribune	San▲Diego▲Union–Trib.
San Fernando Valley Law Review	San▲Fern.▲V.▲L.▲Rev.

Periodical Name	Abbreviation
★San Francisco Attorney	S.F. Att'y
★San Francisco Chronicle	S.F. Chron.
Santa Clara Computer & High Technology Law Journal	Santa Clara Computer & High Tech. L.J.
Santa Clara Journal of International Law	Santa Clara J. Int'l L.
Santa Clara Law Review	Santa Clara L. Rev.
Was: Santa Clara Lawyer (Vol. 1–Vol. 15)	Santa Clara Law.
Saskatchewan Law Review	Sask. L. Rev.
Scholar: St. Mary's Law Review on Minority Issues, The	Scholar
School	Sch.
★School Law Bulletin	Sch. L. Bull.
Scien(ce, ces, tific)	Sci.
Scientific American	Sci. Am.
Scottish	Scot.
★Scribes Journal of Legal Writing, The	Scribes J. Legal Writing
★Scrivener	Scrivener
★Search and Seizure Law Report	Search & Seizure L. Rep.
Seattle University Law Review	Seattle U. L. Rev.
Was: University of Puget Sound Law Review (Vol. 1–Vol. 17)	U. Puget Sound L. Rev.
Section	Sec.
Securities	Sec.
Securities and Federal Corporate Law Report	Sec. & Fed. Corp. L. Rep.
Securities Law Review	Sec. L. Rev.
Securities Regulation Law Journal	Sec. Reg. L.J.
Sentencing	Sent'g
Seton Hall Circuit Review	Seton Hall Cir. Rev.
Seton Hall Constitutional Law Journal	Seton Hall Const. L.J.
Seton Hall Journal of Sports and Entertainment Law	Seton Hall J. Sports & Ent. L.
Was: Seton Hall Journal of Sports Law	Seton Hall J. Sports L.
Seton Hall Law Review	Seton Hall L. Rev.
Was: Seton Hall Law Journal (1968–1969)	Seton Hall L.J.
Seton Hall Legislative Journal	Seton Hall Legis. J.
Signs	Signs

SMU Law Review—*see* Southern Methodist University Law Review

Social	Soc.
Social Responsibility: Business, Journalism, Law, Medicine	Soc. Resp.
Was: Social Responsibility: Journalism, Law, Medicine (Vol. 1–Vol. 9)	Soc. Resp.
Social Service Review	Soc. Serv. Rev.
Society	Soc'y
Sociolog(ical, y)	Soc.

Software Law Journal—*see* John Marshall Journal of Computer & Information Law, The
South Carolina Environmental Law Journal—*see* Southeastern Environmental Law Journal

Periodical Name	Abbreviation
South Carolina Journal of International Law and Business	S.C.▲J.▲Int'l▲L.▲&▲Bus.
South Carolina Law Review	S.C.▲L.▲Rev.
Was: South Carolina Law Quarterly, The (Vol. 1–Vol. 14)	S.C.▲L.Q.
★South Carolina Lawyer	S.C.▲Law.
South Dakota Law Review	S.D.▲L.▲Rev.
South Texas Law Review	S.▲Tex.▲L.▲Rev.
Was: South Texas Law Journal (Vol. 1–Vol. 26)	S.▲Tex.▲L.J.
Southeastern Environmental Law Journal	Southeastern▲Envtl.▲L.J.
Was: South Carolina Environmental Law Journal (Vol. 1–Vol. 10)	S.C.▲Envtl.▲L.J.
Southern	S.
Southern California Interdisciplinary Law Journal	S.▲Cal.▲Interdisc.▲L.J.
Southern California Law Review	S.▲Cal.▲L.▲Rev.
Southern California Review of Law and Social Justice	S.▲Cal.▲Rev.▲L.▲&▲Soc.▲Just.
Was: Southern California Review of Law and Women's Studies (Vol. 1–Vol. 15, no.1)	S.▲Cal.▲Rev.▲L.▲&▲Women's▲Stud.
Southern Illinois University Law Journal	S.▲Ill.▲U.▲L.J.
Southern Law Quarterly—*see* Tulane Law Review	
Southern Methodist University Law Review	SMU▲L.▲Rev.
Was: Southwestern Law Journal (1948–Spring 1992)	Sw.▲L.J.
Was: Texas Law and Legislation (1947)	Tex.▲L.▲&▲Legis.
Southern Regional Black Law Students Association Law Journal	S.▲Regional▲BLSA▲L.J.
Southern University Law Review	S.U.▲L.▲Rev.
Southwestern Journal of International Law	Sw.▲J.▲Int'l▲L.
Southwestern Journal of Law and Trade in the Americas	Sw.▲J.L.▲&▲Trade▲Ams.
Southwestern Law Journal—*see* SMU Law Review	
Southwestern Law Review	Sw.▲L.▲Rev.
Was: Southwestern University Law Review (Vol. 3–Vol. 37, no. 2)	Sw.▲U.▲L.▲Rev.
Was: Southwestern Law Review (Vol. 1–Vol. 2)	Sw.▲L.▲Rev.
Southwestern Legal Foundation Institute on Oil and Gas Law and Taxation	Sw.▲Legal▲Found.▲Inst.▲on▲Oil▲&▲Gas▲L.▲&▲Tax'n
Sports Lawyers Journal, The	Sports▲Law.▲J.
St. John's Journal of Legal Commentary	St.▲John's▲J.▲Legal▲Comment.
St. John's Law Review	St.▲John's▲L.▲Rev.
St. Louis Law Review—*see* Washington University Law Quarterly	
St. Mary's Law Journal	St.▲Mary's▲L.J.
Was: St. Mary's Law Review (Vol. 1–Vol. 24)	St.▲Mary's▲L.▲Rev.

Periodical Name	Abbreviation
★St. Petersburg Times	St. Pete. Times
St. Thomas Law Review	St. Thomas L. Rev.
Was: St. Thomas Law Forum/Saint Thomas University, School of Law (Vol. 1–Vol. 3)	St. Thomas L.F.
Standard(s)	Stand.
Stanford Environmental Law Journal	Stan. Envtl. L.J.
Was: Stanford Environmental Law Annual (Vol. 1–Vol. 5)	Stan. Envtl. L. Ann.
Stanford Journal of Civil Rights and Civil Liberties	Stan. J. C.R. & C.L.
Stanford Journal of International Law	Stan. J. Int'l L.
Was: Stanford Journal of International Studies (Vol. 3–Vol. 15)	Stan. J. Int'l Stud.
Stanford Journal of Law, Business & Finance	Stan. J.L. Bus. & Fin.
Stanford Law & Policy Review	Stan. L. & Pol'y Rev.
Stanford Law Review	Stan. L. Rev.
Volumes 5–8 are nonconsecutively paginated	
Stanford Technology Law Review	Stan. Tech. L. Rev.
★Star–Ledger (Newark, N.J.)	Star–Ledger (Newark, N.J.)
★Star Tribune (Minneapolis, Minn.)	Star Trib. (Minneapolis, Minn.)
State	St.
State Bar of Texas Environmental Law Journal	St. B. Tex. Envtl. L.J.
Statistic(al, s)	Stat.
Stetson Law Review	Stetson L. Rev.
★Student Lawyer	Student Law.
Was: ★Student Lawyer Journal (Dec. 1967–June 1972)	Student Law. J.
Was: ★Student Lawyer of the American Bar Association (Sept. 1967–Nov. 1967)	Student Law. ABA
Was: ★Student Lawyer Journal of the American Law Student Association (Oct. 1955–Aug. 1967)	Student Law. J. Am. L. Student Ass'n
Studies	Stud.
Studies in Law, Politics, and Society	Stud. L. Pol. & Soc'y
Was: Research in Law, Deviance and Social Control (Vol. 4–Vol. 9)	Res. L. Deviance & Soc. Control
Was: Research in Law and Sociology (Vol. 1–Vol. 3)	Res. L. & Soc.
Suffolk Journal of Trial & Appellate Advocacy	Suffolk J. Trial & App. Advoc.
Suffolk Transnational Law Review	Suffolk Transnat'l L. Rev.
Was: Suffolk Transnational Law Journal (Vol.1–Vol. 15)	Suffolk Transnat'l L.J.
Suffolk University Law Review	Suffolk U. L. Rev.
★Sun–Sentinel (Ft. Lauderdale, Fla.)	Sun-Sent. (Ft. Lauderdale, Fla.)
Supreme Court Economic Review	Sup. Ct. Econ. Rev.

Supreme Court Historical Society—*see* Journal of Supreme Court History

Periodical Name	Abbreviation
Supreme Court Review	Sup. Ct. Rev.
Survey	Surv.
Sustainable Development Law & Policy	Sustainable Dev. L. & Pol'y
Was: International and Comparative Environmental Law (Vol. 1–Vol. 2, no.1)	Int'l & Comp. Envtl. L.
Sydney Law Review	Sydney L. Rev.
Syracuse Journal of International Law and Commerce	Syracuse J. Int'l L. & Com.
Syracuse Journal of Legislation & Policy	Syracuse J. Legis. & Pol'y
Syracuse Law Review	Syracuse L. Rev.
Syracuse Science and Technology Law Reporter	Syracuse Sci. & Tech. L. Rep.
Was: Syracuse Law and Technology Journal (2000–2004)	Syracuse L. & Tech. J.
System	Sys.
Tax	Tax
Tax Adviser	Tax Adviser
Tax Executive	Tax Exec.
Tax Law Review	Tax L. Rev.
Tax Lawyer	Tax Law.
Was: Bulletin of the Section of Taxation, American Bar Association (Vol. 1–Vol. 20, no. 4)	Bull. Sec. Tax'n
Tax Management Estates, Gifts and Trusts Journal	Tax Mgmt. Est. Gifts & Tr. J.
Was: ★Estates, Gifts and Trusts Journal, The (July/Aug. 1976–Nov./Dec. 1983)	Est. Gifts & Tr. J.
Tax Management International Journal	Tax Mgmt. Int'l J.
★Tax Management Memorandum	Tax Mgmt. Memo.
Tax Management Real Estate Journal	Tax Mgmt. Real Est. J.
Tax Notes	Tax Notes
Tax Notes International	Tax Notes Int'l
Taxation	Tax'n
Taxation for Lawyers—*see* Practical Tax Strategies	
★Taxes: The Tax Magazine	Taxes
Techn(ical, ique, ology)	Tech.
Telecommunication(s)	Telecomm.
Temple Environmental Law & Technology Journal	Temp. Envtl. L. & Tech. J.
Temple International and Comparative Law Journal	Temp. Int'l & Comp. L.J.
Temple Journal of Science, Technology and Environmental Law	Temp. J. Sci. Tech. & Envtl. L.
Was: Temple Environmental Law & Technology Journal (Vol. 3–Vol. 23)	Temp. Envtl. L. & Tech. J.
Was: Outlook Environmental Law Journal (Vol. 1–Vol. 2)	Outlook Envtl. L.J.
Temple Law Review	Temp. L. Rev.
Was: Temple Law Quarterly (Vol. 19, no. 3–Vol. 60)	Temp. L.Q.

Periodical Name	Abbreviation
Was: Temple University Law Quarterly (Vol. 13–Vol. 19, no. 2)	Temp. U. L.Q.
Was: Temple Law Quarterly (Vol. 1–Vol. 12)	Temp. L.Q.
Temple Political and Civil Rights Law Review	Temp. Pol. & C.R. L. Rev.
★Tennessee Bar Journal	Tenn. B.J.
Tennessee Journal of Law and Policy	Tenn. J.L. & Pol'y
Tennessee Journal of Practice and Procedure	Tenn. J. Prac. & Proc.
Tennessee Law Review	Tenn. L. Rev.
Texas Bar Journal	Tex. B.J.
Texas Forum on Civil Liberties and Civil Rights	Tex. F. on C.L. & C.R.
Texas Hispanic Journal of Law & Policy	Tex. Hisp. J.L. & Pol'y
Was: Hispanic Law Journal: The University of Texas School of Law (Vol. 1–Vol. 3)	Hispanic L.J.
Texas Intellectual Property Law Journal	Tex. Intell. Prop. L.J.
Texas International Law Journal	Tex. Int'l L.J.
Was: Texas International Law Forum (Vol. 1, no. 2–Vol. 6, no. 2)	Tex. Int'l L.F.
Was: Journal of the University of Texas International Law Society, The (Jan. 1965)	J. U. Tex. Int'l L. Soc'y
Texas Journal of Business Law	Tex. J. Bus. L.
Texas Journal on Civil Liberties and Civil Rights	Tex. J. on C.L. & C.R.
Texas Journal of Oil, Gas, & Energy Law	Tex. J. Oil Gas & Energy L.
Texas Journal of Women and the Law	Tex. J. Women & L.
Texas Law Review	Tex. L. Rev.
Texas Review of Law and Politics	Tex. Rev. L. & Pol.
Texas Southern University Law Review—*see* Thurgood Marshall Law Review	
Texas Tech Journal of Texas Administrative Law	Tex. Tech J. Tex. Admin. L.
Texas Tech Law Review	Tex. Tech L. Rev.
Texas Wesleyan Law Review	Tex. Wesleyan L. Rev.
Third World Legal Studies	Third World Legal Stud.
Thomas Jefferson Law Review	T. Jefferson L. Rev.
Was: San Diego Justice Journal (Winter 1993–Summer 1995)	San Diego Just. J.
Was: Criminal Justice Journal (1976–1992)	Crim. Just. J.
Thomas M. Cooley Journal of Practical and Clinical Law	T.M. Cooley J. Prac. & Clinical L.
Thomas M. Cooley Law Review	T.M. Cooley L. Rev.
Was: Cooley Law Review (Vol. 1–Vol. 7)	Cooley L. Rev.
Thurgood Marshall Law Review	T. Marshall L. Rev.
Was: Texas Southern University Law Review (Vol. 2–Vol. 6)	Tex. S.U. L. Rev.
Tilburg Law Review	Tilburg L. Rev.
Was: Tilburg Foreign Law Review (Vol. 1–Vol. 13)	Tilburg Foreign L. Rev.
Toledo Journal of Great Lakes' Law, Science & Policy, The	Tol. J. Great Lakes' L. Sci. & Pol'y
Tort Trial and Insurance Practice Law Journal	Tort Trial & Ins. Prac. L.J.

Periodical Name	Abbreviation
Was: Tort & Insurance Law Journal (Vol. 1–Vol. 37)	Tort▲&▲Ins.▲L.J.
Touro Environmental Law Journal	Touro▲Envtl.▲L.J.
Touro International Law Review	Touro▲Int'l▲L.▲Rev.
Was: Touro Journal of Transnational Law (Vol. 1–Vol. 4)	Touro▲J.▲Transnat'l▲L.
Touro Law Review	Touro▲L.▲Rev.
Trade	Trade
Trademark	Trademark
Trademark Reporter, The	Trademark▲Rep.
Absorbed: Bulletin of the United States Trademark Association (before 1911)	Bull.▲U.S.▲Trademark▲Ass'n
Transnational	Transnat'l
Transnational Law & Contemporary Problems	Transnat'l▲L.▲&▲Contemp.▲Probs.

Transnational Lawyer, The—*see* Pacific McGeorge Global Business and Development Law Journal

Transportation	Transp.
Transportation Law Journal	Transp.▲L.J.

Transportation Practitioners Journal—*see* Journal of Transportation Law, Logistics, and Policy

★Trauma	Trauma
Trial	Trial
★Trial	Trial
Trial Advocate Quarterly	Trial▲Advoc.▲Q.
Trial Lawyer, The	Trial▲Law.
Was: Trial Diplomacy Journal (Spring 1978–May/June 1998)	Trial▲Dipl.▲J.
Trial Lawyer's Guide, The	Trial▲Law.▲Guide
★Trial Lawyers Quarterly	Trial▲Law.▲Q.
Nonconsecutively paginated since Volume 118	
Tribune	Trib.
Trust(s)	Tr.
Trusts & Estates	Tr.▲&▲Est.
Was: Trust Companies (Vol. 1–Vol. 67)	Tr.▲Cos.
Tulane Environmental Law Journal	Tul.▲Envtl.▲L.J.
Tulane European and Civil Law Forum	Tul.▲Eur.▲&▲Civ.▲L.F.
Was: ★Tulane Civil Law Forum	Tul.▲Civ.▲L.F.
Note: Suspended 1977–1987; ceased with Volumes 6/7, issued 1991–1992	
Tulane Journal of International and Comparative Law	Tul.▲J.▲Int'l▲&▲Comp.▲L.
Tulane Journal of Law and Sexuality	Tul.▲J.L.▲&▲Sexuality
Tulane Law Review	Tul.▲L.▲Rev.
Was: Southern Law Quarterly (Vol. 1–Vol. 3)	S.▲L.Q.
Tulane Maritime Law Journal	Tul.▲Mar.▲L.J.
Was: Maritime Lawyer, The (Vol. 1–Vol. 11)	Mar.▲Law.
Tulsa Journal of Comparative & International Law	Tulsa▲J.▲Comp.▲&▲Int'l▲L.

Periodical Name	Abbreviation
Tulsa Law Review	Tulsa L. Rev.
Was: Tulsa Law Journal (Vol. 1–Vol. 34)	Tulsa L.J.
UCLA–Alaska Law Review—*see* Alaska Law Review	
UCLA Bulletin of Law and Technology	UCLA Bull. L. & Tech.
UCLA Entertainment Law Review	UCLA Ent. L. Rev.
UCLA Journal of Environmental Law & Policy	UCLA J. Envtl. L. & Pol'y
UCLA Journal of International Law and Foreign Affairs	UCLA J. Int'l L. & Foreign Aff.
UCLA Journal of Law and Technology	UCLA J.L. & Tech.
UCLA Law Review	UCLA L. Rev.
UCLA Pacific Basin Law Journal	UCLA Pac. Basin L.J.
UCLA Women's Law Journal	UCLA Women's L.J.
UMKC Law Review	UMKC L. Rev.
Was: University of Missouri at Kansas City Law Review (Vol. 32–Vol. 34)	U. Mo. Kan. City L. Rev.
Was: University of Kansas City Law Review: A Journal of the University of Kansas City (Vol. 7–Vol. 31)	U. Kan. City L. Rev.
Was: Kansas City Law Review (Vol. 1–Vol. 6)	Kan. City L. Rev.
UN Monthly Chronicle	UN Monthly Chron.
Unbound: Harvard Journal of the Legal Left	Unbound
Uniform Commercial Code Law Journal	UCC L.J.
Uniform Commercial Code Reporter–Digest	UCC Rep.–Dig.
United States	U.S.
United States Air Force Academy Journal of Legal Studies	U.S. A.F. Acad. J. Legal Stud.
United States Air Force JAG Law Review—*see* Air Force Law Review	
United States–Mexico Law Journal	U.S.–Mex. L.J.
Universit(ies, y)	U.
University of Arkansas at Little Rock Law Review	U. Ark. Little Rock L. Rev.
Was: University of Arkansas at Little Rock Law Journal (1978–1998)	UALR L.J.
University of Baltimore Intellectual Property Law Journal	U. Balt. Intell. Prop. L.J.
University of Baltimore Journal of Environmental Law	U. Balt. J. Envtl. L.
Was: Environmental Perspectives	Envtl. Persps.
University of Baltimore Law Forum	U. Balt. L.F.
University of Baltimore Law Review	U. Balt. L. Rev.
University of Bridgeport Law Review—*see* QLR	
University of California Davis Journal of International Law and Policy	U.C. Davis J. Int'l L. & Pol'y
University of California Davis Law Review	U.C. Davis L. Rev.
University of California Irvine Law Review	U.C. Irvine L. Rev.
University of Chicago Law Review	U. Chi. L. Rev.
University of Chicago Legal Forum	U. Chi. Legal F.
University of Chicago Law School Roundtable, The	U. Chi. L. Sch. Roundtable

Periodical Name	Abbreviation
University of Cincinnati Law Review	U.▲Cin.▲L.▲Rev.
University of Colorado Law Review	U.▲Colo.▲L.▲Rev.
Was: Rocky Mountain Law Review/University of Colorado (Vol. 1–Vol. 34)	Rocky▲Mtn.▲L.▲Rev.
University of Dayton Law Review	U.▲Dayton▲L.▲Rev.
Was: University of Dayton Intramural Law Review (1976)	U.▲Dayton▲Intramural▲L.▲Rev.
University of Denver Water Law Review	U.▲Denv.▲Water▲L.▲Rev.
University of Detroit Mercy Law Review	U.▲Det.▲Mercy▲L.▲Rev.
Was: University of Detroit Law Review (Vol. 62–Vol. 68)	U.▲Det.▲L.▲Rev.
Was: University of Detroit Journal of Urban Law (Vol. 54–Vol. 61)	U.▲Det.▲J.▲Urb.▲L.
Was: Journal of Urban Law (Vol. 44–Vol. 53)	J.▲Urb.▲L.
Was: University of Detroit Law Journal (Vol. 1–Vol. 43)	U.▲Det.▲L.J.
University of the District of Columbia David Clarke School of Law Law Review	UDC/DCSL▲L.▲Rev.
Was: University of the District of Columbia Law Review, The (Vol. 4–Vol. 6)	U.D.C.▲L.▲Rev.
Was: District of Columbia Law Review (Vol. 1–Vol. 3)	D.C.▲L.▲Rev.
University of Florida Journal of Law and Public Policy	U.▲Fla.▲J.L.▲&▲Pub.▲Pol'y
University of Hawaii Law Review	U.▲Haw.▲L.▲Rev.
University of Illinois Journal of Law, Technology and Policy	U.▲Ill.▲J.L.▲Tech.▲&▲Pol'y
University of Illinois Law Review	U.▲Ill.▲L.▲Rev.
Was: University of Illinois Law Forum (1949–1980)	U.▲Ill.▲L.F.
University of Kansas Law Review	U.▲Kan.▲L.▲Rev.
University of La Verne Law Review	U.▲La▲Verne▲L.▲Rev.
Was: Journal of Juvenile Law (Vol. 1–Vol. 28)	J.▲Juv.▲L.
University of Louisville Journal of Family Law—*see* Brandeis Law Journal	
University of Louisville Law Review	U.▲Louisville▲L.▲Rev.
Was: Brandeis Law Journal (Vol. 37–Vol. 45)	Brandeis▲L.J.
Was: Brandeis Journal of Family Law (Vol. 36, no. 1–Vol. 36, no. 4)	Brandeis▲J.▲Fam.▲L.
Was: University of Louisville Journal of Family Law (Vol. 31–Vol. 35)	U.▲Louis.▲J.▲Fam.▲L.
Was: Journal of Family Law (Vol. 1–Vol. 30)	J.▲Fam.▲L.
University of Maryland Law Journal of Race, Religion, Gender and Class	U.▲Md.▲L.J.▲Race▲Religion▲Gender▲&▲Class
University of Massachusetts Law Review	U.▲Mass.▲L.▲Rev.
University of Memphis Law Review	U.▲Mem.▲L.▲Rev.
Was: Memphis State University Law Review (Vol. 1–Vol. 24)	Mem.▲St.▲U.▲L.▲Rev.
University of Miami Business Law Review	U.▲Miami▲Bus.▲L.▲Rev.
University of Miami Entertainment & Sports Law Review	U.▲Miami▲Ent.▲&▲Sports▲L.▲Rev.

Periodical Name	Abbreviation
Was: Entertainment & Sports Law Journal (Vol. 1–Vol. 5)	Ent. ▲&▲ Sports ▲L.J.
University of Miami Inter–American Law Review, The	U. ▲Miami ▲Inter–Am. ▲L. ▲Rev.
Was: Lawyer of the Americas (Vol. 1–Vol. 15)	Law. ▲Ams.
University of Miami International and Comparative Law Review	U. ▲Miami ▲Int'l ▲&▲ Comp. ▲L. ▲Rev.
Was: University of Miami Yearbook of International Law (Vol. 1–Vol. 6)	U. ▲Miami ▲Y.B. ▲Int'l ▲L.
University of Miami Law Review	U. ▲Miami ▲L. ▲Rev.
Was: Miami Law Quarterly (Vol. 1–Vol. 11)	Miami ▲L.Q.
University of Michigan Journal of Law Reform	U. ▲Mich. ▲J.L. ▲Reform
Was: Journal of Law Reform (Vol. 4–Vol. 5)	J.L. ▲Reform
Was: Prospectus (Vol. 1–Vol. 3)	Prospectus
University of New Brunswick Law Journal	U. ▲New ▲Bruns. ▲L.J.
University of New South Wales Law Journal	U. ▲New ▲S. ▲Wales ▲L.J.
University of Pennsylvania Journal of Business and Employment Law	U. ▲Pa. ▲J. ▲Bus. ▲&▲ Emp. ▲L.
Was: University of Pennsylvania Journal of Labor and Employment Law (Vol. 1–Vol. 9)	U. ▲Pa. ▲J. ▲Lab. ▲&▲ Emp. ▲L.
University of Pennsylvania Journal of Business Law	U. ▲Pa. ▲J. ▲Bus. ▲L.
University of Pennsylvania Journal of Constitutional Law	U. ▲Pa. ▲J. ▲Const. ▲L.
University of Pennsylvania Journal of International Law	U. ▲Pa. ▲J. ▲Int'l ▲L.
Was: University of Pennsylvania Journal of International Economic Law (Vol. 17–Vol. 28)	U. ▲Pa. ▲J. ▲Int'l ▲Econ. ▲L.
Was: University of Pennsylvania Journal of International Business Law (Vol. 9–Vol. 16)	U. ▲Pa. ▲J. ▲Int'l ▲Bus. ▲L.
Was: Journal of Comparative Business and Capital Market Law (Vol. 5–Vol. 8)	J. ▲Comp. ▲Bus. ▲&▲ Cap. ▲Mkt. ▲L.
Was: Journal of Comparative Corporate Law and Securities Regulation (Vol. 1–Vol.4)	J. ▲Comp. ▲Corp. ▲L. ▲&▲ Sec. ▲Reg.
University of Pennsylvania Journal of Law and Social Change	U. ▲Pa. ▲J.L. ▲&▲ Soc. ▲Change
University of Pennsylvania Law Review	U. ▲Pa. ▲L. ▲Rev.
Was: University of Pennsylvania Law Review and American Law Register (Vol. 56–Vol. 93)	U. ▲Pa. ▲L. ▲Rev. ▲&▲ Am. ▲L. ▲Reg.
Was: American Law Register, The (Vol. 46–Vol. 55)	Am. ▲L. ▲Reg.
Was: American Law Register and Review, The (Vol. 40–Vol. 45)	Am. ▲L. ▲Reg. ▲&▲ Rev.
Was: American Law Register, The (Vol. 1–Vol. 39)	Am. ▲L. ▲Reg.
University of Pittsburgh Law Review	U. ▲Pitt. ▲L. ▲Rev.

University of Puget Sound Law Review—*see* Seattle University Law Review

Periodical Name	Abbreviation
University of Richmond Law Review	U. Rich. L. Rev.
Was: University of Richmond Law Notes (Vol. 1–Vol. 2)	U. Rich. L. Notes
University of San Francisco Law Review	U.S.F. L. Rev.
University of San Francisco Maritime Law Journal	U.S.F. Mar. L.J.
University of St. Thomas Journal of Law and Public Policy	U. St. Thomas J.L. & Pub. Pol'y
University of St. Thomas Law Journal	U. St. Thomas L.J.
University of Tasmania Law Review	U. Tas. L. Rev.
University of Toledo Law Review	U. Tol. L. Rev.
Was: University of Toledo Intramural Law Review (Vol. 1)	U. Tol. Intramural L. Rev.
University of Toronto Faculty of Law Review	U. Toronto Fac. L. Rev.
University of Toronto Law Journal	U. Toronto L.J.

University of Washington Law Review—*see* Washington Law Review

Urban	Urb.

Urban Law Annual—*see* Washington University Journal of Law & Policy

Urban Lawyer, The	Urb. Law.
U.S.–Mexico Legal Review	U.S.–Mex. Legal Rev.
★USA Today	USA Today
★Utah Bar Journal	Utah B.J.
Utah Law Review	Utah L. Rev.
Utilit(ies, y)	Util.
UWLA Law Review: University of West Los Angeles School of Law	UWLA L. Rev.
Was: University of West Los Angeles Law Review (Vol. 1–Vol. 13)	UWLA L. Rev.
Valparaiso University Law Review	Val. U. L. Rev.
Vanderbilt Journal of Entertainment and Technology Law	Vand. J. Ent. & Tech. L.
Was: Vanderbilt Journal of Entertainment Law & Practice (Vol. 1–Vol. 7)	Vand. J. Ent. L. & Prac.
Vanderbilt Journal of Transnational Law	Vand. J. Transnat'l L.
Vanderbilt Law Review	Vand. L. Rev.
★VBA News Journal	VBA News J.
Was: ★Virginia Bar Association Journal (Jan. 1975–Spring 1998)	Va. B. Ass'n J.
Vermont Journal of Environmental Law	Vt. J. Envtl. L.
Vermont Law Review	Vt. L. Rev.
Villanova Environmental Law Journal	Vill. Envtl. L.J.
Villanova Information Law Chronicle, The	Vill. Info. L. Chron.
Villanova Journal of Law and Investment Management	Vill. J.L. & Inv. Mgmt.
Villanova Law Review	Vill. L. Rev.
Villanova Sports & Entertainment Law Journal	Vill. Sports & Ent. L.J.
Was: Villanova Sports & Entertainment Law Forum (Vol. 1–Vol. 2)	Vill. Sports & Ent. L.F.
Virginia Environmental Law Journal	Va. Envtl. L.J.

Periodical Name	Abbreviation
Was: Virginia Journal of Natural Resources Law (Vol. 1–Vol. 8, no. 1)	Va. ▲ J. ▲ Nat. ▲ Resources ▲ L.
Virginia Journal of International Law	Va. ▲ J. ▲ Int'l ▲ L.
Was: Journal of the John Bassett Moore Society of International Law (Vol. 1–Vol. 2)	J. ▲ John ▲ Bassett ▲ Moore ▲ Soc'y ▲ Int'l ▲ L.
Virginia Journal of Law and Technology	Va. ▲ J.L. ▲ & ▲ Tech.
Virginia Journal of Social Policy & the Law, The	Va. ▲ J. ▲ Soc. ▲ Pol'y ▲ & ▲ L.
Virginia Law & Business Review	Va. ▲ L. ▲ & ▲ Bus. ▲ Rev.
Virginia Law Review	Va. ▲ L. ▲ Rev.
Virginia Sports and Entertainment Law Journal	Va. ▲ Sports ▲ & ▲ Ent. ▲ L.J.
Was: Virginia Journal of Sports and the Law (Vol. 1–Vol. 3, no. 1)	Va. ▲ J. ▲ Sports ▲ & ▲ L.
Virginia Tax Review	Va. ▲ Tax ▲ Rev.
Wake Forest Law Review	Wake ▲ Forest ▲ L. ▲ Rev.
★Wall Street Journal	Wall ▲ St. ▲ J.
Washburn Law Journal	Washburn ▲ L.J.
Washington and Lee Journal of Civil Rights and Social Justice	Wash. ▲ & ▲ Lee ▲ J. ▲ C.R. ▲ & ▲ Soc. ▲ Just.
Was: Washington and Lee Race and Ethnic Ancestry Law Journal (2000–2004)	Wash. ▲ & ▲ Lee ▲ Race ▲ & ▲ Ethnic ▲ Ancestry ▲ L.J.
Was: Race and Ethnic Ancestry Law Journal (1998–1999)	Race ▲ & ▲ Ethnic ▲ Ancestry ▲ L.J.
Was: Race Ethnic Law Digest (1995–1997)	Race ▲ Ethnic ▲ L. ▲ Dig.
Washington and Lee Law Review	Wash. ▲ & ▲ Lee ▲ L. ▲ Rev.
Washington Law Review	Wash. ▲ L. ▲ Rev.
Was: University of Washington Law Review (Vol. 41, no. 2–Vol. 42)	U. ▲ Wash. ▲ L. ▲ Rev.
★Washington Lawyer, The	Wash. ▲ Law.
Was: ★District Lawyer (1976–July/Aug. 1985)	District ▲ Law.
Was: ★D.C. Bar Journal (Nov. 1966–1973)	D.C. ▲ B.J.
Was: ★Journal of the Bar Association of the District of Columbia (1934–Oct. 1966)	J.B. ▲ Ass'n ▲ D.C.
★Washington Monthly	Wash. ▲ Monthly
★Washington Post	Wash. ▲ Post
★Washington State Bar News	Wash. ▲ St. ▲ B. ▲ News
Washington University Global Studies Law Review	Wash. ▲ U. ▲ Global ▲ Stud. ▲ L. ▲ Rev.
Washington University Journal of Law & Policy	Wash. ▲ U. ▲ J.L. ▲ & ▲ Pol'y
Was: Washington University Journal of Urban and Contemporary Law (Vol. 1–Vol. 55 (1999))	Wash. ▲ U. ▲ J. ▲ Urb. ▲ & ▲ Contemp. ▲ L.
Was: Urban Law Annual (Vol. 1 (1968)–Vol. 23 (1982))	Urb. ▲ L. ▲ Ann.
Washington University Law Review	Wash. ▲ U. ▲ L. ▲ Rev.
Was: Washington University Law Quarterly (Vol. 22–Vol. 83)	Wash. ▲ U. ▲ L.Q.
Was: St. Louis Law Review (Vol. 1–Vol. 21)	St. ▲ Louis ▲ L. ▲ Rev.
Wayne Law Review	Wayne ▲ L. ▲ Rev.
Week	Wk.
Weekly	Wkly.

Periodical Name	Abbreviation
Welfare	Welfare
West(ern)	W.
West Virginia Law Review	W. ▲ Va. ▲ L. ▲ Rev.
Was: West Virginia Law Quarterly and the Bar (Vol. 25–Vol. 51)	W. ▲ Va. ▲ L.Q. ▲ & ▲ B.
Was: ★Bar, The (Vol. 3–Vol. 24)	Bar ▲ (W. ▲ Va.)
Was: West Va. Bar, The (Vol. 1–Vol. 2)	W. ▲ Va. ▲ B.
Was: West Virginia Bar, The (1894–1895)	W. ▲ Va. ▲ B.
Western Legal History	W. ▲ Legal ▲ Hist.
Western New England Law Review	W. ▲ New ▲ Eng. ▲ L. ▲ Rev.

Western Reserve Law Review—*see* Case Western Reserve Law Review

Western State University Law Review	W. ▲ St. ▲ U. ▲ L. ▲ Rev.
Was: Western State Law Review (Vol. 1, no. 2–Vol. 2, no. 1)	W. ▲ St. ▲ L. ▲ Rev.
Was: Law Review (Anaheim) (Vol. 1, no. 1)	L. ▲ Rev. ▲ (Anaheim)
Whittier Journal of Child & Family Advocacy	Whittier ▲ J. ▲ Child ▲ & ▲ Fam. ▲ Advoc.
Whittier Law Review	Whittier ▲ L. ▲ Rev.
Widener Law Journal	Widener ▲ L.J.
Was: Widener Journal of Public Law	Widener ▲ J. ▲ Pub. ▲ L.
Widener Law Review	Widener ▲ L. ▲ Rev.
Was: Widener Law Symposium Journal (Vol. 1, no. 1–Vol. 9, no. 2)	Widener ▲ L. ▲ Symp. ▲ J.
Willamette Journal of International Law & Dispute Resolution	Willamette ▲ J. ▲ Int'l ▲ L. ▲ & ▲ Disp. ▲ Resol.
Was: Willamette Bulletin of International Law & Policy (Vol. 1–Vol. 4)	Willamette ▲ Bull. ▲ Int'l ▲ L. ▲ & ▲ Pol'y
Willamette Law Review	Willamette ▲ L. ▲ Rev.
Was: Willamette Law Journal (Vol. 1–Vol. 14)	Willamette ▲ L.J.
William & Mary Bill of Rights Journal	Wm. ▲ & ▲ Mary ▲ Bill ▲ Rts. ▲ J.
William & Mary Business Law Review	Wm. ▲ & ▲ Mary ▲ Bus. ▲ L. ▲ Rev.
William & Mary Environmental Law and Policy Review	Wm. ▲ & ▲ Mary ▲ Envtl. ▲ L. ▲ & ▲ Pol'y ▲ Rev.
Was: William and Mary Journal of Environmental Law (Vol. 15–Vol. 18)	Wm. ▲ & ▲ Mary ▲ J. ▲ Envtl. ▲ L.
Was: ★Environmental Practice News (Vol. 1–Vol. 14)	Envtl. ▲ Prac. ▲ News
William & Mary Journal of Women and the Law	Wm. ▲ & ▲ Mary ▲ J. ▲ Women ▲ & ▲ L.
William & Mary Law Review	Wm. ▲ & ▲ Mary ▲ L. ▲ Rev.
Was: William and Mary Review of Virginia Law (Vol. 1–Vol. 2)	Wm. ▲ & ▲ Mary ▲ Rev. ▲ Va. ▲ L.
William Mitchell Law Review	Wm. ▲ Mitchell ▲ L. ▲ Rev.
Wisconsin Environmental Law Journal	Wis. ▲ Envtl. ▲ L.J.
Wisconsin International Law Journal	Wis. ▲ Int'l ▲ L.J.
Wisconsin Journal of Law, Gender & Society	Wis. ▲ J.L. ▲ Gender ▲ & ▲ Soc'y
Was: Wisconsin Women's Law Journal (Vol. 1–Vol. 22)	Wis. ▲ Women's ▲ L.J.
Wisconsin Law Review	Wis. ▲ L. ▲ Rev.
★Wisconsin Lawyer, The	Wis. ▲ Law.

Periodical Name	Abbreviation
Was: ★Wisconsin Bar Bulletin, The (Vol. 22–Vol. 61)	Wis.▲B.▲Bull.
Was: Bulletin of the Wisconsin Bar Association (Vol. 21, no. 3–Vol. 21, no. 4)	Bull.▲Wis.▲B.▲Ass'n
Was: Bulletin of the State Bar Association of Wisconsin (Vol. 1–Vol. 21, no. 2)	Bull.▲St.▲B.▲Ass'n▲Wis.
Women	Women
Women & Criminal Justice	Women▲&▲Crim.▲Just.
★Women's Rights Law Reporter	Women's▲Rts.▲L.▲Rep.
Nonconsecutively paginated since Volume 3	
World	World
Wyoming Law Journal—*see* Wyoming Law Review	
Wyoming Law Review	Wyo.▲L.▲Rev.
Was: Land and Water Law Review (1966–2000)	Land▲&▲Water▲L.▲Rev.
Absorbed: Wyoming Law Journal (Dec. 1946–Fall 1965)	Wyo.▲L.J.
Yale Human Rights & Development Law Journal	Yale▲Hum.▲Rts.▲&▲Dev.▲L.J.
Yale Journal of Health Policy, Law, and Ethics	Yale▲J.▲Health▲Pol'y▲L.▲&▲Ethics
Yale Journal of International Law	Yale▲J.▲Int'l▲L.
Was: Yale Journal of World Public Order, The (Vol. 7–Vol. 9)	Yale▲J.▲World▲Pub.▲Ord.
Was: Yale Studies in World Public Order, The (Vol. 1–Vol. 6)	Yale▲Stud.▲World▲Pub.▲Ord.
Yale Journal of Law and Feminism	Yale▲J.L.▲&▲Feminism
Yale Journal of Law and Liberation	Yale▲J.L.▲&▲Liberation
Yale Journal of Law and the Humanities	Yale▲J.L.▲&▲Human.
Yale Journal of Law & Technology	Yale▲J.L.▲&▲Tech.
Yale Journal on Regulation	Yale▲J.▲on▲Reg.
Yale Law & Policy Review	Yale▲L.▲&▲Pol'y▲Rev.
Yale Law Journal	Yale▲L.J.
Yearbook (or Year Book)	Y.B.
★Young Lawyer	Young▲Law.
Was: ★Barrister (Feb. 1974–Fall 1996)	Barrister
Zoning and Planning Law Report	Zoning▲&▲Plan.▲L.▲Rep.

Appendix 6　Federal Taxation Materials

Appendix 6 addresses statutory, judicial, and administrative sources of federal taxation materials. Cite tax treaties and secondary sources relating to taxation— such as treatises, books, legal periodicals, and looseleaf services—using the general rules for those sources in the *Guide*.

This appendix is divided into the following sections:

A. Statutory Compilations
B. Tax Courts and Reporters
　1. Trial Courts Where Federal Tax Cases Are Heard
　2. Appellate Courts for Federal Tax Cases
　3. Unreported Opinions
C. Administrative Materials
　1. Administrative Announcements
　2. I.R.S. Compilations
　3. Officially Published I.R.S. Pronouncements
　4. Taxpayer Forms and Publications
　5. Other I.R.S. and Treasury Materials

6(A)　Statutory Compilations

Although the Internal Revenue Code is located in Title 26 of the *United States Code*, tax courts and practitioners typically cite it by reference to the Internal Revenue Code. To cite a statute in the Internal Revenue Code, begin with the abbreviation "I.R.C.," followed by a section symbol, one space, and the section number. Enclose the date in parentheses. Practitioners often omit the year when citing the *current* version of the I.R.C.; however, using a date is encouraged. If citing an unofficial version of the I.R.C., such as in the *United States Code Annotated* or the *United States Code Service*, add the publisher's name before the date.

To cite a provision of the I.R.C. that is no longer in effect, enclose in an initial parenthetical the year of the I.R.C. version under which the section was

---

SIDEBAR A6.1　Versions of the Internal Revenue Code

The current Internal Revenue Code (I.R.C.) was enacted in 1986 and applies to transactions occurring after October 22, 1986. Other versions since 1900 were the I.R.C. of 1939 (applying to most transactions between January 1, 1939, and August 16, 1954) and the I.R.C. of 1954 (until the 1986 I.R.C. was enacted, applying to income tax transactions that occurred on or after January 1, 1954; to estate tax matters that occurred after August 16, 1954; and to gift tax transactions that occurred on or after January 1, 1955).

promulgated. In a second parenthetical, indicate the year of repeal. See **Sidebar A6.1** for additional information on versions of the Internal Revenue Code.

Examples

Official version:	I.R.C. § 165(g).
Unofficial version:	I.R.C. § 212 (West 2008).
Repealed section:	I.R.C. § 275(c) (1939) (repealed 1954).

6(B) Tax Courts and Reporters

When the Commissioner of Internal Revenue is a party, use the abbreviation "Comm'r" (italicized in practice-based documents). Do not abbreviate as "C.I.R." Cite tax cases to official reporters where available, following **Rule 12** in general. Consult **Rule 12.19** for short citation formats. For citations in academic footnotes, see **Rule 12.2(a)(2)(FN)**. In addition, because many tax cases are reported in unofficial looseleaf services or published only online, you may also need to refer to **Rules 24**, **31**, and **32**.

(1) Trial Courts Where Federal Tax Cases Are Heard

United States District Courts

Cases are reported in the *Federal Reporter* (F., F.2d) through 1931 and the *Federal Supplement* (F.▲Supp., F.▲Supp.▲2d) after 1931; cite cases to one of these reporters if therein. Cases are also published in looseleaf publications: *American Federal Tax Reports* (A.F.T.R., A.F.T.R.2d) (published by Research Institute of America (RIA)) and *United States Tax Cases* (U.S.T.C.) (published by Commerce Clearing House (CCH)). Cite A.F.T.R. cases by initial and pinpoint page numbers (**Rule 5**); note that newer A.F.T.R. cases have hyphenated page numbers beginning with the year of the decision. Cite U.S.T.C. cases by paragraph number as well as pinpoint page number (**Rule 24.1(e)** and **Sidebar 24.1**).

Examples

Beard v. Comm'r, 107 A.F.T.R.2d 2011–552, 2011–556 (7th Cir. 2011).

Bell A. Corp. v. United States, 99-1 U.S.T.C. ¶ 50,119, at 87,041 (E.D. Pa. 1998), *aff'd*, 224 F.3d 200 (3d Cir. 2000).

United States Tax Court (1942 to present)

The United States Tax Court is a federal trial court specializing in tax disputes. It issues three types of decisions: Regular Decisions, Memorandum Decisions, and Summary Decisions. Prior to 1942, the court was known as the United States Board of Tax Appeals (see below).

The Tax Court publishes its Regular Decisions in its official reporter, *Reports of the United States Tax Court* (T.C.). These decisions generally concern novel and important tax issues. Because no other court publishes its opinions in the official reporter, omit the court abbreviation from the date parenthetical (see **Rule 12.6(a)**). Regular decisions dating back to September 25, 1995, are available at http://ustaxcourt.gov.

Example

Weber v. Comm'r, 138 T.C. 348, 356 (2012).

Regular decisions are also available in several looseleaf reporters, such as *Tax Court Reporter* (CCH) and *Tax Court Reported Decisions* (RIA). See **Rule 24.1** for additional information on citing case materials in looseleaf services, and consult **Chart 24.1** for abbreviations for names of looseleaf publishers.

Examples

Estate of Saunders, Tax Ct. Rep. (CCH) 58,610 (2011).

Estate of Saunders, Tax Ct. Rep. Dec. (RIA) ¶ 136.18 (2011).

Tax Court Memorandum Decisions (T.C.▲Memo. or T.C.M.) are Tax Court opinions typically concerning fact-based cases with well-settled legal issues. Memorandum decisions are not officially reported. Unofficial versions are published by CCH, Prentice-Hall (PH) (before April 15, 1991), and RIA (after April 15, 1991). Memorandum decisions dating back to September 25, 1995, are available at http://ustaxcourt.gov.

Examples

Leyshon v. Comm'r, T.C. Memo. 2012-248 (2012).

Leyshon v. Comm'r, 104 T.C.M. (CCH) 243 (2012).

Tax Court Summary Opinions (T.C.▲Summ.▲Op.) are from the small case division; the taxpayer can elect this division for controversies valued at $50,000 or less. These decisions cannot be appealed or used as precedent. Provide a parallel citation to an electronic database, website, or looseleaf service. Summary opinions going back to January 1, 2001, are available on the Tax Court website, http://www.ustaxcourt.gov.

Example

Sjoberg v. Comm'r, T.C. Summ. Op. 2008-162, 2008 Tax Ct. Summary LEXIS 160 (Dec. 23, 2008).

United States Board of Tax Appeals (1924–1942)

The United States Board of Tax Appeals is the predecessor of the United States Tax Court. Its official reporter is *United States Board of Tax Appeals Reports* (B.T.A.).

Examples

Am. Cigar Co. v. Comm'r, 21 B.T.A. 464 (1930).

Standard Oil Co. v. Comm'r, 43 B.T.A. 973, 998 (1941), *aff'd*, 129 F.2d 363 (7th Cir. 1942).

Two unofficial reporters are *Board of Tax Appeals Memorandum Decisions* (B.T.A.▲Memo.▲Dec.▲(PH)) and *Board of Tax Appeals Service* (B.T.A.▲Serv. ▲(CCH)).

Example

Kilpatrick's Estate v. Comm'r, 11 B.T.A. Memo. Dec. (PH) ¶ 42,335 (1942).

United States Court of Federal Claims (Oct. 29, 1992, to present)

The official reporter is the *Federal Claims Reporter* (Fed.▲Cl.). Unofficial reporters for the court are *American Federal Tax Reports* (A.F.T.R., A.F.T.R.2d) and *United States Tax Cases* (U.S.T.C.). Omit the court abbreviation when citing the official reporter.

Examples

Pereira v. United States, 84 Fed. Cl. 597, 600 (2008).

BP Exploration & Oil, Inc. v. United States, 2000-1 U.S.T.C. ¶ 50,460, at 84,493 (Fed. Cl. 2000).

SIDEBAR A6.2   Case Names in Older Tax Authorities

Some sources use the administrative style of the case—the plaintiff's full name in place of the adversarial case name. In these situations, it is preferable to convert the case name to an adversarial style, such as the hypothetical *Plaintiff v. Comm'r*.

United States Claims Court (1982–Oct. 28, 1992)

The United States Claims Court is the predecessor to the United States Court of Federal Claims. The official reporter is the *United States Claims Court Reporter* (Cl.▲Ct.). Unofficial reporters include *American Federal Tax Reports* (A.F.T.R., A.F.T.R.2d) and *United States Tax Cases* (U.S.T.C.). Omit the court abbreviation when citing the official reporter.

Examples

> *Shook v. United States*, 26 Cl. Ct. 1477 (1992).
>
> *Kircher v. United States*, 61 A.F.T.R.2d 88-1182, 88-1183 (Cl. Ct. 1988).

Court of Claims (1855–1982)

This court of original jurisdiction preceded the United States Claims Court. Its official reporter is *Court of Claims Reports* (Ct.▲Cl.). These cases also can be found in the appropriate *Federal Reporter* (F., F.2d) or *Federal Supplement* (F.▲Supp.). The unofficial reporter is *United States Tax Cases* (U.S.T.C.). Omit the court abbreviation when citing the official reporter.

Example

> *Henry v. United States*, 139 Ct. Cl. 362 (1957).

(2) Appellate Courts for Federal Tax Cases

Decisions of United States District Courts and the United States Tax Court are appealed to the appropriate United States Court of Appeals—whose cases are reported in the *Federal Reporter* (F., F.2d, F.3d)—and ultimately to the United States Supreme Court. Cases from the circuit courts of appeal and Supreme Court cases are unofficially reported by *American Federal Tax Reports* (A.F.T.R., A.F.T.R.2d) and *United States Tax Cases* (U.S.T.C.). When citing a United States Supreme Court case to one of these unofficial reporters, provide the court abbreviation (U.S.) in the date parenthetical.

Examples

> *Comm'r v. Simmons*, 646 F.3d 6 (D.C. Cir. 2011).
>
> *Grogan v. Garner*, 70 A.F.T.R.2d 92-5639, 92-5640 (U.S. 1991).
>
> *Crisp v. United States*, 2002-2 U.S.T.C. ¶ 50,765, at 85,791 (9th Cir. 2000).

(3) Unreported Opinions

To cite unreported opinions available only in a separately paginated slip opinion, refer to **Rules 12.12** and **12.19(f)**. Use **Rule 12.13(b)** to cite a case that is unreported but available on an electronic database such as Lexis Advance or WestlawNext.

6(C) Administrative Materials

(1) Administrative Announcements

Treasury Regulations (Treas.▲Reg.)

Although Treasury Regulations are published in Title 26 of the *Code of Federal Regulations*, do not cite them like other regulations (**Rule 18.1**). Instead, begin with the abbreviation "Treas. Reg." followed by a section symbol, the section number, and in parentheses, the year of the regulation's promulgation. For temporary regulations, add the abbreviation "Temp." before "Treas. Reg." For proposed treasury regulations, add the abbreviation "Prop." and use the exact date of the regulation's proposal; if possible, add a parallel citation to the *Federal Register* (**Rule 18.3**).

Examples

> Treas. Reg. § 1.409A-1(b)(4) (2007).
>
> Temp. Treas. Reg. § 1.482 (2006).
>
> Prop. Treas. Reg. § 301.7701-2(a), 4 Fed. Reg. 75,709 (Apr. 4, 2008).

(2) I.R.S. Compilations

Internal Revenue Bulletin (I.R.B.)

The I.R.B. is a weekly publication containing I.R.S. pronouncements such as Revenue Rulings, Revenue Procedures, Treasury Decisions, Notices, and Announcements. Until 2008, it served as the advance sheet for the *Cumulative Bulletin* (for more on the *Cumulative Bulletin*, see below). Although the I.R.S. ceased publishing the *Internal Revenue Bulletin* in print in March 2013, it is available online at http://www.irs.gov/Forms-&-Pubs. Each issue is numbered sequentially by year and week of issue, separated by a hyphen. Provide an initial page number, and if appropriate, a pinpoint page number.

Examples

> I.R.S. Notice 2012-31, 2012-20 I.R.B. 906, 908–09.
>
> I.R.S. Ann. 2009-53, 2009-25 I.R.B. 1107.

Cumulative Bulletin (C.B.)

The *Cumulative Bulletin* was published semiannually from 1919 until 2008, compiling the weekly *Internal Revenue Bulletin* described above. I.R.B. bulletins 1 through 26 were republished in the first *Cumulative Bulletin* each year, and I.R.B. bulletins 27 through 52 were republished in the second *Cumulative Bulletin* each year. Begin a citation to a *Cumulative Bulletin* with its volume number (composed of the year, a hyphen, and the compilation number (usually 1 or 2)), followed by its abbreviation, the initial page, and if relevant, a pinpoint page number.

Examples

> Rev. Proc. 92-59, 1992-2 C.B. 411.
>
> Rev. Rul. 74-330, 1974-2 C.B. 278.

> ### SIDEBAR A6.3   Document Numbers Before and After 2000
>
> Before 2000, many tax sources are numbered using two initial digits, such as 87- or 99-. After 2000, many tax sources are numbered using four digits, such as 2000- or 2001-.

(3) Officially Published I.R.S. Pronouncements (in alphabetical order)

Acquiescence

The I.R.S. reviews tax decisions made by the courts and issues its own opinion about whether it agrees with the decision. The opinion is published as either an acquiescence (*acq.*,), meaning that the I.R.S. will not contest the point in later cases; a nonacquiescence (*nonacq.*,), meaning that the I.R.S. will not appeal but will not follow the decision with other taxpayers; or an acquiescence in result (*acq. in result,*), in which the I.R.S. agrees with the result of the decision, but disagrees with one or more stated reasons. Append the acquiescence information to the case citation, using the relevant abbreviation, followed by a comma and a citation to the opinion in C.B. or I.R.B.

Examples

Lemmen v. Comm'r, 77 T.C. 1326, 1348 (1981), *acq.*, 1983-1 C.B. 1.

Dean v. Comm'r, 35 T.C. 1083 (1961), *nonacq.*, 1973-2 C.B. 4.

Announcements (I.R.S.▲Ann.)

Cite by year and number of issue, separated by a hyphen. Provide a parallel citation to C.B. or I.R.B. You may use an announcement's title as the first component of the citation.

Examples

I.R.S. Ann. 2013-12, 2013–11 I.R.B. 651.

Mutual Agreement on U.K. Pension Arrangements, I.R.S. Ann. 2005-30, 2005-18 I.R.B. 988.

Delegation Orders (I.R.S.▲Deleg.▲Order)

Cite by order number and, when available, revision number (Rev.). Provide a parallel citation to C.B., I.R.B., the *Internal Revenue Manual* (IRM), or the *Federal Register* (Fed.▲Reg.).

Examples

I.R.S. Deleg. Order 42 (Rev. 12), 1979-2 C.B. 482.

I.R.S. Deleg. Order 5 (Rev. 18), 2000-51 I.R.B. 587.

Notices (I.R.S.▲Notice)

Cite by year and sequential number of issue, separated by a hyphen. Provide a parallel citation to C.B. or I.R.B. It is appropriate to include the title of a notice in the citation.

Examples

I.R.S. Notice 2009-21, 2009-13 I.R.B. 724.

Weighted Average Interest Rate Update, I.R.S. Notice 99-7, 1999-1 C.B. 351.

Revenue Procedures (Rev.▲Proc.)

Cite by year and sequential number of issue, separated by a hyphen. Provide a parallel citation to C.B. or I.R.B.

Example

Rev. Proc. 99-25, 1999-1 C.B. 1117.

Revenue Rulings (Rev.▲Rul.)

Cite by year and sequential number of issue, separated by a hyphen. Provide a parallel citation to C.B. or I.R.B.

Example

Rev. Rul. 2004-52, 2004-1 C.B. 973.

Treasury Decisions (T.D.)

Treasury Decisions are proposed and final treasury regulations pertaining to tax matters and are issued by the Secretary of Treasury. Proposed regulations are identified by a REG prefix followed by a project number. Provide a parallel citation to I.R.B., C.B., *Treasury Decisions Under Internal Revenue Laws* (Treas.▲Dec.▲Int.▲Rev.), or *Federal Register* (Fed.▲Reg.).

Examples

REG-112815-12, 2013-35 I.R.B. 162.

T.D. 4723, 34 Treas. Dec. Int. Rev. 4 (1937).

Treasury Directives (Treas.▲Dir.)

Cite by directive number and provide a parallel citation to C.B. or I.R.B.

Example

Treas. Dir. 15-42, 1995-41 I.R.B. 32.

Treasury Orders (Treas.▲Order)

Cite by order number and provide a parallel citation to C.B. or I.R.B.

Example

Treas. Order 150-02, 1994-1 C.B. 721.

(4) Taxpayer Forms and Publications

Taxpayer Forms (I.R.S.▲Form)
Cite by form number. For forms that are issued or revised annually, enclose the year in parentheses. For forms that are not issued or revised annually, enclose the date of last revision in parentheses, preceded by the designation "last rev."

Examples

I.R.S. Form 1040 (2008).

I.R.S. Form 1040 sched. R (2009).

I.R.S. Form 1000 (last rev. Dec. 2005).

Taxpayer Publications (I.R.S.▲Pub.)
Cite by italicized title, I.R.S. publication number, pinpoint page if available, and year of publication.

Examples

Farmer's Tax Guide, I.R.S. Pub. No. 225, at 19 (2012).

(5) Other I.R.S. and Treasury Materials

General Counsel Memoranda (I.R.S.▲Gen.▲Couns.▲Mem.)
These memoranda are numbered sequentially but without reference to the year of issue; enclose the exact date of issue in parentheses. It is appropriate to provide a parallel citation to an electronic database, website, or looseleaf service.

Example

I.R.S. Gen. Couns. Mem. 39,892 (Nov. 26, 2002), 2002 IRS GCM LEXIS 1.

Internal Revenue Manual (IRM)
The IRM is cited in decimal format. The first digit is the part number, the second number is the chapter number, the third number is the section number, and the fourth number is the subsection number. Sub-subsections are set off by an additional decimal. If citing the official version published by the I.R.S., enclose the year of issue in parentheses. If citing an unofficial version, include the publisher and the year of publication.

Examples

IRM 5.7.5 (1996).

IRM 5.7.5.4 (RIA 2001).

News Releases (I.R.S.▲News▲Release)

Cite by year and sequential release number, separated by a hyphen; enclose the exact date in parentheses. It is appropriate to include the title of the release in italics and to provide a parallel citation to an electronic database, website, or looseleaf service.

Example

I.R.S. News Release 2009-77 (Aug. 25, 2009).

Private Letter Rulings (I.R.S.▲Priv.▲Ltr.▲Rul.)

Cite by year followed by a hyphen, the week of release followed by a hyphen, and the three-digit sequential item number for the week; enclose the exact date of issue in parentheses. Prior to the year 2000, numbers for Private Letter Rulings refer to to the last two digits; beginning in 2000, use all digits of the year. It is appropriate to provide a parallel citation to an electronic database, website, or looseleaf service.

Examples

I.R.S. Priv. Ltr. Rul. 90-31-022 (May 7, 1990).

I.R.S. Priv. Ltr. Rul. 2005-29-001 (July 22, 2005), 2005 WL 1707488.

Technical Advice Memoranda (I.R.S.▲Tech.▲Adv.▲Mem.)

Cite by year followed by a hyphen, the week of release followed by a hyphen, and the three-digit sequential item number for the week; enclose the exact date of issue in parentheses.

Example

I.R.S. Tech. Adv. Mem. 87-14-008 (Dec. 17, 1986).

Appendix 7 Federal Agencies

7(A) Selected Official Federal Administrative Reporters and Publications

Appendix 7 lists major official federal administrative publications and their abbreviations. For tax sources, use **Appendix 6**. Required spaces are indicated by triangles (▲). The presence or absence of periods in these abbreviations reflects agency practice.

Reporter/Publication	Abbreviation
Administrative Decisions Under Employer Sanctions, Unfair Immigration-Related Employment Practices and Civil Penalty Document Fraud Laws of the United States	OCAHO
Administrative Decisions Under Immigration and Nationality Laws	I.▲&▲N.▲Dec.
Agriculture Decisions	Agric.▲Dec.
Civil Aeronautics Board Reports	C.A.B.
Copyright Decisions	Copy.▲Dec.
Cumulative Bulletin	C.B.
Customs Bulletin and Decisions	Cust.▲B.▲&▲Dec.
Decisions and Orders of the National Labor Relations Board	N.L.R.B.
Decisions of the Commissioner of Patents	Dec.▲Comm'r▲Pat.
Decisions of the Comptroller General of the United States	Comp.▲Gen.
Decisions of the Department of the Interior	Interior▲Dec.
Decisions of the Department of the Interior and General Land Office in Cases Relating to Public Lands	Pub.▲Lands▲Dec.
Decisions of the Federal Labor Relations Authority	F.L.R.A.
Decisions of the National Mediation Board	N.M.B.
Decisions of the United States Merit Systems Protection Board	M.S.P.B.
Environmental Administrative Decisions	E.A.D.
Equal Opportunity Employment Commission Decisions	E.E.O.C.▲Dec.
Federal Communications Commission Reports	F.C.C.
	F.C.C.2d
Federal Energy Guidelines: FERC Reports	F.E.R.C.
Federal Maritime Commission Reports	F.M.C.
Federal Mine Safety and Health Review Commission Decisions	FMSHRC
Federal Power Commission Reports	F.P.C.
Federal Service Impasses Panel Releases	Fed.▲Serv.▲Imp.▲Pan.▲Rels.
Federal Trade Commission Decisions	F.T.C.
Internal Revenue Bulletin	I.R.B.
Interstate Commerce Commission, Motor Carrier Cases	M.C.C.
Interstate Commerce Commission Reports	I.C.C.
	I.C.C.2d

Reporter/Publication	Abbreviation
National Transportation Safety Board Decisions	N.T.S.B.
Nuclear Regulatory Commission Issuances	N.R.C.
Ocean Resources and Wildlife Reporter	O.R.W.
Official Gazette of the United States Patent Office	Off.▲Gaz.▲Pat.▲Office
Official Gazette of the United States Patent and Trademark Office	Off.▲Gaz.▲Pat.▲&▲Trademark▲Office
Securities and Exchange Commission Decisions and Reports	S.E.C.
Social Security Rulings, Cumulative Edition (indicate year of edition)	S.S.R.▲(Cum.▲Ed.▲Year)
Surface Transportation Board Reporter	S.T.B.

7(B)   Selected Federal Agency Abbreviations

Armed Services Board of Contract Appeals	A.S.B.C.A.
Benefits Review Board	Ben.▲Rev.▲Bd.
Board of Patent Appeals and Interferences	B.P.A.I.
Civilian Board of Contract Appeals	CBCA
Department of Agriculture	USDA
Department of Commerce, National Oceanic and Atmospheric Administration	NOAA
Department of Commerce, Patent and Trademark Office	USPTO
Department of Energy, Nuclear Regulatory Commission	NRC
Department of Labor	Dep't▲of▲Labor
Environmental Appeals Board	EAB
Environmental Protection Agency	EPA
Equal Employment Opportunity Commission	EEOC
Federal Aviation Administration	FAA
Federal Communications Commission	FCC
Federal Energy Regulatory Commission	FERC
Federal Labor Relations Authority	FLRA
Federal Mine Safety and Health Review Commission	FMSHRC
Federal Trade Commission	FTC
Government Accountability Office	GAO
Interior Board of Contract Appeals	IBCA
Interior Board of Indian Appeals	IBIA
Interior Board of Land Appeals	IBLA
International Trade Commission	USITC
Interstate Commerce Commission	ICC
Merit Systems Protection Board	MSPB
National Labor Relations Board	NLRB
National Mediation Board	NMB
National Transportation Safety Board	NTSB
Occupational Safety and Health Review Commission	OSHRC
Office of Dispute Resolution for Acquisition	ODRA
Securities and Exchange Commission	SEC
Small Business Administration	SBA
Social Security Administration	SSA
Surface Transportation Board	STB
Trademark Trial and Appeal Board	T.T.A.B.

Index

Unless otherwise noted, references are to rule numbers.

Paragraphs (cont.)
span, 6.3(a)
subparagraphs, citing, 6.1(a)
symbols, 6.2
textual reference, 6.6
unnumbered, 6.5
Parallel citations
advisory opinions, state, 18.16
agency decisions, 18.5(b)
cases not yet available, 12.12
commercial databases, in, 12.12, 32.1,
   32.2(b), Chart 30.1
court abbreviations, omission of, 12.6(d)
case reports, generally, 12.4(c)
definition, 12.4(c)
executive materials, 18.9(e), 18.17
Fast Formats p. 58
id., 12.19(d)
legislative materials, 15.1(g), 15.2(b),
   15.4(a), 15.4(b)(2), 15.7(f), 15.13(f)
local court rules, 12.4(b)(1), App. 2
locating parallel citations, Sidebar 12.4
microformed sources, 28.6(a), 28.6(b)
neutral citations, 12.17
online availability, 31.1, 31.4
page numbering in, 12.4(b)(4), 12.5(a),
   12.5(c)
pinpoint references, 12.5(c), 12.19(d)
reporters, 12.4(b)(1), 12.4(c)
session laws, 14.6(d)
short citations, 12.19(d)
table cases, 12.11
treaties, 19.1(g)
United States Supreme Court cases,
   12.4(c)
unpublished works, 29.2(f)
Parentheticals
concurring opinion, 12.10(a), Chart 12.5
construction of, 37.3
court abbreviation, 12.6
dates for case citations, 12.7
dissenting opinions, 12.10(a), Chart
   12.5
emphasis added, 39.4(a)
internal cross-reference, 10.2(b)
plurality opinion, 12.10(a)
prior history, use with, 12.9

reference to weight of authority,
   12.10(b)
subsequent history, use with, 12.8(g)
uses of, 12.10(c), 37.4
See also Explanatory parentheticals;
   entries for specific sources
Party names
anonymous, 12.2(d)(3)
business designations, 12.(e)(1), Chart
   12.1
cities, 12.2(j)
Commissioner of Internal Revenue,
   12.2(l)
companies, 12.2(e)(1), Chart 12.1
contrasted with case names, 12.2(b),
   12.2(c)
family names, 12.2(d)(2)
foreign names, 12.2(d)(2)
geographic locations, 12.2(h), 12.2(i),
   App. 3(B)
government, 12.2(e), 12.2(k), 12.2(l),
   12.2(m), Sidebar 12.2
government officials, 12.2(m), Sidebar
   12.2
individuals, 12.2(d), 12.2(o)
initials, 12.2(d)(3)
municipalities, 12.2(j)
organizations, 12.2(e)(1), Chart 12.1
procedural phrases, 12.2(p)
property, 12.2(n), 12.2(p)
relators, 12.2(c), 12.2(o)
short citations, 12.19(b), 12.19(c)
states, 12.2(h), App. 3(B)
"the," in, 12.2(e), 12.2(i), 12.2(j),
   12.2(r)
unions, 12.2(e), 12.2(f)
United States, 12.2(g)
***Passim*, 5.6**
Patents, 18.12
Pattern jury instructions, Fast Formats
   p. 158, 16.3
PDF, 30.1(b), Sidebar 30.2, 31.2(c), 31.4,
   31.5
People of, case name, 12.2(h)
Per curiam, 12.10(b)
Periodicals
abbreviation, 21.2(e), 21.3(c), App. 5